States United, Arthur Harry Bissell

The Postal Laws and Regulations of the United States of America

States United, Arthur Harry Bissell

The Postal Laws and Regulations of the United States of America

ISBN/EAN: 9783337236434

Printed in Europe, USA, Canada, Australia, Japan

Cover: Foto ©Suzi / pixelio.de

More available books at **www.hansebooks.com**

THE

POSTAL LAWS AND REGULATIONS

OF THE

UNITED STATES OF AMERICA,

PUBLISHED IN ACCORDANCE WITH THE

ACT OF CONGRESS

APPROVED MARCH 3, 1879.

COMPILED AND EDITED BY

ARTHUR H. BISSELL,

Law Clerk of the Post-Office Department,

AND

THOMAS B. KIRBY,

Private Secretary to the Postmaster-General.

WASHINGTON:

GOVERNMENT PRINTING OFFICE.

1879.

ORDER OF THE POSTMASTER-GENERAL.

POST-OFFICE DEPARTMENT,
Washington, D. C., July 1, 1879.

The regulations herein contained are issued by my authority and have my official sanction. All former regulations and rulings in conflict, or at variance with those herein contained, are hereby abrogated. All postmasters and other postal officers and employés are required to return to the Post-Office Department all copies of former editions of the Postal Laws and Regulations immediately upon the receipt of the present volume.

D. M. Key

Postmaster-General.

IMPORTANT.

The laws and regulations herein contained must be carefully read by every postmaster and other person employed in the postal service, as no breach of the law or regulations will be excused on the plea of ignorance.

When any law in this book is repealed or amended by Congress, or any regulation is altered or abrogated by direction of the Postmaster-General, through instructions issued by circular or in the United States Official Postal Guide, the postmaster must make the necessary alteration in this book, and add a note referring to the date of the law or order of the Postmaster-General by which the change was made. (See page 353.)

In this volume the regulations follow immediately after the laws upon which they are based.

The laws are printed in long-primer type.

The regulations, executive orders, decisions of the courts, and opinions of the Attorney-General and of the Assistant Attorney-General for the Post-Office Department are printed in brevier type.

The following must be signed by every postmaster:

I have read these laws and regulations, and I will take care that all the persons employed under me shall be made acquainted with the sections thereof affecting their respective duties.

——————— ———————,
Postmaster at ———————.

——————— day of ——————, 18——.

ERRATA.

Page 34, section 5, for "June 19" read "June 17;" for "20 Stat., p. 201," read "20 Stat., p. 141."

Page 42, section 34, for "their respective use" read "the respective use."

Page 84, section 247, for "19 Stat." read "18 Stat."

Page 90, section 276, for "end of each month" read "end of each week."

Page 91, section 288, for "Return Letter Office" read "Dead Letter Office."

Page 101, section 361, for "addressed to box-holders" read "addressed to box numbers."

Page 107, section 414, for "Division Superintendents" read "their Division Superintendent."

Page 114, section 443, line 8, for "*d*" read "*c*."

Page 115, section 449, line 2, strike out the word "only."

Page 117, section 462, for "see section 442" read "see section 472."

Page 143, change the foot-note to read as follows:

"By the act of June 12, 1879 (see page 354), the time is extended to one year."

Page 147, section 627, paragraph 4, line 2, for "of their depots" read "from their depots."

Page 167, for "section 227" read "section 727."

Page 170, for "section 557" read "section 757."

Page 172, section 787, for "attendance book" read "record of arrivals and departures."

Page 183, section 865, for "return-registry-receipt" read "registry-return-receipt."

Page 314, section 1247, for "(R. S. 5434" read "R. S. 5534"; section 1248, for "R. S. 5435" read "R. S. 5535."

Page 318, line 8, for "5265" read "5266."

Page 319, line 1, for "tables" read "topographer."

Page 320, add "American Rapid Telegraph Company, 41 Wall street, New York, received and filed April 12, 1879."

Postmasters and other postal officers and employés must make these corrections in the proper places in the book as soon as they receive it.

TABLE

OF

TITLES AND CHAPTERS.

CONTAINED IN THE

POSTAL LAWS AND REGULATIONS.

TITLE I.

THE POST-OFFICE DEPARTMENT.

TITLE II.

POST-OFFICES AND POSTMASTERS.

TITLE III.

TRANSPORTATION OF THE MAILS.

TITLE IV.

THE RAILWAY MAIL SERVICE.

Pages.

TITLE V.

THE REGISTRY SYSTEM OF THE UNITED STATES.

TITLE VI.

THE MONEY-ORDER SYSTEM OF THE UNITED STATES.

TITLE VII.

EXCHANGE OF CORRESPONDENCE WITH FOREIGN COUNTRIES.

TITLE VIII.

AUDITING POSTAL ACCOUNTS.

TITLE IX.

TITLE X.

TITLE XI.

EXECUTIVE ORDERS AFFECTING THE POSTAL ORGANIZATION.

TITLE XII.

OPINIONS OF THE ASSISTANT ATTORNEY-GENERAL FOR THE POST-OFFICE DEPARTMENT.

TITLE XIII.

SPECIAL INSTRUCTIONS TO POSTMASTERS.

---

1. All necessary blanks and post-office supplies authorized by the law and regulations will be furnished to postmasters upon application to the First Assistant Postmaster-General, Blank Agency, unless specially instructed in the regulations to make application for certain blanks to another office.

2. The Department will furnish postmasters with blank forms for "Publishers' Temporary Permit" and "Formal Notice of Entry," under sections 196 and 199 of the Postal Laws and Regulations. Application for the same should be made to the First Assistant Postmaster-General, Blank Agency.

3. In addressing communications to the Department never write on more than one subject in a letter, and always address letters to the bureau having charge of the subject-matter, as indicated in section 27. Never address letters to the Postmaster-General which are to be acted upon by a bureau officer.

4. Postmasters at free-delivery post-offices will be required to pay special attention to the requirements of section 345. When trial is made it should be done by card or otherwise, and the letter retained in the post-office subject to call at the general delivery.

5. Postmasters at "special post-offices" (see section 76) must promptly notify the Second Assistant Postmaster-General and the Superintendent of Railway Mail-Service for their division (see section 707) when they change the point of supply for their post-offices.

6. Postmasters and mail-carriers are exempted by section 1629 of the Revised Statutes from militia duty. They are not exempt from jury and road duty, and must obey summons thereto, leaving their post-offices in charge of a competent assistant as prescribed by section 518.

7. The new law and regulations for the classification of mail-matter differ radically from former laws and regulations, and must be carefully studied by postmasters.

8. Matter which is in writing, or other matter containing a written inscription in the nature of a personal correspondence, and matter which is sealed against inspection, are, by their nature and the intent of the law, first-class matter.

9. Second-class matter remains as defined by the former law, except that sample copies of second-class matter may now be sent at the pound rates, and that the postage is uniform for all second-class publications at two cents per pound.

10. Third-class matter includes all printed matter not embraced in the second-class. Particular attention should be given to the definition of printed matter, section 219. Books and music are third-class matter, and so are unmounted chromos; but chromos mounted on cloth or pasteboard are fourth-class matter.

11. The new law admits of written inscriptions upon third-class matter not in the nature of personal correspondence. See section 232.

12. Postmasters should consider the presumption to be in favor of the admission of all unsealed printed matter subject to inspection at third-class rates, and should not rate it up on account of written inscriptions thereon unless the inscription is clearly in the nature of a personal correspondence.

13. Fourth-class matter includes everything not included in the other three classes, which is not by law and regulations excluded from the mails. Many articles, which under the old law were rated with letter-postage, as matter to which no specific rate of postage was attached, belong now to the fourth class, and are subject to a postage charge of one cent per ounce. Such are, for instance, drawings, plans, designs, original paintings in oil or water-colors, etc.

14. Special attention is called to the law and regulations requiring the use of postage-due stamps, sections 271–274, for the collection of postage on the delivery of all insufficiently prepaid or unpaid matter. They are to be used upon ship and foreign letters, soldiers' and sailors' letters, as well as upon ordinary domestic letters, and upon matter of the third and fourth-classes when it inadvertently reaches its destination without full prepayment. They must never be put upon matter which is forwarded, returned to writer, or sent to the Dead-Letter Office, except at free-delivery post-offices.

15. Postmasters are required to keep a complaint-book, in which all letters reported to them as lost or missing are entered; and, after making examination in their post-offices, they are required to report the loss, with all particulars, without delay, to the Chief Special Agent of the Post-Office Department, Washington, D. C. These books are not furnished by the Department, but must be provided by postmasters at their own expense.

16. When complaint is made of delay in the receipt of letters beyond the time required by ordinary course of mail, as shown by the postmarks, postmasters should procure the envelopes of such letters and send them, with a statement of the facts, to the Division Superintendent of Railway Mail-Service.

17. Before approving applications for the establishment of new post-offices, postmasters should consult the Postal Guide and see that the name selected has not already been given to a post-office or to a county in the same or an adjoining State.

18. Complaints frequently arise on account of the inaccuracy of the letter-balances in use at post-offices. Postmasters are therefore instructed to have their letter-balances tested and adjusted at least twice a year. For this purpose post-offices of the first and second class, and all Special Agents of the Department, will be furnished with a set of standard weights. Postmasters at other post-offices wishing to test their letter-balances will make application to the nearest Special Agent or postmaster furnished with standard weights. The standards will be sent by mail, registered, to postmasters so applying, and must be returned in the same manner to the postmaster or Special Agent from whom they were received, as soon as the balances have been tested. When the balances are found by the test to be out of order, postmasters should not attempt to adjust them, but should report the facts to the First Assistant Postmaster-General, Blank Agency, when they will be furnished with correct balances.

19. All questions submitted by the public or arising in practice in regard to the construction of postal laws and regulations should be decided by postmasters, in the first instance, subject to appeal to the Postmaster-General.

20. Postmasters are notified that hereafter every number of the United States Official Postal Guide will contain a list of the orders which have been issued during the preceding quarter against persons or firms engaged in conducting schemes for the purpose of obtaining money through the mails under false pretenses; and whenever any of such persons or firms make application at any post-office for the payment of money-orders, or for registered letters addressed to them, the postmaster at such post-office should immediately report the case to the Postmaster-General.

21. Any printed circulars issued from the Post-Office Department must be treated as official written letters; postmasters should acknowledge their receipt, enter their substance opposite the proper section of the Postal Laws and Regulations, edition of 1879, and file the circulars in a book to be kept for that purpose.

22. Postmasters will hereafter preserve all waste-paper and twine at their post-offices until enough is accumulated to fill a mail-bag, when, after careful examination to see that no letters or packages are concealed therein, they will dispatch the same by mail to the postmaster at New York City, N. Y., by whom the same will be sold. Duplicate statements of the amount of waste-paper and twine received and the price for which it was sold will be sent quarterly by the postmaster at New York to each postmaster of the fourth class, to be used as a basis for estimating his compensation. One copy of this statement must in all cases accompany the quarterly account current of each postmaster as a voucher.

SUGGESTIONS TO THE PUBLIC.

1. Mail all letters, etc., as early as practicable, especially when sent in large numbers, as is frequently the case with newspapers and circulars. The trouble of the post-office is much diminished if letters, when mailed in large numbers, are tied in bundles, with the addresses all in one direction.

2. Make the address legible and complete, giving the name of the post-office, county, and State. The name of the street and number of the house should also be given on letters addressed to cities where letter-carriers are employed; while the letter will eventually reach its destination without a number, the omission is often a cause of hesitation and delay. In the case of letters for places in foreign countries, and especially in Canada, in which country there are many post-offices having the same names as post-offices in the United States and in England, the name of the country as well as the post-office should be given in full. Letters addressed, for instance, merely to "London," without adding "England," are frequently sent to London, Canada, and *vice versa*, thereby causing delay, and often serious loss. Letters addressed to Burlington, N. S. (Nova Scotia), often go to Burlington, New York, on account of the resemblance between S. and Y. when carelessly written.

3. Avoid using, as much as possible, cheap envelopes, made of thin paper, especially where more than one sheet of paper, or any other article than paper, is inclosed. Being often handled, and even in the mail-bags subject to pressure, such envelopes not unfrequently split open, often giving cause of complaint against officials who are entirely innocent in the matter.

4. Never send money or any other article of value through the mail, except either by means of a money-order or in a registered letter. Any person who sends money or jewelry in an unregistered letter not only runs a risk of losing his property, but exposes to temptation every one through whose hands his letter passes, and may be the means of ultimately bringing some clerk or letter-carrier to ruin.

5. Provide, in cities where letter-carriers are employed, letter-boxes at places of business or private residences, thereby saving much delay in the delivery of mail-matter.

6. See that every letter contains the full name and post-office address of the writer, with county and State, in order to secure the return of the letter, if the person to whom it is directed cannot be found. A much larger portion of the undelivered letters could be returned if the names and addresses of the senders were always fully and plainly written or printed inside or on the envelopes. Persons who have large correspondence find it most convenient to use "special request envelopes," but those who only mail an occasional letter can avoid much trouble by writing a request to "return if not delivered," etc., on the envelope.

7. When dropping a letter, newspaper, etc., into a street mailing-box, or into the receptacle at a post-office, always see that the packet falls into the box and does not stick in its passage; observe, also, as a finality, whether the postage-stamps remain securely in their places.

8. Postage-stamps should be placed on the upper right-hand corner of the address side of all mail-matter.

9. Postmasters are not obliged to accept in payment of postage-stamps or stamped envelopes, wrappers, etc., any currency which may be so mutilated as to be uncurrent, or the genuineness of which cannot be clearly ascertained. They are not obliged to receive more than twenty-five cents in copper or nickel coins. They are not obliged to affix stamps to letters, nor are they obliged to make change except as a matter of courtesy. Neither should they give credit for postage.

10. In using postal cards, be careful not to write or have anything printed on the side to be used for the address, except the address: also be careful not to paste, gum, or attach anything to them. They are unmailable as postal cards when these suggestions are disregarded.

11. To insure a letter being forwarded in the mails, it must have not less than three cents in postage-stamps affixed. The word "Paid" indorsed on a letter is not regarded at the post-office of delivery; letters so marked, and not having any stamp affixed, are treated as unpaid.

12. Letters cannot be carried out of the mail except in postage-stamped-envelopes. There is no objection to a person who is not acting as a common carrier carrying a sealed letter, whether in a stamped-envelope or not; but to continue the practice, or receive money for so doing, would subject the party to a penalty of one hundred and fifty dollars. Newspapers, magazines, and periodicals may be carried out of the mail for sale or distribution to subscribers, but if they are put into a post-office for delivery the postage must be paid thereon.

13. Mail-matter deposited in any receptacle erected by the Post-Office Department, such as street mailing-boxes for the reception of mail-matter to be collected by letter-carriers, or boxes in railroad depots for the reception of matter to be collected by employés of the railway mail-service, cannot be reclaimed by any one under any circumstances. On all such receptacles erected in railroad depots a notice should be affixed that the same are not intended for the reception of matter for city delivery. Persons depositing letters therein, intended for city delivery, do so at their own risk and cannot reclaim them except through the Dead-Letter Office.

14. A subscriber to a newspaper or periodical who changes his residence and post-office, should at once notify the publisher and have the publication sent to his new address.

15. The delivering of letters is not controlled by any statutory provision, but by the rules and regulations of the Post-Office Department; and the object of the Department is to insure and facilitate such delivery to the person for whom they are intended. In the case of money-orders and registered letters, the parties applying for them, if not known, should be required to prove their identity in the same manner as in banking institutions, where parties presenting drafts, checks, etc., who are not known, are required to prove their identity. In the case of advertised letters, parties applying should be questioned as to the place or places from whence they may be expecting correspondence. In the general delivery of a post-office, the postmaster should exercise a sound discretion in the delivery of letters to persons claiming to be the persons named in the address, and who may not be known to him.

16. Publishers and news agents posting second-class matter in quantities will facilitate its distribution and often hasten its dispatch by separating such matter by States and Territories and the larger cities.

17. Hotel matter must be returned to the post-office as soon as it is evident that it will not be claimed.

18. Proprietors of hotels, officers of clubs and of boards of trade or exchanges, should not hold unclaimed letters longer than ten days, except at the request of the person addressed. When such letters are returned to the post-office they should be redirected for forwarding, and in the absence of more definite information as to where the person addressed may be found, the new address may be taken from the hotel register.

19. First-class matter upon which one full rate of postage has been prepaid and all other fully-prepaid matter may be forwarded from one post-office to another at the request of the party addressed; but matter of the second, third, and fourth class can only be returned to the sender when the postmaster at the post-office of its destination is furnished with return postage. A request may be written or printed upon such matter that the postmaster will notify the sender of non-delivery and of the amount of postage which must be forwarded to insure its return. A request to return such matter cannot be regarded.

20. All inquiries, whether from postmasters or the public, relative to lost or missing mail-matter of every description, both foreign and domestic, ordinary and registered, should be addressed to the Chief Special Agent, Post-Office Department, Washington, D. C., to whom all losses or irregularities should be reported as soon as knowledge is had of their occurrence.

21. All inquiries or communications relative to mail-matter which is known to have been sent to the Dead-Letter Office should be addressed to the Third Assistant Postmaster-General.

22. In both cases the letter of inquiry must state to whom and what post-office the article was addressed, and give the name and full address of the writer or sender, the date and place of mailing, and a brief description of the contents. If it is known when the missing matter was sent to the Dead-Letter Office, the date and the reason should be given. If registered, the number should also be furnished.

23. If all losses are promptly reported it will be the means of correcting irregularities, and the interests of the public, as well as the efficiency of the postal service, will be enhanced in a most important degree.

24. Packages of third and fourth class matter, except single books, may weigh not exceeding four pounds.

25. Packages of mutilated currency addressed to the Treasurer of the United States for redemption may be registered free of charge for registry, but the postage thereon must be prepaid at letter rates.

26. It is much to be desired that the management of newly completed lines of railroad should consult the Post-Office Department in regard to the names of stations; if the names of stations in all cases correspond with those of the post-offices in whose delivery they are, much confusion and annoyance will be saved to the Department and the public.

27. Letters addressed to persons temporarily sojourning in a city where the free-delivery system is in operation should be marked TRANSIENT or GENERAL DELIVERY, if not addressed to a street and number, or some other designated place of delivery.

TITLE I.

THE POST-OFFICE DEPARTMENT.

CHAPTER ONE.

ORGANIZATION AND GENERAL PROVISIONS.

Sec. 1. Establishment of the Post-Office Department.—There shall be at the seat of Government an Executive Department to be known as the Post-Office Department, and a Postmaster-General, who shall be the head thereof, and who shall be appointed by the President, by and with the advice and consent of the Senate, and who may be removed in the same manner; and the term of the Postmaster-General shall be for and during the term of the President by whom he is appointed, and for one month thereafter, unless sooner removed. (R. S., § 388.)

Sec. 2. Assistant Postmasters-General.—There shall be in the Post-Office

3 P L

Department three Assistant Postmasters-General, who shall be appointed by the President, by and with the advice and consent of the Senate, and who may be removed in the same manner. (R. S., § 389.)

Sec. 3. Who may act as Postmaster-General.—In case of the death, resignation, absence, or sickness of the head of any Department, the first or sole assistant thereof shall, unless otherwise directed by the President,* perform the duties of such head until a successor is appointed, or such absence or sickness shall cease. (R. S., § 177.)

EXECUTIVE MANSION,
Washington, October 1, 1878.

It is hereby directed that the Second and Third Assistant Postmasters-General be, and are hereby, respectively authorized to act as Postmaster-General upon the conditions following, to wit:

The Second Assistant Postmaster-General during the absence of the Postmaster-General and the First Assistant Postmaster-General.

The Third Assistant Postmaster-General during the absence of the Postmaster-General and of the First and Second Assistant Postmasters-General.

R. B. HAYES.

Sec. 4. Assistant Attorney-General for the Post-Office Department.—There shall be employed in the Post-Office Department one Assistant Attorney-General, who shall be appointed by the Postmaster-General. (R. S., § 390.)

Sec. 5. Other officers of the Post-Office Department.—The following officers of the Post-Office Department, to be appointed by the Postmaster-General, are appropriated for in the act of June 19, 1878 (20 Stat., p. 201), in addition to the clerks of the several classes and other employés (see, also, R. S., § 393):

One Chief Clerk.

One Stenographer to the Postmaster-General.

One Law Clerk (office of Assistant Attorney-General for the Post-Office Department).

One Topographer.

One Appointment Clerk.

One Chief of Division of Mail Depredations.

One Chief of Special Agents. (Act March 3, 1879, 20 Stat., p. 356).

One Disbursing Clerk and Superintendent of the Building.

Three Chief Clerks to the Assistant Postmasters-General.

One Superintendent of Blank Agency (office of First Assistant Postmaster-General).

One Superintendent of Free Delivery (office of First Assistant Postmaster-General).

One Chief of Division of Inspection (office of Second Assistant Postmaster-General).

One Chief of Division of Dead Letters (office of Third Assistant Postmaster-General).

---

* As provided by section 179, Revised Statutes.

One Chief of Division of Postage-stamps (office of Third Assistant Postmaster-General).

One Superintendent of Foreign Mails.

One Chief Clerk to the Superintendent of Foreign Mails.

One Superintendent of the Money-Order System.

One Chief Clerk to the Superintendent of the Money-order System.

One Superintendent of Railway Mail Service. (Act June 17, 1878, 20 Stat., p. 140).

Sec. 6. Special Agents and their salaries.—The Postmaster-General may employ two special agents for the Pacific coast, and such number of other special agents as the good of the service and safety of the mail may require. (R. S., § 4017.)

Section 4017 of the Revised Statutes provided that Special Agents should be entitled to a salary at the rate of not more than $1,600 a year each, and that each should be allowed for traveling and incidental expenses while actually employed in the service a sum not exceeding $5 per day. But by the act of June 17, 1878, 20 Stat., p. 140, the following was enacted:

That hereafter the per diem pay of all special agents appointed under section 4017, Revised Statutes, shall only be allowed for their actual and necessary expenses not exceeding five dollars per diem when they are actually engaged in traveling on the business of the department, except such, not exceeding ten in number, as are appointed by the Postmaster-General to duty at such important points as he may designate, and nine assistant superintendents of railway mail service, who may be detailed to act as superintendents of division of railway mail service, who shall each receive a salary of two thousand five hundred dollars per annum and no more.

By the act of March 3, 1879 (20 Stat., p. 356), the Superintendent of Railway Mail Service and Chief of Special Agents are paid their actual expenses while traveling on the business of the Department.

Sec. 7. Acting Special Agents.—The Postmaster-General may employ, when the service requires it, the Assistant Postmasters-General and superintendents in his Department as special agents; and he may allow them therefor not exceeding the amount expended by them as necessary traveling expenses while so employed. (R. S., § 4019.)

Sec. 8. Special Agents authorized to administer Oaths.—Any officer or clerk of any of the Departments lawfully detailed to investigate frauds or attempts to defraud on the Government, or any irregularity or misconduct of any officer or agent of the United States, shall have authority to administer an oath to any witness attending to testify or depose in the course of such investigation. (R. S., § 183.)

Sec. 9. Superintendent of Railway Mail Service.—The Postmaster-General may appoint one agent only to superintend the postal railway service, who shall be paid, out of the appropriation for the transportation of the mail on railways, a salary at the rate of three thousand five hundred dollars a year, and his actual expenses while traveling on the business of the department. (Act June 17, 1878, 20 Stat., p. 140 as amended by act of March 3, 1879, § 1, 20 Stat., p. 356.)

See Title IV, *The Railway Mail Service.*

Sec. 10. Payment of Special Agents.—The (*Sixth*) Auditor [of the Treasury for the Post-Office Department] shall charge to the appropriation for mail transportation the salary and per diem of the assistant superintendents of the postal railway service; and to the appropriation for the free-delivery system, the salary and per diem of the special agent detailed for that service; and the salary and per diem of the special agents employed in the money-order service shall be paid out of the proceeds of that service. (R. S., § 4020.)

Sec. 11. Bond required of Special Agents.—Whenever a special agent is required to collect or disburse any public money, he shall, before entering upon such duty, give bond in such sum and form, and with such security as the Postmaster-General may approve. (R. S., § 4018.)

All Special Agents are required to give bond, with two sureties, in the sum of five thousand dollars, which must be filed before they enter upon their duties.

Sec. 12. Assignments of Special Agents.—The Special Agents appointed under section 6 embrace the force proper, who are attached to the office of the Postmaster-General, and those assigned to the office of the Superintendent of the Money-order System, the Free-delivery Service, and the office of the Second Assistant Postmaster-General, as Assistant Superintendents of the Railway Mail Service. These latter officers receive their instructions from the various offices to which they are assigned, and to whose appropriations their compensation and expenses are also chargeable. The force proper of Special Agents receive their instructions from the Chief Special Agent through whose office cases for investigation and reports of Special Agents upon the same pass and are recorded.

Sec. 13. Authority and Powers of Special Agents.—All Special Agents are intrusted with keys to the several mail locks in use, and are, by virtue of their commissions, authorized to open and examine the mails whenever and wherever they may find it necessary to do so. They are also empowered to enter and examine any post-office when the safety of the mails requires it, or the general interests of the service demand such examination. And by virtue of their commissions, all contractors, postmasters, and others in the service of this Department are bound to respect and obey the authority thus conferred.

Sec. 14. Special Agent's Communications Confidential.—Official communications marked *Confidential* from the special agents of this Department will be held as confidential. But no communication should be so marked unless it relates solely to business of the Department, and its interest, and is made in pursuance of confidential instructions. The contents of such communication cannot be divulged except by the permission of the Postmaster-General.

Sec. 15. Jurisdiction over Offenses against the Postal Laws.—When an arrest is made for an offense against the postal laws, the prisoner should be put in charge of the regular law officers of the United States as early as possible. If his examination cannot conveniently be had before a Judge or Commissioner of the United States, he should be taken before the nearest justice of the peace, or other State authority competent to examine and bind him over for trial. As justices of the peace have in many cases declined to issue warrants or to enter upon examination, from a doubt as to their jurisdiction, the special agent may remove such doubt by referring them to the provisions of the law on this subject contained in the following section. See also section 52.

Sec. 16. Preliminary Proceedings before Whom.—For any crime or offense against the United States, the offender may, by any justice or judge of the United States, or by any commissioner of a circuit court to take bail, or by any chancellor, judge of a supreme or superior court, chief or first judge of common pleas, mayor of a city, justice of the peace, or other magistrate, of any State where he may be found, and agreeably to the usual mode of process against offenders in such State, and at the expense of the United States, be arrested and imprisoned, or bailed, as the case may be, for trial before such court of the United States as by law has cognizance of the offense. Copies of the process shall be returned as speedily as may be into the clerk's office of such court, together with the recognizances of the witnesses for their appearance to testify in the case. And where any offender or witness is committed in any district other than that where the offense is to be tried, it shall be the duty of the judge of the district where such offender or witness is imprisoned, seasonably to issue, and of the marshal to execute, a warrant for his removal to the district where the trial is to be had. (R. S., § 1014.)

Sec. 17. When Witnesses must give Bond.—The recognizances of witnesses themselves shall be sufficient, except in cases where it is feared that they will not attend the trial. In the latter case, sureties must be required. When an arrest is made, Special Agents or postmasters are required to immediately inform the Chief Special Agent, in a special report, of all the facts in relation thereto. This report must show the name and official position of the party arrested (if an employé of the Department), where, when, and by whom arrested, the offense, and the exact *status* of the case at date of such report. They are also required to keep the Department fully advised in relation to the progress of trials of persons arrested for violation of the postal laws in their respective districts. Special reports should be made, from time to time, of the progress in each case to its final conclusion, and the result. It is important that these instructions should be complied with so far as it is practicable to do so.

Sec. 18. Special Agents, how related to Postmaster-General.—The Postmaster-General considers Special Agents of the Department as his representatives, and, as such, all postmasters, contractors, and others in the service are subordinate to them. They are responsible for their official acts only to him. In the discharge of their duties they are required to act with the single purpose of advancing the interests of the public, and the efficiency and security of the Department. The elementary details of the postal service must receive their unremitting attention, to the end that the purpose for which the Post-Office establishment was created shall, as far as they may be concerned, have a faithful and complete fulfillment. Instructions for their guidance are furnished them in a separate volume.

Sec. 19. Resident Foreign Mail Agencies.—The Postmaster-General may establish resident mail-agencies at the ports of Panama and Aspinwall in New Granada; Havana in Cuba; at Saint Thomas, and at such other foreign ports at which United States mail-steamers touch to land and receive mails, as may, in his judgment, promote the efficiency of the foreign mail service; and may pay the agents employed by him at such ports, out of the appropriation for transportation of the mail, a reasonable compensation for their services, and the necessary expenses for office-rent, clerk-hire, office-furniture, and other incidentals to be allowed him at each of such agencies. (R. S., § 4021.)

Sec. 20. Mail Agents on Ocean Steamers.—The Postmaster-General may appoint an agent in charge of the mail on board of each of the mail-steamers on the routes between San Francisco, Japan, and China; between San Francisco and Honolulu, in the Hawaiian Islands; and between New York and Rio Janeiro, who shall be allowed, out of the appropriation for transportation of the mail, an annual salary of two thousand dollars each. (R. S., § 4022.)

Sec. 21. Postal Agencies in China and Japan.—The Postmaster-General may establish, in connection with the mail steamship service to Japan and China, a general postal agency at Shanghai, in China, or at Yokohama, in Japan, with such branch agencies at any other ports in China and Japan as he shall deem necessary for the prompt and efficient management of the postal service in those countries; and he may pay the postal agents employed thereat a reasonable compensation for their services, in addition to the necessary expenses for rent, furniture, clerk-hire, and incidental expenses. (R. S., § 4023.)

Sec. 22. Route Agents, Employment of.—The Postmaster-General may employ as many route agents as may be necessary for the prompt and safe transportation of the mail, each of whom shall be paid out of the appropriation for transportation of the mail, at the rate of not less than nine hundred nor more than one thousand two hundred dollars a year each. (R. S., § 4024.)

See Title IV, *The Railway Mail-Service.*

Sec. 23. Railway Postal Clerks.—The Postmaster-General may appoint clerks for the purpose of assorting and distributing the mail in railway post-offices, each of whom shall be paid out of the appropriation for transportation of the mail, at the rate of not more than one thousand four hundred dollars a year each to the head clerks, nor more than one thousand two hundred dollars a year each to the other clerks. (R. S., § 4025.)

See Title IV, *The Railway Mail-Service.*

Sec. 24. Oath of Office.—Before entering upon their duties, and before they shall receive any salary, the Postmaster-General, and all persons employed in the postal service, shall respectively take and subscribe before some magistrate or other competent officer authorized to administer oaths by the laws of the United States, or of any State or Territory, the following oath or affirmation: "'I, A. B. do solemnly swear (or affirm, as the case may be,) that I will faithfully perform all the duties required of me and abstain from everything forbidden by the laws in relation to the establishment of post-offices and post-roads within the United States; and that I will honestly and truly account for and pay over any money belonging to the said United States which may come into my possession or control; and I also further swear (or affirm) that I will support the Constitution of the United States; So help me God.'" (Act of June 8, 1872, § 15, as amended by 18 Stat., p. 19; see also R. S., § 391.)

Sec. 25. Who may Administer Oath.—And this oath or affirmation may be taken before any officer civil or military, holding a commission under the United States, and such officer is hereby authorized to administer and certify such oath or affirmation. (18 Stat., p. 19.)

A contractor for carrying the mail cannot draw pay from the Department for services rendered or work done prior to his taking the oath. (11 Opin., p. 498.)

Sec. 26. Authority of Postmaster-General to Prescribe Regulations.—The head of each Department is authorized to prescribe regulations, not inconsistent with law, for the government of his Department, the conduct of its officers and clerks, the distribution and performance of its business, and the custody, use, and preservation of the records, papers, and property appertaining to it. (R. S., § 161.)

Sec. 27. Distribution of the Business of the Department.—That the business of the Department may be conveniently arranged and prepared for the final action of the Postmaster-General, it is distributed among its several officers as follows:

THE OFFICE OF THE POSTMASTER-GENERAL.—The duties of this office are under the immediate supervision of the CHIEF CLERK of the Department, and relate to the miscellaneous correspondence of the Department not specially connected with its other offices; the appointment of Department employés; the recording of orders promulgated by the Postmaster-General; the fixing of rates for the transmission of government telegrams; the supervision of the advertising, and management of the general work of the Department not otherwise assigned. To it is attached the office of the TOPOGRAPHER, charged with the duty of keeping up the maps in constant use in the Department proper, with the preparation and publication of new and revised post-route maps, with supplying maps to all branches of the postal service,* and with furnishing information for the settlement of all governmental mileage and telegraph accounts: the office of the SUPERINTENDENT AND DISBURSING CLERK, to which is assigned the supervision of all repairs, the care of the public property in and the furnishing of the Departmental building, and the disbursement of the salaries of the officers and employés of the Department; the office of the CHIEF SPECIAL AGENT, to which are referred all cases of losses or irregularities in the mails, and all reported violations of the postal law; and the DIVISION OF SPECIAL AGENTS AND MAIL DEPREDATIONS, to which are referred all accounts of Special Agents for salary, per diem, and allowance.

THE OFFICE OF THE FIRST ASSISTANT POSTMASTER-GENERAL.—To this office is assigned the duty of preparing all cases for the establishment, discontinuance, and change of name or site of post-offices, and for the appointment of all postmasters, and employés of the railway mail service, and all correspondence incident thereto; the duty of readjusting the salaries of postmasters, and the consideration of allowances for rent, fuel, and lights, clerk-hire, and miscellaneous expenditures; of receiving and recording appointments, of receiving, entering, and filing bonds and oaths of postmasters and issuing their commissions. This office is also charged with the correspondence with postmasters and the public upon questions relating to the character and classification of mail-matter and the rates of postage thereon, under the direct supervision of the Law Clerk of the Department. To it is attached the DIVISION OF FREE DELIVERY, having in charge the preparation of cases for the inauguration of the system in cities, the appointment of letter-carriers, and the regulation of allowances for incidental expenses, as well as the general supervision of the free-delivery system throughout the United States; and also the BLANK AGENCY, to which is assigned the

* The Postmaster-General may authorize the sale of one or more of these maps to individuals at the cost thereof; the proceeds to be applied as a further appropriation towards the preparation and publication of post-route maps (including the miscellaneous expenses of the Topographer's office). It is impliedly understood that sales can only be made from surplus copies, after the immediate wants of the Department are supplied; postmasters and others in the service being furnished with these maps only in cases deemed needful by the Department. For tariff of prices and other information, application should be made to the Topographer of the Post-Office Department.

duty of supplying the post-offices entitled thereto with blanks, wrapping-paper and twine, letter-balances, and canceling-stamps, and the Department with stationery.

THE OFFICE OF THE SECOND ASSISTANT POSTMASTER-GENERAL.—To this office is assigned the business of arranging the mail service of the United States, and placing the same under contract, embracing all correspondence and proceedings respecting the frequency of trips, mode of conveyance, and times of departures and arrivals on all the routes; the course of the mails between the different sections of the country, the points of mail distribution, and the regulations for the government of the domestic mail service of the United States. It prepares the advertisements for mail proposals, receives the bids and has charge of the annual and miscellaneous mail lettings, and the adjustment and execution of the contracts. All applications for mail service or change of mail arrangements and for mail messengers should be sent to this office. All claims should be submitted to it for transportation service. From this office all postmasters at the end of routes receive the statement of mail arrangements prescribed for the respective routes. It reports weekly to the Auditor all contracts executed and all orders affecting the accounts for mail transportation; prepares the statistical exhibits of the mail service and the reports to Congress of the mail lettings, giving a statement of each bid; also, of the contracts made, the new service originated, the curtailments ordered, and the additional allowances granted within the year. The rates of pay for the transportation of the mails on railroad routes, according to the amount and character of the service, are adjusted by this office. It also directs the weighing of the mails on the same, and authorizes new service on railroad routes. The issuing of mail-locks and keys, mail-pouches and sacks, and the supervision of the construction of mail-bag-catchers is also in charge of this office. To it is attached the DIVISION OF INSPECTION, to which is assigned the duty of receiving and inspecting the monthly registers of arrivals and departures, reporting the performance of mail service; also special reports of failures or delinquencies on the part of mail contractors or their agents, and of noting such failures or delinquencies, and preparing cases of fines or deductions by reason thereof; of conducting the correspondence growing out of reports of failures or delinquencies in the transportation of the mails; of reporting to the Auditor of the Treasury for the Post-Office Department, at the close of each quarter, by certificate of inspection, the fact of performance or non-performance of contract or recognized mail service, noting therein such fine or deduction as may have been ordered; of authorizing the payment of all employés of the railway mail service; also the payment of such acting employés as may be employed by this office through the Superintendent of Railway Mail Service in cases of emergency, and of authorizing the Auditor to credit postmasters with sums paid by them for such temporary service; and such other duties as may be necessary to secure a faithful performance of the mail service. All complaints against mail contractors or their agents, relating to failures or other irregularities in the transportation of the mails, whether made by postmasters or others, should be promptly forwarded to the Second Assistant Postmaster-General, marked "DIVISION OF INSPECTION."

THE OFFICE OF THE THIRD ASSISTANT POSTMASTER-GENERAL.—This office is charged with the duty of issuing drafts and warrants in payment of balances reported by the Auditor to be due to mail-contractors or other persons; the superintendence of the collection of revenue at depository, draft, and depositing post-offices, and the accounts between the Department and Treasurer and Assistant Treasurers and specially designated depositories of the United States. It receives all accounts, monthly or quarterly, of the depository or draft post-offices, and certificates of deposit from depositing post-offices. This office is also charged with the duty of preparing instructions for the guidance of postmasters respecting registered matter, and all correspondence connected with the REGISTRY SYSTEM OF THE UNITED STATES. To it is attached the DIVISION OF POSTAGE STAMPS AND STAMPED ENVELOPES AND POSTAL CARDS, having charge of the issuing of postage-stamps, stamped-envelopes, newspaper-wrappers, and postal-cards, and the supplying of postmasters with envelopes for their official use, and registered-package-envelopes and seals; the DIVISION OF DEAD LETTERS (so designated in the law but more properly called THE RETURN LETTER OFFICE), having assigned to it the examination and return to the writers of undelivered mail-matter and all correspondence relating thereto. The agencies having the supervision of the manufacture of postage-stamps, stamped-envelopes, and postal-cards are also under the direction of this office.

OFFICE OF THE SUPERINTENDENT OF THE MONEY-ORDER SYSTEM.—The general supervision and control of the postal money-order system throughout the United States and the superintendence of the international money-order correspondence with foreign countries is exercised by this office.

OFFICE OF THE SUPERINTENDENT OF THE FOREIGN MAILS.—To this office are assigned all foreign postal arrangements and correspondence connected with the foreign mail service and the supervision of the ocean mail-steamship service.

OFFICE OF THE SUPERINTENDENT OF THE RAILWAY MAIL SERVICE.—To this office are intrusted the distribution and dispatch of mails on all railroads and inland steamboat mail lines, the management of the postal-car service, and the general direction of the mail service on railroads and inland steamboats after that service has been contracted for or recognized under the law by the Postmaster-General, and the general direction of the distribution and dispatch of mails from all post-offices.

OFFICE OF THE AUDITOR OF THE TREASURY FOR THE POST-OFFICE DEPARTMENT.—This is a bureau of the Treasury, which for convenience is located in the General Post-Office building, to which is assigned the duty of auditing the accounts of the Post-Office Department, including those of postmasters, mail-contractors, and other agents or employés of the Department.

OFFICE OF THE ASSISTANT ATTORNEY-GENERAL FOR THE POST-OFFICE DEPARTMENT.—To this office are referred, when deemed advisable by the Postmaster-General and the heads of the several offices of the Department, questions concerning the construction of the laws and regulations which may arise in the administration of the business of the Department.

Sec. 28. Seal of the Post-Office Department.—The Postmaster-General shall keep the seal heretofore adopted for his Department, which shall be affixed to all commissions of postmasters and others, and used to authenticate all transcripts and copies which may be required from his Department. (R. S., § 395.)

Sec. 29. Duties of the Postmaster-General.—It shall be the duty of the Postmaster-General:

First. To establish and discontinue post-offices.

Second. To instruct all persons in the postal service with reference to their duties.

Third. To decide on the forms of all official papers.

Fourth. To prescribe the manner of keeping and stating accounts.

Fifth. To enforce the prompt rendition of returns relative to accounts.

Sixth. To control, according to law, and subject to the settlement of the (*Sixth*) Auditor [of the Treasury for the Post-Office Department], all expenses incident to the service of the Department.

Seventh. To superintend the disposal of the moneys of the Department.

Eighth. To direct the manner in which balances shall be paid over; issue warrants to cover money into the Treasury; and to pay out the same.

Ninth. To superintend generally the business of the Department, and execute all laws relative to the postal service. (R. S., § 396.)

Possessing the power to discontinue post-offices, the Postmaster-General may exercise it, notwithstanding that the postmasters have been appointed by the President by and with the advice and consent of the Senate, and under a statute which enacts that the appointee shall hold his office for the term of four years, unless sooner removed by the President. The office of postmaster at that place is in such case gone. (Ware *vs.* The United States, 4 Wall., 617.)

The head of a Department has not a right to review the decision of his predecessor allowing a credit, except to correct some error of calculation; if he is of opinion that the allowance was wrongful he must have a suit brought. (United States *vs.* Bank of Metropolis, 15 Peters, 377.)

Where the Postmaster-General is authorized and required by act of Congress to adjust a particular claim, nothing but a new authority emanating from Congress will enable one of his successors to open his adjustment upon the ground that he adopted an erroneous basis of settlement. (Chorpenning Case, 12 Opinions, 355.)

Sec. 30. Property in charge of the Department..—The Postmaster-General shall make out and keep, in proper books, full and complete inventories and accounts of all the property belonging to the United States in the buildings, rooms, offices, and grounds occupied by him and under his charge; and shall add thereto, from time to time, an account of such property as may be procured subsequently to the taking of the same, and also an account of the sale or disposal of any such property, and to report the same to Congress during the first week of each annual session. But this section shall not apply to the supplies of stationery and fuel. (R. S., § 397.)

Sec. 31. Postal Arrangements with Foreign Countries.—For the purpose of making better postal arrangements with foreign countries, or to counteract their adverse measures affecting our postal intercourse with them, the Postmaster-General, by and with the advice and consent of the President, may negotiate and conclude postal treaties or conventions, and may reduce or increase the rates of postage on mail-matter conveyed between the United States and foreign countries. (R. S., § 398.)

Sec. 32. Publication of Postal Conventions.—The Postmaster-General shall transmit a copy of each postal convention concluded with foreign governments to the Secretary of State, who shall furnish a copy of the same to the Congressional Printer for publication; and the printed proof-sheets of all such conventions shall be revised at the Post-Office Department. (R. S., § 399.)

Sec. 33. Blank Agency at Washington.—The Postmaster-General may establish a blank agency for the Post-Office Department to be located at Washington, District of Columbia. (R. S., § 400.)

Sec. 34. Foreign Dead Letters.—The action of the Post-Office Department respecting foreign dead letters shall be subject to conventional stipulations with their respective foreign administrations. (R. S., § 401.)

Sec. 35. Orders, Contracts, etc., to be truly Dated.—Every order, entry, or memorandum whatever, on which any action is to be based, allowance made, or money paid, and every contract, paper, or obligation made by or with the Post-Office Department, shall have its true date affixed to it; and every paper relating to contracts or allowances filed in the Department shall have the date when it was filed indorsed upon it. (R. S., § 402.)

Sec. 36. Form of Bonds and Contracts.—All bonds taken and contracts entered into by the Post-Office Department shall be made to and with the United States of America. (R. S., § 403.)

Postmaster-General *vs.* Early, 12 Wheat. 49.
Dox *vs.* Postmaster-General, 1 Peters, 318.

Sec. 37. Copies of Mail Contracts for the Auditor.—The Postmaster-General shall deliver to the (*Sixth*) Auditor [of the Treasury for the Post-Office Department] within sixty days after the making of any contract for carrying the mail, a duplicate copy thereof. (R. S., § 404.)

Sec. 38. Orders to be Certified to the Auditor.—All orders and regulations of the Postmaster-General which may originate a claim, or in any manner affect the accounts of the postal service, shall be certified to the Auditor of the Treasury for the Post-Office Department. (R. S., § 405.)

Sec. 39. Credits for Payments by Postmasters.—Upon the certified quarterly statement by the (*Sixth*) Auditor [of the Treasury for the Post-Office Department] of the payments by postmasters on account of the postal service, the Postmaster-General shall issue his warrant to the Treasurer to carry the amount to the credit of the postal revenues and to the debit of the proper appropriations upon the books of the Auditor. (R. S., § 406.)

Sec. 40. Fines, Penalties, Forfeitures, etc., how Remitted.—In all cases of fine, penalty, forfeiture, or disability, or alleged liability for any sum of money by way of damages or otherwise, under any provision of law in relation to the officers, employés, operations, or business of the postal service, the Postmaster-General may prescribe such general rules and modes of proceeding as shall appear to be expedient, for the government of the (*Sixth*) Auditor [of the Treasury for the Post-Office Department] in ascertaining the fact in each case in which the Auditor shall certify to him that the interests of the department probably require the exercise of his powers over fines, penalties, forfeitures, and liabilities; and upon the fact being ascertained, the Auditor may, with the written consent of the Postmaster-General, mitigate or remit such fine, penalty, or forfeiture, remove such disability, or compromise, release, or discharge such claim for such sum of money and damages, and on such terms as the Auditor shall deem just and expedient. (R. S.. § 409.)

Sec. 41. Discharge of Imprisoned Judgment Debtors.—The Postmaster-General may discharge from imprisonment any person confined in jail on any judgment in a civil case, obtained in behalf of the Department, if it be made to appear that the defendant has no property of any description. (R. S., § 410.)

Sec. 42. Such Discharge no Bar to Execution.—The release provided for by the preceding section shall not bar a subsequent execution against the property of the defendant on the same judgment. (R. S.. § 411.)

Sec. 43. Postal Employes may not be Interested in Contracts.—No person employed in the Post-Office Department shall become interested in any contract for carrying the mail, or act as agent, with or without compensation, for any contractor or person offering to become a contractor, in any business before the Department; and any person so offending shall be immediately dismissed from office, and shall be liable to pay so much money as would have been realized from said contract, to be recovered in an action of debt, for the use of the Post-Office Department. (R. S., § 412.)

See section 599.

Sec. 44. Prescribed Annual Reports of the Postmaster-General.—The Postmaster-General shall make the following annual reports to Congress:

First. A report of all contracts for carrying the mail made within the preceding year, giving in each case the name of the contractor; the date and duration of the contract; the routes embraced therein, with the length of each; the time of arrival and departure at the ends of each route; the mode of transportation; and the price to be paid, together with a copy of the recorded abstracts of all proposals for carrying the mail, as provided by section 588 (*three thousand nine hundred and forty-eight*) [of the Revised Statutes].

Second. A report of all land and water mails established or ordered within the preceding year, other than those let to contract at the annual letting, giving in each case the route or water-course on which the mail is established; the name of the person employed to transport it; the mode of transportation; the price to be paid; and the duration of the order or contract.

Third. A report of all allowances made to contractors within the preceding year above the sums originally stipulated in their respective contracts, and the reasons for the same, and of all orders made whereby additional expense is incurred on any route beyond the original contract price, giving in each case the route; the name of the contractor; the original service provided for by the contract; the original price; the additional service required; and the additional allowance therefor.

Fourth. A report of all curtailments of expenses effected within the preceding year, giving in each case the same particulars as in the preceding report.

Fifth. A report of the finances of the Department for the preceding year, showing the amount of balance due the Department at the beginning of the year; the amount of postage which accrued within the year; the amount of engagement and liabilities; and the amount actually paid during the year for carrying the mail, showing how much of said amount was for carrying the mail in preceding years.

Sixth. A report of the fines imposed on, and the deductions from the pay of contractors, made during the preceding year, stating the name of the contractor; the nature of the delinquency; the route on which it occurred; when the fine was imposed; and whether the fine or deduction has been remitted; and for what reason.

Seventh. A copy of each contract for carrying the mail between the United States and foreign countries, with a statement of the amount of postage derived under the same, so far as the returns of the Department will enable it to be done.

Eighth. A report showing all contracts which have been made by the Department, other than for carrying the mail, giving the name of the contractor; the article or thing contracted for; the place where the article was to be delivered or the thing performed; the amount paid therefor; and the date and duration of the contract.

Ninth. A report on the postal business and agencies in foreign countries.

Tenth. A report of the amount expended in the Department for the preceding fiscal year, including detailed statements of expenditures made from the contingent fund.

And the Postmaster-General shall cause all of such reports to be printed at the Public Printing Office, either together or separately, and in such numbers as may be required by the exigencies of the service or by law. (R. S., § 413.)

Sec. 45. Annual Reports of the Auditor.—The annual reports of the Auditor of the Treasury for the Post-Office Department to the Postmaster-General shall show the financial condition of the Post-Office Department at the close of each fiscal year, and be made a part of the Postmaster-General's annual report to Congress for that fiscal year. (Act of July 12, 1876, § 4, 19 Stat., p. 80.)

Sec. 46. Annual Estimates of the Postmaster-General.—The Postmaster-General shall submit to Congress at each annual session an estimate of the amount that will be required for the ensuing fiscal year, under each of the following heads:

First. Transportation of the mails.
Second. Compensation of postmasters.
Third. Compensation of clerks in post-offices.
Fourth. Compensation of letter-carriers.
Fifth. Compensation of blank-agents and assistants.
Sixth. Mail depredations and special agents.
Seventh. Postage-stamps and envelopes.
Eighth. Ship, steamboat, and way letters.
Ninth. Dead letters.
Tenth. Mail-bags.
Eleventh. Mail locks, keys, and stamps.
Twelfth. Wrapping-paper.
Thirteenth. Office-furniture.
Fourteenth. Advertising.
Fifteenth. Balances to foreign countries.
Sixteenth. Rent, light, and fuel for post-offices.
Seventeenth. Stationery.
Eighteenth. Miscellaneous.

Such estimates shall show the sums paid under each head, and the names of the persons to whom payments are made out of the miscellaneous fund; but the names of persons employed in detecting depredations on the mail, and of other confidential agents, need not be disclosed. (R. S., § 3668.)

Hereafter, in making his estimates for railway mail service, the Postmaster-General shall separate the estimate for postal-car service from the general estimates; and in case any increase or diminution of service by postal cars shall be made by him, the reasons therefor shall be given in his annual report next succeeding such increase or diminution. (Act of March 3, 1879, § 1, 20 Stat., p. 356.)

Sec. 47. Estimates to be furnished the Secretary of the Treasury.—The Postmaster-General shall furnish a copy of his annual estimates to the Secretary of the Treasury prior to the first of October in each year, which shall be reported to Congress by the latter in his regular printed estimates. (R. S., § 414, as amended by act March 3, 1875, § 3, 18 Stat., p. 370.)

Sec. 48. Contracts signed by the First Assistant.—The bonds of all postmasters may by the direction of the Postmaster-General be approved and accepted, and the approval and acceptance signed by the First Assistant Postmaster-General in the name of the Postmaster-General; and all contracts for stationery, wrapping-paper, letter-balances, scales, and street letter-boxes, for the use of the postal service may be signed in like manner by the First Assistant Postmaster-General in the place and stead of the Postmaster-General, and his signature shall be attested by the seal of the Post-Office Department. (Act March 3, 1877, § 2, 19 Stat., p. 335.)

Sec. 49. Contracts signed by the Second Assistant.—The Second Assistant Postmaster-General on the order of the Postmaster-General may sign with his name, in the place and stead of the Postmaster-General and attest his signature by the seal of the Post-Office Department, all contracts made in the said Department for mail transportation and for supplies of mail-bags, mail-catchers, mail-locks, and keys and all other articles necessary and incidental to mail-transportation. (Act March 3, 1877, § 3, 19 Stat., p. 335.)

Sec. 50. Contracts signed by the Third Assistant.—The Third Assistant Postmaster-General, when directed by the Postmaster-General, may also sign, in his name, in the place and stead of the Postmaster-General, and attest his signature by the seal of the Post-Office Department, all contracts for supplies of postage-stamps, stamped envelopes, newspaper-wrappers, postal cards, registered-package envelopes, locks, seals, and official envelopes for the use of postmasters, and return of dead letters, that may be required for the postal service. (Act March 3, 1877, § 4, 19 Stat., p. 335.)

Sec. 51. Omission to take Oath not to affect Liability, etc.—Every person employed in the postal service shall be subject to all penalties and forfeitures for violation of the laws relating to such service whether he has taken the oath of office or not. (R. S., § 3832.)

Sec. 52. Suits and Prosecutions in State courts.—All causes of action arising under the postal laws may be sued, and all offenders against the same may be prosecuted, before the justices of the peace, magistrates, or other judicial courts of the several States and Territories having competent jurisdiction by the laws thereof, to the trial of claims and demands of as great value, and of prosecutions where the punishments are of as great extent; and such justices, magistrates, or judiciary shall take cognizance thereof, and proceed to judgment and execution as in other cases. (R. S., § 3833.)

Sec. 53. Disbursements for the Topographer's Office, how made.—The disbursements of the moneys appropriated for the preparation and publication of post-route maps shall be made by a regular bonded disbursing-officer of the Post-Office Department, according to the laws, rules, and customs as recognized by the accounting-officers of the Treasury Department. The pay-rolls of the draughtsmen, clerks, messengers, and other employees of the topographer's office, shall be regularly made out by the chief of the topographer's office, examined and checked by the appointment-clerk of the Post-Office Department, and the payments thereof made by a bonded disbursing-officer of the Post-Office Department. All expenditures made by the chief of the topographer's office for the preparation and publication of post-route maps shall be accounted for by vouchers, accompanied by affidavit, and the moneys therefor shall be disbursed by a disbursing-officer of the Post-Office Department; and all of the above disbursements shall be paid out of the appropriation for the preparation and publication of post-route maps. (Act of June 17, 1878, § 2, 20 Stat., p. 143.)

Sec. 54. No Employé to Receive Fees.—No person employed in the postal service shall receive any fees or perquisites on account of the duties to be performed by virtue of his appointment. (R. S., § 3858.)

CHAPTER TWO.

ACCOUNTS, REVENUES, AND DEPOSITS.

Sec. 55. Manner of Keeping Accounts.—The accounts of the postal service shall be kept in such a manner as to exhibit separately the amount of revenue derived from the following sources respectively:

First. Letter-postage.

Second. Book, newspaper, and pamphlet postage.

Third. Registered letters.

Fourth. Box-rents and branch offices.

Fifth. Postage-stamps and envelopes.

Sixth. Dead letters.

Seventh. Fines and penalties.

Eighth. Revenue from money-order business.

Ninth. Miscellaneous.

And they shall exhibit separately the amount of expenditure made for each of the following objects respectively:

First. Transportation of the mail.

Second. Compensation of postmasters.

Third. Compensation of letter-carriers.

Fourth. Compensation of clerks for post-offices.

Fifth. Compensation of blank-agents and assistants.

Sixth. Mail depredations and special agents.

Seventh. Postage-stamps and envelopes.

Eighth. Ship, steamboat, and way letters.

Ninth. Dead-letters.

Tenth. Mail-bags.

Eleventh. Mail locks and keys.

Twelfth. Post-marking and canceling stamps.

Thirteenth. Wrapping-paper.

Fourteenth. Twine.

Fifteenth. Letter-balances.

Sixteenth. Office-furniture.

Seventeenth. Advertising.

Eighteenth. Balances to foreign countries.

Nineteenth. Rent, light, and fuel for post-offices.

Twentieth. Stationery.

Twenty-first. Miscellaneous. (R. S., § 4049.)

Sec. 56. Miscellaneous and Money-order Receipts.—Unclaimed money in dead letters for which no owner can be found; all money taken from the mail by robbery, theft, or otherwise, which may come into the hands of any agent or employé of the United States, or any other person whatever; all fines and penalties imposed for any violation of the postal laws, except such part as may by law belong to the informer or party prosecuting for the same; and all money derived from the sale of waste paper or other public property of the Post-Office Department, shall be deposited in the Treasury, under the direction of the Postmaster-General, as part of the postal revenue. And the Postmaster-General shall cause to be placed to the credit of the Treasurer of the United States, for the service of the Post-Office Department, the net proceeds of the money-order business; and the receipts of the Post-Office Department derived from this source during each quarter shall be entered by the (*Sixth*) Auditor [of the Treasury for the Post-Office Department] in the accounts of such Department, under the head of "revenue from money-order business." (R. S., § 4050.)

Sec. 57. Postal Revenues to be Accounted for.—All postages, box-rents, and other receipts at post-offices, shall be accounted for as part of the postal revenues; and each postmaster shall be charged with and held accountable for any part of the same, accruing at his office, which he has neglected to collect, the same as if he had collected it. (R. S., § 4051.)

Sec. 58. Revenues to be Appropriated for Postal Service.—The money required for the postal service in each year shall be appropriated by law out of the revenues of the service. (R. S., § 4054.)

Sec. 59. Payments, how Made; Advances.—All payments on account of the postal service shall be made to persons to whom the same shall be certified to be due by the (*Sixth*) Auditor [of the Treasury for the Post-Office Department]; but advances of necessary sums to defray expenses may be made by the Postmaster-General to agents employed to investigate mail depredations, examine post routes and offices, and on other like services, to be charged to them by the Auditor, and to be accounted for in the settlement of their accounts. (R. S., § 4055.)

Sec. 60. Transfer of Debts to Contractors.—The Postmaster-General may transfer debts due to the Department from postmasters and others to such contractors as have given bonds, with security, to refund any money that may come into their hands over and above the amount found due them on the settlement of their accounts; but such transfers shall only be in satisfaction of legal demands for which appropriations have been made. (R. S., § 4056.)

Sec. 61. Suits to recover Wrongful or Fraudulent Payments.—In all cases where money has been paid out of the funds of the Post-Office Department under the pretense that service has been performed therefor, when, in fact, such service has not been performed, or as additional allowance for increased service actually rendered, when the additional allowance exceeds the sum which, according to law, might rightfully have been allowed therefor, and in all other cases where money of the Department has been paid to any person in consequence of fraudulent representations, or by the mistake, collusion, or misconduct of any officer or other employé in the postal service, the Postmaster-General shall cause suit to be brought to recover such wrong or fraudulent payment or excess, with interest thereon. (R. S., § 4057.)

Sec. 62. Delivery of Stolen Money to Owner.—Whenever the Postmaster-General is satisfied that money or property stolen from the mail, or the proceeds thereof, has been received at the Department, he may, upon satisfactory evidence as to the owner, deliver the same to him. (R. S., § 4058.)

Sec. 63. Disposal of Fines, Penalties, and Forfeitures; Moieties.—All penalties and forfeitures imposed for any violation of law affecting the Post-Office Department for its revenue or property shall be recoverable, one-half to the use of the person informing and prosecuting for the same, and the other half to be paid into the Treasury for the use of the Post-Office Department, unless a different disposal is expressly prescribed. All fines collected for violations of such laws shall be paid into the Treasury for the use of the Post-Office Department. (R. S., § 4059.)

Sec. 64. Accounts to be Preserved Two Years.—The Postmaster-General may dispose of any quarterly returns of mails sent or received, preserving the accounts-current and all accompanying vouchers, and use such portions of the proceeds as may be necessary to defray the cost of separating and disposing of them; but the accounts shall be preserved entire for at least two years. (R. S., § 4060.)

Sec. 65. Restrictions on Payments on Account of Postal Service.—Payments of money out of the Treasury on account of the postal service shall be in pursuance of appropriations made by law, by warrants of the Postmaster-General, registered and countersigned by the Auditor for the Post-Office Department, and expressing on their face the appropriation to which they should be charged. (R. S., § 3674.)

Sec. 66. Postal Revenues and Collections to be paid into Treasury.—The postal revenues and all debts due to the Post-Office Department shall, when collected, be paid into the Treasury of the United States, under the direction of the Postmaster-General; and the Treasurer, assistant treasurer, or designated depositary receiving such payment, shall give the depositor duplicate receipts therefor. (R. S., § 407.)

Sec. 67. Deposits; how Brought into the Treasury.—All deposits on account of the postal service shall be brought into the Treasury by warrants of the Postmaster-General, countersigned by the Auditor; and no credit shall be allowed for any deposit until such warrant has been issued. (R. S., § 408.)

Sec. 68. Transfer of Postal Deposits.—The Postmaster-General may transfer money belonging to the postal service between the Treasurer, assistant treasurers, and designated depositaries, at his discretion, and as the safety of the public money and the convenience of the service may require. (R. S., § 3641.)

Sec. 69. Accounts of Postal Deposits.—Every depositary shall keep his account of the money paid to or deposited with him, belonging to the Post-Office Department, separate and distinct from the account kept by him of other public moneys so paid or deposited. (R. S., § 3642.)

Sec. 70. Entry of each Deposit, Transfer, and Payment.—All persons charged by law with the safe-keeping, transfer, and disbursement of the public moneys, other than those connected with the Post-Office Department, are required to keep an accurate entry of each sum received and of each payment or transfer. (R. S., § 3643.)

Sec. 71. Public moneys in Treasury subject to draft of Treasurer.—All moneys paid into the Treasury of the United States shall be subject to the draft of the Treasurer. And for the purpose of payments on the public account the Treasurer is authorized to draw upon any of the depositaries, as he may think most conducive to the public interest and to the convenience of the public creditors. Each depositary so drawn upon shall make returns to the Treasury and Post-Office Departments of all moneys received and paid by him, at such times and in such forms as shall be directed by the Secretary of the Treasury or the Postmaster-General. (R. S., § 3644.)

Sec. 72. Money to be Safely Kept.—Postmasters shall keep safely, without loaning, using, depositing in an unauthorized bank, or exchanging for other funds, all the public money collected by them, or which may come into their possession, until it is ordered by the Postmaster-General to be transferred or paid out. (R. S., § 3846.)

Sec. 73. Custody of Government Money in hands of Postmasters.—Any postmaster, having public money belonging to the Government, at an office within a county where there are no designated depositaries, treasurers of mints, or Treasurer or assistant treasurers of the United States, may deposit the same, at his own risk and in his official capacity, in any national bank in the town, city, or county where the said postmaster resides; but no authority or permission is or shall be given for the demand or receipt by the postmaster, or any other person, of interest, directly or indirectly, on any deposit made as herein described; and every postmaster who makes any such deposit shall report quarterly to the Postmaster-General the name of the bank where such deposits have been made, and also state the amount which may stand at the time to his credit. (R. S., § 3847.)

Sec. 74. Frequent Deposits of Revenues.—The postmaster at Washington, and postmasters at cities where there is an assistant treasurer, shall deposit the postal revenues, and all money accruing at their office, with such assistant treasurer, as often as once a week at least, and as much oftener as the Postmaster-General may direct. (R. S., § 3848.)

Sec. 75. No money to be paid Directly into the Department.—No moneys are to be paid directly into the Department, neither are any paid out directly by it. The proceeds of postage, or moneys received for postage-stamps, stamped-envelopes, newspaper-wrappers, or postal-cards sold, will, therefore, never be remitted by postmasters to the Department, nor be paid to any of its officers or agents, without due authority from the Postmaster-General. When money is sent to the Department in violation of this regulation it will be returned at the risk of the person so sending it.

Sec. 76. Post-offices Financially Designated and Classified.—For convenience in collecting and disbursing the revenues of the Post-Office Department, post-offices are designated and classed as follows, viz:

1. SPECIAL POST-OFFICES.—Those post-offices not located on a regular mail-route, but which are supplied by a special carrier, whose compensation is fixed at two-thirds of the salary of the postmaster. See section 548.

2. DEPOSITING POST-OFFICES.—Such as are directed to deposit, at some designated point, their surplus funds, quarterly or oftener.

3. DEPOSITORY AND DRAFT POST-OFFICES.—Those which are directed to retain their own funds, the surplus funds of depositing post-offices and funds received by collection-drafts on hand to meet drafts drawn by the Third Assistant Postmaster-General, and countersigned by the Auditor.

4. COLLECTION POST-OFFICES.—Those which are required to pay over their net proceeds quarterly to the mail carrier named in their special instructions, upon the production by him, from time to time, of the proper orders and receipts sent to him by the Department. No receipts other than the printed forms furnished to contractors by the Department will be recognized. All manuscript receipts are illegal. Upon the presentation of the order to the postmaster by the contractor, or his agent named in the order, the postmaster must pay over all money in his hands due to the United States for that quarter, from whatever source derived (except money-order funds), whether for drafts collected from postmasters and others, postage-stamps, stamped envelopes, newspaper-wrappers, postal cards, waste-paper, box-rents, or other emoluments of the post-office. The amount due the mail-messenger, if employed, is also excepted from this regulation.

Sec. 77. Post-offices transferred from one Class to Another.—Post-offices are transferred, from time to time, from one to another of these classes, to meet the necessities of the service. When such changes are made postmasters will be duly notified.

Sec. 78. Postmasters to transfer their Deposits Promptly.—When a postmaster has been directed to deposit quarterly, he will, as soon as practicable after the close of a quarter, not delaying more than fifteen days, deposit the whole amount due by him to the Department (as shown by his general account) in such funds as are receivable by law, taking an original and duplicate certificate for the same. The original must be transmitted in a letter addressed to the Third Assistant Postmaster-General, and the duplicate retained as a voucher. If it be not convenient for him to attend to it in person, it is expected that he will embrace the first safe opportunity for transferring the funds by private hands to the point designated, without incurring expense or risk to the Department.

Sec. 79. Letter of Transmittal should State what.—A letter of transmittal should accompany each deposit, giving full name of the postmaster, the name of his post-office, county, and State, and the quarter for which the amount is due.

Sec. 80. Postmasters may Transfer Funds free.—Postmasters desiring to do so may trasmit funds for deposit by registered letter, in official penalty-envelopes furnished by the Department, and omit the fee for registration. See section 812.

Sec. 81. Postmasters to report Amounts paid Mail Messengers, etc.—Postmasters at depositing post-offices who pay mail-messengers or special mail-carriers will report the amount so paid each quarter to the Third Assistant Postmaster-General, and deposit the balance, if any, at the point designated.

Sec. 82. Postmasters to report Cause of Failure to Deposit.—Postmasters at post-offices specified by section 78, failing to deposit within a month after the close of a quarter, must report the cause of failure to the Third Assistant Postmaster-General, or they will be treated as delinquent.'

Sec. 83. Want of funds Not accepted as Excuse.—Want of funds will not be accepted as an excuse for failing to pay or to deposit. The postmaster is not permitted to give credit for postages, which are regarded as cash in his hands. In like manner, he is prohibited from using, loaning, investing, or exchanging moneys received for postages, on pain of criminal prosecution.

Sec. 84. Collection-drafts Must be Paid.—A postmaster cannot refuse to pay a draft or collection-order because the contractor is indebted to him, nor because there is an unsettled private account between them, nor upon any other pretext; and such refusal is made by the law (section 1249) *prima-facie* evidence of embezzlement, subjecting him to punishment.

Sec. 85. Failure to deposit Cause for Removal, Unless.—A failure either to deposit according to instructions, or to pay a draft when presented, or to pay over to a contractor upon the production of the proper collection orders and receipts, will be followed by the removal of the delinquent postmaster, unless satisfactory explanation is made to the Postmaster-General.

Sec. 86. Postmasters to Pay over Balance at end of Quarter.—Postmasters at collection post-offices must be ready to pay over the balance of postal funds due to the United States at the end of each quarter after paying all officers and employés of the Post-Office Department authorized by circular No. 3000, and will transmit the contractor's receipt by the very first mail after payment is made. Such payments must include the whole amount of money on hand (except money-order funds), whether arising from the postages of the quarter or any preceding quarters, from sales of postage-stamps, stamped-envelopes, newspaper-wrappers, or postal-cards, or from moneys collected by or deposited with the postmaster. The absence of the postmaster from his post-office when the contractor presents the collection-order will not be accepted as a good reason for non-payment. The receipts must never be put up with the quarterly returns, but should be sent in a separate envelope, addressed to the Auditor of the Treasury for the Post-Office Department.

Sec. 87. Postmasters at Special Post-offices to report Balance.—Every postmaster of a "special post-office" will report to the Postmaster-General, at the end of each quarter, the balance in his hands over and above the sums due the carrier for supplying his post-office with the mail, in order that the Department may make a proper disposition of such balances.

Sec. 88. Postmasters at Special Post-offices to transmit Receipts promptly.—Postmasters at "special post-offices," when under orders to pay their respective carriers, will not only pay promptly, but lose no time in transmitting to the Auditor of the Treasury for the Post-Office Department the receipts taken for their quarterly payments.

Sec. 89. Payments to Department must be in what.—All payments to the Department, whether upon drafts or otherwise, must be in specie, United States Treasury notes, or notes of the national banks; and postmasters, in receiving payment of postages or other dues to the Department, should always bear in mind that they are bound to pay them over in the legal currency of the United States.

Sec. 90. No allowance made for Expenses for Payments, etc.—No allowance will be made to any postmaster for expenses incurred in paying over moneys due by him to the Department; neither will any allowance be made for expenses incurred in collecting moneys due the Department.

Sec. 91. Counterfeit money to be replaced.—Postmasters receiving counterfeit money will be required to replace the same with genuine current funds.

Sec. 92. Postmasters at draft-offices not to pay for other post-offices.—Postmasters at draft post-offices must not pay drafts drawn upon other post-offices. Credit for such payments will not be allowed.

Sec. 93. Postmasters not Required to redeem Mutilated Currency.—Postmasters are not required by law to redeem, or accept in payment of post-office dues, money-orders, stamps, or stamped-envelopes, any currency which may be so mutilated as to be uncurrent; nor is it any part of their duty to receive and transmit to the Treasury, for redemption, mutilated currency belonging to individuals, except as regular mail-matter, forwarded in the usual manner at the risk of the owner.

Sec. 94. Postmasters to Refuse Mutilated Coins.—The Treasury Department having declined to receive any coins which have been mutilated (perforated or abraded), postmasters should refuse all such coins, and thus avoid trouble and expense.

Sec. 95. All funds to be kept in Current Money.—The necessities of the postal service are such that all funds received by postmasters must be kept in current and passable money, so as to be immediately available for paying the drafts of the Department, money-orders, and expenses of the service.

Sec. 96. Postmasters to sign Certificates in Person.—Postmasters at depository post-offices must sign certificates of deposit in person, unless necessarily absent or sick, in which case they may be signed as follows:

A—— B——, *P. M.*,
By C—— D——, *Assistant P. M.*

Sec. 97. Postmasters not to Receive foreign Coins.—Foreign gold and silver coins are not a legal tender in the United States, and postmasters should not receive them in payment of postal dues or stamps.

TITLE II.

POST-OFFICES AND POSTMASTERS.

CHAPTER ONE.

ESTABLISHMENT OF POST-OFFICES AND APPOINTMENT OF POST-MASTERS.—OF BONDS AND SURETIES.

Sec. 98. Establishment of Post-offices.—The Postmaster-General shall establish post-offices at all such places on post-roads established by law as he may deem expedient, and he shall promptly certify such establishment to the (*Sixth*) Auditor [of the Treasury for the Post-Office Department.] And every person who, without authority from the Postmaster-General, sets up or professes to keep any office or place of business bearing the sign, name, or title of post-office, shall, for every such offense, be liable to a penalty of not more than five hundred dollars. (R. S., § 3829.) See sections 76, 548.

Sec. 99. Discontinuance of Post-offices.—The Postmaster-General may discontinue any post-office where the safety and security of the postal service and revenues are endangered from any cause whatever, or where the efficiency of the service requires such discontinuance, and he shall promptly certify such discontinuance to the (*Sixth*) Auditor [of the Treasury for the Post-Office Department.] (R. S., § 3864.)

Sec. 100. Classification of Postmasters.—Postmasters shall be divided into four classes, as follows: The first class shall embrace all those whose annual salaries are three thousand dollars or more than three thousand dollars; the second class shall embrace all those whose annual salaries are less than three thousand dollars, but not less than two thousand dollars; the third class shall embrace all those whose annual salaries are less than two thousand dollars, but not less than one thousand dollars; the fourth class shall embrace all postmasters whose annual compensation, exclusive of their commissions on the money-order business.

of their offices, amounts to less than one thousand dollars. (Act July 12, 1876, § 5, 19 Stat., p. 80.)

Sec. 101. Appointment and term of office of Postmasters.—Postmasters of the first, second, and third classes shall be appointed and may be removed by the President by and with the advice and consent of the Senate, and shall hold their offices for four years unless sooner removed or suspended according to law; and postmasters of the fourth-class shall be appointed and may be removed by the Postmaster-General, by whom all appointments and removals shall be notified to the Auditor (of the Treasury) for the Post-Office Department. (Act July 12, 1876, § 6, 19 Stat., p. 80.)

Sec. 102. Appointments by First Assistant Postmaster-General.—All appointments of postmasters are issued by direction of the Postmaster-General from the office of the First Assistant Postmaster-General.

Sec. 103. Postmasters' Commissions to be Recorded and Countersigned.—Hereafter the commissions of all postmasters appointed by the President, by and with the advice and consent of the Senate, shall be made out and recorded in the Post-Office Department, and shall be under the seal of said Department, and countersigned by the Postmaster-General, any laws to the contrary notwithstanding: *Provided*, That the said seal shall not be affixed to any such commission until after the same shall have been signed by the President of the United States. (Act March 18, 1874, § 1, 18 Stat., p. 23.)

Sec. 104. Residence of Postmasters.—Every postmaster shall reside within the delivery of the office to which he is appointed. (R. S., § 3831.)

A postmaster until the action of the Postmaster-General does not vacate his office by remaining out of the neighborhood of the post-office. If he keep the post-office by an assistant he is still responsible to the Department and to individuals. (2 McLean, 14.)

Sec. 105. Bonds of Postmasters.—Every postmaster, before entering upon the duties of his office, shall give bond, with good and approved security, and in such penalty as the Postmaster-General shall deem sufficient, conditioned for the faithful discharge of all duties and trusts imposed on him either by law or the rules and regulations of the Department; and where an office shall be designated as a money-order office, the bond of the postmaster shall contain an additional condition for the faithful performance of all duties and obligations in connection with the money-order business. On the death, resignation, or removal of a postmaster, his bond shall be delivered to the (*Sixth*) Auditor [of the Treasury for the Post-Office Department.] The bond of any married woman who may be appointed postmaster shall be binding upon her and her sureties, and she shall be liable for misconduct in office as if she were sole. (R. S., § 3834.)

The bond of a deputy postmaster takes effect and speaks from the time that it reaches the Postmaster-General, and not from the day of its date nor from the time when it is deposited in the post-office to be forwarded. (Boody *vs.* United States, 1 Wood & Min., 150.)

The bond does not constitute a binding contract until approved and accepted by the Postmaster-General. The reception and detention of an official bond by the Postmaster-General for a considerable time without objection is a sufficient proof of its acceptance. (The Postmaster-General *v.* Norvel, Gilpin, D. C. R., 131.)

Sec. 106. Application of Payments after Giving new Bond.—Whenever any postmaster is required to execute a new bond, all payments made by him after the execution of such new bond may, if the Postmaster-General or the (*Sixth*) Auditor [of the Treasury for the Post-Office Department] deem it just, be applied first to discharge any balance which may be due from said postmaster under his old bond.

Hereafter, when a deficiency shall be discovered in the accounts of any postmaster, who after the adjustment of his accounts fails to make good such deficiency, it shall be the duty of the (*Sixth*) Auditor of the Treasury [for the Post-Office] Department to notify the Postmaster-General of such failure, and upon receiving such notice the Postmaster-General shall forthwith deposit a notice in the post-office at Washington, District of Columbia, addressed to the sureties respectively upon the bond of said postmaster, at the office where he or they may reside, if known; but a failure to give or mail such notice shall not discharge such surety or sureties upon such bond. (R. S., § 3835, as amended by act of Feb. 4, 1879, 20 Stat., p. 281.)

Sec. 107. Commissions not issued to Postmasters before Approval of Bonds.—Upon the appointment of a postmaster, he is furnished with a letter of appointment, the blank form of the oath required, and a blank bond. The person designated for appointment will execute the bond as directed, take the prescribed oath of office, and transmit the bond and oath to the First Assistant Postmaster-General. A commission will be issued when the bond shall be approved by the Postmaster-General, upon the receipt of which, and not before, the new appointee is authorized to take charge of the post-office. The bond must be signed, in the presence of suitable witnesses, by himself and at least two sureties, the sufficiency of each of whom, for the payment of the sum inserted therein, must be shown by the certificate of the magistrate who administers the oath, whose signatures to the same must be attested by the clerk of a court of record in the county or State where the magistrate resides.

Sec. 108. Who may be appointed Postmaster.—No person can be appointed postmaster who cannot legally execute a bond and take the prescribed oath of office. Minors are, by law, incapable of holding the office of postmaster; but the law provides that married women may be appointed postmasters, and bonds executed by them, as such officers, are declared to be valid. See section 105.

Sec. 109. When new Bond is Required.—In case of the death, removal from the State, insolvency, or any other disability of one or both of the sureties, the postmaster must report the fact to the Department, in order that a new bond may be executed.

Sec. 110. Limit of time of Sureties' Liability.—Whenever the office of any postmaster becomes vacant, the Postmaster-General or the President shall supply such vacancy without delay, and the Postmaster-General shall promptly notify the (*Sixth*) Auditor [of the Treasury for the Post-Office Department] of the change; and every postmaster and his sureties shall be responsible under their bond for the safe-keeping of the public property of the post-office, and the due performance of the duties thereof, until the expiration of the commission, or until a successor has been duly appointed and qualified, and has taken possession of the office; except that in cases where there is a delay of sixty days in supplying a vacancy, the sureties may terminate their responsibility by giving notice, in writing, to the Postmaster-General, such termination to take effect ten days after sufficient time shall have elapsed to receive a reply from the Postmaster-General; and the Postmaster-General may, when the exigencies of the service require, place such office in charge of a special agent until the vacancy can be regularly filled; and when such special agent shall have taken charge of such post-office, the liability of the sureties of the postmaster shall cease. (R. S., § 3836.)

Sec. 111. Responsibility of sureties after Postmaster's death.—Whether the appointment be from the President or the Postmaster-General, in the event of death, the responsibility of the sureties will continue for the fidelity of the person left in charge of the post-office, until a successor is appointed and qualified, and has taken possession of the post-office; and they or any one of them may perform the duties of postmaster until a successor is appointed and takes possession. The person performing such duties must, before entering on the discharge thereof, take the required oath.

Sec. 112. Renewal of Bond.—Whenever any of the sureties of a postmaster notify the Postmaster-General of their desire to be released from their suretyship, or when the Postmaster-General deems a new bond necessary, he shall require the postmaster to execute such new bond with security. When accepted by the Postmaster-General, the new bond shall be as valid as the bond given upon the original appointment of such postmaster, and the sureties in the prior bond shall be released from responsibility for all acts or defaults of the postmaster which may be done or committed subsequent to the last day of the quarter in which such new bond shall be executed and accepted. (R. S., § 3837.)

For the security of the sureties bound in the previous obligation, the date of the acceptance should be indorsed on the bond; yet the sureties to the new bond are bound by the acceptance in fact of their bond by the Postmaster-General, and this acceptance may be shown as any other fact is required to be. (4 Opin., 187; *vide* Bank of U. S. *vs.* Dandridge, 12 Wheat., 64.)

Sec. 113. Application of Sureties for Release, to Whom made.—The office of the First Assistant Postmaster-General being charged with the duty of examining and recording the bonds of postmasters, all applications of sureties to be released from their liability as sureties should be addressed to the First Assistant Postmaster-General.

Sec. 114. Changing Name of post-office Necessitates new Bond.—When the Postmaster-General shall change the name of a post-office without a change of postmaster, the postmaster will be required to execute a new bond, and will be recommissioned. The order changing the name will take effect on the first day of the quarter next succeeding the date of such new bond; but if a change is made both in the postmaster and the name of the post-office, the name designated by the Postmaster-General will be used from the date upon which the new postmaster enters upon the discharge of his duties.

Sec. 115. Sureties on Bonds, how Released.—If on the settlement of the account of any postmaster it shall appear that he is indebted to the United States, and suit therefor shall not be instituted within three years after the close of such account, the sureties on his bond shall not be liable for such indebtedness. (R. S., § 3838.)

CHAPTER TWO.

SALARIES OF POSTMASTERS AND EXPENDITURES AT POST-OFFICES.

Sec. 116. Salaries of Postmasters at Presidential Post-Offices.—The respective compensation of postmasters of the first, second, and third classes shall be annual salaries, assigned in even hundreds of dollars, and payable in quarterly payments, to be ascertained and fixed by the Postmaster-General from their respective quarterly returns to the Auditor [of the Treasury] for the Post-Office Department, or copies or duplicates thereof, for four quarters immediately preceding the adjustment or readjustment, by adding to an amount of the box-rents of the office received or estimated not exceeding thirteen hundred and fifty dollars when the boxes are supplied and owned by the postmaster, and two-thirds of the box-rents, and not to exceed one thousand dollars, when the boxes are not supplied and owned by the postmaster, commissions on all the other postal revenues of the office to an amount not exceeding thirteen hundred and fifty dollars, at the following rates, namely: On the first one hundred dollars per quarter, sixty per centum; on all over one hundred dollars and not over three hundred dollars per quarter, fifty per centum; on all over three hundred dollars and not over seven hundred dollars per quarter, forty per centum; and thirty per centum on all revenues exceeding seven hundred dollars per quarter, but the aggregate of the said commissions not to exceed thirteen hundred and fifty dollars; and at all offices where the total revenues exceed, respectively, four thousand dollars per annum, there shall be added to the compensation hereinbefore provided from box-rents and commissions a percentage of the gross revenues at the following rates, namely: One per centum on all sums over four thousand dollars and not exceeding ten thousand dollars; nine-tenths of one per centum on all sums over ten thousand dollars and not exceeding twenty thousand dollars; eight-tenths of one per centum on all sums over twenty thousand dollars and not exceeding forty thousand dollars; six-tenths of one per centum on all sums over forty thousand dollars and not exceeding eighty thousand dollars; five-tenths of one per centum on all sums over eighty thousand dollars and not exceeding one hundred and sixty thousand dollars; four-tenths of one per centum on all sums over one hundred and sixty thousand dollars and not exceeding three hundred and twenty thousand dollars; three-tenths of one per centum on all sums over three hundred and twenty thousand dollars and not exceeding six hundred and forty thousand dollars; two-tenths of one per centum on all sums over six hundred and forty thousand dollars and not exceeding one million two hundred and eighty thousand dollars: and one-tenth of one per centum on all sums exceeding one million two hundred and eighty thousand dollars; and in order to ascertain the amount of the postal receipts of each office, the Postmaster-General may require postmasters to furnish duplicates of their quarterly returns to the Auditor at such times and for such periods as he may deem necessary in each case: *Provided,* That at offices where the letter-carrier system is now, or may hereafter be, established, the box-rents, in fixing the compensation of the respective postmasters at such offices, shall be estimated at not less than one thousand dollars per annum; but at all such offices where the compensation is now four thousand dollars, they shall be estimated at an amount which, with the commissions and percentages hereby allowed, will make the salaries of the postmasters thereat not less than three thousand dollars. (Act July 12, 1876, § 7, 19 Stat., p. 80.)

Sec. 117. Salaries of Fourth-Class Postmasters.—The compensation of postmasters of the fourth class shall be the whole of the box-rents collected at their offices and commissions upon the amount of the canceled postage-due stamps, provided for in sec. 270, on amounts received from waste-paper, dead newspapers, printed matter, and twine sold, and on postage-stamps, stamped envelopes, postal cards, and newspaper and periodical stamps canceled on matter actually mailed at their offices, at the following rate, namely: On the first one hundred dollars or less per quarter, sixty per centum; on all over one hundred dollars and not over three hundred dollars per quarter, fifty per centum; and on all over three hundred dollars per quarter, forty per centum; the same to be ascertained and allowed by the Auditor in the settlement of the accounts of such postmasters, upon their sworn quarterly returns: *Provided,* That when the compensation of any postmaster of this class shall reach one thousand dollars per annum, exclusive of commissions on money-order business, and when the returns to the Auditor for four quarters shall show him to be entitled to a compensation in excess of that amount under the [preceding] section (*seven of the act of July twelfth, eighteen hundred and seventy-six,*) the Auditor shall report such fact to the Postmaster-General, who shall assign him to his proper class, and fix his salary as provided by said section: *Provided further,* That in no case shall there be allowed to any postmaster of this class a compensation greater than two hundred and fifty dollars in any one quarter, exclusive of money-order commissions. (Act June 17, 1878, 20 Stat., p. 142, and act of March 3, 1879, § 26, 20 Stat., p. 361.)

See sections 270–274.

Sec. 118. Penalties for False Returns, Unlawful Sales of Stamps, etc.—In any case where the Postmaster-General shall be satisfied that a postmaster has made a false return of business, it shall be within his discretion to withhold commissions on such returns, and to allow any compensation that under the circumstances he may deem reasonable: *Provided*, That the form of affidavit to be made by postmasters upon their returns shall be such as may be prescribed by the Postmaster-General; and any postmaster who shall make a false return to the Auditor, for the purpose of fraudulently increasing his compensation under the provisions of this or any other act, shall be deemed guilty of a misdemeanor, and, on conviction thereof, shall be fined in a sum not less than fifty nor more than five hundred dollars, or imprisoned for a term not exceeding one year, or punished by both such fine and imprisonment, in the discretion of the court; and no postmaster of any class, or other person connected with the postal service, intrusted with the sale or custody of postage-stamps, stamped envelopes, or postal cards, shall use or dispose of them in the payment of debts or in the purchase of merchandise or other salable articles, or pledge or hypothecate the same, or sell or dispose of them except for cash, or sell or dispose of postage-stamps or postal cards for any larger or less sum than the values indicated on their faces, or sell or dispose of stamped envelopes for a larger or less sum than is charged therefor by the Post-Office Department for like quantities, or sell or dispose of postage-stamps, stamped envelopes, or postal cards otherwise than as provided by law and the regulations of the Post-Office Department; and any postmaster, or other person connected with the postal service, who shall violate any of these provisions shall be deemed guilty of a misdemeanor, and, on conviction thereof, shall be fined in any sum not less than fifty nor more than five hundred dollars, or be imprisoned for a term not exceeding one year. (Act June 17, 1878, 20 Stat., 142.)

Sec. 119. Biennial Readjustment of Salaries.—The salaries of postmasters of the first, second, and third classes shall be readjusted by the Postmaster-General once in two years, and in special cases, on the application of the postmaster, as much oftener as the Postmaster-General may deem expedient. (Act July 12, 1876, § 9, 19 Stat., p. 82.)

Sec. 120. Orders affecting Salaries to be Reported to the Auditor.—The Postmaster-General shall make all orders assigning or changing the salaries of postmasters in writing, and record them in his journal, and notify the change to the Auditor; and any change made in such salaries shall not take effect until the first day of the quarter next following such order: *Provided*, That in cases of not less than fifty per centum increase or decrease in the business of any post-office, the Postmaster-General may adjust the salary of the postmaster at such office to take effect from the first day of the quarter or period the returns for which form the basis of readjustment.* (Act July 12, 1876, § 10. 19 Stat., p. 82.)

Sec. 121. Allowance for Clerks at Separating Post-Offices.—The Postmaster-General may designate offices at the intersection of mail-routes as distributing or separating offices; and where any such office is of the third or fourth class, he may make a reasonable allowance to the postmaster for the necessary cost of clerical services arising from such duties. (Act of July 12, 1876, § 11, 19 Stat., p. 82.)

Sec. 122. Limit of Salaries.—No salary of any postmaster (*under this act*) shall exceed the sum of four thousand dollars per annum, except in the city of New York, which salary shall remain as now fixed by law [to wit. $8,000]; and no salary of any postmaster where the appointment is now presidential shall be reduced by the compensation herein established until the next readjustment below the sum of one thousand dollars per annum. (Act of July 12, 1876, § 12, 19 Stat., p. 82.

Sec. 123. Applications for Readjustment of Salaries.—Applications for special readjustment of salary must be made to the First Assistant Postmaster-General, and must state fully the facts upon which such application is based, and if found to come within the rule prescribed by the law, an order will be made readjusting the salary of the postmaster.

Sec. 124. Allowance for Clerks and Incidental Expenses.—The Postmaster-General may allow to the postmaster at New York City, and to the postmasters at offices of the first and second classes, out of the surplus revenues of their respective offices, that is to say, the excess of box-rents and commissions over and above the salary assigned to the office, a reasonable sum for the necessary cost of rent, fuel, lights, furniture, stationary, printing, clerks, and necessary incidentals to be adjusted on a satisfactory exhibit of the facts, and no such allowance shall be made except upon the order of the Postmaster-General. (R. S., § 3860.)

Sec. 125. Allowances for Extraordinary Business.—Whenever unusual business accrues at any post-office, the Postmaster-General shall make a special order allowing reasonable compensation for clerical service, and a proportionate increase of salary to the postmaster during the time of such extraordinary business. (R. S., § 3863.)

Sec. 126. Allowances to be Fixed by Order.—Expenditures for clerk-hire, rent, fuel, and light, in the case of the post-office at New York city, and of post-offices of the first and second classes, will be fixed by an order, and shall remain until otherwise ordered: and other items of expense for furniture, stationery, &c., under this section, in the case of the same class of post-offices, must be made only under special authority from the Postmaster-General.

Sec. 127. Allowances cannot Exceed Surplus Revenue.—Allowances for expenses at first and second class post-offices are made out of the surplus revenue of the post-office, that is to say, the excess of box-rents and commissions over and above the salary assigned to the post-office. And in no case will an allowance be made in excess of such surplus revenue.

*The language of this section to the proviso is the same as the first sentence of section 3856 of the Revised Statutes. The remainder of that section reads as follows: "But in cases of an extraordinary increase or decrease in the business of any post-office, the Postmaster-General may adjust the salary of the postmaster at such post-office, to take effect from the first day of the quarter or period the returns for which form the basis of readjustment."

Sec. 128. Receipts Required for Pay of Clerks employed.—Application for allowance for clerk-hire at separating post-offices must be made to the First Assistant Postmaster-General. Such allowance must not be understood as an increase of the salary of the postmaster, but as a compensation for clerical services arising from the duties of separating the mails for other post-offices. The amount of such clerk-hire will not be allowed by the Auditor unless the receipt of the person employed as such clerk shall accompany the quarterly account-current.

Sec. 129. Extra Allowances to first and second class Post-Offices.—Rent, lights, fuel, and stationery are allowed only to post-offices of the first and second class.

Sec. 130. Appointment of Clerks in Post-Offices.—Except as provided in section 413, all clerks and employés in post-offices are appointed by and are under the direct supervision of the postmaster, and all postmasters are held responsible for the acts of their subordinates.

Sec. 131. Roster of Clerks; their Duties and Salaries.—The power will be exercised by the Postmaster-General to fix the number and grades of clerks and their compensation in all post-offices where an allowance for clerk-hire is made. The postmaster at each post-office of the first and second class must submit to the First Assistant Postmaster-General for approval the plan of the organization of his post-office, with a list of all the clerks and other persons employed, showing their respective compensations and the duties performed by each. The approval by the First Assistant Postmaster-General of this roster will be necessary before any allowance for clerk-hire will be made for the ensuing fiscal year. After the roster of clerks and other persons employed has once been approved at the Department the number or compensation of those employed must not be changed without authority from the Department, and postmasters must report all removals and new appointments as soon as made to the First Assistant Postmaster-General. The rosters must be submitted annually, on the first day of January.

Sec. 132. Salaries and Expenses may be Deducted from Receipts.—The salary of a postmaster, and such other expenses of the postal service authorized by law as may be incurred by him, and for which appropriations have been made, may be deducted out of the receipts of his office, under the direction of the Postmaster-General. (R. S., § 3861.)

Sec. 133. Vouchers for Deductions to be sent to the Auditor.—Vouchers for all deductions made by a postmaster out of the receipts of his office, on account of the expenses of the postal service, shall be submitted for examination and settlement to the (*Sixth*) Auditor [of the Treasury for the Post-Office Department], and no such reduction shall be valid unless found to be in conformity with law. (R. S., § 3862.)

Sec. 134. No Postmaster to Retain more than his Salary, etc.—No postmaster shall, under any pretense whatever, have, receive, or retain for himself, in the aggregate, more than the amount of his salary and his commission on the money-order business as hereinafter provided. (R. S., § 3857.) See section 968.

Sec. 135. Compensation of Postmasters pro tem.—Any person performing the duties of postmaster, by authority of the President, at any post-office where there is a vacancy for any cause, shall receive for the term for which the duty is performed the same compensation to which he would have been entitled if regularly appointed and confirmed as such postmaster; and all services heretofore rendered in like cases shall be paid for under this provision. (Act of March 3, 1879, § 31, 20 Stat., p. 362.)

CHAPTER THREE.

POSTAGE-STAMPS, STAMPED ENVELOPES, AND POSTAL CARDS.

☞ For provisions respecting cancellation of stamps, see Chapter nine, Title II.

☞ For provisions respecting misuse of stamps, see Title IX.

Sec. 136. Postage-stamps for Prepayment of Postage.—The Postmaster-General shall prepare postage-stamps of suitable denominations, which, when attached to mail-matter, shall be evidence of the payment of the postage thereon. (R. S., § 3914.)

Sec. 137. Postage-stamps, Denominations of.—Of postage-stamps, three kinds, each consisting of various denominations, are provided, viz: Ordinary stamps, which are used to prepay postage on ordinary mail-matter of the first, third, and fourth classes; postage-due stamps, which are used for the collection of unpaid postage; and newspaper and periodical stamps, which are used to pay postage on second-class matter.

Sec. 138. Stamped-envelopes to be Provided.—The Postmaster-General shall provide suitable letter and newspaper envelopes, with such water-marks or other guards against counterfeits as he may deem expedient, and with postage-stamps with such device and of such suitable denominations as he may direct impressed thereon; and such envelopes shall be known as "stamped envelopes," and shall be sold, as nearly as may be, at the cost of procuring them, with the addition of the value of the postage-stamps impressed thereon; but no stamped envelope furnished by the Government shall contain any lithographing or engraving, nor any printing except a printed request to return the letter to the writer. Letters and papers inclosed in such stamped envelopes shall, if the postage-stamp is of a denomination sufficient to cover the postage properly chargeable thereon, pass in the mail as prepaid matter. [The Postmaster-General shall cause to be prepared a special stamp or stamped envelope, to be used only for official mail-matter, for each of the Executive Departments; and said stamps and stamped envelopes shall be supplied by the proper officer of said Departments to all persons under its direction requiring the same for official use; and all appropriations for postage made prior to March third, eighteen hundred and seventy-three, shall no longer be available for said purpose; and all stamps and stamped envelopes shall be sold or furnished to said several Departments or clerks only at the price for which stamps and stamped envelopes of like value are sold at the several post-offices.] (R. S., § 3915.)

See sections 249–251.

Sec. 139. Stamped-envelopes, of how many Kinds.—Of stamped-envelopes, two kinds, each consisting of various sizes, qualities, and denominations, are provided, viz: Ordinary, which may be either plain or bear a blank request to return; and special-request, which bear a printed request for the return of unclaimed letters, with the name and post-office address printed in full, and which are furnished by the Department without extra charge for such printing.

Sec. 140. Postal-cards to be Provided.—To facilitate letter correspondence, and to provide for the transmission in the mails, at a reduced rate of postage, of messages, orders, notices, and other short communications, either printed or written in pencil or ink, the Postmaster-General is authorized and directed to furnish and issue to the public, with postage-stamps impressed upon them, "postal cards," manufactured of good stiff paper, of such quality, form, and size as he shall deem best adapted for general use; which cards shall be used as a means of postal intercourse, under rules and regulations to be prescribed by the Postmaster-General, and when so used shall be transmitted through the mails at a postage charge of one cent each, including the cost of their manufacture. (R. S., § 3916.)

Sec. 141. Postal-cards for use in Postal Union correspondence.—The Postmaster-General is hereby authorized to furnish and issue to the public postal cards with postage-stamps impressed upon them, for circulation in the mails exchanged with foreign countries under the provisions of the Universal Postal Union Convention of June first, eighteen hundred and seventy eight, at a postage charge of two cents each, including the cost of their manufacture. (Act of March 3, 1879, § 1, 20 Stat., p. 357.)

Sec. 142. Exclusive issue of Postal-cards by the Department.—Postal-cards are issued exclusively by the Department. Cards issued by private parties, which contain any written matter having the nature of personal correspondence other than the address cannot be passed through the mails at less than letter postage, as they are not "postal-cards" within the meaning of the law. See sections 181, 237.

Sec. 143. Letter-sheet Envelopes, double Postal-cards, etc.—The Postmaster-General is hereby authorized to take the necessary steps to introduce and furnish for public use a letter-sheet envelope, on which postage-stamps of the denominations now in use on ordinary envelopes shall be placed. And the Postmaster-General is also authorized to introduce and furnish for public use a double postal card, on which shall be placed two one-cent stamps, and said card to be so arranged for the address that it may be forwarded and returned, said cards to be sold for two cents apiece; and also to introduce and furnish for public use a double-letter envelope, on which stamps of the denominations now in use may be placed, and with the arrangement for the address similar to the double postal card; said letter-sheet and double postal card and double envelope to be issued under such regulations as the Postmaster-General may prescribe. No money shall be paid for royalty or patent on any of the articles named. (Act of March 3, 1879, § 32, 20 Stat., p. 362.)

Sec. 144. Improvements in Stamps and Envelopes.—The Postmaster-General may, from time to time, adopt such improvements in postage-stamps and stamped envelopes as he may deem advisable; and when any such improvement is adopted it shall be subject to all the provisions herein respecting postage-stamps or stamped envelopes. (R. S., § 3917.)

Sec. 145. Sale of Stamps at Post-Offices.—Postage-stamps and stamped envelopes shall be furnished by the Postmaster-General to all postmasters, and shall be kept for sale at all post-offices; and each postmaster shall be held accountable for all such stamps and envelopes furnished to him. (R. S., § 3918.)

Sec. 146. Postmasters to keep a Supply of Stamps.—Stamps, stamped-envelopes, newspaper-wrappers, and postal-cards are furnished only to postmasters for sale. Postmasters who fail to supply themselves from the Department must purchase temporary supplies from the nearest post-offices. They are not required to render to the Department an account of such purchases.

Sec. 147. Requisitions for Stamps, etc., how to be Made.—Requisitions for postage-stamps, stamped-envelopes, newspaper-wrappers, postal-cards, and official penalty-envelopes are required to be made upon printed forms furnished by the First Assistant Postmaster-General, Blank Agency. Care must be taken to fill out the blank form with the name of the post-office, county, and State, the date of the order, the number and amount of each of the several descriptions wanted, the number and amount of each on hand, together with the average monthly requirement. The requisition must be signed by the postmaster himself, unless he be sick or necessarily absent, when it may be signed by the assistant or deputy, who will write the postmaster's name above his own. Requisitions when thus completed, must be forwarded to the Third Assistant Postmaster-General.

Sec. 148. Requisitions, when to be Made.—Postmasters are expected to keep themselves fully supplied with such stamps, stamped-envelopes, newspaper-wrappers, postal-cards, and official penalty-envelopes as are needed at their post-offices, and generally to order in such quantities as, on a careful estimate, may be deemed a sufficient supply for three months from the date of the order. They are not required to make their requisitions at any particular period during the quarter, but should order whenever their supplies are about to become exhausted.

Sec. 149. Requisitions for Special-Request Envelopes.—Requisitions for special-request envelopes must be made by postmasters immediately upon receiving orders from parties wanting them, at whatever time in the quarter it may be, and if possible should always be accompanied by a printed card showing the matter desired to be printed. No order is to be taken on credit, except at the postmaster's own risk, and in no case for less than five hundred of any specified denomination to bear the same printing.

Sec. 150. Postmasters not Supplied with Stamps until Commissioned.—No postmaster will be supplied with stamps, stamped-envelopes, and postal-cards until his bond and oath of office shall have been placed on file, and his commission duly issued.

Sec. 151. Postmasters to Count Supplies when Received.—Upon receiving supplies of postage-stamps, stamped-envelopes, newspaper-wrappers, or postal-cards, postmasters are required to open and count them in the presence of a disinterested witness, to date and sign the receipt, and transmit the same to the Third Assistant Postmaster-General. In case of any deficiency, the affidavit of the postmaster and that of the witness, stating the amount of such deficiency, with all the facts in the case, will be necessary in order to obtain credit therefor; and in every such case the wrapper, label, and box, or wooden case in which the supplies were sent, should also be returned and a record kept of the number, date, address, and all other marks on the same. Receipts must be signed in the same manner as requisitions.

Sec. 152. Damaged Supplies, how to be Treated.—If any portion of a parcel be damaged, the postmaster will sign the receipt for the whole amount of the parcel, and having written across the face of the receipt the number and amount of stamps, envelopes, wrappers, or cards unfit for use, he will return the same, together with the receipt, to the Third Assistant Postmaster-General, who will give credit for the amount returned. But if the damage be total, the entire number should be returned, with the receipt not signed, in order that others may be sent in their place. The package must be registered, and the postmaster must also be able to prove the act of mailing by a disinterested witness. Postmasters failing to register such packages will not receive credit for the amount alleged to have been returned, in case the same fails to reach the Department.

Sec. 153. Mistakes in Printing Special-Request Envelopes.—Special-request envelopes, which may be refused by the parties ordering them, on account of misprinting or other mistake, should be returned registered to the Third Assistant Postmaster-General. If the mistake has occurred through the fault of the Department, credit for the full value of the envelopes will be given in the postmaster's account, and the requisition will be refilled; if otherwise, credit for the postage value only of the envelopes will be given, and the postmaster should forward a new and correct requisition. In no case should a postmaster endeavor to dispose of special-request envelopes to any other party than the one for whose use they were ordered.

Sec. 154. Postmaster to Charge himself with Stamps, etc.—Every postmaster will, at the end of each quarter, charge himself in his quarterly account-current with the amount of such stamps, stamped-envelopes, newspaper-wrappers, and postal-cards as remained on hand at the close of the preceding quarter, or (if he has entered into office during the quarter) with the amount of such articles received from his predecessor, adding thereto the amounts received from the Department during the quarter just ended, and deducting the amount then remaining on hand, together with the amount of damaged stamps, envelopes, or cards returned for credit. The balance of the account thus stated will represent the amount sold, which must be added on the debit side of the quarterly account-current to the amounts due from other sources.

Sec. 155. No quarterly Returns, no Stamps.—Postmasters who have failed to duly render their quarterly returns to the Auditor will not be supplied with postage-stamps, stamped-envelopes, newspaper-wrappers, or postal-cards until the delinquency has been corrected.

Sec. 156. Postage-due-stamps; newspaper and periodical-stamps.—The postage-due-stamps, the newspaper and periodical-stamps, and the special-request envelopes, will all be accounted for in the same manner and together with the ordinary stamps, stamped-envelopes, newspaper-wrappers, and postal-cards.

Sec. 157. Moneys received for sale of Stamps, how Paid over.—Postmasters receiving postage-stamps, stamped-envelopes, newspaper-wrappers, and postal-cards from the Department for sale, will pay over the money by them received for such as may be sold, together with other moneys that may be due the Department at the times and in the manner required by their special instructions. Inclosing money to the Department to pay for stamps, stamped-envelopes, newspaper-wrappers, and postal-cards is prohibited.

Sec. 158. Postage-due-stamps, how used, etc.—Postage-due-stamps are to be used for matter of the first, third, and fourth classes which has passed through the mails and arrived at destination with the postage partly or wholly unpaid. The general manner of using these stamps, and the course to be pursued by postmasters, at post-offices of free delivery only, for obtaining credit for such as may be attached to matter of which no delivery can be made, is fully explained in sections 270–274.

Sec. 159. Newspaper and Periodical-stamps, how used.—Newspaper and periodical-stamps are to be used only for the payment of postage on newspaper and periodical publications, mailed from a known office of publication or news agency to regular subscribers or news agents, known as second-class matter. All matter of this kind intended to be mailed must be brought to the post-office of mailing, where it will be weighed in bulk, and the postage prepaid, according to the weight of the matter to be mailed, by the newspaper and periodical stamps. Ordinary postage-stamps cannot be used for such matter, nor can the newspaper and periodical stamps be used for any other purpose. After weighing the mail matter thus received, and immediately collecting the proper amount of postage thereon, the postmaster will give a receipt to the party mailing from a book of forms to be furnished by the Department. The stamps will then be affixed to the stub of the receipt, and at once effectually canceled. Stamps so used must be accounted for as sold. The stub-books are to be kept permanently in the post-office, ready to be produced whenever demanded by the Department. The stamps attached thereto must never be removed, nor the books disposed of otherwise than as directed by the Department. Postmasters should never neglect to attach to the stub-book the necessary amount to cover all postage collected on newspaper and periodical matter. Failure to attach stamps to the stub-book will subject the offending postmaster to the penalty provided by law for embezzlement.

Sec. 160. When supply Exhausted how to Proceed.—Should the supply of newspaper and periodical stamps at any time become exhausted, the postage on newspaper and periodical matter should be collected in money, and the necessary stamps afterwards attached when they are obtained from the Department. This course should also be pursued in the case of postmasters at whose post-offices such matter is mailed for the first time. In either case, however, no delay should be made in ordering a full supply of stamps.

Sec. 161. Postmasters to report Postage collected from Publishers, etc.—Postmasters will be required to render promptly to the Third Assistant Postmaster-General, at the close of each quarter, on blanks furnished for the purpose, a statement of postage collected from each publisher and news-agent during the whole quarter. In rendering his first statement a new postmaster will state, separately, the amount collected by himself and that collected by his predecessor in the same quarter, giving the exact date, also, when the change of postmasters took effect.

Sec. 162. Monthly reports by Postmasters at Presidential Post-Offices.—Postmasters at post-offices of the first, second, and third classes are required to make monthly reports to the Third Assistant Postmaster-General of the amounts of postage-stamps, stamped-envelopes, newspaper-wrappers, and postal-cards received from the Department, the amount sold, and that remaining on hand at the close of the month.

Blanks for this purpose will be supplied by the First Assistant Postmaster-General, Blank Agency.

Sec. 163. Postmaster to turn over Supplies to Successor.—Upon surrendering a post-office to his successor, the late postmaster, or his representative, will turn over to such successor all the stamps, stamped envelopes, newspaper-wrappers, postal-cards, then on hand, take duplicate receipts for the same, and transmit the original forthwith to the Auditor, that the account of the late postmaster may be credited accordingly. These stamps, envelopes, wrappers, and cards must not be sent to the Department, but should be retained for sale by the postmaster, who will charge himself with the amount in the quarterly account-current. In such receipt will also be included all postage-due stamps that may, at free delivery post-offices only, be attached to matter not delivered to the parties to whom the matter belongs.

Sec. 164. Discontinued post-office, Disposition of Supplies.—If a post-office be discontinued, the postmaster will deliver all stamps, stamped-envelopes, newspaper-wrappers, and postal-cards to the postmaster to whom he is directed to deliver the other post-office property, and will take duplicate receipts, one of which he will transmit to the Auditor as above.

Sec. 165. No percentage to Postmasters for Sale of Stamps, etc.—The law allows no compensation to postmasters for the sale of postage-stamps, stamped-envelopes, newspaper-wrappers, or postal-cards.

Sec. 166. Rules governing Sale of Stamps, etc.—Stamps, envelopes, wrappers, and cards are to be sold only for cash at the prices stated in the receipt which is sent with them to each post-office. In making sales of envelopes and wrappers postmasters are expected to evince a due spirit of accommodation, but they are not required to lose the fraction of a cent in selling small quantities; and if a postmaster cannot readily make change, the purchaser must tender the exact amount for the number wanted.

Sec. 167. Affidavit claiming Credit for Stamps Destroyed.—Whenever a postmaster claims credit for postage-stamps, stamped-envelopes, newspaper-wrappers, or postal-cards alleged to have been lost in the mails, burnt or otherwise destroyed, his own affidavit, stating the circumstances and amount of loss, together with all the other proof which in the particular case he can produce, is required to be forwarded to the Third Assistant Postmaster-General. Upon the receipt of such affidavit and additional testimony, which should be sent with the least possible delay, the claim will be duly considered.

Sec. 168. No credit allowed where Post-office is Robbed of Stamps.—Credit will not be allowed in cases where post-offices have been robbed of stamps or stamped-envelopes, newspaper-wrappers, or postal-cards. In an opinion of a former Attorney-General the following occurs: "If the stamps should be stolen or lost, and get into the hands of those who may use them, and thus deprive the government of so much revenue, the postmaster should be held for them. One who has the custody of public money or property, and is paid for taking care of it, cannot get rid of his responsibility by showing a theft or accidental loss. He is an insurer of its safety against al perils of that kind.".

Sec. 169. Exchange of Postage-stamps Prohibited.—The exchange of postage-stamps or stamped-envelopes for those of other denominations to accommodate private parties is prohibited. Postmasters will not be permitted to return to the Department unserviceable stamps or stamped-envelopes that may be acquired in this way.

Sec. 170. Postage on Spoiled Stamped-envelopes, etc., when Refunded.—The amount of the postage only on stamped envelopes and newspaper-wrappers spoiled in directing may be refunded in stamps or stamped envelopes by a postmaster if satisfied that they have never been used, and that the misdirection occurred at the place where the redemption is claimed; also, provided that such envelopes and wrappers shall be presented in a whole condition. In no case is an envelope or wrapper to be redeemed at the post-office to which it is directed, except in the case of envelopes for drop-letters, which are to be redeemed upon the foregoing conditions.

Sec. 171. Postal-cards when Spoiled to be Redeemed.—Postmasters may also redeem in stamps or stamped envelopes such postal-cards as have been spoiled in printing or by other causes, and have never been used, at the rate of four cents in stamps or stamped-envelopes for every five cards in whatever quantities presented.

Sec. 172. Stamps, etc., redeemed to be sent to Department with letter.—Stamped-envelopes, newspaper-wrappers, and postal-cards redeemed under the two foregoing sections must be sent with a special letter to the Third Assistant Postmaster-General, stating the number and amount. The package must be registered, and the postmaster must be able to prove the act of mailing by a disinterested witness. Postmasters failing to register such packages will not receive credit for the amount alleged to have been returned, in case the same fails to reach the Department. A postmaster need not return spoiled envelopes or wrappers to the Department oftener than once in each quarter.

Sec. 173. Postmasters held to strict Accountability for Stamps, etc.—Postmasters will be held to a strict accountability for all packages of postage-stamps, stamped-envelopes, newspaper-wrappers, and postal-cards passing through their hands: and the value of any package that may be lost or stolen while in transit will be charged to the postmaster through whose fault the loss or robbery occurred. Concerning the treatment of registered packages of postage-stamps, stamped envelopes, and postal cards arriving at or in transit to post-offices reference is made to Title V, *The Registry System of the United States.*

Sec. 174. Stamped envelopes, etc., to be sold at cost.—No stamped envelopes or newspaper-wrappers shall be sold by the Post-Office Department at less (in addition to the legal postage) than the cost, including all salaries, clerk hire, and other expenses connected therewith.* (Act of July 12, 1876, § 14, 19 Stat., p. 82.)

Sec. 175. Postage-stamps sold at Discount to designated Agents.—Postage-stamps and stamped envelopes may be sold at discount to certain designated agents, who will agree to sell again without discount, under rules to be prescribed by the Postmaster-General; but the quantities of each sold to any one agent at one time shall not exceed one hundred dollars in value, and the discount shall not exceed five per centum on the face value of the stamps, nor the same per centum on the current price of the envelopes when sold in less quantities. (R. S., § 3919.)

* Section 3920 R. S., not specifically repealed by section 174, is as follows:

Postage-stamps shall not be sold for any larger sum than the value indicated on their face, nor stamped envelopes for more than is charged therefor by the Post-Office Department for like quantities. Any person connected with the postal service who shall violate this provision shall be punishable by a fine of not less than ten dollars nor more than five hundred.

CHAPTER FOUR.

CLASSIFICATION OF DOMESTIC MAIL-MATTER AND RATES OF POSTAGE THEREON.

☞ For classification of matter addressed to foreign countries, see Title VII.

Sec. 176. Mail-matter Divided into four Classes.—Mail-matter shall be divided into four classes:

First. Written matter.

Second. Periodical publications.

Third. Miscellaneous printed matter.

Fourth. Merchandise. (Act March 3, 1879, § 7, 20 Stat., p. 358.)

Sec. 177. First-class Matter.—Mailable matter of the first class shall embrace letters, postal cards, and all matter wholly or partially in writing, except as hereinafter provided. (Act March 3, 1879, § 8, 20 Stat., p. 358.)

See sections 231 and 232.

Sec. 178. Postage on first-class Matter.—On mailable matter of the first class, except postal cards and drop-letters, postage shall be prepaid at the rate of three cents for each half ounce or fraction thereof; postal cards shall be transmitted through the mails at a postage charge of one cent each, including the cost of manufacture; and drop-letters shall be mailed at the rate of two cents per half ounce or fraction thereof, including delivery at letter-carrier offices, and one cent for each half ounce or fraction thereof where free delivery by carrier is not established. The Postmaster-General may, however, provide, by regulation, for transmitting unpaid and duly certified letters of soldiers, sailors, and marines in the service of the United States to their destination, to be paid on delivery. (Act March 3, 1879, § 9, 20 Stat., p. 358.)

Sec. 179. Soldiers', sailors', and marines' unpaid Letters Forwarded.—Letters written by non-commissioned officers and privates in the military service, or in the naval service (embracing the Marine Corps), on which the postage is not prepaid, must be plainly marked on the outside, over the address, "Soldier's letter," "Sailor's letter," or "Marine's letter" (as the case may be), and this certificate signed with his official designation by a field or staff officer of the regiment to which the soldier belongs, or by the officer in command of his detachment or of the post, or by a surgeon or chaplain at a hospital. In the Navy or Marine Corps, the certificate must be signed by the officer in command of the vessel, or by a chaplain or surgeon on board, or by the officer commanding a detachment of marines on shore. All unpaid letters of soldiers, sailors, or marines, duly certified, must be forwarded to their destination charged with the amounts of postage due at single rates only, to be collected on delivery.

Sec. 180. Prepayment required on Officers' Letters.—Letters written by commissioned officers in the military, naval, or marine service cannot be certified as letters of soldiers, sailors, or marines.

Sec. 181. Postage on Delivered Postal-Cards Reposted.—When a postal-card has once been delivered to the person to whom it is addressed it loses its character as a postal-card; and if it is offered for mailing again it must be prepaid either at letter or third class rates, as indicated by the nature of the printing or writing thereon.

Sec. 182. Other than first-class Matter must be open to Examination.—The Postmaster-General may prescribe, by regulation, the manner of wrapping and securing for the mails all packages of matter not charged with first-class postage, so that the contents of such packages may be easily examined; and no package the contents of which cannot be easily examined shall pass in the mails or be delivered at less rate than for matter of the first class. (Act of March 3, 1879, § 24, 20 Stat., p. 361.)

Sec. 183. Sealed Packages, etc., to pay Letter Rates.—Whenever any package offered for mailing to any point within the United States is sealed or otherwise closed against inspection, or contains or bears writing which is not allowed by law, such package is subject to postage at letter rates, and is, in all respects, to be treated as a letter; *i. e.*, if one full rate (3 cents) is paid, it is to be forwarded rated up with the deficient postage; if less than one full rate, it is to be treated as a short-paid letter. See sections 231, 232, and 233.

Sec. 184. Second-class Matter.—Mailable matter of the second class shall embrace all newspapers and other periodical publications which are issued at stated intervals, and as frequently as four times a year, and are within the conditions named in the next succeeding section. (Act March 3, 1879, § 10, 20 Stat., p, 359.)

Sec. 185. Essential characteristics of Second-class Matter.—The conditions upon which a publication shall be admitted to the second class are as follows:

First. It must regularly be issued at stated intervals, as frequently as four times a year, and bear a date of issue, and be numbered consecutively.

Second. It must be issued from a known office of publication.

Third. It must be formed of printed paper sheets, without board, cloth, leather, or other substantial binding, such as distinguish printed books for preservation from periodical publications.

Fourth. It must be originated and published for the dissemination of information of a public character, or devoted to literature, the sciences, arts, or some special industry, and having a legitimate list of subscribers: *Provided, however*, That nothing herein contained shall be so construed as to admit to the second-class rate regular publications designed primarily for advertising purposes, or for free circulation, or for circulation at nominal rates. (Act March 3, 1879, § 14, 20 Stat., p. 359.)

Sec. 186. A Known Office of Publication defined.—A known office of publication is a public office for the transaction of the business of the periodical, where orders may be received for subscriptions and advertising during the usual business hours. Publications issued without disclosing the office of publication must not be forwarded unless prepaid at the rate of third-class matter.

Sec. 187. Advertising Sheets Defined.—"Regular publications, designed primarily for advertising purposes," within the intendment of section 185, are defined to be—

First. Those owned and controlled by one or several individuals or business concerns, and conducted as an auxiliary, and essentially for the advancement of the main business or calling of those who own or control them.

Second. Those which, having no genuine or paid-up subscriptions, insert advertisements free, on the condition that the advertiser will pay for any number of papers which are sent to persons whose names are given to the publisher.

Third. Those which do advertising only, and whose columns are filled with long editorial puffs of firms or individuals who buy a certain number of copies for distribution.

Fourth. Pamphlets containing market quotations, and the business cards of various business houses opposite the pages containing such quotations.

Sec. 188. Decision upon Doubtful Publications.—Whenever a postmaster is in doubt as to the character of a publication offered for mailing as second-class matter, he will submit a copy of the same to the First Assistant Postmaster-General, and accompany it with a statement of such facts as he may be in possession of respecting the publication and the reasons for his inability to decide as to its character. The First Assistant Postmaster-General will also decide any appeal from the decision of a postmaster by publishers whose publications have been excluded from the second class by the action of the postmaster.

Sec. 189. Postmaster's Record of Second-class Publications.—Postmasters must keep a record of all the publications of the second class mailed at their post-offices, and submit a duplicate thereof to the office of the Third Assistant Postmaster-General, and must report on the first day of every month any changes made therein.

Sec. 190. Postage on Second-class Matter.—Publications of the second class, except as provided in section 239, when sent by the publisher thereof, and from the office of publication, including sample copies, or when sent from a news agency to actual subscribers thereto, or to other news agents, shall be entitled to transmission through the mails at two cents a pound or fraction thereof, such postage to be prepaid, as now provided by law. (Act of March 3, 1879, § 11, 20 Stat., p. 359.) See section 192.

Sec. 191. Weighing of Second-class Matter.—Periodical publications on their receipt at the post-office of mailing shall be weighed in bulk, and postage paid thereon by a special adhesive stamp, to be devised and furnished by the Postmaster-General, which shall be affixed to such matter, or to the sack containing the same, or upon a memorandum of such mailing, or otherwise, as the Postmaster-General may, from time to time, provide by regulations. (Act of June 23, 1874, § 6, 18 Stat., p. 233.)

Sec. 192. Manner of Prepaying second-class Matter.—Publishers and news agents must tender their newspapers and periodicals intended to be sent through the mails at the post-office of mailing, so that they may be weighed in bulk. The postage thereon must then be prepaid, according to the weight of the matter to be mailed, by special adhesive stamps, known as newspaper and periodical stamps, which are furnished by the Department to postmasters for that purpose. Unbound back numbers of a regular second-class publication may be sent at the rate of two cents per pound. See section 159.

Sec. 193. "Regular Subscribers" Defined.—A regular subscriber is a person who has actually paid, or undertaken to pay, a subscription price for a newspaper, magazine, or other periodical, or for whom such payment has been made, or undertaken to be made, by some other person. But, in the latter case, such payment must have been made or undertaken with the consent or at the request of the person to whom such newspaper, magazine, or periodical is sent. Consent is to be implied in the absence of objection by the party to whom the publication is sent.

Sec. 194. Evidence of Subscription-list may be Required.—If a postmaster has reason to doubt that a publication offered for mailing as second class matter has a legitimate list of subscribers, he may require the publisher thereof to satisfy him that it has, before permitting such publication to be mailed at the rates prescribed in section 190.

Sec. 195. Sample copies at Second-class Rates.—By section 185 subscribership is made one of the tests of the *bona fide* character of a publication. A publication having no legitimate list of subscribers cannot be admitted to the second class except as provided in section 196. When once determined to be entitled to transmission as second-class matter, the distinction in favor of subscribership in the circulation of second-class matter, which was made necessary by former laws, is by section 190 abandoned, and sample copies of second-class publications may, when sent from an office of publication, or a news agency, be forwarded in the mails at the same rates as to subscribers, to wit, at two cents per pound or fraction thereof.

Sec. 196. Admission of New Publications to Second-class Rates.—A temporary permit, in writing, shall be granted by a postmaster to a publication when the first issue of the same shall be presented, accompanied by an affidavit from the publisher thereof that the publication is published for the purposes named in section 185, unless the postmaster shall be satisfied from internal evidence furnished by the publication itself that it comes within the proviso of that section. When such temporary permit shall be granted, the publication shall be entitled to pass in the mails at the rate of two cents per pound or fraction thereof. Such temporary permit shall be revoked by the postmaster in case the publication shall have so changed its character as to make it no longer within the conditions named in section 185. A duplicate of such temporary permit shall be forwarded to the First Assistant Postmaster-General whenever issued.

Sec. 197. Penalty for submitting false evidence as to a publication.—Any person who shall submit, or cause to be submitted (*for transportation in the mails*) any false evidence to the postmaster relative to the character of his publication, shall be deemed guilty of a misdemeanor, and upon conviction thereof in any court of competent jurisdiction, shall for every such offense be punished by a fine of not less than one hundred dollars nor more than five hundred dollars. (Act of March 3, 1879, § 13, 20 Stat., p. 359.)

Sec. 198. Postmasters to report the Submission of false Evidence.—Whenever a postmaster is of opinion that a publisher has submitted to him any false statements respecting the character of his publication, either as to its office of publication, or as to its list of subscribers, or as to any other fact which the postmaster may have deemed it his duty to ascertain, in order to determine whether the publication was entitled to admission to the second class, he should report the case, with all the evidence in his possession, to the First Assistant Postmaster-General and await his instructions.

Sec. 199. Entry of Second-class Publications.—After a publication has been determined to be of the second class, the publisher thereof may, if he desire, formally enter the same at the post-office where mailed, and print upon each copy thereof the words "Entered at the post-office at —— as second-class matter." Publications so entered, and having printed upon each copy the words of entry, may be exchanged at second-class rates, with other second-class publications, and may be regularly sent at second-class rates, as complimentary, to customers, or business agents of the publication, and to other persons solely in the interest of the publication itself or of its publishers or employés as such. The formal entry will consist in a written notification of the publisher's desire to the postmaster, who will forward a copy of such entry to the First Assistant Postmaster-General. The unauthorized printing by a publisher of the words of entry herein prescribed, or their equivalent, will render him liable to the penalty prescribed in section 197. Postmasters should take pains to call the attention of publishers to this section and invite them to enter their publications as herein set forth.

Sec. 200. News-agents Applying for Second-class Rates must make and file with the postmaster at their post-office of mailing a statement signed by them showing the names of the periodicals which they thus mail, the post-offices, respectively, to which they are directed, and the number of such subscribers to each, with the dates to which their respective subscriptions extend. On all packages of second-class matter mailed by news-agents to news-dealers the word news-dealer must form part of the address.

Sec. 201. Evidence Required of News-agents.—In order to enable news-agents to transmit matter of the second class at pound rates, which is not published within the delivery of the post-office of mailing, they must furnish evidence that the periodical so offered has been inspected and admitted to the second class by the postmaster at the post-office of publication. The most satisfactory evidence of such inspection and approval will be when, in some conspicuous portion of its title page or cover, the periodical bears the printed words of entry prescribed in section 199.

Sec. 202. News-agents Defined.—No person is a news-agent within the contemplation of the law by virtue of his acting simply as a local or traveling agent for a publication. He must be engaged in business as a news-dealer or bookseller in order to be entitled to send newspapers and periodicals at the pound rates.

Sec. 203. Sample Copies Defined.—Sample copies of publications of the second class, which are entitled to transmission through the mails at two cents a pound, are defined to be copies sent to persons not subscribers, for the purpose of inducing them either to subscribe for or to advertise in the publication, or to agents, or to persons desiring to become agents, or whom the publisher may wish to induce to act as agents, to be used by them in procuring subscriptions and advertising. Any number of copies of any number of different editions of a second-class publication may be sent at any one time as sample copies. The primary design of a publisher in sending out sample copies is to increase the subscription-list and advertising patronage of his publication, and the law permits him to send such copies at the most favored rates, in the expectation that the correspondence resulting therefrom, and the increased circulation of the publication to regular subscribers, will augment the postal revenues. See section 195.

Sec. 204. Extra Numbers not Sample Copies.—Publishers will not be permitted, however, to use the exceptional advantages given to them by the law so as to defraud the Postal Department by mailing as sample copies extra numbers of their publications ordered by advertisers, or by campaign committees, or by other persons, to be sent to specified addresses, and apparently intended, from the nature of the contents or of marked portions thereof, to serve the business, political, or personal interests of the person or persons ordering the same. Such copies are third-class matter, and must be prepaid by stamps at the rate of one cent for each two ounces or fractional part thereof.

Sec. 205. Sample Copies to be Mailed Separately.—Sample copies of second-class publications should be put up in single wrappers, and each package addressed to a person or firm should be plainly marked, in printing or writing, SAMPLE COPY.

Sec. 206. Supplements Admitted as Second-class Matter.—Publishers of matter of the second class may, without subjecting it to extra postage, fold within their regular issues a supplement; but in all cases the added matter must be germane to the publication which it supplements, that is to say, matter supplied in order to complete that to which it is added or supplemented, but omitted from the regular issue for want of space, time, or greater convenience, which supplement must in every case be issued with the publication. (Act of March 3, 1879, § 16, 20 Stat., p. 359.)

Sec. 207. Definition of Supplements.—A supplement is held to be matter proper to be inserted in the publication to which it is added, but not inserted for want of space, or want of time, or because it is more convenient regarding space or time, or either, that it should be printed on a separate sheet. It is not indispensable or necessary that the sheet should be printed at the office of the publication to which it is intended to be a supplement; but if printed there or elsewhere, to be considered or treated as a supplement, it must be printed with the intention and purpose only of supplying an integral portion of the publication to which it professes to be a supplement, and not for another distinct and separate use. It should have direct relation to the publication supplemented, so that without it the publication supplemented would be incomplete.

Sec. 208. Handbills and Posters not Supplements.—The two preceding sections cannot be construed to admit "handbills" or "posters" as supplements. Handbills and posters are subject to the rate of postage of one cent for each two ounces or fraction thereof; and when such matter is inclosed in a newspaper and sent to regular subscribers it subjects the package to postage at the higher rate of one cent for each two ounces. Should the package reach the post-office of delivery without any evidence of prepayment, double the prepaid rate must be charged.

Sec. 209. Examination of Second-class Matter.—Matter of the second class may be examined at the [post-]office of mailing, and if found to contain matter which is subject to a higher rate of postage, such matter shall be charged with postage at the rate to which the inclosed matter is subject: *Provided*, That nothing herein contained shall be so construed as to prohibit the insertion in periodicals of advertisements attached permanently to the same. (Act of March 3, 1879, § 12, 20 Stat., p. 359.)

Sec. 210. Prohibited Advertisements in Second-class Matter.—Advertisements in the form of separate sheets in the body of periodical publications which are inserted for convenience and are for the purpose of being removed and put to separate use, are not "attached permanently" to such periodical within the meaning of the preceding section, and when so inserted will subject the periodicals in which they are found to the rate of one cent for each two ounces or fraction thereof; but this must not be held to apply to bills, receipts, and orders for subscription to such periodicals, which are permitted by the proviso to section 233.

Sec. 211. Detention of Suspected Second-class Matter.—When the postmaster at the post-office of mailing shall have reason to believe that any publisher or news-agent has violated the provisions of section 209 by depositing third-class matter in any post-office, for transmission through the mails as matter of the second class, he may, at his discretion, retain the suspected matter, notifying the publisher or news agent at once of his action, and report the facts to the Postmaster-General. If such third-class matter shall by inadvertence reach its destination, the postmaster at the post-office of destination must collect the postage due thereon as prescribed by law.

Sec. 212. Foreign Publications admitted as Second-class Matter.—Foreign newspapers and other periodicals of the same general character as those admitted to the second class in the United States, may, under the direction of the Postmaster-General, on application of the publishers thereof or their agents, be transmitted through the mails at the same rates as if published in the United States. Nothing in this act shall be so construed as to allow the transmission through the mails of any publication which violates any copyright granted by the United States. (Act of March 3, 1879, § 15, 20 Stat., p. 359.)

Sec. 213. Examination of Foreign Publications.—Agents of foreign publications, who may desire to secure the benefits of the second-class rates of postage for the transmission of such publications in the domestic mails should make application to the postmaster at the post-office where they desire the same to be mailed, and if the postmaster is of opinion, after an examination of the publications submitted, that they are in their essential features similar to domestic publications transmitted in the mails at the second-class rates, he will, upon their complying with the provisions of section 200, and filing an affidavit that the publications submitted come within the first and second conditions of section 185, and that they have a legitimate list of subscribers in the country where they are published, admit them to the mails on the same terms as domestic publications.

Sec. 214. Infringement of Copyright by Foreign Publications.—Whenever the owner of any copyright granted by the United States, or his authorized representative, author, or publisher, shall make complaint to a postmaster that any foreign publication admitted to the mails at the second-class rates is or has violated such copyright, such postmaster will cause such owner or representative to submit to him in writing the name of the publication thus offending, where the same is published, who are the agents for the same, if there be agents in the United States, and to accompany such statement with a certified copy of the title or description furnished such author or publisher by the Librarian of Congress. The postmaster will then forward such statement and certified copy to the First Assistant Postmaster-General and await his instructions.

Sec. 215. Third-class Matter and Postage thereon.—Mail-matter of the third class shall embrace books, transient newspapers, and periodicals, circulars, and other matter wholly in print (not included in section 184), proof-sheets, corrected proof-sheets, and manuscript copy accompanying the same, and postage shall be paid at the rate of one cent for each two ounces or fractional part thereof, and shall fully be prepaid by postage-stamps affixed to said matter. (Act of March 3, 1879, § 17, 20 Stat., p. 359.)

Sec. 216. Proof-sheets Defined.—The provisions of the preceding section relative to "proof-sheets" should not be construed so as to limit the corrections to be made to those of a typographical or merely verbal nature, such as the use of wrong letters, nor to the exclusion of any new matter which the author may desire to insert in order to put the intended publication in the form in which he desires it to be published. Any correction or change of words or sentences, or the insertion of entirely new sentences, if made for that purpose, does not affect its character as a corrected proof-sheet, nor subject it to a higher rate of postage. All marginal notes necessary to the execution of the work are allowable; but they should not extend beyond it and embrace matter of the nature of personal correspondence.

Sec. 217. Circulars Defined.—The term "circular" is defined to be a printed letter, which, according to internal evidence, is being sent in identical terms to several persons. A circular shall not lose its character as such when the date and the name of the addressed and of the sender shall be written therein, nor by the correction of mere typographical errors in writing. (Act of March 3, 1879, § 18, 20 Stat., p. 360.)

Sec. 218. Circulars mailed in bulk for Postmasters to Distribute.—When circulars, handbills, advertising sheets, transient newspapers, or any other printed matter of the third class, is sent in bulk from one post-office to another, with the intention of having them distributed throughout the boxes, or general delivery of the post-office to which they are addressed, or by letter-carriers, the bulk-package must not exceed four pounds in weight, and must be fully prepaid at the rate of one cent for each two ounces or fraction thereof, and the proper drop rate at the post-office of destination must be affixed by the sender to each separate circular or package.

Sec. 219. Printed Matter Defined.—"Printed matter" within the intendment of the law is defined to be the reproduction upon paper, by any process except that of handwriting, of any words, letters, characters, figures, or images, or of any combination thereof, not having the character of an actual and personal correspondence. (Act of March 3, 1879, § 19, 20 Stat., p. 360.)

Sec. 220. Manifolding and Type-writing not Printing.—No description of matter prepared by the "manifold process" or the "type-writer," can be regarded as a reproduction, and hence such matter cannot be transmitted in the mails at the rate for third-class matter.

Sec. 221. Fourth-class Matter.—Mailable matter of the fourth class shall embrace all matter not embraced in the first, second, or third class, which is not in its form or nature liable to destroy, deface, or otherwise damage the contents of the mail-bag, or harm the person of any one engaged in the postal service, and is not above the weight provided by law, which is hereby declared to be not exceeding four pounds for each package thereof, except in case of single books weighing in excess of that amount, and for books and documents published or circulated by order of Congress, or official matter emanating from any of the Departments of the Government, or from the Smithsonian Institution, or which is not declared non mailable under the provision of section [225] (*thirty-eight hundred and ninety-three of the Revised Statutes, as amended by the act of July* 12, 1876), or matter appertaining to lotteries, gift concerts, or fraudulent schemes or devices. (Act March 3, 1879, § 20, 20 Stat., p. 360.)

Sec. 222. Unmailable Matter.—Liquids, poisons, explosive and inflammable articles, fatty substances easily liquefiable, live or dead animals (not stuffed), live insects, and reptiles, fruits or vegetable matter liable to decomposition, comb honey, pastes or confections, guano, and other substances exhaling a bad odor, are regarded as in themselves, either from their form or nature, within the inhibitions of the preceding section, and under no circumstances must they be admitted to the mails.

Sec. 223. Precautions against Injury to the Mails.—Other articles of the fourth class which, unless properly secured, might destroy, deface, or otherwise damage the contents of the mail-bag, or harm the person of any one engaged in the postal service, may be transmitted in the mails when they conform to the following conditions:

1st. They must be placed in a bag, box, or removable envelope made of paper, cloth, or parchment.

2d. Such bag, box, or envelope must again be placed in a box or tube made of metal or some hard wood, with sliding, clasp, or screw lid.

3d. In case of articles liable to break, the inside box, bag, or envelope must be surrounded by sawdust, cotton, or spongy substance.

4th. In case of sharp-pointed instruments, the points must be capped or encased, so that they may not by any means be liable to cut through their inclosure, and where they have blades, such blades must be bound with wire, so that they shall remain firmly attached to each other.

5th. The whole must be capable of easy inspection. Seeds, or other articles not prohibited, which are liable, from their form or nature, to loss or damage, unless specially protected, may be put up in sealed envelopes, provided such envelopes are made of material sufficiently transparent to show the contents clearly, without opening.

Sec. 224. Postmasters Responsible for Admission of Improper Matter.—Postmasters will be expected to exercise the greatest care respecting the admission of articles of the fourth class to the mails. Whenever any article shall be offered for mailing which is not specially declared unmailable by the provisions of section 222, but which postmasters may regard as liable to injure the mails or harm the persons of those handling the same, even when complying with the conditions of the preceding section, they will refuse to receive such article for mailing.

Sec. 225. Obscene Matter Prohibited in the Mails.—Every obscene, lewd, or lascivious book, pamphlet, picture, paper, writing, print, or other publication of an indecent character, and every article or thing designed or intended for the prevention of conception or procuring of abortion, and every article or thing intended or adapted for any indecent or immoral use, and every written or printed card, circular, book, pamphlet, advertisement, or notice of any kind giving information directly or indirectly, where, or how, or of whom, or by what means, any of the hereinbefore mentioned matters, articles, or things may be obtained or made, and every letter upon the envelope of which, or postal card upon which, indecent, lewd, obscene, or lascivious delineations, epithets, terms, or language may be written or printed, are hereby declared to be non-mailable matter, and shall not be conveyed in the mails, nor delivered from any post-office nor by any letter-carrier; and any person who shall knowingly deposit, or cause to be deposited, for mailing or delivery, anything declared by this section to be non-mailable matter, and any person who shall knowingly take the same, or cause the same to be taken, from the mails for the purpose of circulating or disposing of, or of aiding in the circulation or disposition of the same, shall be deemed guilty of a misdemeanor, and shall for each and every offense be fined not less than one hundred dollars nor more than five thousand dollars, or imprisoned at hard labor not less than one year nor more than ten years, or both, at the discretion of the court. (R. S., § 3893, as amended by act of July 12, 1876, 19 Stat., p. 90.)

Sec. 226. Lottery Circulars Prohibited in the Mails.—It shall not be lawful to convey by mail, nor to deposit in a post-office to be sent by mail, any letters or circulars concerning lotteries, so-called gift concerts, or other similar enterprises offering prizes, or concerning schemes devised and intended to deceive and defraud the public for the purpose of obtaining money under false pretenses; and a penalty of not more than five hundred dollars, nor less than one hundred dollars, with costs of prosecution, is hereby imposed upon conviction, in any Federal courts, of the violation of this section. (R. S., § 3894, as amended by act of July 12, 1876, 19 Stat., p. 90.)

Sec. 227. Lottery Advertisements in Second-class Publications.—When a lottery advertisement is inserted in the columns of a regular issue of a newspaper, and sent from the office of publication or a news agency to *bona-fide* subscribers, such paper cannot be excluded from the mails under the law in regard to lotteries; but a part of such paper, or a supplement or extra thereof, or any other printed matter evidently issued and offered for mailing for the purpose of circulating a lottery advertisement, should be excluded from the mails.

Sec. 228. Postmasters Responsible for Admitting Obscene Matter to the Mails.—Postmasters will be expected to rigidly exclude from the mails any and all of the articles enumerated in section 225, and the Department will hold them accountable for any dereliction of duty respecting the plain provisions of that section. Whenever a postmaster is in doubt as to whether a publication, print, picture, pamphlet, book, or writing comes within the statute, he will submit the same to the First Assistant Postmaster-General and await his instructions.

Sec. 229. Postage on Fourth-class Matter.—All matter of the fourth class shall be subject to examination and to a postage charge at the rate of one cent an ounce or fraction thereof, to be prepaid by stamps affixed.—(Act March 3, 1879, § 21, 20 Stat., p. 360.)

Sec. 230. Treatment of Unmailable Matter Reaching its Destination.—If any matter excluded from the mails [*by the preceding section of this act*], except that declared non-mailable by section [225] (*thirty eight hundred and ninety-three of the Revised Statutes as amended*) shall, by inadvertence, reach the office of destination, the same shall be delivered in accordance with its address: *Provided*, That the party addressed shall furnish the name and address of the sender to the postmaster at the office of delivery, who shall immediately report the facts to the Postmaster-General. If the person addressed refuse to give the required information, the postmaster shall hold the package subject to the order of the Postmaster-General. All matter declared non-mailable by section 225 [*thirty-eight hundred and ninety-three of the Revised Statutes as amended*], which shall reach the office of delivery, shall be held by the postmaster at the said office subject to the order of the Postmaster-General. (Act of March 3, 1879, §. 21, 20 Stat., p. 360.)

See section 475.

Sec. 231. Permissible Additions to other than First-class Matter.—Mailable matter of the second class shall contain no writing, print, mark or sign thereon or therein, in addition to the original print, except as herein provided, to wit, the name and address of the person to whom the matter shall be sent, and index figures of subscription book, either written or printed, the printed title of the publication, the printed name and address of the publisher or sender of the same, and written or printed words or figures, or both, indicating the date on which the subscription to such matter will end. Upon matter of the third class, or upon the wrapper inclosing the same, the sender may write his own name or address thereon, with the word "from" above and preceding the same, and in either case may make simple marks intended to designate a word or passage of the text to which it is desired to call attention. There may be placed upon the cover or blank leaves of any book or of any printed matter of the third class a simple manuscript dedication or inscription that does not partake of the nature of a personal correspondence. Upon any package of matter of the fourth class the sender may write or print his own name and address, preceded by the word "from," and there may also be written or printed the number and names of the articles inclosed; and the sender thereof may write or print upon or attach to any such articles by tag or label, a mark, number, name, or letter, for purpose of identification. (Act of March 3, 1879, § 22, 20 Stat., p. 360.)

Sec. 232. Personal Correspondence Negatively Defined.—The character of personal correspondence referred to in the preceding section cannot be ascribed to the following, viz: 1st. To the signature of the sender or to the designation of his name, of his profession, of his rank, of the place of origin, and of the date of dispatch. 2d. To a dedication or mark of respect offered by the sender. 3d. To the figures or signs merely intended to mark the passage of a text, in order to call attention to them.

4th. To the prices added upon the quotations or prices current of exchange or markets, or in a book. 5th. To all printed commercial papers filled out in writing, such as papers of legal procedure, deeds of all kinds, way bills, or bills of lading, invoices, and the various documents of insurance companies, circulars, handbills, &c. 6th. To instructions or requests to postmasters to notify the sender in case of the non-delivery of other than first-class matter, so that he may send postage for its return. See section 465.

Sec. 233. Letter-postage and Penalty for Prohibited Writing or Printing.—Matter of the second, third, or fourth class, containing any writing or printing other than indicated in [*the preceding*] section [231 and 232], or made in the manner other than therein indicated shall not be delivered except upon the payment of postage for matter of the first class, deducting therefrom any amount which may have been prepaid by stamps affixed to such matter; and any person who shall conceal or inclose any matter of a higher class in that of a lower class, and deposit, or cause the same to be deposited, for conveyance by mail, at a less rate than would be charged for both such higher and lower class matter, shall, for every such offense, be liable to a penalty of ten dollars: *Provided, however*, That nothing herein contained shall be so construed as to prevent publishers of the second class and news-agents from inclosing, in their publications, bills, receipts, and orders for subscription thereto; but such bills, receipts, and orders shall be in such form as to convey no other information than the name, location, and subscription price of the publication or publications to which they refer. (Act of March 3, 1879, § 23, 20 Stat., p. 361.)

Sec. 234. Form of Bills Accompanying Second-class Matter.—Bills printed or written in substantially the following form are held by the Department to be within the intendments of the preceding section:

NEW YORK, ——, 187 .

Office of
The —— Weekly,
37 Park Row. P. O. Box, 4295.

To the —— Weekly, Dr.

Subscription, postage included, $3.20 in advance. Terms cash.
Remittances should be made by postal money order or draft on New York in name of

---

Received payment, 1879, for the —— Weekly.

No objection can be urged to a bill which includes the names of more than one publication, and their terms of subscription, provided they are all published by the same individual or company, or sent by the same news-agent. The bill may include any period of subscription or any number of shipments to a news-agent.

Sec. 235. Newspapers to be Wrapped and Sufficiently Dried.—No newspapers shall be received to be conveyed by mail unless they are sufficiently dried and inclosed in proper wrappers. (R. S., § 3883.)

Sec. 236. Manner of Presenting Second-class Matter for Mailing.—In mailing publications of the second class they should in all cases be properly dried, folded, and addressed. It is certainly no part of the duty of a postmaster or his assistants to fold newspapers so that they can be placed in the boxes, &c., for delivery; and in case a publisher persists in sending them without being properly folded, after being notified to put them up so that they can be promptly assorted and delivered, the postmaster would be justified in not distributing them with the regular mail.

Newspapers folded to the size of 9 by 12 inches are considered sufficiently folded so that they could be placed in the boxes of a post-office with little or no inconvenience.

Sec. 237. Manner of Presenting Third-class Matter for Mailing.—Printed matter must be either placed under band, upon a roller, between boards, in a case open at one side or at both ends, or in an unenclosed envelope, or simply closed in such a manner as not to conceal the nature of the packet, or, lastly, tied by a string easy to unfasten.

Address cards, and all printed matter presenting the form and consistency of an unfolded card, may be forwarded without band, envelope, fastening, or fold.

Sec. 238. What a Package of Third-class Matter May Contain.—A package of third-class matter may contain any number of articles of that class. All legitimate binding, mounting, or covering of a book, &c., or of a portion thereof, is permissible whether such binding, &c., be loose or attached; as also rollers in the case of prints or maps, markers (whether of paper or otherwise), in the case of books, pens, or pencils, in the case of pocketbooks, &c., and, in short, whatever is necessary for the safe transmission of such articles, or usually appertains thereto; but the binding, rollers, pens, or pencils, &c., must not be sent as separate packages at third-class rates.

Sec. 239. Free County Publications.—Publications of the second class, one copy to each actual subscriber residing in the county where the same are printed, in whole or in part, and published, shall go free through the mails; but the same shall not be delivered at letter-carrier offices, or distributed by carriers, unless postage is paid thereon at the rate prescribed in section [190]: *Provided*, That the rate of postage on newspapers (excepting weeklies) and periodicals not exceeding two ounces in weight, when the same are deposited in a letter-carrier office for delivery by its carriers, shall be uniform at one cent each; periodicals weighing more than two ounces shall be subject, when delivered by such carriers, to a postage of two cents each, and these rates shall be prepaid by stamps affixed. (Act of March 3, 1879, § 25, 20 Stat., p. 361.)

Sec. 240. Postage on Second-class Matter at Free-Delivery Post-Offices.—Mailable matter of the second class deposited in a letter-carrier post-office for local delivery shall be delivered through boxes or the general delivery on prepayment of postage at the rate of two cents per pound, but when delivered by carriers the following rates must be prepaid by postage-stamps affixed: on newspapers (except weeklies) one cent each without regard to weight; on periodicals not exceeding two ounces in weight, one cent each; on periodicals exceeding two ounces in weight, two cents each. The rate on weekly newspapers of the second class deposited by the publisher in a letter-carrier post-office for local delivery is two cents per pound, whether the same are delivered by carriers or through boxes or the general delivery.

Sec. 241. Second-class Matter at Free-Delivery Offices, how Separated.—Second-class matter for city delivery, where the carrier system is established, should be separately made up at the office of publication—that for delivery by the carriers of a post-office being put in one package or bundle—each article of mail-matter therein properly stamped, and that for delivery through the boxes of the post-office by itself. If the separation is not made at the office of publication, each paper or periodical not properly stamped must be placed in the boxes or at the general delivery for delivery therefrom.

Sec. 242. Free County Publications must be Mailed by Themselves.—When a publisher of a newspaper sends in the mails a package of his papers, a portion intended for subscribers residing within the county in which the paper is printed (in whole or in part) and published, and the remainder intended for subscribers residing in another county, he must pay postage on the entire package at the pound rates. The publisher should make two packages, one for the subscribers residing in the county and one for those out of the county, the former to go free under section 239.

Sec. 243. Publications with Offices in two Counties Free in Neither.—No publication of the second class claiming more than one office of publication in different counties is entitled to pass in the mails free in either county, unless the publisher elect which office he will regard as his office of publication. In that event the publication shall go free in that county only. The postmaster at the post-office thus selected should notify the postmaster at the other post-office of such selection. The provisions of this section are not applicable, however, to publications claiming or having more than one office of publication which do not claim free county circulation.

Sec. 244. Sample Copies of Free County Publications Subject to Postage.—Nothing in the act of March 3, 1879, can be so construed as to permit "sample copies" of any publication to be mailed free in the county where the same is printed or published; they must be prepaid at the rate of two cents for each pound.

Sec. 245. Congressional Documents Free of Postage.—Senators, Representatives, and Delegates in Congress, the Secretary of the Senate, and Clerk of the House of Representatives, may send and receive through the mail free, all public documents printed by order of Congress; and the name of each Senator, Representative, Delegate, Secretary of the Senate, and Clerk of the House shall be written thereon with the proper designation of the office he holds, and the provisions of this section shall apply to each of the persons named herein until the first Monday of December following the expiration of their respective terms of office. (Act of March 3, 1879, § 1, 20 Stat., p. 356.)

Sec. 246. Congressional Record, and Extracts therefrom, Free.—The Congressional Record, or any part thereof, or speeches or reports therein contained, shall, under the frank of a member of Congress, or delegate, to be written by himself, be carried in the mail free of postage under such regulations as the Postmaster-General may prescribe. (Act March 3, 1875, § 5, 19 Stat., p. 343.)

Sec. 247. Seeds and Reports from Agricultural Department Free.—Seeds transmitted by the Commissioner of Agriculture, or by any member of Congress or delegate receiving seeds for distribution from said Department, together with agricultural reports emanating from that Department, and so transmitted, shall, under such regulations as the Postmaster-General shall prescribe, pass through the mails free of charge. And the provisions of this section shall apply to ex-members of Congress and ex-delegates for the period of nine months after the expiration of their terms as members and delegates. (Act of March 3, 1875, § 7, 19 Stat., p. 343.)

Sec. 248. Remailing of Congressional Documents after one Delivery.—It is competent for Senators and Representatives and other persons entitled to the franking privilege to send, when properly franked under the provisions of the law, packages of unaddressed free matter in bulk to any person by mail, to be separately addressed and remailed from another post-office. But such remailing can only be done once, unless it becomes necessary to forward in order to reach the party addressed, in which case the regulations relating to the forwarding of prepaid letters shall apply to the franked package. Except in the case of free matter sent in franked packages in bulk to a person himself entitled to the franking privilege, each book, document or package entitled to be sent free in the mails must separately bear the frank of a Senator, Representative, or other person vested with the franking privilege.

Sec. 249. Letters, etc., on Government Business Free.—It shall be lawful to transmit through the mail, free of postage, any letters, packages, or other matters relating exclusively to the business of the Government of the United States: *Provided*, That every such letter or package to entitle it to pass free shall bear over the words "Official business" an indorsement showing also the name of the Department, and, if from a bureau or office, the names of the Department and bureau or office, as the case may be, whence transmitted. And if any person shall make use of any such official envelope to avoid the payment of postage on his private letter, package, or other matter in the mail, the person so offending shall be deemed guilty of a misdemeanor, and subject to a fine of three hundred dollars, to be prosecuted in any court of competent jurisdiction. (Act of March 3, 1877, § 5, 19 Stat., 335.)

Sec. 250. Penalty Envelopes for Official Matter.—For the purpose of carrying this act into effect, it shall be the duty of each of the Executive Departments of the United States to provide for itself and its subordinate offices the necessary envelopes; and in addition to the indorsement designating the Department in which they are to be used, the penalty for the unlawful use of these envelopes shall be stated thereon. (Act of March 3, 1877, § 6, 19 Stat., 335.)

Sec. 251. Extension of the two Preceding Sections.—The provisions of the [two preceding] [*fifth and sixth*] sections [*of the act entitled "An act establishing post-routes, and for other purposes," approved March third, eighteen hundred and seventy-seven*] for the transmission of official mail-matter, be, and they are hereby, extended to all officers of the United States Government, and made applicable to all official mail-matter transmitted between any of the officers of the United States, or between any such officer and either of the executive departments or officers of the government, the envelopes of such matter in all cases to bear appropriate indorsements containing the proper designation of the office from which the same is transmitted, with a statement of the penalty for their misuse. And the provisions of said fifth and sixth sections are hereby likewise extended and made applicable to all official mail-matter sent from the Smithsonian Institution: *Provided*, That this act shall not extend or apply to pension-agents or other officers who receive a fixed allowance as compensation for their services, including expenses for postage. (Act of March 3, 1879, § 29, 20 Stat., p. 362.)

The penalty-envelopes prescribed under this and the two preceding sections must be furnished by the various Departments at Washington to their subordinate officers throughout the country. Official penalty-labels to be affixed to mail matter may also be furnished in lieu of or in addition to the official penalty-envelopes. The effect of these three sections is to substitute for official postage-stamps and official stamped-envelopes furnished by the Post-Office Department, official penalty-envelopes and official penalty-labels furnished by each Department to its own subordinates.

CHAPTER FIVE.

SHIP AND STEAMBOAT LETTERS.

Sec. 252. Letters on Vessels to and from Foreign Ports.—The master of any vessel of the United States, bound from any port therein to any foreign port, or from any foreign port to any port of the United States, shall, before clearance, receive on board and securely convey all such mails as the Post-Office Department, or any diplomatic or consular office of the United States abroad, shall offer; and he shall promptly deliver the same, on arriving at the port of destination, to the proper officer, for which he shall receive two cents for every letter so delivered; and upon the entry of every such vessel returning from any foreign port, the master thereof shall make oath or affirmation that he has promptly delivered all the mail placed on board said vessel before clearance from the United States; and if he shall fail to make such oath or affirmation, the said vessel shall not be entitled to the privileges of a vessel of the United States. (R. S., § 3976.)

Sec. 253. Letters on Inland Steamboats.—The master of any steamboat passing between ports or places in the United States, and arriving at any such port or place where there is a post-office, shall deliver to the postmaster, within three hours after his arrival, if in the day-time, and if at night, within two hours after the next sunrise, all letters and packets brought by him, or within his power or control and not relating to the cargo, addressed to or destined for such port or place, for which he shall receive from the postmaster two cents for each letter or packet so delivered, unless the same is carried under a contract for carrying the mail; and for every failure to so deliver such letters and packets, the master or owner of said steamboat shall be liable to a penalty of one hundred and fifty dollars. (R. S. § 3977.)

Sec. 254. Payment for Ship-Letters.—The Postmaster-General may pay to the master or owner of any vessel not regularly employed in carrying the mail two cents for each letter carried by such vessel between ports or places in the United States, or from any foreign port to any port in the United States; but all such letters shall be deposited in the post-office at the port of arrival. (R. S., § 3978.)

Sec. 255. Double Postage on Ship-Letters.—All letters conveyed by vessels not regularly employed in carrying the mail shall, if for delivery within the United States, be rated with double postage, to cover the fee paid to the vessel. (R. S., § 3913.)

Sec. 256. Definition of Ship-Letters.—The terms *ship-letters* and *packets* embrace the letters and packets brought into the United States from foreign countries, or carried from one port in the United States to another, in any private ship or vessel not regularly employed in carrying the mail, and in the latter case over a route where the mail is not regularly carried, before such letters have been mailed.

Sec. 257. Manner of Collecting Ship-Fees.—The rates of postage are not to be increased on letters and packets carried in a private ship or vessel, from one port in the United States to another, though a part of the voyage be over a water declared to be a post-road. Thus, the Mississippi River, from New Orleans to the mouth, is a post-road; yet letters carried by ship between New Orleans and any other sea-port in the United States are subject to the usual ship-letter postage. But if the whole of the water between any two ports be a post-road by law, then inland postage will be charged. It is the special duty of the postmaster at a port where vessels may enter to see that this section is strictly observed and enforced. Every such postmaster will obtain from the master of the ship or vessel a certificate specifying the number of letters, with the name of the ship or vessel, and place from which she last sailed; and upon each letter which has not been before mailed, and which shall be delivered into his post-office for mailing or delivery, he shall pay to the said master or owner two cents, and take his receipt therefor.

Sec. 258. Rating up Postage on Ship-Letters.—At the post-office where deposited such letters will be charged with double rates of postage, to be collected at the office of delivery; that is to say, six cents for the single weight if mailed, and four cents the single weight if delivered at the post-office; but if such letter has been prepaid by United States stamps at such double rate of postage, no additional charge will be made, and all United States postage stamps affixed thereto will be recognized to the extent of their value as part payment.

Sec. 259. No Fee on Foreign-addressed Letters.—If such letter is addressed to any point in a foreign country, no fee will be allowed thereon by the postmaster to the carrier. Such letters, however, should all be marked "*Ship.*"

Sec. 260. No Fees to Passengers or Sailors.—If the letters be delivered into the post-office by a passenger or sailor, and not in behalf of the master, nothing is to be paid for them; they are, nevertheless, to be charged with double postage, and the number entered in the account of ship-letters, with the name of the vessel in which they were brought. They will then be forwarded as other ship-letters, the postage to be collected at the post-office of delivery.

Sec. 261. Letters on Mail-steamboats, how Disposed of.—All letters placed on a mail-steamboat, on which the mails are in charge of a route-agent, should go into the hands of such agent; and on these letters the master of the vessel is not entitled to receive any compensation. None but letters on which at least one full rate of postage has been paid should be received on such steamboat, and these should be duly mailed. But should any chance to be unpaid, they should be deposited by the route-agent in the post-office at the terminal point of his route, where the postmaster will treat them in all respects as other unpaid letters.

Sec. 262. Account of Ship and Steamboat Letters to be kept.—Letters brought by steamboats should be marked "Steamboat" at the time of receiving them, and postmasters will keep an account of both ship and steamboat letters received, stating the sums paid for them and the postage chargeable thereon.

Sec. 263. No Fees to Mail-Vessels.—No fees will be allowed to any vessel or to any person on board any vessel which carries the mail, nor to any mail-carrier on any mail-route by land or water.

Sec. 264. Printed Ship-Matter, how to be Treated.—Printed matter delivered to a postmaster by the master of a vessel arriving from a foreign port, and not regularly engaged in carrying the mail, which is wholly unpaid, shall be forwarded by such postmaster to its post-office of destination charged with double third-class rates of domestic postage, to be collected on delivery. No fee, however, shall be paid for such matter.

CHAPTER SIX.

DELIVERY OF ORDINARY MAIL-MATTER.—WITHDRAWAL BY SENDER FROM POST-OFFICE OF MATTER BEFORE ITS DISPATCH.

Sec. 265. Opening of Mails; Placing Matter on Delivery.—Upon the arrival of the mail at any post-office, the mail sacks and pouches, or the packages in a mail-bag addressed to that post-office, and none other, should be opened. Every postmaster, immediately upon the receipt of the mail, will, if possible, place the postmark of his post-office upon every letter received in the mail, showing the date and the hour of the day when the letters were received. He will then look over the letters or packages thus received to see if the postage thereon has been properly prepaid, noting on each letter or parcel the amount, if any, which is found to be due thereon, after which he will place the mail on delivery.

Sec. 266. Postmasters may Remove Wrappers of Packages.—Postmasters at the office of delivery may remove the wrappers and envelopes from mail-matter not charged with letter-postage, when it can be done without destroying them, for the purpose of ascertaining whether there is upon or connected with any such matter anything which would authorize or require the charge of a higher rate of postage thereon. (R. S., § 3882.)

Sec. 267. Double Postage on Unpaid Matter.—If any mail-matter, on which by law the postage is required to be prepaid at the mailing [post] office, shall by inadvertence reach its destination without such prepayment, double the prepaid rates shall be charged and collected on delivery. (R. S., § 3898.)

Sec. 268. Matter Cannot be Delivered until Postage Due is Paid.—No mail-matter shall be delivered until the postage due thereon has been paid. (R. S., § 3900.)

Sec. 269. Weight of Matter Determined at Post-Office of Mailing.—Inasmuch as, through evaporation or other cause, mail-matter not infrequently loses weight in transit, so that upon its arrival at the post-office of destination its weight may not correspond with that indicated by the postage rated up at the post-office of mailing, postmasters are instructed that the weight at time of mailing determines the rate of postage, and they should collect the postage marked due accordingly.

Sec. 270. Postage-due Stamps for Insufficiently-paid Matter.—All mail-matter of the first-class upon which one full rate of postage has been prepaid shall be forwarded to its destination, charged with the unpaid rate, to be collected on delivery; but postmasters, before delivering the same, or any article of mail-matter upon which prepayment in full has not been made, shall affix, or cause to be affixed, and canceled, as ordinary stamps are canceled, one or more stamps equivalent in value to the amount of postage due on such article of mail-matter, which stamp shall be of such special design and denomination as the Postmaster-General may prescribe, and which shall in no case be sold by any postmaster nor received by him in prepayment of postage. That in lieu of the commission now allowed to postmasters at [post] offices of the fourth class upon the amount of unpaid letter-postage collected, such postmaster shall receive a commission upon the amount of such special stamps so canceled, the same as now allowed upon postage stamps, stamped envelopes, postal cards, and newspaper and periodical stamps canceled as postages on matter actually mailed at their [post] offices: *Provided*, The Postmaster-General may, in his discretion, prescribe instead such regulation therefor at the [post] offices where free delivery is established as in his judgment the good of the service may require. (Act March 3, 1879, § 26, 20 Stat., p. 361.)

Sec. 271. Penalty for Failing to affix Postage-due Stamps.—Any postmaster or other person engaged in the postal service who shall collect, and fail to account for, the postage due upon any article of mail-matter which he may deliver, without having previously affixed and canceled such special stamps, as hereinbefore provided, or who shall fail to affix such stamp, shall be deemed guilty of a misdemeanor, and, on conviction thereof, shall be punished by a fine of fifty dollars. (Act March 3, 1879, § 27, 20 Stat., p. 362.)

Sec. 272. Time of affixing Postage-due Stamps.—At all post-offices where the free-delivery service has not been established, postmasters will not affix the postage-due stamps until the delivery of the matter has been requested. At all free-delivery post-offices, matter which has not been sufficiently prepaid will be rated up, and postage-due stamps of the necessary denominations will be affixed as soon as the matter is received at the post-office, unless an order is on file for a letter to be forwarded, in which case it will be forwarded without affixing the postage-due stamp.

Sec. 273. Treatment of Undelivered Matter with Postage-due Stamps thereon.—After the postage-due stamps have been affixed at free-delivery post-offices, such matter as may be refused, unclaimed, or cannot be delivered must be treated as required by the regulations. When sent to the Dead-Letter Office, credit must be claimed on the dead-letter bill for "postage-due stamps canceled on undelivered mail-matter." When returned to writer or redirected to another post-office within the United States, a numbered postage-due bill, stating amount due and name of person from whom it is to be collected, must be attached to and sent with each letter.

Sec. 274. Postage-due Stamps on Forwarded Letters, how Refunded.—When a returned or forwarded letter, with postage-due stamps affixed and bill attached, is received at any post-office from a free-delivery post-office, the receiving postmaster must detach the bill and return it by next mail, with required amount of uncanceled stamps inclosed, to the issuing postmaster. In case of failure to get a return of a bill or stamps after a reasonable delay, postmasters at free-delivery post-offices may obtain the proper credit and expose the delinquent receiving postmaster by making a duplicate bill (from the stub of the original), which they will attach to and incorporate in their regular dead-letter bill. This duplicate must be indorsed, in the blank space at the end, DUPLICATE, ORIGINAL NOT RETURNED, or ORIGINAL RETURNED WITHOUT STAMPS. In forwarding to foreign countries mail-matter on which postage-due stamps have been canceled, the original bill, indorsed FOREIGN LETTER FORWARDED, must be attached to and incorporated in the regular dead-letter bill.

Sec. 275. What Persons are entitled to receive Mail-matter.—The persons entitled to articles of mail-matter received by mail are those whose names are in the address, and the delivery should be either to the person addressed, or according to his or her order. The order is in some cases implied, as where a person is in the habit of receiving his mail through his son, clerk, or servant, and of recognizing the delivery to him. Mail-matter addressed to a firm may be delivered to any member of the firm, and, if addressed to several persons, may be handed to any one of them.

Sec. 276. Letters addressed to Fictitious Persons, etc.—Letters and packages addressed to fictitious persons or firms, to initials, or to no particular person or firm, unless directed to be delivered at a designated place, as a post-office box, street and number, or to the care of a certain person or firm, or other certain place of delivery, within the delivery of the post-office to which they are addressed, must be returned at the end of each month to the Dead-Letter Office.

Sec. 277. Proof of Identity required in Doubtful Cases.—A postmaster should, in all cases of doubt, require satisfactory proof of the identity of persons claiming mail-matter addressed for delivery at the post-office. Great care must be especially taken where such matter appears to be of value, and if the person calling for it be not the person addressed, or a member of his immediate family, it is safest to require a written order for its delivery.

Sec. 278. Letters "Opened through Mistake."—If there be two or more persons of the same name, and a letter intended for one is delivered to another, and returned by him, the postmaster will reseal the letter in the presence of the person who opened it, and request him to write upon it the words, OPENED BY ME THROUGH MISTAKE, and sign his name; he will then replace the letter in the post-office.

Sec. 279. Mail-matter addressed to other Post-Offices not Deliverable.—Postmasters cannot deliver mail-matter which may be addressed to and deliverable from other post-offices, except in cases of matter addressed to a discontinued post-office nearest the post-office where such matter is held for delivery. Exception to this rule may be made in special cases, as when a letter arrives from a foreign country directed to a post-office other than that at the port of arrival, and the person addressed is about to leave the country, or desires to answer at once by mail from that port. In such cases the postmaster, on being satisfied of the identity of the applicant, may deliver the letter. Exceptions may also be made in the case of ambassadors and other diplomatic representatives of foreign governments who may be temporarily residing elsewhere than within the delivery of the post-office to which their correspondence is directed. In the exceptional cases above provided for, the postmaster who delivers the letters shall report his action to the postmaster of the post-office to which they are directed.

Sec. 280. Mail-matter addressed in Care of Another.—Where mail-matter reaches a post-office addressed to a person in care of another, it is the duty of the postmaster to deliver such matter to the person addressed, if so requested by him, rather than to the person to whose care it was addressed.

Sec. 281. Letters from the Pension Office.—It is not proper to deliver a letter from the Pension Office to any one other than the person addressed, or to a member of his or her family, or to a legal guardian of the pensioner, and under no circumstances is it allowable to deliver such letters to an attorney, claim-agent, or broker.

Sec. 282. Under no Pretext are Letters in the Mail to be opened.—A letter once placed in the post-office is in the custody of the Department for transmission and delivery to the party addressed. Neither postmasters nor officers of the law have any authority to open it under the pretext that there might be something improper or even criminal in it, or that would aid in the detection, or furnish evidence for the conviction, of offenders against the law. A letter of a criminal must, therefore, be delivered to him unless he may otherwise direct.

Sec. 283. Mail-Matter to be delivered according to Official Designation.—Mail-matter directed to a public official by his title, or to an officer of a corporation, or person holding a position therein having an official designation, should be delivered to the person actually holding the office or other position designated in the address, notwithstanding the name of another person may also appear therein, the presumptive intention of the sender being that the article of mail-matter shall reach the officer, etc., addressed rather than the individual named.

Sec. 284. Mail-Matter addressed to Minors.—In the case of minor children residing with their parents, and dependent upon them for maintenance and support, such parents are entitled to control the correspondence of the aforesaid minors by directing the disposition to be made of mail-matter addressed to them, and where such minors reside temporarily away from their parents, the latter may delegate to another the right to receive mail-matter addressed to such minors, but such person must show to the postmaster written authority to receive the same before it can be delivered to him.

Sec. 285. Mail-Matter addressed to Deceased Persons.—Mail-matter addressed to a deceased person must in the first instance be delivered to his legal representatives. In case there are no legal representatives the letters should be delivered to the widow, if there be one, unless there are other claimants for the same, in which event the postmaster should report the case with all the facts to the First Assistant Postmaster-General and await his instructions.

Sec. 286. Mail-Matter to be delivered to Assignees, etc.—When the business of a firm has been placed in the hands of an assignee or receiver, its letters should be delivered to the latter, on his presentation of proof of his appointment by a court or other competent authority.

Sec. 287. Mail-Matter addressed to a Defunct Firm or Corporation.—Mail-matter addressed to a firm or corporation which has ceased to exist must be delivered to the legal representatives.

Sec. 288. Postmaster to require Appointment of Receiver.—When a firm or company dissolves partnership, and contention arises as to whom the mail-matter addressed to the former business firm or company, or its officials, shall be delivered, a postmaster, being forbidden by one party to deliver to another, should require the appointment of a receiver, retaining all mail-matter until said receiver is appointed; and if no such receiver is appointed, or no agreement between the contending parties is reached, before the expiration of thirty days from the date when delivery ceased, the letters in dispute, and all that may arrive thereafter (until an agreement is made or receiver appointed), shall be sent to the Return-Letter Office marked IN DISPUTE.

Sec. 289. Decision of Disputed Claims to Mail-matter.—A postmaster is not required to decide disputes between members of a dissolved or existing firm as to the delivery of its mail-matter. If the firm is not dissolved, he should, if its mail has habitually been delivered by carrier, continue such delivery, instructing the carrier to hand the mail-matter to any of its members. If the delivery is through box or general delivery, he will place the mail-matter therein to await the call of any authorized person. If the firm is dissolved, he will be governed in his action by the provisions of the preceding section.

Sec. 290. Injunction of Courts to be respected.—Where mail-matter may be addressed to a firm which has ceased to exist, and having reached its destination through the mails is claimed by different parties, and some of the claimants in order to determine their rights in the premises subsequently institute a suit against the others in the local courts, and obtain an order from the court enjoining the postmaster from delivering the mail-matter to either party, the postmaster should respect the order of the court by retaining the same and delivering it to the parties who shall be finally determined by the court to be legally entitled to it.

Sec. 291. Withdrawal of Letters from Mailing Post-office.—To prevent fraud the postmaster must not permit any letter put into his post-office for transmission by mail to be withdrawn by any person except the writer thereof, or, in case of a minor child, the parent or guardian of the same; and the utmost care must be taken to ascertain that the person applying for such letter is really the writer, parent, or guardian.

Sec. 292. Proof of Identity of Letter required.—To enable him to know that the person applying for the withdrawal of a letter is the writer, the postmaster may require him, or his messenger, to exhibit to him the same superscription and seal that are upon the letter. And if the postmaster is satisfied that the handwriting and seal are the same, he will permit the letter to be withdrawn, taking a receipt, and preserving it with the paper containing the superscription, and the order, if one were sent. If the person applying for the letter is the parent or guardian of the minor, the postmaster must require him to identify the particular letter by extrinsic evidence satisfactory to the postmaster.

Sec. 293. When to refuse Application for Withdrawal.—Postmasters should refuse all applications for the withdrawal of letters in cases where the necessary search would involve the delay of a mail, or retard the regular work of the post-office.

Sec. 294. Mail-matter beyond Mailing Post-office cannot be withdrawn.—After a letter, or any other article of mail-matter, has passed from the mailing post-office, the delivery of it cannot be prevented or delayed by any one except upon the order of the Postmaster-General, to whom direct application must be made by the writer.

CHAPTER SEVEN.

LETTER-BOXES IN POST-OFFICES.

Sec. 295. Postmasters may erect Boxes at their own Expense.—Any postmaster in other than a building owned by the United States may erect boxes in his post-office at his own expense. These boxes are neither owned nor repaired by the Department, but the revenues thereof must be reported quarterly to the Auditor of the Treasury for the Post-Office Department.

Sec. 296. Lock-boxes, etc., for Box-holders at their Expense.—Postmasters may allow box-holders who desire to do so to provide lock-boxes or drawers for their own use, at their own expense, which lock-boxes or drawers, upon their erection in any post-office, shall become the property of the United States, and be subject to the direction and control of the Post-Office Department, and shall pay a rental at least equal to that of other boxes in the same [post] office, or, if there be no other boxes in such [post] office, of boxes in other [post] offices of the same class, which rental shall be accounted for as other box-rents. (R. S., § 4052.)

Sec. 297. Friends of Owner of Box to use same, when.—Letters addressed to the friends of the owner of a box stopping temporarily with him may also be placed in the box, if directed to his care or to the number of the box. But letters addressed to other persons residing in the same place, and living and doing business separate and apart from a box-holder, should *not* be placed in such box.

Sec. 298. Postmasters to keep a List of Box-holders.—Each postmaster must keep a list of all box-holders, with the number of the box assigned to each, and the time during which he has used it. This list will be examined by special agents, and be delivered to his successor in office. The postmaster must state in his quarterly returns the amount of box-rents collected in or on account of each quarter.

• **Sec. 299. Failure of Postmasters to make Report of Box-rents.**—The salaries of postmasters are based upon a sworn statement of the operations of their post-offices for the four quarters immediately preceding the adjustment or readjustment furnished to the First Assistant Postmaster-General. When the postmaster fails to make any report, or reports a less amount of box-rents than that included in his salary, he is charged in the adjustment of his quarterly return, by the Auditor, with the full amount of box-rents included in his quarterly salary.

Sec. 300. Rent of Boxes to be prepaid.—No box at any post-office shall be assigned to the use of any person until the rent thereof has been paid for at least one quarter in advance, for which the postmaster shall give a receipt. (R. S., § 3901.)

Sec. 301. Payment for Boxes must be Quarterly.—Postmasters must rent the boxes and drawers in their post-offices for one quarter (three months) only, the money to be paid in advance. The Department will insist upon a strict compliance with this regulation. Boxes remaining unpaid for ten days from the expiration of a quarter will be declared vacated.

Sec. 302. Box to be restricted to Use of one Family, etc.—A person renting a post-office box is entitled to have the letters of his family put into it. Each box must be restricted to the use of one family, firm, or corporation.

Sec. 303. Postmaster to leave Record of Box-receipts with Successor.—When a postmaster retires from office he must leave in the hands of his successor a record of receipts given for payment of box-rents. In the absence of this record, the postmaster will require the parties claiming to have paid their box-rents to show their receipts, or produce other satisfactory evidence of such payment. When an individual holds a receipt from the late postmaster for box-rent paid, it is the duty of the new postmaster to furnish a box for the time specified in the receipt.

Sec. 304. Postmaster should refuse to rent Box for Improper Purpose.—A postmaster should refuse to rent a box or drawer to any person whom he has reason to suspect would use the same for the promotion of any indecent or illegal purpose. Whenever he shall find that any person to whom he has rented a box or drawer is using the same for the promotion of any such purpose, he should withhold its further use from him, returning to him at the same time a proportionate amount of the rent for the unexpired portion of the quarter.

Sec. 305. Rent for Private Boxes.—So long as persons who own boxes in post-offices permit them to remain, it is the duty of the postmaster to collect rent for those that are used.

Sec. 306. Postmasters not to disclose Names of Boxholders.—Postmasters are strictly prohibited from disclosing to any person the names of the persons owning or renting boxes in their post-offices.

CHAPTER EIGHT.

CARRIERS, FREE DELIVERY AND BRANCH OFFICES, AND STREET MAILING-BOXES.

☞ For provisions respecting postage on second-class matter at carrier post-offices, see Title II, Chapter Four.

☞ For provisions for the collection of unpaid postage at such post-offices, see Title II, Chapter Six.

Sec. 307. Letter-carrier Post-offices.—Letter-carriers shall be employed for the free delivery of mail-matter as frequently as the public convenience may require, at every place containing a population of fifty thousand within the delivery of its post-office, and may be so employed at every place containing a population of not less than twenty thousand within its corporate limits, and at post-offices which produced a gross revenue for the preceding fiscal year of not less than twenty thousand dollars: *Provided*, This act shall not affect the free delivery in towns and cities where it is now established. (Act of February 21, 1879, § 5, 20 Stat., p. 317.)

Sec. 308. Districting of Cities.—Cities must be so districted as to secure the full, equal, and most advantageous employment of the carriers, and the earliest practicable delivery and collection of the mails.

Sec. 309. Classification of Carriers.—For the more equitable compensation of letter-carriers there shall be in all cities which contain a population of seventy-five thousand or more two classes of letter-carriers, to be fixed by the Postmaster-General. (Act February 21, 1879, § 1, 20 Stat., p. 317.)

Sec. 310. Salaries of Carriers.—The salaries of carriers of the first class, who shall have been in service at least one year, shall be one thousand dollars per annum, and the salaries of the carriers of the second class shall be eight hundred dollars per annum. In all cities containing a population of less than seventy-five thousand there shall be one class of letter-carriers, who shall receive a salary of eight hundred and fifty dollars per annum.* (Act February 21, 1879, § 2, 20 Stat., p. 317.)

Sec. 311. Auxiliary Carriers.—Upon the recommendation of the postmaster of any city, the Postmaster-General may establish a third grade of letter-carriers known as auxiliaries, who shall be paid at the rate of four hundred dollars per annum. (Act February 21, 1879, § 3, 20 Stat., p. 317.)

Sec. 312. Appointments and Promotions.—Appointments of letter-carriers in cities having two or more classes shall be made to the class having the minimum rate of pay, and promotions from the lower grades in said cities shall be made to the higher grades to fill vacancies, after one or more years' services, on certificate of the postmaster to the efficiency and faithfulness of the candidate during the preceding year: *Provided, however*, That at no time shall the number of carriers in the first class, receiving the maximum salary of one thousand dollars, be more than two-thirds or less than one-half the whole number of carriers actually in service in the city in which they are employed: *Provided, further*, That no boxes for the collection of mail-matter by carriers shall be placed inside of any building except a public building or railroad station. (Act Feb. 21, 1879, § 4, 20 Stat., p. 317.)

Sec. 313. Public Buildings Described.—No street mailing-box shall be placed inside any building which is not at all hours open to the public and accessible to the carriers. Postmasters may (subject to the above conditions) in their discretion

* Until an appropriation shall be made, in accordance with the provisions of section 310, the following regulation will remain in force:

The salaries of letter-carriers are fixed by the Postmaster-General at the time of their appointment. Increased pay is granted to carriers, from time to time, when the appropriation will justify it, on application of the postmaster to the First Assistant Postmaster-General, setting forth the diligence, fidelity, and experience of the carrier in whose behalf the application is made.

place such boxes within the halls or corridors on the ground-floor of large hotels, and in commercial exchanges, but are forbidden to place them within club-houses, private residences, stores, or offices of business corporations.

Sec. 314. Number of Carriers Limited.—It shall be the duty of the Postmaster-General to carefully inquire into the number of carriers employed in the several cities where the free delivery of mail-matter is established, and to reduce the number of carriers, and the number of deliveries of mails by such carriers for each day to the reasonable requirements of the public service. (Act of March 3, 1877, 19 Stat., p. 384.)

Sec. 315. Letter-carriers' Bonds.—Every letter-carrier shall give bonds, with sureties to be approved by the Postmaster-General, for the safe custody and delivery of all mail-matter, and the faithful account and payment of all money received by him. (R. S., § 3870.)

Sec. 316. Applications for the Carrier System.—Application for the establishment of the carrier system, or for additional carriers, must be made to the First Assistant Postmaster-General, with the reasons therefor.

Sec. 317. How Carriers are Appointed.—Letter-carriers are appointed by the Postmaster-General, on the nomination and recommendation of the local postmaster

Sec. 318. Qualifications for Appointment.—Persons nominated for appointment as letter-carriers must be over twenty-one years of age and under thirty-five. They must be intelligent, temperate, and physically fitted for the service, and must be able to read and write and understand the fundamental rules of arithmetic.

Sec. 319. Form of Application for Appointment.—Applications for the appointment of carriers must state the name in full (plainly written), age, previous occupation, proposed time of commencing service, and the qualifications required in the preceding section.

Sec. 320. Return of Oaths and Bonds.—Blank oaths and bonds sent with the letter of appointment of carriers must be promptly and correctly executed, and returned to the First Assistant Postmaster-General.

Sec. 321. Appointment of Substitutes.—Substitute letter-carriers are appointed when postmasters so advise, at a nominal salary of one dollar a year, and receive the pro-rata pay of the carrier whose route they may be called upon to serve, without regard to the cause of the absence of the regular carrier or his salary. Substitutes appointed by the Department are paid out of the salary of the absent carrier.

Sec. 322. Postmasters may Fill Temporary Vacancies.—Vacanies occurring by death, illness, or other unavoidable causes, may be filled temporarily by postmasters, when the exigencies of the service demand it; but a full statement of the facts must be immediately forwarded to the First Assistant Postmaster-General. Carriers must, however, in every instance, take the oath of office before entering on duty.

Sec. 323. Employment of Additional Carriers.—Additional letter-carriers must not be employed until postmasters are notified of their appointment, and they have qualified by executing the oath and bond required by law.

Sec. 324. Duties of Carriers generally.—Carriers shall be employed in the delivery and collection of mail-matter, or, during the intervals between their trips, may be employed in the post-office in such manner as the postmaster may direct.

Sec. 325. Leaves of Absence without Pay.—Postmasters may grant leave of absence to carriers without pay in cases of illness, disability received in the service, or other urgent necessity, to continue only during the urgency of the case, provided it shall in no instance exceed thirty days. For a longer time, application, setting forth all the circumstances, must be made to the First Assistant Postmater-General.

Sec. 326. Penalty for Absence without Leave.—A carrier absenting himself without leave will forfeit his pay during the time of such absence, and will be reprimanded by the postmaster, or reported to the First Assistant Postmaster-General for removal, as the circumstances may require.

Sec. 327. Carriers' Uniform, and Penalty for Wearing it Unlawfully.—The Postmaster-General may prescribe a uniform dress to be worn by letter-carriers, and any person not connected with the letter-carrier branch of the postal service who shall wear the uniform which may be prescribed shall, for every such offense, be punishable by a fine of not more than one hundred dollars, or by imprisonment for not more than six months, or both. (R. S., § 3867.)

Sec. 328. The Uniform prescribed for Carriers.—The Postmaster-General, under the preceding section, prescribes the following uniform dress, to be invariably worn while on duty, viz:

FOR WINTER WEAR.

First. A single-breasted sack-coat of "cadet-gray," or, technically, "blue-mixed cadet cloth," terminating two-thirds the distance from the top of the hip-bone to the knee, with a pocket at each side, and one on left breast—all outside—with flaps two and three-fourths to three inches wide, with length to suit, say six and a half to seven inches; coat to be bound entirely around with good plain black alpaca binding one inch wide, to be put over half edges, with five brass buttons, with the design of the seal of this Department (post-rider, with mail-bag across the saddle, with the letters P. O. D. beneath), down the front, to button up to the neck, and one-half inch black braid round the sleeves two and a half inches from the bottom.

Second. Pants of same material and color, with fine black broadcloth stripe one inch wide down the outside seam.

Third. A single-breasted vest of the same material and color, with seven oval brass buttons (vest size), with the letters P. O. upon the face.

Fourth. Cap of the same material and color (Navy pattern), bound round with a fine black-cloth band one and one-half inches wide, with small-size buttons at the sides, of the same material and design as those on the vest, and glazed cover for wet weather.

Fifth. A reversible cape (detached from the coat) reaching to the cuff of the coat sleeve when the arm is extended, of the same material and color on one side, and gutta-percha cloth on the other side, with five buttons, the same as on the coat, down the front, and bound entirely round with plain black alpaca binding one inch wide, put half over edges; or an overcoat of the same material and color, trimmed to correspond with the coat, with five brass buttons, of the same size and design as the coat button, down the front. It shall not be obligatory on the carriers to wear either, but whenever additional covering is needed, the postmaster of each city will decide, in accordance with the wishes of a majority of the carriers, which they shall wear, as both must not be worn in the same city.

FOR SUMMER WEAR.

First. Coat, single-breasted, skeleton sack, of gray flannel, terminating two-thirds the distance from the top of the hip-bone to the knee; with lapels (medium roll) made to button over the breast; three pockets, outside, without flaps, one on each side, and one on left breast. Coat to be bound entirely round with plain black alpaca binding one inch wide, put half over edges, and three buttons of present regulation style down front.

Second. Pants, same material and color, with stripe of black alpaca binding one inch wide down the outside seam.

Third. Vest, same material and color, bound same as coat, with collar cut to roll same height as coat, and five regulation buttons down front.

Fourth. Panama hat.

Sec. 329. Carriers Supply their own Uniforms.—Letter-carriers must procure the uniforms at their own expense, but the postmaster is expected to give his personal attention to the matter, and afford the "trade" an opportunity to furnish them at the least expense to the carriers, consistent with a proper execution of the requirements of the above section.

Sec. 330. Behavior required of Carriers.—Carriers must invariably appear on duty in their uniforms, and must wear their satchels while on their rounds. They must be civil, prompt, and faithful in the discharge of their duties.

Sec. 331. Carriers not to Contract Debts on their Routes.—Carriers who borrow money on their routes, or otherwise contract debts, which they are unable to pay, will render themselves liable to severe censure or dismissal from the service, according to the aggravation of the case.

Sec. 332. Carriers not to Solicit Contributions, etc.—Letter-carriers are forbidden to solicit contributions of money, gifts, or presents, in person or through others; to issue addresses, complimentary cards, prints, publications, or any substitute therefor, intended or calculated to induce the public to make them gifts or presents; to sell tickets on their routes to theaters, concerts, balls, fairs, picnics, excursions, or places of amusement or entertainment of any kind, or to deliver any matter while on their routes, except such as may be intrusted to them in the regular course of business.

Sec. 333. Establishment of Street Mailing-boxes.—The Postmaster-General may establish, in places where letter-carriers are employed, and in other places where, in his judgment, the public convenience requires it, receiving-boxes for the deposit of mail-matter, and shall cause the matter deposited therein to be collected as often as public convenience may require. (R. S., §3868.) See section 312.

Sec. 334. Penalty for Injuring Street Mailing-boxes.—Every person who willfully and maliciously injures, tears down, or destroys any letter-box, pillar-box, or other receptacle established by the Postmaster General for the safe deposit of matter for the mail or for delivery, or who willfully and maliciously assaults any letter-carrier, when in uniform, while engaged on his route in the discharge of his duty as a letter-carrier, and every person who willfully aids or assists therein, shall for every such offense be punishable by a fine of not less than one hundred dollars, and not more than one thousand, or by imprisonment for not less than one year and not more than three. (R. S., §3869.)

Sec. 335. Carriers must report Injuries to Street Mailing-boxes.—Carriers will report to the postmaster the commission of any of the offenses provided against in the preceding section which may come to their knowledge, who, if he deems it of sufficient importance, will confer with the United States attorney and take such steps as he may advise.

Sec. 336. Establishment of Branch Post-offices.—The Postmaster-General, when the public convenience requires it, may establish within any post-office delivery one or more branch offices for the receipt and delivery of mail-matter and the sale of stamps and envelopes; and he shall prescribe the rules and regulations for the government thereof. But no letter shall be sent for delivery to any branch office contrary to the request of the party to whom it is addressed. (R. S., 3871.)

Sec. 337. No Carriers' Fee permitted.—No extra postage or carriers' fee shall be charged or collected upon any mail-matter collected or delivered by carriers. (R. S., § 3873.)

Sec. 338. The general Delivery to be Discouraged.—Persons calling at the stations for their mails must be requested to leave their address, and informed that their letters will be promptly sent to them by carrier, free of charge. But as instances may occur in which this rule might work great inconvenience, the superintendent, or, in his absence, the officer in charge, may in such cases deliver letters to the party calling.

Sec. 339. Accounts at Carrier Post-offices.—All expenses of letter-carriers, branch offices, and receiving-boxes, or incident thereto, shall be kept and reported in a separate account, and shall be shown in comparison with the proceeds from postage on local mail-matter at each office, and the Postmaster-General shall be guided in the expenditures for this branch of the service by the income derived therefrom. (R. S., § 3874.)

Sec. 340. Postmasters' reports of Operations.—Postmasters must forward a report of the operations of the carrier system, as required by the preceding section, as early after the close of each month as practicable, to the First Assistant Postmaster-General. The blanks furnished for this purpose must be used.

Sec. 341. Postmasters' Reports of Expenses.—Postmasters will report quarterly to the Auditor of the Treasury for the Post-Office Department, and monthly to the First Assistant Postmaster-General, on blanks furnished by the Department, the several items of expense enumerated in section 339. The pay-roll of letter-carriers, and the account of incidental expenses of the system, must be promptly transmitted to the Auditor at the close of each quarter, accompanied by a voucher for each bill paid, together with an affidavit that the expenditures were necessary, and the prices paid reasonable. The carriers' pay-roll must state the names of the substitute carriers (other than those appointed by the Department), or carriers employed temporarily, for whom and how long they served, the necessity for their employment, and the amount paid them, with a voucher for each payment.

Sec. 342. Rules for Delivery of Matter.—The mails must be assorted and the carriers started on their first daily trip as early as practicable. Mail-matter directed to box-numbers must be delivered through the boxes. Mail-matter directed to street and number must be delivered by carriers, unless otherwise directed. Mail-matter directed neither to a box-holder nor to a street and number, must be delivered by carrier if its address is known or can be ascertained from the city directory; otherwise, at the general delivery.

Sec. 343. Matter not to be Delivered at Unoccupied Premises.—Carriers must not deliver letters in boxes or other receptacles at premises not occupied, in whole or in part, by the persons to whom the letters are addressed, except by the special order of the postmaster.

Sec. 344. Matter not to be Delivered in the Street.—A mail-carrier is forbidden to deliver mail-matter in the streets, even to the owners, but must deliver all matter at the houses to which it is addressed.

Sec. 345. Transient or "to-be-called-for" Letters, how treated.—Letters having as a part of their address the words "transient," "to be called for," or other words indicating that they are intended for transient persons, must be sent to the general delivery, to be delivered on application after proper identification. Letters so directed shall not be delivered by letter-carriers unless on an order from the party addressed. Other letters without street and number or box number, shall be considered as transient, and sent to the general delivery, unless addressed to some person whose address is known to the distributing clerks or to the carriers. While trial search, by directory or otherwise, is being made, the letter shall be subject to inquiry and delivery through the general delivery, and should not be delayed by taking it from the post-office.

Sec. 346. City Directory to be Used to Ascertain Addresses, when.—In cities where a directory is published it must be used when necessary to ascertain the address of persons to whom letters are directed (and it should also be used in the case of transient newspapers and other matter of the third and fourth classes, where the error in or omission of street address is evidently the result of inadvertence or ignorance); but when circulars, printed postal cards, or other matter (except letters) shall arrive at any post-office in large quantities, which have apparently all been sent by the same person or firm, and from which the street addresses have been purposely omitted, the directory need not be used to supply such omission, and all of such circulars, etc., which cannot be readily delivered through boxes or by carriers shall be sent to general delivery to await call.

Sec. 347. Carriers to Receive Letters for Mailing.—Carriers are required, while on their rounds, to receive all letters prepaid by postage-stamps that may be handed to them for mailing, but are strictly forbidden to delay their deliveries by waiting for such letters, or to receive money to pay postage on letters handed them for mailing.

Sec. 348. What Carriers may not do.—Carriers are forbidden to deliver any mailable matter which has not passed through the post-office or station with which they are connected, or to exhibit any mail-matter intrusted to them (except on the order of the postmaster or some one authorized to act for him) to persons other than those addressed, or to deviate from their respective routes, or to carry letters in their pockets, or to engage in any business not connected with this service during their hours of business.

Sec. 349. Return of Undelivered Matter.—Every letter or package that cannot be delivered shall be returned to the post-office or station by the carrier, who shall write upon it the reason for its non-delivery, the initials of his name, and the number of his district.

Sec. 350. Holiday and Evening Delivery.—The windows in connection with the carriers' department must be opened for the delivery of mail-matter during office-hours on Sundays, holidays, and in the evening after the last street delivery.

Sec. 351. Tests of Carriers' Efficiency.—The delivery and collection of mail-matter must be tested at frequent and irregular intervals, and carriers must be held to a strict accountability for any omission or neglect in these particulars.

Sec. 352. Prompt and Frequent Deliveries Required.—The number of daily delivery and collection trips by carriers must not be reduced without the authorization of the Department. Letters must be frequently and promptly delivered by the carriers, so that citizens may have no inducement to call at the post-office. Citizens supplied by carriers should be induced to provide receiving-boxes at their houses and places of business.

Sec. 353. Limited Sale of Stamps by Carriers.—Postmasters must not require nor permit carriers to sell postage-stamps or stamped-envelopes, except in limited quantities; but under no circumstances must they delay their deliveries or collections to make change.

Sec. 354. Branch Post-offices or Postal Stations.—Application for the establishment of branch post-offices or postal stations must be made to the First Assistant Postmaster-General, setting forth in full the necessity and expense thereof.

Sec. 355. Mails between Stations and the General Post-Office.—The mails from the post-office to the stations, and return, must be conveyed with the greatest practicable dispatch, and by the most expeditious routes.

Sec. 356. Advertised Letters.—The advertised list of letters must designate those remaining at the post-office, and those remaining at each station. Such letters must be delivered when called for, and the addressees informed that, if they will leave their address, their letters will in future be promptly sent to them by carriers, free of charge.

Sec. 357. Care of Street Mailing-Boxes.—Street mailing-boxes must be kept in repair, and in a neat condition, and firmly fastened to the post. A list must be kept in the post-office of their number and location.

Sec. 358. Postmasters to inspect Stations.—The stations must be frequently visited by the postmaster, or by some one designated by him, who shall see that these regulations are enforced, and that proper order and discipline are maintained.

Sec. 359. Carriers' Daily Return of Property and Mail.—After the last daily delivery, the carriers must return their satchels, keys, and all the mail-matter they cannot deliver to the post-office or station with which they are connected. Carriers must be held to the strictest accountability for the keys to the street mailing-boxes intrusted to them, the loss of which will be regarded as a grave offense, and render them liable to removal.

Sec. 360. Carriers must not return Deposited Letters.—Carriers are forbidden, under any circumstances, to return to any person whatever letters deposited in the street mailing-boxes.

Sec. 361. Delivery of Registered Letters by Carriers.—Postmasters will hand to the letter-carriers, for delivery, all registered letters (excepting those addressed to box-holders), requiring them first to sign their names in the last column of the record-of-registered-matter-received-and-delivered. The carriers will, on the delivery of every such letter, require the person receiving it to sign the registry-return receipt, and also a receipt for the same in the carriers'-registry-delivery-book. Carriers must exercise the utmost caution in the delivery of these letters to the party addressed, or to some responsible person whom they know to be authorized to receive them. See also sections 866–870.

Sec. 362. Postmasters to supervise Carrier Service.—Postmasters will see that the superintendents of carriers' stations, and the carriers and clerks connected with this service, are informed of the highly responsible character of the duties required of them. They will issue, from time to time, such orders and instructions as may be found necessary to carry out these regulations and to maintain proper order. The carrier disobeying such orders will be reprimanded by the postmaster, or reported for removal to the First Assistant Postmaster-General, as the case may require.

Sec. 363. Arrest of Persons found Tampering with Boxes.—Postmasters will arrange with the police authorities of their several cities for the arrest of all persons in citizens' dress found tampering with or collecting from the street mailing-boxes; also, of all persons wearing the carriers' uniform (including the carriers), found tampering with or collecting from the boxes at other than the usual and regular collection rounds, of which the police authorities must be kept informed.

Sec. 364. "Cave Canem"—"Beware of the Dog."—Carriers are not required to run the risk of being bitten by dangerous dogs in delivering mail-matter. Persons keeping such dogs must call at the post-office for their mail, or if they wish it delivered at their houses, must satisfy the postmaster that it is safe for the carrier to so deliver it.

Sec. 365. Supplies for Carrier Post-Offices.—Street mailing-boxes, blank-books, blank-forms, and carriers' satchels will be furnished on application to the First Assistant Postmaster-General; and locks and keys for street mailing-boxes on application to the Second Assistant Postmaster-General. All other letters relating to this branch of the service must be addressed to the First Assistant Postmaster-General.

Sec. 366. Manner of Keeping Books.—Blank books furnished for this branch of the service must be correctly and neatly kept according to their design, and be at all times subject to examination by the Special Agents of this Department.

CHAPTER NINE.

DISTRIBUTION AND DISPATCH OF ORDINARY DOMESTIC MAIL-MATTER.

☞ For instructions as to the distribution and dispatch of registered matter, see Title V.
☞ For instruction as to the dispatch of foreign mails, see Title VII.

Sec. 367. Postmasters to Receive and Dispatch Mail-matter.—Every postmaster shall keep an [post] office in which one or more persons shall be on duty during such hours of each day as the Postmaster-General may direct, for the purpose of receiving, delivering, making up, and forwarding all mail-matter received thereat. (R. S., § 3839.)

Sec. 368. Time of Closing the Mails.—All letters brought to any post-office half an hour before the time for the departure of the mail shall be forwarded therein; but at [post] offices where, in the opinion of the Postmaster-General, more time for making up the mail is required, he may prescribe accordingly, not exceeding one hour. (R. S., § 3840.)

Sec. 369. Preference given to Letters over other Mail-matter.—When the amount of mail-matter to be carried on any mail-route is so great as to seriously retard the progress or endanger the security of the letter-mail, or materially increase the cost of carriage at the ordinary rate of speed, the Postmaster-General may provide for the separate carriage of the letter-mail at the usual rate of speed; but the other mail-matter shall not be delayed any more than is absolutely necessary, having due regard to the cost of expedition and the means at his disposal for [*affecting*] [effecting] the same. (R. S., § 3994.)

Sec. 370. Penalty for Unlawfully Detaining Mail-matter.—Any postmaster who shall unlawfully detain in his [post] office any letter or other mail-matter, the posting of which is not prohibited by law, with intent to prevent the arrival and delivery of the same to the person to whom it is addressed, shall be punishable by a fine of not more than five hundred dollars, and by imprisonment for not more than six months, and he shall be forever thereafter incapable of holding the office of postmaster. (R. S., § 3890.)

Sec. 371. Prepaid Matter to be Forwarded if Requested.—Prepaid letters shall be forwarded from one post-office to another, at the request of the party addressed, without additional charge for postage. (R. S., § 3940.)

All letters upon which one full rate of postage has been prepaid shall, and all other fully prepaid matter may be forwarded at the request of the party addressed, without additional charge for postage.

Sec. 372. Erroneously Delivered, Redirected Matter to be Forwarded.—When any article of mail-matter is taken from the post-office, or delivered by a carrier, the connection of the post-office has presumptively terminated. If, however, such matter shall have been erroneously delivered, or being addressed to the care of another person shall be immediately returned by him redirected, it shall be the duty of the postmaster to forward or redeliver such matter without extra charge.

Sec. 373 Letters mailed under cover to Postmaster—how treated.—Inasmuch as by law all first-class matter on which one full rate of postage is prepaid must be forwarded, it is the duty of a postmaster to forward such mail-matter which may reach him under cover from any other post-office with or without request to mail the same. Before forwarding such matter he should cancel the stamps and indorse in writing on the reverse side of such matter the following: "RECEIVED AT ——, UNDER COVER FROM THE POST-OFFICE AT ——, TO BE FORWARDED IN THE MAIL."

Sec. 374. Postmasters to Receipt for Copyright Matter.—The postmaster to whom any [*such*] copyright book, title, or other article is delivered, shall, if requested, give a receipt therefor; and when so delivered he shall mail it to its destination. (R. S., § 4961.)

Sec. 375. Postage-stamps to be Canceled.—Postage-stamps affixed to all mail-matter or the stamped envelopes in which the same is inclosed shall, when deposited for mailing or delivery, be defaced by the postmaster at the mailing [post] office, in such manner as the Postmaster-General may direct; and if any mail-matter shall be forwarded without the stamps or envelopes being so defaced, the postmaster at the office of delivery shall deface them, and report the delinquent postmaster to the Postmaster-General. (R. S., § 3921.)

Sec. 376. Return Stamps on Postal-cards and Letter-envelopes.—Should return postal cards and return letter envelopes be issued by the Department, the return stamps must not be canceled until the matter is deposited in some post-office for return to the sender. See section 143.

Sec. 377. Manner of Canceling Stamps.—The cancellation or defacing required by section 375 must be effected by the use of black printing-ink, wherever that material can be obtained; and where it cannot, the operation should be performed by making several heavy crosses or parallel lines upon each stamp, with a pen dipped in good black writing-ink. The use of the office rating or postmarking stamp as a canceling instrument is positively prohibited, inasmuch as the postmark, when impressed on the postage-stamp, is usually indistinct, and the cancellation effected thereby is imperfect.

Sec. 378. Treatment of Matter Bearing Canceled or Improper Stamps.—When matter bearing previously-used stamps is deposited for mailing, and the postmaster can identify the mailing party without violating the seal of such matter, it is his duty to bring the case to the notice of the United States district attorney, that the offender may be prosecuted. If the person mailing such matter cannot be identified as above, then it should be treated as held for postage. Mail-matter bearing stamps other than postage-stamps, or stamps cut from stamped envelopes, newspaper wrappers, or from postal cards, should be treated as held for postage. Mutilated stamps and fractional parts of postage-stamps and postage-due stamps cannot be recognized in prepayment of postage. For example, a letter or package to which one two-cent stamp and the half of another two-cent stamp are affixed cannot be considered as having been prepaid three cents, but only two cents; and a letter or package on which eighteen cents postage is chargeable cannot be prepaid in full by affixing a six-cent stamp and the half of a twenty-four-cent stamp.

Sec. 379. All Mail-matter other than Second Class to be Postmarked.—All mailable matter (except that of the second class) deposited in any post-office for mailing or delivery must bear a postmark giving the name of the post-office and an abbreviation of the name of the State (and on first-class matter the date of deposit); and all letters received from other offices or post-offices for delivery or for redistribution to other offices or post-offices must be postmarked on the reverse side, with the date and, when possible, the hour on which they are received. But in the case of packages of letters from other offices or post-offices, received to be forwarded intact to the post-offices of final destination, the facing-slips only will be postmarked at the post-offices through which they pass. Missent matter of any class, received at any post-office, must be postmarked with the date of receipt before the same is forwarded to its proper destination. First-class post-offices may be exempted from the operations of this section if upon evidence satisfactory to the Postmaster-General they shall show it to be impracticable to comply with its provisions.

Sec. 380. Impressions to be taken of the Dated Stamp.—The figures of the dated stamp must be carefully adjusted at the beginning of each day; and as soon as this has been done, a clear impression must be made in a book specially provided for the purpose, so as to afford evidence of the correct discharge of this duty: special care must be taken not to omit the Sunday impression of the stamp. If the stamp is fitted with letters and figures indicating the hour at which any letter arrives or is dispatched, care must be taken to change them punctually at the appointed periods. If this is not done, the postmaster may often be blamed for a delay which has not occurred at his post-office. An impression must be made in the book provided of every dated stamp used by the postmaster throughout the day, and each impression should be taken immediately a change is made either in the date or hour.

Sec. 381. How to secure Legible Stamping. It is necessary, not only that the impression of every official stamp should be legible, but that it should be perfect in every particular; so that each letter and figure of the stamp may be quite clear. To effect this, attention must be paid to the following points: The stamp must be kept perfectly clean, which may be done most effectually by brushing it with a brush slightly wetted and dipped in powdered potash or soda. Type which has been used must be cleaned before it is replaced in the box. The stamp should be held firmly in the hand and struck upon the letter with a light sharp blow; care being taken not to let the stamp fall upon the impression made at another post-office. It is in the power of any person, by attention and practice, to become a good and rapid stamper.

Sec. 382. Treatment of First-class Matter received in bad order.—All mail-matter of the first class deposited in or received at any post-office unsealed or in a mutilated or otherwise bad condition must be stamped or marked with the name of the post-office, date, and the words "Received unsealed" or "Received in bad order," as the case may be, and be resealed before being forwarded or delivered.

Sec. 383. Distribution and Dispatch of Mails.—In the distribution and dispatch of mails, all postmasters will be governed by orders from the General Superintendent of Railway Mail Service, or from the Division Superintendent of railway mail service acting under him, excepting foreign mails outward from exchange post-offices, which are under the control of the Superintendent of Foreign Mails. In the absence of other instructions, every postmaster whose post-office is situated upon a railroad, will mail all matter direct to the cars, unless it be addressed to post-offices directly connected with his own by star or steamboat routes. Postmasters at other post-offices will mail to the nearest post-office upon a railroad all matter which cannot be sent direct to its destination by star or steamboat route. See section 707.

Sec. 384. No Changes except in Emergency.—No change in distribution or dispatch must be made without first obtaining such an order, except in cases of emergency; and in all such cases an immediate report, giving the reasons for such change, must be made to the Superintendent of Railway Mail Service for the division in which the post-office may be situated.

Sec. 385. Distribution of Mails by Schemes.—Postmasters will carefully distribute and make up mails by the official schemes which may be furnished them, and will conform to any changes that may be made in same by the Superintendent of the Division, and will make up and exchange only such pouches as may be ordered by him. But such post-offices may be excepted from the requirements of this section as the General Superintendent may direct.

Sec. 386. What States should be Distributed.—A distribution or separation should be made of mail only for such States or portions of States as can be advanced or expedited by reason of such distribution.

Sec. 387. Mail to be made up by States.—All mail for States of which no distribution is made must be made up "by States" (and facing-slips used, in accordance with section 396); that is, letter and circular mail for each State must be made up in packages, and newspaper mail in canvas sacks, by itself, and the name of the State marked on the slip covering the package or tag attached to the sack.

Sec. 388. Local Mail for Railroad and Steamboat Lines.—Mail to be forwarded to local post-offices on railroad or steamboat lines should be made up in packages, addressed to the proper railway or steamboat office, and containing only the local mail supplied by that line, as given in the official schemes.

Sec. 389. Other than Local Mail Sent to Railroad and Steamboat Lines.—All other mail, not local, sent to or via such lines, should be made by States, if sufficient to do so, and if not, then put all in one package, addressed with the name of the railway (or steamboat) office in whose pouch it is forwarded, adding "State of ——," to indicate that it contains other than local.

Sec. 390. Making up Local Mail for Railway Lines.—Post-offices on railroad lines, in making up local mail for such line, will make two packages, one for the train going north or south, east or west, as the case may be, and, in addressing the packages, will add the direction in which it is intended to be sent.

Sec. 391. Make Direct Packages for Horse-routes.—In making up mail to be forwarded by a horse or stage route, a direct package should be tied out for each post-office, including the last one, on such route, so as to facilitate the handling of the mail by the intermediate post-offices.

Sec. 392. Making up Mail beyond last Post-office on Stage-route.—Mail from a post-office on and to be forwarded by a horse or stage route and beyond the last post-office on such route, should be made up "by States," as far as possible, or if not sufficient to do so, then in one package, marking the name of such last post-office on the slip covering the same and adding the abbreviation "Dis.," to indicate that the package is for distribution.

Sec. 393. Letters for Delivery and Distribution in Separate Packages.—Letter and circular mail for delivery and mail for distribution at a post-office must always be made up in separate packages.

Sec. 394. Direct Packages.—Making a direct package is placing all letters for one post-office in a package by themselves, with a plainly-addressed letter for such post-office faced out on each side.

Sec. 395. Letters must not be placed in Pouch Loose.—Letter and circular mail must always be properly "faced up" and tied in packages, and never placed in the pouch loose.

Sec. 396. Facing-slips to be used.—Facing-slips must be placed upon all packages of letters and circulars, and in each canvas sack of newspapers, the same to be securely tied on the package, or if newspapers, placed in the sack, and have on each the address or destination of the package or sack, the post-mark, with date and time of close or dispatch, and the name of the person making up the same.

Sec. 397. Checking Errors.—All errors found in the distribution of a package of letters or in a sack of newspapers must be noted on the reverse side of the slip covering or inside of the same, giving the name of the post-office and State, and the county, when included in the superscription, adding thereto the name of the person noting the errors, and postmark with date.

Sec. 398. Disposition of Slips received.—All slips received upon packages of letter or circular mail or in sacks of newspaper mail must be preserved and forwarded to the Division Superintendent. First and second class post-offices will forward such slips daily, and all other post-offices at the end of each week. Slips on which errors are checked should be forwarded in sealed official penalty-envelopes.

Sec. 399. Absence of Slips on Packages or in Sacks.—If no slips are received on the packages or in sacks, notify Division Superintendents, stating, if possible, the office or post-office from which the mail was received, and if newspaper mail, forward the label received on the sack.

Sec. 400. Slips and Schemes furnished.—Postmasters can obtain facing-slips from the Superintendent Railway Mail Service in whose division their post-offices are located; also, official schemes of distribution, or any information relating to the same.

Sec. 401. Report of Unworked Mail received.—Postmasters will report to the Division Superintendent all mail sent to their post-offices which should have been distributed and made up by railway mail employés, forwarding with report the slips covering the same, or if newspaper mail, the labels received on the sacks.

Sec. 402. Report of all Irregularities.—They will also promptly report to the Division Superintendent any and all irregularities in the receipt of mails for or at their post-offices, and any other irregularity affecting the proper dispatch or forwarding of mails which may be brought to their attention.

Sec. 403. No Through Pouches by Mail-trains.—Postmasters will not make any through pouches to be forwarded by mail-trains unless specially instructed to do so. The mail should be properly made up and placed in the pouch for the railway mail employé.

Sec. 404. Changes in Forwarding Mails.—Any changes which postmasters think should be made in the forwarding of mail from their post-offices should be reported to the Division Superintendent for attention.

Sec. 405. Hooks prohibited in Handling Mail-bags.—The use of hooks in handling mail-bags is forbidden.

Sec. 406. Letters with Stamps canceled not to be returned.—After canceling the stamps a postmaster must not return the letter to the person mailing it for him to take to the train. It must be forwarded in the pouch, as railway mail employés are prohibited from receiving it; and any person offering such letter to an employé for mailing is guilty of a misdemeanor under the law. See section 1252.

Sec. 407. Letters not to be placed under Strap of Pouches.—After pouches are closed and dispatched from a post-office letters must not be placed under the strap or attached to the outside of the pouch. If this is done at the depot inform the mail messenger, and have the practice discontinued.

Sec. 408. Printed Labels furnished to be Returned.—Printed wooden labels for sacks of newspaper mail and printed slide-labels for pouches must be taken off when the sacks or pouches are opened, and returned by first mail to the post-office or line from which they were received, the wooden labels to be classed with newspaper mail and the slide-labels as letter mail. Under no circumstances are any of such labels to be defaced or destroyed.

Sec. 409. Application for Printed Labels.—Postmasters will send to Division Superintendent lists of such printed wooden or slide labels as may be needed for use at their post-offices.

Sec. 410. Time of Closing Mails.—Mails at first-class post-offices are to be closed not more than one hour and at all other offices not more than half an hour before the schedule time of departure of trains, unless such departure is between the hours of 9 p. m. and 5 a. m., when they can be closed at 9 p. m. The post-office at New York City is excepted from the requirement of this section.

Sec. 411. Pouches to be examined.—When a pouch or canvas is opened it should be carefully examined to see that no mail is left therein.

Sec. 412. Mail stopping overnight.—When the mail stops overnight where there is a post-office, it must be kept in the post-office, except at points where otherwise ordered by the Department.

CHAPTER TEN.

SUPERINTENDENTS OF MAILS AT POST-OFFICES OF THE FIRST AND SECOND CLASS.

Sec. 413. Appointment of Superintendent of Mails.—The General Superintendent of the Railway Mail Service of the Post-Office Department shall designate post-offices of the first and second classes at which clerks shall be appointed to superintend the distribution of mails, and to be known by the title of "Superintendent of Mails," who shall be appointed upon the nomination of said General Superintendent of Railway Mail Service, approved by the Postmaster-General.

Sec. 414. General Duties of Superintendents of Mails.—Where superintendents of mails are designated, they will have entire charge of the distribution and dispatch of all mails at such post-offices. They will see that the distribution of the post-office is done in accordance with the latest official schemes; that such schemes are kept corrected to date, as per changes issued by Division Superintendents; that case examinations of distributing clerks on the official schemes of distribution are kept up.

Sec. 415. Record and Report of Errors in Distribution.—Superintendents of mails will keep a record of the errors made by each distributing clerk in a post.office and report the same to the postmaster at the end of each month, or oftener, if he desires. He will also report all case examinations had in like manner.

Sec. 416. Examination of Slips.—Superintendents of mails will examine the slips on which errors in distribution have been noted, returned to the post-office by the Division Superintendent, and will, after making a record of the same, return them to the clerks by whom the distribution was made.

Sec. 417. Postmasters to be Furnished With the Record of Errors.—The superintendent of mails must work in harmony with the other departments of the post-office at which he is designated, and endeavor by every means to promote its efficiency as well as that of the service. He will also keep the postmaster advised of the record both of errors in distribution and of the result of case examinations, as well as the general efficiency of each clerk under his supervision.

CHAPTER ELEVEN.

CASE EXAMINATION OF POST-OFFICE CLERKS.

Sec. 418. Case Examinations of Distributing Clerks.—With the view of having distributing clerks become familiar with schemes of distribution, and thereby increase their knowledge of the distribution as well as the efficiency of the service, postmasters at first and second class post-offices will require distributing clerks in their post-offices to be examined from time to time on schemes of such States as are required to be distributed at their post-offices.

Sec. 419. Nature of Case Examinations.—These examinations will consist of the distribution, from memory, and into a case for that purpose, of cards, representing the counties or post-offices of any State of which distribution is made, and in accordance with the official schemes. After the cards have been distributed they must be examined by some person thoroughly acquainted with the distribution of such State.

Sec. 420. Verbal Examination of Clerks.—Clerks should also be sharply questioned as to the proper routes to which mails are dispatched from their post-offices after they are made up, and also respecting such orders relating to the making up and dispatch of mails as may have, from time to time, been given them.

Sec. 421. Postmasters' Order-Book.—Postmasters at first and second class post-offices will keep an order-book, in which all orders relating to the making up and dispatch of mails at their post-offices, all official changes in schemes which are received from Division Superintendent, are to be inserted by record or otherwise, and require distributing clerks to examine the same daily.

Sec. 422. Orders to be Signed by Clerks.—Each order should be signed by all the distributing clerks as an indication that it has been examined.

Sec. 423. Slips with Errors noted to be Compared with Schemes.—All slips on which errors are noted which have been returned to the postmaster by the Division Superintendent must be carefully compared with the schemes and orders by which the distribution was made and a record kept of the same, the slips being returned to the clerk making such distribution.

Sec. 424. Monthly Reports of Case Examinations.—A report must be made at the end of each month to the General Superintendent of the Railway Mail Service for the information of the Department, of the result of all case examinations and the record of errors of each distributing-clerk in the post-office.

Sec. 425. Incompetent Distributing-clerks to be Removed.—When the record of case examinations and errors made in the distribution and forwarding of the mails by any clerk in the post-office is below what is required for the correct performance of such duties, such clerk must not be continued in that position, but a more competent person must be assigned to the place.

CHAPTER TWELVE.

RECEIVING AND DISPATCHING MAILS AT CATCHER POST-OFFICES.

Sec. 426. Cranes and Catcher-Pouchers.—For the purpose of exchanging mails at certain way and flag stations between the post-offices at these places and the railway offices, without an abatement or loss of speed of the train, the Post-Office Department has introduced the use of a "mail-catcher," causing the erection at each of such stations of a "crane" on which the pouch to be exchanged by the postmasters is to be hung, and has furnished a supply of canvas pouches with rings attached to both top and bottom, and strap with buckle attached to the center; these pouches to be used only in making such exchanges.

Sec. 427. How to Prepare Pouches and Hang them on the Crane.—1st. The pouch or mail-bag should be prepared in the following manner. If only a small mail is to be sent let it remain in the bottom of the pouch, but if a large mail is to be sent divide it, put part in the top, but most in the bottom. Buckle the strap around the center of pouch M. In case the strap is gone, tie the middle of the pouch, as seen in the diagram. It is worse than useless to hang up a bag crammed full like a bag of grain.

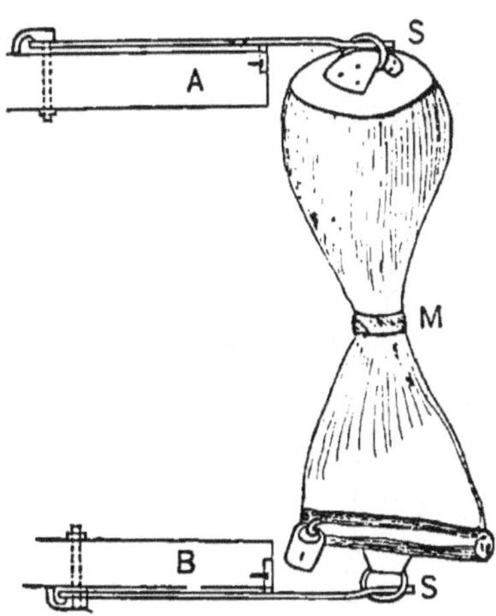

2d. Hang the bottom of the pouch on the upper iron S of the crane A, turn all directly to the track, then lift lower arm B and place the iron S in the ring of the pouch, slip the socket down the stem until there is sufficient strain on the pouch to hold it from blowing down. If a strong wind is blowing, tie the pouch to the two irons S, by the rings, with one strand of ordinary post-office twine. Hang the pouch lock end down.

3d. When the service occurs in the night, or between sunset and sunrise, hang a light on or near the crane. This is important.

Sec. 428. Catcher-pouches to be Used for no other Purpose.—These canvas pouches were manufactured expressly and only for such exchanges, and must be used for no other purpose. It is absolutely necessary that a prompt and regular exchange of the same pouches be always kept up, and employés of the Railway Mail Service are instructed to report to their Division Superintendent every case where a postmaster fails to return to the railway office the pouch last given him.

Sec. 429. Only Fifty Pounds of Mail allowed in Catcher-pouches.—The catchers are especially designed to take on the trains for distribution and dispatch letter-mail, but paper and other mail may be inclosed to a maximum weight of fifty pounds. If more than this weight is to be sent, as at post-offices where papers are published, the paper mail should be sacked and sent by local train to the nearest express stop, thence placed in the mail-cars.

Sec. 430. Special Instructions to Postmasters Served by Catchers.—Postmasters at post-offices at which mail-trains do not stop, and which are supplied by "catcher service," will carefully comply with the following instructions:

1st. See that none but "catcher"-pouches are used.

2d. After the mail is placed in the pouch and locked, see that the pouch is securely strapped or tied around the middle.

3d. See that the pouch is securely suspended on the crane, with the lock downward, not exceeding ten minutes before the schedule time of arrival of the train.

4th. If from any cause the pouch should not be caught by the train and a pouch is put off, return the extra pouch to the next mail-train by securing it to the pouch in which the mail is sent and strapping or tying the two pouches together at the middle as one pouch.

5th. Under no circumstances should "catcher"-pouches be sent out upon any stage or horseback routes, or used for any other purpose than to exchange mails where trains do not stop.

6th. Postmasters must not permit "catcher"-pouches to accumulate at their post-offices, but must return them to the mail-trains at once.

7th. If the crane at your station should get out of position or repair so as to interfere with the exchange of mails, report the fact at once to the Division Superintendent, so that the attention of the railroad company can be called to the matter.

CHAPTER THIRTEEN.

DISPOSAL OF UNMAILABLE, UNDELIVERED, AND DEAD MAIL-MATTER.

Sec. 431. Unmailable Matter to be Sent to the Dead-Letter Office.—All domestic letters, deposited in any post-office for mailing, on which the postage is wholly unpaid or paid less than one full rate as required by law, except letters lawfully free, and duly certified letters of soldiers, sailors, and marines in the service of the United States, shall be sent by the postmaster to the Dead-Letter Office in Washington. But in large cities and adjacent districts of dense population having two or more post-offices within a distance of three miles of each other, any letter mailed at one of such [post] offices and addressed to a locality within the delivery of another of such [post] offices, which shall have been inadvertently prepaid at the drop or local letter rate of postage only, may be forwarded to its destination through the proper [post] office, charged with the amount of the deficient postage, to be collected on delivery. (R. S., § 3937.)

Sec. 432. Definition and Classification of Unmailable Matter.—Unmailable matter includes all matter which is by law, regulation, or treaty stipulation prohibited from being transmitted through the mails; or which, by reason of illegible, incorrect, or insufficient address, it is found impossible to forward to destination. For convenience it is divided into the following classes:

(*a*) *Held for postage;* or that matter which is insufficiently prepaid to entitle it to be forwarded in the mails. This includes all domestic matter of the first class coming under the provisions of the preceding section, and all domestic matter of the third and fourth classes which is not fully prepaid, and all insufficiently prepaid matter addressed to foreign countries not embraced in the Universal Postal Union, to which full prepayment is obligatory. (For rates of postage and conditions of payment on matter addressed to foreign countries, see Foreign Postage Table in any recent number of United States Postal Guide. See also Title VII.)

(*b*) *Misdirected;* or that matter which is so incorrectly, insufficiently, or illegibly addressed that it cannot be forwarded to the person for whom it is intended.

(*c*) *Excess of weight and size;* or those packages of domestic third and fourth class matter weighing more than four pounds each, except single books exceeding that weight, and of foreign matter which are in excess of the weight or size fixed by treaty stipulation as the maximum for such matter. (For regulations in regard to weight and size of matter addressed to foreign countries, see any recent number United States Postal Guide. See also Title VII.)

(*d*) *Destructive* matter; or that matter which, from its harmful nature, is forbidden to be in the mails. (See also section 222 and Rulings published quarterly in the United States Postal Guide.)

(*e*) *Coin and jewelry;* or that matter, to wit, coins, jewelry, or precious articles, which is by treaty stipulation prohibited from being sent in the mails to certain foreign countries. (See latest United States Postal Guide and Title VII.)

(*f*) *Obscene;* or that matter which is by section 225 prohibited from being sent in the mails.

(*g*) *Lottery;* or that matter which is by section 226 prohibited from being sent in the mails.

(*h*) *Mutilated;* or that matter which is recovered from wrecked or burned mail cars or vessels, or which has been so damaged by any means whatever that it cannot be forwarded to its destination. This includes also all matter recovered from depredation on the mails.

Sec. 433. Definition and Classification of Dead Matter.—Dead matter is such matter as, having reached the post-office of destination, is either unclaimed or refused by the party addressed; or which, from its nature, or because of indefinite or fictitious address, cannot be delivered. For convenience it is divided into the following classes:

(*i*) *Unclaimed,* or that which is not called for by the parties addressed, or cannot be delivered.

(*k*) *Refused,* or that which for any reason the parties addressed decline to receive.

(*l*) *Obscene,* or that which is by section 225 forbidden to be sent in the mails, and which the postmaster at the mailing post-office has failed to intercept.

(*m*) *Lottery,* or that which is by section 226 forbidden to be sent in the mails, because it relates to lotteries, etc., and which the postmaster at the mailing post-office has failed to intercept.

(*n*) *Fictitious,* or that which is addressed to fictitious or assumed names or to initials; or in any manner so that the person or persons for whom it is intended cannot be identified. (See section 276.)

(*o*) *Hotel,* or that which has been delivered at a hotel or public institution, or to a consul, agent, or other public officer or individual who is in the habit of receiving mail for transient persons, and has been returned to the post-office by such consignee as unclaimed.

(*p*) *Fraudulent,* or that (registered matter only) which the Postmaster-General has specially ordered to be withheld from delivery and returned to the writer, because the parties addressed are engaged in obtaining money under false pretenses by the use of the mails. Mail-matter not registered must never be treated as fraudulent. See section 875.

Sec. 434. First-class Matter not to be Held Unmailable on mere Suspicion.—Postmasters are specially warned that they have no right to detain first-class matter upon the mere suspicion that it contains articles forbidden to be sent in the mails. Neither will they, under any circumstances, be justified in breaking the seal of any letter or package to ascertain whether or not unmailable matter is inclosed. See section 530.

Sec. 435. Unmailable Matter from Railway Offices, how Treated.—Postmasters receiving any article of unmailable matter from a railway office will dispose of it in the same manner as if it had been deposited in their own post-offices for mailing.

Sec. 436. Unmailable Matter Inadvertently Forwarded, how Treated.—If any matter which should have been detained as "held for postage," "excess of weight and size," "coin," or as "lottery" (see *a*, *c*, *e*, and *g*, section 432), shall have, through inadvertence, been forwarded from the post-office of mailing, it must not be stopped in transit. Such as bears a foreign address will be intercepted by the postmaster at the exchange post-office and treated as hereinafter provided. (See section 443.) Misdirected, destructive, and obscene matter (see *b*, *d*, and *f*, section 432), and all matter found loose in the mails, should, however, be detained by any postmaster into whose hands it may fall.

Sec. 437. Postmasters to Return Unmailable Matter to Senders.—It is the duty of postmasters at whose post-offices any mail-matter is detained as unmailable under any of the classes enumerated in section 432 (except *f* and *g*), to make all reasonable efforts to ascertain the person mailing the same, and, if such person can be found, to either require of him full prepayment of postage, if the matter is held for postage, or else return to him the letter or package. But in returning mail to the senders, postmasters are expected to use great care to avoid the possibility of wrong delivery, and must only return matter to senders beyond the delivery of their post-offices, as prescribed in the following section.

Sec. 438. Matter Returned to Senders at Other Post-Offices.—Under no circumstances whatever is any one except a postmaster permitted to return any such matter direct to the sender; and postmasters must not do so if the sender lives beyond the delivery of their post-offices, except in case of prepaid first-class matter which bears the card or request of the sender, and misdirected second-class matter ("nixes"). These two classes should be appropriately indorsed, stamped on the back with the name of the post-office and date, and immediately returned to the sender without postage charge. Destructive matter will be disposed of as provided in section 440.

Sec. 439. Held-for-Postage Matter that Cannot be Returned to Sender.—When held-for-postage matter which cannot be returned to the persons mailing the same, as provided for in the two preceding sections, is addressed to a person residing within the delivery of the post-office where mailed, he shall be notified of its detention, by circular or otherwise, and upon the payment of the amount of postage due, the necessary stamps will be affixed and canceled, and the matter delivered. If such matter is not claimed within thirty days after notification as above, or is refused by the party addressed, it shall be sent to the Dead-Letter Office in the next regular return of ordinary dead matter, classed as unclaimed or refused, as the case may be. When such matter is addressed to persons living beyond the delivery of the post-office where it is detained, it must be sent to the Dead Letter Office.

Sec. 440. Disposition of Destructive Unmailable Matter.—Postmasters receiving any article of destructive mail-matter from the hands of any railway mail employé, or finding it deposited in their own post-offices, must not send the same to the Dead-Letter Office, but will notify the person mailing such package, whether he live within the delivery of their post-offices or not, that some other means than the mail must be provided for its transportation. If the mailing party is not known, then the postmaster should notify the party addressed of the detention of the package, that it cannot be transmitted in the mails, and that he must provide some other means for its being forwarded at his own expense outside the mails. If, after this, such packages are not disposed of within thirty days, the postmaster should report the facts to the Third Assistant Postmaster-General, and await instructions from him.

Sec. 441. Send Unmailable Matter promptly to Dead-Letter Office.—Unmailable matter must not be held over to be advertised. Post-offices of the first class must make daily, and all other post-offices weekly, returns to the Dead-Letter Office of all unmailable matter except destructive matter. Each return must include all the matter of this class on hand at the time, except that addressed to persons within the delivery of the post-office, who have been notified to pay the postage thereon, as required in section 439.

Sec. 442. How Matter Must be Sent to the Dead-Letter Office.—Every piece of mail-matter sent to the Dead-Letter Office, for whatever cause, must have plainly written or stamped upon the address side the reason of its being sent there, as

UNMAILABLE, stating also whether the matter is held for postage, misdirected, in excess of proper weight or size, or containing coin or jewelry; or UNCLAIMED, giving specific reason for failure to deliver the matter; or REFUSED; or FICTITIOUS; or HOTEL; and upon the reverse side it must bear the name of the post-office from which sent, and the date of sending. *Unmailable* matter must be sent to the Dead-Letter Office in returns entirely separate from the dead matter. The return must be labeled as prescribed in section 474, and addressed "*Dead-Letter Office, Washington, D. C.*," and must be plainly indorsed "RETURN OF UNMAILABLE MATTER FROM" (here add the name of the post-office). *Held-for-postage*, *misdirected*, and *excess-of-weight* matter may be sent in the same return; but when there is any considerable amount of third or fourth class matter to be sent (say more than five or six pieces) the first-class matter should be sent in one parcel or pouch, and the third and fourth class in another. Whenever the amount of matter of either class is so great that it cannot be easily and securely tied into a parcel, it should be sent in a suitable pouch directed and indorsed as above stated.

Sec. 443. How to Make Up and Transmit Returns of Unmailable Matter.— Each return of unmailable matter must be accompanied by a list made on Form 1522, giving as nearly as possible the full name and address of each article. Valuable matter of the third and fourth class must be entered on a list separate from the first class. Miscellaneous printed matter of no obvious value must be sent with the return, but need not be entered on the list, except a memorandum showing the number of pieces included. The matter must be further separated into the classes as indicated in *a*, *b*, and *d*, section 432, and, in addition, the *Held for Postage* (*a*) must be subdivided into that of domestic and foreign address. Each class and division must be arranged alphabetically and entered on the lists accordingly, and every piece of matter and its entry on the list must be numbered to correspond. *Coin* matter must be sent in special returns to the Dead-Letter Office accompanied by a list made upon the same form and in the same manner as lists of *Held for Postage* matter. Returns of this matter should always be registered. *Obscene* and *Lottery* matter must also be sent in special returns to the Dead-Letter Office accompanied by lists the same as *coin* matter. *Mutilated and damaged* matter must also be sent specially to the Dead-Letter Office, and must be accompanied by a letter addressed to the Third Assistant Postmaster-General detailing all the facts in the case and giving a full list of the articles. Lists must in every case be inclosed with the matter to which they refer. They must not be sent in a separate envelope or package. Postmasters must retain duplicates of all lists and statements sent to the Dead-Letter Office for the purpose of reference in making searches for missing matter.

Sec. 444. Advertisement of Unclaimed and Undelivered Matter.— The Postmaster-General may direct the publication of the list of non-delivered letters at any post-office by a written list posted in some public place, or, when he shall deem it for the public interest, he may direct the publication of such list in the daily or weekly newspaper regularly published within the post-office delivery which has the largest circulation within such delivery; and where no daily paper is published within the post-office delivery, such list may be published in the daily newspaper of any adjoining delivery having the largest circulation within the delivery of the post-office publishing the list; and in case of dispute as to the circulation of competing newspapers, the postmaster shall receive evidence and decide upon the fact. Such list shall be published as frequently as the Postmaster-General may deem proper, but not oftener than once a week. (R. S., § 3930.)

A postmaster is not liable to suit by the publisher of a newspaper for refusing to give to him the publication of the list of letters uncalled for, even though he acted maliciously. A public duty is not enforceable by a private action, except when it has been specifically given by statute. (Foster *vs.* McKibben, 14 Penn. St. R., 168; also Strong *vs.* Campbell, 11 Barb., 135.)

In United States *ex rel vs.* Smallwood, Judge Darriel held that under the acts of 1845 and 1863 (containing substantially these provisions) the publication was in the discretion of the Postmaster-General, but when the discretion is once exercised and publication ordered, it must be through the columns of the paper having the largest circulation within the delivery of the post-office. (Am. Law Times Reports, vol. 2, 109.)

Sec. 445. Advertising Foreign Letters.—The list of non-delivered letters addressed to foreign-born persons may be published in a newspaper printed in the language most used by them, which shall be selected in the manner prescribed in the preceding section. (R. S., § 3931.)

Sec. 446. Displaying Lists of Advertised Letters.—Every postmaster shall [*post*] [display] in a conspicuous place in his office a copy of each list of non-delivered letters immediately after its publication. (R. S., § 3933.)

Sec. 447. Pay for Advertising Letters.—The compensation for publishing the list of non-delivered letters shall in no case exceed one cent for each letter so published. (R. S., § 3934.)

Sec. 448. Charge on Advertised Letters.—All letters published as non-delivered shall be charged with one cent in addition to the regular postage, to be accounted for as part of the postal revenue. (R. S., § 3935.)

The charge provided for by this section is only to be made when compensation is paid for advertising letters by virtue of an order of the Third Assistant Postmaster-General in accordance with section 444. See also section 452.

Sec. 449. Advertisement of Unclaimed Matter.—At post-offices of the fourth class unclaimed matter of the first class only, except "card" and "request" letters, and all valuable matter of the third and fourth classes shall be advertised monthly, and when practicable such advertising should take place upon the first day of the month. At all other post-offices such matter shall be advertised weekly, and where practicable such advertising should take place on Monday.

Sec. 450. Matter that should not be Advertised.—Each advertisement should include all the matter indicated in the preceding section on hand at the time of advertising, except such as is intended for persons who call regularly at the post-office, or where it is indorsed TO BE HELD UNTIL CALLED FOR, POSTE RESTANTE, or words to that effect; or where the postmaster has special reason to believe that it will be called for, or where he has been requested by the party addressed to retain it. In such cases it may be held for a period not exceeding two months, after which it should be advertised. But whenever any matter is so held it must be plainly marked "*Specially held for delivery.*"

Sec. 451. Form of the Advertisement.—The advertising of unclaimed matter shall be effected by placing conspicuously in the post-office one or more printed or manuscript lists of the names of the persons to whom such matter is addressed. The names on such list or lists shall be arranged alphabetically, and where there is any considerable number the names of the ladies and gentlemen shall be in separate lists. The third and fourth class matter should always be advertised in a list separate from the letters, with appropriate headings.

Sec. 452. Advertisements in Newspapers.—If the publisher of any newspaper desires to publish such advertised list gratuitously, it shall be the duty of postmasters to furnish a copy for that purpose, and if more than one publisher desires to do so a copy should be furnished to all simultaneously. No expense must be incurred in the advertising of unclaimed matter, nor any fee charged upon delivery of the same except by special permission from the Third Assistant Postmaster-General.

Sec. 453. Advertised Matter to be so Marked.—Every letter or parcel advertised must have plainly written or stamped upon the address side the word ADVERTISED together with the date of advertising.

Sec. 454. Letters from Dead-Letter Office to be Advertised.—Letters and other matter returned from the Dead-Letter Office direct to the sender, should be advertised, and, if not called for, be treated as ordinary unclaimed matter.

Sec. 455. Fictitious Matter not to be Advertised.—Fictitious matter should not be advertised, but should be sent to the Dead-Letter Office weekly from all post-offices to which it is addressed. Such matter must not be detained at the mailing post-office. This matter should be sent in returns entirely separate from other classes of matter, and the packet should be plainly indorsed, RETURN OF FICTITIOUS MATTER. Each return of this matter must be accompanied by a list giving the addresses of the matter included in the return, and the number of pieces to each address. This list may be made on Form 1522 by changing the word "*unmailable*" to "*fictitious.*"

Sec. 456. Request Matter.—When the writer of any letter on which the postage is prepaid shall indorse upon the outside thereof his name and address, such letter shall not be advertised, but after remaining uncalled for at the office to which it is directed thirty days, or the time the writer may direct, shall be returned to him without additional charge for postage, and if not then delivered shall be treated as a dead letter. (R. S., § 3939.)

Sec. 457. Card Matter.—Whenever any unclaimed matter of the first class bears the name and address of the sender or some designated place to which it can be returned, as post-office box, street and number, etc., without a request that the same be returned if not delivered, such matter will not be advertised, but must be returned to the sender at the expiration of thirty days, or such other period as may have been specified on the envelope, from the date of its arrival at the post-office of destination. Under the present postal arrangements with Canada all unclaimed request letters originating in either country are treated in the manner herein provided for domestic request letters.

Sec. 458. Postage must be Prepaid on Card and Request Matter.—No letter or other article of matter of the first class shall be returned to the sender, as provided in the two preceding sections, unless at least one full rate of postage was originally prepaid thereon.

Sec. 459. Unclaimed Official Matter to be Treated as Card Matter.—Unclaimed letters and other matter originating in any of the Executive Departments of the Government or inclosed in official penalty-envelopes, and matter mailed under the frank of Senators and Members or officers of Congress, is to be returned to the post-office of origin under the provisions of section 457 the same as other *card* and *request* matter. If the post-office of origin cannot be ascertained it should be returned to post-office, Washington, D. C.

Sec. 460. Postmasters' Letters to be Treated as Card Letters.—Letters written by postmasters upon official business should be treated as *card* letters, and if unclaimed should be returned to the post-office of origin as indicated by the envelope. If the post-office of origin cannot be determined, then they should be sent to the Dead-Letter Office in the regular return of *unclaimed* matter.

Sec. 461. Date of Arrival and Return of Card Matter.—Every unclaimed *card* or *request* letter must bear the stamp of the post-office indicating the date of its arrival, and a postmark showing the date of its return to the writer.

Sec. 462. Collection of Postage on Short-paid Returned Card Matter.—Unclaimed *card* and *request* letters which are short-paid, but upon which one full rate of postage was prepaid when mailed, are to be returned to the post-office of origin for delivery to the writer, who will be required to pay the amount originally due. If payment is refused, the matter will be indorsed as REFUSED and treated accordingly. See section 442.

Sec. 463. Local Letters not Returned to Another Post-Office.—A request upon a local or drop-letter for its return to the writer at some other post-office, if unclaimed, cannot be respected except in the case of such as may have been prepaid with at least one full (three-cent) rate of postage.

Sec. 464. Disposition of Hotel-card Letters.—Unclaimed letters bearing the card of a hotel, a school, or college, or other public institution which has evidently been placed upon the envelope to serve as a mere advertisement, should not be returned to the place designated in such card unless there is also a special request that they be so returned.

Sec. 465. Return of other than First-Class Card and Request Matter.—Unregistered matter other than that of the first class cannot be returned free to the sender, even if a request to that effect be written or printed thereon, except first-class rates of postage be prepaid thereon. When, therefore, matter of other than the first class is deposited in a post-office for mailing, bearing a request to return to the sender if not delivered, it shall be the duty of the postmaster to retain it and notify the sender at once, by return of matter or otherwise, and call his attention to this regulation. Senders of matter other than first class are permitted and should be encouraged by postmasters to write or print upon parcels sent by them the following notice or the substance thereof to the postmaster at the post-office of delivery, to wit: IF NOT DELIVERED WITHIN —— DAYS, THE POSTMASTER IS REQUESTED TO NOTIFY THE SENDER, SPECIFYING THE AMOUNT OF POSTAGE WHICH MUST BE REMITTED TO INSURE THE RETURN OF THE PARCEL TO ——(giving the name and address of the sender). It is the duty of postmasters receiving matter with this request written or printed thereon to comply therewith as promptly as in the case of first-class matter; and such matter should be stamped as provided in section 461.

Sec. 466. Matter Unclaimed after Return to Sender.—When matter returned to the sender under the provisions of the preceding sections is not claimed, it should be treated in all respects as other ordinary unclaimed matter.

Sec. 467. Disposition of Missent Matter.—Postmasters at whose post-offices letters which have evidently been misdirected may arrive should not forward them to other post-offices for the purpose of trial, on the supposition that they may reach the parties named in the address. If they know the proper direction to be given the letters, they may forward them without additional postage, but otherwise they should be sent to the Dead-Letter Office as *misdirected* matter, as directed in section 442. In either case the letter should be stamped MISDIRECTED, and bear the name of the post-office and the date of disposition.

Sec. 468. Authority of Postmaster-General to Kill Letters.—The Postmaster-General may regulate the period during which undelivered letters shall remain in any post-office and when they shall be returned to the Dead-Letter Office; and he may make regulations for their return from the Dead-Letter Office to the writers, when they cannot be delivered to the parties addressed. (R. S., 3936.)

Sec. 469. Final Disposition of Unclaimed Matter.—Unclaimed matter at post-offices of the first, second, and third classes must be sent to the Dead-Letter Office at the expiration of four weeks after the date of advertisement; and at post-offices of the fourth class one month after advertisement. In this way post-offices that advertise weekly will make a return of dead letters to the Department weekly, and at post-offices where the advertisement is done monthly, the return will be made monthly.

Sec. 470. Undelivered Matter to show Reason for Non-delivery.—Upon every undelivered article of mail-matter must appear the reason for non-delivery, such as

REMOVED, DEAD, REFUSED, FIRM DISSOLVED, &c. The specific reason should always be given, if possible, as the information is often of great value to the writer; but when that cannot be ascertained, it will be sufficient to mark them UNCLAIMED.

Sec. 471. Disposition of Refused Second-class Matter.—Postmasters shall notify the publisher of any newspaper, or other periodical, when any subscriber shall refuse to take the same from the office or neglect to call for it for the period of one month. (R. S., § 3885.)

Sec. 472. Disposition of other Refused Matter.—*Refused* matter should be sent to the Dead-Letter Office with the unclaimed matter, and should be entered on the statement (Form 1523) under its appropriate head. A list giving the address of each piece of matter should accompany the return. These lists should be made in two parts, one for the first-class matter and another for the third and fourth class. Refused matter should not be held in a post-office beyond the time for making the next regular return of unclaimed matter.

Sec. 473. Return of No unclaimed and refused matter.—Whenever it happens that there is no *unclaimed* or *refused* matter to be sent to the Dead-Letter Office at the regular time for making the return of such matter, a statement (Form 1523), properly headed and dated, and the words NO MATTER TO SEND noted thereon, should be sent to the Dead-Letter Office.

Sec. 474. Statements of Unclaimed Matter.—Each return of *unclaimed* matter must be accompanied by a statement made on Form 1523 (suitable blanks, printed on white paper for use at fourth-class post-offices, and on yellow for all others, will be furnished upon application to the Superintendent of Blank Agency, Post-Office Department), and also by a copy of the advertised list. The matter which has been delivered or otherwise disposed of since advertising should be indicated by having the names marked off the list. Both statement and advertised list must always be inclosed with the return, and not sent in a separate envelope or package. Returns of unclaimed matter should be addressed to the Dead-Letter Office, Washington, D. C., and must be plainly indorsed RETURN OF UNCLAIMED MATTER FROM ——— (here insert the name of the post-office). For this purpose an official penalty-envelope will be used as a label, either pasted or securely tied to the package. No postage will be required.

Sec. 475. Disposition of Unmailable Matter Reaching Destination.—When any matter classed as unmailable on account of its harmful nature has, through inadvertence, reached its destination and has been refused, after being treated as prescribed in section 230, it should not be sent to the Dead-Letter Office, but must be detained, and a statement giving a description of contents, name of the addressee, etc., be sent to the Third Assistant Postmaster-General, who will issue instructions as to its final disposition in each case. *Obscene* matter which, through inadvertence of the postmaster at the mailing place, reaches the post-office of destination, should be withheld from delivery and at once sent to the Dead-Letter Office, accompanied by a special letter of advice addressed to the Third Assistant Postmaster-General. *Lottery* matter which has, through the inadvertence of the postmaster at the mailing post-office, reached the post-office of destination, should be withheld from delivery and sent to the Dead-Letter Office, with a letter of advice addressed to the Third Assistant Postmaster-General.

Sec. 476. Hotel Matter without Card or Request.—Hotel matter returned to the post-office not redirected and bearing no "card" or "request" will be sent to the Dead-Letter Office weekly from all post-offices, with a complete list, giving the full name and address of each article. The entries in the list must be arranged alphabetically, and the articles and entries numbered to correspond. The list may be made on Form 1522, changing the word *unmailable* to *hotel*. Returns of this matter must be made separate from other classes of matter, and the words RETURN OF HOTEL MATTER FROM ——— (here add the name of the post-office) must be plainly indorsed upon the outside of the package. Whenever hotel matter is returned to a post-office redirected by the proprietor of a hotel or by other consignee, and in good order, it shall be the duty of the postmaster to forward it accordingly without postage charge therefor: *Provided*, He shall have, at the time of its return, no contrary instructions from the addressee: *And provided further*, That such new address is to any place to which such matter might be forwarded under the provisions of section 371, or is to any place in a foreign country to which prepayment of postage is optional. Hotel letters bearing a special request for their return, and letters bearing the name and address or the business card of the writer, are, of course, excepted from the above requirements, and will be treated as provided in sections 456 and 457.

Sec. 477. All Hotel Matter to be Stamped.—Postmasters should be careful to stamp upon all hotel matter the date of the original delivery and also the date of its return to the post-office.

Sec. 478. Disposition of Dead Printed Matter.—The Postmaster-General may provide, by regulations, for disposing of printed and mailable matter which may remain in any post-office, or in the Department, not called for by the party addressed; but if the publisher of any refused or uncalled-for newspaper or other periodical shall pay the postage due thereon, such newspaper or other periodical shall be excepted from the operation of such regulations. (R. S., § 4061.)

Sec. 479. Dead Foreign Printed Matter.—All foreign printed matter when unclaimed the usual time must be sent to the Dead-Letter Office as part of the regular return, but no entry thereof need be made on the bill except of that upon which postage may be due.

Sec. 480. Dead Domestic Printed Matter.—Domestic miscellaneous printed matter, without obvious value, including printed postal-cards, is not to be sent to the Dead-Letter Office when unclaimed, except that upon which postage may be due, but must be sold as waste-paper at the expiration of each quarter and the proceeds taken up and accounted for as other postal revenue.

Sec. 481. Dead Postal Cards.—Unclaimed postal cards wholly written will be sent to the Dead-Letter Office with the regular return at the expiration of thirty days. Foreign postal cards must be tied in a package by themselves.

Sec. 482. Return of Dead Matter.—In making up the return all matter sent should be securely wrapped and tied together in one package. At post-offices of the first, second, and third classes the foreign matter should be separated from the domestic. When the number of letters to be sent in a single return is large, they should be tied up in packets of one hunderd each, and then the whole return should be bound together in one parcel, or put into a suitable pouch properly addressed and indorsed. If there be third or fourth class matter to accompany the return in sufficient quantity to make it inconvenient to tie the whole in one parcel, a pouch must be used, so that all the matter will be received together.

Sec. 483. Record of Valuable Dead Letters.—Dead letters containing valuable inclosures shall be *registered* [recorded] in the Dead-Letter Office; and when they cannot be delivered to the party addressed nor to the writer, the contents thereof shall be disposed of, and a careful account shall be kept of the amount realized in each case, which shall be subject to reclamation by either the party addressed or the sender for four years from the *registry* [recording] thereof; and all other letters of value or of importance to the party addressed or to the writer, and which cannot be returned to either, shall be disposed of as the Postmaster-General may direct. (R. S., § 3938.)

Sec. 484. Return of Dead Letters Containing Money to Owners.—When dead letters containing money are sent from the Department to a postmaster for delivery to the owners, every effort must be made to discover the proper party to whom they may be delivered, and to this end these letters are inclosed to the postmaster open, that he may be enabled to identify the owner or claimant. The strictest secrecy must be maintained as to the contents. Under no circumstances whatever can a postmaster, or any other person through whose hands such letters pass, be allowed to make any exchange for other funds of the money originally contained therein.

Sec. 485. Return of Dead Money Letters back to Dead-Letter Office.—When such letters cannot be delivered after holding them thirty days from the date on which they were received, the postmaster will indorse the reason for non-delivery on the circular which accompanies each, and return the whole to the Department with duplicate lists (one of which will be verified and returned to the post-office) giving the Department letter, number, and book. The package will be plainly indorsed DEAD REGISTERED MATTER FROM ——— (here add name of post-office) and be addressed "*Dead-Letter Office, Washington, D. C.*"

Sec. 486. Returned Dead Money Letters must be Registered.—If a postmaster neglects to register packages containing such dead letters when returning them to the Department, and they are lost, he will be held responsible for the value of the contents.

Sec. 487. Other than Money Dead Letters need not be Registered.—Letters containing articles of value other than money are not to be registered when returned to the Department, unless they were received registered; but they must be inclosed in a sealed envelope or package and addressed to the "*Dead-Letter Office, Washington, D. C.*" No other kind of letters must be sent in the same package.

Sec. 488. Valuable Dead Letters must not be Forwarded.—Dead letters containing money or other inclosures, sent from the Department to a postmaster for delivery to the owners, must never be forwarded to another post-office, but must be returned to the Department with all the information obtainable as to the present whereabouts of the writer or owner; nor must they be retained by the postmaster longer than one month, unless he has been specially authorized by the Third Assistant Postmaster-General to hold them for a longer period.

Sec. 489. Dead letters not Valuable may be Forwarded.—Dead letters without valuable inclosures, when returned direct to writers (*i. e.*, not under cover to the postmaster), may be forwarded to another post-office for delivery, if necessary.

CHAPTER FOURTEEN.

LOST LETTERS AND MAIL DEPREDATIONS.

Sec. 490. Postmasters to report Lost Mail-Matter to Chief Special Agent.—It is the duty of postmasters to report promptly to the Chief Special Agent every complaint which is made to them or comes to their knowledge of the loss in the mails of letters or articles of value, whether registered or not.

Sec. 491. What Facts such Report must State.—In every case of loss by mail the Chief Special Agent should be immediately informed of all the circumstances connected with it, such as the name of the post-office in which the letter was posted and the date of mailing; whether by the writer himself or by another person; the names of the writer and the person addressed; the amount and a description of the inclosure; the post-office to which addressed: and whether registered or unregistered, and if registered the registry number, with any other particulars that may aid in making a thorough investigation.

Sec. 492. Postmasters to immediately Report Robbery of Post-Office.—Whenever a post-office has been robbed the postmaster will immediately report all the facts to the Chief Special Agent, and to the nearest resident Special Agent. This report must state as fully as possible all the circumstances connected with the robbery, giving the date and extent of the loss. He must be careful to state whether the loss consists of stamps, stamped-envelopes, postal-cards, letters (stolen or rifled), postal or money-order funds, or government property. If the loss includes the mail-key the number should be given; and if registered or ordinary mail-matter, he must be particular to state whether the same was rifled or taken from the post-office. He must give all the information in his possession relating to each lost or rifled registered letter, such as post-office where mailed, date of mailing, number of letter and registered-package envelope, by whom written, to whom addressed, and contents. For the value of registered or ordinary mail lost by robbery of post-offices postmasters will be held responsible if, upon investigation, it appears that due care was not taken to secure the mail-matter from depredation.

Sec. 493. Cases of Mail-Robbery to be Reported at once.—Cases of mail-robbery should at once be reported to the Chief Special Agent, and information given from time to time of any new facts which may be developed in regard to them.

Sec. 494. Report Arrest of Criminals to United States District Attorney.—When a criminal is apprehended, the United States attorney for the district in which the offense was committed must be promptly informed of the facts, and his advice, and, if possible, his personal attention, be obtained. If from any cause the services of the district attorney cannot be had, and it shall become necessary to employ another attorney, the compensation of such attorney must be agreed upon before engaging in the case, subject to the approval of the Postmaster-General; and it will only be paid upon recommendation of the Special Agent who may have charge of the case.

Sec. 495. Examination of Persons Arrested.—Persons arrested for mail depredations should be taken before a district or circuit judge, or a United States commissioner, for examination or commitment.

Sec. 496. Robbery of Mail in Vicinity of Post-Office.—If a postmaster has reason to believe that a mail has been stolen, in whole or in part, in the vicinity of his post-office, he shall at once examine into the evidence, and if satisfied that such robbery or theft has actually occurred, he shall take immediate and energetic measures for recovering the mail and for apprehending and prosecuting the offender, and shall notify the Chief Special Agent of the facts and of his action.

Sec. 497. Moneys Recovered from Mail Robbers.—All moneys recovered from mail robbers, &c., will be forwarded at once through the office of the Chief Special Agent to the Postmaster-General, who will, upon satisfactory evidence, return t same to the owners. See section 62.

CHAPTER FIFTEEN.

PAYMENT OF EMPLOYES OF THE RAILWAY MAIL SERVICE BY POSTMASTERS.

Sec. 493. Record of Arrivals and Departures to be Examined daily.—Postmasters will examine the record of arrivals and departures daily, when the same is kept at their post-offices, and report to the Division Superintendent at once all failures of employés to sign the same, and also all cases of advance signature. When the record of arrivals and departures are kept away from the post-office, they must be examined daily by some person designated by Division Superintendent, and all cases of failures to sign or of advance signature must be reported daily to him.

Sec. 499. Pay Withheld for Failure to Sign Record.—The paying postmaster shall withhold not exceeding one day's pay for each failure on part of an employé to record his arrival or departure, or to perform service, until the matter is reported to the Division Superintendent and instructions received from Second Assistant Postmaster-General. Whenever a failure to record or to perform service is reported by a paying postmaster he shall consider such report as a preliminary notice and shall withhold payment, as specified above, until specific instructions are received from the Second Assistant Postmaster-General.

Sec. 500. Preliminary Notice to Paying Postmaster.—In case of death, resignation, removal, suspension, or change of paying post-office of an employé, the Division Superintendent will at once send a preliminary notice to the paying postmaster.

Sec. 501. Notice to Second Assistant Postmaster-General.—On receipt of each report of failure by the Division Superintendent, he will at once report the same to the Second Assistant Postmaster-General, through the General Superintendent, and at the same time will send a copy of said report to the paying postmaster as a preliminary notice to him to withhold payment, as provided in section 499, until instructions are received from the Second Assistant Postmaster-General.

Sec. 502. Absences more than 30 Days to be Reported.—When an employé has been absent from duty more than thirty consecutive days, on account of sickness or other cause, the Division Superintendent will report the same to the Second Assistant Postmaster-General through the General Superintendent, and also send a preliminary notice to the paying postmaster.

Sec. 503. Partial Suspension of Pay, pending final Instructions.—In all cases where preliminary notice has been received from the Division Superintendent, the paying postmaster will withhold from the pay of the employé a sufficient sum to cover all stoppages, fines, and forfeitures of which he has been notified until final instructions in each case have been received from the Second Assistant Postmaster-General.

Sec. 504. The Cause of Deduction of Pay, etc., how Noted.—The cause of every deduction of pay, and the authority for making the same, must always be noted on pay-roll.

Sec. 505. "No Signature" and "Advance Signature," how Noted.—Whenever an employé fails to sign the record, the postmaster will write the words NO SIGNATURE in the line where the name should have been signed. In case of ADVANCE SIGNATURE, the same will be noted on the same line with the signature.

Sec. 506. Keys and Records must be Turned in before final Settlement.—On the resignation, transfer, suspension, or removal of an employé, final settlement with such employé will be deferred until the paying postmaster has received from the Division Superintendent in whose division such employé last performed service a certificate that all mail-keys, records, and other property of the Department have been turned over to him.

Sec. 507. Record of Arrivals and Departures sent Division Superintendent—At the end of each month postmasters will promptly forward the record of arrivals and departures, duly certified, to the Division Superintendent for inspection; after which they will be returned to the postmaster, who will see that they are carefully preserved.

Sec. 508. No Discretion to be used in Reporting Failures.—No discretion should be exercised by a postmaster, or by any other person in charge of a record of arrivals and departures, in reporting any failures on account of any peculiar circumstances attending the case. The failure should be reported promptly for reference to the Department, for decision upon the merits of the case.

Sec. 509. Instructions as to Paying Employés, from whom Received.—All instructions to postmasters relative to paying employés in the railway mail service must come from the Second Assistant Postmaster-General, Division of Inspection. Any payments made to employés contrary to the regulations and his instructions will be disallowed to the paying postmaster.

Sec. 510. Payments to be made promptly at end of Month.—Postmasters will be prepared to pay employés within three days after the expiration of the month in which the service was performed, but no payments shall be made until the month has expired, and no payment shall be made to employés after entry into service until the paying postmaster has been advised that the oath of office of such employé has been received by the General Superintendent of Railway Mail Service.

Sec. 511. Distinction between Substitute and Acting Employés.—Postmasters will observe the distinction between a substitute and an acting employé. A substitute is a person employed for or by a regular employé to perform his duties for him during his temporary absence from duty. An acting employé is a person employed temporarily to fill a vacancy caused by the death, removal, resignation, etc., of a regular employé. All sums paid to a substitute employé must be receipted for by the principal for or by whom the substitute was employed; but sums paid to an acting employé must be receipted for by such acting employé himself.

Sec. 512. Authority for Paying Acting Employés.—No payment shall be made to acting employés without specific authority from the Second Assistant Postmaster-General.

Sec. 513. Manner of Paying Acting Employees.—A receipt evidencing payment to an acting employé must be taken on a separate blank form furnished by the First Assistant Postmaster-General, Blank Agency. And these vouchers must be forwarded direct to the Second Assistant Postmaster-General, Division of Inspection, for necessary credit. The paying postmaster will also note on said receipts his authority for making the payment. Acting employés should never be put upon the regular pay-roll.

CHAPTER SIXTEEN.

MISCELLANEOUS PROVISIONS RESPECTING DUTIES OF POSTMASTERS.

Sec. 514. Records at Post-Offices of Property and Supplies.—Every Postmaster shall keep a record, in such form as the Postmaster-General shall direct, of all postage-stamps, envelopes, postal books, blanks, and property received from his predecessor, or from the Department or any of its agents; of all receipts in money for postages and box-rents, and of all other receipts on account of the postal service, and of any other transactions which may be required by the Postmaster-General; and these records shall be preserved and delivered to his successor, and shall be at all times subject to examination by any special agent of the Department. (R. S. § 3842.)

Sec. 515. Inventories of Public Property to be Made in Duplicate.—On taking charge of the post-office, each postmaster will make, in duplicate, inventories of the public property belonging to it, as follows:

1. Of all postage-stamps, stamped-envelopes, newspaper-wrappers, and postal-cards, and newspaper and periodical-stamps, and postage-due-stamps.

2. Of all Postal Guides, books of Postal Laws and Regulations, circulars, orders, rating-stamps, etc.

3. Of all desks, cases, and other furniture or fixtures, books, maps, blanks, and stationery allowed or furnished by the Department.

4. Of all locks, keys, and mail-bags.

Sec. 516. Duplicates, how to be Disposed of.—He will deliver one of these duplicates, with his receipt thereon, to his predecessor, and transmit the other as follows: No. 1, to the Auditor of the Treasury for the Post-Office Department; Nos. 2 and 3, to the First Assistant Postmaster-General; and No. 4, to the Second Assistant Postmaster-General.

Sec. 517. Postmaster not to Receive Money from Predecessor, unless.—Each postmaster, on taking charge of his post-office, will not receive from his predecessor any money belonging to the Department, unless specially instructed so to do. When the accounts of the outgoing postmaster have been finally settled he will be notified by the Auditor, and directed in what manner and to whom the balance due the Department shall be paid.

Sec. 518. Assistants to be Appointed.—Precaution should be taken by each postmaster to appoint an assistant, to prevent the post-office from being left without a duly qualified person to perform its duties in case of the necessary absence, the sickness, resignation, or death of the postmaster.

Sec. 519. Oath of Office to be Sent to Department.—Each postmaster will forward the oaths of his assistant, and of the clerks and employés of his post-office to the First Assistant Postmaster-General before they enter upon their duties.

Sec. 520. Who to have Access to Mail-matter in Post-office.—A postmaster will suffer no person whatever, except his duly sworn assistant, clerks, letter-carriers, and Special Agents of the Post-Office Department to have access to the letters, newspapers, and packets in his post-office, or to whatever constitutes a part of the mail, or to the mail locks or keys. This prohibition extends to all persons who may be employed on other duties than handling the mails. He should especially exclude mail contractors and their drivers.

Sec. 521. Mails not to be Opened in Reach of Unauthorized Persons.—Mails must not be opened or made up by the postmaster or his assistants within the reach of persons not authorized to handle them. The postmaster will, therefore, while discharging these duties, if a room be appropriated to the use of his post-office, exclude from it all persons except his assistants regularly employed and sworn.

Sec. 522. Postmasters must Collect and Examine Waste Paper, etc.—The postmaster, or one of his assistants, before the post-office is swept or cleared, should collect and examine the waste paper which has accumulated therein, in order to guard against the possibility of loss of letters or other mail-matter which may have fallen on the floor or have been intermingled with such waste paper during the transaction of business. The observance of this rule is strictly enjoined upon all postmasters. Postmasters should be careful to use, in mailing letters or packets, all wrapping-paper fit to be used again.

Sec. 523. No Post-office to be Located in Bar-room.—No post-office shall be located in a bar-room, or in any room directly connected therewith; nor must any mail be opened or any mail-matter delivered in any room in which liquor is sold at retail, except such liquors are sold by a druggist for medicinal purposes only.

Sec. 524. Loungers not to be Permitted in Post-office.—A postmaster must not allow his post-office to become the resort for loungers or disorderly persons, and whenever necessary he should invoke the aid of the civil authorities to enable him to free his post-office from the same. He is also required to keep his post-office in such a clean and orderly condition that it may be visited by women and children and others without impropriety and embarrassment.

Sec. 525. Business Hours at Post-offices.—Each postmaster will keep his post-office open for the dispatch of business every day, except Sunday, during the usual hours of business in the place, and attend at such other hours as may be necessary to receive and dispatch mails. When the mail arrives on Sunday, he will keep his post-office open for one hour or more after the arrival and assortment thereof, if the public convenience requires it, for the delivery of the same only. If it be received during the time of public worship, the opening of the post-office will be delayed until services have closed.

Sec. 526. Transaction of other Business at Fourth-class Post-offices.—Postmasters at post-offices of the fourth-class will be permitted to transact other business in the same room in which the post-office is located, provided such other business is kept separate and distinct from that of the post-office.

Sec. 527. Changing Site of Post-offices.—No postmaster should change the site or location of his post-office without permission from the Department. In making application for such change, the postmaster should state whether it involves any additional expense for transportation of the mail and is approved by the patrons of his post-office. The distance and direction of the proposed site from the present one should be also stated.

Sec. 528. Receiving Box for Mail at Third and Fourth Class Post-offices.—

LETTER BOX.

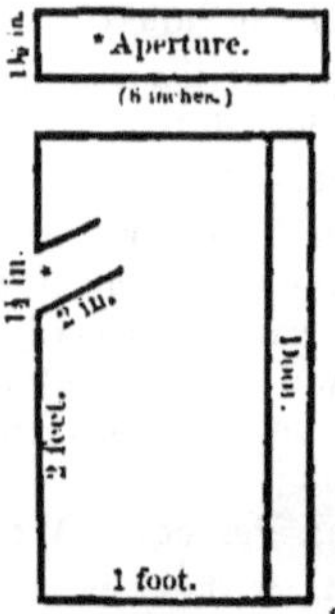

1½ in. *Aperture. (6 inches.)

1½ in. 2 in. 2 feet. Door. 1 foot.

A letter-box must be provided at third and fourth class post-offices, and must be constructed in the post-office window or in the wall; the aperture for the posting of letters must be horizontal, as shown in the margin, and must measure six inches by an inch and a half, and must be easily accessible to the public. The words "Letter-box" must be painted above the aperture. The box must be at least two feet in depth from the lower edge of the aperture, and not less than one foot wide and one foot from back to front; and directly underneath the aperture, on the inside, there should be a ledge, about two inches in width, inclining upwards, as shown in the margin, to prevent persons from seeing the contents of the box, and also to prevent letters from being drawn out of the box. The box should be shut by means of a door forming the entire back or side of the box. The door must always be securely locked, and the key kept in a safe place.

Sec. 529. Place for Mail-matter awaiting Delivery and for Stamps, etc.—At fourth-class post-offices a press or drawer must be provided to hold letters, &c., awaiting delivery, and a separate drawer to hold official papers (including instructions), which should never be placed with the letters. A drawer must be provided in which to keep postage stamps, and a box or till with a secure lock in which to place official cash, which must be kept entirely separate from the postmaster's private money.

Sec. 530. Sanctity of Seals Inviolable.—The several enactments of law defining crimes and offenses against the post-office establishment, to which reference should be frequently made by Special Agents, admonish every person in the employ of the Department that the law-making power intends to throw around the privity of correspondence the solemn sanction of its protection. One of the highest obligations of the Department to the people is to preserve, by all the means in its power, the absolute sanctity of a seal. The enactments referred to are entirely explicit. Special Agents are required to impress on postmasters and their subordinates, at all times, that the Postmaster-General will visit with punishment to the full extent of the law any violation of the law in this particular.

Sec. 531. Postmasters not to give Information respecting Mail-matter.—Postmasters and all others in the service are forbidden to furnish information concerning mail-matter received or delivered, except to the persons to whom it is addressed or to their authorized agents. The messages on postal cards must not be read, except when necessary to facilitate their delivery, or for the purpose of determining whether the same are unmailable by reason of the presence of obscene words or pictures thereon, nor made known to others. A disregard of this regulation will be considered a violation of official trust, and will render the offender liable to removal. Postmasters may, however, when the same can be done without interference with the regular business of the post-office, furnish to officers of the law, to aid them in discovering a fugitive from criminal justice, information concerning the postmarks and addresses of letters, but must not delay or refuse their delivery to the persons addressed.

Sec. 532. Postmasters Powerless to Remit Overcharges on Mail-matter.—

A postmaster has no discretionary power for the remission of penalties or overcharges on mail-matter. Under special circumstances cases will undoubtedly occur in which the strict observance of a general rule may inflict more or less injustice upon individuals. In such cases the postmaster should advise the party to appeal directly to the First Assistant Postmaster-General, he himself keeping, if possible, a record of the facts, so that he may verify or disprove the statement of the party appealing. The mail-matter upon which the appeal may be taken should remain in the possession of the post-office until after the decision of the First Assistant Postmaster General, though circumstances may present themselves where the matter should be delivered pending a decision.

Sec. 533. Official Correspondence, Return of Official Papers.—Applications and inquiries addressed to an officer of the Department become official papers, and when a paper is referred to the postmaster for any purpose, it must on no account be retained by him, but must be carefully returned, as speedily as possible, together with the report that may be required, to the officer from whom it has been received. Under no circumstances may official papers be allowed to pass into the hands of the public without express instructions to that effect.

Sec. 534. How Postmasters should Reply to Official Correspondence.—No official paper of any kind, whether requiring a reply or not, should be returned by the postmaster without some observations denoting that it has been received; and such observations should be written, if possible, directly following the communication to which they refer, in order that the questions and answers, or observations or rejoinders, may appear in consecutive order, according to their dates, and so that the papers may be read as the pages of a book. The postmaster must not fail to sign and date the papers containing every observation or reply that he may make, and the name of his post-office should also be added thereto.

Sec. 535. Postal Guide Supplied Officially and to be Consulted.—A copy of the United States Postal Guide is officially supplied to every postmaster, and he must consider the Guide as an instruction, to be carefully perused and attended to by himself and by his assistants, as well as a book of reference for the public.

Sec. 536. Postmasters in Doubt as to Law to Ask Instructions.—Whenever a postmaster is in doubt as to any provision of the law or regulations, he should, before making a decision or taking any action, address the proper office of the Department for instructions; and no expenditure of any kind must be made without the consent of the Department has been first obtained.

Sec. 537. Attention to be Given to Official Printed Circulars.—Postmasters are required to give the same attention to instructions contained in printed circulars sent from the different bureaus of the Department as to official manuscript letters.

Sec. 538. How Postmasters are to Address the Department.—Every postmaster, in addressing the Department, should write the name of his post-office, county, and State at the head of his letter, and avoid writing upon more than one subject in the same letter. Postmasters will be expected to obey this instruction to the letter. Letters must be plainly addressed to the proper office of the Department.

Sec. 539. Public Documents and Property to be Turned over to Successor.—All instructions, circulars, and orders received by a postmaster from any officer of the Department are to be filed in the post-office and turned over to his successor. In like manner he will turn over to his successor, or, in the event of the discontinuance of the post-office, deliver to the postmaster designated by the First Assistant Postmaster-General, as public property, all safes, desks, cases, and other furniture and fixtures, and all books, office records (such as duplicate pay-rolls, records of arrivals and departures of mails, and of employés of the railway mail service), all maps, blanks, stationery, copies of this book, and other articles which have either been furnished to him as postmaster or have been charged and allowed at any time, and which may remain on hand when the vacancy or discontinuance occurs.

Sec. 540. Credentials of Special Agents to be Demanded.—Postmasters should always insist upon the exhibition of the credentials of persons representing themselves to be Special Agents of the Department unless personally known to them to be such. A Special Agent's credentials are always signed by the Postmaster-General himself.

Sec. 541. Postmasters not to Act as Lottery Agents.—No postmaster shall act as agent for any lottery office, or under any color of purchase, or otherwise vend lottery tickets; nor shall he receive or send any lottery scheme, circular, or ticket free of postage. For any violation of this section the offender shall be liable to a penalty of fifty dollars. (R. S., § 3851.)

TITLE III.

TRANSPORTATION OF THE MAIL.

CHAPTER ONE.

DESIGNATION OF POST-ROADS OVER WHICH THE MAIL MAY BE CARRIED.

Sec. 542. What are Post-roads.—The following are established post-roads:

All the waters of the United States, during the time the mail is carried thereon.

All railroads or parts of railroads which are now or hereafter may be in operation.

All canals, during the time the mail is carried thereon.

All plank-roads, during the time the mail is carried thereon.

The road on which the mail is carried to supply any court-house which may be without a mail, and the road on which the mail is carried under contract made by the Postmaster-General for extending the line of posts to supply mails to post-offices not on any established route, during the time such mail is carried thereon.

All letter-carrier routes established in any city or town for the collection and delivery of mail matters. (R. S., § 3964.)

Sec. 543. The Postmaster-General may Establish Service on Post-roads.—The Postmaster-General shall provide for carrying the mail on all post-roads established by law, as often as he, having due regard to productiveness and other circumstances, may think proper. (R. S., § 3965.)

Sec. 544. All Court-houses to be Supplied with Mail.—The Postmaster-General shall cause a mail to be carried from the nearest post-office on any established post-road to the court-house of any county in the United States which is without a mail. (R. S., § 3966.)

Sec. 545. Carrying the Mail on Canals.—The Postmaster-General may contract for carrying the mail on the navigable canals of the several

States, when, in his opinion, the public interest or convenience requires it. (R. S., § 3967.)

Sec. 546. Carrying the Mail on Plank-roads.—The Postmaster-General may contract for carrying the mail on any plank-road in the United States, when the public interest or convenience requires it. (R. S., § 3968.)

Sec. 547. Carrying the Mail on Waters of the United States.—The Postmaster-General may cause the mail to be carried in any steamboat or other vessel used as a packet on any of the waters of the United States. (R. S., § 3969.)

Sec. 548. Extending Mail Facilities to Special Post-Offices.—The Postmaster-General may enter into contracts for extending the line of posts to supply mails to post-offices not on any established route, and, as a compensation for carrying the mail under such contracts, may allow not exceeding two-thirds of the salary paid to the postmaster at such special [post] offices. (R. S., § 3971.)

See "Special instructions to postmasters."

Sec. 549. Selecting Post-roads.—When there is more than one road between places designated by law for a post-road, the Postmaster-General may direct which shall be considered the post-road. (R. S., § 3972.)

Sec. 550. When Terminus of Post-roads may be Changed.—The Postmaster-General may change the terminus of post-roads connecting with or intersecting railways when the service can be thereby improved. (R. S., § 3973.)

Sec. 551. Discontinuing Service on Post-roads.—Whenever, in the opinion of the Postmaster-General, the postal service cannot be safely continued, the revenues collected, or the laws maintained on any post-road, he may discontinue the service on such road or any part thereof until the same can be safely restored. (R. S., § 3974.)

Sec. 552. Authority of Postmaster-General to Establish Post-roads.—The Postmaster-General may, when he deems it advisable, contract for the transportation of the mails to and from any post-office; but where such service is performed over a route not established by law, he shall report the same to Congress at its meeting next thereafter, and such service shall cease at the end of the next session of Congress, unless such route is established a post-route by Congress. (R. S., § 3975.)

Sec. 553. Penalty for Obstructing the Mail.—Any person who shall knowingly and willfully obstruct or retard the passage of the mail, or any carriage, horse, driver, or carrier carrying the same, shall, for every such offense, be punishable by a fine of not more than one hundred dollars. (R. S., § 3995.)

The temporary detention of the mail, caused by the arrest of its carrier upon an indictment for felony, does not come within the provisions of this section, but a mail-carrier on his route cannot be detained by civil process. (U. S. *vs.* Kirby, 7 Wallace, 482.)

A city may prohibit by ordinance the passage of trains through its limits at a rate of speed not exceeding six miles per hour, and not conflict with this section. (5 Opins. 554.)

Sec. 554. Delaying Mail at a Ferry, Penalty.—Any ferryman who shall delay the passage of the mail by willful neglect or refusal to transport the same across any ferry shall, for every ten minutes such mail may be so delayed, be liable to a penalty of ten dollars. (R. S., § 3996.)

CHAPTER TWO.

CARRIAGE OF THE MAIL A GOVERNMENT MONOPOLY.—UNLAWFUL CARRIAGE OF MAIL-MATTER OUTSIDE OF THE MAILS.—SEIZURE AND DETENTION OF UNLAWFUL MATTER IN THE MAILS.

Sec. 555. Prohibition of Private Expresses.—No person shall establish any private express for the conveyance of letters or packets, or in any manner cause or provide for the conveyance of the same by regular trips or at stated periods, over any post-route which is or may be established by law, or from any city, town, or place to any other city, town, or place between which the mail is regularly carried; and every person so offending, or aiding or assisting therein, shall for each offense be liable to a penalty of one hundred and fifty dollars. *Provided*, Nothing herein contained shall be construed as prohibiting any person from receiving and delivering to the nearest post-office or postal car mail-matter properly stamped. (R. S., § 3982, as modified by act of March 3, 1879, § 1, 20 Stat., p. 356.)

The term packet, as used in this and the following sections of the law, is restricted to mailable matter of the first class. (Opin. No. 14, Ass't Att'y-Gen. P. O. Dept.—Spence.)

A person who intends to make the carrying of letters periodically for hire his regular business, or part of his business, in opposition to the public carriers, is legally incapable of receiving authority to take letters out of the post-office for that purpose, however such authority may be attempted to be conferred. (9 Opins., 161.)

Sec. 556. Private Carriers Forbidden at Carrier Post-Offices.—Postmasters at letter-carrier post-offices will under no circumstances deliver first-class mail-matter to a private carrier, no matter what credentials he may present, whether it be a joint order from all of his employers, or a separate order from each one, a permanent standing order, or an order renewed every day.

Sec. 557. Penalty for Carrying Persons Acting as Express.—The owner of every stage-coach, railway-car, steamboat, or other vehicle or vessel, which shall, with the knowledge of any owner, in whole or in part, or with the knowledge or connivance of the driver, conductor, master, or other person having charge of the same, convey any person acting or employed as a private express for the conveyance of letters or packets, and actually in possession of the same for the purpose of conveying them, contrary to the spirit, true intent, and meaning of this title, shall, for every such offense, be liable to a penalty of one hundred and fifty dollars. (R. S., § 3983.)

Sec. 558. Penalty for Sending Letters by Private Express.—No person shall transmit by private express or other unlawful means, or deliver to any agent of such unlawful express, or deposit, or cause to be deposited, at any appointed place, for the purpose of being transmitted, any letter or packet; and for every such offense the party offending shall be liable to a penalty of fifty dollars. (R. S., § 3984.)

Sec. 559. Penalty for Carrying Letters out of the Mails.—Any person concerned in carrying the mail, who shall collect, receive, or carry any letter or packet, or cause or procure the same to be done, contrary to law, shall, for every such offense, be punishable by a fine of not more than fifty dollars. (R. S., § 3981.) No stage-coach, railway-car, steamboat, or other vehicle or vessel which regularly performs trips at stated periods on any post-route, or from any city, town, or place to any other city, town, or place, between which the mail is regularly carried, shall carry, otherwise than in the mail, any letters or packets, except such as relate to some part of the cargo of such steamboat or other vessel, or to some article carried at the same time by the same stage-coach, railway-car, or other vehicle, except as provided in section [568] [*three thousand nine hundred and ninety-three*]; and for every such offense the owner of the stage-coach, railway-car, steamboat, or other vehicle or vessel shall be liable to a penalty of one hundred dollars; and the driver, conductor, master, or other person having charge thereof, and not at the time owner of the whole or any part thereof, shall for every such offense be liable to a penalty of fifty dollars. (R. S., § 3985.)

Sec. 560. Penalty for Carrying Letters on Board a Mail-Vessel.—No person shall carry any letter or packet on board any vessel which carries the mail otherwise than in such mail, except as provided in section [568] [*three thousand nine hundred and ninety-three*], and for every such offense the party offending shall be liable to a penalty of fifty dollars. (R. S., § 3986.)

Sec. 561. Foreign Letters only to be Received from a Post-Office.—No vessel departing from the United States for any foreign port shall receive on board or convey any letter or packet originating in the United States which has not been regularly received from the post-office at the port of departure, and which does not relate to the cargo of such vessel, except as provided in section [568] [*three thousand nine hund red and ninety three*]; and every collector, or other officer of the port empowered to grant clearances, shall require from the master of such vessel, as a condition of clearance, an oath that he has not received on board, has not under his care or control, and will not receive or convey any letter or packet contrary to the provisions of this section. (R. S., § 3987.)

Sec. 562. Vessels to Deliver all Letters at Post-Office.—No vessel arriving within any port or collection-district of the United States shall be allowed to make entry or break bulk until all letters on board are delivered at the nearest post-office, and the master thereof has signed and sworn to the following declaration, before the collector or other proper customs officer:

"I, A. B., master of the ——, arriving from ——, and now lying in the port of ——, do solemnly swear (or affirm) that I have, to the best of my knowledge and belief, delivered, at the post-office at ——, every letter, and every bag, packet, or parcel of letters, which were on board the said vessel during her last voyage, or which were in my possession or under my power or control."

And any master who shall break bulk before he has delivered such letters shall be liable to a penalty of not more than one hundred dollars, recoverable, one-half to the officer making the seizure, and the other to the use of the United States. (R. S., § 3988.)

Sec. 563. Special Agents to Search Vessels for Letters.—Any special agent of the Post-Office Department, when instructed by the Postmaster-General to make examinations and seizures, and the collector or other customs officer of any port, without special instructions, shall carefully search all vessels for letters which may be on board or which have been conveyed contrary to law. (R. S., § 3989.)

Sec. 564. Seizing and Detaining Letters.—Any special agent of the Post-Office Department, collector, or other customs officer, or United States marshal or his deputy, may at all times seize all letters and bags, packets or parcels, containing letters which are being carried contrary to law on board any vessel or on any post-route, and convey the same to the nearest post-office, or may, by the direction of the Postmaster-General or Secretary of the Treasury, detain them until two months after the final determination of all suits and proceedings which may, at any time within six months after such seizure, be brought against any person for sending or carrying such letters. (R. S., 3990.)

Sec. 565. Forfeiture of Seizures to the United States.—Every package or parcel seized by any special agent of the Post-Office Department, collector, or other customs officer, or United States marshal or his deputies, in which any letter is unlawfully concealed, shall be forfeited to the United States, and the same proceedings may be had to enforce the forfeiture as are authorized in respect to goods, wares, and merchandise forfeited for violation of the revenue laws; and all laws for the benefit and protection of customs officers making seizures for violating revenue laws shall apply to officers making seizures for violating the postal laws. (R. S., § 3991.)

See Title xxxiv, chap. 10, Rev. Stat.

Sec. 566. Letters Seized may be Returned to Senders.—All letters, packets, or other matter which may be seized or detained for violation of law shall be returned to the owner or sender of the same, or otherwise disposed of as the Postmaster-General may direct. (R. S., § 3895.)

Sec. 567. Letters Conveyed Without Compensation.—Nothing herein contained shall be construed to prohibit the conveyance or transmission of letters or packets by private hands without compensation, or by special messenger employed for the particular occasion only. (R. S., § 3992.)

Sec. 568. Letters in Stamped Envelopes.—All letters inclosed in stamped envelopes, if the postage-stamp is of a denomination sufficient to cover the postage that would be chargeable thereon if the same were sent by mail, may be sent, conveyed, and delivered otherwise than by mail, provided such envelope shall be duly directed and properly sealed, so that the letter cannot be taken therefrom without defacing the envelope, and the date of the letter or of the transmission or receipt thereof shall be written or stamped upon the envelope. But the Postmaster-General may suspend the operation of this section upon any mail-route where the public interest may require such suspension. (R. S., § 3993.)

Sec. 569. Postmasters must Report Violations of Postal Monopoly.—Whenever a postmaster receives information or has good reason to believe that letters are illegally brought to or sent from any city, town, landing, station, or place, near his post-office, whether by steamboat, railroad, private carrier for hire, or any other mode of conveyance, or in any way in violation of the preceding section, he will give immediate notice of such violation of law to the Postmaster-General, with all the facts concerning it in his possession.

Sec. 570. Searches Authorized.—The Postmaster-General may, by a letter of authorization under his hand, to be filed among the records of his Department, empower any special agent or other officer of the Post-Office Establishment to make searches for mailable matter transported in violation of law; and the agent or officer so authorized may open and search any car or vehicle passing, or having lately before passed, from any place at which there is a post-office of the United States to any other such place, or any box, package, or packet, being, or having lately before been, in such car or vehicle, or any store or house, other than a dwelling-house, used or occupied by any common carrier or transportation company, in which such box, package, or packet may be contained, whenever such agent or officer has reason to believe that mailable matter, transported contrary to law, may therein be found. (R. S., § 4026.)

Sec. 571. Newspapers may be Carried out of the Mail.—Contractors or mail-carriers may convey out of the mail newspapers for sale or distribution to subscribers. (R. S., § 3888.)

Sec. 572. On such Papers Deposited in Post-Office Postage must be Paid.—If newspapers which have been carried outside of the mail are placed in a post-office for delivery, postage must be charged and collected. Contractors and other persons may also convey books, pamphlets, magazines, and newspapers (not intended for immediate distribution), done up in packages as merchandise, and addressed to some *bona-fide* news-agent or bookseller.

CHAPTER THREE.

ADVERTISEMENTS, PROPOSALS, AND CONTRACTS FOR CARRYING THE MAIL.

Sec. 573. Advertisement of General Mail-Lettings.—The Postmaster-General shall cause advertisements of all general mail-lettings of each State and Territory to be conspicuously posted up in each post-office in the State and Territory embraced in said advertisements for at least sixty days before the time of such general letting; and no other advertisement of such letting shall be required; but this provision shall not apply to any other than general mail-lettings. (Act March 3, 1879, § 1, 20 Stat., p. 356.) See R. S., § 3941; see 19 Stat., 78, 383.)

See also section 578.

Sec. 574. Division of the United States into Contract Sections.—The United States is divided into four contract sections. A general letting for one of these sections occurs every year, and contracts are made at such general lettings for four consecutive years, commencing on the first day of July. The sections and their current contract terms are—

1. Maine, New Hampshire, Vermont, Massachusetts Rhode Island, Connecticut, New York, New Jersey, Pennsylvania, Delaware, Maryland, District of Columbia, Virginia, and West Virginia; current term, July 1, 1877, to June 30, 1881.

2. North Carolina, South Carolina, Georgia, Florida, Alabama, Mississippi, Tennessee, Kentucky, Ohio, and Indiana; current term, July 1, 1876, to June 30, 1880.

3. Illinois, Michigan, Wisconsin, Minnesota, Iowa, and Missouri; current term, July 1, 1879, to June 30, 1883.

4. Arkansas, Louisiana, Texas, Indian Territory, Kansas, Nebraska, Dakota, Montana, Wyoming, Colorado, New Mexico, Arizona, Utah, Idaho, Washington, Oregon, Nevada, and California; current term, July 1, 1878, to June 30, 1882.

Sec. 575. Advertisement of Routes Omitted in General Letting.—Whenever by reason of any error, omission, or other cause any route which should properly be advertised for the regular letting is omitted, it shall be the duty of the Postmaster-General to advertise the same as soon as the error or omission shall be discovered, and the proposals for such route shall be opened as soon as possible after the other proposals in the same contract section; and the contract made under such supplementary advertisement shall run, as nearly as possible, from the beginning to the end of the regular contract term, and during the time necessarily lost by reason of such error, omission, or other cause, the Postmaster-General shall provide for the carrying of the mail on such route at as low rate as possible, without advertising. (R. S., § 3957.)

Sec. 576. Notice of Intention to Change Terms of Contract.—Whenever it becomes necessary to change the terms of an existing contract for carrying the mail otherwise than as provided in (*the preceding*) section [618 and 619], notice thereof shall be given and proceedings had thereon the same as at the letting of original contracts. (R. S., § 3958.)

Sec. 577. Miscellaneous Mail-Lettings Defined.—The lettings for service upon new mail-routes established by Congress in any contract division of the United States during a contract term, and upon routes where the contractor has failed or abandoned his contract, are denominated miscellaneous mail-lettings. Such lettings are made under advertisement to cover the mail service on such routes until the expiration of the contract term, when the service, if continued, is embraced in the general mail-letting.

Sec. 578. Advertisement of Miscellaneous Mail-Lettings.—Before making any contract for inland mail transportation, other than by railroads and steamboats, except for temporary service, as provided for in [sections 603–605] [*an act approved August eleventh, eighteen hundred and seventy-six, amendatory of sub-sections two hundred and forty-six and two hundred and fifty-one of section twelve of an act approved June twenty-third, eighteen hundred and seventy-four*] the Postmaster-General shall cause to be published, in not exceeding ten newspapers published in the State or

Territory in which such service is to be let, one of which shall be published at the seat of government of such State or Territory, once a week, for six consecutive weeks, preceding the time of letting, a notice in displayed type, not to exceed six inches of space in one column of a newspaper of the following purport:

MAIL LETTINGS.

NOTICE TO CONTRACTORS.

POST-OFFICE DEPARTMENT,
Washington, D. C., ——, —, 18—.

Proposals will be received at the Contract Office of this Department until — a. m., of ———, ——, 18—, for carrying the mails of the United States upon the routes, and according to the schedule of arrival and departure, specified by the Department, in the State (or Territory) of ———, from ——, 18—, to ——, 18—. Lists of routes, with schedules of arrivals and departures, instructions to bidders, with forms for contracts and bonds, and all other necessary information, will be furnished upon application to the Second Assistant Postmaster-General.

——— ———,
Postmaster-General.

and no other advertisement of miscellaneous lettings shall be required: *Provided*, That said contracts for mail letting shall not take place in less than sixty days after the first publication. (Act May 17, 1878, § 1, 20 Stat., p. 61.)

Sec. 579. Rates to be Paid for Advertisements.—Hereafter all advertisements, notices, proposals for contracts, and all other forms of advertising required by law for the Post-Office Department may be paid for at a price not to exceed the commercial rates charged to private individuals with the usual discounts, such rates to be ascertained from sworn statements to be furnished to the Postmaster-General by the proprietors of the newspapers proposing to so advertise. But the Postmaster-General may secure lower terms at special rates, whenever the public interest requires it. (Act May 17, 1878, § 4, 20 Stat., p. 61.)

Sec. 580. Proposals for Carrying the Mail, how Delivered and Opened.—Proposals for carrying the mail shall be delivered sealed, and so kept until the bidding is closed, and shall then be opened and marked in the presence of the Postmaster-General, and one of the Assistant Postmasters-General, or of two of the Assistant Postmasters-General, or of any other two officers of the Department, to be designated by the Postmaster-General; and any bidder may withdraw his bid at any time before twenty-four hours previous to the time fixed for the opening of proposals, by serving upon the Postmaster-General, or the Second Assistant Postmaster-General, notice in writing of such withdrawal. (R. S., § 3944.)

Sec. 581. Proposals Accompanied by Bonds Approved by Postmasters.—

Every proposal for carrying the mail shall be accompanied by the bond of the bidder, with sureties approved by a postmaster, and in cases where the amount of the bond exceeds five thousand dollars, by a postmaster of the first, second, or third class, in a sum to be designated by the Postmaster-General in the advertisement of each route; to which bond a condition shall be annexed, that if the said bidder shall, within such time after his bid is accepted as the Postmaster-General shall prescribe, enter into a contract with the United States of America, with good and sufficient sureties, to be approved by the Postmaster-General, to perform the service proposed in his said bid, and, further, that he shall perform the said service according to his contract, then the said obligation to be void, otherwise to be in full force and obligation in law; and in case of failure of any bidder to enter into such contract to perform the service, or, having executed a contract, in case of failure to perform the service, according to his contract, he and his sureties shall be liable for the amount of said bond as liquidated damages, to be recovered in an action of debt on the said bond. No proposal shall be considered unless it shall be accompanied by such bond, and there shall have been affixed to said proposal the oath of the bidder, taken before an officer qualified to administer oaths, that he has the ability, pecuniarily, to fulfill his obligations, and that the bid is made in good faith, and with the intention to enter into contract, and perform the service in case his bid is accepted. (R. S., § 3945, as amended by act June 23, 1874, § 12, 18 Stat., p. 235.)

Sec. 532. Sureties on Bidders' Bonds must Qualify.—Before the bond of a bidder provided for in the aforesaid section is approved, there shall be indorsed thereon the oaths of the sureties therein, taken before an officer qualified to administer oaths, that they are owners of real estate, worth, in the aggregate, a sum double the amount of the said bond, over and above all debts due and owing by them, and all judgments, mortgages, and executions against them, after allowing all exemptions of every character whatever. Accompanying said bond, and as a part thereof, there shall be a series of interrogatories in print or writing, to be prescribed by the Postmaster-General, and answered by the sureties under oath, showing the amount of real estate owned by them; a brief description thereof, and its probable value; where it is situated; in what county and State the record evidence of their title exists. And if any surety shall knowingly and willfully swear falsely to any statement made under the provisions of this section, he shall be deemed guilty of perjury, and, on conviction thereof, be punished as is provided by law for commission of the crime of perjury. (R. S., § 3946, as amended by act August 11, 1876, 19 Stat., p. 129.)

Sec. 533. Amount of Bond Required Stated in Advertisement.—The amount of bond required with bids, and the present pay when it exceeds ($5,000) five thousand dollars, are stated in the advertisement under the appropriate route.

Sec. 534. Qualification of Sureties on More than One Bond.—When the same persons are sureties on more than one bond such real estate must equal in value not less than one-fourth the aggregate of all the bonds on which they are sureties. A married woman will not be accepted as surety, either on the bond of a bidder or contractor.

Sec. 585. Bids to be Accompanied by a Certified Check or Draft.—Hereafter all bidders upon every mail route for the transportation of the mails upon the same, where the annual compensation for the service on such route at the time exceeds the sum of five thousand dollars, shall accompany their bids with a certified check or draft, payable to the order of the Postmaster-General, upon some solvent national bank, which check or draft shall not be less than five per centum on the amount of the annual pay on said route at the time such bid is made, and, in case of new or modified service, not less than five per centum of the amount of the bond of the bidder required to accompany his bid, if the amount of the said bond exceeds five thousand dollars. (In case any bidder, on being awarded any such contract, shall fail to execute the same with good and sufficient sureties, according to the terms on which such bid was made and accepted, and enter upon the performance of the service to the satisfaction of the Postmaster-General, such bidder shall, in addition to his liability on his bond accompanying his bid, forfeit the amount so deposited to the United States, and the same shall forthwith be paid into the Treasury for the use of the Post-Office Department; but if such contract shall be duly executed and the service entered upon as aforesaid, said draft or check so deposited, and the checks or drafts deposited by all other bidders, on the same route, shall be returned to the respective bidders making such deposits.) No proposals for the transportation of the mails where the amount of the bond required to accompany the same shall exceed five thousand dollars shall be considered, unless accompanied with the check or draft herein required, together with the bond required by a preceding section: *Provided*, That nothing in this act shall be construed or intended to affect any penalties or forfeitures which may have heretofore accrued under the provisions of the sections hereby amended. (R. S., § 3953, as amended by act June 23, 1874, § 12, 18 Stat., p. 236.)

Sec. 586. Time of Returning Drafts to Unsuccessful Bidders.—The checks or drafts required to be deposited by the preceding section will be retained until after the contract has been duly executed and the service commenced by the accepted bidder. Checks and drafts of unsuccessful bidders will be returned to them by mail on the written request of the bidders, or delivered to any one on their order. See section 598.

Sec. 587. Penalty for Illegally Approving Bonds.—Any postmaster who shall affix his signature to the approval of any bond of a bidder, or to the certificate of sufficiency of sureties in any contract before the said bond or contract is signed by the bidder or contractor and his sureties, or shall knowingly, or without the exercise of due diligence, approve any bond of the bidder with insufficient sureties, or shall knowingly make any false or fraudulent certificate, shall be forthwith dismissed from office, and be thereafter disqualified from holding the office of postmaster, and shall also be deemed guilty of a misdemeanor, and, on conviction thereof, be punished by a fine not exceeding five thousand dollars, or by imprisonment not exceeding one year, or both (R. S., § 3947, as amended by act June 23, 1874, § 12, 18 Stat., p. 235.)

Sec. 533. All Proposals to be Recorded and Filed.—The Postmaster-General shall have recorded, in a book to be kept for that purpose, a true and faithful abstract of all proposals made to him for carrying the mail, giving the name of the party offering, the terms of the offer, the sum to be paid, and the time the contract is to continue; and he shall put on file and preserve the originals of all such proposals. (R. S., § 3948.)

Sec. 589. Combinations to Prevent Bids, Penalty.—No contract for carrying the mail shall be made with any person who has entered, or proposed to enter, into any combination to prevent the making of any bid for carrying the mail, or who has made any agreement, or given or performed, or promised to give or perform, any consideration whatever to induce any other person not to bid for any such contract; and if any person so offending is a contractor for carrying the mail, his contract may be annulled; and for the first offense the person so offending shall be disqualified to contract for carrying the mail for five years, and for the second offense shall be forever disqualified. (R. S., § 3950.)

See section 601.

Sec. 590. Caution to Postmasters Signing Bidders' Bonds.—Postmasters are cautioned, under penalty of removal, not to sign the approval of the bond of any bidder before the proposal is completed and the bond is signed by the bidder and his sureties, and not until entirely satisfied of the sufficiency of the sureties. They are also cautioned not to divulge to any one the amount of any proposal certified by them. Doing so will be sufficient cause for their removal.

Sec. 591. What are Legal Bids.—Bids that propose to transport the mails with "celerity, certainty, and security," having been decided to be the only legal bids, are construed as providing for the entire mail, however large, and whatever may be the mode of conveyance necessary to insure its "celerity, certainty, and security," and have the preference over all others, and no others are considered, except for steamboat routes.

Sec. 592. Bidders Must Inform Themselves as to Character of Service.—The distances stated in the advertisements for mail proposals are given according to the best information; but no increased pay will be allowed should they be greater than advertised, if the points to be supplied are correctly stated. Bidders must inform themselves on this point, and also in reference to the weight of the mail, the condition of roads, hills, streams, etc., and all toll-bridges, ferries, or obstructions of any kind by which expense may be incurred. No claim for additional pay, based on such grounds, can be considered; nor for alleged mistakes or misapprehension as to the degree of service; nor for bridges destroyed, ferries discontinued, or other obstructions increasing distance, occurring during the contract term. Post-offices established during a contract term are to be visited without extra pay, if the distance be not increased, and at *pro rata* pay for any increase of distance.

Sec. 593. Special Instructions to Bidders.—Bidders should first propose for service strictly according to the advertisement, and then, if they desire, separately for different service; and if the regular bid be the lowest offered for the advertised service, the other propositions may be considered.

There should be but one route bid for in a proposal. Consolidated or combination bids ("proposing one sum for two or more routes") cannot be considered.

The route, the service, the yearly pay, the name and residence of the bidder (that is, his usual post-office address), and the name of each member of a firm where a company offers, should be distinctly stated.

Bidders are requested to use, as far as practicable, the printed proposals furnished by the Department, to write out in full the sum of their bids, and to retain copies of them.

Sec. 594. Alterations and Modifications of Bids Prohibited.—Bids altered in the route, the service, the yearly pay, the name of the bidder, or any material part of the bond, by erasures or interlineations, should not be submitted; and if so submitted will not be considered in awarding the contracts.

A modification of a bid in any of its essential terms is tantamount to a new bid, and cannot be received so as to interfere with regular competition. Making a new bid in proper form is the only way to modify a previous one, and such previous bid must be withdrawn if it is desired that it shall not be considered.

No withdrawal of a bid will be allowed unless the withdrawal is received twenty-four hours previous to the time fixed for opening the proposals.

Sec. 595. Bidders Must be of Legal Age.—No bidder will be accepted who is under twenty-one years of age, or who is a married woman.

Sec. 596. Bids which Cannot be Received.—Bids received after the time named in an advertisement will not be considered. Neither can bids be considered which are without the bond, oath, and certificate required by section 581 and section 582.

Sec. 597. Bids which may be Rejected.—The Postmaster-General reserves the right to reject all bids on any route whenever in his judgment the interests of the service require it. See sections 589 and 601.

Sec. 598. Bidders not Released from Bonds until Service is Commenced.—No bidder for carrying the mails shall be released from his obligation under his bid or proposal, notwithstanding an award made to a lower bidder, until a contract for the designated service shall have been duly executed by such lower bidder and his sureties, and accepted, and the service entered upon by the contractor to the satisfaction of the Postmaster-General. (R. S., § 3952.)

Sec. 599. Persons who may not be Interested in Mail Contracts.—No postmaster, assistant postmaster, or clerk employed in any post-office shall be a contractor or concerned in a contract for carrying the mail. (R. S., § 3850.)

See section 43.

Postmasters are also liable to dismissal from office for acting as agents of contractors or bidders, with or without compensation, in any business, matter, or thing relating to the mail service. They are the trusted agents of the Department, and cannot consistently act in both capacities.

Sec. 600. Bidders may not Assign or Transfer their Bids.—Bids or interests in bids cannot be transferred or assigned to other parties. Bidders will, therefore, take notice that they will be expected to perform the service awarded to them through the whole contract term.

Sec. 601. Contracts in Name of United States, and Awarded to Lowest Bidder.—All contracts for carrying the mail shall be in the name of the United States, and shall be awarded to the lowest bidder tendering sufficient guarantees for faithful performance, without other reference to the mode of transportation than may be necessary to provide for the due celerity, certainty, and security thereof; but the Postmaster-General shall not be bound to consider the bid of any person who has willfully or negligently failed to perform a former contract. (R. S., § 3949.)

Sec. 602. New Sureties on Contracts may be Required or Accepted.—The Postmaster-General, whenever he may deem it consistent with the public interest, may accept or require new surety upon any contract existing or hereafter made for carrying the mails, in substitution for and release of any existing surety. (R. S., § 3955, as amended by act of March 3, 1879, § 30, 20 Stat., p. 362.)

Sec. 603. Bidder Failing, Contract with other Persons Authorized.—After any regular bidder whose bid has been accepted shall fail to enter into contract for the transportation of the mails according to his proposal, or, having entered into contract, shall fail to commence the performance of the service stipulated in his or their contract, as therein provided, the Postmaster-General shall proceed to contract with the next lowest bidder or bidders in the order of their bids, for the same service, who will enter into a contract for the performance thereof, unless the Postmaster-General shall consider such bid or bids too high, and in case each of said bids shall be considered too high, then the Postmaster-General shall be authorized to enter into contract, at a price less than that named in said bids, with any person, whether a bidder or not, who will enter into contract to perform the service in accordance with the terms and provisions prescribed for the execution of other contracts for similar service; and in case no satisfactory contract can be thus obtained, he shall readvertise such route. (R. S., § 3951, as amended by act August 11, 1876, 19 Stat., p. 129.)

Sec. 604. Contractor failing, Contracts with Other Persons Authorized.—And if any bidder whose bid has been accepted, and who has entered into a contract to perform the service according to his proposal, and in pursuance of his contract has entered upon the performance of the service, to the satisfaction of the Postmaster-General, shall subsequently fail or refuse to perform the service according to his contract, the Postmaster-General shall proceed to contract with the next lowest bidder for such service, under the advertisement thereof, (unless the Postmaster-General shall consider such bid too high) who will enter into contract and give bond, with sureties to be approved by the Postmaster-General, for the faithful performance thereof, in the same penalty and with the same terms and conditions thereto annexed as were stated and contained in the bond which accompanied his bid; and in case said next lowest bidder shall decline to enter into contract for the performance of such service, then the Postmaster-General may award the service to, and enter into contract with, any person, whether a bidder on said route or not, who will enter into contract to perform the service and execute a bond of like tenor and effect as that required of bidders, in a penalty to be prescribed, and with sureties to be approved by the Postmaster-General, for the performance of the service contracted to be performed at a price not exceeding that named in the bid of the said next lowest bidder; and if no contract can be secured at the price named in said next lowest bid, then the Postmaster-General shall proceed to secure a contract, at a price not considered too high, with any person who will execute such contract in accordance with the law applicable thereto, giving, in all cases, the preference to the regular bidders on the list whose bids do not exceed the price at which others will contract therefor; and if no satisfactory contract can be thus secured the route shall be readvertised. (*Ibid.*)

Sec. 605. Temporary Contracts Authorized at last Contract Price.—Whenever an accepted bidder shall fail to enter into contract, or a contractor on any mail-route shall fail or refuse to perform the service on said route according to his contract, or when a new route shall be established or new service required, or when, from any other cause, there shall not be a contractor legally bound or required to perform such service, the Postmaster-General may make a temporary contract for carrying the mail on such route, without advertisement, for such period as may be necessary, not in any case exceeding six months,* until the service shall have commenced under a contract made according to law: *Provided, however*, That the Postmaster-General shall not employ temporary service on any route at a higher price than that paid to the contractor who shall have performed the service during the last preceding contract term. "And in all cases of regular contracts hereafter made, the contract may, in the discretion of the Postmaster-General, be continued in force beyond its express terms for a period not exceeding six months, until a new contract with the same or other contractors shall be made by the Postmaster-General." (*Ibid.*)

Sec. 603. Penalty for Making Straw Bids.—Any person or persons bidding for the transportation of the mails upon any route which may be advertised to be let, and receiving an award of the contract for such service, who shall wrongfully refuse or fail to enter into contract with the Postmaster-General in due form to perform the service described in his or their bid or proposal, or having entered into such contract shall wrongfully refuse or fail to perform such service, shall, for any such failure or refusal, be deemed guilty of a misdemeanor, and be punished by a fine of not more than five thousand dollars, and by imprisonment for not more than twelve months. And the failure or refusal of any such person or persons to enter into such contract in due form, or having entered into such contract, the failure or refusal to perform such service shall be *prima facie* evidence in all actions or prosecutions arising under this section that such failure or refusal was wrongful. (R. S., § 3954, as amended by act August 11, 1876, 19 Stat., p. 129.) See 13 Opin., 473.

Sec. 607. Contracts made without Advertisement.—The Postmaster-General may enter into contracts for carrying the mail, with railroad companies, without advertising for bids therefor. (R. S., § 3942.) When from any cause it may become necessary to make a new contract for

* A bill is pending (May, 1879) in Congress to make the time one year.

carrying the mails upon any water route between ports of the United States, upon which mail service has previously been performed, the Postmaster-General may contract with the owner or master of any steamship, steamboat or other vessel plying upon the waters or between ports of the United States, for carrying the mail upon said route for any length of time not exceeding four years and without advertising for proposals therefor whenever the public interest and convenience will thereby be promoted; but the price paid for such service shall in no case be greater than the average price paid under the last preceding or then existing regular contract upon the same route. And the Postmaster-General may contract with the owners or masters of steamships, steamboats or other vessels plying upon the waters or between ports of the United States for carrying the mails upon such routes where no mail service has previously been performed, without advertising for proposals therefor; but no contract for such new service shall be for a longer time than one year. No contract for carrying the mails between the United States and any foreign port shall be for a longer time than two years, unless otherwise directed by Congress. (R. S., §§ 3943, 3956, 3970, as amended by act May 17, 1878, § 5, 20 Stat., p. 61.)

Sec. 608. Mail Apartments to be Furnished on Mail Steamboats.—On routes where steamboat service is required, the contractor will be required to furnish steamboats which are safe, suitable, and satisfactory to the Postmaster-General.

As route-agents will be placed on each boat who will take entire charge of the mails and all mail matter, the contractor will be required to fit up, on each boat employed in the service, a room suitable for an office, with a sleeping apartment attached, for the exclusive use of the route-agent, and to furnish first-class board to such agent without charge.

Sec. 609. Contracts to be Executed in Duplicate.—Each contractor is required to execute, with his sureties, contracts in duplicate, both to be returned to the Second Assistant Postmaster-General. A copy will be furnished to the contractor if requested.

Sec. 610. Term of Contracts.—No contract for carrying the mails shall be made for a longer term than four years. (R. S., § 3956.)

See section 607.

Sec. 611. Time of Executing Contracts.—Contracts are to be executed and filed in the Department by or before the day specified in the advertisement for proposals, otherwise the accepted bidder will be considered as having failed, and the Postmaster-General may proceed to contract for the service with other parties according to law.

Sec. 612. Payment on Contracts.—No person whose bid for carrying the mail is accepted shall receive any pay until he has executed his contract according to law and the regulations of the Department. (R. S., § 3959.)

Payments will be made by collections from, or drafts on, postmasters or otherwise, after the expiration of each quarter—say in November, February, May, and August, provided that required evidence of service has been received.

Sec. 613. Causes for which Contracts may be Annulled.—The Postmaster-General may annul a contract for repeated failures to run agreeably to contract; for assigning the contract; for violating the post-office laws, or disobeying the instructions of the Department; for refusing to discharge a carrier when required by the Department to do so; or for transporting persons or packages conveying mailable matter out of the mail.

Sec. 614. Contractors to Carry all Mails and Care for Mail-Bags.—Contractors are required, in all cases, to carry the entire mail, and are not permitted to leave bags of newspapers and pamphlets on their routes. They must give due attention to the preservation of mail-bags, and must not allow them to be dragged about or otherwise injured.

Sec. 615. Special Agents and Postal Supplies to be Carried Free.—On routes where the mode of conveyance admits of it, the special agents of the Post-Office Department, also post-office blanks, mail-bags, locks and keys, are to be conveyed without extra charge.

Sec. 616. When Postmasters may Employ Temporary Service.—When any contractor fails to commence the service stipulated in his contract, or abandons the same, it is the duty of the postmaster at the head of the route (*i. e.*, the post-office first named in the advertisement and contract) to employ temporary service at the lowest rate possible, but in no case at a higher rate than that paid under the last preceding regular contract, and to report the facts to the Second Assistant Postmaster-General immediately.

Sec. 617. After Contracts Expire Postmasters may not Pay for Service.—After the expiration of a contract, and until the Postmaster-General has decided upon a new contract, or upon the expediency of discontinuing the post-office, postmasters cannot make any contract or payment for service unless expressly authorized to do so by the Postmaster-General.

Sec. 618. Increase of Compensation for Increased Service.—Compensation for additional service in carrying the mail shall not be in excess of the exact proportion which the original compensation bears to the original service, and when any such additional service is ordered the sum to be allowed therefor shall be expressed in the order, and entered upon the books of the Department; and no compensation shall be paid for additional regular service rendered before the issuing of such order. (R. S., § 3960.)

Sec. 619. Increase of Compensation for Increased Celerity.—No extra allowance shall be made for any increase of expedition in carrying the mail unless thereby the employment of additional stock and carriers is made necessary, and in such case the additional compensation shall bear no greater proportion to the additional stock and carriers necessarily employed than the compensation in the original contract bears to the stock and carriers necessarily employed in its execution. (R. S., § 3961.)

Sec. 620. Determination of Compensation for Increased Celerity.—When it becomes necessary to increase the speed on any route, the contractor will be required to state, under oath, the number of horses and men required to perform the service according to contract schedule and the number required to perform it with the proposed increase of speed.

Sec. 621. Decreased Compensation for Decreased Service.—The Postmaster-General may discontinue or curtail the service on any route, in whole or in part, in order to place on the route superior service, or whenever the public interests, in his judgment, shall require such discontinuance or curtailment for any other cause; he allowing, as full indemnity to contractor, one month's extra pay on the amount of services dispensed with, and a *pro rata* compensation for the amount of services retained and continued.

Sec. 622. Changes of Schedule-time of Arrival and Departure.—The Postmaster-General may change schedules of departures and arrivals in all cases, and particularly to make them conform to connections with railroads, without increase of pay, provided the running time be not abridged. But an application for schedule change cannot be granted—

1. Without the assent of the postmasters at the ends of the route, except in case of manifest necessity.
2. Unless agreed to by the contractor, except in cases where the propriety of the change is clearly shown.
3. If more running-time is asked than is given in the contract schedules.
4. If it breaks connection with any other route.
5. If it puts the mail on a wrong day for the newspapers circulated over the route.
6. If it prevents or lessens any other special accommodation to the public.
7. If it fails to show a good reason for the change.

Sec. 623. Contracts cannot be Assigned or Transferred.—No contractor for transporting the mail within or between the United States and any foreign country shall assign or transfer his contract, and all such assignments or transfers shall be null and void. (R. S., § 3963.)

Sec. 624. Contracts not Sublet without Consent of Postmaster-General.—Hereafter no subletting or transfer of any mail contracts shall be permitted without the consent in writing of the Postmaster-General; and whenever it shall come to the knowledge of the Postmaster-General that any contractor has sublet or transferred his contract, except with the consent of the Postmaster-General as aforesaid, the same shall be considered as violated and the service may be again advertised as herein provided for; and the contractor and his securities shall be liable on their bond to the United States for any damage resulting to the United States in the premises. (Act May 17, 1878, § 2, 20 Stat., p. 61.)

It has been decided by the Attorney-General that the word "transfer" in this section only applies to the transfer of such an interest in the contract as may be necessary to secure the subcontractor as provided in the following section, and that this section does not, therefore, repeal the preceding section, but affects only the conflicting portion of section thirty-seven hundred and thirty-seven of the Revised Statutes, which prohibits the transfer of any interest in any contract.

Sec. 625. Subcontracts Permissible with Consent of Postmaster-General.—When any person or persons being under contract with the Government of the United States for carrying the mails, shall lawfully sublet any such contract, or lawfully employ any other person or persons to perform the service by such contractor agreed to be performed, or any part thereof, he or they shall file in the office of the Second Assistant Postmaster-General a copy of his or their contract; and thereupon it shall be the duty of the Second Assistant Postmaster-General to notify the Auditor of the Treasury for the Post-Office Department of the fact of the filing in his office of such contract. Said notice shall embrace the name or names of the original contractor or contractors, the number of the route or routes, the name or names of the subcontractor or subcontractors, and the amount agreed to be paid to the subcontractor or subcontractors. And upon the receipt of said notice by the Auditor of the Treasury for the Post-Office Department, it shall be his duty to retain, out of the amount due the original contractor or contractors, the amount stated in said notice as agreed to be paid to the subcontractor or subcontractors, and shall pay said amount, upon the certificate of the Second

Assistant Postmaster-General, to the subcontractor or subcontractors, under the same rules and regulations now governing the payments made to original contractors: *Provided*, That upon satisfactory evidence that the original contractor or contractors have paid off and discharged the amount due under his or their contract to the subcontractor or subcontractors, it shall be the duty of the Second Assistant Postmaster-General to certify such fact to the Auditor of the Treasury for the Post-Office Department; and thereupon said Auditor shall settle with the original contractor or contractors, under the same rules as are now provided by law for such settlements. (Act May 17, 1878, § 3, 20 Stat., p. 61.)

Sec. 626. Regulations under which Subcontracts may be Made.—Contractors must in all cases secure the permission of the Postmaster-General before making a subcontract on any route. The application to sublet must be made separately for each route, specifying the number and terminal points thereof.

A subcontract must not embrace more than one route, and should specify the amount to be paid under it in case the service shall be changed, and whether fines and deductions are to be deducted from pay of contractor or subcontractor.

The evidence of payment of a subcontractor by a contractor, provided for in the preceding section, must be the receipt of the subcontractor, attested by a postmaster at a terminus of the route sublet, on a form furnished by the Second Assistant Postmaster-General.

A subcontractor, in order to avail himself of the benefits of the preceding section and receive payment from the Post-Office Department direct, must file a copy of his subcontract in the office of the Second Assistant Postmaster-General, furnishing therewith his post-office address. No subcontractor can be paid by the Department for service prior to the beginning of the quarter in which he files his contract, nor at a greater rate than that named in the original contract, and to secure such payment the subcontract must be filed at least ten days before the end of the quarter.

The copy of subcontract filed must be certified to be a true copy of the original by a postmaster at one of the termini of the route therein sublet.

No subcontract can be recognized unless made with the original contractor.

Sec. 627. Mail-Messenger Service.—In connection with railroad and steamboat routes, mail-messengers are designated to carry the mail to and from post-offices not at the termini of routes when such post-offices are more than eighty rods (one-quarter of a mile) from the steamboat landing or railroad station.

(1) Whenever it is necessary to secure such service, the postmaster at the post-office to be supplied is authorized, by special instructions in each case, to advertise for sealed proposals for five or ten days, with instructions to forward to the Second Assistant Postmaster-General (unopened and in one envelope) all proposals received, accompanying them with a copy of the notice posted and a report of his action in the matter.

(2) The proposals are then opened by the Second Assistant Postmaster-General, and the lowest bidder is designated by an order as mail-messenger (unless the postmaster shall have reported that he is dishonest or incapable), and the postmaster is directed to pay him quarterly.

(3) Mail-messengers are not required to execute a contract, and are not designated for a definite period, but are expected to serve at the compensation proposed at least one year, or until otherwise ordered by the Postmaster-General.

(4) Railroad and steamboat contractors are to have the service performed at all post-offices not more than a quarter of a mile of their depots, stations, or landings, as well as at the terminal post-offices of their routes.

(5) A postmaster cannot be allowed any compensation for this service performed by himself.

(6) A mail-messenger cannot be employed without express authority from the Second Assistant Postmaster-General.

(7) He must be paid in full by the postmaster before any payment is made to the contractor or before making deposit.

(8) He should be paid promptly at the close of every quarter out of any funds in the hands of the postmaster belonging to the United States, except money-order funds.

(9) If not paid, the reason should be stated by the postmaster. If paid, the receipt should be transmitted at once to the Auditor.

(10) If the original has been sent and lost, the postmaster should forward the duplicate, retaining an exact copy.

(11) The payment must be made and the receipts taken to correspond with the regular quarters, which end on the 31st of March, the 30th of June, the 30th of September, and the 31st of December.

(12) Two receipts must be taken ("orignal" and "duplicate"). The original must be sent by the first mail to the "Auditor of the Treasury for the Post-Office Department." The duplicate should be retained until sent for.

(13) These receipts must be signed by the appointed mail-messenger himself, not by an agent.

(14) If signed by a mark, they must be witnessed; if illegibly signed, the name must be plainly written underneath.

(15) Deductions must be made for lost trips and noted on the face of the receipt.

(16) The postmaster's name, not the assistant's, should be written in the body of the receipt.

(17) Altered receipts will not be credited. Blank receipts will be supplied by the First Assistant Postmaster-General, Blank Agency.

(18) The receipt must never be inclosed with the quarterly returns or with other papers. It should be sent in an envelope by itself.

(19) The name of the postmaster and of the post-office must be written plainly.

(20) Receipts must not be sent for amounts not actually paid.

(21) If the postmaster has not sufficient funds to pay the whole amount due, he must pay what he has, send on the receipt for the amount paid, state the balance claimed to be due, and apply for a draft on some other office to pay it.

(22) In making application for a draft a blank form must be used, which will be furnished by the Auditor if requested.

(23) Drafts are not sent until applied for, nor for very small balances, except to close an account.

(24) Advances made for this service will be refunded on application.

(25) Payments for this service must be charged in the "general account," and not in the "quarterly account-current."

(26) Mail-messengers must take the usual oath of office, and transmit it to the Second Assistant Postmaster-General, Division of Inspection. See sections 24 and 25.

Sec. 628. Mail-carriers to receive Mail for Delivery at next Post-office.—Every route-agent, postal clerk, or other carrier of the mail shall receive any mail-matter presented to him, if properly prepaid by stamps, and deliver the same for mailing at the next post-office at which he arrives; but no fees shall be allowed him therefor. (R. S., § 3980.)

See Title IV, *The Railway Mail-Service;* see, also, section 555.

When any properly-prepaid mail-matter is presented to an employé of the railway-mail service, he complies with the provisions of this section by depositing it in his mail-car, as all postal cars and mail apartments in cars and steamboats have been designated by the Postmaster-General as post-offices for the distribution of mail in transit. See section 708.

CHAPTER FOUR.

ADJUSTMENT OF COMPENSATION TO RAILROADS FOR CARRYING THE MAILS.

Sec. 629. Conditions of Railway service and Rates of Pay for same.—The Postmaster-General is authorized and directed to readjust the compensation hereafter to be paid for the transportation of mails on railroad routes upon the conditions and at the rates hereinafter mentioned:

First. That the mails shall be conveyed with due frequency and speed; and that sufficient and suitable room, fixtures, and furniture, in a car or apartment properly lighted and warmed, shall be provided for route-agents to accompany and distribute the mails.

Second. That the pay per mile per annum shall not exceed the following rates, namely: On routes carrying their whole length an average weight of mails per day of two hundred pounds, fifty dollars; five hundred pounds, seventy-five dollars; one thousand pounds, one hundred dollars; one thousand five hundred pounds, one hundred and twenty-five dollars; two thousand pounds, one hundred and fifty dollars; three thousand five hundred pounds, one hundred and seventy-five dollars; five thousand pounds, two hundred dollars, and twenty-five dollars additional for every additional two thousand pounds, the average weight to be ascertained, in every case, by the actual weighing of the mails for such a number of successive working-days, not less than thirty, at such times, after June thirtieth, eighteen hundred and seventy-three, and not less frequently than once in every four years, and the result to be stated and verified in such form and manner as the Postmaster-General may direct. (R. S., § 4002.)

Sec. 630. Refusals to Provide Post-office Cars.—In case any railroad company now furnishing railway post-office cars shall refuse to provide such cars, such company shall not be entitled to any increase of compensation under the provisions of the next section. (R. S., § 4003.)

Sec. 631. Dimensions of and Additional Pay for Post-office Cars.—Additional pay may be allowed for every line comprising a daily trip each way of railway post-office cars, at a rate not exceeding twenty-five dollars per mile per annum for cars forty feet in length; and thirty dollars per mile per annum for forty-five-foot cars; and forty dollars per mile per annum for fifty-foot cars; and fifty dollars per mile per annum for fifty-five to sixty-foot cars. (R. S., § 4004:) *Provided*, That the Postmaster-General may use such portion of the postal-car service appropriation as may be spared from it to supply any deficiency that may arise from insufficient appropriations in the item for railway transportation. (Act of March 3, 1879, § 1, 20 Stat., p. 357.)

Sec. 632. Cars to be Furnished as Required by the Postmaster-General.—All cars or parts of cars used for the railway mail service shall be of such style, length, and character, and furnished in such manner, as shall be required by the Postmaster-General, and shall be constructed, fitted up, maintained, heated, and lighted by and at the expense of the railroad companies. (Act of March 3, 1879, § 4, 20 Stat., p. 358. See R. S., § 4005.)

Sec. 633. Mails, How and When to be Weighed.—The Postmaster-General is hereby directed to have the mails weighed as often as now provided by law by the employés of the Post-Office Department, and have the weights stated and verified to him by said employés, under such instructions as he may consider just to the Post-Office Department and the railroad companies. (Act of March 3, 1875, § 1; 18 Stat., p. 342.)

Sec. 634. Railroad Companies to Give Notice of their Readiness for Weighing. The transportation of mails is authorized on railroad routes with the understanding that the rate of compensation shall be determined upon returns showing the amount and character of the service, to be made within twelve months from the date of its commencement, or earlier if the Department so elect, and no payment will be made except upon the basis of such returns. The mails should not be weighed until the service is fairly established on the route, and when the company is satisfied that this is accomplished, the fact should be reported to the Second Assistant Postmaster-General, who directs the weighing of mails.

Sec. 635. Compensation of Railroads Reduced Ten Per Centum.—The Postmaster-General is hereby authorized and directed to readjust the compensation to be paid from and after the first day of July, eighteen hundred and seventy-six, for transportation of mails on railroad-routes by reducing the compensation to all railroad companies for the transportation of mails ten per centum per annum from the rates fixed and allowed by [section 629] [*the first section of an act entitled "An act making appropriations for the service of the Post-Office Department for the fiscal year ending June thirtieth, eighteen hundred and seventy-four, and for other purposes," approved March third, eighteen hundred and seventy-three*], for the transportation of mails on the basis of the average weight. (Act of July 12, 1876, § 1, 19 Stat., p. 79.)

This act does not affect the compensation for railway postal cars, provided for in the act of March 3, 1873 (section 631, supra). Opin. Att'y-Gen. Taft, Oct. 7, 1876.

This act was not intended to affect existing contracts. Opin. Att'y-Gen. Taft, Dec. 21, 1876.

Sec. 636. Compensation of Railroads Reduced Five Per Centum More.—The Postmaster-General is hereby authorized and directed to readjust the compensation to be paid from and after the first day of July, eighteen hundred and seventy-eight, for transportation of mails on railroad routes by reducing the compensation to all railroad companies for the transportation of mails five per centum per annum from the rates for the transportation of mails, on the basis of the average weight fixed and allowed by the [preceding section] [*first section of an act entitled "An act making appropriations for the service of the Post-Office Department for the fiscal year ending June thirtieth, eighteen hundred and seventy seven, and for other purposes," approved July twelfth, eighteen hundred and seventy-six*]. (Act of June 17, 1878, § 1, 20 Stat., p. 142.)

Sec. 637. Congress may Fix Compensation to be Paid Land-Grant Railroads.—All railway companies to which the United States have furnished aid by grant of lands, right of way, or otherwise, shall carry the mail at such prices as Congress may by law provide; and, until such price is fixed by law, the Postmaster-General may fix the rate of compensation. (R. S., § 4001.]

For rights and obligations of land-grant roads under this section, vide 13 Opins., 445, 536; 14 Opins., 428, 663, etc.

Sec. 638. Congress does Fix Compensation to be Paid said Railroads.—Railroad companies whose railroad was constructed in whole or in part by a land-grant made by Congress on the condition that the mails should be transported over their road at such price as Congress should by law direct, shall receive only eighty per centum of the compensation authorized by [*this act*] [section 635.] (Act of July 12, 1876, § 13, 19 Stat., p. 82.)

Sec. 639. When Railroad Companies must Deliver Mails to Post-Offices.—Railroad companies are required to take the mails from and deliver them into the terminal post-offices, and to all intermediate post-offices located not over eighty rods from the line of road, and the distances from the terminal depots to the post-offices, where railroad companies deliver the mails, are paid for by the Department as a part of the length of the route.

Sec. 640. Mails not to be Carried beyond Termini without Authority.—In case railroads are extended or trains run beyond the termini of the route on which the transportation of mails is duly authorized, the mails must not be carried beyond the termini of the route until the additional service is ordered by the Second Assistant Postmaster-General.

Sec. 641. Knowledge of Specific Requirements of the Service, how Obtained.—The rates of compensation are computed upon the average weight of mails per day carried the whole length of the route; but the rates fixed by law require not only a certain weight of mails, but also that the mails shall be carried with due frequency and speed, and that suitable room, fixtures and furniture shall be provided in a car or apartment of car, properly lighted and warmed, for route-agents to accompany and distribute the mails as accessories to the weight of mails, in order to entitle a company to the maximum rates of pay. The specific requirements of the service, with regard to these items, will be made known through the General Superintendent of the Railway-Mail Service. The requirement as to due frequency, and the size of the mail-car or apartment, are at all times to be determined by the Department.

Sec. 642. Postmaster-General to Decide what Trains shall Carry the Mail.—The Postmaster-General shall, in all cases, decide upon what trains and in what manner the mails shall be conveyed. (Act of March 3, 1879, § 3, 20 Stat., p. 358.)

Sec. 643. Railway Company must Carry Mails on any Train.—Every railway company carrying the mail shall carry on any trains which may run over its road, and without extra charge therefor, all mailable matter directed to be carried thereon, with the person in charge of the same. (R. S., § 4000.)

Sec. 644. To Carry Supplies and Special Agents.—Railroad Companies are required to convey, without specific charge therefor, all mail-bags, post-office blanks, and stationery supplies. Also, to convey, free of charge, all duly-accredited Special Agents of the Department, on the exhibition of their credentials.

Sec. 645. When Mail may be Carried on Railway Routes by Horse Express.—If the Postmaster-General is unable to contract for carrying the mail on any railway route at a compensation not exceeding the maximum rates herein provided, or for what he may deem a reasonable and fair compensation, he may separate the letter-mail from the other mail, and contract, either with or without advertising, for carrying such letter-mail by horse-express or otherwise, at the greatest speed that can reasonably be obtained, and for carrying the other mail in wagons, or otherwise, at a slower rate of speed. (R. S., § 3999.)

Sec. 646. Railroad Companies Requested to Report Receipts and Expenses.—The Postmaster-General shall request all railroad companies transporting the mails to furnish, under seal, such data relating to the operating, receipts and expenditures of such roads as may, in his judgment, be deemed necessary to enable him to ascertain the cost of mail transportation and the proper compensation to be paid for the same; and he shall, in his annual report to Congress, make such recommendations, founded on the information obtained under this section, as shall, in his opinion, be just and equitable. (Act of March 3, 1879, § 6, 20 Stat., p. 358.)

Sec. 647. Communications Affecting Pay of Railroads, How Addressed.—All communications affecting the pay for carrying the mails, or so intended, must be made in writing at the time the service is rendered for which payment is desired, and must be addressed to the Second Assistant Postmaster-General.

Sec. 648. Auditor to Furnish Instructions Respecting Financial Agent.—As soon as service is commenced on a route, application should be made to the Auditor of the Treasury for the Post-Office Department for instructions respecting the designation of a financial agent to receive and receipt for amounts due for carrying the mail.

CHAPTER FIVE.

FOREIGN MAIL SERVICE.

Sec. 649. Transportation of Domestic Mails Through Foreign Countries.—The Postmaster-General, after advertising for proposals, may enter into contracts or make suitable arrangements for transporting the mail through any foreign country, between any two points in the United States, and such transportation shall be by the speediest, safest, and most economical route; and all contracts therefor may be revoked whenever any new road or canal shall be opened affording a speedier, more economical, and equally safe transportation between the same points; but in case of the revocation of any such contract a fair indemnity shall be awarded to the contractor. (R. S., § 4006.)

Sec. 650. Transportation of Foreign Mails through the United States.—The Postmaster-General may, by and with the advice and consent of the President, make any arrangements which may be deemed just and expedient for allowing the mails of Canada, or any other country adjoining the United States, to be transported over the territory of the United States from one point in such country to any other point in the same, at the expense of the country to which the mail belongs, upon obtaining a like privilege for the transportation of the United States mail through the country to which the privilege is granted; but such privilege may at any time be annulled by the President or Congress from and after one month succeeding the day on which notice of the act of the President or Congress is given to the chief executive or head of the Post-Office Department of the country whose privilege is to be annulled. (R. S., § 4012.)

Sec. 651. Foreign Mails in Transit to be Treated as Domestic.—Every foreign mail shall, while being transported across the territory of the United States under the provisions of the preceding section, be deemed and taken to be a mail of the United States, so far as to make any violation thereof, or depredation thereon, or offense in respect thereto, or any part thereof, an offense of the same grade, and punishable in the same manner and to the same extent as though the said mail was a mail of the United States; and in any indictment for any such offense the mail, or any part thereof, may be alleged to be, and on the trial of any such indictment it shall be deemed and held to be, a mail or part of a mail of the United States. (R. S., § 4013.)

Sec. 652. Contracts for Carrying Foreign Mails.—The Postmaster-General may, after advertising for proposals, enter into contracts for the transportation of the mail between the United States and any foreign country whenever the public interests will thereby be promoted. (R. S., § 4007.) No contract for carrying the mails between the United States and any foreign port shall be for a longer time than two years unless otherwise ordered by Congress. (Act May 17, 1878, § 5, 20 Stat., p. 62.)

See section 607.

Sec. 653. How Foreign Mails may be Carried.—The mail between the United States and any foreign port, or between ports of the United States touching at a foreign port, shall be transported in steamships; but the Postmaster-General may have such transportation performed by sailing-vessels when the service can be facilitated thereby. (R. S., § 4008.)

Sec. 654. Limit of Compensation for Carrying Foreign Mails.—For transporting the mail between the United States and any foreign port, or between ports of the United States touching at a foreign port, the Postmaster-General may allow as compensation, if by a United States steamship, any sum not exceeding the sea and United States inland postage, and if by a foreign steamship or by a sailing-vessel, any sum not exceeding the sea postage, on the mail so transported. (R. S., § 4009.)

Sec. 655. Foreign Mail Contractors may be Fined.—The Postmaster-General may impose fines on contractors for transporting the mail between the United States and any foreign country, for any unreasonable or unnecessary delay in the departure of such mail, or the performance of the trip; but the fine for any one default shall not exceed one-half the contract price for the trip. (R. S., § 4010.)

Sec. 656. Foreign Mail Contracts may be Terminated by Congress.—Every contract for transporting the mail between the United States and any foreign country shall contain, besides the usual stipulation for the right of the Postmaster-General to discontinue the same, the further stipulation that it may be terminated by Congress. (R. S., § 4011.)

CHAPTER SIX.

INSPECTION AND VERIFICATION OF SERVICE RENDERED BY CARRIERS OF THE MAIL—OF FINES AND DEDUCTIONS.

Sec. 657. Record of Arrivals and Departures of the Mail.—The Postmaster-General shall furnish to the postmasters at the termination of each route a schedule of the time of arrival and departure of the mail at their [post-]offices, respectively, to be posted in a conspicuous place in the [post-] office; and he shall also give them notice of any change in the arrival and departure that may be ordered; and he shall cause to be kept and returned to the Department, at short and regular intervals, registers, showing the exact times of the arrivals and departures of the mail. (R. S., § 3841.)

Sec. 658. Postmasters' Report of Arrivals and Departures of the Mails.—Postmasters at the end of every mail-route, and at such other post-offices as the Postmaster-General may direct, will be furnished with blank forms from the office of the Second Assistant Postmaster-General, Division of Inspection, upon which they will report the exact times of the arrival and departures of all the mails which are opened at their post-offices, as required in the preceding section. Particular care should be exercised in filling up the blank forms furnished, giving the name of the post-office, county, and State; the number of the route, the names of the places where it terminates, the schedule days and hours of arrival and departure, the name of the contractor, the name of the carrier, and the mode of carrying the mail. The reports should be fully dated, giving the day of the week, the month, and the year. When there is a failure to arrive or depart, write opposite to its date on the face of the report the word FAILURE; when the arrival is so far behind the schedule time as to fail to connect with a depending mail or mails, write FAILED TO CONNECT; and when the arrival is after the schedule time, causing complaint, although not missing connection, write COMPLAINT. The cause of each failure must be noted upon the back of the report; also whether the carrier makes every proper effort to arrive and depart according to the schedule. Whenever the mail is carried by any other person than the contractor or his authorized agent or carrier, the fact is to be noted on the report.

Sec. 659. Special Reports, when Required.—In addition to the above, special reports are to be made by any postmaster, whether at terminal or intermediate post-offices, when mails are received wet or in otherwise bad condition; also of extraordinary failures, interruptions, or abandonment of routes; and from time to time of all such information as may aid the Department in enforcing the strictest performance of duty on the part of contractors, and securing for the community the greatest possible regularity, safety, and efficiency in the mail service. The special reports should state the number, or, if the number is not known, the termini of the route.

Sec. 660. Disposition of Regular and Special Reports.—The regular and special reports must be forwarded to the Second Assistant Postmaster-General, Division of Inspection, by the first mail after the close of each month. In no case are they to be sent with the quarterly returns. A copy of each report sent to the Department should be kept by the postmaster, that a duplicate may be promptly furnished if called for. Neglect to forward reports, or duplicates thereof, promptly will be considered sufficient cause for the removal of a postmaster, as such neglect prevents the prompt payment of contractors, and seriously obstructs the business of the Department.

Sec. 661. Duplicate Reports to be Preserved in Post-offices.—The duplicates of the reports of the arrivals and departures of mails retained by postmasters are a part of the public records of the Post-Office Department, and must be carefully preserved with the other records of the post-office. In the event of a change of postmasters they must be turned over to the incoming postmaster with the other records.

Sec. 662. Delivery of Mails to Way Post-offices on Star Routes.—When the mail is carried in a vehicle drawn by horses, the driver will not be required to leave his team in order to deliver the mail to way post-offices, except where the carrier remains over night, when the mail must be deposited in the post-office by the carrier. In no case should the mail be thrown upon the ground. Postmasters and carriers of the mail must report to the Second Assistant Postmaster-General, Division of Inspection, any violations of this section by either.

Sec. 663. Postmasters to Report Delinquent Mail-Carriers.—Postmasters shall promptly report to the Postmaster-General every delinquency, neglect, or malpractice of the contractors, their agents or carriers, which may come to their knowledge. (R. S., § 3849.)

Sec. 664. Certain Delinquencies to be Specially Reported.—(1) Every instance in which the mail is brought to a post-office by a person under the age of sixteen years, or by a person who has not been duly sworn, must be reported to the Second Assistant Postmaster-General, Division of Inspection.

(2) If a mail-carrier, having the mail in charge, become intoxicated, the postmaster will instantly dismiss him, employ another at the expense of the contractor, and report the facts to the Second Assistant Postmaster-General, Division of Inspection.

(3) Every instance in which the mail stopping over night at a place where there is a post-office without being kept in the post-office must be reported by the postmaster to the Second Assistant Postmaster-General, Division of Inspection.

(4) If the mail arrive without a lock, the postmaster will ascertain where the fault is, and report it to the Second Assistant Postmaster-General.

(5) He will also carefully observe how mails are carried by any steamers landing near his post-office, and will report every case in which he finds them exposed on deck, or not secured in some proper place under lock and key; and in all cases he will see that the mails, by whatever mode of conveyance they are sent from or received at his post-office, are properly protected from the weather.

Sec. 665. Deductions for Contractors' Failures, Fines for Delinquencies.—The Postmaster-General may make deductions from the pay of contractors for failures to perform service according to contract, and impose fines upon them for other delinquencies. He may deduct the price of the trip in all cases where the trip is not performed; and not exceeding three times the price if the failure be occasioned by the fault of the contractor or carrier. (R. S., § 3962.)

Sec. 666. When Postmasters must Notify Contractors of Failures.—Failures of mails to arrive at the ends of routes and other points within contract time cannot but be known in all cases to contractors or their agents. No notice, therefore, is necessary to be given to contractors of failures to arrive at any post-office on contract time, as reported by postmasters to the Department; but when the failure is caused by the neglect of a carrier employed by the contractor, the postmaster will notify the contractor of the failure, and require him to take measures to prevent its recurrence.

Sec. 667. Contractors to Make Specific Excuses for each Delinquency.—Should a mail at any time fail to arrive at the end of a route, or at any intermediate post-office, where the time of arrival is fixed, within the time specified in the contract or schedule, it will be expected of every contractor immediately, by himself or agent, to send his excuse to the Second Assistant Postmaster-General, Division of Inspection, setting forth particularly the cause of the failure. A specific excuse is required for each delinquency of a contractor, and general allegations will not be admitted. If bad roads be alleged, a specific report must be made of what portion of the road was so bad as to obstruct the mails, and what was its peculiar condition; if high waters, it must be shown what water-courses were impassable; and so of all other excuses. If part of the trip only was performed, the report must show what part, and give the distance traveled.

Sec. 668. Causes for which Forfeitures must Occur.—In all cases there will be a forfeiture of the pay of the trip when the trip is not run—of not more than three times the pay of the trip when the trip is not run and no sufficient excuse for the failure is furnished, and a forfeiture of at least one-fourth part of it when the running or arrival is so far behind time as to lose the connection with a depending mail. These forfeitures may be increased into penalties of higher amount, according to the nature or frequency of the failures and the importance of the mail. Whenever it shall be satisfactorily shown that the contractors, their carriers or agents, have, for the accommodation of passengers, left or put aside the mail, or any portion of it, or have failed to deliver a mail at a post-office immediately upon arrival, they shall forfeit not exceeding a quarter's pay.

Sec. 669. Causes for which Fines will be Imposed.—Fines will be imposed, unless the delinquency be satisfactorily explained in due time, for each of the following causes: Failing to take from or deliver at a post-office the mail or any part of it: for suffering it to be wet, injured, lost, or destroyed; for conveying it in a place or manner that exposes it to depredation, loss, or injury; for refusing, after demand, to convey a mail by any coach, railroad, car, or steamboat, which the contractor regularly runs, or is concerned in running, on the route, beyond the specified number of trips in the contract; for not arriving at the time fixed by the schedule; the penalty to be exacted being equal to a quarter's pay.

Sec. 670. Deductions and Fines upon Railroad Companies.—The Postmaster-General shall deduct from the pay of the railroad companies, for every failure to deliver a mail within its schedule time, not less than one-half of the price of the trip, and where the trip is not performed, not less than the price of one trip, and not exceeding, in either case, the price of three trips: *Provided, however,* That if the failure is caused by a connecting road, then only the connecting road shall be fined. And where such failure is caused by unavoidable casualty, the Postmaster-General, in his discretion, may remit the fine. And he may make deductions and impose fines for other delinquencies. (Act March 3, 1879, § 5, 20 Stat., p. 358.)

CHAPTER SEVEN.

MAIL EQUIPMENTS.

Sec. 671. Term "Mail-bags" Includes, what.—The general term "*mail-*

bags" includes MAIL-POUCHES (used for every mode of conveyance excepting horseback) of five different sizes, the largest being No. 1; HORSE MAIL-BAGS (for horseback service only) of three different sizes, the largest being No. 1; MAIL-CATCHER POUCHES (of one size only), designed exclusively for exchanges of mails on railways by catchers and cranes; CANVAS MAIL-SACKS (not locked, but tied with cord), designed for printed matter only.

Sec. 672. Every Mail-route must be Supplied with Mail-bags.—Every mail-route must always be duly provided with suitable mail-bags and locks, in good and safe condition. Postmasters, especially those at the ends of routes, must see to this, and promptly make application for such as are needed. It is their duty to look constantly to the condition of mail-bags in use, permitting none to be used which are too much worn or otherwise unsafe, and to report any damage discovered to have been done to them, whether through accident, negligence, or design, while in the custody of carriers.

Sec. 673. Applications for Mail-bags must State, what.—Applications for mail-bags should explain why they are needed, and specify the number and size or capacity of each, also the number of the route (or the terminal points thereof), and especially the mode of conveyance thereon.

Sec. 674. Applications for Supplies to Second Assistant Postmaster-General.—Postmasters must obtain requisite supplies of mail-bags by direct application to the office of the Second Assistant Postmaster-General, Division of Mail Equipments, and not by withholding the return of such as were received with mail-matter from other post-offices. Before old mail-bags in use become too much worn for safety, timely application must be made for new ones by postmasters at the ends of the routes where they are used, and the old bags must be sent to the nearest depository, on receipt of new ones.

Sec. 675. Repairs of Mail-bags by Postmasters, etc.—When a mail-bag in use becomes so damaged as to require slight repairs, and the postmaster at the end of the route where it first arrives in that condition has not a good bag to substitute for same, he must immediately have it repaired at a reasonable cost, charging the amount paid therefor in his account of contingent expenses, and sending to the Auditor with his quarterly returns a bill and receipt rendered by the mender of the bag as a proper voucher for the allowance of the money so paid and charged by him. In having repairs of mail-bags done, he should direct the person performing the work to specify in his bill, whenever practicable, the number of each size of every kind of mail-bags repaired, and the nature and price of the repairs done to each.

Sec. 676. Mail-bag in Transit becoming Unsound.—In case a mail-bag in transit becomes too unsound to convey the mail with safety to the end of the route, the postmaster first discovering its bad condition must have it repaired immediately, even if he has no suitable mail-bag to substitute for it, and must therefore detain the mail until the needful repairs can be done. Postmasters whose post-offices are not mail-bag depositories should not have surplus mail-bags repaired, but such bags only as are in demand for immediate use.

Sec. 677. What Mutilation of a Mail-bag may be allowed.—When a mail-bag has a damaged or defective lock upon it, which cannot be opened with the proper key in good order, such lock should be removed without further damage, where there are a bag and lock in good condition to substitute for them, by filing or cutting asunder that staple of the bag to which the lock is fastened. No other mutilation of a mail-bag is admissible under such or any other circumstances whatever. When the staple is cut, the mail-bag must not be used again until a new staple shall have been applied to it. The fastening-strap of a mail-bag must never be cut, and must never be spliced nor repaired in any way, but must be replaced, when necessary, with a new one.

Sec. 678. Sacks Containing Public Documents.—Postmasters, especially those at the resident places of members of Congress (to whose post-offices canvas sacks containing public documents are sent from Washington, D. C.), must see that all such sacks are emptied and sent back to the post-office in the latter place.

Sec. 679. Damaged Mail-bags at Mail-bag Depository Post-offices.—Postmasters whose post-offices are mail-bag depositories are not authorized to have repairs done to mail-bags collected in their post-offices, but are required to forward all damaged mail-bags to the established repair-shops, under such special instructions as may from time to time be received from the Second Assistant Postmaster-General.

Sec. 680. Surplus Mail-bags not to Accumulate.—Surplus mail-bags must not be allowed to accumulate and fall into disuse in any post-office not a depository for mail-bags. All such, whether in good condition or not, must be forwarded to the nearest mail-bag depository.

Sec. 681. Equal Exchange or Reciprocal Return of Locked Pouches.—The use of locked pouches (for letter mails) must be controlled by the rule of equal exchange or reciprocal return: therefore a separate locked pouch must not be made up in any post-office directly for any other, with greater or less frequency than a separate locked pouch is usually received directly therefrom, without special instructions from the Department. Repeated failures to comply with this rule on the part of any post-office must be reported to the Second Assistant Postmaster-General by any postmaster whose supplies of mail-bags may have materially been reduced thereby. The same rule is not applicable to separate tied sacks of printed matter, which may be made up and dispatched without regard to a corresponding return of printed matter; but all such sacks (or a like number of them), received and emptied in post-offices not depositories, are to be promptly returned, duly labeled, to the place whence they were received, whether there shall be printed matter to send back in them or not. Any that may be received from unknown sources, or from places where they are not needed, must not be suffered to fall into disuse, but be forwarded without delay to the nearest mail-bag depository.

Sec. 682. Register of Outgoing and Incoming Mails to be Kept.—In all post-offices where many lock-pouches are sent and received daily, such a register of the outgoing and incoming mails should be kept as will show the places to which separate locked pouches are sent and from which they are received, as well as the number sent to and received from each daily. Postmasters will give particular attention to keeping such registers, and will be guided by the same in correcting all disparities in their exchanges of locked pouches.

Sec. 683. Names of Depositories for Mail Bags and Locks.—The following post-offices are depositories for mail bags and locks, where mail bags and locks, new and old, are collected and distributed, under special instructions from the Second Assistant Postmaster-General: *Portland* and *Bangor, Maine; Concord, New Hampshire; Rutland, Vermont; Boston, Massachusetts; Providence, Rhode Island; Hartford* and *New Haven, Connecticut; New York, Albany,* and *Buffalo, New York; Trenton, New Jersey; Philadelphia, Harrisburgh,* and *Pittsburgh, Pennsylvania; Baltimore, Maryland; Washington, District of Columbia; Richmond, Virginia; Wheeling, West Virginia; Raleigh, North Carolina; Charleston* and *Columbia, South Carolina; Atlanta* and *Savannah, Georgia; Tallahassee, Florida; Mobile* and *Montgomery, Alabama; Jackson, Mississippi; New Orleans, Louisiana; Little Rock, Arkansas; Nashville* and *Memphis, Tennessee; Louisville, Kentucky; Cincinnati* and *Cleveland, Ohio; Detroit, Michigan; Indianapolis, Indiana; Springfield* and *Chicago, Illinois; Saint Louis, Missouri; Milwaukee, Wisconsin; Des Moines* and *Dubuque, Iowa; Saint Paul, Minnesota; Galveston, Texas; San Francisco, California; Portland, Oregon; Salt Lake City, Utah Territory; Lawrence, Kansas;* and *Omaha, Nebraska.*

Sec. 684. Accounts of Depository Post-offices to be Rendered.—It is the duty of every postmaster whose post-office is a depository for mail bags and locks to render to the office of the Second Assistant Postmaster-General, Division of Mail Equipments, an account at the end of every month showing the number of each kind of mail-locks and of each size of the several kinds of mail-bags on hand at the beginning of and received during the month, of those furnished to other post-offices, of those in actual use in his post-office, and of those remaining on hand not in use, but ready for distribution. Blanks for this purpose will be furnished from time to time on application to the Second Assistant Postmaster-General, Division of Mail Equipments.

Sec. 685. Surplus Stock to be Kept apart from the Current Stock.—Each postmaster at a depository for mail bags and locks must be careful to keep apart from the mail bags and locks required for current use of his post-office all surplus articles of that kind, and to consider them as deposited for distribution in such manner as may be directed by the Department. For all mail bags and locks so distributed he will obtain receipts, which are to be transmitted immediately to the Department. He may withdraw mail bags and locks from the surplus stock on deposit to supply wants of his own post-office, but not to supply other post-offices, without special instructions, except in emergencies admitting of no delay. For mail-bags so withdrawn from deposit, his certificate in the former case, and receipts in the latter, must be transmitted to the Department, where, when received, they will be entered to his credit.

Sec. 686. Legitimate Use of Mail-bags Restricted to what.—The legitimate use of mail-bags is restricted to the transmission of mailable matter while under the care, custody, and control of the Post-Office Department, through its postmasters and other authorized agents. Their application to any other uses than those of this Department is illegal and strictly forbidden. The stealing, purloining, converting from proper use, or conveying away, to the detriment of the service, of any mail-bags, is an offense by law, punishable with fine and imprisonment. See section 1241.

Sec. 687. Canvas Sacks may be Taken by Publishers, when.—Whenever, in any post-office in the large towns and cities, there is an extreme necessity of extending to publishers the privilege of taking canvas sacks to their printing-offices to be there filled with printed matter for the mails, the postmaster must keep an exact account with each publisher of the number of sacks taken from and returned to his post-office on every occasion. Besides the account kept in the post-office for that purpose, pass-books should be used between the several printing-offices and the post-office. No sacks should be delivered for any publisher, except on presentation of his pass-book, in which he is to be debited with the number of sacks intrusted to him and credited with the number returned; and for the due return of all sacks so intrusted to him each publisher shall be held responsible.

Sec. 688. Waste or Abuse of Mail-bags to be Prevented.—It is the duty of postmasters and other agents of this Department to prevent, whenever in their power, any waste or abuse of mail-bags; to reclaim them from improper hands; and to give information of every instance of theft or illegal use of mail-bags coming to their knowledge.

Sec. 689. Mail-bags not to be Purchased by Postmasters.—Mail-bags of every description are required by law to be purchased by the Postmaster-General, under contract made with the lowest bidder, after advertisement for proposals. They are not to be purchased by postmasters or mail-contractors, and no allowance will be made for mail-bags purchased by them without special instructions from the Department.

Sec. 690. Mail-catchers, how Furnished.—Mail-catchers (for use where they are allowed by the Department) are furnished on application to the office of the Second Assistant Postmaster-General, Division of Mail Equipments.

Sec. 691. Application for Mail-bags, etc., to State Reasons.—Every application for mail-bags and mail-catchers must state fully the reasons which make an additional supply necessary.

Sec. 692. Mail Locks and Keys, by whom Furnished.—Mail locks and keys are furnished from the office of the Second Assistant Postmaster-General, Division of

Mail Equipments. Applications for mail locks or keys must always assign the reasons therefor.

Sec. 693. Care of Mail-keys—Penalty for Loss.—The careful use of mail-locks and the safe-keeping of mail-keys are essential to the integrity of the postal service. The mail-key must never be exposed to public observation nor placed where it may be lost or stolen. It must not be suffered to pass, even for a moment, into the hands of any person not a sworn officer of the Post-Office Department. The safe-keeping of the mail-key is one of the expressed conditions of the official bond of every postmaster. The loss of a mail-key, as it may afford peculiar facilities for stealing from the mails, is an act of carelessness likely to be more pernicious to the service than almost any other a postmaster or agent of the Department can commit. It is therefore deemed sufficient cause for removing the postmaster or agent so offending, enforcing the penalty of the official bond of the former, and even in certain cases for discontinuing the post-office.

Sec. 694. Mail-keys to have a Specific Number.—The mail-keys bear, each of them, a different number stamped upon them. Every postmaster or employé to whom such keys are intrusted will be charged therewith and held to a strict account therefor. On the receipt of any such mail-key by a postmaster, he should make a record, to be kept in his post-office, of the date of its receipt and of the number stamped upon it. Whenever such or any other mail-key shall afterwards be referred to, in any communication to the Department, its number must invariably be specified. Every casualty whatever concerning a mail-key must be promptly reported.

Sec. 695. Exchange of Mail-keys by Railway Mail Employés.—In all cases of an exchange of routes between employés of the Railway Mail Service, there must also be an exchange of mail-keys between them, so that every mail-key shall always be retained in the particular office for which it was originally furnished by the Department, and never be taken away for use elsewhere.

Sec. 696. Receipts to be always Taken for Mail-keys.—No mail-key shall be transferred or exchanged except to a successor in office, nor be furnished nor loaned without special instructions from the Department. No such key, not obtained directly from the Department or from a predecessor in office, shall be kept or detained, but promptly returned to the Department, with a full report of facts in relation to it. If a mail-key be received from a discontinued post-office, or elsewhere, it must be sent without delay to the Department by the postmaster receiving it, stating when and from whom it was received by him. Whenever a retiring postmaster turns over a mail-key, he must obtain and transmit to the Second Assistant Postmaster-General a receipt for the same, specifying the number stamped upon it, in order that he may receive due credit on the books of the Department, and he and his sureties be released from all further responsibility therefor.

Sec. 697. Repairing Mail-locks and Keys Forbidden.—No attempt shall be made to have a mail-key or a mail-lock repaired; nor to pry into the internal mechanism of any mail-lock. No damaged or defective mail-key shall be kept in post-offices, but each one, as soon as it becomes damaged or defective, must be promptly returned to the Department with an explanatory letter. With every application for a new mail-key in lieu of one broken, the broken parts must be inclosed, and the number of the broken key stated.

Sec. 698. Defective Keys to be Reported to the Department.—When a mail-key is perceived to be much worn and becoming defective, timely notice should be given of the fact, always stating the number of the key, so that a new one may be furnished before the old one becomes entirely useless; the latter to be returned to the Department. Whenever extra keys are furnished they should be kept in reserve for an emergency, and be locked up in a safe place in the post-office, accessible to the postmaster and his assistant only.

Sec. 699. Brass Locks not to be Sent to Iron-Lock Post-offices.—In those post-offices where the use of the brass locks and keys is allowed for through mails, it will be deemed very reprehensible if sufficient care be not always taken to prevent such locks being used, instead of iron locks, on bags dispatched to post-offices where their use is not allowed, and where, of course, there is no key to open them. If, however, a bag secured with a brass lock be received at a post-office where there is no brass key allowed, the lock should not be broken or tampered with, nor the bag be mutilated; but it should either be returned unopened to the post-office whence it came, or be sent to some nearer post-office using the brass key, with the request to substitute an iron lock for the brass one. But in either case, the postmaster at whose post-office the irregularity occurred must be advised of it, and, if there be a repetition of it, be reported to the Second Assistant Postmaster-General.

Sec. 700. Proper Course when Defective Key will not Open Mail-lock.—If the only mail-key in a post-office be broken or so defective as not to open all the locks, the bags should be passed, unopened, to the nearest post-office, with a request to the postmaster to take out the letters, &c., for the post-office where the lock could not be opened, and send them back by the mail-carrier outside the bag, in a sealed package, until another key be received from the Department. In such case any mutilation of the bag is inexcusable.

Sec. 701. Proper Course when Defective Lock cannot be Opened.—When a postmaster cannot open a lock securing a bag, because of a defect in the lock, and not of his key, he will then cut that staple of the bag to which the lock is attached, provided he has another bag and lock to substitute for them; but if he has no other bag and lock, he will pass the bag, unopened, to the next post-office, as in the case indicated in the preceding section.

Sec. 702. Fastening-Strap Never to be Cut.—The fastening-strap of a mail-bag should never be cut; but if ever done, the strap must not afterwards be spliced, but a new one put on instead of the strap cut. When the staple is cut asunder, the bag should have a new one applied before being used again.

Sec. 703. Economy in the Use of Mail-locks.—The mail-locks must be used with care and economy. Care must also be taken to equalize the exchange of locked pouches, and thereby secure to every post-office a return of the same number of locks sent from it. If at any post-office (not a depository) locks from unknown sources should accumulate in excess of its current wants, all such surplus locks must be forwarded with an explanatory letter to the Department.

Sec. 704. Unlawful Use of Mail-bags to be Reported to the Department.—It is the duty of postmasters and agents of the Department to reclaim and transmit to the office of the Second Assistant Postmaster-General, Division of Mail Equipment, all mail locks and keys found to be in improper hands, or applied to any other than their lawful use, and to see that the law (section 1241) is enforced in every case of its violation known to them, by exerting due diligence always in collecting and reporting to the Department the facts and proofs to sustain a prosecution against the offender.

Sec. 705. How to Address Communications on Mail Equipments.—All communications required by this chapter to be sent to the Department must be addressed to the Second Assistant Postmaster-General, Division of Mail Equipments. Such communications must invariably give the name of the post-office, county, and State from which they are sent, and must not embrace any other subject.

TITLE IV.

THE RAILWAY MAIL SERVICE.

CHAPTER ONE.

ORGANIZATION AND GENERAL PROVISIONS.

Sec. 706. The General Superintendent of Railway Mail Service.—The Postmaster-General has vested the general supervision of the distribution and dispatch of mails at post-offices and in transit upon railroad and steamboat routes in the General Superintendent of Railway Mail Service, with headquarters at Washington, D. C., and in the Superintendents under his directions.

Sec. 707. Division Superintendents.—For the purpose of securing efficiency in the dispatch and distribution of mails, the United States has been divided into nine divisions, each of which is in charge of a Superintendent, as follows:

FIRST DIVISION.—Comprising the New England States.—*Headquarters of Superintendent, Boston, Mass.*

SECOND DIVISION.—Comprising New York, New Jersey, Pennsylvania, Delaware, and the Eastern Shore of Maryland.—*Headquarters of Superintendent, New York, N. Y.*

THIRD DIVISION.—Comprising Maryland (excluding the Eastern Shore), North Carolina, Virginia, West Virginia, and the District of Columbia.—*Headquarters of Superintendent, Richmond, Va.*

FOURTH DIVISION.—Comprising South Carolina, Georgia, Florida, Alabama, Mississippi, and Louisiana.—*Headquarters of Superintendent, Atlanta, Ga.*

FIFTH DIVISION.—Comprising Ohio, Indiana, Kentucky, and Tennessee.—*Headquarters of Superintendent, Cincinnati, Ohio.*

SIXTH DIVISION.—Comprising Wisconsin, Illinois, Iowa, Nebraska, Minnesota, and Upper Peninsula of Michigan, and the Territories of Dakota and Wyoming.—*Headquarters of Superintendent, Chicago, Ill.*

SEVENTH DIVISION.—Comprising Missouri, Kansas, Arkansas, Texas, Colorado, the Indian Territory, and New Mexico.—*Headquarters of Superintendent, Saint Louis, Mo.*

EIGHTH DIVISION.—Comprising California, Nevada, Oregon, and the Territories of Alaska, Arizona, Idaho, Montana, Utah, and Washington.—*Headquarters of Superintendent, San Francisco, Cal.*

NINTH DIVISION.—Comprising the through mails via Buffalo, Suspension Bridge, Toledo, and Detroit, the lines of the Lake Shore and Michigan Southern Railroad, and the Lower Peninsula of Michigan.—*Headquarters of Superintendent, Cleveland, Ohio.*

Sec. 708. "Offices"—Post-offices for Distributing Mail in Transit.—The Postmaster-General has designated all railway postal cars and mail apartments in cars and steamboats as post-offices for the distribution of mail-matter in transit. To distinguish these traveling post-offices from ordinary post-offices, they are designated in the regulations as "Offices."

Sec. 709. Employés of Railway Mail Service.—In the Postal Regulations the word "employés" is used to designate all railway post-office clerks, route-agents, and mail-route messengers. Local mail-agents retain their present designation.

Sec. 710. Appointment of Employés.—Appointments to the railway mail service are made upon the recommendation of the General Superintendent. All appointments are originally made for six months only, and at the expiration of that time, if the record and final examination of the person temporarily appointed are satisfactory, he receives a permanent appointment. All promotions are made upon the recommendation of the General Superintendent, based upon the report of the Division Superintendent as to good conduct, faithful service, and efficiency, and all such reports must be accompanied by the employé's full record, including case examinations and facing-slips.

Sec. 711. Uniform for Railway Mail Employés.—Postal clerks, route-agents, and mail-route messengers shall not be required to wear uniform other than a cap or badge. (Act of March 3, 1879, section 1, 20 Stat., p. 357.)

The uniform cap required by this section of the law to be worn by employés is regulation navy, three inches deep, 1¾ inch front, with black corded silk band; cloth to be full indigo dark navy blue; lining of cap to be silesia, and oil-glazed cover; the cap to bear upon its front the letters "R. M. S." in silver, surrounded by a gold wreath.

The Postmaster-General is satisfied that the adoption of a uniform for the railway mail service has been productive of great good to the service by elevating its tone and inspiring a feeling of manly pride in the corps, which has greatly increased its efficiency. While the law forbids him to require any uniform to be worn other than a cap or badge, and no distinction can be made between those who wear the entire uniform and those who do not, he believes that the interests of the service will be promoted and the safety of the mails increased if all the employés, of their own free will and accord, continue to wear the entire uniform formerly required—a uniform which any man should be proud to wear in view of the honorable record which the railway mail service of the United States has made since its organization.

Sec. 712. Division Superintendents not to recommend Appointments.—Division Superintendents must confine themselves in their recommendations for promotions in the railway mail service to the fact as to whether, in their opinion, the person recommended would make an efficient employé, and must not recommend, directly or indirectly, any person for appointment.

Sec. 713. Assignment of Chief Head Clerks.—Division Superintendents may assign to duty (when necessary, subject to the approval of the General Superintendent) as chief head clerks of railway mail service, such employés as in their judgment are best qualified to discharge the duties expected of them, and the duties of such chief head clerks will be to make examination of the men under their charge; to see that they perform all the duties required of them promptly and thoroughly; to see that the schemes furnished are kept corrected, and that all orders issued by the Division Superintendent are promptly executed. All irregularities, insubordination, inefficiencies, and lax morality occurring on routes under their charge must be reported to their Division Superintendent at once.

CHAPTER TWO.

INSTRUCTIONS TO EMPLOYÉS HANDLING ORDINARY MAIL-MATTER.

☞ For instructions as to handling registered matter, see Title V, *The Registry System of the United States.*

Sec. 714. Employés to Carry Instructions with Them.—Each employé, when on duty, must have with him either the volume of Postal Laws and Regulations of the latest edition, or so much thereof as relates to the railway mail-service and registry system of the United States, copies of current "Orders" affecting his line, "Schemes of distribution," latest "Postal Guide," and copy of "Schedule of mail-trains."

Sec. 715. Employés to Report Errors Discovered in the Postal Guide.—Every employé detecting errors in the United States Official Postal Guide must report the same at once to his Division Superintendent, in order that it may be reported to the Department for correction.

Sec. 716. Employés to be Examined in the Postal Laws and Regulations.—At each examination of employés they will be required to answer questions touching the postal laws and regulations, and they must be thoroughly instructed on the rates of postage and in the regulations of their own service and of the registry system of the United States. They must also be informed as to the duties of postmasters, so far as those duties affect the railway mail service.

Sec. 717. One Employé to have Charge of Office.—Where there is more than one employé assigned to duty in an Office, one of the number will be designated to take charge of the same.

Sec. 718. Accountability of Employé in Charge of Office.—The one so designated will have charge of and be accountable for all property belonging in or pertaining to the Office, and he will for the time being have full charge of the same. It will be his duty to see that all necessary reports are made, that all distribution in the Office is correct, and that all mails are properly made up and put upon the proper route to their destination.

Sec. 719. Assistants to Obey Employé in Charge.—It will be the duty of his assistants to implicitly obey orders of the employé in charge, and no one on duty will consider his labors ended until the whole mail has been properly distributed, pouched, and transmitted.

Sec. 720. Receiving Mail at Cars; Cancelled Stamps to be Refused.—Letters and other properly-prepaid mail-matter must be received at the Offices, and all employés who are required to open letter-boxes at stations and take mail therefrom must visit the boxes the last moment before leaving; but employés are strictly prohibited from receiving from the public for mailing, matter on which the stamps have been canceled.

Sec. 721. Cancellation of Postage-Stamps.—Postage-stamps affixed to letters, packets, or parcels of any description, and all stamped envelopes, newspaper wrappers, and postal cards, must be immediately and effectually canceled in the Office in which they may be deposited for transmission. The cancellation must be effected by the use of black printing-ink wherever that material can be obtained; and where it cannot, the operation should be performed by making several heavy crosses or parallel lines upon each stamp with a pen dipped in good black writing-ink.

Sec. 722. Post-marking Stamps not to be Used for Cancellaton.—The use of the Office rating or postmarking stamp as a canceling instrument is positively prohibited, inasmuch as the postmark when impressed on the postage-stamp is usually indistinct, and the cancellation effected thereby is imperfect. The postage-stamp must, therefore, be effectually canceled with a separate instrument.

Sec. 723. Receiving and Delivering Second-class Mail at Cars.—The Postmaster-General may provide by order the terms upon which route-agents may receive from publishers or any news agents in charge thereof, and deliver the same as directed, if presented and called for at the mail-car or steamer, packages of newspapers and other periodicals not received from or intended for delivery at any post-office. (R. S., § 3889.)

Employés are prohibited from receiving newspapers and periodicals from publishers and news-agents, unless the same are accompanied by a certificate from the postmaster that the postage has been paid.

Sec. 724. Mail to be Made up by States.—All mail for States of which no distribution is made must be made up "by States" and facing-slips used, in accordance with section 728; that is, letter and circular mail for each State must be made up in packages, and newspaper mail in canvas sacks, by itself, and the name of the State marked on the slip covering the package or tag attached to the sack.

Sec. 725. Separate Mail for Delivery and Mail for Distribution.—Mail for delivery and mail for distribution at a post-office must always be made up in separate packages.

Sec. 726. Direct Packages.—Making a direct package is placing all letters for one Office or post-office in a package by themselves, with a plainly-addressed letter for such Office or post-office faced out on each side.

Sec. 227. Letters must not be Placed in Pouch Loose.—Letter and circular mail must always be properly "faced up" and tied in packages, and never placed in the pouch loose.

Sec. 728. Facing-slips to be Used.—Facing-slips must be placed upon all packages of letters and circulars (except those made up direct for delivery, when the slip should be placed inside of each package, and be postmarked and bear the name of the person making the package and the direction moving), and in each canvas sack of newspapers, the same to be securely tied on the package, or if newspapers, placed in the bag, and have on each the address or destination of the package or sack, the postmark, with date, direction moving, and the name of the person making up the same.

Sec. 729. Checking Errors.—All errors found in the distribution of a package of letters or in a sack of newspapers must be noted on the reverse side of the slip-covering or inside of the same, giving the name of the post-office and State, and the county when included in the superscription, adding thereto the name of the person noting the errors, and postmark with date.

Sec. 730. Disposition of Slips Received.—All slips received upon packages of letter or circular mail or in sacks of newspaper mail must be preserved and forwarded to the Division Superintendent.

Sec. 731. Distribution of Mails by Schemes.—Employés will carefully distribute and make up mails by the official schemes which may be furnished them, and will conform to any changes that may be made in the same by the Superintendent of the Division, and will make up and exchange only such pouches as may be ordered by him.

Sec. 732. Open and Distribute One Pouch or Sack at a Time.—Employés will complete the distribution of the contents of one pouch or sack before opening another, so that any errors in distribution or missent mail may be correctly noted and reported.

Sec. 733. Absence of Slips on Packages or in Sacks.—If no slips are received on the packages or in sacks, notify Division Superintendents, stating, if possible, the line or post-office from which the mail was received, and if newspaper mail, forward the label received on the sack.

Sec. 734. Sack to be Turned Inside Out.—Whenever a sack of newspaper mail is emptied the sack must be turned inside out, to make sure that no mail is left in it.

Sec. 735. Pouches to be Examined.—In emptying a pouch great care must be taken that no mail is left therein; and to be certain of this, it must be held so that the whole interior can be seen and looked into, in each case, in addition to thoroughly shaking it.

Sec. 736. Printed Labels to be Returned.—Printed wooden labels for sacks of newspaper mail and printed slide-labels for pouches must be taken off when the sacks or pouches are opened, and returned by first mail to the post-office or Office from which they were received, the wooden labels to be classed with newspaper mail and the slide-labels as letter mail. Under no circumstances are any of such labels to be defaced or destroyed.

Sec. 737. Trip Reports to be Forwarded.—Trip reports, together with all slips received, must be properly filled out and promptly forwarded to the Division Superintendent at end of each trip. Be particular to give all the information called for by the trip report.

Sec. 738. Vigilance Required in Guarding Mails.—All employés are expected to use extraordinary vigilance in guarding the mails under their charge, which must not be left for a moment exposed, day or night, and especially in making transfers where there is considerable portage between trains. Should they become aware that the mails are so exposed at any time or place, they are required to note the same upon their trip-report, for the information of the Division Superintendent. When accompanying the mails on other than regulation wagons, one of the employés should always sit in such position as to be able to instantly detect the loss of a pouch or sack.

Sec. 739. Waste Paper and Twine to be Examined.—Waste paper and twine must be preserved and turned in at terminal post-office, but carefully examined before being sent from the car, and the sack containing the same shall bear the words "Waste paper," and the postmark, with date of time of sending it into the terminal post-office.

Sec. 740. Disposition of Unmailable Matter Found in the Mails.—Any employé in whose Office shall be deposited for mailing domestic letters wholly unpaid, or on which less than one full rate of postage is paid, letters or packages bearing stamps that have been previously used, or stamps cut from stamped envelopes or wrappers, or packages of third or fourth class matter not fully prepaid, shall detain the same and turn them over to his Division Superintendent. It shall also be his duty to intercept and withdraw from the mail all letters or packages of the second, third, or fourth class so incorrectly, illegibly, or insufficiently addressed that they cannot be forwarded to the persons for whom they are intended, or the addresses of which have become detached or erased; all articles found loose in any pouch or sack, and any article which, by the rulings of the Department, has been declared unmailable because of its harmful nature, and forward the same to his Division Superintendent, with a statement giving the date and name of the post-office or other source from which such matter was received. Employés must not change the address upon such matter, and no indorsement upon a letter, or addition thereto in pencil or ink or any other way, will be permitted.

Sec. 741. Unmailable Matter Forwarded to Superintendent.—All such matter forwarded to the Division Superintendent must be accompanied by a slip addressed to the Superintendent, and bearing the name of the employé forwarding the same, and the postmark of his Office with date.

Sec. 742. Mailable Matter Turned in as Unmailable to be Checked as Errors.—Any such mail-matter, the address on which is found in the latest current "Postal Guide," will be noted as errors on the slip accompanying the same and charged against the employé.

Sec. 743. Unmailable Matter to be Postmarked.—Unmailable matter of the first and second class sent to the Division Superintendent must be postmarked on the back.

Sec. 744. Soldiers' and Sailors' Letters.—Soldiers' and sailors' letters, duly certified, should be forwarded the same as prepaid matter.

Sec. 745. Change of Schedules to be Reported.—Employés are directed to notify the Superintendent of the Division of all changes of schedules or running of trains upon their respective routes.

Sec. 746. Letters Outside of Pouches to be Reported.—Employés will report to the Division Superintendent each instance of finding letters under the strap or attached to the outside of a pouch, giving name of Office or post-office from which received.

Sec. 747. No Employé to be Absent without Leave.—No employé is allowed to absent himself from his line, or to exchange runs with an employé on the same or any other line, without the written permission of the Division or General Superintendent of Railway Mail Service. And any employé to whom a leave of absence is granted will be required to furnish a suitable and competent substitute, at his own expense, unless he can make a satisfactory arrangement with the other employés on his line to perform his duties during his absence; such arrangement to be evidenced by a memorandum, in writing, signed by all the parties concerned, and to be filed with the Division Superintendent. But no employé shall be absent for a period aggregating more than sixty days in any one year (computing from January first) nor more than thirty consecutive days without special authority from the Department. See sections 502, 503, *Instructions to Paying Postmasters.*

Sec. 748. In Case of Disability, Employé must Send Certificate.—In case an employé shall be disabled while in the actual discharge of his duties as such by a railroad or other accident, he shall forward to his Division Superintendent a sworn certificate of his attending physician or surgeon, setting forth the nature, extent, and cause of his disability and the probable duration of the same. This certificate should be sworn to before a notary public, justice of the peace, or other officer authorized to administer an oath who uses a seal. On receipt of this certificate, leave of absence, with pay, may be granted to the disabled employé or employés on application to the Second Assistant Postmaster-General, Division of Inspection. But no leave of absence, with pay, granted under such circumstances, shall cover a period exceeding ninety days from the date the disability was received. But if at the expiration of ninety days from said date the employé be unable to resume duty, further leave, without pay, may be granted by the Second Assistant Postmaster-General on recommendation of the General Superintendent of Railway Mail Service.

Sec. 749. Employés' Record of Arrivals and Departures.—A record of arrivals and departures will be kept at each terminal post-office, or at some other place at each terminus of a run, to be designated by the Division Superintendent, in which each employé is required to sign in his own handwriting his name and the day and hour of the schedule arrival and departure of the train, and of his own arrival at and departure from the post-office or other place where the record is kept. Failure to do so will be regarded as a failure to perform service without excuse, and the employé will forfeit one day's pay for each failure to so sign, but such forfeiture shall not exceed one day's pay for any number of failures to sign on any one day. See section 499.

Sec. 750. Posting Record-Book.—The person in charge of the record of arrivals and departures must fill up the blank spaces at the head of each page before the page is signed upon.

Sec. 751. Partial Duty to be Noted on Record.—In case an employé does not perform duty over the whole length of the route, the portion over which he performed duty must be noted on the record. In case of a substitute, he will sign, in addition to his own name, that of the employé for whom he is performing service.

Sec. 752. Employés Paid for Daily Service.—The Department pays each employé for daily service whether he is on duty or not, and therefore has a right to demand service of him at any time.

Sec. 753. Address of Employés.—Employés must keep the Division Superintendent advised of their full address.

Sec. 754. Period of Duty.—Employés must remain on duty the whole length of their allotted runs.

Sec. 755. Employés must Accompany Mails to and from Post-Offices.—It is the duty of each employé to accompany the mails to and from the initial and terminal post-offices of their respective runs.

Sec. 756. Employés must Examine Offices at the End of Runs.—Employés will thoroughly examine their Offices before leaving, to see that no mail is left therein, and that every precaution for the proper protection of the Office has been taken.

Sec. 557. Replies to Official Communications.—Each employé is required to date and sign with his official signature all replies to official inquiries and other communications.

Sec. 758. Who may have Access to Offices.—The Office is for the exclusive accommodation of the mails and the persons specially appointed to take charge of the same. It is strictly private, not to be entered by any person except regular Special Agents of the Post-Office Department and persons who may be authorized by the General Superintendent and Superintendents of the Railway Mail Service. The conductor of the train, however, will have access to the Office in the performance of his duties, and, in case of necessity, other railway employés may pass through, but none of them shall be allowed to remain therein.

Sec. 759. Trip Permits to Ride in Offices.—Permits, signed by the General Superintendent Railway Mail Service, and countersigned by one of the Division Superintendents, will be required (except for Special Agents of the Post-Office Department) as authority for riding in Offices. Without such permit no person except Special Agents of the Post-Office Department, who will be required by the employé in charge to show their commissions, will be allowed to ride in an Office. This applies to all employés in the service passing over lines to which they are not assigned.

Sec. 760. All but Annual Permits to be Taken up.—Permits will be taken up by the employé in charge of the Office, who will affix his postmark, with date, also his name, on the reverse side, and forward to his Division Superintendent with his trip report, noting on the same the points between which the person rode in his Office. If it is an annual permit, it should not be taken up, but the number of it should be noted on the trip report, and also the points between which the holder rode in the Office.

Sec. 761. Permits not good for Transportation.—A permit is in no way to be considered as furnishing transportation to the person holding it, but simply as authority to ride in the Office, and the conductor must be notified, so that he may take up ticket, or pass, or collect fare.

Sec. 762. Sale of Postage-Stamps by Employés.—Employés are required to keep constantly on hand a supply of postage-stamps of the denomination of three cents, for the accommodation of the public at the Office. Applicants should make their own change. It is a penal offense for an employé to demand for a postage-stamp a sum exceeding that expressed on its face.

Sec. 763. Employés on Duty not to Traffic.—Traffic in merchandise by employés, while on duty or the active engagement, at any time, in any occupation of profit or emolument, is strictly prohibited. They must confine themselves wholly to the duties imposed upon them by the Department. The time while off actual duty is for rest and study.

Sec. 764. Must not Impart Information to unauthorized Persons..—No information must be imparted, voluntarily or otherwise, concerning letters or other mail-matter passing through the hands of employés in the process of distribution, excepting to those who may be officially authorized to receive information, and when information may be desired by them.

Sec. 765. Turning over Property of Department.—On the resignation, suspension, or removal of an employé, he shall turn over the mail-keys and all other property and records (including the records of registered packages received and forwarded) in his possession to the Superintendent of Railway Mail Service of the Division in which he last performed service. A refusal to deliver all or either of the above articles of property, on demand, is an indictable offense under the statutes of the United States.

Sec. 766. Forwarding of Resignations.—Resignations must be forwarded to the Department through the Superintendent of the Division, and should be sent as long prior to the date on which they are intended to take effect as possible.

Sec. 767. No Information to be Given Concerning Vacancies.—Information regarding vacancies or probable vacancies in the service must not be imparted by employés, nor must they take any part in procuring appointments.

Sec. 768. Intoxicating Liquors Prohibited.—The use of intoxicating liquors when on duty is absolutely prohibited.

Sec. 769. Mail in Transit not to be Delivered.—Employés are specially instructed not to make a delivery at the Office of letters in transit, which come into their hands for distribution, to any person whatever (except an authorized Special Agent of the Department), although it be personally known to them that the applicant is the person named in the address. The act of delivery is devolved by law and the regulations of the Department on the postmaster at the post-office to which the letters are addressed.

Sec. 770. Public Property not to be Used for Private Purposes.—The use of any property of the Department for personal purposes is strictly prohibited.

Sec. 771. Exchange of Pouches.—Exchange of letter-mails must always be made in locked pouches, and, whether there is any letter-mail or not, a pouch, duly locked, must be furnished whenever one is due.

Sec. 772. Mail must not be Delivered at Places not Post-Offices.—Under no circumstances should mail be delivered at any place not a regularly established post-office; and wherever a post-office is discontinued, the mail for it should be delivered into the nearest established post-office.

Sec. 773. List to be kept of Exchange Pouches.—Each employé in charge of an Office must keep a list of all exchange pouches that should be dispatched and received by him, and on each run each pouch received must be "checked off" at the time it is received. Any failures to receive any regular exchange must be reported to the Division Superintendent on the "trip report."

Sec. 774. Irregularities to be Reported.—Every serious irregularity in the forwarding of mails should be specially reported, and in making these reports, where letters are concerned, give the exact postmark, including the hour. In the case of newspapers, state whether received in a pouch or a sack, and, if in a sack, whether it contained all second class, all third class, or mixed matter; and if all one publication, give the name and date of it. In addition to the above, the date, place, exact time of receipt, and train by which received, should be given. In all cases, the tag on a missent pouch or sack must be forwarded with the report to the Division Superintendent.

Sec. 775. Missent Matter to be so Stamped.—Each letter or paper missent to an Office must be plainly stamped MISSENT, and the postmark of the Office also stamped plainly thereon. This also applies particularly to registered mail.

Sec. 776. Mutilation of Property Prohibited.—Any mutilation of property furnished for the use and convenience of the employés of the service is strictly prohibited.

Sec. 777. Employés must Examine Order-Book.—Employés must, immediately previous to starting out upon each run, invariably examine all order-books or orders left for their guidance.

Sec. 778. Second Class and other Matter outside of Mail-Bags.—Mail-matter must under no consideration be carried outside of the regular mail-bags, except second-class matter designed and marked for outside delivery, or matter the form of which prevents it from being carried in the mail-bag.

Sec. 779. Reading Mail-Matter in Transit Forbidden.—Employés must not remove newspapers or periodicals in the mail from their wrappers, packages, or bundles for the purpose of reading them.

Sec. 780. Case Exminations.—Case examinations of employés will be had, from time to time, upon the official schemes of distribution furnished them, the connection of trains as shown in the "schedule" of mail-trains, and such other instructions and orders as relate to the service.

Sec. 781. Examination of Employés on their Instructions.—Employés will be examined as to their knowledge of the "Instructions to Employés of the Railway Mail Service" at each case examination. The questions asked will be such as will require an answer giving the substance of each section of the instructions, and the result of the examination will be reported to the Department.

Sec. 782. Probationary Appointees to be Examined Monthly.—All probationary appointees will be examined monthly during their probationary term. These examinations will consist of a knowledge of the instructions, the schemes of distribution which may be furnished them, and railway connections at the various junctions, as given in the schedule of mail-trains. The result of each examination will be reported to the Department, and on the result of these examinations and their efficiency in their work will depend their permanent appointment in the service.

Sec. 783. Employés on Night Lines.—The special attention of employés on night lines is called to the following: When there is any mail to be distributed or work to be done, every employé must be awake and do his full share.

When the distribution is entirely finished and all of the work done, there is no objection to a part of the crew going to sleep, but at least one employé must always be wide awake and on duty.

This precaution is absolutely necessary for the proper protection of the registered and other mail against accident, fire, or robbery, as well as for the personal safety of the employés on duty.

Sec. 784. Securing Mail-Locks and Mail-Key.—Employés when on duty must always wear the mail-key securely attached to their clothing by the safety-chain. Under no circumstances will employés on vacating their Offices leave mail-locks therein.

Sec. 785. Notify Division Superintendent of Changes Needed in Offices.—Employés should notify their Division Superintendent of any changes or alterations needed in their cars, and must not go to the railroad company with any requests or suggestions as to what alterations or changes they think should be made.

Sec. 786. Employés must Assist Special Agents.—In all cases Special Agents of the Post-Office Department, presenting proper credentials, must be given any assistance or facility they may ask, and in no case must the fact of a Special Agent being on the train be communicated by one employé to another. No excuse will be taken for any violation of this section.

Sec. 787. Presence of Special Agents not to be Reported.—No entry should be made in the attendance book of the fact that any Special Agent has ridden in the Office.

Sec. 788. Accidents to Mail-Trains to be Reported.—When any accident occurs to any mail-train, the employé in charge of the mail will at once make a full report of the same to his Division Superintendent. This is in addition to notation on trip report.

Sec. 789. Hooks Prohibited in Handling Mail-Bags.—The use of hooks in handling mail-bags is forbidden.

Sec. 790. Courtesy to Public Enjoined.—Employés must observe, in their official intercourse with the public and with each other, the strictest courtesy; and must endeavor, by active and intelligent effort, to promote the positive interest of the service and of the public.

Sec. 791. Delivery of Mails at Catch-Stations.—At catch-stations, where cranes are erected for the exchange of mails without slacking the speed of trains, the pouch must never be kicked off, but must be thrown off by hand to a distance of at least ten feet from the track, so as to prevent the pouch from being drawn under the train.

Sec. 792. Rules of Railway Companies Observed.—The rules and regulations of the railway companies, not in conflict with these instructions, must be respected and obeyed.

Sec. 793. Ignorance of Rules no Excuse for Violations.—Ignorance of the foregoing instructions will not be considered an excuse for the violation of the same, and the violation thereof will be considered a sufficient cause for immediate removal.

CHAPTER THREE.

LOCAL AGENTS AND THEIR DUTIES.

Sec. 794. Local Agents under Supervision of Supt. R. M. S. only.—Local agents are entirely under the supervision of the Superintendent of Railway Mail Service of the Division in which the point at which they are stationed is located, and will look to him only for all instructions. Division Superintendents will keep a record of all errors in forwarding mail made by local agents in the same manner as that of errors made by employés is kept. They will send to each local agent in their division a slip such as is sent to other employés, stating the errors which the local agent has made in forwarding the mail from the point at which he is stationed.

Sec. 795. Transfer and Delivery of Mails.—Local agents are required to superintend and assist in the transfer and delivery of all mails at the points where they are stationed, as far as possible; to inform themselves thoroughly in relation to the routes over which mails should pass that are transferred at that point, and of designations of routes and mails generally, in order that they may be able, in cases where mails are missent or incorrectly put off, to dispatch them by the proper trains; to keep themselves correctly informed of the hours of arrival and departure of all trains upon which mails are carried, and to notify the Division Superintendent of Railway Mail Service, in writing, of any change of schedule whereby railroad connections may be made or missed, to the end that the quickest possible dispatch of mails may be secured.

Sec. 796. Vigilance in Guarding Mails.—Local agents are expected to use extraordinary vigilance in guarding the mails under their charge, which must not be left for a moment exposed, day or night, and especially in making transfers where there is a considerable portage between trains; they should accompany the mails upon the wagon in all cases possible, where there is no authorized employé in charge of the same, and sit in such position at all times as to be able to instantly detect the loss of a pouch or sack. Frequent losses have been occasioned by a disregard of this latter requirement.

Sec. 797. Supervision of Messenger Service.—Local agents will report to their Division Superintendents every irregularity in the messenger service at their stations which may come to their knowledge.

Sec. 798. Checking Mails in Transit.—Special effort should be made to check off all mail-bags in transit so that it may be known with certainty, both at the time and at any subsequent period, exactly what mails are transferred at the station; and it is hoped that an actual notation of this at the time of the transfer can be made to advantage by having lists prepared in convenient form of all the mails to be transferred, with columns on either side in which a check mark opposite each name of a sack or pouch will be all the record that need be taken at the actual time of making the transfer; this to be afterward entered in the permanent book of record.

Sec. 799. Daily Reports.—Local agents should keep a daily record of the arrival and departure of mails, mail-trains, and mail-wagons at their stations, and make a daily report to the Superintendent of Railway Mail Service for the Division in which their station is situated of all failures of railroads to make their regular mail connections, of all irregularities in the transmission of the mails, and in the service by mail wagon. A daily report regarding each of these features should be made whether there is a failure or not.

Sec. 800. Examinations of Local Agents.—Examinations will be made of local agents from time to time: First of all, concerning their knowledge of the current titles and numbers of trains arriving at and departing from their stations; the mails to be transferred and the arrival of mail-trains; subsequently, when deemed desirable, concerning distribution and other information more particularly applicable to employés on duty on the routes. It should also be noted whether they are thoroughly informed as to the correct terminal titles of routes concerning which they ought to be conversant.

Sec. 801. Arrivals and Departures must be Recorded.—A record of arrivals and departures must be kept at each local mail agency, in which each local mail-agent and assistant will sign his exact time of going on duty and leaving duty at station each day. At the end of each month this record will be sent to the Division Superintendent for inspection.

Sec. 802. Handling Registered Matter.—In special cases local agents may be required to receipt for, transfer, and deliver registered packages; in which case the registers must be entered in a book of record, which will be furnished for that purpose, and a receipt obtained from the postmaster, or employé to whom the packages are delivered. Local agents are positively prohibited from transferring registered matter except as above instructed.

Sec. 803. Absence.—Each local agent is forbidden to absent himself from duty, or to exchange duties with other employés in other branches of the service, or to employ and transfer his duties to a substitute without written permission from the Superintendent Railway Mail Service for his Division, and when such leave is granted, he will be required to furnish a suitable and competent substitute (who must be sworn), at his own expense, to perform his duties during his absence, such arrangement to be evidenced by memorandum in writing, signed by all the parties concerned, and to be filed with the Division Superintendent. But no local agent shall be absent for a period aggregating more than sixty days in any one year (computing from January first), nor more than thirty consecutive days, without special authority from the Department.

See sections 502, 503. *Instructions to Paying Postmasters.*

Sec. 804. Courtesy Enjoined.—It is especially enjoined upon all local agents to observe in their official intercourse with the public and railroad officials or employés the strictest courtesy, and endeavor by active and intelligent effort to promote the positive interest of the service and the public.

Sec. 805. Local Agents Governed by General Instructions to Employés.—In addition to these special instructions to local mail-agents, they will also be governed by the general instructions to employés of the railway mail service when applicable.

TITLE V.

THE REGISTRY SYSTEM OF THE UNITED STATES.

CHAPTER ONE.

RECEIVING, TRANSMITTING, AND DELIVERING REGISTERED DOMESTIC MAIL-MATTER.

Sec. 806. Registry System Authorized.—For the greater security of valuable mail-matter, the Postmaster-General may establish a uniform system of registration. But the Post-Office Department or its revenue shall not be liable for the loss of any mail-matter on account of its having been registered. (R. S., § 3926.)

Sec. 807. Object of the Registry System.—The registry system is intended to secure to valuable mail-matter in its transmission through the mails the utmost security within the province of the Post-Office Department.

Sec. 808. Means Employed to Attain Safety.—The manner in which security over ordinary mail-matter is obtained is by the use of a distinctive cover, retention in special custody, systematic receipts and records showing any transfer from receipt until delivery, affording a continuous trace from the sender in its course through the mails until its delivery into the hands of the addressee.

Sec. 809. Postmaster's Duty to Encourage Registration.—Postmasters are obliged to register all mailable matter offered for registration, and should advise the public to register valuable mail-matter, so as to enable the Post-Office Department to keep it under this strict supervision, which cannot be given to the transmission of ordinary mail matter.

Sec. 810. What Mail-Matter can be Registered.—First-class matter, or matter on which letter rates of postage has been paid, which matter must always be sealed. Third-class matter and fourth-class matter, unsealed, fully prepaid at the proper rates and conforming to all requirements. No matter excluded by law from the mails can be registered. See Title II, Chapter Three.

Sec. 811. No Registration on Sunday.—Postmasters are not required to receive letters or other matter for registration on Sundays or legal holidays.

Sec. 812. Limit of Fee for Registration.—No Fee on Official Matter.—Mail-matter shall be registered only on the application of the party posting the same, and the fee therefor shall not exceed twenty cents in addition to the regular postage, to be, in all cases, prepaid; and all such fees shall be accounted for in such manner as the Postmaster-General shall direct. But letters upon the official business of the Post-Office Department which require registering shall be registered free of charge and pass through the mails free of charge. (R. S., § 3927.)

Sec. 813. Registration Fee.—The fee on any registered matter, domestic or foreign, is fixed at ten cents on each letter or parcel, to be affixed in stamps, in addition to the postage. Two or more letters or parcels addressed to, or intended for, the same person cannot be tied or otherwise fastened together and registered as one.

Sec. 814. Rules for Sender of Registered Letters.—Postmasters before receiving a letter for registration must require the sender to have it fully and legibly addressed; to have his or her name and address indorsed across the end; to have placed all its contents in a firmly sealed envelope; and affixed the necessary stamps to pay postage and fee.

Sec. 815. Rules for Sender of Third and Fourth Class Matter.—Postmasters before receiving third and fourth class matter for registration must require full address, indorsement, and prepayment of fee and postage, as stated in preceding section, and further require that such matter shall be marked THIRD CLASS or FOURTH CLASS, as the case may be, and shall be so put up as to safely bear transportation, and admit of an examination of contents, to ascertain that it is admissible to the mails as such matter. See sections 223, 237, and 238.

Sec. 816. Postmasters must not Address and Seal Letters.—Postmasters and their employés are forbidden to address a registered letter for the sender, to place contents in letter, or to seal the letter, or to affix the stamps. This must, in all cases, be done by the sender, as required in section 814. No inquiry must be made further than to ascertain that the matter is mailable, and no statement can appear on the receipt as to the contents of any registered letter, except letters containing currency, registered under the following section:

Sec. 817. Registry of Letters Containing Currency for Redemption.—Under such regulations as the Postmaster-General may prescribe, all postmasters are authorized to register in the manner prescribed by law, but without payment of any registration fee, all letters containing fractional or other currency of the United States, which shall be by them sent by mail to the Treasurer of the United States for redemption; and the postmaster at the city of Washington, in the District of Columbia, shall register, in like manner, without charge, all letters containing new currency returned for currency redeemed, which shall be received by him from the Treasurer, in sealed packages, marked with the word "register" over the official signature of the said Treasurer. (R. S., § 3932.)

Sec. 818. Special Instructions for Registering Currency.—Whenever letters containing currency for redemption are offered for registration, postmasters will be governed by the following instructions:

First. They must require the contents of every such letter to be exhibited to them, with a descriptive list of contents, giving an accurate and detailed description of the money to be remitted. In case of fractional currency, the number and denomination of pieces will be sufficient; but of currency of the denomination of one dollar and upward, the letter, number of series, and date of each note, as well as the denomination, must be given.

Second. The list must be carefully examined and compared with the money to be remitted, and when found to be correct will be filed in the office, to be subject at all times to the inspection of proper agents of the Post-Office Department.

Third. The money must then be inclosed and the letter sealed in the presence of the postmaster, who will then give the usual registry-receipt therefor.

Fourth. The letter must then be disposed of in the manner provided for other registered letters; but, for the sake of further security, the postmaster must be ready to prove beyond question in every case, by a disinterested witness, that such letter was duly mailed in the mode prescribed for registered letters; otherwise, should the letter or package be lost, he will be held responsible therefor.

Sec. 819. Receiving Mail-Matter for Registration.—When a letter or parcel is presented for registration the postmaster will first examine it to see that the sender has complied with requirements of sections 814 and 815, and, if such be the case, he will then enter on the book of registration the name and address of sender, address and destination of letter or parcel, registered number and date of mailing, filling out alike the stub of the book and registry receipt. He will number the letter or parcel to correspond with number on stub and registry receipt, sign the receipt, separate it from the stub, and give it to the sender.

NOTE.—Postmasters will erase the word LETTER or PARCEL on receipt and stub, so that it will read according to the character of article registered.

Sec. 820. Number Registered Matter and Registered-Package Envelopes.—The registration-book must be commenced each quarter with No. 1, and continued consecutively through the quarter, and the letters or parcels registered correspondingly numbered. Registered-package envelopes are also to be numbered consecutively, commencing each quarter with No. 1.

Sec. 821. Matter becomes Registered after a Receipt is given Therefor.—After a receipt has been given therefor, and the matter has been numbered as prescribed in the preceding sections, the letter or parcel becomes a registered letter or parcel, and must be guarded with the utmost care, and kept separate from ordinary mail-matter.

Sec. 822. Cancellation of Stamps, Registry-Mark, and Postmark.—All stamps on registered matter will be effectually canceled, and the letter or parcel marked plainly REGISTERED, and plainly postmarked.

Sec. 823. Registered Matter to be kept Secure.—All registered matter must be kept separate from ordinary matter, and in that part of the post-office most secure from accident or theft, and to which no access can be had by any one unauthorized by the postmaster, who must account for all registered matter coming into his post-office.

Sec. 824. Receipt to be Taken upon Delivery of Registered Matter.—A receipt shall be taken upon the delivery of any registered mail-matter, showing to whom and when the same was delivered, which shall be returned to the sender, and be received in the courts as *prima-facie* evidence of such delivery. (R. S., § 3928.)

Sec. 825. The Registry-Return-Receipt.—A registry-return-receipt of the new card form must be filled out for each domestic letter or parcel (*i. e.*, addressed to any post-office in the United States or Territories). The registry-return-receipt must on its face have written the name of sender, street and number, or post-office box, name of post-office, county, and State (the space for stamp of post-office is reserved for post-office of delivery). On the other side enter date of mailing, registry number, mailing post-office and State, and address of the registered letter or parcel.

Sec. 826. The Registry-Bill.—A registry-bill, of the new card form, must be prepared to accompany the registered letter or parcel, which bill must, on its face, be filled out with the name of the mailing post-office, county, and State (the place for stamp is reserved for post-office of destination); on the other side, in the heading, the date of mailing, mailing post-office, post-office of destination, county, and State, number of registered-package envelope in which it is to be inclosed, and in proper columns in body of bill the registry number of letter or parcel, class, whether first, third, or fourth, name of addressee, and the bill must be signed by the postmaster on the lower left corner.

NOTE.—The above section mentions only one letter or parcel, but it is not intended that postmasters shall use a separate bill for each letter or parcel sent by one mail to the same post-office; all domestic registered letters or parcels for the same post-office are to be entered on one bill and inclosed in one registered-package envelope when practicable. When this cannot be done, a separate registry bill must be made out for the contents of each registered-package envelope. Special bills in sheet form (old style) may be used by large post-offices when necessary.

Sec. 827. Registered-Package Envelope.—A registered-package envelope is to be used for no other purpose than covering registered mail-matter in its transmission from the receiving post-office to post-office of delivery. They must securely cover the registered matter they convey, be plainly addressed to post-office of destination, county, and State, be distinctly numbered, and legibly postmarked with the postmark of the mailing post-office and date of mailing.

Sec. 828. Preparing Registered Matter for Dispatch.—The registered letter or parcel with registry-bill and registry-return-receipt must be placed together in a registered-package envelope, addressed to the same post-office as the letter or parcel. The registered-package envelope must then be firmly sealed.

Sec. 829. Matter too Large to go in Registered-Package Envelopes.—When a registered letter or parcel too large to place inside of a registered-package envelope is received, it must, together with the registry-bill and registry-return-receipt, be wrapped, and a registered-package envelope, cut open so as to expose address and record of transit, be securely tied thereon, or be gummed or sealed to the wrapped package so that it cannot be detached or the contents interfered with.

Sec. 830. Registered-Package Receipt.—After a registered package has been made up for dispatch, a registered-package receipt must be filled out with name of mailing post-office, date of mailing, number and address of registered package. This registry-receipt is to be signed and returned without delay by the postmaster or employé of the Railway Mail Service who next receives the registered package after it leaves the mailing postmaster.

Sec. 831. Dispatching a Registered Package.—If a registered package is to be delivered direct to an employé of the Railway Mail Service for transmission, the postmaster will hand to him the package and obtain his signature on the package receipt. Where a registered package cannot be delivered direct, as above, it must be deposited in the mail-pouch, never in a newspaper or tie sack, the package receipt being placed in the letter package which is to be first distributed by the employé receiving the same. The pouch must be locked, and the lock must be tried to ascertain if it has been securely fastened.

Sec. 832. Registered Matter not to be Tied with Ordinary Mail-Matter.—Postmasters must not wrap or tie registered packages with any ordinary mail-matter, but should place them separately in the mail-pouch, so that their presence can be observed at once by the person opening the pouch.

Sec. 833. Mail-Carriers not to Handle Registered-Matter.—Under no circumstances can a registered package be intrusted to a mail-carrier or a mail-messenger outside of the locked pouch, nor should the pouch be intrusted to any but a sworn officer or employé of the Department.

Sec. 834. Certifying to Proper Dispatch of Registered Matter.—The postmaster, his deputy, or a duly-qualified clerk must be prepared at any time to make affidavit that any particular registered package was either given to an employé of the railway mail service or left the post-office in a pouch properly locked and labeled, and was forwarded by the proper route; and in all cases where practicable two persons should be present at the mailing of a registered package, and be prepared to testify as above, in case it should be required.

Sec. 835. Sending Registered Matter to an Office from Distant Post-Offices.—When a registered package that is to pass into an Office is to be sent from a post-office located on a route at any distance from the railway or steamboat line, the postmaster must so pouch the package that it will be received and receipted for by the postmaster at a post-office connecting with the Office. If the sending postmaster makes up a direct pouch to the Office and another to the connecting post-office the registered packages must not be placed in the pouch for the Office, if the pouch passes through any other post-office before reaching the Office.

Sec. 836. Never send Registered Matter Direct over Railway Mail Routes.—In no case must a postmaster dispatch a registered package in a direct pouch over a route upon which there is railway mail service. Registered matter on such routes must be held for the Office and pouched or delivered to the employé in charge, as the safety of registered matter must be considered before celerity in its dispatch. If the dispatching post-office is not on a railroad or steamboat line the requirements of the preceding section must be observed.

Sec. 837. Receiving Registered Packages in Pouches for a Post-Office.—Postmasters opening a pouch and finding registered packages therein addressed to their post-offices will sign the package receipts which they will find in the bundles of letters, examine the registered packages, and note the condition and date of arrival on the package receipt, which they will return by first mail to the sending postmaster or employé of the railway mail service.

Sec. 838. Postmasters Receiving Registered Packages in Transit.—If a registered package received in a way-pouch is addressed to a post-office beyond his own on the same route, the postmaster will sign the accompanying registered-package-receipt and fill up another package-receipt, inserting the name of his post-office, and, after indorsing the package, replace it in the pouch with the package-receipt placed in the bundle of letters for the next post-office on the route.

Sec. 839. Recording Packages in Transit and Returning Receipts.—From the package-receipt he received with a transit package the postmaster must make the proper entry in the record-of-registered-matter-in-transit, and then return the receipt by first mail to the Office or post-office whence it came.

Sec. 840. Continuous Examination, Record and System of Receipts.—The process of examination, indorsement, record, filling out package-receipts anew and depositing in pouch, must be repeated by every postmaster opening the pouch until it reaches its destination.

Sec. 841. Record-of-Registered-Matter-in-Transit.—Postmasters at all post-offices where pouches containing mail-matter for other post-offices are opened must make on the record-of-registered-matter-in-transit a full statement (as per heading of columns) of every registered package, registered postal-card package, registered stamped-envelope package, registered postage-stamp package, or through-registered-pouch passing through their post-offices, showing particulars of arrival and disposal of each such package or pouch. They must at all times be prepared to make prompt reply to any inquiry from a Special Agent or postmaster concerning such registered packages or pouches. The registered packages are so conspicuous that their presence among the contents of any mail-pouch cannot fail to be observed, and an omission to make record of them will not be excused. This record of transit must be carefully preserved in good order and be at all times open to the inspection of Special Agents of the Post-Office Department.

Sec. 842. When Registered Packages should go in Way-Pouches.—Where through-pouches and way-pouches are sent over routes on which there is no railway mail service, the registered packages must be sent in the way-pouches, and not in the through-pouches, except when the through-pouches are sent under brass locks and special instructions given to forward registered mail in the same.

Sec. 843. Registered Packages must be Sent by the most Secure Route.—Postmasters must dispatch registered packages by the most secure route, and endeavor, especially when they have to be sent long distances, to have them reach a railway Office or through-registered-pouch-office as soon as possible, even though such registered packages traverse a longer distance to destination than that taken by ordinary mail-matter; it being desirable that registered matter should be in the hands of responsible agents of the service, as far as practicable avoiding the exposure and handling necessitated by the frequent opening of pouches at way post-offices. For list of through-registered-pouch-offices see the latest Official Postal Guide.

Sec. 844. Postmasters must Observe the Registry Schemes.—When registry schemes and schedules of routes and times for the dispatch of registered matter are furnished to postmasters by the General Superintendent or Division Superintendent of Railway Mail Service, they will comply with such schemes and schedules until otherwise directed by the General Superintendent of Railway Mail Service, or by the Division Superintendent.

Sec. 845. Indorsing Registered Packages.—When a postmaster or railway-mail employé signs a receipt for a registered package, he will carefully examine the package, and indorse thereon in the spaces provided therefor a statement of its condition, the date of its receipt, the name of his post-office or Office and his signature; also indorse statement of condition on package-receipt.

Sec. 846. Checking Return of Package Receipts and Bills.—On the return of a registered-package receipt and registry-bill, the postmaster will note the date on the stub of the registration-book and file them for future reference.

Sec. 847. Failure to Return Registered-Package Receipt.—In case a registered-package receipt is not promptly returned by the postmaster, or employé of the railway mail service, to whom it was sent with the package, the postmaster who sent it must fill out a duplicate, noting date of such duplicate on registration-book. Failure of duplicate to return in due season must be reported to Third Assistant Postmaster-General.

Sec. 848. Failure to Return Registry Bill.—In case the registry bill fails to come back to the mailing post-office in reasonable time, a *Circular of inquiry for registered matter*, giving particulars of the package and its contents, must be sent to the post-office to which the registered package was addressed.

Sec. 849. Circular of Inquiry Returned Indorsed "Not Received."—If the circular of inquiry is returned stating the registered package has not reached its destination, a full report of the case must be made to the Chief Special Agent Post-Office Department, Washington, D. C., for investigation, and, in addition, to such Special Agents for certain States and Territories as may be designated by the Chief Special Agent.

Sec. 850. Misdirected Registered Packages in Transit not to be Opened.—Misdirected registered packages, except those mentioned in next section, must be returned to the mailing post-office for better directions. The postmaster detecting the error must indorse it "RETURNED FOR BETTER DIRECTION," place the misdirected registered package under cover of a regularly numbered registered-package envelope, duly postmarked and addressed to the mailing post-office, and sealed, making due note of the fact on his record-of-registered-matter-in-transit. Registered packages in transit or addressed to another post-office must not be opened.

Sec. 851. Misdirected Registered Postage-Stamp Packages, etc.—Postmasters at through-registered-pouch-offices, or separating post-offices, on receiving a registered package of stamps, envelopes, or postal cards bearing an incorrect or imperfect address, should hold the package and at once notify the Third Assistant Postmaster-General, STAMP DIVISION, giving the registered number, date of postmark, and full address of the package, and await instructions in regard to its disposal.

Sec. 852. Registered Packages Found in Bad Order or Damaged in Transit.—In case a registered package becomes damaged it must be placed in a new registered-package envelope at the post-office where the injury occurs or is discovered; or, when damaged in the hands of an employé of the railway mail service, at the post-office at the terminus of his route. The original registered-package envelope must not be removed, but, before it is inclosed in the new one, it must be indorsed with a statement of its exact condition, signed by the postmaster or railway-mail employé from whom received. The new registered-package envelope must bear the address, registry number, and name of the post-office of origin, and also the postmark of the post-office at which the package is re-enveloped. The fact of reinclosure must be noted on the Record-of-registered-matter-in-transit. Employés of the railway mail service finding in their Offices registered packages in bad order or damaged must deliver them to the postmaster at the terminal post-office for treatment as prescribed in this section. See section 855.

Sec. 853. Postmasters to Receive Registered Matter from Employés.—Postmasters at terminal post-offices of routes on which there is railway mail service must at all times be prepared to receive and properly receipt for registered packages brought to their post-offices by emplo s of the railway mail service. No delay of trains or unreasonable hours of arrival will authorize a deviation from this regulation.

Sec. 854. Rules for Registered Packages Uniform for all Classes.—The rules given for the treatment of registered packages apply equally to registered postage-stamp packages, postal-card packages, and stamped-envelope packages, except where special rules are given for the treatment of such matter in certain contingencies.

Sec. 855. Registered Postage-Stamp Packages Damaged in Transit.—Registered postage-stamp packages, registered postal-card packages, or registered stamped-envelope packages which have been damaged in transit must be securely wrapped and sealed by the postmaster discovering the damage, or at the terminal post-office to which such matter is delivered by railway-mail employés. After indorsing the package as provided in section 852, the postmaster will attach to it a label, "Registered postage-stamp package," "Registered postal-card package," or "Registered stamped-envelope package," as the case may be, will mark the original address and registry number on the wrapper, indorsed as follows: "PLACED UNDER COVER AT ——— POST-OFFICE. ———, 18—." He will then enter the package upon the record-of-registered-matter-in-transit, forward it to its destination as other registered matter, noting the fact of its being damaged and placed under cover, and send a full report of the facts to the Third Assistant Postmaster-General, STAMP DIVISION.

Sec. 856. Receiving Registered Matter at a Post-Office for Delivery.—On the arrival of a mail at any post-office the pouch must be opened only by the postmaster, his deputy, or a sworn clerk. If a registered package addressed to the postmaster is found in the pouch, the registered-package receipt must be first returned, as required in section 837; the registered package will be opened by cutting the end, and the addresses, etc., of the registered letters or parcels contained therein compared with the entries on the registry-bill. If these are found to correspond, the postmaster will examine the letters or parcels as to their condition, postmark them on the back, enter or the Record-of-registered-matter-received-and-delivered, date of arrival, the number and postmark of the registered package, and the number and addresses of the registered letters or parcels, and attach the return-receipts to the letters or parcels by bands or thread. The registry-bill is then to be signed, postmarked on the proper place, and remailed without cover. Postmasters receiving registered-stamp packages, postal-card packages, or envelope-packages, addressed to their post-offices, must enter such packages on Record-of-registered-matter received-and-delivered, and sign for them in delivery column.

Sec. 857. Omissions on Registry-Bill and Return-Receipt to be Supplied.—If the sending postmaster has failed to properly fill up his registry-bill or registry-return-receipt, the receiving postmaster must supply the omission. Before returning the registry-bill, he will note any irregularity thereon over his signature.

Sec. 858. Failure to Send Registry-Bill or Registry-Return-Receipt.—If, on opening a registered package, no bill is found, the receiving postmaster must fill out a bill and indorse it NO BILL RECEIVED, sign it, address it properly, postmark it, and forward it without cover to the mailing post-office. If no registry-return-receipt accompanies a registered letter or parcel, the postmaster opening the package must fill one out, attach it to the letter or parcel, and mail it to the sender when signed. A report of every such case must be made to the Third Assistant Postmaster-General, in order that the delinquent postmaster may be specially advised.

Sec. 859. Treatment of Registered Letters Arriving in bad Order.—If, on opening a registered package, a registered letter is found in bad order, the postmaster will indorse the letter, RECEIVED IN BAD ORDER, and sign his name. He will then inclose the letter in an ordinary official envelope, seal the envelope, and address it to the person to whom the registered letter is addressed, indorsing on the envelope, HAVE THIS EXAMINED ON DELIVERY, and make proper entry thereof, as required in section 856. On delivery of this letter the addressee should be requested to open the envelope in presence of the postmaster, delivery-clerk, or letter-carrier, and if there should be any of its original contents missing, the original envelope of the letter should be obtained from the addressee, with his indorsement thereon as to the deficiency; and this envelope, with the registered-package envelope, should be sent to the Chief Special Agent for investigation.

Sec. 860. Registered Letters found Unsealed.—If a registered letter arrive unsealed, the postmaster will indorse it RECEIVED UNSEALED, and sign his name. He will then place it in an official envelope, and deliver it as directed in the preceding section, obtaining from the addressee the original envelope of the letter, with the indorsement of the addressee thereon, stating whether the contents are correct or incorrect. If the contents are found correct, a report must be made of the case to the Third Assistant Postmaster-General, accompanied by the envelope. If incorrect, the case should be reported and the envelope of the letter and the registered-package envelope sent to the Chief Special Agent.

Sec. 861. No Charge to be Made on the Delivery of Registered Matter.—The law, section 812, requires full prepayment of registry fee and postage, which is to be affixed by stamps to letter or parcel when presented for registration; postmasters, therefore, receiving registered letters or parcels for delivery will deliver them to the addressee even if the requisite amount of stamps to cover postage and fee are not affixed, first examining them to see if the postmaster at the mailing post-office has performed his duty in this respect, and noting any cases where it has been neglected.

Sec. 862. Report when Stamps do not cover Postage and Fee.—A report of all cases where the postage stamps upon registered matter do not cover the postage and registration fee, showing number of letter or parcel, date of mailing, post-office of origin, and amount of deficiency, must be made weekly to the Third Assistant Postmaster-General, that it may be recovered from the mailing postmaster who has failed to comply with the law. See section 812.

Sec. 863. Registry-Notices to be Sent.—On receipt of a registered letter or parcel at a post-office (not a free-delivery post-office), the postmaster must notify the addressee of its arrival, using for that purpose a "Registry-notice," which notice must be delivered to the addressee in the same manner as ordinary mail-matter. This "Registry-notice" may also be used at free-delivery post-offices for registered letters or parcels too large to send out by carrier.

Sec. 864. A Box-Holder to be Notified when Registered Matter Arrives.—Box-holders must be advised of the arrival of a registered letter or parcel addressed to their boxes, by depositing in the boxes the proper notices, as provided in the preceding section.

Sec. 865. Delivery of Registered Letter or Parcel.—On application for a registered letter or parcel, the applicant proving to be the proper person to receive it, the postmaster will require signature to be given on the record-of-registered-matter-received-and-delivered; also on the return-registry-receipt which accompanies the registered letter or parcel.

Sec. 863. Delivery of Registered Matter by Carriers.—Postmasters at free delivery post-offices must deliver through the carriers all registered letters and parcels addressed to street and number, requiring the carriers to receipt for such letters on the record-of-registered matter-received-and-delivered or on a special receipt-book. The carriers must, on the delivery of any registered letter or parcel, require the person receiving it to sign the return receipt, and also receipt in the book furnished for the purpose.

Sec. 867. Name of Carrier Delivering Registered Matter must Appear.—Carriers' registry-delivery-books must show the name of the carrier who delivers each registered letter or parcel.

Sec. 868. Utmost Care Required in Delivery.—Registered letters or parcels must never be delivered to any person but the one to whom they are addressed, or on the written order of addressee. Identification should be required when the applicant is unknown, and written orders should be verified and placed on file as vouchers.

Sec. 869. Responsibility for Wrong Delivery.—Postmasters will be held responsible for the wrong delivery of any registered matter, and must, therefore, take the requisite measures to ascertain the proper person to receive it.

Sec. 870. Proper Signature Required.—When a person other than the addressee signs for a registered letter or parcel, the names of both addressee and recipient must appear on the receipts.

Sec. 871. Registry-Return-Receipt to be Remailed to the Sender.—As soon as any registered matter has been delivered and the registry-return-receipt therefor has been properly signed, the receipt must be postmarked with date of delivery (which is also the mailing postmark), and sent by next mail, without cover of an envelope, to the address of the sender which is written on the registry-return-receipt.

Sec. 872. No Postage on Registry-Bills and Registry-Return-Receipts.—The registry-bills and registry-return-receipts, after signature, require no postage thereon; they are to be simply postmarked and mailed without delay.

Sec. 873. Registered Matter for Delivery to Insane or Dead Persons.—If, on the receipt of a registered letter or parcel, the person addressed is dead, it may be delivered to the legal representative of the deceased, who must be either the executor of the will or the administrator of the deceased, and who produces proof of the fact. In some States the residuary legatee named in a will is allowed, on giving bonds for the proper fulfillment and execution of its provisions, to become the executor. In any such case such person is, upon presentation of the necessary proof, to be considered the legal representative of the deceased. Registered matter addressed to persons who have been declared insane by competent authority should be treated as above; but in the absence of any legal representative, all such domestic registered matter must be returned to the mailing post-office for delivery to the sender.

Sec. 874. Attachment of Registered Letters.—A registered letter is not subject to attachment in the hands of a postmaster before its delivery, as the Department holds it in *custodia legis* for delivery to the person addressed, or to his or her order. A postmaster acting in virtue of his office, and refusing to deliver letters on a process issued by a State court, will readily be purged of any alleged contempt of such process; and in case of any conflict with the State law, he, acting in the line of his duty, will have protection by the law which governs the transmission of registered matter.

Sec. 875. Fraudulent Registered Letters may be Returned.—The Postmaster-General may, upon evidence satisfactory to him that any person is engaged in conducting any fraudulent lottery, gift-enterprise, or scheme for the distribution of money or of any real or personal property, by lot, chance, or drawing of any kind, or in conducting any other scheme or device for obtaining money through the mails by means of false or fraudulent pretenses, representations, or promises, instruct postmasters at any post-offices at which registered letters arrive directed to any such person, to return all such registered letters to the postmasters at the [post] offices at which they were originally mailed, with the word "fraudulent" plainly written or stamped upon the outside of such letters; and all such letters so returned to such postmasters shall be by them returned to the writers thereof, under such regulations as the Postmaster-General may prescribe. But nothing contained in this title shall be so construed as to authorize any postmaster or other person to open any letter not addressed to himself. (R. S., §3929.)

Sec. 876. Return Undelivered Registered Matter to Mailing Post-Office.—If a domestic registered letter or parcel cannot be delivered within thirty days after its arrival, or within such time as may be named in a request indorsed on its face, or in case delivery is prohibited by the Postmaster-General in accordance with the preceding section, the postmaster must indorse on it the cause of non-delivery and return it to the post-office whence it was mailed. It must be marked RETURNED TO WRITER, renumbered, and entered in registration-book, as if mailed at his post-office (counted as free in his quarterly report of registered letters and parcels), placed in a registered-package envelope with a registry bill, and a note of such return with date thereof made in receipt column of record-of-registered-matter-received-and-delivered. The address of letter or parcel must be changed only as to destination, and R. W. marked on registry bill, indicating return to writer. On arrival at the original mailing post-office it must be treated as if it were an original registered letter or parcel received for delivery. Fraudulent matter of foreign origin must be sent to the Dead-Letter Office, accompanied by a letter of advice addressed to the Third Assistant Postmaster-General, explaining the character of the matter, and giving the date of the order of the Postmaster-General forbidding its delivery.

Sec. 877. Refused Registered Letters or Parcels.—In case of addressee simply refusing to receive a registered letter or parcel, it must be retained the proper length of time before return, as prescribed in the preceding section.

Sec. 878. Original Record to Show Return of a Letter or Parcel.—Note must be made on the original record of every registered letter or parcel returning to a mailing post-office, stating its return and date.

Sec. 879. When Sender of Returned Registered Matter is not found.—In case a domestic returned registered letter or parcel cannot be delivered to sender, it must be retained thirty days and be then forwarded (properly registered) to the Dead-Letter Office, after due notice to sender by advertisement or otherwise.

Sec. 880. Sending Registered Letters or Parcels to the Dead-Letter Office.—When registered letters or parcels are sent to the Dead-Letter Office they must be postmarked with date of sending, indorsed with reason for so forwarding, be accompanied with duplicate bills showing the sending post-office and the number and address of each registered article, and placed under cover of an official envelope addressed to Third Assistant Postmaster-General, Dead-Letter Office, Washington, D. C., indorsed INCLOSING REGISTERED MATTER. The packet must be registered as a free registered letter and placed with registry-bill and registry-return-receipt under cover of a registered-package envelope addressed to the postmaster, Washington, D. C.

Sec. 881. Forwarding Registered Letters or Parcels.—Should a registered letter or parcel be received addressed to a person who has removed, or who from any other cause wishes it forwarded to him at another post-office or returned to writer, it may be so forwarded or returned, at his written request, without additional charge for postage or fee. In such cases the postmaster must enter it on his delivery-book, and make in the record of-registered-matter-received-and-delivered, in delivery column, a memorandum showing when and where forwarded. He must alter the address of the registered letter or parcel as to destination only, and indorse it FORWARDED. It must then be entered in registration-book as if mailed at his post-office, counted as free in quarterly report registered matter, numbered anew, and forwarded in a registered-package envelope, with a registry-bill, accompanied by the original registry-return-receipt. The order for forwarding or returning must be filed as a voucher.

Sec. 882. Missent Registered Letters or Parcels Received.—If on opening a registered package addressed to his post-office a postmaster finds a registered letter or parcel inclosed addressed to another post-office, he will indorse the bill MISSENT, sign and remail it, file the registered-package envelope, and enter the letter or parcel on his record-of-registered-matter-received-and-delivered, making a note in delivery column, *Missent and forwarded*, and re-register it from his post-office as in preceding section.

Sec. 883. Writer cannot Control Registered Letter after its Dispatch.—After a registered letter has been transmitted from the mailing post-office, it cannot be recalled by the sender, but must be sent to the destination named in its address. If not delivered it will be returned in accordance with section 876. Before dispatch a registered letter can only be reclaimed by writer under extraordinary circumstances. He must give satisfactory reasons to the postmaster for such action, produce a fac-simile of the envelope, fully identify himself, and return the registration-receipt endorsed with his name, which the postmaster will paste opposite the entry in the registration book, endorsing the entry RETURNED TO WRITER BY ME, ———, P. M. The registered letter, before return, must be endorsed WITHDRAWN BY WRITER FROM ——— POST-OFFICE, ——— P. M.

Sec. 884. Response to Inquiries.—Inquiries or tracers regarding registered packages, letters, or parcels must receive immediate attention from postmasters as also all inquiries on registered business.

Sec. 885. Tracers for Stamp, Envelope, or Postal-Card Packages.—When a registered package of stamps, envelopes, or postal cards has been forwarded, and no acknowledgment therefor is received by due course of mail, or bill returns marked NOT RECEIVED or BAD ORDER, a coupon tracer will be sent to ascertain whether the package reached its destination in safety, or at what point and through whose fault it disappeared or was tampered with. If, through this means, it should be ascertained that the package reached its destination in good order, the tracer may be retained when it returns; but if it appears that the package was received in bad condition, or was lost or stolen in transit, the tracer must then be forwarded to the Third Assistant Postmaster-General. Should the tracer not be returned in due season, a duplicate must be sent to the post-office whence last coupon was returned or special inquiry sent until package is accounted for or loss ascertained, when the tracer with full report of loss must be sent to Third Assistant Postmaster-General.

Sec. 886. Registered Matter found among Ordinary Mail-Matter.—Matter which has once been registered can never lose its character as such until it has been delivered to the rightful owner. When a postmaster discovers any registered letter or parcel among ordinary mail-matter, he must enter it upon his record-of-registered-matter-received-and-delivered, and treat the registered letter or parcel as directed by the regulations. If the registered letter or parcel is addressed to his own post-office, he will deliver it to the person for whom it was intended, and if addressed to another post-office he will inclose it in a registered-package envelope and forward it. He will in each case report all the facts immediately to the Third Assistant Postmaster-General.

Sec. 887. Report to Chief Special Agent Missing Registered Matter.—Every case of missing registered packages, registered letters, or registered parcels must be reported without delay to the Chief Special Agent, Post-Office Department, Washington, D. C., giving full particulars, as also all cases of alleged abstraction of contents of registered letters or parcels; and also to Special Agents, as stated in section 849.

Sec. 888. Quarterly Reports to Third Assistant Postmaster-General.—At the expiration of each quarter postmasters must forward to the Third Assistant Postmaster-General a report showing separately the number of domestic and foreign letters registered at their post-offices, together with the number of parcels of third and fourth class matter, domestic and foreign, registered during the quarter.

Sec. 889. Omit in Account-Current Fees on Registered Matter.—The postage and registry fee on a registered letter or parcel is required by law to be prepaid and affixed to the letter or parcel in stamps and the stamps canceled, and no special entry of such items should be made on the quarterly account-current rendered by postmasters to the Auditor of the Treasury for the Post-Office Department; the money received for stamps sold for this purpose should be included in the general postal account under the head of *Amount of stamps sold during the quarter.*

Sec. 890. Accounts of Registered Matter.—No accounts or records in relation to registered letters or parcels are to be forwarded to the Department other than the quarterly report stated in section 888. All other accounts and records are to be carefully preserved by the postmasters for future reference.

Sec. 891. Disposition of Used Registered-Package Envelopes.—Registered-package envelopes which have been emptied of their contents, those spoiled by misdirection, or in any way rendered unfit for use (cutting and resealing is not permissible), must be retained on file one year and then sold for the highest attainable price, and the proceeds of such sales taken up in account-current under head of *Amount received for waste-paper, etc.*; provided, however, if they cannot be sold at small post-offices, they may be sent in a lot to the postmaster at the nearest large post-office having facilities for the sale of waste-paper.

Sec. 892. Blanks Used in Registration.—The following blanks required for use in the registry system are furnished on application to the Superintendent Blank Agency, office First Assistant Postmaster-General, Washington, D. C.:

Registration-book, showing matter registered and dispatched	Form No. 1549
Registry-bill	1550
Registry-return-receipt	1548
Registered package receipt	1556
Record-of-registered-matter-received-and-delivered	1547
Record-of-registered-matter-in-transit	1553
Carriers'-registry-delivery-books	1560
Railway-mail-registry-books	1539
Registry-notices	1525
Registry-circular-of-inquiry	3856
Registry quarterly report	3848
Requisition for registered-package envelopes	3204
Registry deficiency report	3846
Registry-tracer	1536

Sec. 893. Envelopes Used in Registry Business.—The envelopes used will be furnished on requisition addressed to the Third Assistant Postmaster-General.

1. *Ordinary official penalty-envelopes.*
2. *Registered-package envelopes.*

Sec. 894. Registry Supplies to be Kept Up.—Postmasters must not allow their supply of registered-package envelopes or any of the blanks required in the registry business to become exhausted. Requisition must always be made in time to receive a new supply before those on hand are entirely used.

Sec. 895. Postmasters take Special Interest in Success of Registry System.—In order to make the registry system as efficient as possible, it is necessary that it should receive not only the attention, but the hearty co-operation, of every postmaster, who should feel that he has an interest in the improvement of the service as well as a desire to promote the public good. Special attention should be paid to secure legibility of addresses and postmarks on registered-package envelopes, and all entries upon registry blanks and records should be neatly and distinctly written. Postmasters are particularly enjoined to report promptly to the Third Assistant Postmaster-General any neglect or violation of the registry regulations which may come to their knowledge, in order that the officer in fault may be called to account for his misconduct.

Sec. 896. Postmasters not to Reprimand other Postmasters.—Postmasters are positively forbidden to reprimand other postmasters for neglect or violation of these regulations. It is the province of the Department to instruct postmasters as to their duties and to take cognizance of their neglect or refusal to obey instructions.

Sec. 897. Postmasters in Doubt as to their Duty as to any requirements of the regulations of the registry system, must submit the matter in doubt to the Third Assistant Postmaster-General. Ignorance of the law or regulations will not be accepted as an excuse for their violation or for neglect of duty.

CHAPTER TWO.

RESPECTING REGISTERED LETTERS AND PARCELS ADDRESSED TO, OR ORIGINATING IN, FOREIGN COUNTRIES.

Sec. 898. Registered Correspondence for Foreign Countries.—Registered letters or parcels addressed to foreign countries are governed in their transportation within and through the United States by the same rules and regulations as domestic registered matter, except that no domestic registry-return-receipt is to be made out by the mailing postmaster and sent with such foreign registered correspondence, and the registered-package envelope is to be addressed to the proper exchange post-office in the United States designated to dispatch registered correspondence to foreign countries. See section 1125.

Sec. 899. Registration Fee to Foreign Countries.—The registration fee to all countries where registration is permissible is ten cents on each letter or parcel, to be prepaid by stamps, in addition to the postage. See sections 813–816.

Sec. 900. Postmasters Registering Foreign Matter Consult Postal Guide.—All classes of mail-matter may be registered to countries and colonies in the Universal Postal Union, but to certain countries and colonies not in the Universal Postal Union registration of letters only is permissible. To some parts of the world there is no means of forwarding registered matter; postmasters are therefore specially enjoined to consult the foreign postal table in the latest issue of the United States Official Postal Guide to ascertain the proper rates of postage, and whether the matter presented is entitled to registration, as will be shown by the ten-cents fee appearing in the columns headed "Registered matter" in said table; absence of the fee in both columns headed "Registration fee on letters" and "Registration fee on other articles" indicates that no registration exists; presence of fee in letter column alone indicates letters only can be registered; postmasters must, therefore, refuse to register any mail-matter addressed to countries to which there is no registration or to register other mail-matter to countries where registration is confined to letters.

Sec. 901. Registered Packages Misdirected to Foreign Post-Offices.—If a registered package is received in transit addressed to a post-office in a foreign country, it should be sent to the post-office designated to exchange registered matter with such foreign country, where the registered package will be opened and the contents properly forwarded.

Sec. 902. Sender may Demand a Foreign Registry-Return-Receipt.—The sender of a registered letter or parcel addressed to countries in the Universal Postal Union may, by writing on the face of the letter or parcel, RETURN RECEIPT DEMANDED, have a return receipt sent back to him from the foreign post-office of delivery.

Sec. 903. Registry-Return-Receipts to Foreign Countries.—The return receipt will be made out by the exchange post-office which dispatches the registered matter to the foreign country on a specially provided form.

Sec. 904. Matter which Cannot be Registered to Foreign Countries.—It is forbidden to send by mail to countries of the Universal Postal Union—

a. Letters or parcels containing gold or silver substances, pieces of money, jewelry, or precious articles.

b. Any parcel whatever containing articles liable to customs duty.

c. Articles of a nature likely to soil or injure other matter in the mail.

d. Parcels of samples of merchandise which have a salable value, or which exceed two hundred and fifty grams (eight and three-fourth ounces) in weight, or measure more than twenty centimeters (eight inches) in length, ten centimeters (four inches) in breadth, and five centimeters (two inches) in depth.

e. Parcels of commercial papers and printed matter of all kinds the weight of which exceeds two kilograms (four pounds and six ounces).

f. Any letter which has declared value, *i. e.*, an inscription stating the value of contents.

g. Any matter excluded from the domestic mails as unmailable.

The articles excluded above in paragraphs *c* and *g* are also prohibited from transmission in the mails exchanged with foreign countries other than those of the Universal Postal Union.

In the mails exchanged with Canada, it is forbidden to transmit the articles mentioned in paragraphs *c* and *f* and *g*, and also samples of merchandise in excess of eight ounces in weight.

Sec. 905. Mark Registered Packages Inclosing Foreign Matter, "Foreign."—In order to facilitate the handling and dispatch of foreign registered matter at an exchange post-office, postmasters will mark on the registered-package-envelopes containing foreign matter, beside the address, the word FOREIGN. They will also make out a registry-bill for the foreign registered letters separate from the bill on which is entered domestic registered matter for delivery (in case foreign and domestic letters or parcels are placed together in the same registered-package-envelope), writing the country after name of addressee in the body of the bill.

Sec. 906. Registered Matter from Foreign Countries.—Postmasters receiving from exchange post-offices registered packages containing letters or parcels originating in foreign countries will treat the package and contents as instructed in section 856 respecting registered letters received for delivery.

Sec. 907. Registry-Return-Receipts of Foreign Origin.—When a foreign registry-return-receipt accompanies a registered letter or parcel from a foreign country, the registry-return-receipt must be properly signed by recipient of letter when delivery is made, postmarked, and properly returned, under cover of an official penalty-envelope, addressed to the postmaster at the United States exchange post-office from which the registered package containing it was received. Great care must be taken that any foreign postage-stamps attached to a foreign registry-return-receipt do not become detached therefrom.

Sec. 908. Undelivered Foreign Registered Letters or Parcels.—Should a foreign letter or parcel remain undelivered at the expiration of thirty days (except specially directed to be held for delivery) it must, even though indorsed with the name and address of the sender, or a return request, be forwarded to the Dead-Letter Office in the manner prescribed for sending registered matter to the Dead-Letter Office, in section 880. Request registered letters originating in Canada are excepted from this regulation. They should be returned to writer as requested.

Sec. 909. Foreign Registry-Return-Receipts not Sent to Dead-Letter Office.—If a Registry-return-receipt is attached to a foreign registered letter or parcel that cannot be delivered, the Registry-return-receipt must be indorsed with the cause of non-delivery, postmarked with date, and returned to the exchange post-office in the United States whence it came.

Sec. 910. Registered Matter Supposed to be Liable to Customs-Duty.—Regulations respecting ordinary matter subject to customs duty, section 1133, govern registered matter also, except that the receipt of the addressee must first be obtained by the postmaster before any opening of the registered letter or parcel is permitted by the addressee. If the addressee refuses to sign a receipt for any such supposed dutiable registered matter, it must be marked REFUSED, held the proper length of time, and sent to the Dead-Letter Office.

Sec. 911. Foreign Registered Matter Specially Held for Delivery.—When the postmaster has good reason to believe that registered letters or parcels from a foreign country can be delivered to addressee, he may mark them SPECIALLY HELD FOR DELIVERY, and retain them not to exceed three months before sending to Dead-Letter Office. Registered letters addressed POSTE RESTANTE, or TO BE CALLED FOR, or to a passenger or sailor on a vessel to arrive, must also be held not to exceed three months.

Sec. 912. Forwarding Registered Matter in the Universal Postal Union.—Registered letters or parcels received from foreign countries in the Postal Union may be forwarded to any other country in the Postal Union, or to any post-office in the United States, without additional charge for postage or registry fee.

Sec. 913. Postmark Foreign Registered Matter at Exchange Post-Offices.—All registered letters or parcels sent to or received from foreign countries must be postmarked at exchange post-offices with the registry postmarking stamp, showing date of dispatch or receival.

Sec. 914. Do not Write to Foreign Postmasters.—Postmasters of post-offices (not exchange post-offices) are instructed not to address correspondence to foreign post-offices on registry business.

CHAPTER THREE.

THE TRANSMISSION OF THROUGH-REGISTERED-POUCHES.

Sec. 915. Object of this Branch of the Registry System.—By the system of through-registered-pouches the Department has been enabled to keep pace with the growth of registry business in consolidating the registered packages under cover of special pouches at certain post-offices termed through-registered-pouch-offices, relieving the railway-mail service by preventing too great an accumulation of registered packages on the several lines of postal cars, preventing risks at transfers, and placing the work where better opportunity offers for its correct performance.

Sec. 916. Mode of Carrying on Through-Registered-Pouch-Service.—Certain post-offices are designated by the Third Assistant Postmaster-General as through-registered-pouch-offices, and provided with through-registered-pouches, special registered locks, keys, labels, and disks, and instructed to make exchanges only with such through-registered-pouch-offices and at such times as they may be directed by the Third Assistant Postmaster-General. For list of such post-offices with their exchanges, see the latest Official Postal Guide.

Sec. 917. Exchanges Directed to be Made Invariably.—Postmasters will make the directed dispatches of through-registered-pouches whether there is any registered matter to be sent in them or not. In case there is no registered matter to be sent in a through-registered-pouch dispatched, a pouch-bill marked NO PACKAGES SENT, properly filled up, signed, copied, and postmarked, must be placed in the pouch and the pouch locked and regularly dispatched.

Sec. 918. Through-Registered-Pouch-Office Supplies, How used and kept.—The through-registered-pouches, locks, labels, and disks, having been made expressly for the registry system, must not be used for any other purpose, and must be securely kept, the locks and keys in the safe, and the pouches, labels, disks, and bills in that part of the post-office set apart for the transaction of the business of the registry system, and under no circumstances must any other pouches, locks, labels, or disks be used in transmitting registered matter to post-offices with which through-registered-pouches are exchanged.

Sec. 919. Additional Supplies.—Timely notice of the need of additional through-registered-pouches, locks, labels, and disks must be given to the Third Assistant Postmaster-General, in order that they may be sent before the supply is exhausted. Requisition for through-registered-pouch-bills, through-registered-pouch blanks, and through-registered-pouch press-books must be made of the Superintendent of the Blank Agency, Post-Office Department, office of the First Assistant Postmaster-General.

Sec. 920. Registered Matter Dispatched in Through-Registered-Pouches.—In the through-registered-pouches for each through-registered-pouch-office must be placed all the registered matter addressed to that post-office, and to post-offices on routes beyond it as shown by the through-registered-pouch schemes; but packages too large to be inclosed in the pouch must be dispatched by the hands of the proper railway-mail employé.

Sec. 921. Preparation of Matter for Through-Registered-Pouches.—Before dispatching a through-registered-pouch there must be entered on the through-registered-pouch-bill the number of the bill, commencing each quarter with No. 1, the date of dispatch, the name of the post-office to which the pouch is to be sent, numb. r of the lock to be used in fastening the pouch, which number is to be considered the number of the pouch, the numbers, postmarks, and addresses of the registered packages to be sent in the pouch, and at the foot the number of registered packages sent in that pouch, the total number of through-registered-pouches to be sent to that post-office by that mail, and the total number of registered packages sent in those pouches. At those post-offices where it is usual to dispatch two or more through-registered-pouches to the same post-office by the same mail, the entry of the total number of pouches sent, and of the total number of packages sent in such pouches, may be omitted on the pouch-bills of all the pouches, except the pouch-bill of the pouch last closed, as the disks show the total number of through-registered-pouches.

Sec. 922. Signing the Pouch-Bill and Copying.—The pouch-bill must then be signed by two dispatching clerks, copied in the through-registered-pouch press-book provided for that purpose, postmarked, and placed in the pouch with the registered packages.

Sec. 923. Inspection before Closing.—Before closing a through-registered-pouch for dispatch, the dispatching clerks must assure themselves beyond any doubt that all the packages advised to the pouch-bill are inclosed.

Sec. 924. Labeling and Locking.—The through-registered-pouch must be properly labeled before any packages are placed therein, and the packages, tied together in bundles in order of entry on bill, and marked with name of through-registered-pouch-office, should be compared with the bill and with the label of the pouch, lock number proved correct, and bill and packages then placed in the pouch, which must be securely locked and the proper entries made on the record of through-registered-pouches dispatched, and on delivery to the railway-mail employé a receipt taken therefor.

Sec. 925. Indicating Dispatch of Extra Through-Registered-Pouches.—When two through-registered-pouches are sent from a post-office by the same dispatch to the same post-office, a registry-disk bearing the figure "2" must be attached to each pouch by passing the link of the lock through the ring of the disk. If three pouches are to be sent by the same mail, a disk bearing the figure "3" must be used, and so on, attaching the disk bearing the figure which corresponds with the total number of pouches sent on each separate pouch.

Sec. 926. Object of the Registry-Disk.—The registry-disk is attached to the through-registered-pouches to inform employés of the service whose duty it is to receive and receipt for them how many through-registered-pouches are included in any one dispatch; they must, therefore, at any transfer of the through-registered-pouches, examine the registry-disks and ascertain before receipting that the full complement of pouches from each post-office indicated by the registry-disks have been delivered to them. Whenever the letter B appears on the registry-disk, in addition to the number, a box must accompany the pouch or pouches for each B appearing on the registry-disk. The letters indicate the number of boxes, and the figures the total of boxes and pouches.

Sec. 927. Return Extra Through-Registered-Pouches, etc., Promptly.—In order that each through-registered-pouch-office may preserve its proper complement of through-registered-pouches, locks, and disks, the extra number when received must be returned by next dispatch, inside of the regular pouch, duly entered on the pouch-bill.

Sec. 928. Through-Registered-Pouch in Bad Order.—On the arrival of a through-registered-pouch at a through-registered-pouch-office, the receiving clerk must, before receipting to the railway-mail employé, assure himself of the good condition of both pouch and lock. If either appears to have been tampered with or is in bad order, the receipt for the pouch must be withheld until its contents have been carefully examined, and found not only to correspond with the entries on the pouch-bill, but to be in good order and condition. Proper facilities should be allowed the railway mail employé to be present at such examination, and if the contents are not in good order the receipt given him must state that fact. A minute of the case must also be placed in the files of the through-registered-pouch-office, in case any loss of contents should afterward be charged.

Sec. 929. Checking Contents of Through-Registered-Pouch.—A through-registered-pouch must be opened by two clerks, and its contents must be compared with the entries on the pouch-bill. After proper entries of the packages on the books of the through-registered-pouch-office, the pouch-bill must be signed by both clerks, postmarked, and returned to the sending post-office in the next through-registered-pouch dispatched to that post-office. Each pouch must be thoroughly shaken, and its interior inspected, to ascertain that it has been completely emptied.

Sec. 930. Safety of Registered Keys and Locks.—When a through-registered-pouch is opened at the post-office of destination the lock must be at once placed in the safe of the registry branch of the post-office, where it must be kept until needed for immediate use again. The keys used in opening the registered locks must be attached to the safe by a chain, and must not be detached therefrom or be handled by any one save the clerk in charge thereof. Under no circumstances must the registered keys or locks be exhibited to any one.

Sec. 931. Through-Registered-Pouches in Transit, when to be Opened.—If by reason of missing a connection, or for other cause, a through-registered-pouch, labeled and intended for another through-registered-pouch-office, is brought into a post-office authorized to exchange through-registered-pouches, it must be receipted for in the same manner as if addressed to that post-office. It must then be opened, the contents examined, and compared with the pouch-bill, which must be indorsed, POUCH DELIVERED TO THIS POST-OFFICE BECAUSE OF ———. CONTENTS [*correct or incorrect, as case may be, the disagreement being stated*]. ———, and signed by two clerks. The registered packages called for on the pouch-bill must be entered on the record-of-registered-matter-in-transit, and the pouch, with its bill and original contents therein, must be fastened by the same lock (unless the pouch or lock is damaged, in which event it will be replaced by a good one, such action being noted on the bill), and be dispatched by the next mail to the post-office for which it was intended.

Sec. 932. Discrepancy in Contents of Through-Registered-Pouch.—If the contents of a through-registered-pouch do not agree with the pouch-bill, the fact must be immediately noted thereon, and a report sent by mail to the Third Assistant Postmaster-General. In addition, in cases where there are entries on the bill for which no corresponding registered packages are found, the discrepancy must be telegraphed to the dispatching post-office, in order that the error may be rectified or immediate action taken concerning the loss.

Sec. 933. Record of Delays to be Kept.—Postmasters must keep a full record of all delays and miscarriages of through-registered-pouches, reporting the facts in each case to the Third Assistant Postmaster-General.

Sec. 934. Damaged Registered Locks and Keys.—Damaged registered locks and keys must be securely enveloped, and sent, registered, to the "Mail Equipment Division, Office of Second Assistant Postmaster-General, Washington, D. C." Damaged pouches should be labeled DAMAGED POUCH, FROM POST-OFFICE AT———, RETURNED TO SECOND ASSISTANT POSTMASTER-GENERAL; and should be forwarded, unlocked, in the through-registered-pouch for Washington, D. C. If the sending post-office does not exchange through-registered pouches with Washington, it must be sent in the through-registered-pouch for the post-office nearest that point with which such pouches are exchanged, and will be forwarded in same manner from that post-office. A letter of advice must always be transmitted to both the Second and Third Assistant Postmasters-General concerning damaged registered locks or pouches returned.

Sec. 935. Through-Registered-Pouch or Blank must be Delivered.—Railway mail employés must ascertain what through-registered-pouches are to be daily transmitted over their routes, and must in no case leave their terminal post-offices without demanding the regular pouches, or that the blank used stating the reason for absence of pouch be given them. Either the pouch must be delivered or the blanks stating reason for failure. If they are not sent, the railway mail employé must note on his railway-mail-registry-book the reason why. This course must also be pursued with regard to such through-registered-pouches as they should regularly receive from connecting Offices. By such means the post-office at which the pouch is due will be informed of the cause of the delay by the railway mail employé whose duty it is to bring it in.

Sec. 936. Non-delivery of Through-Registered-Pouches.—In case of failure in arrival of a through-registered-pouch when due, without satisfactory reason for its absence, report must be made immediately to the Third Assistant Postmaster-General.

Sec. 937. Through-Registered Pouches Taken to Terminal Post-Offices.—Railway mail employés must, in every case where possible, deliver the through-registered-pouches direct to the connecting Office. But if connection with other Offices is not made, the pouches must be taken into the terminal post-offices and receipt obtained for them.

Sec. 938. Disposition of Through-Registered-Pouches in Bad Order in Transit. When a through-registered-pouch is delivered to a railway mail employé, he must, before receipting for the same, assure himself that the registered lock and pouch are in good order. If either is not, his receipt must show that fact, and the pouch must be taken by him into the terminal post-office of his route, if such post-office exchanges through-registered-pouches. If the terminal post-office of his route is not a through-registered-pouch-office, or if there is no through-registered-pouch-office on his route, the pouch must be forwarded until it reaches a through-registered-pouch-office, care being taken that none of its contents are lost. Railway mail employés must keep a record of the facts in all such cases for future reference.

CHAPTER FOUR.

THE HANDLING OF REGISTERED MATTER BY RAILWAY MAIL EMPLOYÉS.

Sec. 939. Registered Packages between Post-Office and Office to be Pouched. Railway mail employés must place their registered packages under cover of a leather pouch (as far as the size of the packages will permit) in conveying them to and from the terminal post-office and the Office, and must keep this pouch in their personal charge, and accompany the wagon on which it is conveyed to the train.

Sec. 940. Railway-Mail-Registry-Books.—Railway mail employés will be furnished by their Division Superintendent with railway-mail-registry-books, provided by the Department, for the purpose of keeping a record of all registered matter passing through their hands.

Sec. 941. Record of Registry Matter kept.—An entry of the number, postmark, date, and address of every registered package, registered-stamp package, registered-postal-card package, and stamped-envelope package, as well as every through-registered-pouch passing through their hands, must be made in the railway-mail-registry-book by every railway-mail employé, and where it is possible the receipt on delivery of these packages must be taken direct, in the proper column of the book.

Sec. 942. Receiving Registered Matter at terminal Post-offices.—Before leaving the terminal post-office the proper railway-mail employé must receive and receipt for all through-registered-pouches and registered packages tendered him by the postmaster or proper clerk, and become personally responsible for their care until their delivery into the hands of the proper postmaster or other authorized agent of the Department, or their disposal as required by the regulations of the registry system.

Sec. 943. Receipt for Registered Matter.—Employés will in all cases obtain a receipt for each registered package from the person to whom it is delivered. In the delivery of registered-package envelopes they should be arranged in the same order in which they are entered on the railway-mail-registry-book.

Sec. 944. Postmarking and Returning Registered Package Receipts.—To protect themselves against fraud in the matter of receipts given to postmasters and others for registered mail, employés will affix the imprint of the postmarking stamp on each receipt as many times as there may be packages, and return the package receipts by next mail to the sending postmaster or employé of the railway-mail service.

Sec. 945. Registered Matter not to be delivered to Employés of Railroads.—Employés must not deliver registered mail to messengers employed by the railroad company, nor to any mail-messenger, unless specially instructed. It must be placed in the pouch, together with a receipt, to be signed and returned.

Sec. 946. Receipting for Registered Matter.—The Department does not authorize employés to stamp their names in receipting for registered matter. They must sign their names with pen or pencil.

Sec. 947. Illegible Postmark on Registered Packages.—The first recipient of a registered package with illegible postmark should write on the package the name of the Office or post-office from which it was received.

Sec. 948. Examination of Condition of Registered Packages.—When a registered package is handed to a railway mail employé by an employé on a connecting Office or a postmaster, he must examine the package, make the proper indorsement showing its condition, sign, date, and hand the receipt back. He must then make proper indorsement on the package and enter it in his railway-mail-regis try-book. See section 852.

Sec. 949. Registered-package Receipts to be properly Filled Out.—Receipts for registered packages must be properly filled up by the sending postmaster or railway-mail employé. If this duty is not performed, the employé will report the delinquent to his Division Superintendent.

Sec. 950. Forward Registered Mail in a Pouch.—When the delivery of any registered matter cannot be made direct to the postmaster or a connecting Office, and it has to be placed in a pouch for a post-office, a package-receipt for the same, properly filled up, must be placed in the package of letters for such post-office, to be signed and returned to the employé. The package must always be placed in the pouch, and the pouch securely locked.

Sec. 951. Check return of Registered-Package Receipt.—On the return of a registered-package receipt, properly indorsed and signed, the railway-mail employé must check its return on his railway-mail-registry-book and preserve it for future reference. In case it fails to return in due season, he must prepare a duplicate and send it to the postmaster. If the duplicate fails to return in proper time the railway-mail employé must report the case, with all particulars, to his Division Superintendent.

Sec. 952. Registered Matter for Through-Registered-Pouch-Offices.—Registered matter that can be properly forwarded in through-registered-pouches, coming into the hands of railway mail employés, must be delivered into their terminal post-offices, when such post-offices are through-registered-pouch-offices, to be forwarded thence under cover of through-registered-pouches. Such registered packages should be kept in the order of their entry on the railway-mail-registry-book, so as to facilitate delivery.

Sec. 953. Registered Matter for Delivery to Connecting Office.—When a railway-mail employé arrives at the terminus of his route, he must deliver to a connecting railway-mail employé all registered matter deliverable on the route of such connecting employé when practicable. If he fails to meet such employé he must deliver the registered pouches or packages into the terminal post-office with the registered matter deliverable at such post-office.

Sec. 954. Get Receipt for Registered Matter and Registry-Book.—Railway mail employés must not leave registered matter at terminal post-offices, under any circumstances, without first obtaining proper receipt therefor, nor must they allow their railway-mail-registry-books to go out of their possession until they can no longer be used.

Sec. 955. Turn over Registry-Book when Full to Division Superintendent.—When a railway mail employé has filled his registry-book with entries, and all the package-receipts have been returned and checked, he will turn over his book and receipts to his Division Superintendent for filing at his headquarters and receive a receipt showing date of first and final entry in book and the total number of package-receipts, and the book will be placed on file for reference. The package-receipts should be arranged in the order of their entry on the railway-mail-registry-book. Any inquiry or tracer received respecting registered packages entered in such registry-books will be referred to the Division Superintendent with indorsed slip, stating RECORDED IN BOOK, DATED (*from first to last date, as shown on receipt.*)

The Division Superintendent will fill the tracer from the record on the registry-book and forward tracer.

TITLE VI.

THE MONEY-ORDER SYSTEM OF THE UNITED STATES.

CHAPTER ONE.

ESTABLISHMENT AND GENERAL PROVISIONS.

Sec. 956. Establishment of the Money-Order System.—To promote public convenience, and to insure greater security in the transfer of money through the mail, the Postmaster-General may establish and maintain, under such rules and regulations as he may deem expedient, a uniform money-order system, at all suitable post-offices, which shall be designated as "money-order offices." (R. S., 4027.)

Sec. 957. Object of the Money-Order System.—The money-order system is intended to promote public convenience and to secure safety in the transfer through the mails of small sums of money. The principal means employed to attain safety consist in leaving out of the money-order the name of the payee or person for whom the money is intended. In this respect a money-order differs from an ordinary bank draft or check. An advice, or notification, containing full particulars of the money-order, is transmitted without delay by the issuing postmaster to the postmaster at the post-office of payment. The latter is thus furnished, before the money-order itself is presented, with information which will enable him to prevent its payment to any person not entitled thereto, provided the remitter complies with the regulation of the Department which prohibits him from sending the same information in a letter inclosed with his money-order.

Sec. 958. Design of Congress in Establishing Money-Order System.—The following is the construction given by the late Attorney-General (Williams) to the statute creating the money-order system:

Congress designed to give money-orders, in some respects, the character of ordinary negotiable instruments, to the end that they might be received with full credit, and their usefulness, in a business point of view, be thus promoted.

The statute does not contemplate that the remitter of the money-order shall be at liberty to revoke it and demand back his money against the will of the payee after it comes into the possession of the latter; since, to enable the former to obtain a repayment of the funds deposited, he must produce the money-order.

The payee of the money-order, upon complying with the requirements of the law and of the regulations of the Post-Office Department, is entitled to payment of the money on demand, and the remitter of the money-order cannot, previous to its being paid, by any notice that he may give to the post-office at which it is payable, forbid the payment thereof to the payee. (14 Opinions, 119.)

Sec. 959. Postmasters to Issue Money Orders. Responsibility therefor.—The postmaster of every city where branch post-offices or stations are established and in operation, subject to his supervision, is authorized, under the direction of the Postmaster-General, to issue, or cause to be issued, by any of his assistants or clerks in charge of branch post-offices or stations, postal money-orders, payable at his own or at any other money-order office, or at any branch post-office or station of his own, or of any other money-order office, as the remitters thereof may direct; and the postmaster and his sureties shall, in every case, be held accountable upon his official bond for all moneys received by him or his designated assistants or clerks in charge of stations, from the issue of money-orders, and for all moneys which may come into his or their hands, or be placed in his or their custody by reason of the transaction by them of money-order business. (R. S., § 4029.)

Sec. 960. Issue of Money-Orders by Clerks. Postmasters' Responsibility.—In case of the sickness or unavoidable absence from his office of the postmaster of any money-order post-office, he may, with the approval of the Postmaster-General, authorize the chief clerk, or some other clerk employed therein, to act in his place, and to discharge all the duties required by law of such postmaster; and the official bond given by the principal of the office shall be held to cover and apply to the acts of the person appointed to act in his place in such cases; and such acting officer shall, for the time being, be subject to all the liabilities and penalties prescribed by law for the official misconduct in like cases of the postmaster for whom he shall act. (R. S., 4031.)

Sec. 961. Postmasters to Designate Clerks to Sign Money-Orders, when.—In case of the sickness or unavoidable absence for a length of time from his post-office of the postmaster at a money-order post-office, he should apply to the Postmaster-General for permission to put a designated clerk in his place to discharge his duties, upon the condition that the bond of the postmaster shall cover and apply to the acts of such clerk.

Sec. 962. Signature by Clerks for Postmasters and by Acting Postmasters.—It is desirable that money-orders and other official papers should in all cases be signed by the postmaster himself; but when, by reason of his unavoidable absence, it may be necessary for the assistant postmaster or designated clerk to sign the money-orders, the postmaster's name must be written, and beneath it the name and designation of the writer, thus:

"JOHN DOE,
"*Postmaster*,
"By RICHARD ROE,
"*Assistant Postmaster (or Clerk)*."

It may also happen that in case of the death, the absconding, or the arrest of a postmaster, a person may be placed by the sureties in charge of the post-office as "acting postmaster" for them until a new postmaster is appointed by the Department. The person thus placed in charge should sign money-orders and other official papers as "acting postmaster."

Sec. 963. Classification of Money-Order Post-Offices.—Money-order post-offices are divided into two classes. Post-offices of the first class are depositories, in which those of the second class deposit their surplus money-order funds. This classification does not in any manner refer to that established by section 100. The names of money-order post-offices of the first class are printed in the United States Official Postal Guide in *italics*. Any post-office in either class may draw upon any other post-office in the list of money-order post-offices.

Sec. 964. New Bonds Required at Post-Offices Made Money-Order Offices.—Postmasters whose post-offices are designated as money-order post-offices are required, before commencing the money-order business, to give a new bond to the government, with at least two sureties, which is conditioned for the faithful performance of the duties and obligations imposed upon them by the laws relating to the postal as well as to the money-order business.

Sec. 965. Books, Circulars, Blanks Furnished Money-Order Post-Offices.—When a post-office is designated as a money-order office, the postmaster will be furnished with the books required to be kept, and with the necessary blank forms for conducting the money-order business. Postmasters should be careful not to suffer their stock of these blanks to become exhausted, but to make a timely application for a new supply. The utmost economy in the use of blanks is always to be observed. The registers and the cash-book, being the property of the Department, must be carefully preserved by the postmaster, and must be delivered up when called for, or upon his going out of office. All circulars and instructions sent to a postmaster must be kept on file in his post-office, permanently for reference.

Sec. 966. Duty of Retiring Postmaster at a Money-Order Post-Office.—In case of the appointment of a new postmaster at a money-order post-office, it will become the duty of the late postmaster to render a statement of the business transacted up to the date on which he ceased to be responsible, even should it be for a fractional part of a week only. Upon giving up charge of the post-office, he will deposit with his successor the balance of money-order funds remaining in his hands, taking duplicate receipts therefor, one of which he will transmit to the Superintendent of the Money-Order System, together with his final statement, in the "Summary" of which he will take credit for the amount thus deposited. The late postmaster will also turn over to his successor the money-order books, blanks, and all circulars and instructions which have been sent to the post-office by the Department, and also all advices on hand of money-orders drawn upon him, whether paid or unpaid, and he will obtain therefor, as in the preceding case, duplicate receipts, one of which he will transmit to the Department; the receipt must distinctly state the number and description of the blanks, and must designate the first and the last number of the money-order and advice forms delivered, as, "From No. 183 to No. 500, inclusive." The late postmaster will, therefore, obtain from his successor two separate and distinct sets of receipts—one for the money-order funds only, and one for the money-order blanks.

Sec. 967. Duty of Incoming Postmaster at a Money-Order Post-Office.—Upon taking charge of a money-order post-office, the postmaster will obtain from his predecessor full information as to the condition of the accounts of the post-office, the place of deposit, etc., and he will debit himself in the money-order cash-book, and in his first weekly statement, with the amount of funds received from his predecessor. If the latter had been furnished with a credit on the postmaster at New York, he will apply at once to the Department for a transfer to himself of the unexpended balance of such credit, or, if there be no balance, for a renewal thereof in his favor.

Sec. 968. Extra Compensation for Issuing and Paying Money-Orders.—Postmasters at money-order offices may be allowed, as compensation for issuing and paying money-orders, not exceeding one-third of the whole amount of the fees collected on orders issued and one-fourth of one per centum on the gross amount of orders paid at their respective offices, provided such compensation, together with the postmaster's salary, shall not exceed four thousand dollars per annum, except in the case of the postmaster at New York City. (R. S., § 4047.)

Sec. 969. Payment for Stationery and Incidentals out of Money-Order Proceeds.—The Postmaster-General may pay out of the proceeds of the money-order business the cost of stationery and such incidental expenses as are necessary for the transaction of that business. (R. S., § 4048.)

Sec. 970. Surplus Money-Order Proceeds. Limit of Clerk-Hire.—If the entire receipts from the rates of compensation allowed by section 968 for the money-order business at any post-office should, when added to the annual salary of the postmaster, exceed the sum of $4,000 per annum, or $1,000 per quarter, he must account to the Department for the surplus of such receipts. At the close of each quarter postmasters will be duly notified by the Auditor of the amount allowed for commissions, and instructed as to the proper entry to be made thereof. Postmasters whose total compensation from all sources amounts to $4,000 per annum can receive nothing in addition thereto for the transaction of the money-order business, but may be allowed by the Postmaster-General a fixed sum for the necessary clerical force actually employed in that business. Postmasters are strictly prohibited from employing in the transaction of their money-order business any portion of the time of their clerks paid for out of the allowance from postal funds for clerk-hire.

Sec. 971. Special Permission Required for All Expenditures.—Postmasters are not authorized to incur, without special permission from the Department, any expense whatever on account of the money-order business, except for necessary stationery to be used exclusively in that business; but they will bear in mind that all blank-books and blanks required in the transaction of the money-order business are not to be purchased by them, but will be furnished by the Department, upon application therefor to the Superintendent of the Money-Order System. They will take credit for all authorized expenses incurred on money-order account in the cash-book, and in the summary of the weekly statement, under the head of "incidental expenses," and will be careful to forward with the statement proper vouchers for the credits claimed therein. Such vouchers must specifically state that the said expense was incurred on money-order account. Upon application to the Third Assistant Postmaster-General, postmasters at money-order post-offices will be supplied by the Department with a sufficient number of envelopes of the size required in the transaction of the money-order business.

Sec. 972. Postmasters to Recommend the Money-Order System to the Public.—It is expected of postmasters that they will use a legitimate influence in recommending the money-order system, and, by courteous attention to the inquiries of applicants, exhibit its superiority as a safe method of transmitting small sums of money through the mails.

Sec. 973. Postmasters must Conform Strictly to Regulations.—The success of the money-order system will greatly depend upon the attention, promptitude, and accuracy of postmasters; and it is expected, therefore, that every postmaster will carefully study the regulations and strictly conform to them. Postmasters are also required to report to the Superintendent of the Money-Order System all cases of repeated failure in the receipt by them of advices from any one post-office. Negligence in forwarding advices cannot be tolerated. It causes delay in payment, and thereby often inflicts great hardship upon the payee. It, moreover, tends to derange and discredit the money-order system.

Sec. 974. No Money-Order Business on Sunday.—Postmasters are not permitted to transact any money-order business on Sunday.

Sec. 975. Letters on Money-Order Business to be Forwarded Separately.—All letters addressed by postmasters to the Department, or the Superintendent of the Money-Order System, should be forwarded separately, and are not, under any circumstances, to be inclosed in envelopes with the weekly statements.

Sec. 976. Postmaster-General makes Foreign Money-Order Conventions.—The Postmaster-General may conclude arrangements with the post departments of foreign governments with which postal conventions have been, or may be, concluded, for the exchange, by means of postal orders, of small sums of money, not exceeding fifty dollars in amount, at such rates of exchange, and compensation to postmasters, and under such rules and regulations as he may deem expedient; and the expenses of establishing and conducting such system of exchange may be paid out of the proceeds of the money-order business. (R. S., § 4028.)

Sec. 977. Books to be Kept at Money-Order Post-Offices.—The books to be kept, and which, to insure uniformity, will be furnished to all the money-order post-offices by the Department, upon application to the Superintendent of the Money-Order System, are:

1. A register of money-orders issued, in which must be recorded, daily, the particulars of all orders issued.
2. A register of advices received, which will be used for the record of advices.
3. A cash-book, showing the debit and credit transactions of each day.

They should contain a complete record of the money-order business of the post-offices to which they are furnished, and must be fully written up before the close of each day.

The headings of the registers, together with the instructions contained in Chapter Five of this Title, will so effectually direct postmasters that no mistakes need occur in keeping these books.

CHAPTER TWO.

ISSUE OF DOMESTIC MONEY-ORDERS.

Sec. 978. Blank Forms of Application to be Supplied.—The Postmaster-General shall supply money-order [post] offices with blank forms of application for money-orders, which each applicant shall fill up with his name, the name and address of the party to whom the order is to be paid, the amount and the date of application; and all such applications shall be preserved by the postmaster receiving them for such time as the Postmaster-General may prescribe. (R. S., § 4033.)

Sec. 979. Postmasters not to Fill up Money-Order Applications.—When a money-order is applied for, the postmaster will furnish the applicant with a printed form of application (Form No. 6001), in which the latter must enter, himself, all the particulars of amount, name, address, &c., required to be stated in the money-order and advice. Postmasters and money-order clerks are strictly prohibited from filling up the application.

Sec. 980. Printed Forms to be Furnished for Money-Orders.—The Postmaster-General shall furnish money-order [post] offices with printed or engraved forms for money-orders, and no order shall be valid unless it be drawn upon such form. (R. S., § 4034.)

Sec. 981. Money-Order Advices.—The postmaster issuing a money-order shall send a notice thereof by mail, without delay, to the postmaster on whom it is drawn. (R. S., § 4035.)

Sec. 982. No Money-Order to be Issued on Credit.—Any postmaster who issues a money-order without having previously received the money therefor shall be deemed guilty of a misdemeanor, and shall be fined not less than fifty nor more than five hundred dollars. (R. S., § 4030.)

Postmasters are not permitted to receive in payment of money-orders issued by them, or to pay out for money-orders drawn upon them, any money that is not a legal-tender by the laws of the United States, except national bank notes. Check, drafts, or promissory notes are not to be received under any circumstances for money-orders.

Sec. 983. Fees upon Money-Orders. No Order for more than Fifty Dollars.—On and after the first day of July, eighteen hundred and seventy-five, the fees on money-orders shall be, for orders not exceeding fifteen dollars, ten cents; exceeding fifteen and not exceeding thirty dollars, fifteen cents; exceeding thirty and not exceeding forty dollars, twenty cents; exceeding forty and not exceeding fifty dollars, twenty-five cents; and no money-order shall be issued for a sum greater than fifty dollars. (R. S., § 4032, as amended by act of March 3, 1875, 18 Stat., p. 351.)

Sec. 984. Fractional Parts of a Cent not to be Included.—A single money-order may include any amount from one cent to fifty dollars, but such money-order must not contain a fractional part of a cent.

Sec. 985. Only Three Fifty-Dollar Orders to one Person for same Payee.—When a larger sum than fifty dollars is required, additional money-orders to make it up must be obtained. But postmasters are instructed to refuse to issue in one day, to the same remitter and in favor of the same payee, more than three money-orders payable at the same post-office. The plain evasion of this rule by the substitution of a different remitter for every three of a large number of money-orders issued in one day, in favor of the same payee, should not be tolerated by postmasters.

Sec. 986. Issuing Money-Orders and Transmitting Advices.—From the items contained in the application, the postmaster will make out the money-order required in conformity therewith, and also the corresponding form of advice. The money-order, when completed, is to be handed to the applicant upon payment of the sum expressed therein and of the fee chargeable thereon, which fee must invariably be paid in money, postage-stamps not being receivable therefor. By the first mail dispatched to the post-office of payment after the issue of a money-order, the postmaster must transmit, in a sealed envelope, the corresponding advice to the postmaster at the post-office upon which it is drawn. In forwarding advices he must use only such envelopes as bear the printed letters M. O. B. or the words *Money Order Business*. Delay and mistakes in sending advices cause difficulty in payment and tend to discredit the system. Their repetition will lead to the removal of the negligent postmaster. The utmost accuracy must be observed in writing both the money-order and the advice, neither of which should be "post-dated," but each should in every instance bear the stamp of the actual date of issue. The application must be numbered to correspond with the money-order issued, and filed for future reference.

Sec. 987. Stamping Money-Orders and Advices.—To insure at all times a clear impression, a special stamp must be employed for stamping money-orders and advices, which should never be used for stamping letters. Such stamp is not to contain the postmaster's name, but only the name of the post-office and State or Territory, with the date of impression and the letters M. O. B.

Sec. 988. Persons Procuring Money-Orders must Carefully Examine them.—Parties procuring money-orders should examine them carefully to see that they are properly filled up and stamped. This caution will appear the more necessary when it is understood that any defect in this respect will throw difficulties in the way of payment.

Sec. 989. Signature of Postmaster on Money-Orders must be Written.—The signature of the postmaster or designated clerk who issues a money-order must invariably be written and not stamped thereon.

Sec. 990. When Errors are made New Orders must be made out.—If an error of any kind be made in filling up a money-order, and it be discovered at the time of issuing or before the advice has been dispatched, a new money-order must be made out, as no alterations or erasures are permitted. The special attention of postmasters is called to this important regulation.

Sec. 991. How to Use Blank Money-Orders and Advices.—Postmasters will observe that the forms for money-orders and advices are numbered, consecutively, from 1 to 500 or 1,000, or to higher numbers, according to the requirements of the issuing post-office. This is intended as a safeguard against the improper use of the blanks; and therefore when, through mistake or from any other cause, any of them have been spoiled, the words NOT ISSUED must be written or stamped across both the money-order and the advice. The spoiled money-order, with the corresponding advice, must be transmitted to the Superintendent of the Money-Order System with the weekly statement, and must be entered therein in its proper numerical order, with the words NOT ISSUED written opposite, the particulars and amount of the money-order being left blank. A similar entry must be made against the corresponding number in the register of money-orders issued. No departure from this rule will be permitted, as the Postmaster-General imperatively requires that every blank form of a money-order sent to a postmaster shall be accounted for at the end of the week in which it is used, or canceled as spoiled and not issued.

Sec. 992. Omitted and Defective Blanks to be Reported.—Money-order and advice forms should be carefully examined by the postmaster immediately upon their receipt, and all irregularities reported. Should a blank money-order be omitted in the book supplied to a post-office, the postmaster will make a note thereof opposite the proper number in the weekly statement in which the money-order would have appeared if supplied. He will also make a similar memorandum in his register of money-orders issued. Should any of these blanks be defective or mutilated, the postmaster will cut out and return the same to the Superintendent of the Money-Order System, and treat the blank or blanks as "Not issued." Should any of the blank money-orders be duplicated, it will only be necessary to cut out the extra one and return it to the Department.

Sec. 993. Postmasters Responsible for Loss of Money-Order Forms.—Postmasters should keep their stock of blank money-order forms and advices in their own custody, under lock and key, in some place of security to which unauthorized persons cannot have access, and they will be held responsible for any loss which the Department may suffer arising from fraud made possible through a disregard of this regulation.

Sec. 994. How Postmasters should make out Advices.—The given names of both remitter and payee must be entered in the advice in full when possible; and a married woman must be described by her own name, and not by that of her husband, it the former name is known to the remitter. Thus, the appellation "Mrs. *William* Brown" is defective, as it does not accurately describe the payee, whose true name may be Mrs. *Mary* Brown. Both names and sums must be written so legibly as to effectually guard against errors. When an applicant is unable to state the initials of the given name or names of an individual to whom he desires to send a money-order, the postmaster must refuse to issue the money-order. A money-order should always be made payable to one person or to one firm only, and not to either of two or more designated persons or firms.

Sec. 995. When Second Advices should be Issued.—When a second or duplicate advice is required, in consequence of the original advice having been spoiled in issuing a money-order or when the original advice is stated not to have reached its destination, or when it is necessary to readvise for any reported discrepancy in number, name, or amount, one of the spare advice forms headed "Second advice" must be used. Whenever the issuing postmaster receives a "Letter of inquiry" from the postmaster at the post-office of payment, in "case of discrepancy between the advice and the statement of the payee," the former will carefully examine the original "application," and if it agrees with the statement of the payee, he will fill up a "second advice" from the application. If, however, the application agrees with the first advice, he will, when practicable, ascertain from the remitter what correction, if any, is required in the application, and fill up the "second advice" accordingly. But in case the remitter cannot readily be found, the postmaster will simply fill up from the application a "second advice," and write thereon the words, REMITTER NOT FOUND.

Sec. 996. Amount of Money-Order to be in Writing.—When money-orders are issued for sums less than one dollar, or for any amount in complete dollars, the spaces for "dollars" or "cents," as the case may be, both at the head and in the body of the money-order, must be filled up with a heavy dash, so as in all cases effectually to prevent any subsequent alteration. The amount in the body of the money-order must invariably be expressed in writing, and not in figures.

Sec. 997. Money-Orders may be Drawn upon what Post-Offices.—Money-orders can only be drawn upon such post-offices as are enumerated in the list of money-order post-offices contained in the United States Official Postal Guide. In issuing money-orders, the name of the post-office drawn upon must not be abbreviated, but must be written in full upon advices as well as upon money-orders.

Sec. 998. Notice Money-Order Post-Offices Discontinued.—On receipt by postmasters of each number of the Postal Guide they are directed to read carefully the list of money-order offices discontinued, which is placed at the top of the list of money-order post-offices.

Sec. 999. Postmasters to Instruct Applicants on what Post-Office to Draw.—It is expected of postmasters that they will exercise their judgment with respect to the selection of the post-office upon which a money-order may be drawn, as the applicant, from lack of information, is liable to mistakes as to locality which may be productive of inconvenience to the payee. Therefore, when occasion requires, postmasters will endeavor to ascertain which is the money-order post-office most conveniently situated for the purpose of the remitter, and to advise him that the money-order be drawn thereon.

Sec. 1000. Money-Orders to be Recorded when Issued.—Upon the issue of a money-order, the postmaster will record all the particulars thereof in the "register of money-orders issued," as directed by the headings; and if any subsequent action should be taken in reference thereto (such, for instance, as repayment, the issue of a duplicate, etc.), he will note the alteration opposite the entry in the register under the head of "Remarks."

Sec. 1001. Report $300 Drawn upon other than First-Class Post-Offices.—When the aggregate amount of money-orders issued by any money-order post-office in one day, upon a post-office of other than the first class, equals or exceeds $300, the issuing postmaster will be required to send by the first mail a special notice of the fact, stating the amount drawn for, to the Superintendent of the Money-Order System. (See Form No. 6037.) Postmasters are required to pay strict attention to this rule, as a neglect of the duty it enjoins may result in delay of payment, and consequent inconvenience to the payee.

Sec. 1002. Advices to be Checked to Insure Correctness.—Postmasters are strictly enjoined to check their advices carefully before dispatching them, so as to be sure that they are correctly addressed.

Sec. 1003. Reissue of Money-Orders. New Fee Required.—After a money-order has been issued, if the purchaser desires to have it modified or changed, the postmaster who issued the order shall take it back and issue another in lieu of it, for which a new fee shall be exacted. (R. S., § 4038.)

Sec. 1004. Rules for Reissuing Money-Orders.—When the remitter of a money-order desires to change the place of payment of the same, or when a mistake has been made in drawing a money-order through error of the remitter, the issuing postmaster is authorized, with the above restrictions, to take back the first money-order, which he will repay, and issue another in lieu thereof, for which a second fee must be charged and exacted as on a new transaction, in accordance with the preceding section. If the advice has gone forward to the post-office upon which the original money-order was drawn, he will, by the first mail, dispatch a special notice, informing the postmaster at that post-office of the repayment of said money-order. The special advice is not to be used instead of the proper accompanying advice of the new money-order, but is additional to it. Under no circumstances must a postmaster issue a new money-order in lieu of another until the original money-order shall have been returned to him. Should the mistake be made by the postmaster he will be held responsible therefor, and must charge himself with the fee for issuing the new money-order. If the original advice has not been mailed to the paying post-office, the money-order should be treated by the postmaster as "spoiled" or not "issued," in accordance with section 991 of these regulations.

Sec. 1005. Issue of Duplicate Money-Orders.—Whenever a money-order has been lost, the Postmaster-General, upon the application of the remitter or payee of such order, may cause a duplicate thereof to be issued, without charge, providing the party losing the original shall furnish a certificate from the postmaster by whom it was payable that it has not been, and will not thereafter be, paid; and a similar certificate from the postmaster by whom it was issued that it has not been, and will not thereafter be, repaid. (R. S., § 4040.)

Sec. 1006. Duplicate Money-Orders Issued only by the Superintendent.—In case a money-order is lost in transmission, or otherwise, a duplicate will be issued by the Superintendent of the Money-Order System, on the receipt of an application therefor from either the remitter, the payee, or the indorsee of the original. Such application should be made on Form No. 6002, and should be forwarded to the Department by the issuing or the paying postmaster. The duplicate can be made payable only to the payee, or, in case of indorsement, to the indorsee of the original, unless the written consent of the payee or indorsee to the repayment of the money-order, by duplicate, to the remitter, shall have been obtained by the latter, and duly filed in the Department. Such written consent must bear a certificate as to its genuineness from the postmaster at the place where the payee resides. It is the duty of the issuing and of the paying postmaster to aid the remitter, as far as they may be able, in obtaining the consent required by this section. If the payee is dead, the remitter must obtain the written consent of his legal representative, who should be required to exhibit to the postmaster, who certifies to such consent, the proper documentary evidence of his authority to act in that capacity. If the owner of the money-order (whether the payee or indorsee), or his legal representative, cannot, after the lapse of a reasonable time, be found, the remitter should forward to the Department satisfactory evidence of that fact, if he desires repayment. A blank bond of indemnity, in a penal sum of double the amount of the lost money-order, will then be sent him, to be executed by himself and two sureties, and returned to the Department: the condition of such bond being that if, after the issue and payment of a duplicate money-order to the remitter, any other person establishes a valid adverse claim to the original money-order, the amount so paid by duplicate shall be refunded to the Post-Office Department. Upon full compliance with the above requirements, the remitter thus situated will receive a duplicate of the lost money-order.

Sec. 1007. Duty of Postmaster Applying for Duplicate Money-Order.—When a postmaster has been informed by the remitter, payee, or indorsee of a money-order that the same has been lost or destroyed, he will cause the said remitter, payee, or indorsee to sign a statement, setting forth the loss or destruction thereof, and containing a request for the issue of a duplicate. If the applicant is the indorsee of the original, his application must be accompanied by a certificate to that effect from the payee, the genuineness of which must be attested by the postmaster at the latter's place of residence. The postmaster before whom the application is made will complete the application by enumerating the particulars of the lost money-order, and by stating to whom the duplicate is to be made payable, whether to the payee or to the indorsee, and also the full address of such person. He will thereupon execute the proper certificate relative to the payment or repayment of the original money-order, and dispatch the form to the issuing or to the paying postmaster, as the case may be, for his certificate. The latter should be requested to forward the paper, when completed, to the Superintendent of the Money-Order System.

Sec. 1008. Second Advice Furnished when Needed to get Duplicate.—In case both the money-order and advice are lost, the issuing postmaster will, upon receiving notice of the loss of the latter from the paying postmaster, forward to him a "second advice," embracing all the particulars of the missing advice, so that application may be made through the paying postmaster, and he may be enabled to give his certificate in the manner above described.

Sec. 1009. Original Money-Order may be Paid before Duplicate is Issued.—Should the original money-order alleged to be lost come into the possession of the remitter, payee, or indorsee thereof, and should the postmaster to whom the money-order is presented notify the Department of the fact before a duplicate is issued, special permission will be given him to pay or repay, as the case may be, such original money-order. But if sufficient time has elapsed for the issue of a duplicate, the postmaster to whom the money-order is presented will write across it the words, CANCELED—DUPLICATE APPLIED FOR. If the person who presents it requires the postmaster to return it to him, he may do so; but, if not, the money-order should be sent to the Department.

Sec. 1010. Duty of Postmaster Certifying Non-payment of Money-Order.—When a postmaster signs a certificate that a money-order drawn upon his post-office has not been and will not be paid, he should at once note the same by writing, in red ink, across the face of the advice and under the entry thereof in the register of advices received, the words DUPLICATE APPLIED FOR—ORIGINAL MONEY-ORDER NOT TO BE PAID; and in the case of a money-order issued at his post-office, when he has certified that the original money-order has not been and will not be repaid, he will write under the entry of the said money-order, in the register of money-orders issued, the words DUPLICATE APPLIED FOR—ORIGINAL MONEY-ORDER NOT TO BE REPAID. Neglect of this rule may involve a postmaster in serious trouble, as he will be held strictly accountable should the original money-order be afterward paid or repaid at his post-office.

Sec. 1011. Postmasters cannot issue Duplicates.—Duplicate money-orders will be issued only by the Department. Under no circumstances whatever will a postmaster be allowed to issue them.

Sec. 1012. On what Post-Offices Duplicates can be Drawn.—A duplicate money-order can only be drawn upon the issuing or on the paying post-office of the original money-order, and becomes invalid if it bear more than one indorsement or is not presented for payment within one year after its date.

CHAPTER THREE.

PAYMENT OF DOMESTIC MONEY-ORDERS.

Sec. 1013. Money-Orders Valid only for One Year from Date.—No money-order shall be valid and payable unless presented to the postmaster on whom it is drawn within one year after its date; but the Postmaster-General, on the application of the remitter or payee of any such order, may cause a new order to be issued in lieu thereof. (R. S., § 4036.)

Sec. 1014. Only One Indorsement Allowed on Money-Orders.—The payee of a money-order may, by his written indorsement thereon, direct it to [be] paid to any other person, and the postmaster on whom it is drawn shall pay the same to the person thus designated, provided he shall furnish such proof as the Postmaster-General may prescribe that the indorsement is genuine, and that he is the person empowered to receive payment; but more than one indorsement shall render an order invalid and not payable, and the holder, to obtain payment, must apply in writing to the Postmaster-General for a new order in lieu thereof, returning the original order, and making such proof of the genuineness of the indorsements as the Postmaster-General may require. (R. S., § 4037.)

Sec. 1015. Postmasters must have Payees Identified.—When a money-order is presented for payment at the post-office upon which it is drawn, the postmaster or authorized clerk will use all proper means to assure himself that the applicant is the person named and intended in the advice, or is the indorsee or attorney of the latter; and upon payment of the money-order care must be taken to obtain the signature of the payee, or of the person authorized by him to receive payment, to the receipt on the face of the money-order. The signature to the receipt upon the face of the money-order must be that of the person who presents and receives payment of the same.

Sec. 1016. Money-Orders must not be Paid until Advice is Received.—No money-order must be paid until the corresponding letter of advice has been received.

Sec. 1017. Advices Examined and Filed as Received.—As soon as practicable after the close of each day's business, all advices received during the day must be arranged and filed in alphabetical order according to the name of the issuing post-office, so that, whenever needed, they may be referred to without difficulty. They must be retained on file for a term of four years, at the expiration of which time they are to be disposed of as "waste paper" of the post-office. The postmaster is required to examine each advice when received, to see that it is properly stamped and in all respects regular, and at the same time, if found to be drawn upon his post-office, to enter the particulars thereof in the register of advices received. To avoid errors and to facilitate payment, the "paid" and "unpaid" advices should be kept in separate packages.

Sec. 1018. Advices must be Kept Secret.—Every care should be taken to guard against the loss of these important documents; and with this view, and to prevent their disarrangement, they should be kept under lock and key. Postmasters, assistant postmasters, and money-order clerks are forbidden to reveal to any person the information communicated to them by the advices in their possession of money-orders drawn upon their respective post-offices. Should they do so, in any case, without special permission from the Department, such action will be regarded by the Postmaster-General as sufficient cause for removal.

Sec. 1019. Missent Advices to be Remailed.—In the event of an advice being received of a money-order which is not drawn upon his post-office, the postmaster must transmit it by the first mail to its proper destination, previously noting on the document the circumstance of its having been missent. A strict compliance with this regulation is of the utmost importance to prevent delay in payment.

Sec. 1020. Second Advice to be Entered when Received.—Should a second advice be received, correcting the number, name, or amount of the original, the entry in the register should be altered accordingly, and the second advice be attached to the original, and placed on file.

Sec. 1021. Precautions to be Taken before Paying Money-Orders.—When a money-order is presented for payment, the postmaster will first examine the document to see that it is properly signed, stamped, etc.; he will then compare the date, number, and amount with the advice or with the record thereof in the register of advices received, and satisfy himself that the applicant is the person entitled to payment. Every person who applies for payment of a money-order should be required by the postmaster to prove his identity, unless the applicant is known to be the rightful owner of the money-order. Special caution should be exercised in the payment of money-orders issued in favor of women or of soldiers or sailors. In the event of a money-order having been paid to the wrong person through lack of necessary precaution on the part of the postmaster, he will be held accountable for such payment. Whoever identifies the payee of a money-order should be required, before payment is made, to write his name and residence on the back of the corresponding advice, under a statement that he knows the applicant for payment to be the person he represents himself to be. Care should be taken that the signature of the payee be as full as the name given in the advice, and that it be in no way inconsistent therewith. If the payee be unable to write, he must sign the receipt by making his mark, to be witnessed in writing. The witness should sign his name, with his address, in the presence of the postmaster, and the latter will then certify the payment by adding his own initials. The witness should be known to the postmaster, but it is desirable (though not imperative) that he be not connected with the post-office. In no case should the postmaster act as witness himself. It is not absolutely necessary that the witness should be personally acquainted with the payee. When the payee of a money-order is a bank, railway company, insurance company, municipality, college, newspaper, society, or corporation of any kind, the president, cashier, manager, secretary, treasurer, agent, or the person who has authority to receive payment of moneys due such bank, railway company, &c., must be required to sign the receipt on the money-order in his official capacity, and the paying postmaster may exact satisfactory proof that the applicant for payment is duly authorized to sign and to receive payment of the money-order.

Sec. 1022. Money-Orders not Properly Issued to be Refused Payment.—Should the stamp of the issuing postmaster and the written date be wanting upon a money-order, the postmaster at the post-office upon which it is drawn must decline payment, but a money-order may be paid notwithstanding the absence of the stamp of the issuing post-office, provided the money-order is not defective in any other respect. Money-orders from which the stamp of either post-office has been omitted will be rejected as vouchers by the Department, and will be returned to the postmaster at fault, in order that the omission may be supplied.

Sec. 1023. Inquiry for Missing Advice.—When a money-order is presented for which no advice has been received, one of the printed letters of inquiry for missing advices (Form No. 6006) must at once be dispatched to the postmaster who issued the order. Under no circumstances whatever can an order be paid until the corresponding advice shall have been received.

Sec. 1024. Duty of Postmaster when Money-Orders do not Agree with Advice.—When a money-order is presented which does not agree with the advice, payment must be refused until a second advice can be obtained, unless the difference be evidently accidental and trifling, in which case the postmaster may, if he chooses, pay the money-order; but he will be held responsible if the payment should prove to be incorrect. Every case of difference, however small, between a money-order and an advice should be reported in forwarding the money-order at the end of the week. If the discrepancy is considerable and is not corrected by a second advice, the holder of the money-order should be directed to return it to the remitter, so that the latter may present it to the issuing postmaster for repayment and the issue of a new money-order in lieu thereof. If the latter postmaster is responsible for the error, he must charge himself with the fee for the new money-order. In case, however, the amount stated in the advice is less than that in the money-order, payment of the lesser amount may be made to the payee at once, provided he requests it. The postmaster must then write across the face of the money-order this memorandum: PAID $, AMOUNT OF ADVICE, IN COMPLIANCE WITH PAYEE'S REQUEST; and must send to the issuing postmaster for a second advice. Should the amount of the second advice agree with that of the money-order the postmaster will transmit to the Superintendent of the Money-Order System, in an envelope marked "Special," the paid money-order, together with both advices and a full statement of the case, that he may cause the balance due on the money-order to be paid to the payee. If the second advice agrees in amount with the first, no further action need be taken in the matter.

Sec. 1025. Postmasters Paying Money-Orders must Provide against Delays.—It is the special duty of the postmaster to provide as far as possible against delay in the payment of money-orders on presentation, by making immediate application for funds (using Form No. 6036), whenever the amount of advices received indicates the need of assistance to enable him to pay the corresponding money-orders. He is authorized to defer payment only long enough to procure the requisite funds, and the delay, if he is prompt in making his application, should not exceed five days. Should a postmaster who has sufficient funds of the Department, whether arising from the issue of money-orders or from postages, in his hands, refuse to pay money-orders drawn upon him when duly presented, such refusal will be deemed sufficient cause for his immediate removal.

Sec. 1026. Paid Money-Orders to be Stamped and Recorded.—After payment of a money-order, the date of such payment must immediately be stamped upon the money-order and upon the advice, and likewise entered opposite the record thereof in the register of advices received, with the word PAID written opposite the entry, in the column headed "Remarks."

Sec. 1027. Payment by Duplicate to be Noted.—When a money-order is paid by duplicate, the fact must be noted in the register of advices received, by writing opposite the entry of the advice, in the column of "Remarks," the words PAID BY DUPLICATE NO. — (adding the number and date of payment). The same should be written in red ink under the particulars of the original order in the weekly statement.

Sec. 1028. Payment upon Power of Attorney or to Legal Representative.—Postmasters are prohibited from paying a money-order to a second person without the written indorsement to such second person by the payee on the back of the money-order, unless the payee has, by a duly executed power of attorney, designated and appointed some person to collect moneys due or to become due him, in which case the attorney should be required, before payment is made him, to file at the post-office of payment a certified copy of such power of attorney, or unless the payee has given a written order, addressed to the paying postmaster, which is to be filed with the latter, authorizing a second person to receive payment of and to receipt for any specific money-order or for all money-orders, payable by such postmaster to the payee. Money-orders paid upon a power of attorney, or upon a written order from the payee, should bear upon their face, written or stamped in red ink, the words POWER OF ATTORNEY ON FILE, or WRITTEN ORDER ON FILE, as the case may be.

Where money-orders are paid upon an indorsement, the utmost caution should be exercised, and before paying them the postmaster must be satisfied that the signature to the indorsement is genuine, and that the person presenting the money-order is the one named in the indorsement. The person presenting the money-order should be required, if unknown to the postmaster, to prove his identity. The name of the indorsee to whom a money-order is paid should be entered in the column of "Remarks" in the "register of advices received."

In case of the death of the payee the money-order is to be paid to his "legal representative," whether executor or administrator, who should be required to satisfy the paying postmaster of his authority to act in such capacity, and to sign the receipt to the money-order as executor or administrator, as the case may be. A money-order payable to a firm, bank, or company which has ceased to exist, must be paid to the legal representative thereof.

Sec. 1029. Money-Orders must be Correctly Receipted and Stamped.—Any money-order not correctly receipted, or not stamped with the date of payment, will be disallowed from the weekly account and returned for correction.

Sec. 1030. Payment of Money-Order on Day of Issue.—The Department does not undertake to secure payment of a money-order on the day of its issue, but the postmaster at the post-office drawn upon may, if he has received the corresponding advice, make payment on that day.

Sec. 1031. Department not Responsible after Payment of Money-Order.—After once paying a money-order, by whomsoever presented, provided the required information has been given by the party who presented it, the Department will not hold itself liable to any further claim, but in case of improper payment of a money-order, will endeavor to recover the amount for the owner.

Sec. 1032. How Money-Orders more than a Year Old may be Paid.—Any money-order which is not presented for payment until after the expiration of one year from the date thereof, is declared "invalid and not payable" by section 1013, and the postmaster to whom such money order is presented must refuse payment of the same. In order to obtain payment of such invalid money-order, the holder will be required to forward the same, through the issuing or the paying postmaster, to the Superintendent of the Money-Order System of the Post-Office Department. (See Form No. 6003.) If the Department is satisfied that the money-order has not been paid, a duplicate will be issued payable to the remitter, payee, or indorsee, as may be requested in the application, and the same will be sent to the postmaster for delivery or payment, as the case may be.

Sec. 1033. Examine Advices for Money-Orders over one Year Old.—The register of advices received should be carefully examined at least once a week, with a view to ascertain whether any of the unpaid advices entered therein have become invalid by reason of being more than one year old; and should it be found that any of them have become invalid for the reason stated, the several dates and numbers thereof in the register must be underscored in red ink, and the advices picked out at the close of the week and forwarded to the Department; the envelope containing the same being indorsed ADVICES OF INVALID ORDERS. Under the corresponding entries thereof in the register should be written, INVALID—ADVICE FORWARDED TO THE DEPARTMENT ———, 187—. A strict compliance with this regulation is of the first importance.

Sec. 1034. Payment of Amounts of Money-Orders Illegally Indorsed.—It is provided by law (section 1014) that more than one indorsement upon a money-order shall render the same invalid and not payable. Hence, the postmaster to whom a money-order, whether "original" or "duplicate," thus illegally indorsed is presented, must refuse payment of the same; and the holder thereof, to obtain payment of the money-order, is required to forward the same, with an application for renewal, to the Superintendent of the Money-Order System, and to furnish the statement, under oath or affirmation, of two responsible persons known to the postmaster (whose certificate shall be appended thereto) that the indorsement is genuine, and that the holder is the person named therein. (See Form No. 6003.) Upon his compliance with these requirements, a duplicate of the illegally indorsed money-order will be issued, as above. In all cases of lost or invalid money-orders, the owner of the money-order (whether remitter, payee, or indorsee) may make application, through either the issuing or the paying postmaster, for a duplicate; and it is the duty of the postmaster to whom such application shall be made to fill up and dispatch the proper forms therefor. The duplicate will be issued agreeably to the request contained in the postmaster's letter—*i. e.*, to the remitter, payee, or indorsee—and made payable at the issuing or the paying post-office, as may be desired, and forwarded to the address specified by the applicant.

Sec. 1035. Repayment of Money-Order to Applicant.—The postmaster issuing a money-order shall repay the amount of it upon application of the porson who obtained it, and the return of the order; but the fee paid for it shall not be returned. (R. S., § 4039.)

Sec. 1036. Rules for Repaying Money-Orders.—A postmaster may repay a money-order issued at his own post-office, provided the money-order is presented to him for that purpose, and is less than one year old, and does not bear more than one indorsement; but the repayment must be made to the person who obtained the money-order, except in special cases. (See section 1038.) If the advice has gone forward to the post-office upon which the money-order was drawn, the postmaster will, by the first mail, dispatch a special advice (Form No. 6036) notifying that post-office of the repayment. If the advice has not gone forward, it is to be transmitted to the Superintendent of the Money-Order System, inclosed with the corresponding repaid money-order in the weekly account. The fee must not in any case be refunded.

Sec. 1037. Repaid Money-Orders to be so Stamped.—The word REPAID (and the date) must be written or stamped on the face of every repaid money-order, and a corresponding entry made in the register of money-orders issued, against the particulars of the money-order and in the column headed "Remarks."

Sec. 1038. Repaid Money-Orders to be Signed, by Whom.—Every money-order repaid must be signed by the remitter or person who procured it. But if he should be unable to make application for such repayment in person, it can be made to another party, in which case the remitter will fill up the indorsement upon the back with the name of the person to whom he wishes the payment made, and sign his own name thereto, substituting the word "remitter" for that of "payee," where the latter occurs. But postmasters will exercise the greatest caution in repaying a money-order to a second person. It may occasionally happen that a money-order is presented for payment at the post-office of issue by the payee. The issuing postmaster is at liberty to pay the money-order in such case, and treat it as "repaid," provided he is satisfied as to the identity of the payee, and that the latter has good reasons for presenting the order at his post-office. Across the face of the order should be written these words, viz: REPAID TO THE PAYEE, and a "special advice of repayment" should be forwarded to the post-office on which the money-order was drawn.

Sec. 1039. Repayment by Duplicate.—When a money-order is repaid by duplicate, the fact must be noted in the register of money-orders issued, by writing opposite the entry of the original money-order, in the column of "Remarks," the words REPAID BY DUPLICATE No. — (adding the number and the date of repayment). Special notice must also be sent to the post-office on which the original money-order was drawn. In taking credit for such repayment in the summary of the weekly statement, the postmaster will enter the number of the original money-order, and also that of the duplicate, thus, "By money-order No. 1286 (repaid by duplicate 120), $19.25."

Sec. 1040. Special Notice of Repayment, how Entered.—When a postmaster receives a special notice of the repayment of a money-order by the issuing postmaster, he will write the words REPAID AT —— (naming the place and date) opposite the entry in the register of advices received, and also upon the original advice which, after having attached the special notice thereto, he will place on file.

Sec. 1041. Postmasters Pay only Money-Orders on their Post-Offices.—No postmaster will be permitted to pay a money-order which is not drawn upon his post-office. This, however, does not preclude the repayment of a money-order at the post-office where it was drawn, as specified in section 1036. The postmaster at the post-office drawn upon may also pay a money-order to the remitter thereof, but such payment should be made with great caution, as prescribed in section 1038.

Sec. 1042. Notice to be Sent to Payee of Duplicate.—The postmaster who receives from the Department a duplicate payable by him must forthwith send notice to the payee of such duplicate to call for payment. In paying a duplicate order the postmaster is required to exercise the same precautions as in paying an original order.

Sec. 1043. Postmaster-General may Stop Payment of Money-Orders, when.—

The Postmaster-General may, upon evidence satisfactory to him that any person is engaged in conducting any fraudulent lottery, gift enterprise, or scheme for the distribution of money, or of any real or personal property, by lot, chance, or drawing of any kind, or in conducting any other scheme or device for obtaining money through the mails by means of false or fraudulent pretenses, representations, or promises, forbid the payment, by any postmaster, to any such person of any postal money-order drawn to his order or in his favor, and may provide by regulations for the return, to the remitter, of the sums named in such money-orders. But this shall not authorize any person to open any letter not addressed to himself. (R. S., § 4041.)

Sec. 1044. Payment of Money-Orders to be Withheld, When.—(*a*) Payment of a money-order may be with heldby the paying postmaster, upon the receipt of a written request from the issuing postmaster or the remitter, for a sufficient time to enable the remitter to furnish the paying postmaster with proof that the money-order was procured by him through false representations, or other fraudulent action of the payee, who is furthermore alleged by him to be engaged in conducting a scheme or device for obtaining money through the mails by means of false or fraudulent pretenses, representations, or promises. The case, together with the proof furnished, must be referred to the Department, in order that the Postmaster-General may, under the authority given him by the preceding section, if the evidence is satisfactory to him, forbid the payment of the money-order, and direct the return of the amount thereof to the remitter upon application of the latter for a duplicate.

(*b*) In cases in which payment of a money-order to the payee is not forbidden by the Postmaster-General under the conditions above mentioned, the payee is entitled to payment, "notwithstanding the protest of the remitter of the money-order; and the remitter of a money-order cannot forbid the payment of it by any notice to the post-office at which it is made payable before it has been paid." The above quotation is from volume xiv, page 110, Official Opinions of the Attorneys-General of the United States. The possession of a money-order by the remitter, payee, or indorsee thereof is *prima-facie* evidence of ownership.

(*c*) When a postmaster receives by mail a letter containing a money-order drawn upon him, purporting to be receipted on the face by the payee thereof, or to be made payable to such postmaster by the indorsement of the payee, with a request to transmit to the payee by mail, in money or by draft, the amount of the money-order, the postmaster should decline to comply with this request, and should notify the payee that he will, if the latter consents, forward to him a new money-order, drawn upon any money-order post-office which the payee may designate, for an amount equal to the money-order received, less the fee for the new money-order. If the payee declines, in a case of this kind, to give his consent to the issue of a new money-order, the postmaster will send back to him the receipted or indorsed money-order.

(*d*) When a money-order is presented for payment, in which the only defect is that the name of the State in which the paying post-office is situated is erroneously given, the postmaster is at liberty to pay such money-order at his own risk, provided there is no other obstacle to payment, and that he has on hand the corresponding advice of the same number and date, which advice gives correctly the name of his post-office and of his State. After having paid a money-order of this description, the postmaster will write across the face thereof the following statement: THE CORRESPONDING ADVICE OF THIS MONEY-ORDER IS CORRECTLY DRAWN ON THIS POST-OFFICE, which statement he will duly sign and date.

CHAPTER FOUR.

ISSUE AND PAYMENT OF FOREIGN MONEY-ORDERS.

Sec. 1045. Exchange of Money-Orders with Great Britain.—The exchange of money-orders between the United States and the United Kingdom of Great Britain and Ireland, is to be effected through the agency of two post-offices, termed "international exchange post-offices." The international exchange post-office on the part of the United States is New York, and that on the part of the United Kingdom is London.

Sec. 1046. International Money-Orders, how Drawn.—Certain money-order post-offices in this country, designated for the purpose by the Postmaster-General, are authorized to issue money-orders on the postmaster at New York, payable to beneficiaries in the United Kingdom, and to pay money-orders issued by that postmaster for sums remitted by the Postal Department of the United Kingdom for payment to beneficiaries in the United States. Hence, a postmaster in either country cannot draw an international money-order for an amount deposited with him directly upon a postmaster in the other, but must draw the same upon the international exchange post-office of his own country. An international money-order must not be drawn for a larger sum than $50 in United States currency, and must not contain a fractional part of a cent. The fees for the issue of international money-orders are as follows, viz: On money-orders not exceeding $10, 25 cents; over $10 and not exceeding $20, 50 cents; over $20 and not exceeding $30, 75 cents; over $30 and not exceeding $40, $1; over $40 and not exceeding $50, $1.25. Postmasters are not permitted to receive in payment for international money-orders issued by them, or to pay for such money-orders drawn upon them, any money that is not a legal tender, except national-bank notes.

Sec. 1047. Form of Application for International Money-Order.—A special form of application (Form No. 6201) must be furnished to the applicant for an international money-order payable in Great Britain. On this form he must enter all the particulars of the amount, names, address, etc., and must state the full name and exact residence of the payee, giving the town or village, and county. From the items contained in such application, the issuing postmaster will fill up the international money-order and coupon, both of which he will, by the next outgoing mail, dispatch, without separating them, to the postmaster at New York. The corresponding certificate of the same number and date he will deliver, when completed, to the remitter, as a receipt for the amount paid in by the latter. No "advice" is used at the issuing post-office in this international system, inasmuch as the money-order, instead of being delivered to the remitter for transmission, is forwarded directly by the issuing postmaster to the "exchange" post-office at New York. The particulars of the money-order are to be entered in the register of international money-orders issued, and the application must be retained on file. The general rules in regard to issuing domestic money-orders contained in the domestic money-order instructions are to be observed in the issue of international money-orders, in so far as these rules are applicable. The postmaster, however, must refuse to issue a money-order payable to any person, if the surname and the initial letter of that person's name are not furnished by the applicant, unless the payee be a peer or a bishop, in which case his ordinary title is sufficient. If the payee be a firm, the usual designation of such firm will suffice, such as "Baring Bros.," "Smith & Son," "Jones & Co."; but the mere term "Messrs.," such as "Messrs. Rivington," or the name of a company trading under a title which does not consist of the names of the persons composing such company, as, for example, "The Carron Company," must not be accepted as sufficient by the issuing postmaster, who will decline to issue a money-order on the United Kingdom in favor of such payee, as payment thereof would be refused in that country.

Sec. 1048. Issuing Postmaster not to Decide Coin Value of Currency.—The issuing postmaster must not undertake to decide definitively upon the actual value in United States gold coin of a certain sum in currency for which an international money-order is issued. He is at liberty, however, to advise the remitter as to its approximate value, which may be found to differ materially from the real value, as the latter is to be computed upon the basis of the premium upon gold on the day of the receipt of the money-order by the postmaster at New York. Hence, this Department cannot undertake, on behalf of a remitter in this country, to pay a determinate sum in gold in the United Kingdom. As the premium on gold is variable, it is evident that an international money-order issued for a sum in United States currency may, when received at the exchange post-office at New York, yield a sum in gold greater or less than that considered at the post-office of issue as the equivalent of such money-order. For the same reason, the value in United States currency of a money-order in gold, certified by the exchange office at London to the exchange post-office at New York, would depend upon the premium on gold on the day of the receipt of the list containing such certified order. This Department, therefore, can only agree to cause a payment to be made to a beneficiary in Great Britain of the gold value of any international money-order issued for an amount in United States currency, and to pay to a beneficiary in this country the currency value of an international money-order in gold from Great Britain. To guard against misapprehension, postmasters will be careful to explain this point fully to remitters and to payees.

Sec. 1049. Postmaster of New York Decides Coin Value of Currency.—When the international money-order and coupon are received by the postmaster at New York, the latter will stamp thereon the date of receipt, and insert the items to be filled in by him, viz: "Premium on gold the day of receipt at New York"; "Value of money-order in United States gold"; "Value of money-order in sterling"; "Date and number of list in which money-order was certified to the United Kingdom"; "Current number of certified money-order." When the coupon has been completed by the postmaster at New York, he will return it to the issuing postmaster, who will place it on file with the corresponding application for reference, in case the remitter of the money-order desires information as to the value thereof in gold when received at New York, the amount transmitted, or the date of transmission. It is expected that the issuing postmaster will cheerfully and promptly comply with a request of the remitter for information as to any of these points.

Sec. 1850. Lists of International Money-Orders.—It is the duty of the postmaster at New York to enter the particulars of each British international money-order issued in this country and received by him since his last previous dispatch to Great Britain in a blank form called a "List of international postal orders," which list he transmits by the next transatlantic mail to the exchange post-office at London, together with his certificate that the several amounts of these money-orders have been duly received in the United States for payment in the United Kingdom to the persons named in that list. He also forwards at the same time a money-order drawn by him, in sterling, in favor of and addressed to each payee mentioned in the list, which order the exchange office at London undertakes to send, free of postage, to the payee. The postmaster at New York, therefore, retains on file all international money-orders drawn on him by postmasters in the United States, but forwards to the United Kingdom a descriptive list thereof, together with corresponding money-orders, payable in sterling, made out by him in favor of the several beneficiaries. The exchange post-office at London, in like manner, transmits by each transatlantic mail to the postmaster at the exchange post-office at New York a similar list of international money-orders for sums received in the United Kingdom for payment to beneficiaries in the United States. The receiving exchange post-office at New York immediately issues a money-order in favor of each beneficiary for an amount in United States currency equivalent to that in gold mentioned in the certified list, which money-order is payable by the money-order post-office nearest his place of residence, and is transmitted to the postmaster at such post-office. It is provided by the Convention that each exchange post-office shall, in the certified lists, state the amounts of the money-orders in the denominations of the money of the dispatching and of the receiving country, and that, in the transaction of the international money-order business, the pound sterling of Great Britain shall be considered as equivalent in value to four dollars and eighty-six cents of the gold coin of the United States.

Sec. 1051. Payment of International Money-Orders.—Upon the receipt of an international money-order, issued by the postmaster at New York upon the postmaster of a money-order post-office in this country, the latter will enter the particulars thereof in his register of international money-orders received. He will then send a notification (Form No. 6704) to the payee to apply for payment of the order in person or by his duly authorized agent, who must file with the paying postmaster his written authority from the payee to receive payment of the money-order and execute a receipt therefor, and must prove his identity if required to do so. Such written authority, when given by a payee who does not reside within the delivery of the post-office of payment, should be executed in the presence of the postmaster of his locality, and should bear a certificate from the latter to that effect, as well as the impression of his post-office stamp. The date of payment must immediately be stamped upon the international money-order and likewise entered opposite the record thereof in the register, and the paid money-order must be forwarded to the Department as a voucher with the weekly statement of international money-order business.

Sec. 1052. Inquiry for Missing International Money-Order.—Should inquiry be made at the post-office for a money-order from Great Britain, notice of which had been received by the payee from the remitter, but which had not reached the postmaster, he will send a letter of inquiry upon the subject to the postmaster at New York. The latter, in case an international money-order had been drawn by him upon the postmaster in favor of the payee and had been lost in transmission, will take measures to furnish a duplicate thereof.

Sec. 1053. Repayment of International Money-Orders.—Whenever the remitter of an international money-order, payable in the United Kingdom, makes application to the issuing postmaster for repayment of the amount thereof, the latter should immediately communicate the fact to this Department, whereupon, if the money-order has not already been certified by the exchange post-office at New York to the exchange post-office at London for payment, the issuing postmaster will be authorized to repay the amount of such money-order. But if it has been so certified, this Department will notify the Postal Department of Great Britain that application has been made for its repayment, and, should it not have been paid in that country at the date of the receipt of the notification, it will be recertified to the exchange post-office at New York, in due course of business, for repayment. Authority will then be given the issuing postmaster to repay the same. All money-orders certified to the Postal Department of either country, which for any reason cannot be paid within twelve months from the month of issue, become invalid, and will be recertified to the country of issue for repayment, or other disposal, in accordance with the laws and regulations of that country. Postmasters will therefore take care to forward promptly to this Department all invalid money-orders of this kind, with their weekly statements containing a description thereof.

Sec. 1054. Issue of Duplicate International Money-Orders.—In case the postmaster who issues an international money-order does not receive, after a sufficient lapse of time, the corresponding coupon thereof, duly filled up and stamped by the postmaster at New York, the former should send him a letter of inquiry on the subject, with the request that, if the money-order had not been received at the exchange post-office at New York, the latter would transmit to the issuing post-office a certificate to that effect. Upon the receipt of such a document, the postmaster who issued the original should draw and transmit a new money-order in lieu thereof, for the same amount, and should write across its face, and across the coupon, in red ink, the words IN LIEU OF BRITISH INTERNATIONAL MONEY-ORDER NO. —, NOT RECEIVED BY THE POSTMASTER AT NEW YORK. The certificate of loss should be carefully filed, but it is not necessary to make out and deliver a second receipt to the remitter.

Sec. 1055. Money-Orders on Germany, Switzerland, and Italy.—The international post-office of exchange with the United States, on the part of the German Empire, is Cologne, and on the part of Switzerland, is Basle, and on the part of Italy, is Turin.

Sec. 1056. Fees for Money-Orders on Switzerland and Italy.—The foregoing instructions relative to the international money-order system between Great Britain and this country are, except as provided in section 1058, to be strictly followed by postmasters in the issue of international money-orders payable in Switzerland, Germany, or Italy, and in the payment of money-orders for sums delivered to the postal administration of either of those countries, for transmission to the United States. The fees or rates of commission for the issue of international money-orders, payable in Switzerland or Italy, are the same as are charged for issuing international money-orders on Great Britain.

Sec. 1057. Fees for Money-Orders on Germany.—The fees for the issue of international money-orders payable in Germany are as follows, viz: On money-orders not exceeding $5, 15 cents; over $5 and not exceeding $10, 25 cents; over $10 and not exceeding $20, 50 cents; over $20 and not exceeding $30, 75 cents; over $30 and not exceeding $40, $1; over $40 and not exceeding $50, $1.25.

Sec. 1058. Rules for Money-Orders on Germany, Switzerland, and Italy.—In the issue of international money-orders payable in Germany, Switzerland, or Italy, the mode of procedure differs from that described in section 1047 of the instructions relative to British international money-orders, in this respect, viz: The postmaster at New York transmits, at stated periods, to the exchange post-office at Cologne, or at Basle, or at Turin, as the case may require, a list of international money-orders, for sums received in the United States, for payment by either of those post-offices in their respective countries, but no money-orders are drawn by him in favor of and addressed to the payees, and transmitted to either of those exchange post-offices for delivery, in the manner detailed in section 1049. On the receipt of a "list" from New York by the exchange post-office at Cologne, at Basle, or at Turin, a domestic money-order is immediately issued in favor of each payee mentioned in the list, which order is payable at the money-order post-office nearest his place of residence, and is sent to him or to the postmaster at such post-office.

Sec. 1059. Interchange of Money-Orders with Canada.—The exchange of money-orders between the United States and Canada is to be effected through the agency of certain post-offices in the United States, selected for that purpose, to be known as "international exchange post-offices." Six such exchange post-offices have been agreed upon in the convention between the two countries, viz, Bangor, Me., Buffalo, N. Y., Detroit, Mich., Saint Paul, Minn., Portland, Oreg., Saint Albans, Vt.

Sec. 1060. Issue of Money-Orders on Canada and Newfoundland.—Certain other money-order post-offices in this country, specially selected for this service by the Postmaster-General, and to be known as "inland post-offices," in distinction from the exchange post-offices, are authorized to issue money-orders on any of the above-mentioned international exchange post-offices, payable to beneficiaries in the Dominion of Canada and in the province of Newfoundland, and to pay money-orders, properly certified by postmasters of such exchange post-offices, for sums remitted by postmasters in the Dominion of Canada and in the province of Newfoundland, for payment to beneficiaries in the United States; but each exchange post-office shall also be an inland post-office, the postmaster at which shall have the right to draw orders on his own or on any other exchange post-office for certification in the usual manner. Hence, a postmaster in either country cannot draw an international money-order, for an amount deposited with him, directly upon a postmaster in the other, but must draw the same upon some one of the designated "exchange post-offices" most convenient to the residence of the payee or beneficiary for whom the money is intended. An international money-order must not be drawn for a larger sum than fifty dollars in United States currency, and must not contain a fractional part of a cent. The fees for the issue of international money-orders are as follows, viz: On money-orders not exceeding $10, twenty cents; over $10 and not exceeding $20, forty cents; over $20 and not exceeding $30, sixty cents; over $30 and not exceeding $40, eighty cents; over $40 and not exceeding $50, one dollar. No other money can be received or paid for Canadian money-orders than that which is a legal tender, except national-bank notes.

Sec. 1061. Postmasters not to Decide Value of Currency in Canadian Money.—The Canadian dollar is equivalent in value to the gold dollar of the United States, but the issuing postmaster must not undertake to decide definitely upon the actual value, in United States gold coin (or Canadian money), of a certain sum in currency for which an international money-order is issued by him. He is at liberty, however, to advise the remitter as to its approximate value, which may be found to differ materially from the real value, as the latter is to be computed, on the day the order is received by the exchange post-office, upon the basis of the premium on gold in New York, as last advised by the postmaster of that city. Hence, this Department cannot undertake, on behalf of a remitter in this country, to pay a determinate sum in gold (or Canadian money) in the Dominion of Canada. As the premium on gold is variable, it is evident that an international money-order issued for a sum in United States currency may, when received at such "exchange post-office," yield a sum in gold greater or less than that considered at the post-office of issue as the equivalent of such money-order. For the same reason, the value in United States currency of a money-order in gold, when received for certification by any "exchange post-office," would depend upon the premium on gold in New York on the day of the receipt of the money-order, as shown by the last telegraphic advices from the postmaster thereof to such "exchange post-office." This Department, therefore, can only agree to cause payment to be made to a beneficiary in the Dominion of Canada of the gold value of any international money-order issued for an amount in United States currency, and to pay to a beneficiary in this country the currency value of an international money-order in gold from the Dominion of Canada. To guard against misapprehension, postmasters will be careful to explain this point fully to remitters and to payees.

Sec. 1062. Application for Canadian Money-Order.—A special form of application, form "No. 6401, Canadian," must be furnished to each applicant for an international money-order payable in the Dominion of Canada. On this form he must enter all the particulars of the amount, names, address, &c., and must state the full name and exact residence of the payee, giving the town or village and county. From the items contained in such application the (inland) issuing postmaster will fill up a Canadian international money-order, the advice of the same, the coupon, and the receipt, all of which, after having been properly dated, and stamped with the money-order stamp of his post-office, he will forward, without separating them, to the international exchange post-office nearest the residence of the payee, but he will not undertake to enter upon either of them the name of the post-office in the Dominion of Canada at which such money-order is to be paid. He will also fill up, detach, and deliver to the remitter of such money-order the certificate. Upon the return to him, from the exchange post-office, of the receipt "No. 12*d*," he will place the same on file in his post-office for reference, should the remitter apply for information as to the gold value of the money-order. He will also enter in his "combined register" of money-orders issued the particulars of such money-order, and the application must be retained on file at the issuing post-office.

Sec. 1063. Payment of Canadian Money-Orders.—When a money-order, drawn by a postmaster in the Dominion of Canada, and properly numbered, dated, certified, stamped, signed, and addressed to him by the postmaster a ta duly-authorized international exchange post-office, is presented for payment to the postmaster of an inland post-office, authorized to transact Canadian business, he will compare such money-order with the corresponding advice, which should previously have been received by him, and after having satisfied himself, in the manner required for domestic money-orders (see sections 1013 to 1044, inclusive), that both the advice and money-order are correct, and that the person presenting the money-order is legally entitled to receive the amount due thereon, he will pay the same, and will enter all such paid money-orders upon his combined weekly statement. The postmaster issuing a Canadian money-order should be careful to instruct the sender thereof that he "should at once inform the payee, in Canada, of the full name and address of the remitter," inasmuch as payment thereof cannot be obtained unless the payee is able to furnish that information to the paying postmaster. All applications for duplicates of lost or missing advices, or for corrections of advices, must be made to the exchange postmaster by whom such advices were certified. Postmasters, however, must refuse to issue a money-order payable to any person, if the surname of that person, and his given name or names, or at least the initial letters thereof, are not furnished by the applicant.

Sec. 1034. Daily Reports of Premium on Gold to be Filed.—The postmaster at New York, N. Y., will telegraph at 3 p. m. daily, except Sunday, the rate of premium on gold at that hour in New York to each of the exchange post-offices designated for the certification of international money-orders to and from Canada; and postmasters at exchange post-offices are required to keep on file in their post-offices the telegrams received daily from New York concerning the premium on gold.

Sec. 1035. Canadian Money-Orders to be Stamped at Exchange-Offices.—The postmaster at each of said international exchange post-offices will, whenever he receives a money-order with its corresponding "advice," "coupon," and "receipt," stamp, at once, upon each of these papers the current international number and the date of its receipt at his post-office. He will also enter therein the value of the same in gold (or Canadian currency), if such money-order originated in the United States, or its value in United States currency, if it originated in the Dominion of Canada, as ascertained by calculation, upon the basis of the last telegram received by him from the postmaster at New York, and the name of the post-office in the Dominion of Canada or in the United States, as the case may be, at which he desires the same to be paid, which should be the post-office nearest the residence of the payee or most accessible by him. He will then forward the money-order, inclosed in an envelope, to the payee, and the advice to the postmaster instructed to pay the money-order, and will send back the receipt to the issuing postmaster, but will retain the coupon on file in his post-office for future reference. At the close of each week he will make up, in duplicate, from the coupons on file in his post-office a "weekly list of international money-orders" issued in the United States which have been certified by him during the week for payment in the Dominion of Canada, and "weekly list of international money-orders" issued in the Dominion of Canada which have been certified by him during the week for payment in the United States, and will forward such duplicate "lists," with his weekly statement, to the Superintendent of the Money-Order System at Washington, D. C. He will also furnish, upon the application of postmasters drawn upon, duplicates of lost advices, which must be made up from the corresponding coupons on file in his post-office. When the postmaster at an exchange post-office receives an application from a paying postmaster for a corrected advice, the former will, if necessary, apply to the issuing postmaster for precise information in the premises, and will communicate the same to the postmaster at the post-office of payment.

Sec. 1066. Repayment of Canadian Money-Orders.—When a remitter of an international money-order, payable in the Dominion of Canada or in the United States, makes application to the issuing postmaster for repayment of the amount thereof, the latter should immediately communicate the fact to the postmaster of the exchange post-office on which it was drawn, whereupon, if he has not already certified and forwarded the money-order to the payee, and the advice to the paying postmaster, he will return them to the issuing postmaster for repayment. But if the money-order (in case it is payable in the Dominion of Canada) has been so certified, the issuing postmaster, upon the receipt of notice to that effect from the exchange post-office, will apply to the Superintendent of the Money-Order System at Washington, D. C., for repayment, who will notify the Canadian Postal Department of such application, and request authority for repayment of the money-order. When that authority is received by him, notice will at once be sent to the issuing postmaster to repay the amount of the money-order.

Sec. 1067. Invalid Canadian Money-Orders.—All money-orders certified for payment in either country, which for any reason cannot be paid within twelve months after the month of issue become invalid, and will be recertified to the country of issue for repayment or other disposal in accordance with the laws and regulations of that country. Postmasters will therefore take care to forward promptly to this Department the advices of all invalid money-orders of this kind with their weekly statements and a description thereof.

Sec. 1068. Inquiries about Canadian Money-Orders.—All inquiries from inland postmasters in the United States concerning the issue or the payment in Canada of international money-orders should be addressed to the postmaster of the exchange post-office by whom such money-orders were certified.

Sec. 1069. Issue of Duplicate Canadian Money-Orders.—In case the postmaster who issues an international money-order does not receive, after a sufficient lapse of time, the corresponding receipt thereof, duly filled up and stamped by the postmaster at the exchange post-office drawn upon, the former should send him a letter of inquiry on the subject, with the request that if the money-order and advice have not been received at the exchange post-office the latter would transmit to the issuing post-office, and also to the Superintendent of the Money-Order System at Washington, D. C., a certificate to that effect. Upon the receipt of such a document, the postmaster who issued the originals should at once draw upon and transmit to the same exchange post-office a new money-order, advice, coupon, and receipt in lieu thereof for a like amount, after having written across the face of each of them in red ink the words IN LIEU OF CANADIAN MONEY-ORDER NO. —, NOT RECEIVED BY THE POSTMASTER AT ——— EXCHANGE POST-OFFICE. The certificate of non-receipt should be carefully filed by the issuing postmaster, but it is not necessary for him to furnish remitter with a second receipt. Great caution should be exercised by postmasters at exchange post-offices in certifying such money-orders, as they will be held responsible for all double payments that may occur through their negligence.

Sec. 1070. General Rules for International Money-Order Business.—Postmasters will receive as compensation for transacting international money-order business one fourth of one per cent. on the gross amount of international money-orders issued and paid, and the domestic money-order regulations in regard to incidental expenses and to the transfer of funds and blanks from a late to a newly appointed postmaster are to be followed in the transaction of all international money-order business.

Sec. 1071. When Gold and Paper are at Par.—While the gold coin and the paper currency of the United States are of equal commercial value, so much of those regulations as is based upon the existence of a difference in their value is void and of no effect.

CHAPTER FIVE.

MONEY-ORDER FUNDS AND ACCOUNTS.

Sec. 1072. Transfer of Money-Order Funds.—All payments and transfers to and from money-order offices shall be under the direction of the Postmaster-General. He may transfer money-order funds from one postmaster to another, and from the postal revenue to the money-order funds: and he may transfer money-order funds to creditors of the Department, to be replaced by equivalent transfers from the postal revenues. (R. S., § 4042.)

Sec. 1073. Transfer by Warrant to Money-Order Funds.—The Postmaster-General may transfer to the postmaster at any money-order office, by warrant on the Treasury, countersigned by the [Sixth] Auditor [of the Treasury for the Post Office Department], and payable out of the postal revenues, such sum as may be required over and above the current revenues at his office to pay the money-orders drawn upon him. (R. S., § 4043.)

Sec. 1074. What are Money-Order Funds.—All money received for the sale of money-orders, including all fees thereon, all money transferred from the postal revenues to the money-order funds, all money transferred or paid from the money-order funds to the service of the Post-Office Department, and all money-order funds transferred from one postmaster to another, shall be deemed and taken to be money-order funds and money in the Treasury of the United States. And it shall be the duty of the assistant treasurer of the United States to open, at the request of the Postmaster-General, an account of "money-order funds" deposited by postmasters to the credit of the Postmaster-General, and of drafts against the amount so deposited, drawn by him and countersigned by the [Sixth] Auditor [of the Treasury for the Post-Office Department.] (R. S., § 4045.)

Sec. 1075. Postmasters' Weekly Reports of Money-Order Funds.—The Postmaster-General shall require each postmaster at a money-order office to render to the Post-Office Department weekly, semi-weekly, or daily accounts of all money-orders issued and paid; of all fees received for issuing them; of all transfers and payments made from money-order funds; and of all money received to be used for the payment of money-orders or on account of money-order business. (R. S., § 4044.)

Sec. 1076. Embezzlement of Money-Order Funds, Penalty, Explanation.—Every postmaster, assistant, clerk, or other person employed in or connected with the business or operations of any money-order office who converts to his own use, in any way whatever, or loans, or deposits in any bank, except as authorized by this Title, or exchanges for other funds, any portion of the money-order funds, shall be deemed guilty of embezzlement; and any such person, as well as every other person advising or participating therein, shall, for every such offense, be imprisoned for not less than six months nor more than ten years, and be fined in a sum equal to the amount embezzled; and any failure to pay over or produce any money-order funds intrusted to such person shall be taken to be prima-facie evidence of embezzlement; and upon the trial of any indictment against any person for such embezzlement, it shall be prima-facie evidence of a balance against him to produce a transcript from the money-order account-books of the [Sixth] Auditor [of the Treasury for the Post-Office Department]. But nothing herein contained shall be construed to prohibit any postmaster depositing, under the direction of the Postmaster-General, in a national bank designated by the Secretary of the Treasury for that purpose, to his own credit as postmaster, any money-order or other funds in his charge, nor prevent his negotiating drafts or other evidences of debt through such bank, or through United States disbursing officers, or otherwise, when instructed or required to do so by the Postmaster-General, for the purpose of remitting surplus money-order funds from one post-office to another, to be used in payment of money-orders. Disbursing officers of the United States shall issue, under regulations to be prescribed by the Secretary of the Treasury, duplicates of lost checks drawn by them in favor of any postmaster on account of money-order or other public funds received by them from some other postmaster. (R. S., § 4046.)

Sec. 1077. How to Write up the Cash-Book.—In writing up the cash-book, the balance will first be brought forward. Then, on the debit side must be entered the amount received upon a draft drawn by the postmaster under authority of the Postmaster-General's credit, the amount received for premium upon the same, the amount received on deposit from other postmasters, and the amount transferred from the postage to the money-order account, should any of these transactions have taken place; then the amount received from the issue of money-orders, the amount of fees thereupon, and, lastly, the balance, should there be one. The credit side must embrace the amount transferred to the postage account, the amount remitted or deposited, the amount paid on account of incidental expenses (such as clerk-hire, stationery, etc.), and the amount repaid on money-orders, should any of these transactions have taken place; then the amount paid for money-orders drawn upon the post-office, and, lastly, the balance. The cash-book must be written up and balanced daily at every post-office.

FORM OF CASH-BOOK.

——— ———, postmaster at ———, in account with the money-order office, Post-Office Department, the ——— day of ———, 187—.

DR.			CR.		
To balance brought forward...........	$40	60	By amount paid for money-orders drawn on this office..................	$250	
To amount transferred from postage account..................................	100	00	By certificate of deposit, No. —........	00	
To amount received for money-orders issued, No. — to No. —, inclusive	118	22			
To amount of fees upon same..........	.....	90	By balance..........................	9	72
	259	72		259	72

Sec. 1078. Transferring Postage Funds to Money-Order Account.—It is to be expected that occasionally at some post-offices the postmaster will be called upon to pay money-orders to an amount exceeding that of the money-order funds in his hands. In every such event he will transfer from the postage to the money-order account a sum of money large enough to enable him to pay these orders. In case the postage funds are insufficient for such transfer the postmaster will transfer as large an amount as practicable (provided it be sufficient to pay even one money-order), and must immediately notify the Department (see Form No. 6034), when he will be furnished with a draft for the amount required. Should the payments at any post-office continue to exceed the receipts thereat, the postmaster at such post-office will be furnished with a letter of credit, to be used only when absolutely required for the payment of money-orders.

Sec. 1079. Entry of Transferred Funds in Cash-Book.—In making a transfer of funds (which must in all cases consist of complete dollars only, the introduction of cents into transfers being prohibited), if from the "postage" to the "money-order" account, postmasters will first take credit for the amount of said transfer in their general account with the Post-Office Department. They will then debit themselves therewith in the money-order cash-book, and enter the transaction under its proper head in the weekly statement following such transfer. If from the "money-order" to the "postage" account, the amount must be entered on the credit side of the money-order cash-book and a corresponding entry made on the debit side of the general account, the transfer to be noted in the weekly statement as before. A notification (Form 6024) is, in all cases, to be forwarded to the Superintendent of the Money-Order System immediately after a transfer of funds from either account. A transfer from the money-order to the postage account is only to be made when expressly directed by the Department. No entry of a transfer to the money-order account should be made by a postmaster in his quarterly account of postal business. The proper credit for such transfers will be allowed him by the Auditor upon the settlement of his postal accounts. In order to avoid mistakes the strictest attention should be given to the directions contained in this section.

Sec. 1080. The Fixed Reserve.—At certain money-order post-offices the fluctuating character of the business makes it necessary that a limited sum of money be kept constantly on hand to insure the prompt payment of money-orders when presented. This sum is specified in each instance by direction of the Postmaster-General, and is known as the "fixed reserve." Its amount is determined by the nature and extent of the business of the post-office to which it is allowed, and may be changed from time to time by order of the Department.

Sec. 1081. Daily Remittance of Money-Order Funds.—The money-order accounts must be kept separately from all other accounts, and must be adjusted at the close of each day's business, in order that the balance of money-order funds on hand may be accurately ascertained. Every dollar of money-order funds, in excess of a sum equal to the amount of the unpaid advices on hand less than two weeks, must be remitted daily to the designated post-office of the first class, where the postmaster shall have been instructed to make his deposits; but postmasters to whom a "fixed reserve" is allowed may retain the amount of the "fixed reserve," and no more, except when the amount of such unpaid advices exceeds the "fixed reserve," in which event the postmaster may retain a sum which, when added to the "fixed reserve," will equal the amount of his unpaid advices on hand less than two weeks. For instance, suppose the postmaster's fixed reserve is $100, and that he has advices on hand less than two weeks to the amount of $175; in this case he will be at liberty to withhold from deposit only $75 in addition to his fixed reserve of $100. He will thus have $175 to meet the amount of such unpaid advices.

In the total of unpaid advices on hand less than two weeks is to be included the amount of money-orders, payment of which has been refused, for the reason that the corresponding advices have not been received, but for which second advices have been requested from the issuing postmaster by the postmaster drawn upon.

Sec. 1082. Receipts for Daily Remittances.—The postmaster at the post-office of the first class who receives these deposits will fill up and number consecutively certificates therefor in duplicate, one of which he will transmit to the Superintendent of the Money-Order System, and the other to the depositing postmaster, who will take credit therefor in his weekly statement, entering therein its proper number, date, and amount.

Sec. 1083. No Credit for Remittances until Receipt is Obtained.—Postmasters are prohibited from taking credit in their money-order cash-books or in their weekly statements for the amount of any remittance until they shall have received a certificate of deposit therefor from the designated post-office of the first class to which it was sent. The amount of each remittance for which no certificate has been received, must appear in the money-order cash-book and in the summary of the weekly statement, as a part of the "cash balance on hand," exactly as though no remittance had been made; but it should be entered with its proper date in the blank space, provided for such entries, at the bottom of the weekly statement. A failure to comply with this requirement will be deemed sufficient cause for the removal of the offending postmaster.

Sec. 1084. Daily Reports of Remittances Received.—Postmasters at all money-order offices of the first class are required to forward daily to the Superintendent of the Money-Order System a list of the remittances received by them during the day, by which means the Superintendent is enabled to know precisely the exact date and amount of each remittance of money-order funds made in the United States.

Sec. 1085. Postmasters must Remit and Deposit Promptly.—The dates of the issues of the several money-orders, and also of the deposits, entered in the weekly statements, will clearly show to the Department when the moneys received for such issues and deposits should have been remitted; and postmasters will be held strictly accountable for any failure to remit or to deposit promptly in obedience to these instructions

Sec. 1086. Unpaid Advices Less than Two Weeks Old in Weekly Statements.

Every postmaster is required, in making up his weekly statements, to enumerate, in detail, carefully and accurately, all the unpaid advices which have been in his hands less than two weeks, but he will take no account whatever of unpaid advices that have been on hand two weeks or more. If there is not space enough to include in the weekly statement all the unpaid advices on hand less than two weeks, he will enter only the aggregate amount thereof, but will make a detailed enumeration of these advices on a separate paper, which must be inclosed with the weekly statement, as a voucher for funds withheld from deposit. A blank form for this enumeration of advices will be furnished postmasters who need it, on application to the Department. Postmasters who fail to comply with these requirements will be considered as having improperly withheld the money. In case no unpaid advices are on hand at the close of the week, the fact should be noted in the statement by writing the words NONE ON HAND, under the proper heading.

Sec. 1087. Money-Order Funds not Subject to Rules of Postal Funds.—Postmasters will take notice that the standing instructions which they may receive from the Post-Office Department with respect to the disposal of quarterly balances arising from the sale of postage-stamps, stamped envelopes, etc., due from them to the United States, do not apply to money-order funds in their hands, but only to postal funds.

Sec. 1088. Weekly Statements, how Transmitted.—The weekly statement for each week, together with all vouchers and other papers appertaining thereto, and all correspondence with the Post-Office Department relative to the money-order business, must be addressed to the "SUPERINTENDENT OF THE MONEY-ORDER SYSTEM, WASHINGTON, D. C." It is desirable that each communication should relate to one subject only, and that a memorandum should be written on each envelope stating the nature of its contents.

Sec. 1089. Money-Order Cash must be Kept Separately.—Postmasters should keep their money-order cash apart from all other cash whatsoever, and with this view a special drawer should be provided for it. All receipts of cash on money-order account, whether for money-orders issued and for fees for remittances from other postmasters, or for postage-money transferred, should be deposited therein; and all disbursements, whether payments of money-orders, remittances made to other postmasters, or transfers to postage account, should be made therefrom.

Sec. 1090. Weekly Statements to be Numbered Consecutively.—Postmasters must not fail to number their weekly statements consecutively, beginning with No. 1 for the first statement made in the month of January of each year. The greatest care must be taken to write the names of the remitters and payees of the money-orders so plainly in the statements that they may be easily read.

Sec. 1091. Make up Weekly Statements Every Saturday.—On Saturday evening of each week every postmaster will make up his weekly statement, being careful to state therein all the particulars required by the headings, and to compare the several items with those contained in the registers and cash-book before the statement is forwarded to the Superintendent of the Money-Order System, which must be done by the first mail after the accounts of the week have been closed.

Sec. 1092. Statements of "No Business."—If no business has been transacted during the week the postmaster will be required to send forward the usual form, with a statement of the last balance, and the words NO BUSINESS written across the face of the blank. Copies of the weekly statement should not be retained by the postmaster.

Sec. 1093. Weekly Statements at Close of Quarter.—Postmasters will be careful to enter into their weekly statements neither more nor less than the transactions of one week, and the week must be understood to commence on Monday and to end on Saturday. But at the expiration of each quarter of the year, viz. 31st March, 30th June, 30th September, and 31st December, should either of these days not fall on Saturday or Sunday, a statement must be made up and forwarded of the business transacted from the last Saturday but one in the month, up to the close of the last day of that month and quarter. The next succeeding statement must embrace all the business transacted since the first day of the first month of the next quarter up to the close of the second Saturday of said month. For example, the 30th of September, 1879, falls on Tuesday; hence no statement is to be made on Saturday, the 27th of that month, but a statement must be made on Tuesday, the last day of the month, to include all the business transacted since Saturday, the 20th of the month. In like manner, no statement should be made on Saturday, October 4, 1879, but the statement of the next Saturday, October 11, must embrace all the business transacted since the first day of that month. The object of this regulation is to facilitate the quarterly settlement of the accounts of postmasters, and also to dispense with statements for fractional parts of a week.

Form of summary on weekly statement.

Summary of the week's business.

Date.	Dr.	For use by the post-master.	For use at the Department.
May 3	Balance from statement No. 16	$251 45	
	To cash from orders issued, No. 313 to No. 354, inc	120 20	
	To cash received for fees on the same	1 70	
	To amount of my draft No. on postmaster at N. Y		
	To amount of my draft No. on postmaster at N. Y		
	To amount of my draft No. on postmaster at N. Y		
	To amount of my premium on drafts		
	To cash this day transferred from postage account		
	To cash this day transferred from postage account		
	To cash this day transferred from postage account		
	To cash this day transferred from postage account		
	To cash this day transferred from postage account		
	To cash this day transferred from postage account		
	To errors as per Auditor's circular of , 187		
		376 35	

Date.	Cr.		For use by the post-master.	For use at the Department.
May 3	By 2 orders paid		$10 25	
	By Money-Order No. 324, repaid	$1 00		
	By Money-Order No. 325, repaid	2 00	3 00	
	By Money-Order No. , repaid			
	By cash deposited at , as follows:			
" 6	Certificate No. 7482, amount	$42 00		
7	Certificate No. 7510, amount	50 00		
" 8	Certificate No. 7563, amount	24 00		
" 9	Certificate No. 7608, amount	16 00	132 00	
	Certificate No. , amount			
	Certificate No. , amount			
	By cash paid incidental expenses, as per voucher herewith			
	By cash transferred to postage account			
	By errors as per Auditor's circular of , 187			
	By commissions, as allowed, for the quarter ended			
" 10	By cash on hand at close of the week		231 10	
			376 35	

Advices, on hand not more than two weeks of orders drawn upon this office and not yet presented for payment.

Date of order.	No.	Where issued.		Amount.
		Post-office.	State.	
May 7	6311	Albany	N. Y.	$15 00
May 8	2316	Joliet	Ill	22 00
		Total		37 00

Memorandum of deposits for which credit has not yet been taken:
May 9, 1879. Remitted to P. M. at New York, $100.
May 10, 1879. Remitted at P. M. at New York, $ 91.
, 187 . Will remit to P. M. at $

IMPORTANT.—Postmasters are strictly required to make their deposits in compliance with section 1081 of the Postal Laws and Regulations. In depositing, cents must be omitted.

———, *Postmaster.*

Sec. 1094. Vouchers to Accompany Weekly Statements.—The paid, repaid, and "not issued" money-orders, and the vouchers for incidental expenses must invariably accompany the statements, which will not be considered complete without them.

Postmasters at first-class post-offices are required to send with each weekly statement a transcript of their cash account for the week (Form No. 6018), giving therein the business of each day in detail. Postmasters who remit their surplus money-order funds to the postmaster at San Francisco, Cal., are required to send him a similar transcript, using Form No. 6020, and those who deposit at Portland, Oreg., must forward such transcripts weekly to the postmaster of that city.

Sec. 1095. Credits Allowed on New York.—Whenever it is found necessary, in order to prevent delay or embarrassment in the payment of money-orders, the postmasters at certain post-offices will be allowed a credit for a specific amount with the postmaster at New York, or at some other first-class post-office designated for the purpose, which credit will be used in the following manner: When at any post-office having such credit the funds arising from the money-order business are insufficient to pay the money-orders presented, the postmaster will thereupon be permitted to draw a draft, payable to his own order, against the amount placed to his credit, for such a sum, and no more as may be necessary to meet the requirements of the case. It is therefore apparent that this credit must be drawn by installments; for example, $100, $200, etc., as may be required, and not in one gross sum. The amounts so drawn from time to time must be entered by the postmaster to his debit in the cash-book upon the day they are drawn, and also in the weekly statement. Should the amount of money-orders paid at any one of these post-offices continue to exceed considerably the amount of money-orders issued, this credit will, of course, become exhausted. In that event the postmaster having a credit should make timely application to the Superintendent of the Money-Order System for a renewal thereof (Form No. 6035).

Sec. 1096. Drafts against Credits, how Made.—Special drafts will be supplied to postmasters having these credits, who, in the margin provided for their own use, will state the amount of the credit, and enter and deduct from it the amount drawn by the corresponding draft, by which means they will be constantly reminded of the condition of the fund. Each of these drafts bears a coupon, which the postmaster drawing the draft will fill up, date, and sign, and which the postmaster at the post-office drawn upon will transmit to the Superintendent of the Money-Order System whenever the draft is paid. It rarely happens that any difficulty is experienced by a postmaster in negotiating a draft of this description. For this purpose a form of indorsement is printed upon the back. Should he be unable to obtain the amount of such draft in his vicinity, he will promptly notify the Department. In the negotiation of these drafts, the postmaster is not at liberty to receive any money that is not a legal tender, except national-bank notes, inasmuch as he is prohibited from paying out any other money for money-orders presented. If a premium be received for a draft, the postmaster must charge himself therewith.

Sec. 1097. Special Drafts for Emergencies.—In case of special exigency, where assistance is needed at a post-office the business of which does not require a standing credit, a draft for a designated sum sufficient to meet the unpaid advices will be sent upon application to the Superintendent of the Money-Order System.

Sec. 1098. Drafts must always be on Forms Furnished.—Postmasters are prohibited from drawing drafts in manuscript or upon any other forms than those supplied by the Department, and they must invariably sign the drafts themselves, except in the cases mentioned in section 952.

Sec. 1099. Special Instructions about Remittances.—The postmaster at every money-order post-office will make the deposits required by these instructions (see section 1081) by transmitting the amount to be deposited in a registered package addressed to the postmaster of the post-office named as his depository. Inclosed in this package he will also send a letter (Form 6021), giving in detail an accurate description of the money therein remitted. For the sake of convenience and security, the notes remitted should be of the highest denominations procurable, and the postmaster must keep an exact record of the series, numbers, denominations, and dates of all notes remitted by him in compliance with these instructions. In every case of a remittance of money-order funds made by means of paper money, sent through the mails, the postmaster should be able to prove by at least one disinterested witness, who should, if practicable, be a person not employed in his post-office, that the money was actually inclosed in a properly registered package, addressed to the postmaster at the post-office of the first class, designated to receive the deposit, and furthermore, that said package, with the money inclosed therein, was securely locked in the mail-pouch, and was taken from the post-office out of the postmaster's possession by the contractor, employé of the railway-mail service, mail-carrier, or other person duly authorized to dispatch the same to destination. Should the remitting postmaster fail to comply with the foregoing instructions, he will be required, if the money is lost, to make good the amount. If the remitting postmaster does not receive in due time an acknowledgment of the receipt of the registered package and a certificate of deposit for its contents, he will report the fact to the nearest Special Agent and to the Superintendent of the Money-Order System. These deposits may likewise be made by means of drafts drawn by one national bank upon another national bank of the locality where the first-class post-office named as the depository is situated, provided such drafts can be obtained without cost. Postmasters are instructed that the unauthorized use of any portion of the money-order funds, for which they are accountable, or any failure to remit, or to pay over their surplus money-order funds to the person duly authorized by the Postmaster-General to receive the same, will subject them to the penalties prescribed by law for such offenses. If a remittance of surplus money-order funds should contain any notes which appear to the receiving postmaster to be counterfeit, he should submit such notes to the nearest assistant treasurer of the United States, or to the proper officer of any national bank, for examination, who will, in accordance with instructions from the Treasury, stamp or brand the notes as counterfeit if they should prove to be so. They should then be returned, with a certificate of deposit for the remainder of the remittance, to the postmaster who forwarded them. In case a remittance should contain any notes or drafts, other than those of national banks, the receiving postmaster should report the fact to the Superintendent of the Money-Order System.

Sec. 1100. Postmasters may Deposit in National Banks, when.—Postmasters are also strictly prohibited by law from depositing money-order funds in their charge in any bank except a national bank. See section 73.

Sec. 1101. Importance of Promptly Transmitting Weekly Statements.—Negligence or delay in transmitting the weekly statements, forwarding advices, or in remitting funds for deposit, according to instructions, are serious obstacles to the successful working of the money-order system, and postmasters must be cautious in these respects. As intimated elsewhere, the withholding of money in violation of the regulations, and the illegal use thereof, will subject the offender to severe penalties.

TITLE VII.

EXCHANGE OF CORRESPONDENCE WITH FOREIGN COUNTRIES.

CHAPTER ONE.

THE UNIVERSAL POSTAL UNION.

Sec. 1102. The Convention of Paris.—Universal Postal Union concluded between Germany, the Argentine Republic, Austria-Hungary, Belgium, Brazil, Denmark and the Danish Colonies, Egypt, Spain and the Spanish Colonies, the United States of North America, France and the French Colonies, Great Britain and certain British Colonies, British India, Canada, Greece, Italy, Japan, Luxemburg, Mexico, Montenegro, Norway, the Netherlands and the Netherland Colonies, Peru, Persia, Portugal and the Portuguese Colonies, Roumania, Russia, Servia, Salvador, Sweden, Switzerland, and Turkey.

CONVENTION.

The undersigned, plenipotentiaries of the governments of the countries above enumerated, being assembled in congress at Paris, by virtue of Article 18 of the Treaty constituting the General Postal Union, concluded at Berne on the 9th of October, 1874, have, by mutual agreement, and subject to ratification, revised the said Treaty, conformably to the following stipulations:

ARTICLE 1.

The countries between which the present Convention is concluded, as well as those which may join it hereafter, form, under the title of *Universal Postal Union*, a single postal territory for the reciprocal exchange of correspondence between their post-offices.

ARTICLE 2.

The stipulations of this Convention extend to letters, post-cards, printed matter of all kinds, commercial documents and samples of merchandise, originating in one of the countries of the Union and intended for another of those countries. They also apply, so far as regards conveyance within the Union, to the exchange by mail of the articles above mentioned between the countries of the Union and countries foreign to the Union, whenever that exchange makes use of the services of two of the contracting parties at least.

ARTICLE 3.

The Postal Administrations of neighboring countries, or countries able to correspond directly with each other without using the intermediary of the services of a third Administration, determine, by mutual agreement, the conditions of the conveyance of their reciprocal mails across the frontier, or from one frontier to the other.

Unless there be a contrary arrangement, the direct sea conveyance performed between two countries by means of packets or vessels depending upon one of them, shall be considered as a third service; and such conveyance, as well as any performed between two offices of the same country, by the intermediary of maritime or territorial services maintained by another country, is regulated by the stipulations of the following article.

ARTICLE 4.

The right of transit is guaranteed throughout the entire territory of the Union.

Consequently, the several Postal Administrations of the Union may send reciprocally through the intermediary of one or of several of them, as well closed mails as correspondence in open mails, according to the requirements of trade and the convenience of the postal service.

The correspondence exchanged, whether in open or in closed mails, between two administrations of the Union, by means of the services of one or of several other administrations of the Union, is subject to the following transit charges, to be paid to each of the countries traversed, or whose services participate in the conveyance, viz:

1st. For territorial conveyance, 2 francs per kilogramme of letters or post-cards, and 25 centimes per kilogramme of other articles;

2d. For sea conveyance, 15 francs per kilogramme of letters or post-cards, and 1 franc per kilogramme of other articles;

It is, however, understood—

1st. That wherever the transit is already gratuitous at present, or subject to more advantageous conditions, such condition is maintained, except in the case provided for in paragraph 3, following:

2d. That wherever the rate of sea-transit has hitherto been fixed at 6 francs 50 centimes per kilogramme of letters or post-cards, such rate is reduced to 5 francs;

3d. That every sea-conveyance not exceeding 300 nautical miles is gratuitous if the administration concerned is already entitled, on account of mails or correspondence benefiting by this conveyance, to the remuneration applicable to the territorial transit; in the contrary case payment is made at the rate of 2 francs per kilogramme of letters or post-cards, and 25 centimes per kilogramme of other articles;

4th. That in the case of sea-conveyance effected by two or more administrations, the expenses of the entire transportation cannot exceed 15 francs per kilogramme of letters or post-cards, and 1 franc per kilogramme of other articles. These expenses are in such case shared between the administrations *pro rata* for the distances traversed, without prejudice to other arrangements between the parties interested;

5th. That the rates specified in the present article do not apply either to conveyance by means of services depending upon administrations foreign to the Union, or to conveyance within the Union by means of extraordinary services specially established or maintained by one administration in the interest or at the request of one or several other administrations. The conditions of these two categories of conveyance are regulated by mutual agreement between the administrations interested.

The expenses of transit are borne by the administration of the country of origin.

The general settlement of these expenses takes place on the basis of statements prepared every two years, during a month to be determined on in the Regulation of Execution referred to in Article 14 hereafter.

The correspondence of the postal administrations with each other, articles reforwarded or missent, undeliverable articles, acknowledgments of delivery, post-office money-orders or advices of the issue of orders, and all documents relative to the postal service, are exempt from all transit charges, whether territorial or maritime.

Article 5.

The rates of postage for the conveyance of postal articles throughout the entire extent of the Union, including their delivery at the residence of the addressees in the countries of the Union where a delivery service is or shall be organized, are fixed as follows:

1st. For letters, 25 centimes in case of prepayment, and double that amount in the contrary case, for each letter and for every weight of 15 grammes or fraction of 15 grammes;

2d. For post-cards, 10 centimes per card;

3d. For printed matter of every kind, commercial papers, and samples of merchandise, 5 centimes for each article or packet bearing a particular address; and for every weight of 50 grammes or fraction of 50 grammes, provided that such article or package does not contain any letter or manuscript note having the character of an actual and personal correspondence, and that it be made up in such a manner as to admit of its being easily examined.

The charge on commercial papers cannot be less than 25 centimes per packet, and the charge on samples cannot be less than 10 centimes per packet.

In addition to the rates and minima fixed by the preceding paragraphs, there may be levied:

1st. For every article subjected to the sea transit rates of 15 francs per kilogramme of letters or post-cards and 1 franc per kilogramme of other articles, an additional charge, which may not exceed 25 centimes per single rate for letters, 5 centimes per post-card, and 5 centimes per 50 grammes or fraction of 50 grammes for other articles. As a temporary arrangement, there may be levied an additional charge up to 10 centimes per single rate for the letters subjected to the transit rate of 5 francs per kilogramme.

2d. For every article conveyed by services maintained by administrations foreign to the Union, or conveyed by extraordinary services in the Union giving rise to special expenses, an additional charge in proportion to these expenses.

In case of insufficient prepayment, articles of correspondence of all kinds are liable to a charge equal to double the amount of the deficiency, to be paid by the addressees.

Circulation shall not be given—

1st. To articles other than letters which are not prepaid at least partly, or which do not fulfill the conditions required above in order to enjoy the reduced rate;

2d. To articles of a nature likely to soil or injure the correspondence;

3d. To packets of samples of merchandise which have a salable value, or which exceed 250 grammes in weight, or measure more than 20 centimeters in length, 10 in breadth, and 5 in depth.

4th. Lastly, to packets of commercial papers and printed matter of all kinds, the weight of which exceeds 2 kilogrammes.

ARTICLE 6.

The articles specified in Article 5 may be registered.

Every registered article is liable, at the charge of the sender—

1st. To the ordinary prepaid rate of postage upon the article, according to its nature;

2d. To a fixed registration fee of 25 centimes at the maximum in the European states, and of 50 centimes at the maximum in the other countries, including the issue to the sender of a bulletin of posting.

The sender of a registered article may obtain an acknowledgment of delivery of such article by paying in advance a fixed fee of 25 centimes at the maximum.

In case of the loss of a registered article, and except in case of *force majeure*, there is to be paid an indemnity of 50 francs to the sender, or, at his request, to the addressee, by the administration upon whose territory or in whose maritime service the loss has occurred; that is to say, where the trace of the article has ceased.

As a temporary measure, the administrations of the countries beyond Europe, whose legislation is at present opposed to the principle of responsibility, are permitted to postpone the application of the preceding clause until the time when they shall have obtained from the legislative power authority to subscribe to it. Up to that time, the other administrations of the Union are not bound to pay an indemnity for the loss, in their respective services, of registered articles addressed to or originating in the said countries.

If it is impossible to discover the service in which the loss has occurred, the indemnity is borne in equal proportions between the two corresponding offices.

Payment of this indemnity is made with the least possible delay, and, at the latest, within a year dating from the day of application.

Every claim for an indemnity is excluded if it has not been made within one year from the date on which the registered article was posted.

ARTICLE 7.

Those countries of the Union which have not the franc for their monetary unit fix their postages at the equivalent in their respective currencies of the rates determined by Articles 5 and 6 preceding. Such countries have the option of rounding off the fractions in conformity with the table inserted in the regulation of execution mentioned in Article 14 of the present Convention.

ARTICLE 8.

Prepayment of postage on every description of article can be effected only by means of postage-stamps valid in the country of origin for the correspondence of private individuals.

Official correspondence relative to the postal service, and exchanged between the postal administrations, is alone exempt from this obligation and admitted free.

ARTICLE 9.

Each administration keeps the whole of the sums which it has collected in execution of the foregoing Articles 5, 6, 7, and 8. Consequently, there is no necessity on this head for any accounts between the several administrations of the Union.

Neither the senders nor the addressees of letters and other postal articles are called upon to pay, either in the country of origin or in that of destination, any postage or any postal fee other than those contemplated by the articles above mentioned.

ARTICLE 10.

No additional charge is levied for the reforwarding of postal matter within the interior of the Union.

ARTICLE 11.

It is forbidden to the public to send by mail:

1st. Letters or packets containing gold or silver substances, pieces of money, jewelry, or precious articles;

2d. Any packets whatever containing articles liable to customs duty.

In case a packet falling under one of these prohibitions is delivered by one administration of the Union to another administration of the Union, the latter proceeds according to the manner and forms prescribed by it s legislation or by its interior regulations.

There is, moreover, reserved to the government of every country of the Union the right to refuse to convey over its territory, or to deliver, as well articles liable to the reduced rate, in regard to which the laws, ordinances, or decrees which regulate the conditions of their publication or of their circulation in that country have not been complied with, as correspondence of every kind which evidently bears inscriptions forbidden by the legal enactments or regulations in force in the same country.

ARTICLE 12.

The offices of the Union which have relations with countries beyond the Union admit all the other offices to take advantage of such relations for the exchange of correspondence with the said countries.

The correspondence exchanged *in open mails* between a country of the Union and a country foreign to the Union, through the intermediary of another country of the Union, is treated, as regards the conveyance beyond the limits of the Union, in conformity to the conventions, arrangements, or special provisions governing the postal relations between the latter country and the country foreign to the Union.

The rates chargeable on the correspondence in question consist of two distinct elements, viz:

1st. The Union rate fixed by Articles 5, 6, and 7 of the present Convention.

2d. A rate for the conveyance beyond the limits of the Union.

The first of these rates is assigned—

a. For correspondence originating in the Union and addressed to foreign countries, to the dispatching office in case of prepayment, and to the office of exchange in case of non-prepayment.

b. For correspondence originating in foreign countries and addressed to the Union, to the office of exchange in case of prepayment, and to the office of destination in case of non-prepayment.

The second of these rates is, in every case, assigned to the office of exchange.

With regard to the expenses of transit within the Union, the correspondence originating in or addressed to a foreign country is assimilated to that from or for the country of the Union which maintains relations with the country foreign to the Union, unless such relations imply obligatory and partial prepayment, in which case the said Union country has the right to the territorial transit rates fixed by Article 4 preceding.

The general settlement of the rates chargeable for the conveyance beyond Union limits takes place upon the basis of statements which are prepared at the same time as the statements drawn up by virtue of Article 4 preceding for the calculation of the expenses of transit within the Union.

As regards the correspondence exchanged in *closed mails* between a country of the Union and a country foreign to the Union, through the intermediary of another country of the Union, the transit thereof is subject as follows:

Within the limits of the Union, to the rates fixed by Article 4 of the present Convention.

Beyond the limits of the Union, to the conditions arising from special arrangements concluded or to be concluded for that purpose between the administrations interested.

ARTICLE 13.

The exchange of letters of declared value and that of postal money-orders form the subject of special arrangements between the various countries or groups of countries of the Union.

ARTICLE 14.

The postal administrations of the various countries composing the Union are competent to establish by mutual agreement, in a regulation of execution, all the measures of order and detail which are judged necessary.

The several administrations may, moreover, make among themselves the necessary arrangements on the subject of questions which do not concern the Union generally, provided that these arrangements are not contrary to the present Convention.

The administrations interested are, however, permitted to come to mutual arrangements for the adoption of lower rates of postage, within a radius of 30 kilometers, for the conditions of the delivery of letters by express, as well as for the exchange of post-cards with paid answer. In this latter case, the answer-cards, when sent back to the country of origin, are exempt from the transit charges stipulated by the last paragraph of Article 4 of the present Convention.

ARTICLE 15.

The present Convention involves no alteration in the postal legislation of any country as regards anything which is not provided for by the stipulations contained in this Convention.

It does not restrict the right of the contracting parties to maintain and to conclude treaties, as well as to maintain and establish more restricted Unions, with a view to the improvement of postal relations.

ARTICLE 16.

There is maintained, under the name of the *International Bureau of the Universal Postal Union*, a central office, which is conducted under the superintendence of the Swiss Postal Administration, and the expenses of which are borne by all the administrations of the Union.

This office continues to be charged with the duty of collecting, collating, publishing, and distributing information of every kind which concerns the international postal service: of giving, at the request of the parties concerned, an opinion upon questions in dispute; of making known proposals for modifying the acts of the Congress; of giving notice of the changes adopted, and, in general, of undertaking examinations and labors devolving upon it in the interest of the Postal Union.

ARTICLE 17.

In case of disagreement between two or more members of the Union as to the interpretation of the present Convention, the question in dispute is decided by arbitration. To that end, each of the administrations concerned chooses another member of the Union not directly interested in the matter.

The decision of the arbitrators is given by the absolute majority of votes.

In case of an equality of votes, the arbitrators choose, in order to settle the difference, another administration equally disinterested in the disputed question.

ARTICLE 18.

Countries which have not taken part in the present Convention are admitted to adhere thereto upon their demand.

Notice is given of this adhesion, through the diplomatic channel, to the government of the Swiss Confederation, and by that government to all the countries of the Union.

It implies, as a right, accession to all the clauses and admission to all the advantages stipulated by the present Convention.

It devolves upon the government of the Swiss Confederation to determine, by mutual agreement with the government of the country interested, the share to be contributed by the Administration of this latter country toward the expenses of the International Bureau, and, if necessary, the rates to be levied by that administration in conformity with Article 7 preceding.

ARTICLE 19.

Congresses of plenipotentiaries of the contracting countries, or simple administrative conferences, according to the importance of the questions to be solved, are held when a demand for them is made or approved by two-thirds, at least, of the governments or administrations, as the case may be.

Nevertheless, a Congress must be held at least once every five years.

Each country may be represented either by one or several delegates, or by the delegation of another country. But it is understood that the delegate or delegates of one country can be charged with the representation of two countries only, including the country which they represent.

In the deliberations each country has one vote only.

Each Congress fixes the place of meeting for the following Congress.

For Conferences, the administrations fix the places of meeting upon proposal of the International Bureau.

ARTICLE 20.

In the interval which elapses between the meetings, any postal administration of a country of the Union has the right to address to the other administrations belonging to it, through the intermediary of the International Bureau, proposals concerning the regimen of the Union. But to become executive these propositions must obtain, as follows:

1st. Unanimity of votes, if they involve a modification of the stipulations of Articles 2, 3, 4, 5, 6, and 9 preceding.

2d. Two-thirds of the votes, if they involve a modification of the stipulations of the Convention other than those of Articles 2, 3, 4, 5, 6, and 9.

3d. A simple absolute majority, if they involve the interpretation of the stipulations of the Convention, except in the case of dispute contemplated in Article 17 preceding.

The binding decisions are sanctioned, in the first two cases, by a diplomatic declaration, which the government of the Swiss Confederation is charged to prepare and transmit to all the governments of the contracting countries, and, in the third case, by a simple notification from the International Bureau to all the administrations of the Union.

ARTICLE 21.

The following are considered as forming, for the application of Articles 16, 19, and 20 preceding, a single country, or a single administration, as the case may be:

1st. The Empire of British India;

2d. The Dominion of Canada;
3d. The whole of the Danish Colonies;
4th. The whole of the Spanish Colonies;
5th. The whole of the French Colonies;
6th. The whole of the Netherland Colonies;
7th. The whole of the Portuguese Colonies.

ARTICLE 22.

The present Convention shall be put into execution on the 1st of April, 1879, and shall remain in force during an indefinite period; but each contracting party has the right to withdraw from the Union by means of a notice given, one year in advance, by its government to the government of the Swiss Confederation.

ARTICLE 23.

After the date on which the present Convention takes effect, all the stipulations of the treaties, conventions, arrangements, or other acts previously concluded between the various countries or administrations, in so far as those stipulations are not in accordance with the terms of the present Convention, are abrogated, without prejudice to the rights reserved by Article 15 above.

The present Convention shall be ratified as soon as possible. The acts of ratification shall be exchanged at Paris.

In faith of which, the plenipotentiaries of the countries above enumerated have signed the present Convention at Paris, the first of June, one thousand eight hundred and seventy-eight.

For the United States of America	JAS. N. TYNER. JOSEPH H. BLACKFAN.
For Germany	DR. STEPHAN. GÜNTHER. SACHSE.
For the Argentine Republic	CARLOS CALVO.
For Austria	DEWÉZ.
For Hungary	GERVAY.
For Belgium	J. VINCHENT. F. GIFE.
For Brazil	VICOMTE D'ITAJUBA.
For Denmark and the Danish Colonies	SCHOU.
For Egypt	A. CAILLARD.
For Spain and the Spanish Colonies	G. CRUZADA VILLAAMIL. EMILIO C. DE NAVASQÜES.
For France	LÉON SAY. AD. COCHERY. A. BESNIER.
For the French Colonies	E. ROY.
For Great Britain and the British Colonies	F. O. ADAMS. WM. JAS. PAGE. A. MACLEAN.
For British India	FRED. R. HOGG.

For Canada	F. O. ADAMS. WM. JAS. PAGE. A. MACLEAN.
For Greece	N. P. DELYANNI. A. MANSOLAS.
For Italy	G. B. TANTESIO.
For Japan	NAONOBOU SAMESHIMA. SAML. M. BRYAN.
For Luxembourg	V. DE ROEBE.
For Mexico	G. BARREDA.
For Montenegro	DEWÉZ.
For Norway	CHR. HEFTY.
For the Netherlands and the Netherland Colonies	HOFSTEDE. BARON SWEERTS DE LANDAS-WYBORGH.
For Peru	JUAN M. DE GOYENECHE.
Persia unrepresented	——— ———.
For Portugal and the Portuguese Colonies	GUELHERMENO AUGUSTO DE BARROS.
For Roumania	C. F. ROBESCO.
For Russia	BARON VELHO. GEORGES POGGENPOHL.
For Salvador	J. M. TORRÈS CAÏCEDO.
For Servia	MLADEN F. RADOYCOVITCH.
For Sweden	WM. ROOS.
For Switzerland	DR. KERN. ED. HÖHN.
For Turkey	B. COUYOUMGIAN.

Having examined and considered the provisions of the aforegoing Convention, signed at Paris on the 1st of June, A. D. 1878, revising the Treaty constituting the General Postal Union which was concluded at Berne on the 9th of October, A. D. 1874, the same is by me, in virtue of the powers vested in the Postmaster-General by law, hereby ratified and approved, by and with the advice and consent of the President of the United States.

In witness whereof I have caused the seal of the Post-Office Department of the United States to be hereto affixed, with my signature, this 13th day of August, 1878.

[SEAL.] D. M. KEY,
Postmaster-General.

I hereby approve the above-mentioned Convention, and in testimony thereof I have caused the seal of the United States to be affixed hereto.

[SEAL.] R. B. HAYES.

By the President:
F. W. SEWARD,
Acting Secretary of State.

WASHINGTON, *August* 13, 1878.

FINAL PROTOCOL.

The undersigned, plenipotentiaries of the governments of the countries which have this day signed the Convention of Paris, have agreed as follows:

I. Persia, which forms part of the Union, being unrepresented, will nevertheless be allowed to sign the Convention hereafter, provided that country confirms its adhesion by a diplomatic act with the Swiss government before the 1st of April, 1879.

II. The countries foreign to the Union, which have deferred their adhesion or which have not yet announced their intentions, shall enter the Union on fulfilling the conditions specified in Article 18 of the Convention.

III. In case one or other of the contracting parties should not ratify the Convention, this Convention shall nevertheless be binding on the parties to it.

IV. The various British colonies, other than Canada and British India, which are parties in the Convention, are Ceylon, the Straits Settlements, Labuan, Hong-Kong, Mauritius and dependencies, Bermuda, British Guiana, Jamaica, and Trinidad.

In faith of which the undermentioned plenipotentiaries have drawn up the present final protocol, which shall have the same force and the same value as if the stipulations which it contains were inserted in the Convention itself, and they have signed it in one single instrument, which shall be deposited in the archives of the French government, and a copy of which shall be delivered to each party.

Paris, June 1st, 1878.

For Germany	DR. STEPHAN. GÜNTHER. SACHSE.
For the Argentine Republic	CARLOS CALVO.
For Austria	DEWÉZ.
For Hungary	GERVAY.
For Belgium	J. VINCHENT. F. GIFE.
For Brazil	VICOMTE D'ITAJUBA.
For Denmark and the Danish Colonies	SCHOU.
For Egypt	A. CAILLARD.
For Spain and the Spanish Colonies	G. CRUZADA VILLAAMIL. EMILIO C. DE NAVASQÜES.
For the United States of America	JAS. N. TYNER. JOSEPH H. BLACKFAN.
For France	LEON SAY. AD. COCHERY. A. BESNIER.
For the French Colonies	E. ROY.
For Great Britain and the British Colonies	F. O. ADAMS. WM. JAS. PAGE. A. MACLEAN.

For British India	FRED. R. HOGG.
For Canada	F. O. ADAMS. WM. JAS. PAGE. A. MACLEAN.
For Greece	N. P. DELYANNI. A. MANSOLAS.
For Italy	G. B. TANTESIO.
For Japan	NAONOBOU SAMESHIMA. SAML. M. BRYAN.
For Luxembourg	V. DE RŒBE.
For Mexico	G. BARREDA.
For Montenegro	DEWÉZ.
For Norway	CHR. HEFTY.
For The Netherlands and the Netherland Colonies	HOFSTEDE. BARON SWEERTS DE LANDAS-WYBORGH.
For Peru	JUAN M. DE GOYENECHE.
For Portugal and the Portuguese Colonies	GUELHERMENO AUGUSTO DE BARROS.
For Roumama	C. F. ROBESCO.
For Russia	BARON VELHO. GEORGES POGGENPOHL.
For Salvador	J. M. TORRÉS-CAÏCEDO.
For Servia	MLADEN F. RADOYCOVITCH.
For Sweden	WM. ROOS.
For Switzerland	DR. KERN. ED. HÖHN.
For Turkey	B. COUYOUMGIAN.

Having examined and considered the provisions of the foregoing final protocol, signed at Paris on the 1st of June, A. D. 1878, relative to the Convention of Paris, signed the same day, the same is by me, in virtue of the powers vested in the Postmaster-General by law, hereby ratified and approved, by and with the advice and consent of the President of the United States.

In witness whereof I have caused the seal of the Post-Office Department of the United States to be hereto affixed, with my signature, this 13th day of August, 1878.

[SEAL.]

D. M. KEY,
Postmaster-General.

I hereby approve the above-mentioned protocol, and in testimony thereof I have caused the seal of the United States to be affixed.

[SEAL.]

R. B. HAYES.

By the President:

F. W. SEWARD,
Acting Secretary of State.

WASHINGTON, *August* 13, 1878.

Sec. 1103. Regulations of Detail and Order under the Paris Convention.—Regulations of detail and order for the execution of the Convention concluded between Germany, the Argentine Republic, Austria-Hungary, Belgium, Brazil, Denmark and the Danish Colonies, Egypt, Spain and the Spanish Colonies, the United States of North America, France and the French Colonies, Great Britain and certain British Colonies, British India, Canada, Greece, Italy, Japan, Luxemburg, Mexico, Montenegro, Norway, The Netherlands and the Netherland Colonies, Peru, Persia, Portugal and the Portuguese Colonies, Roumania, Russia, Servia, Salvador, Sweden, Switzerland, and Turkey.

The undersigned, in view of Article 14 of the Convention concluded at Paris June 1st, 1878, for the revision of the fundamental compact of the General Postal Union, have, in the name of their respective administrations, established, by mutual agreement, the following measures to insure the execution of the said Convention:

I.

Direction of the Correspondence.

1. Each administration is bound to forward, by the most rapid routes at its disposal for its own mails, the closed mails and the correspondence in open mails which are delivered to it by another administration.

2. The administrations which avail themselves of the right to levy supplementary charges, as representing the extraordinary expenses attending certain routes, are at liberty not to forward by those routes when other means of communication exist, such of the insufficiently-paid correspondence for which the employment of the said routes has not been expressly requested by the senders.

II.

Exchange in Closed Mails.

1. The exchange of the correspondence in closed mails between the administrations of the Union is regulated by mutual agreement, and according to the needs of the service, between the administrations concerned.

2. If an exchange is to be made through the intermediary of one or several third countries, the administrations of those countries must be informed thereof in due time.

3. It is, moreover, obligatory in this latter case to make up closed mails, whenever the amount of the correspondence is of a nature to impede the operations of an intermediary administration, according to the statement of that administration.

4. In case of alteration in a service of exchange in closed mails established between two administrations through the intermediary of one or more third countries, the administration which has called for the alteration gives notice thereof to the administrations of the countries through whose intermediary the exchange is made.

III.

Extraordinary Services.

The extraordinary services of the Union giving rise to special expenses, the fixing of which is reserved by Article 4 of the Convention for arrangements between the administrations interested, are exclusively—

1st. Those which are maintained for the accelerated territorial conveyance of the mail called Indian;

2d. That which the postal administration of the United States of America maintains upon its territory for the conveyance of closed mails between the Atlantic Ocean and the Pacific Ocean.

IV.

Fixing the Rates of Postage.

1. In execution of Article 7 of the Convention, the administrations of the countries of the Union which have not the franc for monetary unit, levy their rates of postage according to the following equivalents:

Countries.	25 centimes.	10 centimes.	5 centimes.
Germany	20 pfennig	10 pfennig	5 pfennig.
Argentine Republic	8 centavos	4 centavos	2 centavos.
Austria-Hungary	10 kreuzer	5 kreuzer	3 kreuzer.
Brazil	100 reis	50 reis	25 reis.
Denmark	20 öre	10 öre	5 öre.
Danish colonies:			
Greenland	20 öre	10 öre	5 öre.
West Indies	5 cents	2 cents	1 cent.
Egypt	1 piastre	20 paras	10 paras.
United States of America	5 cents	2 cents	1 cent.
Great Britain	2½ pence	1 penny	½ penny.
British India	2 annas	¾ anna	½ anna.
British colonies:			
Jamaica, Trinidad, British Guiana, Labuan, Mauritius and dependencies, Bermudas	2½ pence	1 penny	½ penny.
Ceylon, Straits Settlements, Hong-Kong, Canada	5 cents	2 cents	1 cent.
Japan	5 sen	2 sen	1 sen.
Montenegro	10 soldi	5 soldi	3 soldi.
Norway	20 öre	10 öre	5 öre.
Netherlands and Netherland colonies	12½ cents	5 cents	2½ cents.
Persia	5 shahis	2 shahis	1 shahi.
Portugal and Portuguese colonies	50 reis	20 reis	10 reis.
Russia	7 kopecks	3 kopecks	2 kopecks.
Servia	50 paras	20 paras	10 paras.
Sweden	20 öre	10 öre	5 öre.
Turkey	50 paras	20 paras	10 paras.
Mexico	6 centavos	3 centavos	2 centavos.
Peru	5 centavos	2 centavos	1 centavo.
Salvador	5 centavos de peso.	2 centavos de peso.	1 centavo de peso.

2. In case of change in the monetary system in one of the above-named countries, the administration of that country must have an understanding with the Swiss Postal Administration in order to modify the above equivalents: it devolves upon the latter administration to give notice of this modification to all the other offices of the Union through the intermediary of the International Bureau.

3. Any administration has the right to have recourse, if it deems it necessary, to the understanding provided for in the preceding paragraph, in case of an important modification in the value of its money.

4. The monetary fractions resulting either from the complement of the charge applicable to insufficient prepaid correspondence, or from the combination of the Union postages with the foreign postages, or with the surcharges contemplated by article 5 of the Convention, may be rounded off by the administrations which collect them. But the sum to be added on this account cannot, in any case, exceed the value of one-twentieth of a franc (five centimes).

V.

Correspondence with Countries foreign to the Union.

1. The offices of the Union which have relations with countries foreign to the Union, furnish to the other offices of the Union a table conformable to model C annexed to the present Regulations, and indicating, with the conditions of dispatch, the rates due for the conveyance outside of the Union of the correspondence for or from the aforesaid countries. In the case provided for by the tenth paragraph of Article 12 of the Convention, there may be added five centimes per single rate of letters and two centimes per single rate of other articles.

2. In application of Article 12 of the Convention, there is levied, in addition to the foreign rates indicated in table C:

1st. By the office of the Union forwarding prepaid correspondence for countries outside the Union, the rates of prepayment respectively applicable to correspondence of the same nature for the country of egress from the Union;

2d. By the office of the Union to which is addressed unpaid or partially paid correspondence of foreign origin, as follows:

a. For letters, the rate applicable to the unpaid letters coming from the country of the Union which serves as the intermediary;

b. For other articles, a charge equal to the prepaid rate on similar articles which are addressed from the Union country of destination to the Union country serving as the intermediary.

VI.

Application of Stamps.

1. Correspondence originating in countries of the Union is impressed with a stamp indicating the place of origin and the date of posting.

2. Correspondence originating in countries foreign to the Union is impressed, by the office of the Union which has received it, with a stamp indicating the point and date of entrance into the service of that office.

3. Unpaid or insufficiently prepaid correspondence is, in addition, impressed with the stamp T (tax to be paid), the application of which devolves upon the office of the country of origin in cases of correspondence originating in the Union, and upon the office of the country of entry in cases of correspondence originating in countries foreign to the Union.

4. Registered articles must bear the special mark (label or stamp) adopted for articles of a like nature by the country of origin.

5. The stamps or marks, the employment of which is prescribed by the present article, are placed on the address side of the packet.

6. Every article of correspondence not bearing the stamp T is considered as prepaid and treated accordingly, unless there be an obvious error.

VII.

Indication of the Number of Rates and the Amount of the Foreign Charges.

1. When a letter or other article of correspondence is liable, by reason of its weight, to more than a single rate, the office of origin or of entry into the Union, as the case may be, indicates, at the upper left corner of the address, in ordinary figures, the number of rates paid or to be paid.

2. This regulation is not obligatory for the fully prepaid correspondence.

3. The foreign charges due by virtue of Article 12 of the Convention and of Article V of the present Regulations, for the conveyance outside of the Union of correspondence for or from countries foreign to the Union, are indicated at the lower left corner of the address of each article, as follows:

1st. By the office of the country of origin, in red figures, in case of regularly prepaid correspondence originating in the Union;

2d. By the office of the country of entry into the Union, in blue figures, in case of correspondence of foreign origin to be charged by the Union office of destination.

VIII.

Insufficient Prepayment.

1. When an article is insufficiently prepaid by means of postage-stamps, the dispatching office indicates, in black figures placed at the side of the postage-stamps, the amount of the insufficiency, expressing it in francs and centimes.

2. According to this indication, the exchange office of the country of destination charges the article with double the insufficiency ascertained.

3. In case use be made of postage-stamps not valid for prepayment, no account is taken of them. This circumstance is indicated by the cipher (0) placed at the side of the postage-stamps.

IX.

Letter Bills.

1. The letter bills accompanying the mails exchanged between two administrations of the Union are in conformity with the model A annexed to the present Regulations.

2. The registered articles are entered in table No. I of the letter-bill, with the following details: The name of the office of origin, the name of the addressee, and the place of destination, or simply the name of the office of origin and the number given to the article at that office.

3. When the number of registered articles usually sent from one office of exchange to another requires it, a special and separate list may be used to replace table No. I of the letter bill.

4. In table No. II are to be entered, with the details which this table requires, the closed mails which accompany the direct dispatches.

5. When it is deemed necessary, for certain relations, to make other tables or headings upon the letter-bill, the measure may be accomplished by mutual agreement between the administrations interested.

6. When an exchange office has no article to forward to a corresponding office, it must nevertheless send, in the ordinary form, a mail which is composed solely of the letter bill.

X.

Registered Articles.

1. The registered articles and, if necessary, the special list specified in paragraph 3 of Article IX, are placed together in a separate packet, which must be suitably inclosed and sealed so as to preserve its contents.

2. This packet, with the letter bill around it, is placed in the center of the mail.

3. The presence in the mail of a packet of registered articles, the description of which is given upon the special list mentioned in paragraph 1 above, must be announced by the application at the head of the letter bill, either of a special entry, or of the label, or of the registration stamp in use in the country of origin.

4. It is understood that the mode of making up and transmitting registered articles prescribed by paragraphs 1 and 2 above applies only to ordinary relations. For important relations, it appertains to the administrations interested to prescribe, by mutual agreement, special arrangements, under reservation, in the one case as in the other, of the exceptional measures to be taken by the chiefs of the exchange offices, when they have to assure the transmission of registered articles which, from their nature, their form, or their bulk, cannot be inserted in the mail.

XI.

Indemnity for the Loss of a Registered Article.

The obligation to pay the indemnity in case of the loss of a registered article, devolves upon the administration to which the dispatching office is subordinate, subject to appeal, if necessary, to the administration responsible for the loss.

XII.

Making up the Mails.

1. As a general rule, the articles of which the mails consist must be classified and put up in bundles according to the nature of the correspondence.

2. Every mail, after having been first tied with string, is inclosed in strong paper of sufficient quantity to prevent any injury to the contents, then tied again on the outside and sealed with wax, or by means of a gummed paper label bearing an impression of the seal of the office. The mail is furnished with a printed address bearing, in small characters, the name of the dispatching office, and in larger characters the name of the office of destination: "From ...." "For ...."

3. If the size of the mail requires it, it is inclosed in a bag properly closed, sealed, and labeled.

4. The bags must be returned empty to the dispatching office by the next mail, subject to other arrangement between the corresponding offices.

XIII.

Verification of the Mails.

1. The office of exchange which receives a mail ascertains, in the first place, if the entries upon the letter bill and—the case occurring—upon the list of registered articles, are correct.

2. When it detects errors or omissions, it immediately makes the necessary corrections on the letter bills or lists, taking care to strike out the erroneous entries with a pen, in such a manner as to let the original entries be seen.

3. These corrections are made by the concurrence of two officers. Except in the case of an obvious error, they are accepted in preference to the original statement.

4. A bulletin of verification, in conformity with model B annexed to the present regulations, is prepared by the receiving office and sent without delay, under official registration, to the dispatching office.

5. The latter, after examination, returns it with any observations to which it may give rise.

6. In case of the failure of a mail, of a registered article, of the letter bill, or of the special list, the circumstance is immediately authenticated, in the manner agreed upon, by two officers of the receiving exchange office, and reported to the dispatching exchange office by means of a bulletin of verification. If needful, the latter office may also be advised thereof by telegram, at the expense of the office which sends the telegram.

7. In case the receiving office has not forwarded by the first mail to the dispatching office a note of verification reporting errors or irregu-

larities of any kind, the absence of that document is to be regarded as evidence of the due receipt of the mail and of its contents, until proof to the contrary.

XIV.

Registered Articles.—Conditions of Form and Fastening.

No special condition of form or of fastening is required for the registered articles. Each office has the right to apply to this correspondence the regulations established in its interior service.

XV.

Post Cards.

1. Post-cards must be forwarded without cover. One of the sides is reserved for the address alone. The communication is written on the other side.

2. Post-cards cannot exceed the following dimensions:

Length, 14 centimeters;

Width, 9 centimeters.

3. As far as possible, post-cards issued specially for circulation within the Union, should bear an impressed stamp and the title "Universal Postal Union," followed by the name of the country of origin. This title, when not in the French language, is to be repeated in that language.

4. Post-cards issuing from Union offices are alone admitted to circulation in the international service.

5. It is forbidden to join or to attach to post-cards any article whatsoever.

XVI.

Commercial Papers.

1. The following are considered as commercial papers and admitted as such to the reduced postage sanctioned by Article 5 of the Convention, viz: All instruments or documents written or drawn wholly or partly by hand, which have not the character of an *actual and personal correspondence*, such as papers of legal procedure, deeds of all kinds drawn up by public functionaries, way bills or bills of lading, invoices, the various documents of insurance companies, copies or extracts of deeds under private seal written on stamped or unstamped paper, scores or sheets of manuscript music, manuscripts of works forwarded separately, &c.

2. Commercial papers must be forwarded under band or in an open envelope.

XVII.

Printed matter of all kinds.

1. The following are considered as printed matter, and admitted as such to the reduced postage sanctioned by Article 5 of the Convention,

viz: Newspapers and periodical works, books stitched or bound, pamphlets, sheets of music, visiting-cards, address cards, proofs of printing, with or without the manuscripts relating thereto, engravings, photographs, drawings, plans, geographical maps, catalogues, prospectuses, announcements and notices of various kinds, whether printed, engraved, lithographed, or autographed, and, in general, all impressions or copies obtained upon paper, parchment, or card-board, by means of printing, lithographing, or any other mechanical process easy to recognize, except the copying-press.

2. The following are excluded from the reduced postage, viz: Stamps or forms of prepayment, whether obliterated or not, as well as all printed articles constituting the representative sign of a monetary value.

3. The character of *actual and personal correspondence* cannot be ascribed to the following, viz:

1st. To the signature of the sender or to the designation of his name, of his profession, of his rank, of the place of origin, and of the date of dispatch.

2d. To a dedication or mark of respect offered by the author.

3d. To the figures or signs merely intended to mark the passages of a text, in order to call attention to them.

4th. To the prices added upon the quotations or prices current of exchange or markets.

5th. Lastly, to annotations or corrections made upon proofs of printing or musical compositions, and relating to the text or to the execution of the work.

4. Printed matter must be either placed under band, upon a roller, between boards, in a case open at one side or at both ends, or in an unclosed envelope, or simply folded in such a manner as not to conceal the nature of the packet, or, lastly, tied by a string easy to unfasten.

5. Address cards, and all printed matter presenting the form and consistency of an unfolded card, may be forwarded without band, envelope, fastening, or fold.

XVIII.

Samples.

1. Samples of merchandise are admitted to the advantage of the reduction of postage which is granted to them by Article 5 of the Convention only under the following conditions:

2. They must be placed in bags, boxes, or removable envelopes, in such a manner as to admit of easy inspection.

3. They must not have any salable value, nor bear any manuscript other than the name or profession of the sender, the address of the addressee, a manufacturer's or trade-mark, numbers, and prices.

XIX.

Articles grouped together.

It is permitted to inclose in the same packet samples of merchandise, printed matter and commercial papers, but subject to the following conditions:

1st. That each article taken singly shall not exceed the limits which are applicable to it as regards weight and size.

2d. That the total weight must not exceed two kilogrammes per package.

3d. That the minimum charge shall be 25 centimes when the packet contains commercial papers, and 10 centimes when it consists of printed matter and samples.

XX.

Reforwarded Correspondence.

1. In execution of Article 10 of the Convention, and subject to the exceptions specified in paragraph 2 of the present article, correspondence of every kind circulating in the Union, addressed to persons who have changed their residence, is treated by the delivering office as if it had been addressed directly from the place of origin to the place of new destination.

2. With regard to articles of the interior service of one of the countries of the Union, which enter, in consequence of reforwarding, into the service of another country of the Union, the following rules are observed:

1st. Articles unpaid or insufficiently paid for their first transmission, are treated as international correspondence, and subjected by the delivering office to the charge applicable to articles of the same nature addressed directly from the country of origin to the country in which the addressee may be.

2d. Articles regularly paid for their first transmission, and upon which the remainder of the charge relating to the further transmission has not been paid previous to reforwarding, are subjected, according to their nature, by the delivering office, to a charge equal to the difference between the prepaid rate already paid and that which would have been levied if the articles had been originally dispatched to their new destination. The amount of this difference must be expressed in francs and centimes at the side of the postage stamps by the reforwarding office.

In both cases, the charges contemplated above remain to be defrayed by the addressees, even if, owing to successive reforwardings, the articles should return to the country of origin.

3. Articles of every kind missent are, without delay, reforwarded by the most rapid route to their destination.

XXI.

Undelivered Correspondence.

1. The correspondence of every kind which is not delivered, from whatever cause, must be returned immediately after the expiration of the period for keeping it required by the laws of the country of destination through the intermediary of the respective offices of exchange, and in a special bundle labeled "*Rebuts.*"

2. Nevertheless, undelivered registered correspondence is returned to the exchange office of the country of origin as if it were registered correspondence addressed to that country, except that as regards the descriptive entry in table No. I of the letter bill, or in the separate list, the word "*Rebuts*" is entered in the column of observations by the returning office.

3. As an exception, two corresponding offices may, by mutual agreement, adopt a different mode of returning undelivered correspondence, and may also dispense with the reciprocal return of certain printed matter considered to be without value.

XXII.

Statistics of Transit Expenses.

1. The statistics to be taken once every two years in execution of Articles 4 and 12 of the Convention, for the settlement as well of the expenses of transit within the Union as of the charges relating to the conveyance beyond the limits of the Union, are established according to the provisions of the following articles, during the entire month of May or of November alternately, in such a manner that the first statistics shall take place in November, 1879; the second in May, 1881; the third in November, 1883, and so on.

2. The statistics of November, 1879, shall take effect from the 1st of April in the same year, until the 31st December, 1880. Each subsequent statistical account shall serve as basis for the payments relating to the current year, and to that which follows.

3. If during the period of application of the statistics, a country having important relations should enter the Union, the countries of the Union whose situation might, in consequence of this circumstance, be affected in regard to the payment of transit rates, have the option to demand special statistics relating exclusively to the countries recently admitted.

XXIII.

Correspondence in Open Mails.

1. The office serving as the medium for the transmission of correspondence exchanged in open mails, either between two countries of the Union or between a country of the Union and a country foreign to it, pre-

pares beforehand, for each of its correspondents of the Union, a table in conformity with model D annexed to the present Regulations, and in which it indicates, distinguishing, if needful, the different routes of transmission, the rates of payment by weight due to it for conveyance within the Union of both categories of correspondence by means of the services at its disposal, as well as the rates of payment by weight to be paid, the case occurring, by the office itself to other offices of the Union, for the further conveyance of the said correspondence within the Union. If needful, it communicates in due time with the offices of the countries to be traversed as to the routes the correspondence is to take, and the rates to be applied thereto.

2. A copy of table D is forwarded by the said office to the corresponding office interested, and serves as the basis of a special account to be established between them with reference to the intermediate conveyance in the Union of the correspondence in question. This account is prepared by the office which receives the correspondence, and is submitted to the examination of the dispatching office.

3. The dispatching office prepares, according to the particulars given in the form D, furnished by its correspondent, tables in conformity with model E, hereto annexed, and intended to show for each mail the expenses of intermediate conveyance within the Union of the correspondence, without distinction of origin, comprised in the mail to be forwarded by the intermediary of the said corresponding office. With this view, the dispatching exchange office enters in table No. 1 of a form E, which it joins to its dispatch, the total weight, according to its nature, of the correspondence of this class which it delivers in open mail to the corresponding exchange office, and the latter, after verification, undertakes the further transmission of the correspondence to its destination in mixing it with its own, in respect to the payment, if needful, of the further charges for conveyance.

4. With regard to the expenses of conveyance beyond the limits of the Union of correspondence addressed to or coming from countries foreign to the Union, they are calculated according to the particulars given in the table C mentioned in Article V of the present Regulations, and entered in gross upon the form E, as follows:

In table No. II, in the case of paid correspondence for abroad (expense at the charge of the dispatching office of the Union);

In table No. III, in the case of unpaid correspondence coming from abroad, and of reforwarded or undelivered correspondence marked with foreign charges to be refunded (expense at the charge of the Union office of destination);

5. Any error in the statement of the office of exchange which has dispatched the table E is immediately notified to that office by means of a bulletin of verification, notwithstanding the correction made in the table itself.

6. If there be no correspondence liable to a charge for intermediate

or foreign conveyance, the table E is not prepared. In case of the unexplained omission of this table, the irregularity is equally reported by means of a bulletin of verification to the office in fault, and must be immediately repaired by the latter.

XXIV.

Closed Mails.

1. The correspondence exchanged in closed mails between two offices of the Union, or between an office of the Union and an office foreign to the Union, across the territory, or by means of the services of one or more other offices, forms the object of a statement similar to model F annexed to the present Regulations, and which is prepared according to the following stipulations:

2. As regards the mails from one country of the Union to another country of the Union, the dispatching office of exchange enters in the letter bill for the office of exchange receiving the mail the net weight of the letters and post-cards, and of the other articles, without distinction of the origin or destination of the correspondence. These entries are verified by the receiving office, which prepares, at the end of the period for taking the statistics, the statement above mentioned, in as many copies as there are offices interested, including the office of the place of dispatch.

3. In the four days which follow the close of the statistical operations, the statements F are transmitted by the offices of exchange which have prepared them to the offices of exchange of the administration indebted, in order to be accepted by them. The latter, after having accepted these statements, transmit them to the central administration to which they are subordinate, which is charged with distributing them among the offices interested.

4. As regards the closed mails exchanged between a country of the Union and a country foreign to the Union, by the intermediary of one or several offices of the Union, their conveyance is effected in both directions, at the charge of the said Union country, and the offices of exchange of that country themselves prepare, for each mail dispatched or received, a statement F, which they transmit to the office of departure or of entry, which prepares, at the end of the statistical period, a general statement, in as many copies as there are offices interested, including itself and the debtor office of the Union. A copy of this statement is transmitted to the debtor office, as well as to each of the offices which have participated in the conveyance of the mails.

XXV.

Account of the Expenses of Transit.

1. The tables E and F are incorporated in a special account, in which is shown, in francs and centimes, the annual amount of transit payment

accruing to each office, by multiplying the totals by 12. The duty of preparing this account devolves upon the creditor office, which transmits it to the debtor office.

2. The balance resulting from the reciprocal accounts between two offices is paid by the debtor office to the creditor office in effective francs, and by means of bills drawn upon the capital, or upon a commercial place of the latter office.

3. The preparation, transmission, and payment of the accounts of the expenses of transit belonging to a period of service must be effected with the least possible delay, and at the latest, before the expiration of the first six months of the following period of service. When this time has passed, the amounts due by one office to another office are subject to interest at the rate of five per cent. per annum, dating from the day of the expiration of the said delay.

4. Nevertheless, the option is reserved to the offices interested to make, by mutual agreement, other arrangements than those which are set forth in the present Article.

XXVI.

Exceptions in Matters of Weight.

As an exceptional measure, it is agreed that the States which, in consequence of their interior regulations, are unable to adopt the decimal metrical system of weight, have the right to substitute for it the ounce avoirdupois (28.3465 grammes), by assimilating a half ounce to 15 grammes, and two ounces to 50 grammes, and to raise, if needful, the limit of the single rate of postage on newspapers to four ounces, but under the express condition that, in the latter case, the postage on newspapers be not less than 10 centimes, and that an entire rate of postage be charged for each copy of the newspaper, even though several newspapers be included in the same packet.

XXVII.

Applications for Ordinary Articles which have failed to reach their Destination.

1. Every application respecting an article of ordinary correspondence which has failed to reach its destination gives rise to the following proceeding:

1st. A form similar to the model G hereto annexed, is handed to the applicant, who is requested to fill up as exactly as possible, the portion which concerns him.

2d. The office at which the application originates transmits the form direct to the corresponding office. It is transmitted officially and without any writing.

3d. The corresponding office causes the form to be handed to the addressee or to the sender, as the case may be, with the request that particulars on the subject be furnished.

4th. Supplied with these particulars, the form is sent back officially to the office which prepared it.

5th. In case the application proves to be well founded, it is transmitted to the central administration, to serve as the basis for further investigation.

6th. Unless by agreement to the contrary, the form is drawn up in French, or bears a French translation.

2. Any administration may require, by means of a notification addressed to the International Bureau, that the exchange of applications, so far as it is concerned, be effected through the intermediary of the central administrations, or of an office specially designated.

XXVIII.

Division of the Expenses of the International Bureau.

1. The ordinary expenses of the International Bureau must not exceed the sum of 100,000 francs annually, not including the special expenses to which the meeting of a Congress or of a Conference may give rise.

2. The administration of the Swiss Post Office superintends the expenses of the International Bureau, makes the necessary advances, and prepares the annual account, which is communicated to all the other administrations.

3. For the division of the expenses, the countries of the Union are divided into seven classes, each contributing in the proportion of a certain number of units, viz:

1st class	25 units.
2d "	20 "
3rd "	15 "
4th "	10 "
5th "	5 "
6th "	3 "
7th "	1 "

4. These coefficients are multiplied by the number of countries of each class, and the total of the products thus obtained furnishes the number of units by which the total expense is to be divided. The quotient gives the amount of the unit of expense.

5. The countries of the Union are classified as follows, in view of the division of the expenses:

1st class: Germany, Austria-Hungary, United States of America, France, British India, the whole of the other British colonies except Canada, Great Britain, Italy, Russia, Turkey.

2d class: Spain.

3d class: Belgium, Brazil, Canada, Egypt, Japan, Netherlands, Roumania, Sweden, Spanish colonies or provinces beyond sea, French colonies, Netherland East Indies.

4th class: Denmark, Norway, Portugal, Switzerland, Portuguese colonies.

5th class: Argentine Republic, Greece, Mexico, Peru, Servia.

6th class: Colony of Surinam (or Dutch Guiana), colony of Curaçoa (or Netherland West Indies), Luxemburg, Persia, Danish colonies, Salvador.

7th class: Montenegro.

XXIX.

Communications to be addressed to the International Bureau.

1. The International Bureau serves as the intermediary for the regular and general notifications which concern the international relations.

2. The administrations forming the Union must communicate to each other specially through the medium of the International Bureau:

1st. Information of the additional charges which they levy by virtue of Article 5 of the Convention, in addition to the Union rate, whether for sea-postage or for the expenses of extraordinary conveyance, as well as a list of the countries in relation to which these surcharges are levied, and, if needful, the designation of the routes which cause their collection;

2d. The impression of the special stamp or mark serving to authenticate the registration;

3d. The model of their form of advice of receipt;

4th. The collection of their postage stamps;

5th. Lastly, the tables C, the preparation of which is prescribed by Article V of the present Regulations.

3. Every modification adopted hereafter in regard to one or other of the five points above mentioned, must be notified, without delay, in the same manner.

4. The International Bureau equally receives from all the administrations of the Union, two copies of all the documents which they publish, as well relating to the interior service as to the international service.

5. Moreover, each administration transmits, in the first half of each year, to the International Bureau, a complete series of statistical details relating to the preceding year, in the form of tables filled up according to information from the International Bureau, which distributes for this purpose formulas already prepared.

6. The correspondence addressed by the administrations of the Union to the International Bureau, and *vice versa*, is assimilated, as regards freedom from postage, to the correspondence exchanged between the administrations.

XXX.

Duties of the International Bureau.

1. The International Bureau prepares general statistics for each year.

2. It publishes, by the aid of the documents which are put at its disposal, a special journal in the German, English, and French languages.

3. All the documents published by the International Bureau are distributed to the administrations of the Union in the proportion of the

number of contributing units assigned to each by Article XXVIII preceding.

4. The additional copies and documents which may be applied for by these administrations are paid for, separately, at prime cost.

5. The International Bureau must, besides, hold itself always at the disposal of the members of the Union, for the purpose of furnishing them with any special information they may require upon questions relating to the International Postal Service.

6. The International Bureau makes known demands for the modification or interpretation of the stipulations which govern the Union. It notifies the results of each application, and any modification or resolution adopted is not executive until two months, at least, after its notification.

7. In the questions to be decided by unanimous assent or by the majority of the Union administrations, those administrations which have not sent in their reply within the maximum delay of four months are considered as expressing no opinion.

8. The International Bureau prepares the business to be submitted to the congresses or conferences. It undertakes the necessary copying and printing, the editing and distribution of amendments, journals of proceedings, and other details.

9. The Director of this Bureau attends the sessions of the congresses or conferences, and takes part in the discussions, without the power of voting.

10. There is issued, under his superintendence, an annual report, which is communicated to all the administrations of the Union.

11. The official language of the International Bureau is the French language.

XXXI.

Language.

1. The letter-bills, tables, statements, and other forms used by the administrations of the Union in their reciprocal relations must, as a general rule, be drawn up in the French language, unless the administrations interested arrange otherwise by direct agreement.

2. As regards official correspondence, the present state of things is maintained, unless any other arrangement should subsequently be agreed upon by common consent between the administrations interested.

XXXII.

Jurisdiction of the Union.

The following are considered as belonging to the Universal Postal Union:

1st. The Island of Heligoland, as assimilated to Germany, from a postal point of view.

2d. The Principality of Lichtenstein, as subordinate to the postal administration of Austria.

3d. Iceland and the Faroe Islands, as forming part of Denmark.

4th. The Balearic Isles, the Canary Islands, and the Spanish possessions on the Northern Coast of Africa, as forming part of Spain; the Republic of Andorra and the postal establishments of Spain upon the western coast of Morocco, as subordinate to the Spanish postal administration.

5th. Algeria, as forming part of France; the Principality of Monaco, and the French post-offices established at Tunis, Tangier (Morocco), and at Shanghai (China), as subordinate to the postal administration of France; Cambodia and Tonquin, as assimilated, so far as regards the postal service, to the French colony of Cochin China.

6th. Gibraltar, as well as Malta and its dependencies, as subordinate to the postal administration of Great Britain.

7th. The post-offices which the administration of the English colony of Hong-Kong maintains at Kiung-chow, Canton, Swatow, Amoy, Foochow, Ningpo, Shanghai, and Hankow (China), and Hai-Fung and Hanoi, (Tonquin).

8th. The Indian postal establishments of Aden, Muscat, Persian Gulf, Guadur, and Mandalay, as subordinate to the postal administration of British India.

9th. The Republic of St. Marino, and the Italian offices of Tunis and Tripoli, in Barbary, as subordinate to the postal administration of Italy.

10th. The post-offices which the Japanese administration has established at Shanghai, Chefoo, Chin-Kiang, Hankow, Ning-po, Foo-Chow, Newchwang, Kiukiang, and Tien-Tsin (China), and of Fusampo (Corea).

11th. Madeira and the Azores, as forming part of Portugal.

12th. The Grand Duchy of Finland, as forming an integral part of the Empire of Russia.

XXXIII.

In the interval which elapses between the meetings, every postal administration of a country of the Union has the right to address to the other participating administrations, through the intermediary of the International Bureau, proposals in regard to the stipulations of the present Regulations. But to become binding these proposals must obtain as follows:

1st. Unanimity of votes, if they relate to the modification of the stipulations of the Articles III, IV, V, XI, XXVI, XXXIII, and XXXIV.

2d. Two-thirds of the votes, if they relate to the modification of the stipulations of the Articles I, II, VIII, X, XIII, XIV, XV, XVI, XVII, XVIII, XIX, XX, XXII, XXIII, XXIV, XXV, XXVII, XXXI, and XXXII.

3d. Simply an absolute majority, if they relate to the modification of stipulations other than those above mentioned, or to the interpretation of the various stipulations of the Regulations.

The resolutions adopted in due form are sanctioned by a simple notification from the International Bureau to all the administrations of the Union.

XXXIV.

Duration of the Regulations.

The present Regulations shall be put into execution from the day on which the Convention of the 1st June, 1878, comes into force. They shall have the same duration as that Convention, unless they be renewed by mutual agreement between the parties interested.

Done at Paris, the 1st June, 1878.

For the United States of America.....	JAS. N. TYNER. JOSEPH H. BLACKFAN.
For Germany	DR. STEPHAN. GÜNTHER. SACHSE.
For the Argentine Republic	CÁRLOS CALVO.
For Austria............................	DEWÉZ.
For Hungary..........................	GERVAY.
For Belgium	J. VINCHENT. F. GIFE.
For Brazil	VICOMTE D'ITAJUBA.
For Denmark and the Danish Colonies...	SCHOU.
For Egypt	A. CAILLARD.
For Spain and the Spanish Colonies...	G. CRUZADA VILLAAMIL. EMILIO C. DE NAVASQÜES.
For France	LÉON SAY. AD. COCHERY. A. BESNIER.
For the French Colonies	E. ROY.
For Great Britain and the British Colonies	F. O. ADAMS. WM. JAS. PAGE. A. MACLEAN.
For British India......................	FRED. R. HOGG.
For Canada	F. O. ADAMS. WM. JAS. PAGE. A. MACLEAN.
For Greece........................	N. P. DELYANNI. A. MANSOLAS.
For Italy	G. B. TANTESIO.
For Japan	NAONOBOU SAMESHIMA. SAML. M. BRYAN.
For Luxemburg	V. DE ROEBE.
For Mexico	G. BARREDA.
For Montenegro........................	DEWÉZ.
For Norway............................	CHR. HEFTY.
For the Netherlands and Netherland Colonies	HOFSTEDE. BARON SWEERTS DE LANDAS-WYBORGH.
For Peru	JUAN M. DE GOYENECHE.
For Portugal and the Portuguese Colonies	GUELHERMENO AUGUSTO DE BARROS.

For Roumania .... C. F. ROBESCO.
For Russia .... { BARON VELHO. GEORGES POGGENPOHL.
For Salvador .... J. M. TORRÉS-CAÏCEDO.
For Servia .... MLADEN F. RADOYCOVITCH.
For Sweden .... WM. ROOS.
For Switzerland .... { DR. KERN. ED. HÖHN.
For Turkey .... B. COUYOUMGIAN.

Sec. 1104. Postage and Registration Fee to Postal-Union Countries.—By order dated March 3, 1879, the Postmaster-General has fixed the rates of postage to be levied in the United States to all parts of the Universal Postal Union at those prescribed in article 5 of the Convention of Paris (section 1102, pp. 233, 234), without regard to the rates of sea-transit chargeable thereon. The registration fee chargeable in the United States is fixed, in accordance with article 6, at ten cents; but no fee will be charged for return receipts for registered articles in cases where such receipts are requested.

Sec. 1105. The Metric System of Weights Used for Foreign Mails.—The Postmaster-General shall furnish to the post-offices exchanging mails with foreign countries, and to such other offices as he may deem expedient, postal balances denominated in grams of the metric system, fifteen grams of which shall be the equivalent, for postal purposes, of one-half ounce avoirdupois, and so on in progression. (R. S., 3880.)

Sec. 1106. Countries and Colonies of the Union.—The following are the countries and colonies which, up to the date of this publication, are embraced in the Universal Postal Union:

AUSTRIA-HUNGARY, including the Principality of Lichtenstein.

ARGENTINE REPUBLIC.

BELGIUM.

BERMUDAS.

BRAZIL.

BRITISH COLONIES on West Coast of Africa, (Gold Coast, Lagos, Senegambia, and Sierra Leone.)

BRITISH COLONIES, West Indies, viz: Antigua, Dominica, Montserrat, Nevis, St. Christopher, and the Virgin Isles.

BRITISH GUIANA.

BRITISH HONDURAS.

BRITISH INDIA: Hindostan and British Burmah (Aracan, Pegu, and Tenasserim), and the Indian postal establishments of Aden, Muscat, Persian Gulf, Guadur, and Mandalay.

CANADA. (See sections 1107 and 1108.)

CEYLON.

DANISH COLONIES of St. Thomas, St. Croix, and St. John.

DENMARK, including Iceland and the Faroe Islands.

EGYPT, including Nubia and Soodan.

FALKLAND ISLANDS.

FRANCE, including Algeria, the Principality of Monaco, and French post-office establishments at Tunis, Tangier (Morocco), and at Shanghai (China), Cambodia, and Tonquin.

FRENCH COLONIES.

1. *In Asia:* French establishments in India, (Chandernagore, Karikal, Mahé, Pondicherry, and Yanaon,) and in Cochin China, (Saïgon, Mytho, Bien-Hoa, Poulo-Condor, Vingh-Long, Hatien, Tschandok.)
2. *In Africa:* Senegal and dependencies, (Gorée, St. Louis, Bakel, Dagana,) Mayotte and Nossi-bé, Gaboon, Reunion, (Bourbon,) Ste. Marie de Madagascar.
3. *In America:* French Guiana, Guadaloupe and dependencies, (Désirade or Deseada, Les Saintes, Marie Galante, and the north portion of St. Martin,) Martinique, St. Pierre, and Miquelon.

FRENCH COLONIES—Continued.

4. *In Oceanica:* New Caledonia, Tahiti, Marquesas Islands, Isle of Pines, Loyalty Islands, the Archipelagoes of Gambier, Toubouaï, and Tuamotou, (Low Islands.)

GERMANY, including the Island of Heligoland.

GREAT BRITAIN AND IRELAND, including Gibraltar, Malta, the dependencies of Malta, (Gozzo, Comino, and Cominotto,) and the Island of Cyprus.

GREECE, including the Ionian Isles.

GREENLAND.

HONDURAS, Republic of.

HONG-KONG and the post-offices maintained by Hong-Kong at Kiung-Chow, Canton, Swatow, Amoy, Foo-Chow, Ning-po Shanghai, and Hankow, (China,) and Hai-Fung and Hanoi, (Tonquin.)

ITALY, including the Republic of San Marino, and the Italian offices of Tunis and Tripoli in Barbary.

JAMAICA.

JAPAN and Japanese post-offices at Shanghai, Chee Foo, Chin Kiang, Hankow, Ning-po, Foo-Chow, Newchwang, Kin-Kiang, and Tien-Tsin, (China,) and at Fusam-po, (Corea.)

LABUAN.

LIBERIA.

LUXEMBURG.

MAURITIUS and dependencies (the Amirante Islands, the Seychelles and Rodrigues).

MEXICO.

MONTENEGRO.

NETHERLANDS.

NETHERLAND COLONIES:

1. *In Asia:* Borneo, Sumatra, Java, (Batavia,) Billiton, Celebes, (Macassar,) Madura, the Archipelagoes of Banca and Rhio, (Riouw,) Bali, Lombok, Sumbawa, Flores, the S.W. portion of Timor, and the Moluccas.
2. *In Oceanica:* The N.W. portion of New Guinea, (Papua).

NETHERLAND COLONIES—Continued.

3. *In America:* Netherland Guiana, (Surinam,) Curaçoa, Aruba, Bonaire, part of St. Martin, St. Eustatius, and Saba.

NEWFOUNDLAND.

NORWAY.

PERSIA.

PERU.

PORTUGAL, including the island of Madeira and the Azores.

PORTUGUESE COLONIES:

1. *In Asia:* Goa, Damao, Diu, Macao, and part of Timor.
2. *In Africa:* Cape Verde, Bissao, Cacheo, Islands of St. Thome and Prince's, Ajuda, Mozambique, and the province of Angola.

ROUMANIA, (Moldavia and Wallachia.)

RUSSIA, including the Grand Duchy of Finland.

SALVADOR.

SERVIA.

SPAIN, including the Balearic Isles, the Canary Islands, the Spanish possessions on the north coast of Africa, (Ceuta, Peñon de la Gomera, Alhucemas, Melilla, and the Chaffarine Islands, the Republic of Andorra, and the postal establishments of Spain on the west coast of Morocco, (Tangiers, Tetuan, Larrache, Rabat, Mazagan, Casablanca, Saffi, and Mogadore.)

SPANISH COLONIES:

1. *In Africa:* Islands of Fernando Po, Annobon, and Corisco.
2. *In America:* Cuba and Porto Rico.
3. *In Oceanica:* The Archipelagoes of the Mariana (Ladrone) and the Caroline Islands.
4. *In Asia:* The Philippine Archipelago, (Luzon with Manila, Mindanao, Palawan, Panay, Amar, &c.)

STRAITS SETTLEMENTS, (Singapore, Penang, and Malacca.)

SWEDEN.

SWITZERLAND.

TRINIDAD, W. I.

TURKEY, (European and Asiatic.)

UNITED STATES OF AMERICA.

Sec. 1107. Paris Convention does not Govern Exchange with Canada.—Agreeably to the provisions of Articles XV and XXIII of the Paris Convention, the special postal arrangement between the United States and Canada in force prior to the entrance of the latter country into the Postal Union is continued in operation, excepting that the privilege of registration is accorded to all the correspondence exchanged between the two countries which is also exchangeable registered under the Paris Convention.

Sec. 1108. Rates of Postage and Conditions of Prepayment.—The postages applicable in the United States to correspondence exchanged with the Universal Postal Union (Canada excepted) are as follows:

For prepaid letters, 5 cents per fifteen grams (½ ounce).

For unpaid letters received, 10 cents per fifteen grams (½ ounce).

For insufficiently paid letters or other articles received, a charge equal to double the amount of the deficiency.

For postal cards, 2 cents each.

For newspapers, if not over four ounces in weight, 2 cents each; if over four ounces in weight, 2 cents for each additional four ounces or fraction thereof.

For printed matter of all kinds, commercial papers, and samples of merchandise, 1 cent for each article or packet bearing a particular address, and for every weight of two ounces or fraction thereof; with a minimum charge of 5 cents per packet of commercial papers, and a minimum charge of 2 cents per packet of samples of merchandise; that is to say, for commercial papers not exceeding ten (10) ounces in weight, the postage is five (5) cents, and if above ten ounces in weight, one cent for each two ounces or fraction thereof; for samples not exceeding four ounces in weight, two cents; if above four ounces in weight, one cent for each two ounces or fraction thereof.

For the registration fee on all correspondence, 10 cents.

No fee will be charged for return receipts of registered articles in cases where such receipts are requested.

The prepayment of the Union postage on ordinary letters is optional, but the postage on all other articles (except postal cards, which are necessarily prepaid, and registered letters and other articles registered) must be at least partially prepaid.

Sec. 1109. Mode of Prepayment.—Payment of postage on every description of correspondence can be effected only by means of postage-stamps valid in the country of origin for the correspondence of private individuals.

Sec. 1110. Franking of Official Correspondence.—Official correspondence relative to the postal service, exchanged directly between the respective Postal Administrations of the Union, is alone admitted free of postage.

Sec. 1111. Postmarking.—All classes of correspondence are required to be impressed by the mailing office with a stamp indicating the place of origin and date of posting.

Sec. 1112. Registration.—Any article of mail-matter may be registered, subject to prepayment of the postage upon the article, according to its nature, in addition to the registration fee of 10 cents. For detailed instructions as to registration of foreign matter, see Title V, Chapter Two.

Sec. 1113. Conditions of Form and Weight.—1. Postal cards must be forwarded without cover. One of the sides must be reserved for the address alone, and the communication written on the other side. It is forbidden to join or to attach to postal cards any article whatever.

2. Printed matter must be either placed under band, upon a roller, between boards, in a case open at one side or at both ends, or in an unclosed envelope; or simply folded in such a manner as not to conceal the nature of the packet; or, lastly, tied by a string easy to unfasten.

3. Address cards and all printed matter presenting the form and consistency of an unfolded card may be forwarded without band, envelope, fastening, or fold.

4. The maximum weight of printed matter is fixed at 2 kilograms (4 lbs. 6 ozs.).

5. Commercial papers must be forwarded under band or in an open envelope.

6. The maximum weight of commercial papers is fixed at 2 kilograms (4 lbs. 6 ozs.).

7. Samples of merchandise must conform to the following conditions:

1st. They must be placed in bags, boxes, or removable envelopes in such a manner as to admit of easy inspection.

2d. They must not have any salable value, nor bear any manuscript other than the name or profession of the sender, the address of the addressee, a manufacturer's or trade-mark, numbers and prices.

3d. They must not exceed 250 grams in weight (8¾ ounces), or the following dimensions: 20 centimeters (8 inches) in length, 10 centimeters (4 inches) in breadth, and 5 centimeters (2 inches) in depth.

8. Packets of printed matter, commercial papers, and samples must not contain any letter or manuscript note having the character of an actual and personal correspondence, and must be made up in such manner as to admit of being easily examined.

The character of actual and personal correspondence cannot be ascribed to the following, viz:

1st. To the signature of the sender or to the designation of his name, of his profession, of his rank, of the place of origin, and of the date of dispatch.

2d. To a dedication or mark of respect offered by the author.

3d. To the figures or signs merely intended to mark the passages of a text, in order to call attention to them.

4th. To the prices added upon the quotations or prices current of exchange or markets.

5th and lastly. To annotations or corrections made upon proofs of printing or musical compositions, and relating to the text or to the execution of the work.

It is permitted to inclose in the same packet samples of merchandise, printed matter, and commercial papers, but subject to the following conditions:

1st. That each article taken singly shall not exceed the limits which are applicable to it as regards weight and size.

2d. That the total weight must not exceed 2 kilograms (4 lbs. 6 ozs.) per package.

3d. That the minimum charge shall be 5 cents when the packet contains commercial papers, and 2 cents when it consists of printed matter and samples.

Sec. 1114. Printed Matter Defined.—The following are considered as printed matter, viz: Newspapers and periodical works, books stitched or bound, pamphlets, sheets of music, visiting cards, address cards, proofs of printing, with or without the manuscripts relating thereto, engravings, photographs, drawings, plans, geographical maps, catalogues, prospectuses, announcements and notices of various kinds, whether printed, engraved, lithographed, or autographed, and, in general, all impressions or copies obtained upon paper, parchment, or card-board by means of printing, lithographing, or any other mechanical process easy to recognize, except the copying-press.

Sec. 1115. Commercial Papers Defined.—The following are considered as commercial papers, viz: All instruments or documents written or drawn wholly or partly by hand which have not the character of an actual and personal correspondence, such as papers of legal procedure, deeds of all kinds drawn up by public functionaries, way-bills or bills of lading, invoices, the various documents of insurance companies, copies or extracts of deeds under private seal, written on stamped or unstamped paper, scores or sheets of manuscript music, manuscripts of works forwarded separately, etc.

Sec. 1116. Articles Excluded from Reduced Postage.—The following are excluded from the reduced postage, viz: Stamps or forms of prepayment, whether obliterated or not, as well as all printed articles constituting the representative sign of a monetary value.

Sec. 1117. Articles Excluded from Postal-Union Mails.—It is forbidden to send by mail:

1. Letters or packets containing gold or silver substances, pieces of money, jewelry, or precious articles.

2. Any packet whatever containing articles liable to customs duty.

3. Articles other than letters which are not prepaid at least partly, or which do not fulfill the conditions required in order to enjoy the reduced rate.

4. Articles of a nature likely to soil or injure the correspondence.

5. Packets of samples of merchandise which have a salable value, or which exceed 250 grams (8⅞ ozs.) in weight, or measure more than 20 centimeters (8 inches) in length, 10 centimeters (4 inches) in breadth, and 5 centimeters (2 inches) in depth.

6. Packets of commercial papers and printed matter of all kinds, the weight of which exceeds 2 kilograms (4 lbs. 6 ozs.).

There is, moreover, reserved to the government of every country of the Union the right to refuse to convey over its territory, or to deliver as well, articles liable to the reduced rate in regard to which the laws, ordinances, or decrees which regulate the conditions of their publication or of their circulation in that country have not been complied with, as correspondence of every kind which evidently bears inscriptions forbidden by the legal enactments or regulations in force in the same country.

See also "Miscellaneous Regulations and Suggestions," section 1132, subsections 19, 20, 21.

Sec. 1118. Special Arrangements with Certain Countries.—By the terms of Article XXIII of the Convention of Paris all the stipulations of antecedent special treaties, conventions, arrangements, or other acts previously concluded between the various countries or administrations, in so far as those stipulations are not in accordance with the terms of the Paris Convention, are abrogated. Hence, such of the provisions of antecedent postal conventions as are not inconsistent or at variance with the provisions of the Universal Postal Union Convention, may, by mutual understanding between the administrations parties to such conventions, be considered as remaining in force.

1. A mutual understanding has been had between this Department and the postal administrations of Great Britain and Germany to continue in force the former regulation limiting the dimensions of book-packets and other printed matter to two (2) feet in length and one (1) foot in width or depth.

2. By virtue of a similar understanding between the United States and Great Britain, periodicals published in the United States at intervals of not more than thirty-one days may be sent to Great Britain at newspaper rates of postage.

Sec. 1119. International Postal Card.—A two-cent postal card has been specially prepared and issued by this Department for circulation in the Universal Postal Union mails, and is to be used for card correspondence with the countries of the Postal Union. See section 141.

Sec. 1120. Reforwarding.—1. All mailable matter of Postal Union origin (including such matter from Canada) received in the United States may be reforwarded from the United States post-office of original destination to any other United States post-office, or to any Postal Union country, without charge of additional postage therefor, or, if a registered article, without charge of an additional registry fee.

2. Such matter, however, as has been in the first instance addressed to a post-office in the country of mailing is chargeable on redirection with the same postage, less the sum prepaid, as would have been charged had it been addressed in the first instance to the post-office of ultimate delivery, but, if registered, without additional registry fee.

Sec. 1121. Articles not Transmissible, or Limited in Weight, to Italy.—1. Living plants, and generally any living portion of a vegetable, such as branches, bulbs, or roots, being prohibited entrance by mail in Italy, samples of these articles cannot be sent in the mails to that country.

2. Samples of tobacco, being subject to customs duties in Italy, should not be sent in the mails to that country.

3. Samples of raw or spun silk for Italy are limited to a weight of one hundred grams (3½ ozs.).

Sec. 1122. Addressing Correspondence to Russia.—Correspondence for Russia should have the name of the place of destination added in either English,

French, or German, and if for the smaller towns in Russia, they should bear, as a part of their address, the name of the province or government in which the towns are situated. If these conditions are not complied with the Russian post-office declines to undertake delivery of the correspondence.

Sec. 1123. Newspapers for Russia. Restrictions.—Newspapers and other political publications of foreign origin are not allowed circulation in Russia by mail, except such as are addressed to members of the reigning imperial family, the ministers of the empire, or members of the diplomatic corps. Non-political publications and newspapers are only admitted to circulation by mail when addressed to the Public Imperial Library, the Academy of Sciences, the higher establishments of education, and established bookstores, but any person in Russia may subscribe at the Russian post-offices for foreign newspapers and publications, whether political or not.

Sec. 1124. Letters of Declared Value not Admissible to Union Mails.—The United States not having entered into arrangements with other countries of the Universal Postal Union for the exchange of letters of declared value, it is prohibited to send to any of those countries any registered or other articles marked on the outside with the declared value of the contents.

Sec. 1125. List of Exchange Post-Offices.—The following table and paragraphs appended exhibit the exchange of United States mails with foreign countries.

Where mails for the same countries are made up at more than one United States exchange post-office, ordinary (unregistered) correspondence addressed abroad should be forwarded to that one of the exchange post-offices from which it will have the earliest dispatch; but registered correspondence must always be sent under domestic registration to the United States exchange post-office at the port of embarkation or place of egress of the mails.

Table giving details respecting exchanges of mails from the United States for foreign countries, Canada and Mexico excepted.

Countries and places for which mails are made up.	Countries and places correspondence for which is transmissible in the mails.	United States exchange post-offices which make up the mails.	Route of the mails.	When mails are dispatched.*
1. TRANS-ATLANTIC MAILS.				
Austria-Hungary	Austria, Hungary, and Principality of Lichtenstein	New York	Via England and via Germany	Every Tuesday, Wednesday, Thursday, and Saturday.
Belgium	Belgium	New York	Direct	Irregular.
		...do	Via England	Every Tuesday, Wednesday, Thursday, and Saturday.
		Boston	...do	Every Saturday.
		Philadelphia	Direct	Irregular.
Denmark	Denmark, including Iceland, Faroe Islands, and Greenland.	New York	Via Germany	Every Thursday and Saturday.
		Chicago	Via New York and Germany	do.
France	France, Algeria, China (portions of China not in Postal Union), French colonies in Asia and Africa, French post-offices at Cambodia and Tonquin, and at Tunis and Tangier (Morocco), Madagascar (other than St. Mary's), Principality of Monaco, St. Lucie, W. I.	New York	Direct	Every Wednesday and Thursday.
		...do	Via England	Every Tuesday and Saturday.
		Boston	Direct from New York	Every Wednesday and Thursday.
		...do	Via New York and England	Every Tuesday and Saturday.
Germany	Germany, China (cities of Ourga, Kalgan, Pekin and Tien-Tsin), in Russian mails, Egypt (including Nubia, and Soodan), Heligoland, Greece, and Ionian Isles, Luxemburg, Montenegro, Persia, Roumania, Russia, (including Finland), Servia, Turkey.	New York	Direct	Every Thursday and Saturday.
		...do	Via England	Every Tuesday, Wednesday, Thursday, and Saturday.
		Boston	Direct from New York	Every Thursday and Saturday.
		Philadelphia	...do	do.
		Chicago	...do	do.
		Baltimore	...do	do.
		...do	Direct from Baltimore	Irregular.
		...do	Via New York and England	Every Tuesday, Wednesday, Thursday, and Saturday.
Great Britain	England, Ireland, Scotland, and Wales, Africa (British colonies, west coast of), Argentine Republic, Ascension, Australia, Brazil, British India, Cape of Good Hope, Ceylon, China (portions of, not in Postal Union), Cyprus, island of, Falkland Islands, Gibraltar, Labuan, Liberia, Madagascar (other than St. Mary's), Malta and dependencies, Mauritius and dependencies, Morocco (except Spanish colonies on west coast of), Natal, New Zealand, Paraguay, Patagonia, Portugal (including the Azores and island of Madeira), Portuguese colonies in Africa and Asia, Siam, Spanish colonies in Africa, Asia, and Oceanica, St. Helena, Straits Settlements, Tasmania, Uruguay, and Zanzibar.	New York	Direct	Every Tuesday, Wednesday, Thursday, and Saturday.
		Boston	...do	Every Saturday.
		...do	Direct via New York	Every Tuesday, Wednesday, Thursday, and Saturday.
		Philadelphia	Direct	Irregular; 4, 5, and 6 times each month.
		...do	Direct via New York	Every Tuesday, Wednesday, Thursday, and Saturday.
		Chicago	Direct via Detroit	Weekly.
		...do	Direct via New York	Tri-weekly.
		Detroit	Direct	Weekly.
		...do	Direct via New York	do.
		San Francisco	...do	do.

Italy	Italy, British India, Cabul (Afghanistan), Holkar, and Hyderabad (India), Italian post-offices of Tunis and Tripoli, Kashmir, Ladakh, and Mysore (India), Netherlands colonies in Asia and Oceanica, and Republic of San Marino.	New York	Via England	Every Tuesday, Wednesday, Thursday, and Saturday.
Netherlands	The Netherlands	New York	Direct	Three times each month.
		...do	Via England	Every Tuesday, Wednesday, Thursday, and Saturday.
Norway	Norway	New York	Via Germany	Every Thursday and Saturday.
		Chicago	Via New York and Germany	do.
Spain	Spain, and territory included therewith in the Postal Union, Gibraltar, Portugal, and Portuguese colonies.	New York	Via England	Every Tuesday, Wednesday, Thursday, and Saturday.
Sweden	Sweden	New York	Via England and via Germany	Every Thursday and Saturday.
		Chicago	Via New York and England, and via New York and Germany.	do.
Switzerland	Switzerland	New York	Via England	Every Tuesday, Wednesday, Thursday and Saturday,
2. TRANS-PACIFIC MAILS.				
British India, viz, Bombay, Calcutta, Madras, Rangoon.	The places named and other portions of British India	San Francisco	Via Hong-Kong	Every 15 days.
Ceylon	Ceylon	San Francisco	Via Hong-Kong	Every 15 days.
French colonies in Oceanica.	Tahiti, Marquesas Islands, Isle of Pines, Loyalty Islands, the Archipelagoes of Gambier, Toubouai, and Tuamotou (Low Islands).	San Francisco	Direct	Irregular.
	New Caledonia	...do	Via New South Wales	Monthly.
Fiji Islands	Fiji Islands	San Francisco	Via New South Wales	Monthly.
Hawaii	Hawaii	San Francisco	Direct	Monthly.
Hong-Kong	Hong-Kong, and Hong-Kong post-offices at Amoy, Canton, Foo-Chow, Hankow, Hanoi, Hai-fung, Kiung-Chow, Ning-po, Shanghai, and Swatow; British India, China, French establishments in Cochin China, French post-offices at Cambodia, Shanghai, and Tonquin, Formosa, Labuan, Mauritius, Netherland colonies in Asia, Asia, Philippino Archipelago, Portuguese colonies in Siam.	San Francisco	Direct	Every 15 days.
Japan	Japan and Japanese post-offices at Chee-Foo, Chin-Kiang, Fusampo, Foo-Chow, Hankow, Kiu-Kiang, Newchwang, Ning-po, Shanghai, Tien-Tsin.	San Francisco	Direct	Every 15 days.
Manila	Manila and Philippine Archipelago	San Francisco	Via Hong-Kong	Every 15 days.
New South Wales	New South Wales and Australia, except Queensland and Victoria.	San Francisco	Direct	Monthly.
New Zealand	New Zealand, Chatham Island	San Francisco	Direct	Monthly.
Queensland	Queensland	San Francisco	Via New South Wales	Monthly.
Shangai, China	Shanghai	San Francisco	Via Yokohama	Every 15 days.
Straits Settlements	Straits Settlements (Singapore, Penang, and Malacca)	San Francisco	Via Hong-Kong	Every 15 days.
Victoria	Victoria	San Francisco	Via New South Wales	Monthly.

* For exact dates of dispatches of mails consult the Monthly Steamship Schedule issued by the Post-Office Department.

Table giving details respecting exchanges of mails from the United States, &c.—Continued.

Countries and places for which mails are made up.	Countries and places correspondence for which is transmissible in the mails.	United States exchange post-offices which make up the mails.	Route of the mails.	When mails are dispatched.*
3. MISCELLANEOUS.				
Argentine Republic	Argentine Republic, Paraguay, and Uruguay	New York	Via Brazil	Regular steamer monthly; other services irregular.
Aspinwall	Aspinwall, Costa Rica (east coast), Colombia (United States of), Ecuador, Nicaragua (east coast).	New York	Direct	Every 10 days.
		San Francisco	Via Panama	Twice each month.
Bahamas	The Bahamas	New York	Direct	Irregular.
Barbadoes	Barbadoes	New York	Direct	Irregular.
Bermudas	The Bermudas	New York	Direct	Weekly in May and June. Fortnightly remainder of year.
Brazil	Brazil	New York	Direct	Regular steamer monthly; other services irregular
Colombia (United States of).	United States of Colombia, except Aspinwall and Panama	New York	Direct via Aspinwall	Every 10 days.
Cuba	Cuba, Porto Rico	New York	Direct via Havana	From 8 to 12 times each month.
		Boston	do	Monthly.
		New Orleans	do	Irregular.
		Key West	do	do.
Curaçoa, W. I	Curaçoa, Aruba, Bonaire, Netherlands portion of St. Martin, St. Eustatius, and Saba.	New York	Direct	Irregular.
Ecuador	Ecuador	New York	Direct via Aspinwall	Every 10 days.
		San Francisco	Direct via Panama	Twice each month.
Guadeloupe, W. I	Guadeloupe, Deseada, Les Saintes, Maria Galante, and north portion of St. Martin.	New York	Direct	Irregular.
Greytown (Nicaragua)	Greytown	New York	Direct	Irregular.
Guatemala	Guatemala	New York	Direct via Aspinwall	Every 10 days.
		San Francisco	Direct via Panama	Twice each month.
Hayti	Hayti	New York	Direct	Irregular.
Honduras (British)	British Honduras	New Orleans	Direct	Every 20 days by steamer, and irregular by other services.
Honduras (Republic of)	Republic of Honduras	New York	Direct via Aspinwall	Every 10 days.
		San Francisco	Direct	Twice each month.
		New Orleans	Direct	Every 20 days by steamer, and irregular by other services.
Jamaica	Jamaica, British Honduras, British Guiana, French Guiana, Netherlands Guiana, St. Thomas, St. John, and St. Croix (West Indies.)	New York	Direct and via Jamaica	Twice each month.
Martinique, W. I	Martinique	New York	Direct	Irregular.
Miquelon	Miquelon	Boston	Via Halifax	Fortnightly.
Navassa, W. I	Navassa	New York	Direct	Irregular.
		Baltimore	do	do.

Newfoundland	Newfoundland	New York	Direct via Halifax, by sea and overland.	Fortnightly from Halifax.
		Boston	do	do.
Panama	Panama, Bolivia, Chili, Colombia (United States of), Costa Rica (west coast), Nicaragua (west coast).	New York	Direct via Aspinwall	Every 10 days.
		San Francisco	Direct	Twice each month.
Peru	Peru	New York	Direct via Panama	Every 10 days.
		San Francisco	do	Twice each month.
Porto Rico, W. I.	Porto Rico	New York	Direct	From 8 to 12 times each month.
Salvador	Salvador	New York	Direct via Aspinwall	Every 10 days.
		San Francisco	Direct	Twice each month.
St. Pierre	St. Pierre	Boston	Via Halifax	Fortnightly.
St. Thomas (West Indies.)	St. Thomas, St. John and St. Croix, Antigua, Aspinwall, Barbadoes, Colombia (United States of), Curaçoa and dependencies, Dominica, Guiana (British, French, and Dutch), Guatemala, Guadeloupe, Hayti, Honduras (British), Martinique, Montserrat, Nevis, Nicaragua, Panama, St. Domingo, St. Christopher, St. Bartholomew, Turk's Island, Venezuela, Virgin Isles (West Indies,) British and other West Indies not above named.	New York	Direct and via St. Thomas	Two or 3 times each month.
		New York	Via Bermuda	Monthly.
Trinidad, W. I	Trinidad	New York	Direct	Irregular.
Turk's Island, W. I.	Turk's Island	New York	Direct	Irregular.
Venezuela	Venezuela	New York	Direct	Irregular.
			Via Jamaica	Twice each month.

* For exact dates of dispatches of mails consult the Monthly Steamship Schedule issued by the Post-Office Department.

EXCHANGE OF MAILS WITH CANADA.

The exchange of mails with Canada takes place between the following exchange post-offices:

On the side of the United States.	On the side of Canada.
Albany, N. Y	Hamilton, Ont.; Toronto, Ont.; Montreal, Q.
Bangor, Me	St. John, N. B.
Boston, Mass	Hamilton, Ont.; Toronto, Ont.; Kingston, Ont.; Montreal, Q.; Quebec, Q.; Halifax, N. S.; Yarmouth, N. S. (summer service); St. John, N. B.; Charlottetown, Pr. Ed. I.
Buffalo, N. Y	Great Western Railway, Ont.; Canada Southern Railway Postal Car, Ont.; Buffalo & Lake Huron Railway Postal Car, Ont.; London, Ont.; Fort Erie, Ont.; Hamilton, Ont.; Niagara, Ont.; Toronto, Ont.
Burlington, Vt	Montreal, Q.
Calais, Me	St. Stephen, N. B.; Western Extension Railway Postal Car, N. B.
Canaan, Vt	Hereford, Q.
Canada Roads, Me	Jersey, Q.; Marlow, Q.
Cape Vincent, N. Y	Kingston, Ont.
Chicago, Ill	Great Western Railway Postal Car, Ont.; Hamilton, Ont.; Toronto, Ont.; Grand Trunk Railway (west) Postal Car, Ont.
Cleveland, Ohio	London, Ont.
Derby Line, Vt	Stanstead, Q.
Detroit, Mich	Great Western Railway Postal Car, Ont.; Canada Southern Railway Postal Car, Ont.; Windsor, Ont; Toronto, Ont.; Grand Trunk Railway Postal Car, Ont.; Montreal, Q.
Duluth, Minn	Silver Islet, Ont.; Thunder Bay, Ont.
Eastport, Me	Grand Manan, N. B.; St. Andrews, N. B.; St. John, N. B.
Fort Covington, N.Y	Huntingdon, Q.
Fort Fairfield, Me	Andover, N. B.
Houlton, Me	St. Andrews, N. B.; St. Stephen, N. B.; Woodstock N. B.; Western Extension Railway Postal Car, N. B.
Island Pond, Vt	Montreal, Q.; Montreal & Island Pond Railway Postal Car, Q.
Marine City, Mich	Sombra, Ont.
Morristown, N. Y	Brockville, Ont.
Newport, Vt	Lennoxville, Q.; Massawippi Valley Railway Postal Car, Q.
New York, N. Y	London, Ont.: Hamilton, Ont.; Toronto, Ont.; Kingston, Ont.; Ottawa, Ont.; Montreal, Q.; Quebec, Q.; Halifax, N. S.
Ogdensburg, N. Y	Prescott, Ont.
Oswego, N. Y	Kingston, Ont.
Pembina, Dak	West Lynne, Man.
Portland, Me	Montreal, Q.; St. John, N. B.
Portland, Oreg	Victoria, B. C.
Port Huron, Mich	Sarnia, Ont.
Port Townsend, Wash. Ter	Victoria, B. C. (by steamers).
Richford, Vt	Southeastern Railway Postal Car, Q.
Rochester, N. Y	Port Hope, Ont (by steamer in summer).
Rouse's Point, N. Y	Montreal, Q.; St. John's, Q.
Rutland, Vt	Montreal, Q. (via St. Armand & St. Albans R. P. O. and St. Albans & Boston R. P O.).
Saint Albans, Vt	Montreal, Q.; St. Armand Station, Q.; St. John's, Q.; Vermont Junction Railway Postal Car, Q.; Quebec, Q.
Saint Vincent, Minn	Winnipeg, Man.
San Francisco, Cal	Victoria, B. C.
Sault de Ste. Marie, Mich	Sault de Ste. Marie, Ont.
Suspension Bridge, N. Y	Great Western Railway Postal Car, Ont.; Clifton, Ont.; Toronto, Ont. (for registered letters).

On the side of the United States.	On the side of Canada.
Thousand Island Park, N. Y	Kingston, Ont. (during summer).
Troy, N. Y	Montreal, Q.
Upper Madawaska, Me	Edmundston, N. B.
Vanceborough, Me	Halifax, N. S. (for registered letters); Western Extension Railway Postal Car, N. B.
Waddington, N. Y	Morrisburg, Ont.
Watertown, N. Y	Kingston, Ont.
Detroit & Chicago R. P. O	Toronto, Ont.; Grand Trunk Railway (east) Postal Car, Ont.; Montreal, Q.
Island Pond & Portland agent	Montreal, Q.
Newport & Springfield agent	Montreal, Q.; Massawippi Valley Railway Postal Car, Q., and Stanstead, Q.
New York & Chicago R. P. O., east of Rochester, N. Y	Toronto, Ont.
Richford & Newport agent	Southeastern Railway Postal Car, Q.
Rome, Watertown & Ogdensburg agent	Kingston, Ont.
Rouse's Point & Albany agent	Montreal, Q.
St. Albans & Boston R. P. O	Montreal, Q.; Vermont Junction Railway Postal Car, Q.
St. Paul & St. Vincent agent	Winnipeg and St. Vincent route agents.
Tacoma & Victoria agent	Victoria, B. C.
Vanceborough & Bangor, Me., R. P. O	St. Stephens, St. Andrews, and Woodstock, N. B.

EXCHANGE OF MAILS WITH MEXICO.

The exchange of mails with Mexico takes place between the following exchange post-offices:

1. Between New York and Vera Cruz (by sea).
2. Between New Orleans and Tampico and Vera Cruz (by sea).
3. Between San Francisco and Mazatlan, San Blas, Manzanilla, Acapulco (by sea).
4. Between Brownsville, Tex., and Matamoras.
5. Between Eagle Pass, Tex., and Piedras Negras,
6. Between El Paso, Tex., and Paso del Norte.
7. Between Tucson, Ariz., and Magdalena.

Correspondence for Yucatan, Campeachy, Tobasco, Vera Cruz, Puebla, and the entire eastern and central sections of Mexico is expeditiously forwarded via New York or via New Orleans.

Correspondence for the State of Tamaulipas and northeastern section of Mexico is expeditiously forwarded via Brownsville, Tex., or via New Orleans.

Correspondence for the States of Nueva Leon and Coahuila, up to San Luis Potosi, is expeditiously forwarded via Eagle Pass, Tex.

Correspondence for the State of Chihuahua and central and northwestern sections of Mexico is expeditiously forwarded via El Paso.

Correspondence for the States of Sonora, Sinaloa, Jalisco, and Durango and the Territory of Lower California is expeditiously forwarded via Tucson, Ariz.

Correspondence for ports and places on the Pacific coast and western and southern sections of Mexico is expeditiously forwarded via San Francisco.

CHAPTER TWO.

CORRESPONDENCE UNDER SPECIAL ARRANGEMENTS, AND WITH COUNTRIES NOT IN THE UNIVERSAL POSTAL UNION.

Sec. 1126. Special Postal Conventions and Arrangements.—Special postal conventions are in force with the countries named below.

The principal provisions governing the exchange of correspondence under the respective conventions and arrangements, together with the rates of postage, are stated under each.

CANADA.

The Dominion of Canada embraces all the British North American Provinces, except Newfoundland.

The correspondence exchangeable comprises letters (ordinary and registered), postal cards, newspapers, pamphlets, magazines, books, maps, plans, engravings, drawings, photographs, lithographs, sheets of music, etc., and patterns and samples of merchandise, including grains and seeds.

Patterns and samples are construed to be *bona fide* specimens of goods on hand and for sale, having no intrinsic value aside from their use as patterns and samples. The weight of each package is limited to eight ounces, and the postage charge is ten cents per package, prepayment compulsory. They are subject to the regulations of either country to prevent violations of the revenue laws; must not be closed against inspection, and must be so wrapped and inclosed as to be easily examined.

All articles of mail-matter, except samples, must be fully prepaid at the domestic rates of the country of origin, and are deliverable free of charge in the country of destination.

Newspapers sent from offices of publication in the United States to regular subscribers in Canada are subject to the same rates of postage and conditions of prepayment as when sent to subscribers in the United States.

"Request letters" originating in Canada are returnable directly to the Canadian mailing post-offices, in the event of non-delivery to their addressees within the time specified by the writers.

The regulations respecting the manner of inclosure and limit of weight, governing the transmission of domestic correspondence, are applicable to correspondence exchanged with Canada, patterns and samples excepted.

ECUADOR.

Letters, and manuscript subject by the laws of either country to letter rate of postage, newspapers, and prints of all kinds in sheets, in pamphlets, and in books, sheets of music, engravings, lithographs, photographs, drawings, maps, and plans, comprise the correspondence exchangeable with Ecuador.

All correspondence, except letters, and manuscript subject to letter postage, is transmissible under the same regulations and restrictions as are stated for Guatemala (the limit for books excepted), and is also subject to the laws of each country in regard to its liability to customs duty, if containing dutiable goods.

Correspondence other than letters, received from Ecuador, is liable, on delivery in the United States, to the rates of postage for matter sent to Ecuador.

The rates of postage applicable to correspondence for Ecuador, sent via Panama, are as follows, prepayment compulsory, and on letters in full to destination:

Letters, per ½ ounce, 20 cents.

Newspapers, 2 cents each, if not exceeding 4 ounces in weight.

Other printed matter, not over 1 ounce, 2 cents; over 1 but not over 2 ounces, 3 cents; over 2 but not over 4 ounces, 4 cents.

Newspapers and other printed matter are liable to postage on delivery in Ecuador.

Registration is not permissible and samples are not exchangeable.

GUATEMALA.

Letters, newspapers, unsealed circulars at newspaper rates, pamphlets, periodicals, books, and other kinds of printed matter may be exchanged in the mails with Guatemala.

All printed matter must be sent in narrow bands, open at the sides or ends, and is subject to the laws and regulations of each country, respectively, in regard to its liability to be rated with letter postage when containing written matter, or for any other cause specified in said laws and regulations.

Bound or unbound books weighing over two pounds cannot be sent, except at letter rates of postage.

The rates of postage applicable to correspondence for Guatemala sent via Panama are as follows, prepayment compulsory:

Letters, per ½ ounce, 10 cents.

Newspapers, 2 cents each.

Other printed matter, 1 cent an ounce.

Correspondence of all kinds received from Guatemala is liable, on delivery in the United States, to the rates of postage for matter sent to Guatemala, and on that from the United States sent to Guatemala postage is chargeable on delivery.

Registration is not permissible and samples cannot be sent.

THE HAWAIIAN KINGDOM (SANDWICH ISLANDS).

Letters, newspapers, and printed matter of every kind are exchangeable.

Rates of postage, prepayment compulsory, on correspondence for Hawaii sent in direct mails:

Letters, per ½ ounce, 6 cents.

Newspapers, United States domestic rates.

Other printed matter, 4 cents per 4 ounces or fraction thereof.

On newspapers received in the United States from Hawaii the established rates of the United States domestic postage are chargeable. Articles of printed matter except newspapers are liable, on delivery in the United States, to postage at the rate of 4 cents for each 4 ounces or fraction thereof. The domestic postage rates of the Hawaiian Kingdom are chargeable upon all correspondence, except letters, received there from the United States.

To regular subscribers in the Hawaiian Kingdom newspapers published in the United States may be sent at domestic rates.

Registration is not permissible, and samples cannot be sent.

NEW SOUTH WALES (AUSTRALIA).

Exchangeable correspondence comprises letters (ordinary and registered), newspapers, printed matter of every kind, and patterns and samples.

The provisions relative to unpaid and insufficiently prepaid letters to New Zealand, as below stated, are applicable in the case of New South Wales.

Correspondence of all kinds, if prepaid in full in New South Wales, is delivered free of charge in the United States.

The regulations and conditions governing the exchange of newspapers and printed matter are identical with those stated below for New Zealand.

Rates of postage, prepayment compulsory, and in full to destination, on correspondence for New South Wales sent in direct mails:

Letters, per ½ ounce, 12 cents.

Register fee on letters, 10 cents.

Newspapers, 2 cents each.

Other printed matter and samples, 4 cents per 4 ounces or fraction thereof.

NEW ZEALAND.

For the correspondence exchangeable, see New South Wales above.

Letters may be registered with fee and postage prepaid.

Letters unpaid, or prepaid less than one full rate, cannot be forwarded, but insufficiently paid letters, on which a single rate or more has been prepaid, will be forwarded charged with the deficient postage.

Correspondence of all kinds prepaid in full in New Zealand is delivered free of charge in the United States.

Newspapers, printed matter, and patterns of merchandise are subject to the laws and regulations of each country, respectively, in regard to liability to be rated with letter postage when containing written matter, or for any cause specified in said laws and regulations, as well as in regard to liability to customs duty under the revenue laws.

The rates of postage, register fee, and conditions of prepayment on correspondence for New Zealand sent in direct mails are the same as for New South Wales.

QUEENSLAND (AUSTRALIA).

Exchangeable correspondence comprises letters (ordinary and registered), newspapers, printed matter of every kind, and patterns and samples of merchandise.

The provisions relative to unpaid and insufficiently paid letters to New Zealand, as above stated, are applicable in the case of Queensland.

Correspondence of all kinds prepaid in full in Queensland is delivered free of charge in the United States.

Newspapers, printed matter, and patterns and samples of merchandise are subject to the laws and regulations of each country, respectively, in regard to their liability to be rated with letter postage, when containing written matter, or for any other cause specified in said laws and regulations, as well as in regard to their liability to customs duties.

Postage rates, register fee, and conditions of prepayment for correspondence for Queensland sent in direct mails are as above stated for New South Wales and New Zealand.

VENEZUELA.

The correspondence exchangeable with Venezuela comprises letters and manuscript, subject by the laws of the United States, or Venezuela, to letter rate of postage, newspapers and prints of all kinds in sheets, in pamphlets, and in books, sheets of music, engravings, lithographs, photographs, drawings, maps, and plans.

Mail-matter other than letters must be inclosed in narrow bands or covers, open at the sides or ends, so as to be easily examined, subject to the laws and regulations of each country, respectively.

Rates of postage, prepayment compulsory, for correspondence for Venezuela sent in direct mails:

Letters, per ½ ounce, 10 cents.

Newspapers, United States domestic rates for transient newspapers, with one cent added for each paper.

Other printed matter, United States domestic rates and one cent for each ounce or fraction thereof.

Domestic rates of postage are chargeable on all correspondence received from Venezuela, and correspondence sent is liable on delivery in Venezuela to the inland postage there chargeable.

Registration is not permissible and samples cannot be exchanged.

VICTORIA (AUSTRALIA).

Letters (ordinary and registered), newspapers, printed matter of every kind, and patterns and samples of merchandise are exchangeable with Victoria.

Letters prepaid less than one full rate of postage cannot be forwarded. Those prepaid at single rates or more will be forwarded charged with the deficient postage.

Correspondence fully prepaid in Victoria is delivered free of charge in the United States.

Newspapers, printed matter, and samples of merchandise are subject to the laws and regulations of each country, respectively, in regard to liability to letter postage when containing written matter, or for any other cause specified in said laws and regulations, as well as with reference to liability to customs duties.

Postage rates and register fee upon correspondence for Victoria sent in direct mails are the same as given above for Queensland.

Sec. 1127. Rates of Postage when not Fixed by Convention.—The rate of United States postage on mail-matter sent to or received from foreign countries with which different rates have not been established by postal convention or other arrangement, when forwarded by vessels regularly employed in transporting the mail, shall be ten cents for each half-ounce or fraction thereof on letters, unless reduced by order of the Postmaster-General;* two cents each on newspapers; and not exceeding two cents per each two ounces, or fraction thereof, on pamphlets, periodicals, books, and other printed matter, which postage shall be prepaid on matter sent and collected on matter received; and to avoid loss to the United States in the payment of balances, the Postmaster-General may collect the unpaid postage on letters from foreign countries in coin or or its equivalent. (R. S., § 3912.)

Sec. 1128. Rates, &c., for Non-Convention Countries by Direct Mails.—Correspondence from the United States for foreign countries and places other than those heretofore named, or with which no postal treaties or other postal arrangements have been made by the United States, if forwarded in direct mail by vessels regularly employed in carrying the mails, and not through the intermediary of a country having postal relations with the United States by treaty or other arrangement, is subject to the rates of postage stated in section 1127 and foot-note thereto.

Only ordinary letters, newspapers, pamphlets, periodicals, books, and other printed matter may be sent in these cases, under the regulations and conditions applicable to the same correspondence in the domestic mails.

Prepayment of postage is compulsory for all correspondence, and the prescribed rates are collectible upon delivery in the United States of matter received.

Sec. 1129. List of Principal Non-Convention Countries.—The principal countries and places to which the above rates and conditions at present apply are the

* The Postmaster-General has reduced the rate to five cents. (See next section.)

United States of Colombia, other Central and South American States not embraced in the Universal Postal Union, or not having postal arrangements with the United States; the West India Islands not in the Postal Union; the Fiji and other islands of the Pacific Ocean not in the Postal Union, or with which no postal arrangements have been made; Shanghai, China, and the Australian colonies other than New South Wales, Queensland, and Victoria.

Registered letters may be transmitted to Aspinwall, Panama, and to Shanghai.

Sec. 1130. Rates to Non-Convention Countries on Matter not Sent Direct.—If correspondence for countries not in the Postal Union, or the countries and places mentioned or referred to in the last section, is transmitted in open mails through the intermediary of other countries having postal arrangements with the United States and with the countries of destination, it is liable generally to the combined rates of the United States, as named above for direct transmission, and those applicable in the intermediary country to correspondence for the same destinations, less the domestic interior rate of the intermediary country, and the combined postages are usually required to be prepaid.

Sec. 1131. Postal Guide to be Consulted for Foreign Postage Table.—Reference should be had to the Foreign Postage Table in the latest edition of the United States Official Postal Guide for rates of postage, condition and limit of prepayment, and the classes of correspondence transmissible, in the cases of countries and places not in the Universal Postal Union, or to which correspondence is forwarded in the open mails of intermediary countries.

Sec. 1132. Miscellaneous Regulations and Suggestions.—1. All inquiries relative to foreign mails and mail steamship service between the United States and foreign countries should be addressed to "Superintendent Foreign Mails, Post-Office Department, Washington, D. C."

2. The Post-Office Department is the proper medium for official communication with foreign postal officials respecting postal matters, and United States postmasters should refer all subjects requiring official correspondence with foreign postal administrations or officials to the Superintendent of Foreign Mails at Washington, D. C., through whose office such correspondence is conducted.

3. All articles of correspondence addressed to foreign countries must bear a legible impression of the stamp of the mailing post-office, or inscription in ink, showing the place of mailing and date of dispatch therefrom.

4. In order to avoid the delay consequent upon the return through the Dead-Letter Office of short-paid letters, addressed to countries to which prepayment of postage is compulsory, care should be exercised in the weighing and stamping of such letters. In case of doubt it is safer to prepay at the higher rate. Delay may also be avoided by writing the name and address of the sender on the covers.

5. Make the address legible and complete, giving the name of the country, as well as the name of the post-office or town. Letters addressed merely to "London," without adding "England," may be sent to London, Canada, and *vice versa*, thereby causing delay, and often serious loss. Wherever practicable the name of the street and number of the house should also be given on letters addressed to cities. While the letter may eventually reach its destination without a number, the omission is often a cause of hesitation and delay.

6. See that every letter, newspaper, or other packet sent by mail is securely folded and fastened. In affixing the postage-stamps to the covers of printed matter, see that they do not overlap the covers and adhere in part to the contents, thus, in effect, closing the packet against inspection. Avoid using cheap envelopes, made of thin paper, especially where more than one sheet of paper or any other article than paper is inclosed. Being often handled, and subject to pressure in the mail-bags, such envelopes not unfrequently split open, often giving cause of complaint against officials who are entirely innocent in the matter.

7. It is recommended that some other material than wax be used for closing letters or packets addressed to places in warm climates.

8. Many of the suggestions relative to domestic correspondence apply with equal force to correspondence addressed to foreign countries.

9. Letters for countries to which payment of postage is compulsory, when unpaid or insufficiently prepaid, are sent to the Dead-Letter Office, to be opened and returned to the writers.

10. Undelivered correspondence of foreign origin is returned to the senders in pursuance of the stipulations of postal treaties or conventions in force with foreign countries, or in accordance with special arrangements made with reference thereto.

11. Newspapers and periodicals sent in the mails to foreign countries should be wrapped singly, except those sent by publishers to regular subscribers in Canada and the Hawaiian Kingdom.

12. To avoid possible errors, the route by which the correspondence is desired to be forwarded should be plainly marked on the face of the correspondence, near the address.

13. In the absence of special instruction to the contrary, where correspondence is marked for transmission by a route requiring prepayment, and the amount prepaid is insufficient for that route, it will be sent by some other route by which prepayment of postage is optional; but if there is no such route, and no means of obtaining full prepayment by notice to the sender, the correspondence will be sent to the Dead-Letter Office.

14. Directions given by senders on correspondence for foreign countries respecting routes of transmission desired will be observed whenever practicable.

15. Prepayment of postage on correspondence sent from the United States to foreign countries must be made in United States postage-stamps. On correspondence from foreign countries to the United States prepayment must be made in postage-stamps of the country of mailing.

16. The amount of postage due on unpaid or insufficiently paid correspondence received from foreign countries is plainly marked on the cover by the United States exchange post-office through which the correspondence passes, and only the amount so marked as due should be collected. But in the case of mail-matter other than letters, which is discovered at the office of destination to contain a letter or other communication in writing, the postmaster at such office should levy postage thereon at letter rates for collection on delivery.

17. Senders have no legal claim upon the Post-Office Department for the value of postage-stamps uselessly employed upon mail-matter; but in cases where excessive postage has been paid upon correspondence addressed to foreign countries upon erroneous information given to the sender at mailing post-offices in the United States by postal officials at the time of mailing, the Department will require the overpaid sums to be reimbursed by the postmaster of the mailing post-office.

18. The exchange of postal cards is limited to the Universal Postal Union, including Canada. They can only be sent to, or received from, other countries and places at letter rates of postage.

19. Liquids, poisons, explosive and inflammable articles, fatty substances, live or dead animals, reptiles, fruits or vegetable matter liable to decomposition, confectionery, pastes or confections, and substances exhaling a bad odor, excluded from transmission in domestic mails as being in themselves either from their form or nature liable to destroy, deface, or otherwise injure the contents of the mail-bags or the persons of those engaged in the postal service, are prohibited from transmission in the mails exchanged with foreign countries, as are also obscene, lewd, or lascivious books, pamphlets, etc., and letters and circulars concerning lotteries, so-called gift concerts, etc., also excluded from domestic mails.

20. Certain articles, other than those above mentioned, which from their nature or form are liable to destroy, deface, or injure the contents of the mail-bags or the per-

sons of those engaged in the postal service, may be transmitted as samples in the mails to foreign countries when inclosed in the form prescribed for such matter in domestic mails.

21. All articles prohibited from domestic mails under sections 225 and 226, pages 79 and 80 of this book, are also excluded from circulation in the mails to or from foreign countries.

22. Packets of patterns or samples of merchandise, for dispatch in the mails to foreign countries, are restricted to *bona-fide* trade samples or specimens having no salable or commercial value in excess of that actually necessary for their use as samples or specimens. Goods sent for sale, in execution of an order, or as gifts, however small the quantity may be, are not admissible.

23. Prices-current and trade circulars (unsealed) may be sent to Guatemala at newspaper rate of postage, but to all other countries at the rate of postage for "other printed matter."

24. The domestic regulation requiring notice to be given by United States postmasters, to publishers whose publications are refused or not taken out of the post-office by the persons addressed, does not apply in the case of newspapers and periodicals of foreign origin refused or not taken out of the post-office by their addressees.

25. The public should bear in mind that all matter received in the mails from foreign countries which is subject to customs duties, such as watches, jewelry, lace, silk, etc., is liable to seizure by the officers of the customs.

26. The Post-Office Department assumes no responsibility for the delay, injury, or loss of either registered or ordinary correspondence for or from foreign countries, but it will, at the instance of senders or addressees, use the means at its command for the purpose of ascertaining the causes of such delay, injury, or loss, and preventing the recurrence thereof.

27. Where no special regulation is made relative to the transmission of correspondence, the domestic regulations will govern.

Sec. 1133. Treatment of Dutiable Articles.—When letters, sealed packages, or packages the wrappers of which cannot be removed without destroying them, are received in the United States from a foreign country, and the postmaster of the exchange post-office at which they are received has reason to believe they contain articles liable to customs duties, he shall immediately notify the customs officer of the district in which his post-office is located, or the customs officer designated by the Secretary of the Treasury for the purpose of examining the mails arriving from foreign countries, of the receipt of such letters or packages, and their several addresses; and if any letter or package of this character be addressed to a person residing within the delivery of his post-office, the postmaster shall also, at the time of its arrival, notify the addressee or addressees thereof that such letter or package has been received and is believed to contain articles liable to customs duties, and that he or they must appear at the post-office at a time in said notice to be designated, not exceeding twenty days from the date of said notice, and receive and open said letter or package in the presence of an officer of the customs.

Letters and sealed packages, or packages the wrappers of which cannot be removed without destroying them, which are supposed to contain articles liable to customs duties, and which are addressed to persons residing outside of the delivery of the United States exchange post-office where they were first received from abroad, shall be forwarded, without longer detention than twenty-four hours, to their respective destinations, marked *Supposed liable to customs duties*, and upon their receipt at the post-offices of destination the postmasters thereof shall notify the nearest customs officer and the parties addressed, in the manner and to the same effect as hereinbefore provided in the case of similar letters or packages addressed for delivery at the United States exchange post-office where they were first received.

Provided, however, that nothing hereinabove contained shall authorize or allow customs officers to seize or take possession of any letter or sealed package while the same is in the custody of a postmaster, nor until after its delivery to the addressee; and provided further, that no letter or sealed package shall be detained at the post-office of delivery a longer period than may be necessary for the appearance of a customs officer and the addressee, in pursuance of the notices hereinbefore provided to be given.

Unsealed packages received in the mails from foreign countries, which are found on examination by customs officers to contain articles liable to customs duties, shall be delivered by the postmaster at the exchange post-office of receipt to the proper officer of the customs for the collection of the duties chargeable thereon, with notice of such delivery to the person addressed.

Unsealed packages of samples of merchandise, including grains and seeds, in excess of eight ounces in weight, forwarded to the United States in the mails from Canada contrary to the provisions of the postal arrangement between the two countries, which are declared by customs officers to be dutiable, shall be immediately returned from the United States exchange post-office of receipt to the Canadian exchange post-office from which they were dispatched.

Postmasters are expected to extend to customs officers, specially designated for that duty by the Secretary of the Treasury, such facilities as may be necessary to enable them to examine mail matter arriving in the mails from foreign countries, in order to protect the customs revenue.

Sec. 1134. Dutiable Printed Matter in Foreign Mails.—Printed matter, other than books, received in the mails from foreign countries under the provisions of postal treaties or conventions, shall be free of customs duty, and books which are admitted to the international mails exchanged under the provisions of the Universal Postal Union Convention may, when subject to customs duty, be delivered to addressees in the United States under such regulations for the collection of duties as may be agreed upon by the Secretary of the Treasury and the Postmaster-General. (Act of March 3, 1879, § 17, 20 Stat., p. 360.)

Sec. 1135. Discretional Remission of Duties on Single Books.—From information received by the Postmaster-General from the Secretary of the Treasury, it appears that no books are absolutely exempt from customs duties, except those printed and manufactured more than twenty years; but collectors of customs may, in their discretion, remit duties on importations of single copies of books of less dutiable value than one dollar, when such books are intended for the personal use of the addressees.

Sec. 1136. Consuls may Pay Foreign Postage on Letters for the United States.—The Postmaster-General or the Secretary of State is hereby authorized to empower the consuls of the United States to pay the foreign postage on such letters destined for the United States as may be detained at the ports of foreign countries for the non-payment of postage, which postage shall be by the consul marked as paid by him, and the amount thereof shall be collected in the United States as other postage, on the delivery of the letters, and repaid to said consul, or credited on his account at the State Department. (R. S., § 4014.)

Sec. 1137. Retaliatory Postage on Certain Foreign Matter—The Postmaster-General, under the direction of the President of the United States, is hereby authorized and empowered to charge upon, and collect from, all letters and other mailable matter carried to or from any port of the United States, in any foreign packet-ship or other vessel, the same rate or rates of charge for American postage which the government to which such foreign packet or other vessel belongs imposes upon letters and other mailable matter conveyed to or from such foreign country in American packets or other vessels as the postage of such government, and at any time to revoke the same; and all custom-house officers and other United States agents designated or appointed for that purpose shall enforce or carry into effect the foregoing provision, and aid or assist in the collection of such postage, and to that end it shall be lawful for such officers and agents, on suspicion of fraud, to open and examine, in the presence of two or more respectable persons, being citizens of the United States, any package or packages supposed to contain mailable matter found on board such packets or other vessels or elsewhere, and to prevent, if necessary, such packets or other vessels from entering, breaking bulk, or making clearance until such letters or other mailable matter are duly delivered into the United States Post-Office. (R. S., § 4015.)

Sec. 1138. Letters Brought by Foreign Vessels to be Deposited in Post-Office.—All letters or other mailable matter conveyed to or from any part of the United States by any foreign vessel, except such sealed letters, relating to such vessel, or any part of the cargo thereof, as may be directed to the owners or consignees of the vessel, shall be subject to postage-charge, whether addressed to any person in the United States or elsewhere, provided they are conveyed by the packet or other ship of a foreign country imposing postage on letters or mailable matter conveyed to or from such country by any vessel of the United States; and such letters or other mailable matter carried in foreign vessels, except such sealed letters, relating to the vessel, or any part of the cargo thereof, as may be directed to the owners or consignees, shall be delivered into the United States post-office by the master of such vessel when arriving, and be taken from a United States post-office when departing, and the postage paid thereon, justly chargeable [*by this Title*], and for refusing or failing to do so, or for conveying such letters or any letters intended to be conveyed in any vessel of such foreign country over or across the United States, or any portion thereof, the party offending shall be punishable by a fine of not more than one thousand dollars for each offense. (R. S., § 4016.)

TITLE VIII.

AUDITING POSTAL ACCOUNTS.

CHAPTER ONE.

THE AUDITOR OF THE TREASURY FOR THE POST-OFFICE DEPARTMENT.

Sec. 1139. Auditor, how appointed.—There shall be appointed by the President, by and with the advice and consent of the Senate, an [*Sixth*]* Auditor of the Treasury for the Post-Office Department. (R. S., § 276.)

Sec. 1140. Duties of Auditor generally Stated.—To this office, which is not a bureau of the Post-Office Department, but an office of the Treasury Department, established for the adjustment and preservation of the accounts of the former are assigned the duties of examining the returns of postmasters and of notifying them of errors found therein; of adjusting their accounts; of designating the post-offices from which contractors shall make collections, and of furnishing them the blank orders and receipts necessary for that purpose; and, upon receipt of such collection-orders, together with the acknowledgments of collections and of certificates from the Division of Inspection, Office of the Second Assistant Postmaster-General, of the performance of service, of adjusting the quarterly compensation of contractors for carrying the mail, and of transmitting to them the drafts issued in payment of the balances found due; of adjusting the accounts for advertising, mail-bags, mail locks and keys, stamps, Special Agents, and all other demands properly arising under the laws, contracts, regulations, or orders of the Department; of closing the accounts of the Department quarterly, and of reporting the amounts paid by postmasters pursuant to appropriations made by law; and of registering, charging, and countersigning all warrants upon the Treasury for receipts and payments when warranted by law, as well as all drafts issued in payment or collection of debts. To the Auditor is also assigned the duty of adjusting and settling the money-order accounts of postmasters, and attending to all correspondence relating thereto. It is the duty of the Auditor to report to the Postmaster-General all delinquencies on the part of postmasters in paying over the moneys in their hands, all failures of postmasters to render their quarterly returns according to law, and all failures of appointees to qualify. To the Auditor is also assigned the duty of collecting from

---

*Title, formerly Sixth Auditor, changed by act of March 3, 1875. (18 Statutes at Large, page 397.

late postmasters balances due the United States upon their general postal and money-order accounts; and in cases of failure to collect such balances by drafts in favor of postmasters or other authorized agents of the Department, to prepare and transmit to the Department of Justice certified copies of all accounts and papers necessary for the institution of legal proceedings against such late postmasters and their sureties. To the Auditor should be transmitted all quarterly and general accounts; all vouchers and letters relating thereto; all receipts of postmasters for money and stamps turned over to them by their predecessors or other postmasters; all acknowledgments of drafts issued in payment of balances; all receipts of mail contractors for, and their acknowledgments of, the collections from postmasters; all letters admitting or contesting balances due on the general accounts of postmasters and mail contractors; all receipts for drafts issued in collecting such balances; all letters returning such drafts, or reporting the non-payment thereof; and all letters in relation to the settlement of the money-order accounts of postmasters.

Sec. 1141. Divisions of Auditor's Office.—There are in the office of the Auditor of the Treasury for the Post-Office Department eight divisions, through which the work of the office is distributed. Their names and duties are as follows:

COLLECTING DIVISION.—To this division is assigned the collection of balances due from all postmasters, late postmasters, and contractors; also the payment of all balances due to late and present postmasters, and the adjustment and final settlement of postal acounts.

STATING DIVISION.—The general postal accounts of postmasters and those of late postmasters, until fully stated, are in charge of this division.

EXAMINING DIVISION.—Receives and audits the quarterly accounts-current of all post-offices in the United States. It is divided into four subdivisions, viz, the opening-room, the stamp-rooms, the examining corps proper and the error-rooms.

MONEY-ORDER DIVISION.—Accounts of money-orders paid and received are examined, and paid money-orders are assorted, checked, and filed, remittances of money-order funds are registered and checked and errors corrected by this division.

FOREIGN MAIL DIVISION.—Has charge of the postal accounts with foreign governments, and the accounts with steamship companies for ocean transportation of the mails.

REGISTERING DIVISION.—Receives from the examining division the quarterly accounts-current of all the post-offices in the United States, re-examines and registers them, and exhibits in the register ending June 30 of each year the total amount of receipts and expenditures for the fiscal year.

PAY DIVISION.—The adjustment and payment of all accounts for the transportation of the mails, whether carried by ocean-steamers, railroads, steamboats, or any mail-carrier; the accounts of the railway postal service, railway postal clerks, route-agents, and local agents, mail-depredations, Special Agents, free-delivery system, postage-stamps, postal cards, envelopes, stamps, maps, wrapping-paper, twine, mail-bags, mail locks and keys, advertising, fees in suits on postal matters, and miscellaneous accounts, are assigned to this division.

BOOKKEEPING DIVISION.—The duty of keeping the ledger-accounts of the Department, embracing postmasters, late postmasters, contractors, late contractors, and accounts of a general, special, and miscellaneous character, is performed by this division.

Sec. 1142. The Duties of the Auditor as Prescribed by Statute.—The [*Sixth*] Auditor of the Treasury for the Post-Office Department shall receive all accounts arising in the Post-Office Department, or relative thereto, with the vouchers necessary to a correct adjustment thereof, and shall audit and settle the same and certify the balances thereon to the Postmaster-General. He shall keep and preserve all accounts and vouchers after settlement. He shall close the account of the Department quarterly, and transmit to the Secretary of the Treasury quarterly statements of its receipts and expenditures. He shall report to the Postmaster-General, when required to do so, the manner and form of keeping and stating the accounts of the Department, and the official forms of papers to be used in connection with its receipts and expenditures. He shall report to the Postmaster-General all delinquencies of postmasters in rendering their accounts and returns, or in paying over money-order funds and other receipts at their offices. He shall register, charge, and countersign all warrants upon the Treasury for receipts or payments issued by the Postmaster-General, when warranted by law. He shall perform such other duties in relation to the financial concerns of the Department as may be assigned to him by the Secretary of the Treasury, and make to the Secretary or to the Postmaster-General such reports respecting the same as either of them may require. (R. S., § 277.)

The Auditor of the Treasury for the Post-Office Department has direct official relation to both the Treasury and the Post-Office Department. (7 Opins., 439.)

Sec. 1143. Accounts of Post-Office Department, how to be Kept.—Hereafter the [*Sixth*] Auditor of the Treasury for the Post Office Department shall keep the accounts in his office so as to show the expenditures of the Post-Office Department under each item of appropriation provided by law. (Act of March 3, 1875, § 4; 18 Stats., p. 343.)

Sec. 1144. To Superintend the Collection of Debts Due the Department.—The [*Sixth*] Auditor [of the Treasury for the Post-Office Department] shall superintend the collection of all debts due the Post-Office Department, and all penalties and forfeitures imposed for any violation of the postal laws, and take all such other measures as may be authorized by law to enforce the payment of such debts and the recovery of such penalties and forfeitures. He shall also superintend the collection of all penalties and forfeitures arising under other statutes, where such penalties and forfeitures are the consequence of unlawful acts affecting the revenues or property of the Post-Office Department. (R. S., § 292.)

Sec. 1145. Accounts of the Money-Order Business.—The [*Sixth*] Auditor [of the Treasury for the Post-Office Department] shall keep the accounts of the money-order business separately, and in such manner as to show the number and amount of money-orders issued at each office, the number and amount paid, the amount of fees received, and all the expenses of the money-order business. (R. S., § 293.)

Sec. 1146. Accounts of Expenses Paid by Postmasters to be Stated.—The [*Sixth*] Auditor [of the Treasury for the Post-Office Department] shall state and certify quarterly to the Postmaster-General an account of the money paid by postmasters out of the receipts of their offices, and pursuant to appropriations, on account of the expenses of the postal service; designating the heads under which such payments were made. (R. S., § 294.)

Sec. 1147. Compromise of Judgments to be Made, how.—Whenever a judgment is obtained for a debt or damages due the Post-Office Department, and it satisfactorily appears that such judgment, or so much thereof as remains unpaid, cannot be collected by due process of law, the [*Sixth*] Auditor [of the Treasury for the Post-Office Department] may, with the written consent of the Postmaster-General, compromise such judgment, and accept in satisfaction less than the full amount thereof. (R. S., § 295.)

Sec. 1148. Papers Required in Suits for Delinquencies, etc.—In case of delinquency of any postmaster, contractor, or other officer, agent, or employé of the Post-Office Department, in which suit is brought, the [*Sixth*] Auditor [of the Treasury for the Post-Office Department] shall forward to the Department of Justice certified copies of all papers in his office tending to sustain the claim. (R. S., § 296.)

Sec. 1149. Oaths in Settlement with Auditor.*—Any mayor of a city, justice of the peace, or judge of any court of record in the United States, may administer oaths, in relation to the examination and settlement of the accounts committed to the charge of the [*Sixth*] Auditor [of the Treasury for the Post-Office Department]. (R. S., § 298.)

Sec. 1150. Appeal to First Comptroller from Auditor's Settlement.—Whenever the Postmaster-General or any person whose accounts have been settled by the [*Sixth*] Auditor [of the Treasury for the Post-Office Department] is dissatisfied with the settlement made by the Auditor, he may, within twelve months, appeal to the First Comptroller, whose decision shall be conclusive. (R. S., § 270.)

CHAPTER TWO.

POSTMASTERS' QUARTERLY RETURNS.

Sec. 1151. Quarterly Accounts of Receipts.—Every postmaster shall render to the Postmaster-General, under oath, and in such form as the

* Section 297, Revised Statutes, provides that the several Auditors are empowered to administer oaths to witnesses in any case in which they may deem it necessary for the due examination of the accounts with which they shall be charged.

latter shall prescribe, a quarterly account of all moneys received or charged by him or at his office, for postage, rent of boxes or other receptacles for mail-matter, or by reason of keeping a branch office, or for the delivery of mail-matter in any manner whatever. (R. S., § 3843.)

Sec. 1152. Quarterly Accounts to be Sworn to.—The Postmaster-General may require a sworn statement to accompany each quarterly account of a postmaster, to the effect that such account contains a true statement of the entire amount of postage, box-rents, charges, and moneys collected or received at his office during the quarter; that he has not knowingly delivered, or permitted to be delivered, any mail-matter on which the postage was not at the time paid; that such account exhibits truly and faithfully the entire receipts collected at his office, and which, by due diligence, could have been collected, and that the credits he claims are just and right. (R. S., § 3844.)

Sec. 1153. Neglect to Render Accounts; Penalty.—Whenever any postmaster neglects to render his accounts for one month after the time, and in the form and manner prescribed by law and the regulations of the Postmaster-General, he and his sureties shall forfeit and pay double the amount of the gross receipts at such office during any previous or subsequent equal period of time; and if, at the time of trial, no account has been rendered, they shall be liable to a penalty of such sum as the court and jury shall estimate to be equivalent thereto, to be recovered in an action on the bond. (R. S., § 3845.)

Sec. 1154. Time of Forwarding Quarterly Returns.—Immediately after the close of each quarter, which is on the last day of March, June, September, and December, every postmaster must make up his accounts for the quarter and forward transcripts of them to the Auditor. The originals must be retained by the postmaster, subject to inspection. Quarterly returns must not be addressed to the Third Assistant Postmaster-General.

Sec. 1155. What Composes the Quarterly Return.—The quarterly return is composed of the account-current and the necessary transcripts and vouchers.

Sec. 1156. Manner of Mailing Quarterly Returns.—To insure a correct and expeditious settlement of the quarterly accounts of postmasters, it is indispensable that each return should arrive at the Department in one perfect, unbroken bundle or packet. The packet should be plainly directed to the "Auditor of the Treasury for the Post-Office Department." The words "Quarterly returns" should be plainly written on the package. No letter, receipt, paper, or other thing whatever, not strictly belonging to the quarterly return, should be inclosed with it.

Sec. 1157. Transcripts must Accompany Account-Current.—Postmasters should never send an account-current without the transcripts from which it is made up; and never neglect to send with the transcripts an account-current. The postmaster's signature should be attached to each paper.

Sec. 1158. Written Accounts will not be Audited.—Quarterly returns must be made upon the regular blanks furnished by the First Assistant Postmaster-General. Written accounts will not be audited.

Sec. 1159. Quarterly Returns to Include but One Quarter.—A quarterly return must not include more than the business of one quarter.

Sec. 1160. Printed Labels for Returns from Presidential Post-Offices.—Postmasters at post-offices of the first, second, and third classes will be furnished by the First Assistant Postmaster-General, on application, with printed labels, which they are required to paste upon the package containing their quarterly returns. The use of these labels in transmitting to the Auditor the quarterly returns enables the receiving clerks to distinguish these returns from those of fourth-class post-offices, and very greatly expedites the settlement of the accounts.

Sec. 1161. Detailed Statement from Presidential-Post-Offices.—Postmasters at post-offices of the first, second, and third classes are required to transmit with their quarterly returns, upon the printed blank furnished them for that purpose, a detailed statement of stamps, stamped envelopes, newspaper-wrappers, and postal cards received during the quarter, and also a detailed statement of the vouchers accompanying the account-current.

Sec. 1162. Accounts of Outgoing and Incoming Postmasters.—Where a change of postmaster occurs, the outgoing postmaster will render an account to and including the day upon which the office is delivered to his successor; and the successor will render an account for the remainder of the quarter. At fourth-class post-offices, however, by agreement between the parties, the late postmaster or his successor may render the account for the entire quarter, provided that all postage-stamps, stamped envelopes, postal cards, etc., are duly accounted for in said account-current.

Sec. 1163. Accounts of Deceased Postmasters.—In case of the death of a postmaster, the assistant, deputy, or the sureties may render the account to and including the day upon which the new postmaster enters upon the discharge of his duties. Such account will be duly audited, compensation allowed in the settlement of the same, and credited to the account of the deceased postmaster.

Sec. 1164. Postmaster Giving New Bond; Return not Changed.—The execution of a new bond by a postmaster does not in any way change the manner of rendering the quarterly return, as the sureties upon the former bond are held responsible until the last day of the quarter in which the new bond is executed.

Sec. 1165. Originals must be Retained.—Many postmasters are in the habit of forwarding to the Department, contrary to regulation, their original accounts, keeping no duplicate or copy. This violation of rule cannot be permitted or overlooked. Transcripts or copies only must be sent, and the original accounts must be carefully preserved for inspection by any Special Agent of the Department who may require it.

Sec. 1166. Who must Sign Account-Current.—The quarterly account-current and all other official papers must be signed by the postmaster himself, unless necessarily absent or sick, in which case it may be signed as follows:

A—— B——, *P. M.*,
By C—— D——, *Assistant P. M.*

The blank heading of the account-current must be filled up with the name of the post-office, its county and State.

Sec. 1167. Correction of Errors in Accounts.—The accounts of all postmasters are examined and adjusted by the Auditor as they are received, and the errors, if there be any, are carefully corrected, and the postmasters at post-offices of the first, second, and third classes are notified of the corrections made. Postmasters at all other post-offices are notified of errors which increase by as much as one dollar the balance due to the United States. Postmasters, therefore, will understand that any alteration in the balances of their accounts is occasioned either by the correction of some clerical error, or by some deviation on their part from a strict conformity to the law and the instructions.

Sec. 1168. Record to be Kept of Receipts by Postmasters.—Every postmaster shall keep in a book, separate from his other accounts, a record—

1. Of all postage-stamps, stamped envelopes, newspaper-wrappers, newspaper and periodical stamps, postage-due stamps, and postal cards received by him.

2. Of all postal books, blanks, or other property turned over by his predecessor, or received from the Post-Office Department, or from any of its agents, during his term of office.

3. Of all box-rents. (The entry of money received for box-rents should show the number of the box and the period for which the payment was made.)

4. Of all other rents, emoluments, and moneys received by him as postmaster, or as custodian of the building in which the post-office is located.

Every postmaster will keep the above accounts separately, and charge himself with all receipts thereon. He will make quarterly returns thereof to the Auditor, and turn over his records to his successor.

Sec. 1169. Duty of Postmasters when Returns are Lost in the Mail.—The postmaster, though he may have mailed his returns, will not be considered as discharged from the penalty mentioned in section 1153 unless, after being notified that they have not been received at the Department, he transmits forthwith duplicate transcripts from the original accounts retained in his possession.

Sec. 1170. Unreasonable Delay in Presenting Claims. Inference from.—As the account-current is intended to show the net proceeds of the post-office for the quarter, no balance due on a former quarter, nor any payment to or collection for the Department in a former quarter, is to be inserted in it. All vouchers for expenses charged in the account-current must be transmitted with the said accounts, and if for advertising letters, must state the number of letters. Unreasonable delay not only implies neglect of the public business, but is calculated to bring suspicion upon the claims withheld; and the Department, therefore, reserves to itself the right to reject all such claims after the quarterly accounts have been adjusted.

Sec. 1171. Allowance for Advertising Letters.—When proper authority has been given to the postmaster by the Postmaster-General, one cent will be allowed for advertising each letter, and the printer's receipt must state the number of letters and the amount paid for advertising.

Sec. 1172. Items not to be Entered on the Account-Current.—Items relating to Money Order Business, to expenditures on account of the Free Deli very System and of the Railway Postal Service, must not be entered on the account-current.

Sec. 1173. No Allowance for Expenditures without Vouchers.—No allowance will be made for any expenditure unless accompanied by the proper voucher—that is, a bill receipted.

Sec. 1174. No Allowance for Administering Oaths.—No allowance can be made for fees paid for administering oaths to accounts.

Sec. 1175. Indorsement on Back of Account-Current.—The postmaster must indorse plainly upon the back of the account-current, in the blanks prepared for that purpose, the class and name of the post-office, the name of the State, the period for which the account is rendered, and the name of the postmaster.

Sec. 1176. Blank Forms, how Procured.—Blank forms for quarterly accounts-current are furnished on application to the First Assistant Postmaster-General, Blank Agency; and postmasters should so arrange their orders as to have a supply sufficient for one year constantly on hand.

CHAPTER THREE.

ACCOUNTS-CURRENT AND TRANSCRIPTS—FORMS.

Sec. 1177. Forms for Presidential Post-Offices.—The following forms of accounts-current and transcripts, which are printed upon colored or tinted paper, are prescribed for the use of postmasters at post-offices of the first, second, and third classes:

Quarterly Account-Current.

PRESIDENTIAL POST-OFFICE.

CLASS ——.

Post-office at ——, county of ——, State of ——, in account-current with the United States, for the service of the Post-Office Department from —— to ——, 18—, inclusive.

Column for Auditor.	DR.	Column for Auditor.	Column for postmaster.	Column for postmaster.	CR.	Column for postmaster.	Column for Auditor.
	1. For amount received for waste paper, dead newspapers, printed matter, and twine sold during the quarter......				8. By salary		
	2. For box-rent				9. By ship and steamboat letters paid for this quarter, as per receipts herewith, at cents each		
	3. Amount of postage-stamps, postage-due stamps, stamped envelopes, newspaper wrappers, newspaper and periodical stamps, and postal cards on hand at close of last quarter				10. By expenses, per vouchers herewith		
	4. Amount of postage-stamps, postage-due stamps, stamped envelopes, newspaper wrappers, newspaper and periodical stamps, and postal cards received from the Department this quarter........						
	5. Deduct amount of postage-stamps, postage-due stamps, stamped envelopes, newspaper wrappers, newspaper and periodical stamps, and postal cards now on hand ..						
	6. Deduct damaged stamps and stamped envelopes returned						
	7. Leaving amount of postage-stamps, postage-due stamps, stamped envelopes, newspaper wrappers, newspaper and periodical stamps, and postal cards sold during quarter..				11. Balance due the United States		

I, —— ——, postmaster of ————, do —— that the accounts which I have rendered to the Post-Office Department for the quarter ending ————, 18—, exhibit truly and faithfully the entire receipts of my post-office which have been collected thereat, and the entire sum which could have been, by due diligence, collected thereat, during the period above stated, and that the credits claimed in the said accounts are just and true, as I verily believe; and, furthermore, that during the said period I have not knowingly delivered, or permitted to be delivered, to any person any mail matter on which the postage had not been paid by postage-due stamps at the time of such delivery, in accordance with the provisions of section 26 of the act of Congress approved March 3, 1879, and of sections 270–274 of the Postal Laws and Regulations, edition of 1879.

————Postmaster.

Sworn and subscribed before the undersigned, a —— for the —— of ——, this —— day of ——, A. D. 18—.

—— ——.

Box-rent account.

Quarter-yearly return of all receipts for boxes and drawers by me received as postmaster of ——, State of ——, for the quarter ending ——, 18—.

		No.	Rate.	Dollars.	Cts.
	Rent of boxes				
	Rent of drawers				

I, ——, postmaster of ——, do —— that the above and foregoing is a true and correct account of all receipts for rent of boxes and drawers for the quarter ending ——, 18—.

—— ——, Postmaster.

—— and subscribed before the undersigned, a —— for the —— of ——, this —— day of ——, A. D. 18—.

Detailed statement of stamps, &c., received.

(No. 1511.)

Post Office: ——————————

County of ——————————

State of ——————————

——————————, 18—.

A detailed statement of stamps and stamped envelopes, newspaper wrappers, postal cards, newspaper and periodical stamps, and postage-due stamps received during the quarter ended ——, 18—, and acknowledged in article 4 of the account-current for that quarter.

Date of receipt.	Number of receipt.	Description. (Whether stamps, envelopes, newspaper wrappers, or postal cards.)	Amount.	
			Dollars.	Cents.
		Total		

I certify the above statement to be correct.

—— ——, Postmaster.

Pay-roll of clerks.

We, the undersigned, officers in the post-office at ——, have received of —— ——, post-master the several sums affixed to our names, in full for services to ——, inclusive.

	Names.	Time of service.			Amount.	Signatures.

Expense voucher.

(Form 1526.)

Post Office ____________________, State of ____________________.

To ____________________, Dr.

To		

Received of —— ——, P. M. at ——, State of ——, the above sum of ——$\frac{}{100}$ dollars, for which —— have signed duplicate receipts this —— day of ——, 18—.

—— ——.

Detailed statement of vouchers.

(No. 1559.)

Post Office: ____________________

County of ____________________

State of ____________________

____________________, 18—.

A detailed statement of vouchers accompanying quarterly account-current for the quarter ended ——, 18—, for which credit is claimed in art. 10 of said account-current.

No. of voucher.	To whom paid.	For what expended.	Amount.	
			Dollars.	Cents.
Total				

I certify the above statement to be correct.

—— ——, Postmaster.

Sec. 1178. Forms for Fourth-Class Post-Offices.—The following forms, which are printed upon white paper to distinguish them from those of presidential post-offices, are prescribed for the use of postmasters at fourth-class post-offices:

INSTRUCTIONS.

The special attention of postmasters is directed to the following instructions, and a strict compliance with the same will be required:

ARTICLE 1. Enter the amount received for waste-paper, twine, &c., sold during the quarter.

ARTICLE 2. Enter the amount of box-rent collected during the quarter.

Postmasters are prohibited from collecting or receiving the rent of boxes for more than one quarter in advance.

ARTICLE 3. Enter the exact value of all postage-stamps, postage-due stamps, stamped envelopes, newspaper stamps, newspaper wrappers, and postal cards that remained on hand at the close of the preceding quarter. Where a change of postmasters occurs, the value of stamps, envelopes, cards, etc., received from the outgoing postmaster should also be entered in this article.

ARTICLE 4. Enter the value of all postage-stamps, postage-due stamps, stamped envelopes, newspaper stamps, newspaper wrappers, and postal cards received from the Department during the quarter. Then add together articles 3 and 4, placing their sums directly underneath the line opposite the words "Total amount of stamps, etc."

ARTICLE 5. Enter the exact value of all postage-stamps, postage-due stamps, stamped envelopes, newspaper stamps, newspaper wrappers, and postal cards that remained on hand the last day of the quarter.

ARTICLE 6. Enter the value of damaged stamps, etc., returned to the Department during the quarter; but not until notice of allowance shall be received from the Third Assistant Postmaster-General. This item must be deducted from the value of stamps sold during the quarter, and not from the amount remaining on hand.

ARTICLE 7. Enter the value of all postage-stamps, stamped envelopes, postal cards, etc., sold during the quarter, and of postage-due stamps affixed upon delivery of insufficiently prepaid matter. This item is ascertained by subtracting the amount on hand (article 5) from the sum total of articles 3 and 4. The difference being the amount sold, less any damaged stamps that may have been returned during the quarter.

ARTICLE 8. Compute and enter the commissions on the aggregate amount charged under article 1, and the amount of canceled stamps shown by the transcript accompanying the account-current, at the rates provided by law and as set forth on the inside lower margin of this form. Credit should also be taken under this article for the whole amount of box-rent charged under article 2. (See section 117, Postal Laws and Regulations, edition of 1879.

ARTICLE 9. Enter the number of ship and steamboat letters received and paid for during the quarter, taking credit for the amount paid. No credit will be allowed in this item unless accompanied by vouchers, signed by the master of the ship, showing the name of the vessel and port from which the letters were carried.

ARTICLE 10. Credit should be taken under this article for expenses incurred in the repair of mail-bags, and for office furniture and clerk hire where allowances have previously been granted by the Postmaster-General:

ARTICLE 11. Under this article should be entered the difference between the total footing of the debit side and the sum of the credits claimed under articles 8, 9, and 10 of the credit side of the account-current, as this difference constitutes the balance due the United States.

Credit for payments made to the mail-carrier must not be entered in this account, as such credits are allowed in the general account on the books of the Auditor's office immediately on receipt of the carrier's voucher.

Quarterly Account-Current

CLASS 4.

Post-office at ——, County of ——, State of ——, in account-current with the United States, for the service of the Post-Office Department, from —— to ——, 18 —, inclusive.

DR.

Column for Auditor.		Column for Auditor.	Column for postmaster.	Column for postmaster.
	1. For amount received for waste-paper, dead newspapers, printed matter, and twine sold during the quarter			
	2. Box-rent			
	3. Amount of postage-stamps, postage-due stamps, stamped envelopes, newspaper wrappers, postal cards, and newspaper and periodical stamps on hand at the close of last quarter			
	4. Amount of postage-stamps, postage-due stamps, stamped envelopes, newspaper wrappers, postal cards and newspaper and periodical stamps received from the Department this quarter			
	Total amount of stamps, &c.			
	5. Deduct amount of postage-stamps, postage-due stamps, stamped envelopes, newspaper wrappers, postal cards, and newspaper and periodical stamps now on hand			
	6. Deduct damaged stamps, and stamped envelopes returned to the Department			
	7. Leaving amount of postage-stamps, postage-due stamps, stamped envelopes, newspaper wrappers, postal cards, and newspaper and periodical stamps sold during the quarter			

CR.

	Column for postmaster.	Column for Auditor.
8. By commissions on the aggregate amount of article 1 and canceled stamps, as follows:		
On $ at 60 per cent		
On $ at 50 per cent		
On $ at 40 per cent		
By whole amount of box-rents charged in article 2		
Total compensation		
9. By ship and steamboat letters paid for this quarter, as per receipts herewith, at two cents each		
10. By expenses, per vouchers herewith		
11. Balance due the United States		

Amount of article 1, ——; amount of canceled stamps as per transcript, ——; total, ——.

☞ Postmasters will take credit under article 8 for commissions on the above amount as follows:

On the first $100 or less, 60 per cent.; on the next $200 or less, 50 per cent.; on the excess above $300, 40 per cent.

☞ The amount of compensation is limited to $250 per quarter.

☞ Postmasters will be required to report the entire amount of box-rents collected quarterly. A failure to do so will be considered cause for removal.

I, ———, Postmaster of ———, do —— that the accounts which I have rendered to the Post-Office Department for the quarter ending ——, 188—, exhibit truly and faithfully the entire receipts of my office which have been collected thereat, and the entire sum which could have been, by due diligence, collected thereat, during the period above stated and that the credits claimed in the said accounts are just and true, as I verily believe; and, furthermore, that during the said period, I have not knowingly delivered, or permitted to be delivered, to any person any mail matter on which the postage had not been paid at the time of such delivery, by affixing and canceling postage-due stamps in accordance with sec. 26, act of March 3, 1879, and of sections 270–274, Postal Laws and Regulations, edition of 1879. And, furthermore, that the amount of postage-stamps, stamped envelopes, postal cards, newspaper and periodical stamps canceled as postages on matter actually mailed during the quarter, and of postage-due stamps canceled in payment of undercharged and unpaid postages upon matter delivered during the quarter, upon which commission is claimed, is truly and accurately stated in the transcript accompanying this account.

——— ———, *Postmaster.*

Sworn and subscribed before the undersigned, a —— for the —— of ——, this —— day of ——, A. D. 188—.

——— ——— ———.

Transcript for fourth-class offices.

Account of box-rents collected, and daily transcript of amount of postage-stamps, stamped envelopes, postal cards, and newspaper and periodical stamps canceled as postages on matter actually mailed, and of postage-due stamps canceled in payment of undercharged and unpaid postages upon letters delivered at the post-office at ——, county of —— and State of ——, during the quarter ending ——, 188—.

This transcript forms a part of the quarterly return, and must, in all cases, be inclosed in and transmitted to the Auditor with the quarterly account-current.

Daily transcript of amount of postage-stamps, stamped envelopes, postal cards, and newspaper and periodical stamps canceled as postages on matter actually mailed, and of postage-due stamps canceled in payment of undercharges and unpaid postages upon matter delivered during the quarter.

Month.	Day.	Amount.		Month.	Day.	Amount.		Month.	Day.	Amount.	
		Dolls.	Cts.			Dolls.	Cts.			Dolls.	Cts.
	1				1				1		
	2				2				2		
	3				3				3		
	4				4				4		
	5				5				5		
	6				6				6		
	7				7				7		
	8				8				8		
	9				9				9		
	10				10				10		
	11				11				11		
	12				12				12		
	13				13				13		
	14				14				14		
	15				15				15		
	16				16				16		
	17				17				17		
	18				18				18		
	19				19				19		
	20				20				20		
	21				21				21		
	22				22				22		
	23				23				23		
	24				24				24		
	25				25				25		
	26				26				26		
	27				27				27		
	28				28				28		
	29				29				29		
	30				30				30		
	31				31				31		
Total........$				Total........$				Total........$			

Total amount of stamps, &c., canceled during the quarter, to be carried to account-current, $——.

Box-rent account.

Quarterly account of all receipts for rent of boxes and drawers for the quarter ending ——, 188—.

	Number of boxes rented.	Rate.	Dollars.	Cents.
Rent of boxes..				
Rent of drawers......................................				
Total—to be carried to articles 2 and 8 of the account-current	$			

Post-Office at ______________________

County of ______________________

State of ______________________

I hereby certify, on my official oath as postmaster, that the above and within transcript is a true statement from the records of this office.

—— ——, Postmaster.

CHAPTER FOUR.

THE GENERAL POSTAL ACCOUNT.

Sec. 1179. All Postmasters to keep General Account.—Every postmaster is required to keep in his post-office a general or ledger account with the United States for the service of the Post-Office Department, subject to the inspection of the Postmaster-General, or of any general or Special Agent of the Post-Office Department.

Sec. 1180. Statement to be Sent Quarterly to Auditor.—Postmasters at post-offices of the first, second, and third classes are required to transmit to the Auditor of the Treasury for the Post-Office Department, as soon as possible after the close of each quarter, and not later than the twentieth day of the first month of the succeeding quarter, a statement of their general postal accounts as kept by themselves.

Sec. 1181. Debit Side of Account.—On the debit side of the general postal account the postmaster will charge himself with the balance on the general account, as rendered, for the preceding quarter; with corrections of former quarterly and general account; with the balance on the quarterly account for the current quarter; with drafts collected giving dates when paid, dates of issue, numbers, names of post-offices, and by whom paid; with deposits received, giving dates, names of post-offices, and depositors; with transfers from money-order fund to postal fund, giving dates and amounts.

Sec. 1182. Credit Side of Account.—On the credit side should be entered corrections of former quarterly and general accounts; aggregate amounts, for the quarter, paid to letter-carriers, and to employés of the railway mail service, and for incidental expenses of the railway postal system; amounts and dates of payments to contractors, mail-messengers or special mail-carriers; deposits made, when, where, and with whom; drafts paid, with dates of payment and of issue, numbers, and to whom paid; also, transfers from postal to money-order fund, with amount and date of each.

Sec. 1183. Distinction between Quarterly and General Account.—Particular care should be taken not to include in the quarterly statement of the general postal accounts any items which have been charged or credited in the quarterly accounts-current, and also to enter all the items of the general postal account pertaining to, and all payments on account of, the quarter for which it is rendered.

Sec. 1184. General Accounts to be Sent Separately to Auditor.—The general postal account should not be inclosed with the quarterly account-current, but must be transmitted in a separate envelope addressed to the "Auditor of the Treasury for the Post-Office Department."

Sec. 1185. Vouchers to be kept by Postmasters.—The duplicate quarterly accounts-current, the duplicate certificates of deposit, the duplicate collection orders, and also all instructions, are to be kept on file by the postmaster as vouchers with this account, and be subject to inspection.

Sec. 1186. Postmaster and Auditor to compare Accounts.—The postmaster, upon being furnished with a statement of his general account as kept by the Auditor, will immediately compare it with the account as kept by himself, and at once acknowledge to the Auditor the balance appearing on such statement, or point out specifically the particulars wherein the accounts disagree.

Sec. 1187. Blanks for General Accounts.—Blanks for general accounts will be furnished to postmasters at post-offices of the first, second, and third classes only, on application to the First Assistant Postmaster-General.

Sec. 1188. Fourth-Class Postmasters' General Account.—Postmasters at post-offices of the fourth class are not required to render a statement of their general accounts to the Auditor quarterly, but this regulation does not relieve them from the duty of keeping such general accounts in their post-offices; and the Auditor may at any time, if he deems it necessary, require postmasters at such post-offices to furnish statements of their general accounts for examination and comparison with the accounts as kept in his office.

Sec. 1189. All Payments to be Made for Each Quarter before Transmitting.—The law requires the Auditor to close the accounts of the department quarterly, and to transmit to the Postmaster-General and the Secretary of the Treasury quarterly statements of its receipts and expenditures. That he may be enabled to discharge this duty fully and accurately, postmasters are required to make all payments on account of the free-delivery service, employés of the railway mail service, mail-route messengers, and local-agents service, and all the expenses of their respective post-offices for the quarter just expired, before transmitting their accounts and rolls to the Auditor, which must be done on or before the 20th day of the next quarter.

Sec. 1190. Form of Account for Fourth-Class Post-Offices.—As a guide to postmasters at post-offices of the fourth class, the following form of a general postal account is given:

GENERAL POSTAL ACCOUNT.

James Smith, P. M., Smithville, N. Y., in account with the United States.

Dr.				Cr.	
1879.			1879.		
	To balance due on account-current from July 1 to September 30 1879	$210 15	July 30	By transfer from postal to money order fund	$100 00
			Sept. 30	By amount paid mail messenger for 3d quarter 1879	50 00
			Oct. 4	By amount paid E. Weber, contractor	135 15
Oct. 4	To transfer from money order to postal fund	75 00	" 10	By transfer from postal to money order fund	20 00
	To balance due on account-current from October 1 to December 31, 1879	163 90	" 21	" " " " "	30 00
			Dec. 31	By amount paid mail messenger for 4th quarter 1879	50 00
1880.			1880.		
Jan. 6	To Auditor's draft No. 1020 on L. James, L. P. M.	49 36	Jan. 1	By amount paid E. Weber, contractor	110 00
	To balance due on account-current from January 1 to March 31, 1880	212 60	" 4	By amount deposited with P. M. at Albany, N. Y.	3 26
April 10	To amount received from P. Brown, L. P. M	96	Feb. 12	By transfer from postal to money order fund	110 00
	To balance due on account-current from April 1 to June 30, 1880	223 80	Mar. 31	By amount paid mail messenger for 1st quarter 1880	50 00
			April 4	By amount paid E. Weber, contractor	52 60
			" 28	By transfer from postal to money order fund	20 00
			May 1	" " " " "	25 00
			June 15	" " " " "	29 00
			" 30	By amount paid mail messenger for 2nd quarter 1880	50 00
			July 4	By amount paid E. Weber, contractor	100 76
		935 77			935 77

JAMES SMITH,
Postmaster.

CHAPTER FIVE.

COLLECTION OF DEBTS DUE THE DEPARTMENT.

Sec. 1191. Collection by Contractors' Orders.—When the convenience of the service requires it, contractors are furnished with printed blank orders upon postmasters on their routes, to whom, upon presentation of an order at the end of the quarter, postmasters are required to pay over all moneys due the United States, from whatever source received, except "money-order funds." In such cases no form of order or receipt will be recognized except the printed blank furnished by the Department. A payment made otherwise than strictly according to the regulations is null and void.

Sec. 1192. Collection by Drafts.—Whenever it shall be deemed advisable by the Auditor, drafts will be issued for the collection of balances due by postmasters, late postmasters, and others; and immediately upon the receipt of such drafts by the postmaster in whose favor they are issued, it is his duty to notify the party or parties upon whom such drafts are drawn and demand prompt payment thereof, as instructed by the circulars accompanying the drafts.

Sec. 1193. Postmasters Expected to Honor Drafts.—Upon the receipt of such notice and demand, it is the duty of the postmasters, or other persons upon whom such drafts are drawn, to pay the amount thereof to the postmaster in whose favor they are issued without delay and without risk or expense to the United States.

Sec. 1194. Notification to Auditor of Payment of Draft.—If the draft be collected by the postmaster, he shall immediately notify the Auditor by transmitting his receipt for the amount, as instructed by the circular accompanying the draft, and should charge himself upon his general postal account with the amount of such draft.

Sec. 1195. Notification of Non-Payment.—If the postmaster, late postmaster, or other person upon whom the draft is drawn, fail to respond to the demand within the time named in the Auditor's circular of instructions, the postmaster holding the draft will notify the Auditor by letter of such failure, communicating the reply to his demand, if any be received, when further instructions will be sent by the Auditor.

Sec. 1196. Report of Cause of Failure to Collect.—If the exertions of the postmaster to collect from the party or his sureties prove unavailing, he will communicate to the Auditor the cause of such failure, and also the residence and pecuniary circumstances of all the parties, if alive; or, if dead, the condition of their estates and the names of their administrators or executors.

Sec. 1197. Responsibility for Uncollected Drafts.—If due diligence be not used in making the collection, or if, being unsuccessful, any postmaster fail to return the draft or demand to the Auditor, or otherwise to give notice of such failure, or fail to give any information required in relation to the same, such neglect and want of fidelity will amount to a breach of the condition of his bond, and the draft will be permanently charged to the general account of the postmaster holding it, and he and his sureties will be held responsible for the amount of the same.

Sec. 1198. Postmasters may be Removed for Neglect to Collect.—The failure or refusal of a postmaster to comply strictly with instructions sent him in relation to the collection of drafts will be considered just ground for his removal from office.

Sec. 1199. Suits upon Collection-Drafts.—Upon the return of a collection-draft upon a late postmaster or contractor unpaid, the Auditor will at once prepare and transmit to the Department of Justice certified copies of all the accounts and other papers necessary for the immediate institution of a suit against the principal and sureties for the recovery of the balance due the United States.

Sec. 1200. Collection-Drafts not Issued for Money-Order Funds.—Collection-drafts are not issued upon late postmasters for balances due the United States upon their money-order accounts. If a late postmaster fails to pay to his successor, immediately upon his taking charge of the post-office, the full amount of money-order funds in his hands, as shown by the last statement rendered, the Auditor will instruct the postmaster, by letter, to demand immediate payment of such balance; and if payment be not made promptly, the postmaster will be directed to require payment of the sureties of the late postmaster, as in the case of the collection of drafts for postal balances. Should payment be refused by the sureties, the case will be submitted to the Department of Justice for suit, as provided in the preceding section.

CHAPTER SIX.

RENEWAL OF LOST WARRANTS OR DRAFTS.

Sec. 1201. Indemnity Bond for Duplicate Warrant.—In all cases where application is made for the issue of a duplicate warrant, upon the allegation that the original is lost, every such application must be addressed to the Auditor of the Treasury for the Post-Office Department, who will furnish the applicant with a blank "bond of indemnity," to be filled up in accordance with the conditions specified in the same, which bond, duly executed, must be returned to the Auditor, accompanied by a statement, on oath or affirmation, by the applicant, or the person who is the legal holder thereof, showing the time, place, and all the circumstances attending the loss or destruction of the warrant, with its number, date, and amount; in whose favor it was issued; and if assigned, to whom made payable; together with any other particulars relating to it within the knowledge of the applicant.

Sec. 1202. Certificate of Non-Payment.—The applicant must also produce a letter or certificate from the officer or person on whom the warrant may have been drawn, showing that it has not been paid; also that payment of the same will not thereafter be made to the owner, or any other person whatever.

Sec. 1203. No Bond Required for Duplicate Draft.—When the application is for a duplicate draft, the applicant must conform to the above requirements, except as to the execution of the bond of indemnity.

Sec. 1204. Tenor, Force, and Effect of Duplicate.—The duplicate, when issued, shall have the same tenor, force, and effect as the original, unless, in case of assignment, the assignee of the lost draft or warrant produce due authority from the payee for the issue of the duplicate in his own favor.

Sec. 1205. Renewal of Lost Collection-Drafts.—Where collection-drafts sent to postmasters are lost, the postmasters to whom they are sent are required to make affidavit, either that they have never received the same, or that payment has been requested and refused, or that the draft has been forwarded by mail. The postmaster will be required to make further affidavit that neither the whole nor any part of such draft has been paid to him nor to any other person, so far as he knows or is able to ascertain. Forms for this affidavit will be furnished by the Auditor.

CHAPTER SEVEN.

PROCEEDINGS IN SUITS.

Sec. 1206. Circuit and District Courts, Jurisdiction under Postal Laws.—The circuit courts [of the United States] shall have original jurisdiction as follows: * * * Fourth. * * * of all causes arising under the postal laws. The district courts [of the United States] shall have jurisdiction as follows: * * * Seventh. Of all causes of action arising under the postal laws of the United States. All suits arising under the postal laws shall be brought in the name of the United States. (R. S., § 563, 629, 919.)

Sec. 1207. Attachments in Postal Suits.—In all cases where debts are due from defaulting or delinquent postmasters, contractors, or other officers, agents, or employés of the Post-Office Department, a warrant of attachment may issue against all real and personal property and legal and equitable rights belonging to such officer, agent, or employé, and his sureties, or either of them, in the following cases:

First. When such officer, agent, or employé, and his sureties, or either of them, is a non-resident of the district where such officer, agent, or employé was appointed, or has departed from such district for the purpose of permanently residing out of the same, or of defrauding the United States, or of avoiding the service of civil process.

Second. When such officer, agent, or employé, and his sureties, or either of them, has conveyed away, or is about to convey away his property, or any part thereof, or has removed or is about to remove the same or any part thereof from the district wherein it is situate, with intent to defraud the United States.

And when any such property has been removed, certified copies of the warrant may be sent to the marshal of the district into which the same has been removed, under which certified copies he may seize said property and convey it to some convenient point within the jurisdiction of the court from which the warrant originally issued. And alias warrants may be issued in such cases upon due application, and the validity of the warrant first issued shall continue until the return day thereof. (R. S., § 924.)

Sec. 1208. Application for Warrant; by Whom and how Made.—Application for such warrant of attachment may be made by any district or assistant district attorney, or any other person authorized by the Postmaster-General, before the judge, or, in his absence, before the clerk of any court of the United States having original jurisdiction of the cause of action. And such application shall be made upon an affidavit of the applicant, or of some other credible person, stating the existence of either of the grounds of attachment enumerated in the preceding section, and upon production of legal evidence of the debt. (R. S., § 925.)

Sec. 1209. Issuing Warrant; Duty of Clerk and Marshal.—Upon any such application and upon due order of any judge of the court, or, in his absence, without such order, the clerk shall issue a warrant for the attachment of all the property of any kind belonging to the person specified in the affidavit, which warrant shall be executed with all possible dispatch by the marshal, who shall take the property attached, if personal, into his custody, and hold the same subject to all interlocutory or final orders of the court. (R. S., § 926.)

Sec. 1210. Ownership of Attached Property; Trial.—At any time within twenty days before the return day of such warrant, the party whose property is attached may, on giving notice to the district attorney of his intention, file a plea in abatement, traversing the allegations of the affidavit, or denying the ownership of the property attached to be in the defendants or either of them; in which case the court may, upon application of either party, order an immediate trial by jury of the issues raised by the affidavit and plea; but the parties may, by consent, waive a trial by jury, in which case the court shall decide the issues raised. And any party claiming ownership of the property attached and a specific return thereof, shall be confined to the remedy herein afforded, but his right to an action of trespass, or other action for damages, shall not be impaired hereby. (R. S., § 927.)

Sec. 1211. Proceeds of Attached Property to be Invested.—When the property attached is sold on any interlocutory order of the court or is producing any revenue, the money arising from such sale or revenue shall be invested in securities of the United States, under the order of the court, and all accretions shall be held subject to the orders of the same. (R. S., § 928.)

Sec. 1212. Publication of Attachment.—Immediately upon the execution of any such warrant of attachment, the marshal shall cause due publication thereof to be made, in the case of absconding debtors for two months and of non-residents for four months. The publication shall be made in some newspaper published in the district where the property is situate, and the details thereof shall be regulated by the order under which the warrant is issued. (R. S., § 929.)

Sec. 1213. Holders of Defendant's Property to Account for it.—After the first publication of such notice of attachment as required by law, every person indebted to, or having possession of any property belonging to, the said defendants, or either of them, and having knowledge of such notice, shall account and answer for the amount of such debt and the value of such property; and any disposal or attempt to dispose of any such property, to the injury of the United States, shall be illegal and void. And when the person indebted to, or having possession of the property of, such defendants, or either of them, is known to the district attorney or marshal, such officer shall see that personal notice of the attachment is served upon such person, but the want of such notice shall not invalidate the attachment. (R. S., § 930.)

Sec. 1214. Discharge of Attachment; Bond.—Upon application of the party whose property has been attached, the court, or any judge thereof, may discharge the warrant of attachment as to the property of the applicant, provided such applicant shall execute to the United States a good and sufficient penal bond, in double the value of the property attached, to be approved by a judge of the court, and with condition for the return of said property, or to answer any judgment which may be rendered by the court in the premises. (R. S., § 931.)

Sec. 1215. Accrued Rights not to be Abridged.—Nothing contained in the preceding eight sections shall be construed to limit or abridge, in any manner, such rights of the United States as have accrued or been allowed in any district under the former practice of, or the adoption of State laws by, the United States courts. (R. S., § 932.)

Sec. 1216. Attachments Dissolved in Conformity with State Laws.—An attachment of property, upon process instituted in any court of the United States, to satisfy such judgment as may be recovered by the plaintiff therein, except in the cases mentioned in the preceding nine sections, shall be dissolved when any contingency occurs by which, according to the laws of the State where said court is held, such attachment would be dissolved upon like process instituted in the courts of said State: *Provided*, That nothing herein contained shall interfere with any priority of the United States in the payment of debts. (R. S., § 933.)

Sec. 1217. What Credits Allowed in Suits.—No claim for a credit shall be allowed upon the trial of any suit for delinquency against a postmaster, contractor, or other officer, agent, or employé of the Post-Office Department, unless the same has been presented to the [*Sixth*] Auditor [of the Treasury for the Post-Office Department] and by him disallowed, in whole or in part, or unless it is proved to the satisfaction of the court that the defendant is, at the time of trial, in possession of vouchers not before in his power to procure, and that he was prevented from exhibiting to the said auditor a claim for such credit by some unavoidable accident. (R. S., § 952.)

Sec. 1218. Suits of United States against Individuals. What Credits Allowed.—In suits brought by the United States against individuals, no claim for a credit shall be admitted, upon trial, except such as appear to have been presented to the accounting officers of the Treasury, for their examination, and to have been by them disallowed, in whole or in part, unless it is proved to the satisfaction of the court that the defendant is, at the time of the trial, in possession of vouchers not before in his power to procure, and that he was prevented from exhibiting a claim for such credit at the Treasury by absence from the United States or by some unavoidable accident. (R. S., § 951.)

In U. S. *vs.* Wilkins, 6 Wh., 143, it was decided that under the 3d and 4th sections of the act of March 3, 1797, the defendant is entitled at his trial to the benefit of any credit in his favor whether arising out of the particular transaction for which he was sued, or out of distinct and independent transactions which would constitute a legal or equitable set-off in whole or in part to the debt sued for by the United States. (Vide note to Ware's edition, 1866, p. 84.) U. S. *vs.* Robeson, 9 Peters, 319. U. S. *vs.* Eckford, 6 Wall., 484, and large numbers of decisions cited under this section in Revised Statutes.)

Sec. 1219. Judgment at Return Term, unless.—In suits arising under the postal laws the court shall proceed to trial, and render judgment at the return term; but whenever service of process is not made at least twenty days before the return day of such term, the defendant is entitled to one continuance, if, on his statement, the court deems it expedient; and if he makes affidavit that he has a claim against the Post-Office Department, which has been submitted to and disallowed by the [*Sixth*] Auditor [of the Treasury for the Post-Office Department], specifying such claim in his affidavit, and that he could not be prepared for trial at such term for want of evidence, the court, if satisfied thereof, may grant a continuance until the next term. (R. S., § 958.)

Sec. 1220. Interest on Balances Due Post-Office Department.—In all suits for balances due to the Post-Office Department, interest thereon shall be recovered, from the time of the default, at the rate of six per centum a year. (R. S., § 964.

Sec. 1221. Duties of United States Attorneys.—In the prosecution of any suit for money due the Post-Office Department, the United States attorney conducting the same shall obey the directions which may be given him by the Department of Justice. (R. S., § 381.)

Sec. 1222. Proceedings in Equity, when.—When proceedings at law for money due the Post-Office Department are fruitless, the Department of Justice may direct the institution of a suit in chancery, in any United States district or circuit court, to set aside fraudulent conveyances or trusts, or attach debts due the defendant, or obtain any other proper exercise of the powers of equity to have satisfaction of any judgment against such defendant. (R. S., 382.)

Sec. 1223. Copies of Post-Office Records and of Auditor's Statement of Accounts.—Copies of the quarterly returns of postmasters and of any papers pertaining to the accounts in the office of the [*Sixth*] Auditor [of the Treasury for the Post-Office Department], and transcripts from the money-order account-books of the Post-Office Deparment, when certified by the [*Sixth*] Auditor [of the Treasury for the Post-Office Department] under the seal of his office, shall be admitted as evidence in the courts of the United States, in civil suits and criminal prosecutions; and in any civil suit, in case of delinquency of any postmaster or contractor, a statement of the account, certified as aforesaid, shall be admitted in evidence, and the court shall be authorized thereupon to give judgment and award execution, subject to the provisions of law as to proceedings in such civil suits. (R. S., § 889.)

(See U. S. *v.* Hodge, 13 How., 478; Lawrence *v.* U. S., 2 McLean, 581.)

Sec. 1224. Copies of Statements of Demands by Post-Office Department.—In all suits for the recovery of balances due from postmasters, a copy, duly certified under the seal of the [*Sixth*] Auditor [of the Treasury for the Post-Office Department], of the statement of any postmaster, special agent, or other person, employed by the Postmaster-General or the Auditor for that purpose, that he has mailed a letter to such delinquent postmaster at the post-office where the indebteness accrued, or at his last usual place of abode; that a sufficient time has elapsed for said letter to have reached its destination in the ordinary course of the mail; and that payment of such balance has not been received, within the time designated in his instructions, shall be received as sufficient evidence in the courts of the United States, or other courts, that a demand has been made upon the delipquent postmaster; but when the account of a late postmaster has been once adjusted and settled, and a demand has been made for the balance appearing to be due, and afterward allowances are made or credits entered, it shall not be necessary to make a further demand for the new balance found to be due. (R. S., § 890.)

Sec. 1225. Returns of Marshal to Auditor of the Treasury for the Post-Office Department.—Every marshal to whom any execution upon a judgment in any suit for moneys due on account of the Post-Office Department has been directed, shall make returns to the [*Sixth*] Auditor [of the Treasury] for that Department, at such times as he may direct of the proceedings which have taken place upon the said process of execution. (R. S., § 792.)

TITLE IX.

CRIMES AND MISDEMEANORS AGAINST THE OPERATIONS OF THE POST-OFFICE DEPARTMENT.

Sec. 1226. Forging Postal Money-Orders.—Any person who shall, with intent to defraud, falsely make, forge, counterfeit, engrave, or print, or cause or procure to be falsely made, forged, counterfeited, engraved, or printed, or willingly aid or assist in falsely making, forging, counterfeiting, engraving, or printing, any order in imitation of or purporting to be a money-order issued by the Post-Office Department, or any of its postmasters or agents, or any material signature or indorsement thereon; any person who shall falsely alter, or cause or procure to be altered, or willingly aid or assist in falsely altering any such money-order; any person who shall, with intent to defraud, pass, utter, or publish, or attempt to pass, utter, or publish, as true, any such false, forged, counterfeited, or altered money-order, knowing the same, or any signature or indorsement thereon, to be false, forged, counterfeited, or altered, shall be punishable by a fine of not more than five thousand dollars, or by imprisonment at hard labor for not less than two years and not more than five years. (R. S., § 5463.)

Sec. 1227. Forging or Counterfeiting Postage-Stamps, Dies, etc.—Any person who shall forge or counterfeit any postage-stamp, or any stamp printed upon any stamped envelope, postal card, or any die, plate, or engraving therefor; any person who shall make, or print, or knowingly use or sell, or have in possession, with intent to use or sell, any such forged or counterfeited postage-stamp, stamped envelope, postal card, die, plate, or engraving; any person who shall make, or knowingly use or sell, or have in possession, with intent to use or sell, any paper bearing the water-mark of any stamped envelope, postal card, or any fraudulent imitation thereof; any person who shall make or print, or authorize or procure to be made or printed, any postage-stamp, stamped envelope, or postal card, of the kind authorized and provided by the Post-Office Department, without the special authority and direction of the Department; any person who shall, after such postage-stamps, stamped envelopes, or postal card, have been printed, and with intent to defraud the postal revenue, deliver the same to any person not authorized by an instrument of writing duly executed under the hand of the Postmaster-General and the seal of the Post-Office Department to receive them, shall be punished by a fine of not more than five hundred dollars, or by imprisonment at hard labor not more than five years, or by both such fine and imprisonment. (R. S., 5464.)

Sec. 1228. Forging or Counterfeiting Foreign Postage-Stamps.—Any person who shall forge or counterfeit or knowingly utter or use any forged or counterfeited postage-stamp of any foreign government, shall be punished by imprisonment at hard labor of not less than two nor more than ten years. (R. S., § 5465.)

Sec. 1229. Injuring Mail-Matter in Street Mailing-Box, etc.—Any person who shall willfully or maliciously injure, deface, or destroy any mail-matter deposited in any letter-box, pillar-box, or other receptacle established by authority of the Postmaster-General for the safe deposit of matter for the mail or for delivery, or who shall willfully aid or assist in injuring such mail-matter, shall be punishable by a fine of not more than five hundred dollars, or by imprisonment for not more than three years. (R. S., § 5466.)

Sec. 1230. Embezzlement of Letters Containing Inclosures.—Any person employed in any department of the postal service who shall secrete, embezzle, or destroy any letter, packet, bag, or mail of letters intrusted to him, or which shall come into his possession, and which was intended to be conveyed by mail, or carried or delivered by any mail-carrier, mail-messenger, route-agent, letter-carrier, or other person employed in any department of the postal service, or forwarded through or delivered from any post-office or branch post-office established by authority of the Postmaster-General, and which shall contain any note, bond, draft, check, warrant, revenue stamp, postage-stamp, stamped envelope, postal card, money-order, certificate of stock, or other pecuniary obligation or security of the Government, or of any officer or fiscal agent thereof, of any description whatever; any bank-note, bank post bill, bill of exchange, or note of assignment of stock in the funds; any letter of attorney for receiving annuities or dividends, selling stock in the funds, or collecting the interest thereof; any letter of credit, note, bond, warrant, draft, bill, promissory note, covenant, contract, or agreement whatsoever, for or relating to the payment of money, or the delivery of any article of value, or the performance of any act, matter, or thing; any receipt, release acquittance, or discharge of or from any debt, covenant, or demand, or any part thereof; any copy of the record of any judgment or decree in any court of law or chancery or any execution which may have issued thereon; any copy of any other record, or any other article of value, or writing representing the same; any such person who shall steal or take any of the things aforesaid out of any letter, packet, bag, or mail of letters which shall have come into his possession, either in the regular course of his official duties or in any other manner whatever, and provided the same shall not have been delivered to the party to whom it is directed, shall be punishable by imprisonment at hard labor for not less than one year nor more than five years. (R. S., § 5467.)

An indictment which charges the defendant with unlawfully abstracting a letter containing bank-notes from the mail is good, if it alleges that the letter containing bank-notes was put into the post-office to be conveyed by post, and came into possession of defendant as a driver of the mail-stage. (The United States *vs.* Martin, 2 McLean, 256.)

In an indictment for embezzlement, under this section, it is sufficient to charge "that defendant was a person employed in one of the departments of the Post-Office establishment of the United States." (The United States *vs.* Patterson, 6 McLean, 466.)

It is not necessary to aver in an indictment, under this section, that the letter embezzled was intended to be conveyed to any particular place; an averment that it was intended to be conveyed by post being sufficient. (U. S. *vs.* Okie, 5 Blatch., 576. See also U. S. *vs.* Randall, 1 Deady, 524; U. S *vs.* Hardyman, 13 Pet., 176; U. S. *vs.* Golding, 2 Curtis's C. C., 212; U. S. *vs.* Winter; U. S. *vs.* Jenther, 13 Blatch., 333, 335.)

Sec. 1231. Meaning of Words "Intended to be Conveyed by Mail."—The fact that any letter, packet, bag, or mail of letters has been deposited in any post-office or branch post-office established by authority of the Postmaster-General, or in any other authorized depository for mail-matter, or in charge of any postmaster, assistant clerk, carrier, agent, or messenger employed in any department of the postal service, shall be evidence that the same was "intended to be conveyed by mail" within the meaning of the two preceding sections. (R. S., § 5468.)

Sec. 1232. Penalty for Detaining Letters.—Any postmaster who shall unlawfully detain in his office any letter or other mail-matter, the posting of which is not prohibited by law, with intent to prevent the arrival and delivery of the same to the person to whom it is addressed, shall be punishable by a fine of not more than five hundred dollars, and by imprisonment for not more than six months, and he shall be forever thereafter incapable of holding the office of postmaster. (R. S., § 3890.)

Sec. 1233. Penalty for Detaining, Opening, or Destroying Letters.—Any person employed in any department of the postal service, who shall unlawfully detain, delay, or open any letter, packet, bag, or mail of letters intrusted to him, or which has come into his possession, and which was intended to be conveyed by mail, or carried or delivered by any mail-carrier, mail-messenger, route-agent, letter-carrier, or other person employed in any department of the postal service, or forwarded through or delivered from any post-office or branch post-office established by authority of the Postmaster-General; or who shall secrete, embezzle, or destroy any such letter, packet, bag, or mail of letters, although it does not contain any security for or assurance relating to money or other thing of value, shall be punishable by a fine of not more than five hundred dollars, or by imprisonment for not more than one year, or by both. (R. S., § 3891.)

Sec. 1234. Penalty for Intercepting or Secreting Letters.—Any person who shall take any letter, postal card, or packet, although it does not contain any article of value or evidence thereof, out of a post-office or branch post-office, or from a letter or mail carrier, or which has been in any post-office or branch post-office or in the custody of any letter or mail carrier, before it has been delivered to the person to whom it was directed, with a design to obstruct the correspondence, or to pry into the business or secrets of another, or shall secrete, embezzle, or destroy the same, shall, for every such offense, be punishable by a fine of not more than five hundred dollars, or by imprisonment at hard labor for not more than one year, or by both. (R. S., § 3892.)

See U. S. *vs.* Bond, 2 Curtis, 265; U. S. *vs.* Lancaster, 2 McLean, 431.

Sec. 1235. Stealing or Fraudulently Obtaining Mail, Opening Valuable Letters.—Any person who shall steal the mail, or steal or take from or out of any mail or post-office, branch post-office, or other authorized depository for mail-matter, any letter or packet; any person who shall take the mail, or any letter or packet therefrom, or from any post-office, branch post-office, or other authorized depository for mail-matter, with or without the consent of the person having custody thereof, and open, embezzle, or destroy any such mail, letter, or package which shall contain any note, bond, draft, check, warrant, revenue-stamp, postage-stamp, stamped envelope, money-order, certificate of stock, or other pecuniary obligation or security of the Government, or of any officer or fiscal agent thereof, of any description whatever; any bank-note, bank post-bill, bill of exchange, or note of assignment of stock in the funds; any letter of attorney for receiving annuities or dividends, selling stock in the funds, or collecting the interest thereof; any letter of credit, note, bond, warrant, draft, bill, promissory note, covenant, contract, or agreement whatsoever, for or relating to the payment or the delivery of any article of value, or the performance of any act, matter, or thing; any receipt, release, acquittance, or discharge of or from any debt, covenant, or demand, or any part thereof; any copy of the record of any judgment or decree in any court of law or chancery, or any execution which may have issued thereon; any copy of any other record, or any other article of value, or any writing representing the same; any person who shall, by fraud or deception, obtain, from any person having custody thereof, any such mail, letter, or packet containing any such article of value shall, although not employed in the postal service, be punishable by imprisonment at hard labor for not less than one year and not more than five years. (R. S., § 5469. See also R. S., § 5535.)

This section does not look beyond a possession of letters obtained *wrongfully* from the post-office or from a mail-carrier. After the voluntary termination of the custody of a letter by the post-office or its agents the rights of the real proprietor of the letter are under the guardianship of the local law and not of that of the United States U. S. *vs.* Parsons, 2 Blatch., 104.

To constitute a post-office under this section, the place where the business of keeping, forwarding, and distributing mailable matter is conducted need not be a building set apart for that use, or any apartment or room in a building; but, according to the extent of the business done, may be a desk, or a trunk, or box, carried about a house or from one building to another. (The United States *vs.* Marselis, 2 Blatch., 108.)

A decoy letter, containing money, mailed for the purpose of entrapping a clerk in a post-office, etc., is within this section. (U. S. *vs.* Collingham, 2 Blatch., 470. *Vide* also U. S. *vs.* Pond, 2 Curtis's C. C., 265; U. S. *vs.* Lander, 6 McLean, 598; U. S. *vs.* Fisher, 2 McLean, 23.)

Sec. 1236. Receiving Articles Stolen from the Mails.—Any person who shall buy, receive, or conceal, or aid in buying, receiving, or concealing, any note, bond, draft, check, warrant, revenue-stamp, postage-stamp, stamped envelope, postal card, money-order, certificate of stock, or other pecuniary obligation or security of the government, or of any officer or fiscal agent thereof, of any description whatever; any bank-note, bank post-bill, bill of exchange, or note of assignment of stock in the funds; any letter of attorney for receiving annuities or dividends, selling stock in the funds, or collecting the interest thereof; any letter of credit, note, bond, warrant, draft, bill, promissory note, covenant, contract, or agreement whatsoever, for or relating to the payment of money or the delivery of any article of value, or the performance of any act, matter, or thing; any receipt, release, acquittal, or discharge of or from any debt, covenant, or demand, or any part thereof; any copy of the record of any judgment or decree in any court of law or chancery, or any execution which may have issued thereon any copy of any other record; or any other article of value or writing representing the same, knowing any such article or thing to have been stolen or embezzled from the mail, or out of any post-office, branch post-office, or other authorized depository for mail-matter, or from any person having custody thereof, shall be punishable by a fine of not more than two thousand dollars, and by imprisonment at hard labor for not more than five years. (R. S., § 5470.)

See U. S. *vs.* Hardyman, 13 Pet., 176.

Sec. 1237. Stealing, Detaining, or Destroying Newspapers.—Any person employed in any department of the postal service who shall improperly detain, delay, embezzle, or destroy any newspaper, or permit any other person to detain, delay, embezzle, or destroy the same, or open, or permit any other person to open, any mail or package of newspapers not directed to the office where he is employed, shall be punishable by a fine of not more than fifty dollars. And if any other person shall open, embezzle, or destroy any mail or package of newspapers not being directed to him, and he not being authorized to open or receive the same, he shall be punishable by a fine of not more than twenty dollars. And any person who shall take or steal any mail or package of newspapers from any post-office, or from any person having custody thereof, shall be imprisoned at hard labor for not more than three months. (R. S., § 5471.)

Sec. 1238. Robbery of the Mail.—Any person who shall rob any carrier, agent, or other person intrusted with the mail, of such mail, or any part thereof, shall be punishable by imprisonment at hard labor for not less than five years and not more than ten years; and if convicted a second time of a like offense, or if, in effecting such robbery the first time, the robber shall wound the person having custody of the mail, or put his life in jeopardy by the use of dangerous weapons, such offender shall be punishable by imprisonment at hard labor for the term of his natural life. (R. S., § 5472.)

Sec. 1239. Attempting to rob the Mail.—Any person who shall attempt to rob the mail by assaulting the person having custody thereof, shooting at him or his horse, or threatening him with dangerous weapons, and shall not effect such robbery, shall be punishable by imprisonment at hard labor for not less than two years and not more than ten years. (R. S., § 5473.)

Sec. 1240. Deserting the Mail.—Any person who shall have taken charge of the mail and shall voluntarily quit or desert the same before he has delivered it into the post-office at the termination of the route, or to some known mail-carrier, messenger, agent, or other employé of the Post-Office Department authorized to receive the same, shall be punishable by a fine of not more than five hundred dollars, and by imprisonment for not less than three months nor more than one year. (R. S., § 5474.)

Sec. 1241. Stealing Post-Office Property.—Any person who shall steal, purloin, or embezzle any mail-bag or other property in use by or belonging to the Post-Office Department, or who shall, for any lucre, gain, or convenience, appropriate any such property to his own or any other than its proper use, or who shall, for any lucre or gain, convey away any such property to the hinderance or detriment of the public service; if the value of the property be twenty-five dollars or more, the offender shall be punished by imprisonment at hard labor for not more than three years, and if the value of the property be less than twenty-five dollars, the offender shall be punishable by imprisonment for not more than one year, or by a fine of not less than ten dollars and not more than two hundred dollars. (R. S., § 5475.)

Sec. 1242. Injuring Mail-Bags, etc.—Any person who shall tear, cut, or otherwise injure any mail-bag, pouch, or other thing used or designed for use in the conveyance of the mail, or who shall draw or break any staple, or loosen any part of any lock, chain, or strap attached thereto, with intent to rob or steal any such mail, or to render the same insecure, shall be punishable by a fine of not less than one hundred dollars and not more than five hundred, or by imprisonment at hard labor for not less than one year and not more than three years. (R. S., § 5476.)

Sec. 1243. Stealing or Forging Mail Locks or Keys.—If any person who shall steal, purloin, or embezzle, or obtain by any false pretense, or shall aid or assist in stealing, purloining, embezzling, or obtaining by any false pretense, any key suited to any lock adopted by the Post-Office Department and in use on any of the mails or bags thereof; any person who shall knowingly and unlawfully make, forge, or counterfeit, or cause to be unlawfully made, forged or counterfeited, or knowingly aid or assist in making, forging or counterfeiting any such key; any person who shall have in his possession any such mail lock or key, with the intent unlawfully or improperly to use, sell, or otherwise dispose of the same, or cause the same to be unlawfully or improperly used, sold, or otherwise disposed of; or any person engaged as contractor or otherwise in the manufacture of any such mail locks or keys, who shall deliver, or cause to be delivered, any finished or unfinished lock or key used or designed for use by the Department, or the interior part of any such lock, to any person not duly authorized, under the hand of the Postmaster-General and the seal of the Post-Office Department, to receive the same, unless the person receiving is the contractor for furnishing the same, or engaged in the manufacture thereof in the manner authorized by the contract, or the agent for such manufacturer, shall be punishable by imprisonment at hard labor for not more than ten years. (R. S., § 5477.)

Sec. 1244. Breaking and Entering Post-Office.—Any person who shall forcibly break into, or attempt to break into any post-office, or any building used in whole or in part as a post-office, with intent to commit therein larceny or other depredation, shall be punishable by a fine of not more than one thousand dollars and by imprisonment at hard labor for not more than five years. (R. S., § 5478.)

Sec. 1245. Counterfeiting Bid, Bond, etc.—If any person shall falsely make, alter, forge, or counterfeit, or cause or procure to be falsely made, altered, forged, or counterfeited, or willingly aid or assist in the false making, altering, forging, or counterfeiting any bond, bid, proposal, guarantee, security, official bond, public record, affidavit, or other writing, for the purpose of defrauding the United States; or shall utter or publish as true, or cause to be uttered or published as true, any such false, forged, altered, or counterfeited bond, bid, proposal, guarantee, security, official bond, public record, affidavit, or other writing, for the purpose of defrauding the United States, knowing the same to be false, forged, altered, or counterfeited; or shall transmit to or present at, or cause [*to*] [or] procure to be transmitted to or presented at, the office of any officer of the United States, any such false, forged, altered, or counterfeited bond, bid, proposal, guarantee, security, official bond, public record, affidavit, or other writing, knowing the same to be false, forged, altered, or counterfeited, for the purpose of defrauding the United

States, shall be punishable by a fine of not more than one thousand dollars, or by imprisonment at hard labor for not more than ten years, or by both such punishments. (R. S., § 5479; see, also, R. S., § 5418.)

Sec. 1246. Sending Letters Through the Mails with Intent to Defraud.— If any person having devised or intending to devise any scheme or artifice to defraud, or be effected by either opening or intending to open correspondence or communication with any other person, whether resident within or outside of the United States, by means of the Post-Office Establishment of the United States, or by inciting such other person to open communication with the person so devising or intending, shall, in and for executing such scheme or artifice, or attempting so to do, place any letter or packet in any post-office of the United States, or take or receive any therefrom, such person so misusing the Post-Office Establishment shall be punishable by a fine of not more than five hundred dollars, and by imprisonment for not more than eighteen months, or by both such punishments. The indictment, information, or complaint may severally charge offences to the number of three when committed within the same six calendar months; but the court thereupon shall give a single sentence, and shall proportion the punishment especially to the degree in which the abuse of the Post-Office Establishment enters as an instrument into such fraudulent scheme or device. (R. S., § 5480.)

See also sections 875 and 1043, Postal Laws and Regulations.

Sec. 1247. Accessory to Robbery of the Mail.—Every accessory after the fact to any robbery of the carrier, agent, or other person intrusted with the mail, of such mail, or of any part thereof, shall be fined not more than two thousand dollars, and be imprisoned at hard labor not more than ten years. (R. S., § 5434.)

Sec. 1248. Accessory to Stealing Mail-Matter.—Every accessory after the fact to the offense of stealing or taking any letter or other mail-matter, or any inclosure therein, shall be fined not more than one thousand dollars, and be imprisoned not more than five years. (R. S., § 5435.)

Sec. 1249. Willfully Neglecting to Deposit Postal Revenues.—Any officer, agent, postmaster, clerk, or other person employed in any branch of the postal service having temporary custody of any money taken from dead-letters; any money derived from the sale of waste paper or other public property of the Post-Office Department; or any money derived from any other source which by law is part of the postal revenues, who shall willfully neglect to deposit the same in the Treasury of the United States, or in some other depository authorized to receive the same, shall be deemed guilty of embezzlement, and be subject to a fine of not more than double the sum so retained, or to imprisonment for not more than three years, or both. And any person intrusted by law with the sale of postage-stamps or stamped envelopes, who shall refuse or neglect to account for the same, or who shall pledge or hypothecate or unlawfully dispose of them, for any purpose whatever, shall be deemed guilty of embezzlement, and shall be punishable by like fine and imprisonment as are provided in this section for the embezzlement of money. (R. S., § 4053.)

Sec. 1250. Fraudulent Receipts of Postage.—If any postmaster, or other persons authorized by the Postmaster-General to receive the postage of letters, shall fraudulently demand or receive any rate of postage or gratuity or reward other than is provided by this section for the postage of letters or packets, he shall be punishable by a fine of one hundred dollars. (R. S., § 3899.)

Sec. 1251. Painting upon Vessels, etc., the Words "United States Mail."—Any person who shall paint, print, or in any manner place upon or attach to any steamboat or other vessel, or any stage-coach or other vehicle, not actually used in carrying the mail, the words "United States mail," or any words, letters, or characters of like import; or any person who shall give notice, by publishing in any newspaper or otherwise, that any steamboat or other vessel, or any stage-coach or other vehicle, is used in carrying the mail, when the same is not actually so used, every person so offending, or willfully aiding or abetting therein, shall, for every such offense, be punishable by fine of not less than one hundred dollars, nor more than five hundred dollars. (R. S., § 3979.)

Sec. 1252. Penalty for Using, Washing, Selling Canceled Stamps.—Any person who shall use, or attempt to use, in payment of postage, any canceled postage-stamp or postage-stamps, whether the same have been before used or not, or who shall by any means remove, or attempt to remove, or assist in removing, marks from any postage-stamp or postage-stamps, with intent to use the same in payment of postage, or who knowingly shall have in his possession any postage-stamp or postage-stamps canceled, with intent to use the same, or from which such cancellation marks have been removed, or who shall sell or offer to sell any such stamp or stamps, or who shall use or attempt to use the same in payment of postage, or who shall remove the superscription from any stamped envelope or postal card that has once been used in the payment of postage, with intent to again use the same for a like purpose, shall be deemed guilty of a misdemeanor, and shall, on conviction thereof, be punished by imprisonment for not less than six months nor more than one year, or by a fine of not less than one hundred dollars nor more than five hundred dollars for each offense, or by both such fine and imprisonment, in the discretion of the court. (Act of March 3, 1879, § 28; 20 Stat., p. 362.)

Any person employed in any branch of the postal service who shall willfully and unlawfully remove from any mail-matter any postage-stamp affixed thereto in payment of the postage, shall be punishable by a fine of not more than one hundred dollars, or by imprisonment for not more than six months. (R. S., 3922.)

Any person who shall use or attempt to use, in payment of the postage on any mail-matter conveyed by mail or otherwise, any postage-stamp or stamped envelope, or any stamp cut from any such stamped envelope, which has been before used for a like purpose, shall be liable to a penalty of fifty dollars. (R. S., § 3923.)

If any person employed in any department of the Post-Office Establishment of the United States shall willfully and knowingly use, or cause to be used, in prepayment of postage, any postage-stamp, postal card, or stamped envelope issued, or which may hereafter be issued, by authority of an act of Congress, or of the Postmaster-General, which has already been once used for a like purpose, or shall remove, or attempt to remove, the canceling or defacing marks from any such postage-stamp, or stamped envelope, or postal card, with intent to use or cause the use of the same a second time, or to sell, or offer to sell, the same, or shall remove from letters or other mail matter deposited in or received at a post-office the stamps attached to the same in payment of postage with intent to use the same a second time for a like purpose, or to sell, or offer to sell, the same, every such offender shall be deemed guilty of felony, and shall be imprisoned for not less than one year nor more than three years. (R. S. § 3924.)

If any person not employed in any department of the Post-Office Establishment of the United States shall commit any of the offenses described in the preceding section, every such person shall be deemed guilty of a misdemeanor, and be punishable by imprisonment for not less than six months nor more than one year, or by a fine of not less than one hundred dollars nor more than five hundred dollars, for each offense, or by both. (R. S., § 3925.)

Sec. 1253. Aiding or Abetting in Trading in Obscene Literature, etc.—Whoever, being an officer, agent, or employé of the Government of the United States, shall knowingly aid or abet any person engaged in any violation of any of the provisions of law prohibiting importing, advertising, dealing in, exhibiting, or sending or receiving by mail, obscene or indecent publications, or representations, or means for preventing conception or procuring abortion, or other articles of indecent or immoral use or tendency, shall be deemed guilty of a misdemeanor, and shall for every offense be punishable by a fine of not less than one hundred dollars and not more than five thousand, or by imprisonment at hard labor for not less than one year nor more than ten, or both. (R. S., § 1785; see sections 225 and 228, Postal Laws and Regulations.)

TITLE X.

POSTAL AND OFFICIAL TELEGRAMS.

Sec. 1254. Telegraph Companies Granted Right of Way over Public Domain.—Any telegraph company now organized, or which may hereafter be organized, under the laws of any State, shall have the right to construct, maintain, and operate lines of telegraph through and over any portion of the public domain of the United States, over and along any of the military or post roads of the United States which have been or may hereafter be declared such by law, and over, under, or across the navigable streams or waters of the United States; but such lines of telegraph shall be so constructed and maintained as not to obstruct the navigation of such streams and waters, or interfere with the ordinary travel on such military or post roads. (R. S., § 5263.)

Sec. 1255. Telegraph Companies to Take Materials from Public Lands.—Any telegraph company organized under the laws of any State shall have the right to take and use from the public lands through which its lines of telegraph may pass, the necessary stone, timber, and other materials for its posts, piers, stations, and other needful uses in the construction, maintenance, and operation of its lines of telegraph, and may pre-empt and use such portion of the unoccupied public lands subject to pre-emption through which their lines of telegraph may be located as may be necessary for their stations, not exceeding forty acres for each station; but such stations shall not be within fifteen miles of each other. (R. S., § 5264.)

Sec. 1256. Telegraph Companies may not Transfer above-granted Rights.—The rights and privileges granted under the provisions of the act of July twenty-four, eighteen hundred and sixty-six, entitled "An act to aid in the construction of telegraph lines, and to secure to the Government the use of the same for postal, military, and other purposes," or under this Title, shall not be transferred by any company acting thereunder to any other corporation, association, or person. (R. S., § 5265; see 14 Opinions, 153, 278.)

Sec. 1257. Priority of Official Telegrams; Postmaster-General to fix Rates.—Telegrams between the several Departments of the Government and their officers and agents, in their transmission over the lines of any telegraph company to which has been given the right of way, timber, or station lands from the public domain shall have priority over all other business, at such rates as the Postmaster-General shall annually fix. And no part of any appropriation for the several Departments of the Government shall be paid to any company which neglects or refuses to transmit such telegrams in accordance with the provisions of this section. (R. S., § 5265.)

Sec. 1258. The United States may Purchase Telegraph Lines.—The United States may, for postal, military, or other purposes, purchase all the telegraph lines, property, and effects of any or all companies acting under the provisions of the act of July twenty-fourth, eighteen hundred and sixty-six, entitled "An act to aid in the construction of telegraph lines, and to secure to the Government the use of the same for postal, military, and other purposes," or under this Title, at an appraised value, to be ascertained by five competent, disinterested persons, two of whom shall be selected by the Postmaster-General of the United States, two by the company interested, and one by the four so previously selected. (R. S., § 5267.)

Sec. 1259. To Secure Rights Telegraph Companies must Accept Obligations.—Before any telegraph company shall exercise any of the powers or privileges conferred by law, such company shall file their written acceptance with the Postmaster-General of the restrictions and obligations required by law. (R. S., § 5268.)

Sec. 1260. Penalty for Refusal to Transmit Dispatches at Rates Fixed.—Whenever any telegraph company, after having filed its written acceptance with the Postmaster-General of the restrictions and obligations required by the act approved July twenty-fourth, eighteen hundred and sixty-six, entitled "An act to aid in the construction of telegraph lines, and to secure to the Government the use of the same for postal, military, and other purposes," or by this Title, shall, by its agents or employés, refuse or neglect to transmit any such telegraphic communications as are provided for by the aforesaid act, or by this Title, or by the provisions of section two hundred and twenty-one, Title "THE DEPARTMENT OF WAR," authorizing the Secretary of War to provide for taking meteorological observations at the military stations and other points of the interior of the continent, and for giving notice on the northern lakes and sea-board of the approach and force of storms, such telegraph company shall be liable to a penalty of not less than one hundred dollars and not more than one thousand dollars for each such refusal or neglect. (R. S., § 5269.)

Sec. 1261. Rates for Official Telegrams as Fixed by the Postmaster-General.—The rate for all telegraphic communications, sent otherwise than over circuits established by the Chief Signal-Officer of the Army for the transmission of enciphered weather reports, shall be as follows, viz:

One cent per word for each circuit through which it shall be transmitted, said rate to be computed subject to the following conditions, viz:

A distance of five hundred miles, as computed by the tables of the Post-Office Department,* shall be deemed a circuit, and the shortest practicable route of the company transmitting the message shall in all cases be the basis of computation.

If, in computing circuits, there shall be found one or more circuits and a fraction of a circuit, such fraction shall be deemed a circuit.

If a communication shall be sent a distance less than five hundred miles, that distance shall be deemed a circuit.

All words of the communication transmitted are to be counted, excepting the date and place at which such communication is filed.

All messages of less than twenty-five words, address and signature included, shall be rated as if containing twenty-five words, and all messages exceeding twenty-five words shall be rated by the exact number of words they contain, address and signature included.

Each company will be allowed to charge for messages received from another line at the same rates as if received from the Government direct for transmission over its own line.

Companies forwarding messages to another line will be entitled to compensation at established rates to the terminus of their lines, at the same rates as if for messages transmitted exclusively over their own lines.

The rate for all telegraphic communications known as the Signal-service weather reports shall not exceed three cents for each word of said reports for each circuit over which they may pass, in accordance with the schedule of circuits and plans of the Chief Signal-Officer of the Army, which are now or may hereafter be adopted by him for transmitting these reports, or such parts thereof as he may designate, in such words or ciphers as may from time to time be directed by him. The amount thus estimated is to be taken in full payment for said reports; no additional allowance to be made for drops, office messages, or other services or special facilities required by the Chief Signal-Officer for the correct and prompt transmission of said Signal-service-reports.

If, at any time, from competition or other cause, telegraph rates should be reduced so that a message of ten words may be sent for the public at a less rate than that above mentioned for a twenty-five-word message, then, and in that case, this order shall be changed to meet such lower public rate; it being intended by this proviso that in no case shall the Government be compelled to pay more for a twenty-five-word message, including address and signature, than the public is required to pay for a ten-word message, exclusive of such address and signature.

All officers of the United States Government are requested to report to the Postmaster-General any charges in excess of the above rates.

Sec. 1262. Telegraph Companies Subject to Foregoing Sections.—The following is a list of telegraph companies that have filed their acceptances of the provisions of the preceding sections of this Title up to the first day of June, 1879:

1. The National Telegraph Company of New York, N. Y.
2. The Globe Insulated Lines Telegraph Company of New York.
3. The American Submarine Telegraph Company of New York, N. Y.
4. International Telegraph Company of Portland, Me.
5. The Atlantic and Pacific Telegraph Company of New York, N. Y.
6. The Franco-American Land and Ocean Telegraph Company of New York, N. Y.
7. The Globe Telegraph Company of New York.
8. Mississippi Valley National Telegraph Company of Saint Louis, Mo.
9. Western Union Telegraph Company of New York, N. Y.
10. Northwestern Telegraph Company of Kenosha, Wis.
11. Great Western Telegraph Company of New York, N. Y.
12. The Franklin Telegraph Company of Boston, Mass.
13. The Insulated Lines Telegraph Company of Boston, Mass.
14. Pacific and Atlantic Telegraph Company of Pittsburgh, Pa.

* See section 27, p. 39.

15. The Alantic and Pacific States Telegraph Company of Sacramento, Cal.
16. The Eastern Telegraph Company of Philadelphia, Pa.
17. The Delaware River Telegraph Company, Philadelphia, Pa.
18. Peninsula Telegraph Company, New York City.
19. Cape May and Shore Telegraph Company, New York City.
20. Ocean Telegraph Company of Boston, Mass.
21. The American Cable Company of New York, N. Y.
22. Southern and Atlantic Telegraph Company of Philadelphia, Pa.
23. International Ocean Telegraph Company, New York City.
24. Missouri River Telegraph Company of Sioux City, Iowa.
25. Atlantic and Pacific Telegraph Company of Missouri. Executive Office, 145 Broadway, New York City. Received and filed May 8, 1877.
26. New Jersey and New England Telegraph Company. Received and filed November 21, 1878. Address A. L. Worthington, No. 10 Green street, Trenton, N. J.
27. Central Union Telegraph Company, 145 Broadway, New York. Received and filed May 9, 1879.
28. New York Land and Ocean Telegraph Company. Received and filed May 10, 1879.
29. Deseret Telegraph Company, Salt Lake City, Utah. Received and filed May 19, 1879.

TITLE XI.

EXECUTIVE ORDERS AFFECTING THE POSTAL SERVICE.

1.

EXECUTIVE ORDER IN REGARD TO UNITED STATES OFFICERS HOLDING STATE AND MUNICIPAL OFFICES.

By the President of the United States:

Whereas it has been brought to the notice of the President of the United States that many persons holding civil office by appointment from him, or otherwise, under the Constitution and laws of the United States, while holding such Federal positions, accept offices under the authority of the States and Territories in which they reside, or of municipal corporations, under the charters and ordinances of such corporations, thereby assuming the duties of the State, Territorial, or municipal office at the same time that they are charged with the duties of the civil office held under Federal authority; and

Whereas it is believed that, with few exceptions, the holding of two such offices by the same person is incompatible with a due and faithful discharge of the duties of either office; that it frequently gives rise to great inconvenience, and often results in detriment to the public service, and moreover is not in harmony with the genius of the government:

In view of the premises, therefore, the President has deemed it proper thus and hereby to give public notice that, from and after the fourth day of March, A. D. 1873, except as herein specified, persons holding any Federal civil office by appointment under the Constitution and laws of the United States will be expected, while holding such office, not to accept or hold any office under any State or Territorial government, or under the charter or ordinances of any municipal corporation; and, further, that the acceptance or continued holding of any such State, Territorial, or municipal office, whether elective or by appointment, by any person holding civil office, as aforesaid, under the Government of the United States, other than judicial offices under the Constitution of the United States, will be deemed a vacation of the Federal office held by such person, and will be taken to be, and will be, treated as a resignation by such Federal officer of his commission or appointment in the service of the United States.

The offices of justices of the peace, of notaries public, and of commissioners to take the acknowledgment of deeds, or bail, or to administer oaths, shall not be deemed within the purview of this order, and are excepted from its operation, and may be held by Federal officers. The appointment of deputy marshal of the United States may be conferred upon sheriffs or deputy sheriffs; and deputy postmasters, the emoluments of whose office do not exceed $600 per annum, are also excepted from the operations of this order, and may accept and hold appointments under State, Territorial, or municipal authority, provided the same be found not to interfere with the discharge of their duties as postmaster. Heads of Departments and other officers of the government who have the appointment of subordinate officers are required to take notice of this order, and to see to the enforcement of its provisions and terms within the sphere of their respective Departments or offices, and as relates to the several persons holding appointments under them respectively.

By order of the President:

HAMILTON FISH,
Secretary of State.

WASHINGTON, *January* 17, 1873.

NOTE.—The President has modified the above order so as not to apply to post-offices the salary of which is less than $1,000.

2.

WHO ARE ENTITLED TO HOLD STATE AND MUNICIPAL OFFICES UNDER THE ORDER OF THE PRESIDENT.

DEPARTMENT OF STATE,
Washington, D. C., January 28, 1873.

Inquiries having been made from various quarters as to the application of the Executive order issued on the 17th of January, relating to the holding of State and municipal offices by persons holding civil offices under the Federal government, the President directs the following reply to be made:

It has been asked whether the order prohibits a Federal officer from holding also the office of an alderman, or of a common councilman in a city, or of a town councilman of a town or village, or of appointment under city, town, or village governments. By some it has been suggested that there may be distinction made in case the office be held with or without salary or compensation.

The city or town officers of the description referred to, by whatever names they may be locally known, whether held by election or by appointment, and whether with or without salary or compensation, are of the class which the Executive order intends not to be held by persons holding Federal offices.

It has been asked whether the order prohibits Federal officers from holding positions on boards of education, school committees, public libraries, religious or eleemosynary institutions, incorporated or established or sustained by State or municipal authority.

Positions and service on such boards or committees and professorships in colleges are not regarded as "offices" within the contemplation of the Executive order, but as employments or service in which all good citizens may engage without incompatibility, and in many cases without necessary interference with any position which they may hold under the Federal Government. Officers of the Federal Government may, therefore, engage in such service, provided the attention required by such employment does not interfere with the regular and official discharge of the duties of their office under the Federal Government. The head of the department under whom the Federal office is held will in all cases be the sole judge whether or not the employment does thus interfere.

The question has also been asked with regard to the officers of the State militia.

Congress having exercised the power conferred by the Constitution to provide for organizing the militia, which is liable to be called forth to be employed in the service of the United States, and is thus in some sense under the control of the General Government, and is, moreover, of the greatest value to the public, the Executive order of 17th January is not considered as prohibiting Federal officers from being officers of the militia in the States and Territories.

It has been asked whether the order prohibits persons holding office under the Federal Government being members of local or municipal fire departments; also, whether it applies to mechanics employed by the day in the armories, arsenals, and navy-yards. &c., of the United States.

Unpaid service in local or municipal fire departments is not regarded as an office within the intent of the Executive order, and may be performed by Federal officers, provided it does not interfere with the regular and efficient discharge of the duties of the Federal office, of which the head of the department under which the office is held will in each case be the judge.

Employment by the day as mechanics or laborers in the armories, arsenals, navy-yards, &c., does not constitute an office of any kind, and those thus employed are not within the contemplation of the Executive order. Master-workmen and others who hold appointments from the government or from any Department, whether for a fixed time or at the pleasure of the appointing power, are embraced within the operation of the order.

By order of the President:

HAMILTON FISH,
Secretary of State.

3.

POSTAL OFFICERS FORBIDDEN TO PARTICIPATE IE POLITICAL CAMPAIGNS, ETC.

EXECUTIVE MANSION,
Washington, June 22, 1877.

SIR: I desire to call your attention to the following paragraph in a letter addressed by me to the Secretary of the Treasury, on the conduct to be observed by officers of the general government in relation to the elections:

"No officer should be required or permitted to take part in the management of political organizations, caucuses, conventions, or election campaigns. Their right to vote and to express their views on public questions, either orally or through the press, is not denied, provided it does not interfere with the discharge of their official duties. No assessment for political purposes on officers or subordinates should be allowed."

This rule is applicable to every Department of the civil service. It should be understood by every officer of the general government that he is expected to conform his conduct to its requirements.

Very respectfully,

R. B. HAYES.

To the POSTMASTER-GENERAL.

TITLE XII.

OPINIONS OF THE ASSISTANT ATTORNEY-GENERAL FOR THE POST-OFFICE DEPARTMENT.

NOTE.—Only such opinions as are of general importance are given at length. The numbers in parentheses refer to the docket number. At the close of this Title will be found a full index to all opinions not printed in full in this volume, which are on file in the office of the Assistant Attorney-General for the Post-Office Department.

[Number (6) One.]

Local or Drop Letters.

1. When a drop-letter properly stamped has been deposited in the post-office for delivery, and the person to whom it is addressed requests that it should be forwarded to another post-office, under that request the character of a drop-letter is entirely lost to it, and it assumes the character of a letter deposited "for mailing," without any stamp for that purpose.

2. The postage on a drop-letter must be prepaid, and, to that extent, it falls within the general terms of a prepaid letter, but the prepayment is not such as would entitle the depositor to have it carried beyond the bounds of delivery of the post-office where deposited, or even to be put into the mails.

OFFICE OF THE ASSISTANT ATTORNEY-GENERAL
FOR THE POST-OFFICE DEPARTMENT,
Washington, July 29, 1873.

SIR: I have considered your communication of July 25, 1873, inclosing the letter of Mr. C. W. Bennett, and the envelopes accompanying it, addressed to the postmaster of this city.

Mr. Bennett excepts to the postage charged on the envelopes by the postmaster here. The envelopes appear to have been deposited in this office, addressed to Mr. Bennett at this place, with stamps affixed to them, at the time they were deposited, sufficient to cause them to be received and delivered to their address as drop or local letters.

Upon their receipt at this office as drop or local letters the stamps affixed to them were canceled; and Mr. Bennett having requested that all letters deposited or received at this office to his address should be forwarded to him at another office, through the mails, stamps proper to be charged on such letters, as letters deposited "for mailing," were affixed thereto at this office, and the letters forwarded, as Mr. Bennett requested.

The postmaster here, in affixing the stamps, in order that they should be forwarded through the mails to another office, has charged the postage on them without regard to the postage which had been paid on them as drop-letters. It is to the postage so charged that Mr. Bennett excepts.

The letters forwarded were letters which had been deposited in this office with postage prepaid as local or drop letters. Letters of that character are mentioned in only two sections, the 156th and 157th sections of the act of June 8, 1872, entitled "An act to revise, consolidate, and amend the statutes relating to the Post-Office Department," commonly called the "Postal Code."

In the 156th section although they are recognized as "mail-matter wholly or partly in writing," yet to mark their special and distinctive character they are expressly excepted from the postage of three cents for each half ounce or fraction thereof, which by that section is charged on other letters.

The 157th section describes a local or drop letter, and directs the postage with which such a letter shall be charged, and is in the following terms:

"That letters commonly known as drop or local letters, *delivered through the post-office or its carrier*, shall be charged with postage at the rate of two cents, where the system of free delivery is established, and one cent where such system is not established, for each half ounce or fraction thereof."

The description of a local or drop letter is probably more clearly drawn in the laws which it was the purpose of the Postal Code to "revise, consolidate, and amend," than in these sections of that code. Thus, in the 23d and 22d sections of the act of March 3, 1863, we have the distinction clearly drawn between drop or local letters and other domestic letters. The language in the 22d section is that "the rate of postage on all domestic letters, *transmitted in the mails* of the United States, and not exceeding one-half ounce in weight, shall be uniform at three cents." Of the 23d section it is: "That the rate of postage on all letters not *transmitted through the mails* of the United States, but delivered through the post-office or its carriers, *commonly described as local or drop letters*, not exceeding one-half ounce in weight, shall be uniform at two cents," etc.

In this 23d section we have the character or a local or drop letter defined as a letter *not to be "transmitted through the mails."* In the act of March 3, 1855, section 1, a drop-letter is still more accurately described in different language, but of the same purport, in the following terms: "And all drop-letters or letters placed in any post-office *not for transmission through the mails, but for delivery* only."

From the language of these several statutes there can be no doubt that the local or drop letter intended in the 157th section was a letter deposited in the post-office not to be transmitted through the mails, but for delivery only. All letters deposited in a post-office, whether to be transmitted through the mails or for delivery only, must be prepaid by stamps, according to the purpose for which they are deposited, before they can be officially received; that is, received so as to impose an obligation on the Department to transmit them through the mails or deliver them from the office where deposited, or by its carriers, to their address. The prepayment of postage entitles the person depositing a letter to have it so officially received.

When a letter properly stamped is officially received, the stamp has performed its office, and is canceled, and when canceled is no further available for any purpose.

When a drop-letter, properly stamped, has been deposited in the office for delivery, and the person to whom it is addressed, requests that it should be forwarded to another office under that request, the character of a drop-letter is entirely lost to it, and it assumes the character of a letter deposited "for mailing" without any stamp for that purpose. The stamp affixed to it when deposited was so affixed in order that it should be received for the purpose of delivery only, and was not intended to be, nor was, available for any other purpose.

If the request "to forward" is to be gratified, it can only be by the prepayment of the postage proper to be charged on a letter deposited to be transmitted through the mails to the address contained in the request.

The comprehensive terms of the 199th section are well calculated to mislead if read without regard to other parts of the Code. The terms of the 199th section are, "That prepaid and free letters shall be forwarded from one post-office to another at the request of the party addressed without additional charge for postage." It is evident, however, for many reasons, notwithstanding the comprehensiveness of its terms, that this section was not intended to apply to drop-letters. In the first place, the language of the section clearly implies that the letter to be forwarded under its provisions has been already carried through the mails from one post-office to another, and that postage for that service has been paid. But inasmuch as the prepayment of one full rate of postage entitles the sender to have his letter carried through the mails anywhere where the mails are carried, the right so purchased is *not* exhausted under the provisions of this section until it reached not only the destination which the sender has given to it, but also that further destination which may be given to it by the person to whom it is addressed. But the prepayment to which this right is incident is that which would have carried the forwarded letter to its last destination if it had been so directed when deposited for mailing.

The postage on a drop-letter it is true must be prepaid, and to that extent it falls within the general terms of a prepaid letter, but the prepayment is not such as would entitle the depositor to have it carried beyond the bounds of delivery of the office where deposited, or even to be put into the mails. In the language of the acts of 1855 and 1863 it is placed in the office "not for transmission through the mails."

Hence it cannot be held or considered to be embraced within that class of prepayments to which the right is incident to have the letter carried any and every where where letters are carried through the mails; and that is the prepayment which is clearly contemplated in the 199th section.

Again, from all the provisions of the code relating to this subject, we can come to no other conclusion than that it was the intention of the law that no letter should be carried through the mails from one post-office to another except upon the prepayment by stamps of three cents for each half ounce or fraction thereof, and yet, by a construction different from that which I have given, a letter deposited in an office "*for delivery only*" may be carried across the continent for a postage-stamp of one cent; for if a drop letter on which one cent postage by stamp has been paid, at an office where there is no free delivery, is a prepaid letter, embraced within the intendment of the 199th section, then, on the request of the person to whom the letter is addressed, it must be forwarded "*without additional postage*" to any office he may direct. This was clearly not intended by the law.

For these reasons, I can see no error in the action of the postmaster at Washington in treating the letters, of which the envelopes covering them are before me, as drop letters, not entitled, by any postage which might have been paid on them as such, to be transmitted through the mails, and if transmitted after their official receipt as drop letters at the request of the person to whom they are addressed to another post-office, the postage directed by law to be prepaid on letters deposited for "mailing" must be charged and prepaid on them.

I herewith return the letter of Mr. Bennett, with the accompanying envelopes, sent with your communication.

Very respectfully,

T. A. SPENCE,
Assistant Attorney-General Post-Office Department.

Hon. JOHN A. J. CRESWELL,
Postmaster-General.

[Number (11) Two.]

Delivery of Letters. Effect of Injunction of State Court.

OFFICE OF THE ASSISTANT ATTORNEY-GENERAL
FOR THE POST-OFFICE DEPARTMENT,
Washington, August 11, 1873.

SIR: I have carefully examined the papers transmitted for my consideration with your communication of August 1.

From those papers I infer the following facts: Alvan W. Chase, being the proprietor of the copyright of a book which he had published, and a large steam-printing house, in August 1869, for a valuable consideration sold the said copyright and steam-printing house to Rice A. Beal; and in the contract of sale, among other agreements, the said Chase contracted with the said Beal "that all letters and packages that should thereafter be received at the post-office in said city of Ann Arbor, addressed to the said Chase, whether registered or otherwise, and not having the description by number of his private box, should be delivered to the said Beal;" that the postmaster at the said city of Ann Arbor, having knowledge of the said sale and contract, did, from the time of his appointment to the said office in June, 1870, to September, 1872, deliver to the said Beal all letters and packages addressed to the said Chase, not having thereon the description, by number, of the private box of the said Chase in the said office; that in the month of September, 1872, the said Chase, by his written order, directed the said postmaster, after the date of the said order, to wit, September 19, 1872, to place all letters addressed to him in his box, unless there was something in the address of the letter to indicate that it was intended for the publisher of Dr. Chase's recipes or the proprietor of Dr. Chase's steam-printing house; and thereafter, in compliance with said order, the said postmaster placed in the letter-box of the said Chase, to be delivered to him, or his order, all letters addressed to him, as by the said order directed. That the said Rice A. Beal subsequently, after the order aforesaid of the said Chase to the said postmaster, filed in the circuit court of Washtenaw County, in the State of Michigan, his bill of complaint against the said Alvan W. Chase and others, with a prayer for an injunction. The circuit court for Washtenaw County, on the filing of the said bill of complaint, ordered a writ of injunction as prayed, and, amongst other restraints therein, enjoined the said defendants "from taking or receiving from the post-office in the city of Ann Arbor any letter or letters that may be received at said office addressed to the said Alvan W. Chase which shall not have upon them a designation of the number of said Chase's private letter-box at said office, or in any manner interfering to prevent the delivery of the same to the said complainant, Rice A. Beal, at said post-office;" that the defendants, after service of the said writ of injunction, without having filed a plea or answer to the said bill, but upon affidavits which they filed to be read at the hearing of the motion, moved the court to dissolve the injunction. The motion to dissolve the injunction was heard and considered, and was denied. The court in denying the motion passed the following order:

"The motion to dissolve the injunction is therefore denied, and it is ordered that the modification of the same, as ordered on the 21st of July instant, be, and is hereby, set aside and held for nought, and that the injunction do stand in full force and effect as originally granted, without modification or alteration, until the coming in of the defendant's answer to said bill of complaint, and until the further order of this court, except that the said defendant, Chase, shall not be prevented by said injunction from taking from the post-office any and all letters directed to himself or family which shall be designated by the number of his post-office box, 351, written thereon."

Rice A. Beal, under his purchase from, and contract with, Alvan W. Chase, hereinbefore stated, and this order of the court, now demands of the postmaster at the city of Ann Arbor the letters and packages received at his office addressed to the said

Chase "which shall not be designated by the number of his post-office box, 351, written thereon."

Under these facts the postmaster at the city of Ann Arbor, in his letter accompanying your communication, asks the Postmaster-General to be informed of his duty in the premises; to whom he shall deliver, or what disposition he shall make of the letters addressed to Alvan W. Chase, and now demanded by Rice A. Beal.

After a careful examination of all the facts presented, I can find nothing that would relieve the postmaster from his duty, as clearly and explicitly stated in the 58th and 59th sections of the regulations of 1866 of this Department. Those regulations are as follows.

"Sec. 58. The persons entitled to letters received by mail are those whose names are in the address."

"Sec. 59. The delivery should be either to the person addressed or according to his or her order."

Under this law, making plain the duty of postmasters, and controlling their action, the postmaster at the city of Ann Arbor must deliver to Alvan W. Chase, or to his order, all letters and packages addressed to the said Chase, received at the said post-office, "unless there is something in the address of the letter or package to indicate that it is intended for the publisher of Dr. Chase's recipes or the proprietor of Dr. Chase's steam-printing house"; and he must do so on request, notwithstanding the injunction which enjoins the said Chase from receiving them.

If Alvan W. Chase should take from the post-office the letters he has been enjoined from taking or receiving, he would thereby offend against the order of the court, and may be punished for the contempt; but the postmaster, as such, has not been made a party to the proceeding in equity, referred to, of Beal *vs.* Chase and others; nor is he in any manner controlled by the order of the court; nor would he be protected by it, in violating his duty, as imposed by the regulations of the department referred to.

The postmaster under these rules, in the discharge of his official duties, is bound to respect the written order given him by Alvan W. Chase on the 19th September, 1872, however much in his private judgment such order might be inconsistent with, or violate the contract hereinbefore set out in, the statement of facts, which the said Chase had made with the said Beal in August, 1869.

It is not the duty, nor is it proper, for a postmaster to decide the validity and legal effect of contracts, nor to act on any construction which he may give them, when such action is in direct contravention of the plain law of his duty.

Under the order of Alvan W. Chase, of the 19th September, 1872, it was the duty of the postmaster to place in the private letter-box of the said Chase the letters addressed to him, as by the said order he was directed.

It does not appear, from any of the papers before me, that that order has ever been rescinded; and until it is rescinded, the same duty remains and continues. It is not to be presumed that Alvan W. Chase will offend against the order of the court, and take from the office the letters he has been enjoined from taking; and they will, therefore, remain in the office, and be treated by the postmaster as unclaimed letters, unless specially ordered by the Postmaster-General to hold them for delivery, or to be disposed of under a future order. The present order of the circuit court of Washtenaw County is only temporary; the injunction may be dissolved or made perpetual when the defendants have filed their answer to the bill of complaint and further proceedings shall have been had thereon, or the court may pass other and further orders in the cause, considering that the neglect or refusal of A. W. Chase to rescind the order which controls the action of the postmaster, and prevents R. A. Beal from receiving the letters and packages which under the contract aforesaid, as construed by the court, the said Beal is in equity entitled to have, is a violation of the present order of the court and a contempt of its authority.

In conclusion, I can see nothing in the papers transmitted with your communication which would authorize or justify the postmaster at the city of Ann Arbor in delivering the letters and packages received at this office, addressed to A. W. Chase, to R. A. Beal, in violation of the order aforesaid of the said Chase of the 19th September, 1872, or until that order is in some manner, directly or indirectly, rescinded or annulled.

Yours, respectfully,

T. A. SPENCE,
Assistant Attorney-General, Post-Office Department.

Hon. J. A. J. CRESWELL,
Postmaster-General.

[Number (14) Three.]

Mail-Matter by Express.

1. There is nothing "in any existing statute upon the subject of postal matter" which discriminates in favor of the Departments of the Government in relation to the mode and manner of transmitting mailable matter.
2. Distinction between packet and package discussed.
3. No limit of weight or size for first-class mail-matter.

OFFICE OF THE ASSISTANT ATTORNEY-GENERAL
FOR THE POST-OFFICE DEPARTMENT,
Washington, D. C., August 26, 1873.

SIR: I have carefully considered the letter of the honorable the Secretary of War of the 14th instant, addressed to you, and the papers accompanying it.

Enclosed in the letter of the Secretary is a copy of an order of the War Department in the following words:

"General Orders, No. 80.

"WAR DEPARTMENT, ADJUTANT-GENERAL'S OFFICE,
"*Washington, Aug. 1st, 1873.*

"Where any considerable saving would result, packages of official mail-matter, such as returns, &c., weighty or bulky in character, may be transmitted by express, instead of through the mails as heretofore, the expressage to be paid out of the appropriations for the military service.

"By order of the Secretary of War.

"THOMAS M. VINCENT,
"*Assistant Adjutant-General.*

"Official:
"E. D. TOWNSEND,
"*Adjutant-General.*"

And you are asked if the forwarding of mailable matter by express, as directed by that order, "is considered by the Department in conflict with existing statutes upon the subject of postal matter."

There is nothing "in any existing statute upon the subject of postal matter" which discriminates in favor of the Departments of the Government in relation to the mode and manner of transmitting mailable matter.

The law is general, and since the abolition of the franking privilege by the act of Congress passed January 31, 1873, all of the restrictions and prohibitions of the act passed June 8, 1872, entitled "An act to revise, consolidate, and amend the statutes relating to the Post-Office Department," which apply to the private citizen, are applicable, to the same extent, to an officer of any of the Departments.

If the private citizen, by the provisions of that act, and particularly by the 230th section thereof, is inhibited from using an express, or other unlawful means, for the transmission of mailable matter, so also is the public officer; nor are the inhibitions in any manner affected by the public or private character of the mailable matter.

It will not be supposed that a private citizen would be permitted to violate with impunity the provisions of the 230th section of the act referred to, which provides "that no person shall transmit, by private express or other unlawful means, or deliver to any agent of such unlawful express, or deposit, or cause to be deposited, at any appointed place, for the purpose of being transmitted, any letter or packet, and for every such offense the party so offending shall forfeit and pay fifty dollars," for any consideration of the saving of postage to him for the violation. Much less could it be allowed an officer of a Department to violate the same law for a similar consideration, especially in view of the fact that Congress has provided so liberally by appropriation for the payment of the postage of the several Departments.

It may not be improper in this communication to notice a matter intimately connected with this subject, although not directly responsive to the question propounded in the letter of the Secretary of War. It was the purpose of the 228th, 229th, 230th, and 231st sections of the act of June 8, 1872, to prevent, by penal enactments, the transmission of mailable matter of the first class (all correspondence wholly or partly in writing) by express or other unlawful means. By the 134th section of the same act, it is provided that "*packages* weighing more than four pounds shall not be received for conveyance by mail."

The term *package* in this section, and throughout the law, appears to be used in a different sense and with a different intendment from the term "packet" found in the sections above referred to.

The latter is restricted to mailable matter of the first class; the former is used throughout the law as applicable to mailable matter of the second and third classes. And inasmuch as mailable matter of the second and third classes, under the restrictions of the 134th section, cannot be received into the mails when each of the several proper mailable parcels of such matter, made up in a package, exceeds four pounds in weight, such packages are not within the contemplation of the Postal Code, and may be sent by express, or in any other manner, without a violation of law; but the 134th section not being applicable to mailable matter of the first class, all matter of that class can be conveyed through the mails without regard to its weight, and all the inhibitions of the several sections of the Postal Code, prohibiting its transmission by express or other unlawful means, apply to it.

Very respectfully, yours, &c.,

T. A. SPENCE,
Assistant Attorney-General, Post-Office Department.

Hon. JOHN A. J. CRESWELL,
Postmaster-General.

[Number (24) Four.]

Production of Letters before a Court under Process Duces Tecum.

OFFICE OF THE ASSISTANT ATTORNEY-GENERAL,
FOR THE POST-OFFICE DEPARTMENT,
Washington, D. C., January 24, 1874.

SIR: My opinion is asked as to the duty of the postmaster at Greensburgh, in the State of Indiana, under the following circumstances:

There is in the post-office at Greensburgh, in the said State of Indiana, a letter addressed to Sally Covert; that fact having come to the knowledge of a certain William Denwood, and he desiring to know and be informed of its contents, and to obtain the information, instituted suit in the circuit court of Decatur County, in the State aforesaid, against a certain Nicholas Howard, and caused subpœna to be issued out of the court in which the said suit was brought, commanding the sheriff of said county to summon George H. Dunn (the postmaster at Greensburgh) to produce on the trial a letter in his possession addressed to Sallie Covert, Greensburgh, Indiana, and to appear before the said court to testify in the said suit. The subpœna has been served in due form of law on the said George H. Dunn.

From the subpœna it appears that George H. Dunn has been summoned as an individual, not as an officer, to produce in court a letter which he has in his possession addressed to Sallie Covert. If he has in his possession as an individual, and not in his official character as postmaster, a letter addressed to Sallie Covert, it will be his duty to obey the summons of the court implicitly; but if the letter sought to be obtained is in the post-office at Greensburgh as proper mail-matter, and he is summoned as postmaster, having charge of the said office, to take the letter from the office to produce the same before the circuit court for Decatur County, to be used as evidence, or for any other purpose, he should respectfully decline to obey the summons. The letter addressed to Sallie Covert, having through the mails reached its destination, according to its address, at the post-office at Greensburgh, it is then, until delivered to the person to whom it is addressed or disposed of as the postal laws and regulations direct, in the custody of the Post-Office Department of the government, by its agent or representative, the postmaster of the office. His custody or possession of the mail-matter in the office is purely representative, not personal; and his duties as the representative are clearly and distinctly defined by the laws and regulations governing the postal service. They are to him his only rule of conduct. No mandate or order of any tribunal, judicial or otherwise, directing or commanding him to disobey or disregard them, or to act in contravention to them, will justify him in so doing, or excuse or protect him from any and all penalties which would follow the violation of his official duties.

The government, in receiving the letter addressed to Sallie Covert in the mails, undertook to carry that letter to its destination at the office of delivery, and there to deliver it to the person to whom it is addressed without unnecessary detention or delay. Any act which would or might detain or delay the delivery to the person to whom the letter is addressed would not only be a default in the undertaking, but would be on the part of the postmaster a palpable violation of the Postal Code, for which offense, according to its gravity, the punishment of fine and imprisonment is provided by law. The post-office at the office of delivery is the only proper place of custody of mail-matter until it is delivered; and a postmaster cannot be justified in taking letters from the post-office for any purpose other than for delivery to the person addressed, except in exceptional cases, for greater security.

The postmaster at Greensburgh, in obeying the summons of the circuit court for Decatur County to produce this letter before it for the purposes of evidence, would not only violate his duty as to the proper custody of the letter before its delivery, but he would further violate the plain letter of the law in doing an act naturally tending to detain and delay the delivery of the letter. The circuit court for Decatur County cannot properly interfere with the postmaster at Greensburgh in the lawful and proper discharge of his official duties, nor require him to do that which would violate in their letter or their spirit the laws and regulations relating to the Post-Office Department.

The court may exercise its jurisdiction over individuals, but not to control the officers of the government to a violation of the laws relating to their office. It may, in the proper exercise of its jurisdiction, restrain an individual to whom a letter is addressed from taking it from the post-office, or, if the letter has been delivered, and thereby all connection of the government with it, or relating to it, terminated, the court may then exercise its jurisdiction to compel its production before it, in whosesoever possession it may be found.

But it may be, and probably is, alleged that the address "Sallie Covert" is fictitious, and that the letter under that address is intended for the wife of the plaintiff in this action, William Denwood. If such an allegation was true, it might and would affect the duties of the postmaster as to its disposition, but none the more justify him in obeying the summons of the court which has been served on him. If the address is fictitious, there is no person to whom it can be delivered, and his duty in relation to it is clearly defined by the regulations of the Department. He must return it at the end of the month to the Dead-Letter Office, there to be disposed of as provided by the laws relating to and the regulations of the Department.

I would, therefore, advise that the postmaster at Greensburg be instructed to appear in person before the circuit court of Decatur County on the day named in the writ of summons, but not produce before it the letter which by the said writ he is ordered to produce; and that, if required, he should purge himself of any alleged contempt of the court by the statement that the letter mentioned in the writ is in his custody, not as an individual, but as an officer of the government, and that he cannot obey the summons of the court without violating the laws relating to and the rules and regulations of the Post-Office Department.

Very respectfully, yours,

T. A. SPENCE,
Assistant Attorney-General Post-Office Department.

Hon. JOHN A. J. CRESWELL,
Postmaster-General.

[Number (26) Five.]

Letter-Boxes. Letters Addressed to Fictitious Names; How Disposed of.

OFFICE OF THE ASSISTANT ATTORNEY-GENERAL
FOR THE POST-OFFICE DEPARTMENT,
Washington, D. C., February 4, 1874.

SIR: An opinion on the facts presented by the application of Dr. John M. Dagnall "to have delivered to him a large number of letters addressed to Nathaniel Mayfair, P. O. box 153, Brooklyn, N. Y.," which have been sent by the postmaster at Brooklyn to the Dead-Letter Office of the Department, requires a review of the laws and postal regulations relating to the purpose and use of letter-boxes, the delivery of letters, and the use of a fictitious address on mailable matter.

While letter-boxes are frequently recognized in the Postal Code as a proper part of postal facilities, and as a source of postal revenues, they are never provided at the expense of the Departments, "except when the building is owned by the United States." They may be and are provided by postmasters and individuals. Boxes "put up" by postmasters are the private property of the postmasters, but the rents or revenues thereof must be paid over to the Department. Box-holders may provide lock-boxes or drawers for their own use at their own expense, which upon their erection become the property of the United States, subject to the direction and control of the Departments, and for which a rent is expected equal to that of other boxes in the same office. A letter-box may be considered a particular space in the post office, which for a consideration is set apart for the exclusive use of an individual for the greater facility of the person to whom it is assigned in receiving his mail-matter, and to be a source of revenue to the Department. Its use is subject to and controlled by the regulations of the Department, which have been framed and adopted with a proper regard to the purposes for which it is allowed to be and is erected.

For the convenience of the person renting a box, he is entitled to have put in it the letters of his family, firm, or company, and those of his friends stopping *temporarily* with him, if directed to his care or the number of his box; but to protect the revenues of the Department it is provided, that letters addressed to other persons residing in the same place, and living and doing business separate and apart from a box-holder, should not be placed in the box.

In order to protect the revenues and to prevent the improper use of the privilege of box-holders, postmasters should use proper care that none should have the privilege of the box except those to whom it is allowed under the regulations.

In the exercise of this care, the difficulties and embarrassments that will most frequently occur to postmasters will be the disposition to be properly made of letters addressed to initials or fictitious names.

This embarrassment may be removed by instructions from the renter of the box directing the postmaster that letters so addressed are intended for some of the persons who are allowed to have his or her letters put in his box. All the regulations of the Department in relation to the delivery of letters are framed with care to secure the certain delivery of the letters to the persons to whom they are addressed and to none other.

The Department may be relieved from the duty of delivering them directly to the person to whom they are addressed if the address directs them to be delivered at a designated place within the delivery of the office to which they are addressed. But the question may not unfrequently be asked, Is a box in a post-office a designated place within the intendment of the term as used in the regulations of the Department, and in which letters addressed to fictitious persons, or firms, or to initials, or to no particular person or firm, and, further, addressed to a box of particular number, can be placed? I think not, in the absence of instructions from the renter of the box, satisfactory to the postmaster, that the letters so addressed are intended for some of the persons allowed under the rules to have their letters deposited in that particular box.

If it was otherwise, the restrictions of the regulations to protect the revenue of the Department would be unavailing, as the use of the box would be open to any one who desired to use it, and for that purpose would resort in their correspondence to the use of initials or fictitious names.

When a letter is addressed only to a particular box in a post-office, the presumption is that it is intended for the person who rents the box; but that presumption does not arise when, in addition to the address to the box, there is that of initials or names, which are not the initials or names of persons whose letters, under the regulations, are entitled or allowed to be put in the box. These remarks are not applicable to registerd letters. These regulations provide that such letters "must never be delivered to any person but the one to whom they are addressed, or to a person whom the postmaster *knows* to be authorized to receive them. A receipt for each registered letter delivered must always appear on the sheets provided for that purpose."

In relation to the delivery of letters addressed to fictitious persons or firms, to initials, or to no particular person or firm, the 157th section of the regulations provides that "such letters must be returned at the end of each month to the Dead-Letter Office, unless directed to be delivered at a designated place, or to the care of a certain person or firm, within the delivery of the office to which they are addressed."

Such direction relieves the Department, in the delivery, from the embarrassment arising from the uncertainty of the address.

The term used in this section of the regulations is "fictitious persons or firms," and is not applicable to firms or companies conducting a real and legitimate business under a style or name which is not that of any member of the firm or company, and for that reason might be termed a fictitious name. In such cases letters addressed to the firm or company by its style or name only can be properly delivered to any known member of it. The proper construction of this term of the regulation would limit its application to letters addressed to persons or firms having no real or business existence.

It appears from the statements accompanying your communication that John M. Dagnall rented box No. 153, in the post-office at Brooklyn; that a large number of letters addressed to "Nathaniel Mayfair, P. O. box 153, Brooklyn, N. Y.," arrived at the post-office at the city of Brooklyn for delivery.

From this address the postmaster, in the absence of information to the contrary, would properly presume that "Nathaniel Mayfair" was the name of a real and not a fictitious person, for whom the letters were intended, and, so presuming, could not put them for delivery in the box rented by John M. Dagnall until satisfied that Nathaniel Mayfair, for whom the letters were intended, was a member of his family or a friend stopping temporarily with him. But, if against this presumption, he should be informed that "Nathaniel Mayfair" was a fictitious name, which John M. Dagnall had assumed for a presumed legitimate purpose in his correspondence, and that the letters so addressed were intended for him, then the letters should be put in his box for delivery to him, the address to the box being equal in all respects for the purpose of delivery to an address to his care.

The use of initials and fictitious names, as an address on letters to be sent through the mails for fraudulent and immoral purposes, is much to be deprecated, but they can be and are used extensively for legitimate and proper purposes, and in the absence of express legislation directing it, no further or other restriction or limitation could properly be imposed upon their use than that provided by a fair and proper construction of the 157th regulation hereinbefore referred to.

There is nothing in your communication, aside from the suspicion which attaches itself to the use of a fictitious name under any circumstances, tending to show that the letters under the address of "Nathaniel Mayfair" were used for a purpose which should, under the law, exclude them from the mails; and the statement of John M. Dagnall that "Nathaniel Mayfair" is a fictitious name for himself, that he has assumed in his correspondence for a legitimate purpose, and that statement being confirmed by the address to the box of which he is the renter, and other circumstances, I can see no impropriety in gratifying his request "that the letters now in the Department addressed to "Nathaniel Mayfair, P. O. box 153, Brooklyn," should be delivered to him as the person for whom they were intended.

Respectfully, yours,

T. A. SPENCE,
Assistant Attorney-General, Post-Office Department.

Hon. JOHN A. J. CRESWELL,
Postmaster-General.

[Number (83) Six.]

Sureties upon Contracts. Their Liability, how Tested.

1. No certain and unerring rule can be laid down by which the effect of other liabilities upon the pecuniary responsibility or sufficiency as surety of a person assuming them may be measured or determined; and the only safe rule of conduct, by one who is called upon in the discharge of an official duty to determine the effect and extent of such liabilities, is to act in the case presented as a prudent man would act in a similar case when transacting his own private business.

OFFICE OF THE ASSISTANT ATTORNEY-GENERAL
FOR THE POST-OFFICE DEPARTMENT,
Washington, D. C., March 13, 1876.

SIR: I have carefully considered the questions embodied in the following letter, which you have submitted to me:

"WASHINGTON, *March* 10, 1876.

"SIR: In the matter of sureties on mail contracts, I desire instructions on the following points:

"1st. Is each contract to be considered an independent transaction, and the ability of the sureties to be tested as to its amount without reference to the fact as to whether they have assumed liability on other contracts?

"2d. Where the same sureties have assumed liabilities on more than one contract, shall their responsibility be tested as to the aggregate liability, and their ability be required to be equal to the aggregate of liability assumed on all the contracts? And if not, to what extent?

"Very respectfully, your obedient servant,

"J. M. EDMUNDS,
"*Postmaster.*

"Hon. MARSHALL JEWELL,
"*Postmaster-General.*"

I would state, in reply to the first question, that although each contract is to be considered an independent transaction, yet the ability of the sureties is *not* to be tested as to its amount without reference to the fact as to whether they have assumed liability on other contracts.

As to the second question: The obligation of a surety in the bond of a bidder for mail transportation is not a debt in the ordinary acceptation of the term, yet it is a liability which affects his pecuniary responsibility, and his sufficiency as surety in any other bond is diminished in proportion to the number and extent of such liabilities compared with his property, real and personal.

No certain and unerring rule can be laid down by which the effect of other liabilities upon the pecuniary responsibility or sufficiency as surety of a person assuming them may be measured or determined; and the only safe rule of conduct by one who is called upon in the discharge of an official duty to determine the effect and extent of such liabilities is to act in the case presented as a prudent man would act in a similar case when transacting his own private business.

A prudent man when called upon in the transaction of his private business to determine the sufficiency as a surety of a person offered as such, to secure a debt or the performance of a contract, would properly inquire into the property, real and personal, of the person offered, and the direct and contingent liabilities for which his property might in any event be made responsible. With the same carefulness of inquiry does the law require a postmaster to act before he certifies to the sufficiency of the sureties in the bond or contract of a bidder. The law expressly requires the exercise of due diligence by a postmaster on approving the bond of a bidder, under the penalties of dismissal from office, disqualification from holding a like office in the future, and punishment, on conviction, by fine and imprisonment; that requirement is not complied with without a careful inquiry as to the property and liabilities of the persons offered as sureties, and the exercise of an impartial judgment upon the information obtained by such inquiry.

This is my answer to the second question.

I am, very respectfully,

T. A. SPENCE,
Assistant Attorney-General, Post-Office Department.

Hon MARSHALL JEWELL,
Postmaster-General.

[Number (122) Seven.]

Official Envelopes, Misuse of, by Private Individuals.

OFFICE OF THE ASSISTANT ATTORNEY-GENERAL
FOR THE POST-OFFICE DEPARTMENT,
Washington, D. C., November 8, 1877.

SIR: Your communication of the 2d instant, referring to this office certain interrogatories from Charles H. Coster, has been considered. In reply, I have to suggest that so far as disclosed by the papers submitted, Mr. Coster sustains no such relation to the Department as entitles him to the information sought. If, however, you should deem it proper to answer his communication, I have the honor to advise you that under no circumstances has a postmaster a right to detain a letter upon which the full amount of postage has been paid. He cannot, under any circumstances, be allowed to base his action upon a presumed knowledge of the contents of a sealed letter. The sacredness of a seal is inviolable. The law presumes that the contents of a sealed letter are confidential, except in so far as they may be divulged by the person having the authority to break the seal, and this presumption is conclusive. The postmaster has no right to know and has no authority to inquire into the contents of a sealed letter. If it should come to his knowledge, aside from any information that the letter itself might furnish, that the writer had improperly and illegally used an official stamp or envelope, it would be his duty to report such violation of the law to the proper authorities of the government. It would, however, even in that case, be his duty to deliver the letter, unless restrained from so doing by some competent authority.

Respectfully,

A. A. FREEMAN,
Assistant Attorney-General for the Post-Office Department.

Hon. A. D. HAZEN,
Third Assistant Postmaster-General.

[Number (130) Eight.]

Payment of Money-Orders to Fictitious Address.—Validity of Power of Attorney after Decease of Grantor.

1. Distinction is to be made in the payment of money-orders between those cases where assumed names are made use of to cover a legitimate *bona-fide* business carried on with a legitimate intent, and those where the business itself is questionable and the intent a fraudulent one.
2. Power of attorney is personal, and dies with the party giving it.

OFFICE OF THE ASSISTANT ATTORNEY-GENERAL
FOR THE POST-OFFICE DEPARTMENT,
Washington, D. C., July 16, 1878.

SIR: Your letter of the 8th instant, together with inclosures, has been considered.

The subject-matter of said communication and inclosures may be considered under the three specific interrogatories which you have propounded to me, and which are in the following words, to wit:

"1st. Whether a money-order issued in favor of a person or company having no existence in fact, could properly be paid to one doing business behind the advertised name or style of such pretended person or company; and if so what form of signature would render the order a valid voucher under the provisions of law respecting the issue and payment of money-orders?"

"2d. Where an advertised business conducted under a personal name, such as 'Jos. T. Inman,' has been legally transferred, would it be proper to pay to successors in such business, say 'Allison and Hearne,' an order drawn in favor of Joseph T. Inman; and if so, would a receipt in form like Allison and Hearne, successors to Jos. T. Inman, or Allison & Hearne, doing business under the name of Joseph T. Inman, serve to render the order a sufficient voucher for the payment?"

"3d. Would a power of attorney to collect or to sign be of effect, or could effect be given thereto, under any circumstances in the case of a money-order drawn, or of one presented for payment, after the decease of the person named as payee of such order, and by whom such power of attorney was executed?"

In reply to your first question, as to whether a money-order issued in favor of a person or company having no existence in fact could properly be paid to one doing business behind the advertised name or style of such pretended person or company, I have to advise you that a proper solution of the question depends upon a correct ascertainment of the facts of each particular case as it may arise. Everything, or at least very much, depends upon the *quo animo* of the party using the name. Distinction is to be made between those cases where assumed names are made use of to cover a legitimate *bona fide* business carried on with a legitimate intent and those cases where the business itself is questionable and the intent a fraudulent one. Imaginary or catch titles are often made use of, in this country at least, as a means of advertising a strictly legitimate business.

One of the cases cited by the postmaster at New York, in his letter of the 28th June, will serve as an illustration of this.

J. T. Gilman is a responsible tea merchant, but he does his business under the names of "The Great American Tea Co.," "The Great Atlantic and Pacific Tea Co.," etc. He doubtless finds it to his advantage to thus advertise, and the use of these titles can scarcely subject him to the charge of using a fictitious title within the meaning of the statute. If, however, J. T. Gilman should be an assumed name, and if in addition he should make use of any one or all of these titles, and be not engaged in the trade which these titles indicate, or if he should make use of a legitimate title to cover a fraudulent business or a business of the class denounced in section 3929 of the Revised Statutes, he would clearly come within the scope of your first interrogatory.

In the case which you have particularly referred to this office it appears that Messrs. Allison and Hearne make and sell a medicine which they advertise as the discovery of Rev. Jos. T. Inman. One of the firm personated Jos. T. Inman, in signing money-orders drawn to him or his order, until it was discovered by the New York office that there was no such person as Jos. T. Inman doing business as pretended. It was then alleged by Allison and Hearne that Jos. T. Inman was deceased, and they still claim to be the equitable owners of the orders, entitled, moreover, to sign the orders by virtue of a power of attorney given to Allison by Jos. T. Inman in 1858, but which had since been lost.

It is stated also in the letter of Mr. James, heretofore alluded to, that the business in which these parties are engaged is of a questionable nature.

Under the circumstances of this case I should advise you that the payment of money-orders drawn to the order of Jos. T. Inman should be refused.

As to your second interrogatory, I answer in the affirmative to both branches of it. The postmaster, however, to whom such orders are presented for payment should be satisfied as to the legality of the transfer of the business of the payee and the identity of the persons purporting to be the successors of such payee.

Your third interrogatory is susceptible of but one answer. A power of attorney to collect or to sign a money-order, drawn or presented for payment after the decease of the person named as payee of such order, and by whom such power of attorney was executed, is void and of no effect in law. It is of a personal character, and dies with the person granting it. The papers submitted are herewith returned.

JULY 27, 1878.

SIR: I am in receipt of the letter of Mr. James, postmaster at New York, under date of the 25th instant, and addressed to yourself, relative to my opinion of the 16th instant in the case of Allison and Hearne, submitted by your office under date of July 10th.

In his letter of the 25th Mr. James calls attention to my answer to the second question propounded by you in your former letter, and its probable effect if adopted unqualifiedly as the rule in paying the class of money-orders referred to, in depriving the payee of his heretofore-unquestioned right to all his money-order remittances.

For the sake of connection, I quote again the second interrogatory propounded in your former letter and my answer thereto. The question and answer are as follows:

"When an advertised business, conducted under a personal name, such as Jos. T. Inman, has been legally transferred, would it be proper to pay to successors in such business, say 'Allison and Hearne,' an order drawn in favor of Jos. T. Inman; and, if so, would a receipt in form like 'Allison and Hearne,' successors to Jos. T. Inman, or 'Allison and Hearne' doing business under the name of Jos. T. Inman, serve to render the order a sufficient voucher for the payment?"

To this question the reply was as follows:

"As to your second interrogatory, I answer in the affirmative to both branches of it. The postmaster, however, to whom such orders are presented for payment should be satisfied as to the legality of the transfer of the business of the payee and the identity of the persons purporting to be the successors of such payee."

As a general proposition of law, I have no doubt of the correctness of this view. It must be borne in mind, however, that the money-order sought to be collected by the transferee must be directly connected with the business transferred. The transferee must have a direct interest in the order presented for payment growing out of the transfer. This interest might or might not attach to remittances drawn to the predecessor of the transferee. That would depend upon the nature of the transfer. A. B. may transfer not only his right and title to the business in question to C. D., but the transfer may include all outstanding claims or debts of A. B. If such be the case, C. D., as the successor of A. B., would have the undoubted right to receipt for all money-orders drawn to the order of A. B. in any way connected with the business transferred. If, however, the transfer applied only to the right to continue the business under the title, only such money-orders could be receipted for by C. D. as were incident to the transfer of the title.

It is proper to observe in this connection that after fully considering the letter of the postmaster at New York, and the cases suggested by him, where a strict application of the rule would work injustice, I am satisfied that it would be difficult to lay down any general proposition for his guidance. Each case must stand upon its own merits. The course suggested by Mr. James, to wit, of requiring the payee to either receipt the order or authorizing in writing another to collect and receipt for him, is unquestionably the safest one.

Very respectfully,

A. H. BISSELL,
Acting Assistant Attorney-General, Post-Office Department.

Hon. C. F. McDONALD,
Superintendent Money-Order System.

Approved.

A. A. FREEMAN,
Assistant Attorney-General for the Post-Office Department.

[Number (132) Nine.]

Fraudulent Use of the Mails.

OFFICE OF THE ASSISTANT ATTORNEY-GENERAL
FOR THE POST-OFFICE DEPARTMENT,
Washington, D. C., August 16, 1878.

SIR: The circular, purporting to have been issued by the "Albion Portrait Works," submitted by you for my opinion, is unmailable under section 4041 of the Revised Statutes. That section reads as follows:

"The Postmaster-General may, upon evidence satisfactory to him that any person is engaged in conducting any fraudulent lottery, gift-enterprise, or scheme for the distribution of money, or of any real or personal property, by lot, chance, or drawing of any kind, or in conducting any other scheme or device for obtaining money through the mails by means of false or fraudulent pretenses, representations, or promises, forbid the payment, by any postmaster, to any such person of any postal money-order drawn to his order or in his favor, and may provide by regulations for the return, to the remitter, of the sums named in such money-orders. But this shall not authorize any person to open any letter not addressed to himself."

This is undoubtedly a scheme for the distribution of "money" or "personal property" by "lot" or "chance," and should be stamped as a "fraud" and excluded from the mails. It is evident upon the most casual examination of the circular that the "Albion Portrait Works" (which seems to have an international existence, an office located for one purpose in Canada and a different office for a different purpose in the United States) cannot comply with its undertakings. True, it claims that it can afford to make these immense sacrifices to secure a large circulation, and by that means an extensive advertisement of its paintings. This plea will not avail to cover up the fraud. No honest man would advertise to give away a hundred-dollar gun or a forty-dollar gun in order to sell a twenty-five dollar picture. But admitting that these gifts or prizes are to be distributed as set out in the circular, the author of this scheme shows that they are distributed by *chance*, and explains in detail the mode of distribution, thus bringing his scheme so clearly within the inhibition of the statute as to render comment unnecessary. The objection frequently urged against lotteries is that they are not governed alone by lot or chance. This author, however, is particular to demonstrate that under his scheme it is impossible that anything save the merest chance should control his distribution, not even the sender of the prize or gift being allowed to know what the gift is. It avails nothing to say that the so-called "Premium gift order" is sent unsolicited, and that the recipient has his option to return it accompanied by the additional price of the picture or to retain or destroy the order. If the orders are worth what they purport to be (varying from twenty-five to four hundred per cent. of the price of the painting), then the company cannot afford to give them away. If, on the other hand, they are worthless, as the manner of giving them to every man who is willing to receive them from the postmaster would seem most clearly to demonstrate, then it is a fraud, and ought to be suppressed. If this grand gift concern, alias "The Albion Portrait Works," is engaged, as it purports to be, in, recklessly squandering and giving away its property, it would be a stroke of good fortune to have its business suppressed. If, on the other hand, it is an attempt to defraud the public, then its victims are entitled to the protection afforded them by the restrictions the law has thrown around the use of the mails.

Very respectfully,

A. A. FREEMAN,
Assistant Attorney-General for the Post-Office Department.

Hon. JOS. H. BLACKFAN,
Superintendent Foreign Mails.

[No. (157) Ten.]

Advertising Sheets.—What Constitutes a "Regular Publication, Designed Primarily for Advertising Purposes."

1. In ascertaining the primary purpose of the paper, we are not confined to either its editorial or advertising columns; for it is a fact that will hardly be controverted that by far the most valuable advertisements are those which, in the nature of editorials, call particular attention to that character of business in which the advertiser is engaged. This is especially true when the particular character of business thus advertised can be conducted at but one place, and the editor or proprietor is the only person advertised as engaged in that particular business.

2. A paper owned and controlled by one or several individuals or business concerns and conducted as an auxiliary, and essentially for the advancement of the main business or calling of those who own or control them, is an advertising sheet within the intent of the law.

OFFICE OF THE ASSISTANT ATTORNEY-GENERAL
FOR THE POST-OFFICE DEPARTMENT,
Washington, D. C., March 7, 1879.

SIR: In compliance with your verbal request, I have examined the petition of Mr. **** **** asking that the question of the proper classification of the **** **** a paper published in the city of Washington, D. C., be reopened and reviewed by the Department. Mr. ****** proposes to support his application by substantially the following:

1st. His own affidavit, showing that the **** **** is not published "primarily for advertising purposes"; and, further, that said paper is not published at nominal rates nor for free circulation.

2d. That the Post-Office Department knowingly permits other papers, which are notoriously advertising sheets, to go through the mails at pound rates, citing the "Scientific American," "The Boston Journal of Chemistry," "The Star-Spangled Banner," etc.

3d. That the law officer of the Department stated that the Scientific American was permitted to pass through the mails at the pound rates because of its wide and extensive circulation, while the **** **** has a circulation as large, if not larger, than the Scientific American.

4th. That he is making a profit of $3,000 per year from the subscriptions received.

5th. That the order excluding the **** **** from the pound rates is an unjust discrimination against its subscribers, who are soldiers.

He proposes to show by letters from "tens of thousands of ex-soldiers that they look upon the **** **** as a newspaper, and that they believe themselves outraged by the government in this unjustifiable attempt to interfere with their family paper."

The petition then concludes as follows:

"I propose to prove that the word primarily does not attach to a paper where seventeen-eighteenths of the same is not advertising, but that the whole, or nearly the whole part of the paper must be used for advertising before the word 'primarily' can rightfully attach thereto in the meaning of the law.

"All of which I ask permission to submit, in order to revoke the order excluding the **** **** from its just rights under the laws."

It will be observed, in the first place, that the petitioner does not ask for a review of the ruling of the Department, on the ground that the evidence offered to be submitted is new or that is was not heard when the matter of the classification of the paper was originally before the Department. Before you can be asked to review your action in the premises, I am of the opinion the petitioner ought to submit new facts, or else show in a very satisfactory manner that the original ruling, as based on the facts already adduced, was wrong. This the petitioner does not do. The statement proposed to be made that the **** **** *is not published "primarily for advertising purposes"* is more of the nature of a conclusion of law than a statement of a fact. A paper, the principal object or design of which is to advertise a particular trade or profession, edited and controlled by a person engaged in the particular trade or profession advertised in its columns, falls within the class defined by law to be "regular publications designed primarily for advertising purposes." (Sec. 15, act approved July 12, 1876.)

In ascertaining the primary purpose of the paper, we are not confined to either its editorial or advertising columns; for it is a fact that will hardly be controverted that by far the most valuable advertisements are those which, in the nature of editorials, call particular attention to that character of business in which the advertiser is engaged. This is especially true when the particular character of business thus advertised can be conducted at but one place, and the editor or proprietor is the only person advertised as engaged in that particular business.

I therefore conclude that the matters of fact offered to be set forth in the affidavit of the petitioner might be true, and yet not inconsistent with the judgment already rendered by the Department.

A regular publication, designed primarily for advertising purposes, may possess every characteristic set out in Mr. ****** proposed affidavit. As to the statement that it is not published at nominal rates, that has nothing to do with the question as to whether its primary purpose is that of advertising. Papers that are published for free circulation, or at nominal rates of subscription, form a distinct class. The paper in question may have a large and *bona-fide* subscription list, from which its proprietor may derive a large income; it may possess all the paraphernalia of a newspaper, possessing a known office of publication, issued in regular numbers, conveying intelligence of passing events, &c., and yet be a "regular publication designed primarily for advertising purposes."

I am not called upon to determine whether the paper in question falls within that class; that question has already been determined; and I am called upon to say whether the evidence proposed to be submitted is sufficient of itself to reverse that conclusion.

This question is invested with almost insuperable difficulties.

The 15th section of the act of July 12, 1876, provides that "transient newspapers magazines, and regular publications, designed primarily for advertising purposes, or for free circulation, or for circulation at nominal rates, and all printed matter of the third class except unsealed circulars, shall be admitted to and transmitted through the mails at the rate of one cent for every two ounces or fractional part thereof,"

What is a "regular publication designed primarily for advertising purposes"? In order to arrive at a proper conclusion, it may be necessary to examine critically two words used in the paragraph, namely, "designed" and "primarily." The term design means to intend, to purpose; *i. e.*, a paper, the intention or purpose in the publication of which is to advertise. But this must be its "primary" purpose. The term "primary" here relates not to the order of time when this purpose was formed, but relates to the character of this design, its dignity and importance. It means, therefore, a regular publication, the principal purpose or object of which is to advertise.

But we are told that the principal profit derived from the most of periodical publications is derived from advertisements, and therefore we are asked to conclude that advertising is the principal object of the leading newspapers of the country; and as it was not the design of Congress to include the common current newspapers of the day in this class, that therefore this definition is unsatisfactory.

But we must not confound the "desire" or "wish" of the publisher with his "design." His wish or desire is to make money. His design is to do so by means of publishing a paper. He may conclude to publish a paper having no advertisements at all—such, for instance, as the New York Ledger—or he may conclude to publish one having, like the New York Herald, a large amount of advertisements. In both cases, however, his business is the dissemination of newspaper matter. We buy, subscribe for, and read the Ledger on account of its essays, literature, and stories. We read the Herald on account of the world-wide information as to current events found in its columns, and also on account of the varied business interests it advertises. Whether we look to its advertising or editorial columns we find it full of legitimate newspaper matter. We look in vain through its columns to ascertain who its editor is or what his business is. In fact, there is nothing in either one of the papers I have named, or the thousand of others that might be named (for I have instanced these two as the leading examples of the two different kinds of papers), to indicate that the publishers have any other business than that of publishing the paper. A careful examination of these papers fails to disclose that the editor of either has any other occupation than that of publishing a newspaper. The one advertises for nobody; the other for everybody.

The paper under consideration pursues neither course; the burden of its editorials and general reading matter is directed in a single channel, viz, that of building up the private business of its editor. The paper is devoted to the interests of those having claims, present or prospective, against the government, and the proprietor, and he alone, is advertised as engaged in the business of collecting these claims. To fall within this class it need not be a transient or irregular publication, nor a publication designed for free circulation, nor for circulation at nominal rates; these form, as already stated, a distinct class of their own, and the rate of postage on each is prescribed by law. We find a paper published at a point where a particular trade or profession amounts to a specialty, and we find the columns of said paper largely devoted to a particular trade or profession; its editorials principally on that subject; its correspondence almost exclusively on that or kindred subjects; the burden of its information relating to a particular subject, as, for instance, the collection of claims against the government. When we find the whole make-up of the paper of a character to catch the eye and enlist the interest of only a particular class, we conclude, of course, that it is what is denominated a "class journal." That, however, is not sufficient to exclude it from the pound rates; for very many papers of this class are every day admitted to the mails at pound rates. But when we proceed a step further, and ascertain that, in addition to all this, the paper advertises the *proprietor, and him alone*, as engaged in a business enterprise, in which the particular class of persons whose interests are apparently sought to be promoted are most deeply interested, I think we may well conclude that the primary or principal object of the paper is to advertise the business of the editor.

I am not holding that a lawyer, mechanic, or physician, a claim agent or merchant, may not edit a legitimate newspaper, entitled as such to the pound rates. I do hold, however, that when a person engaged in any of the trades or professions named, or others of similar character undertakes, in addition to and in connection with such occupation or profession, to publish a newspaper, having for its principal object the promotion of the particular class of business in which its proprietor is engaged, conveying through its columns the superior facilities of its editor or proprietor for the transaction of that particular business, in such a manner as to impress even a casual reader with the fact that the entire influence of the paper is devoted to forwarding the professional interests of its editor or proprietor, that such a paper falls within the rule. Nor does it materially alter the case that such a paper contains a large proportion of reading-matter of interest to the general public. It is not the amount of space occupied by what are ordinarily denominated *advertisements* that brings it within the rule. Seventeen-eighteenths of the paper in question may, as the petitioner alleges, be devoted to reading-matter. The rule has been held, and I think correctly, to apply to a paper filled with reading-matter, other than advertisements, containing not a single advertisement in the ordinary sense of that term, for the reason that it made the simple announcement, in a marginal form, that it was published by a firm engaged in a certain trade; as, for instance, "this paper is published by John Smith, the grocer." The most casual examination of the paper under consideration discloses the interest of its publisher in its circulation. He may have, as he says, tens of thousands of subscribers, and all the paraphernalia of a regular newspaper. His paper may be read, and doubtless is read, by thousands of ex-soldiers and others having claims, real or prospective, against the government; but the paper is so apparently, palpably, and notoriously devoted to forwarding the private interest of the proprietor as an attorney or claim agent, that I cannot see how we can avoid the conclusion that the paper is devoted primarily to advertising his business. Suppose instead of seventeen-eighteenths, as is claimed, ninety-nine one hundredths of the space were devoted to matter relating principally to the subject of pensions and other claims, and the paper should contain a simple announcement, in some peculiar and attractive form, that it was issued by John Smith, attorney and counsellor at law and solicitor of claims and patents, is it not apparent that it would fall within the rule?

I have already intimated that it is very difficult to lay down any general rule on this subject. I think, however, we may adopt as a basis for a sound discrimination on this subject the following rule, viz: A paper principally or very largely devoted to a particular interest, as, for instance, the collection of claims against the government or the sale of a particular article of manufacture, or the development of a particular section of country, edited and controlled, in the first instance, at the seat of government by a claim agent, or, in the second instance, by the proprietor of the article advertised in its columns, or, in the third instance, by a real-estate agent in the section of country advertised or proposed to be developed—such a paper may very safely be held to be within the rule. If it should be urged as an objection to this rule that it excludes professional men, merchants, and artisans from the editorial class, I reply by saying that the law interposes no obstacle in the way of either of the classes named, except to say that they may not burden the mails with advertisements of their private interests under the guise of publishing a newspaper devoted to the interests of a particular class of persons or the public.

I am not prepared to say that a person engaged in either of the occupations I have named, or an occupation or profession of kindred character, may not also engage in editing a legitimate newspaper entitled to the pound rates of postage. I am prepared to say, however, in view of the law, that a person so engaging in two occupations having so little legitimate connection ought not (if the paper is devoted to the particular interest in which he is engaged) to advertise himself at all, for if he does he must know that he raises a very strong, if not a conclusive, presumption that the primary or leading object of his paper is to advertise his business. If, for instance, the primary object of the paper under consideration is to serve the interest of the soldier element of the country, it is submitted that the general interest of that element could be equally as well served if the exclusive advertisement of the editor's professional business was left out entirely. It is no more to the interest of the soldier element of the country to know that blanks and forms for prosecuting claims for pensions, &c., can be procured from the proprietor of the ***** *****, and that such claims will be collected by such proprietor, than it is to the general public to know that a certain character of goods can be procured of A. T. Stewart & Co., and yet a copy of such a paper as the New York Ledger containing reading matter for the million, and without a single advertisement, could not go through the mails at pound rates if it contained the simple announcement that it was issued by A. T. Stewart & Co., merchant, etc.

The law could interfere by saying that "notwithstanding your paper is filled with good reading matter; notwithstanding not a single advertisement, in the ordinary sense of that term, is found in your columns, yet the very mode in which you issue the paper—nay, the very fact that advertisements of all business, especially all rival firms, is excluded from your columns, shows that the primary object of issuing the paper is to advertise your business."

I deem it unnecessary to discuss the allegations in the petition that other journals are admitted, which, under the law, ought to be excluded. While not agreeing to the correctness of this statement, it is not at all impossible that, in the construction or application of a statute of this character, mistakes should occur. It is not believed, however, that in any instance has a paper been admitted to the mails at pound rates for the simple reason of its extensive circulation; nor for the reason that it was regarded by a large number of persons as a good paper. There is no other class of persons deserving so much at the hands of the government as the soldier class, but in the absence of any legislation on the subject, the Department can make no distinction in the application of the law fixing the rates of postage on newspapers.

A paper, the primary or principal purpose of which is to advertise the business of a gentleman engaged in the collection of pensions or other claims against the government, is chargeable, under the law, with precisely the same rate of postage required to be paid on a paper the primary purpose of which is to advertise any other business or occupation.

Very respectfully,

A. A. FREEMAN,
Assistant Attorney-General, Post-Office Department.

Hon. D. M. KEY,
Postmaster-General.

[Number (159) Eleven.]

Delivery of Letters, Right of Trustees to Letters addressed to a Firm by whom they were Appointed, Discussed.

OFFICE OF THE ASSISTANT ATTORNEY-GENERAL
FOR THE POST-OFFICE DEPARTMENT,
Washington, D. C., April 5, 1879.

SIR: The papers submitted by you on this day show that on the 3d day of March, 1879, Trufant & Davis, merchants in the city of Boston, executed a deed of trust to George Woods Rice and Stephen M. Crosby. The deed, or so much thereof as relates to the question hereinafter stated, is as follows: * * * "Now, therefore, the said Trufant & Davis, for the purposes herein contained, and in consideration of one dollar to him paid by the said parties of the second part, the receipt whereof is hereby acknowledged, do hereby grant, bargain, sell, assign, and convey to said parties of the second part, all the goods, wares, merchandise, chattels, effects, choses in action, estates and property, real and personal, of every name, nature, and description, wheresoever the same may be, belonging to said parties of the first part, together with all their books of accounts, evidences of debt, and correspondence relating to their business, whether now in their hands or which may hereafter come to them, excepting, however, herefrom their household furniture and effects." * * * *

Under this deed the trustees claim the right to demand and receive all letters addressed to the makers of the deed. I do not think this claim can be maintained. Under all ordinary circumstances the addressee of a letter, and he alone, is entitled to demand it from the postmaster. The exceptions to this rule are very few, and rest upon well-defined principles of natural or commercial necessity.

If the addressee is dead it is physically impossible to make the delivery to him; it must in that case go to his representative. If he is bankrupt he is *civiliter mortuus*, and in like manner incapable of receiving letters relating to the matter of his commercial life, and such letters are, therefore, required to be delivered to the assignee; not to his assignee, but the assignee appointed under the law without his direction. He is civilly dead, and the court has appointed a representative to take charge of his estate. He is incapable of receiving his correspondence, and therefore the law, *ex necessitate rei*, directs its delivery to another person.

Here the case is different. Both parties are alive, physically and commercially. Both are capable of contracting. It is true that the addressees of the correspondence have undertaken to convey the correspondence relating to their business; but this conveyance is limited to the correspondence now in their (the addressees') hands, or which may hereafter come to them. How is it practicable to determine before a letter is opened that it is a "correspondence relating to their business"? The fact that it is addressed to the firm is a very strong circumstance in favor of that presumption, but by no means conclusive.

Under this deed, if the assignee is entitled to receive and open all the correspondence addressed to the assignors, it would be their duty to return such as did not relate to the business. If, on the contrary, the assignors are entitled to receive and open letters addressed to them, it would be their duty to return to the trustees all letters relating to their business.

The postmaster ought not to be required to assume the responsibility of deciding as to the proper party to exercise so delicate a trust.

It would have been an easy matter to so draft the deed as to have made it operate as a direction to the postmaster to deliver all the correspondence to the trustee, if such had been the design of the parties to the deed.

But I am not undertaking to decide as to what was the intention of the parties to the deed. It is enough that the matter is left in doubt, and wherever the least shadow of doubt exists, as to the proper person to receive a letter, the postmaster should follow literally the directions upon the face of the letter.

Very respectfully,

A. A. FREEMAN,
Assistant Attorney-General, Post-Office Department.

Hon. JAMES N. TYNER,
First Assistant Postmaster-General.

List of all Opinions Given by the Assistant Attorney-General for the Post Office Department.

No.	Subject.	Date.
1	Construction of section 5464 Revised Statutes. Bang's photographic postal card.	23 June, 1873.
2	Delivery of letters to members of dissolved partnership	24 June, 1873.
3	Cancellation of official stamps. Construction of section 3855 Revised Statutes.	26 June, 1873.
4	New service. Construction of term	11 July, 1873.
5	Concealment of mail-matter. Construction of section 3887 Revised Statutes.	18 July, 1873.
6	Local or drop letters	27 July, 1873.
7	Mail contractor's oath	30 July, 1873.
8	Bona-fide and regular subscribers. Construction of term	5 Aug., 1873.
9, 10	Moiety to informers	8 Aug., 1873.
11	Delivery of letters. Effect of injunction of State court	11 Aug., 1873.
12	Back numbers. Meaning of term	15 Aug., 1873.
13	Delivery of letters of deceased person	22 Aug., 1873.
14	Sending of mail-matter by express. Packet and package defined.	26 Aug., 1873.
15	Gift enterprises. Sections 3894, 3929, 4041, and 5480 Revised Statutes.	2 Oct., 1873.
16	Obscene publications. Construction of act of March 3, 1873. Section 3893 Revised Statutes.	23 Oct., 1873.
17	Copyright act	12 Nov., 1873.
18	Continental Bank-Note Company. Construction of their contract of January 25, 1873.	8 Dec., 1873.
19	Loss of money in the mails	6 Jan., 1874.
20	Readjustment of compensation for railway mail service	7 Jan., 1874.
21	Delivery of letters of deceased person. Rights of widow, child, and legal representative discussed.	13 Jan., 1874.
22	Neglect of government officials	14 Jan., 1874.
23	Readjustment of compensation for carrying the mails	20 Jan., 1874.
24	Production of letters before a court under process *duces tecum*	24 Jan., 1874.
25	Guarantors of a bidder for mail-contract. Postmaster's certificate as to their responsibility.	29 Jan., 1874.
26	Letter-boxes. Law governing the use of	4 Feb., 1874.
27	Mail contracts. Method of bidding for, and obligation of bidders.	13 Feb., 1874.
28	Return of checks or drafts accompanying bids for mail service.	23 Feb., 1874.
29	Official stamps to be furnished Executive Departments. Construction of section 4, act of March 3, 1873.	25 Feb., 1874.
30	Successful bidder for mail service cannot associate another with him.	6 Mar., 1874.
31	Baltimore and Ohio Railroad. Claim for extra compensation for carrying mail.	16 Mar., 1874.
32	Postmasters' salaries. Readjustment of, in special cases	17 Mar., 1874.
33	Interruption of mail by ferrymen. Mail-carrier's rights in crossing a ferry.	20 Mar., 1874.
34	Carrying the mail. Rights of legal representatives of deceased contractors.	26 Mar., 1874.
35	Carrying the mail. Power of Postmaster-General to contract for.	6 April, 1874.
36	Lottery letters. Disposition of, now in the Dead-Letter Office	9 April, 1874.
37	Effect of discontinuance of post-office upon postmaster appointed by President.	17 April, 1874.
38	Letters addressed to letter-box	22 April, 1874.
39	Supplement. Construction of word	24 April, 1874.
40	Carrying mail without advertisement, when	8 May, 1874.
41	Compensation to railroads for carrying the mails	15 May, 1874.
42	Mail contracts. Construction of section 3951 Revised Statutes	28 May, 1874.
43	Application to reconsider the rejection of the bid of John D. Johnson.	3 June, 1874.
44	Curtailed service, Term discussed	9 June, 1874.
45	Failure of lowest bidder to execute contract by time required	16 June, 1874.
46	Relative to the compromise of the claim of the United States against Lowell, late postmaster at New Orleans.	18 June, 1874.

List of opinions given by Assistant Attorney-General for Post-Office Department—Cont'd.

No.	Subject.	Date.
47	Right and duty of Postmaster-General regarding unfinished investigation of predecessor. Application to reopen case.	11 July, 1874.
48	What advertisements for carrying the mail must contain.......	14 July, 1874.
49	Upon the proposal of Mr. Hinckly to submit the question of compensation to Philadelphia, Wilmington & Baltimore Railroad to arbitration.	21 July, 1874.
50	Official Postal Guide. Before entering into contract for compilation and publication, must there be an advertisement.	24 July, 1874.
51	Use of the mails by persons advertising gift-concerts, etc.......	20 Aug., 1874.
52	Demand for a mail contract as next lowest bidder because of alleged failure of the contractor to perform the service.	8 Sept., 1874.
53	Against award of contract for stamped envelopes and wrappers to Plympton Manufacturing Company. Protest of George H. Reay.	6 Oct., 1874.
54	Against extending time for furnishing stamped envelopes. Protest of Messrs. Raynor & Co.	17 Oct., 1874.
55	Regarding postage on foreign periodicals imported and mailed in the United States.	28 Oct., 1874.
56	Transmission of newspapers to Europe outside of the mails.....	21 Dec., 1874.
57	Sureties of mail contractors. Duties of postmasters certifying to the sufficiency of.	23 Dec., 1874.
58	Newspapers and periodical publications. Construction of section 5, act of June 23, 1874.	15 Feb., 1875.
59	Constitutional powers of President to fill vacancies originating during the session of the Senate and continuing during the recess.	19 Feb., 1875.
60	Contractors for carrying the mails. Section 3943 Revised Statutes, does not restrict contractors to owners or masters of steamboats. Postmaster-General may let contract without advertisement to one who is neither a master nor owner of a steamboat.	2 Mar., 1875.
61	Right of Postmaster-General to compromise judgment against Simms, postmaster at Atlanta, Ga., and sureties.	11 Mar., 1875.
62	What constitutes "corrected proof-sheets"	15 May, 1875.
63	Question of forfeitures considered............................	17 May, 1875.
64	Periodical publication. What constitutes, within the intendment of section 5, act of June 23, 1874.	2 June, 1875.
65	Heirs of Sheldon McKnight. Application to have the case reopened.	5 June, 1875.
66	Liability of postmaster's bond for loss of registered package...	8 June, 1875.
67	Taking or receiving of letters, etc., for the purpose of obstructing the correspondence or prying into the business or secrets of another. Construction of section 3892, Revised Statutes.	26 June, 1875.
68	Power of Postmaster-General to contract with more than one railroad to carry the mails over same route.	14 Aug., 1875.
68½	Denver Pacific Railway and Telegraph Company. Claim for compensation for transportation of mails.	23 Aug., 1875.
69	Application for reward offered September 9, 1874. *In re* J. T. Morris.	27 Aug., 1875.
70	Oregon Steam Navigation Company *vs.* Z. S. Moody..........	25 Oct., 1875.
71	Reweighing of mails on railroad routes. Construction of sections 4002–4005 Revised Statutes.	16 Nov., 1875.
72	Failure of railroads to perform service. Rule of deduction.....	24 Nov., 1875.
73	Postal convention with Canada. Construction of, relative to repayment of money-order to remitter.	20 Dec., 1875.
74	Southern newspapers. Compensation to, under designation of Clerk of House of Representatives.	28 Dec., 1875.
75	Deposit of postal funds by postmasters in cities where there is an assistant treasurer.	19 Jan., 1876.
76	Postal cards. Their character and relation to the postal service.	24 Jan., 1876.
77	Curtailment of service. Rate of compensation................	25 Jan., 1876.
78	"Lap service." Rule of compensation to be paid to Burlington and Missouri Railroad Company.	25 Jan., 1876.

List of opinions given by Assistant Attorney-General for Post-Office Department—Cont'd.

No.	Subject.	Date.
79	Special Agents. Per diem allowance to. Construction of sections 4017, 4019, and 4020, Revised Statutes.	15 Feb., 1876.
80	"Lap service." Compensation to be paid to Pittsburgh, Cincinnati and Saint Louis Railroad Company.	1 Mar., 1876.
81	Electric pen. Circulars written with, may pass through mails as third-class matter.	3 Mar., 1876.
82	Bonds of bidder. Approval of, by clerk in post-office	4 Mar., 1876.
83	Sureties upon contracts. Their liability, how tested	13 Mar., 1876.
84	Claim of Bowling Embry for compensation during time of suspension from office.	14 Mar., 1876.
85	Claim of R. W. Gurley, Superintendent of Free Delivery, for back compensation.	16 Mar., 1876.
86	Pacific Mail Steamship Company. Right of Postmaster-General to pay for performance of service in steamships of greater burden than those mentioned in their proposals.	22 Mar., 1876.
87	Letter boxes in post-offices are under control of postmaster.	23 Mar., 1876.
88	Letters and circulars defined, and their difference shown.	31 Mar., 1876.
89	Claim of George H. Giddings for carrying the mails on route No. 12900.	1 April, 1876.
90	"Lap service." Claim of Rockford, Rock Island and Saint Louis Railroad Company for compensation.	17 April, 1876.
91	Assignment of contract. Effect of..................................	20 April, 1876.
92	Compensation to railroad companies for mail-messenger service. Case of Baltimore and Potomac Railroad.	12 July, 1876.
93	Extension of route from Bellaire to Pittsburgh	12 July, 1876.
94	Railroad companies under contract. Whether subject to the provisions of act of July 12, 1876.	21 July, 1876.
95	Importations through the mails.................................	28 July, 1876.
96	"Lap service." Claim of Alabama Central Railroad Company for compensation.	31 July, 1876.
97	Rate of postage. Effect of autograph signature on printed matter which is incomplete without it.	25 Aug., 1876.
98	"Lap service." Claim of Northern Central Railroad Company for compensation.	26 Aug., 1876.
99	Land-grant railroads. Application of section 13, act of July 12, 1876, to such as are under contract.	1 Sept., 1876.
100	Extension of service. Claim of Cleveland and Pittsburgh and Pittsburgh and Erie Railroad Companies for compensation.	18 Sept., 1876.
101	Compensation to railroads for use of postal cars. Application of act of July 12, 1876.	26 Sept., 1876.
102	Advertisements. Number of papers in District of Columbia...	23 Nov., 1876.
103	Application to Postmaster-General to enter into contract. *In re* Selucius Garfield.	29 Nov., 1876.
104	Application for readjustment of mail pay, under act of July 12, 1876.	22 Dec. 1876.
105	Metric system. Construction of section 3880, Revised Statutes.	9 Feb., 1877.
106	Compensation to railroads for postal-car service not subject to reduction of section 1 of act of July 12, 1876.	17 Mar., 1877.
107	Ante-bellum mail contract. Wilmington and Weldon Railroad Company.	15 Mar., 1877.
108	Contract for furnishing adhesive postage-stamps.—Power of Postmaster-General to limit advertisements, etc., to certain class of persons.	5 April, 1877.
109	"Lap service".—Claim of Memphis and Charleston Railroad Company for compensation.	3 May, 1877.
110	Indians not United States citizens. Right to hold the office of postmaster.	3 May, 1877.
111	Protest against application of act of July 12, A. D. 1876. Saint Paul and Sioux City Railroad.	10 May, 1877.
112	Construction of section 3998, Revised Statutes. Twenty-five per cent. for night service to Lake Shore and Michigan Southern Railroad.	18 May, 1877.
113	Extension of route. Under what circumstances can it be ordered.	24 May, 1877.

List of opinions given by Assistant Attorney-General for Post-Office Department—Cont'd.

No.	Subject.	Date.
114	Regular publications designed primarily for advertising purposes.	7 June, 1877.
115	Construction of contract for furnishing postal cards.	16 June, 1877.
116	Papyrographic process of printing. Newspaper correspondence executed by.	18 June, 1877.
117	Baltimore and Havana Steamship Company. Claim of, for transportation of mails.	21 June, 1877.
118	Claim of G. H. Giddings. One month's pay for discontinuance of service.	23 June, 1877.
119	Sioux City and Saint Paul Railroad Company. Rate of compensation to.	5 July, 1877.
120	Saint Louis Practical Photographer. Insets in publications.	12 July, 1877.
121	Uniforming railway clerks, etc. Right of Postmaster-General to issue order for the.	27 Oct., 1877.
122	Official envelopes. Misuse of, by private individuals.	9 Nov., 1877.
123	Allowance to postmasters for rent. When post-office drops from second to third class.	9 Nov., 1877.
124	New Orleans, Opelousas and Great Western Railroad Company. Construction of section 13, act of July 12, 1876.	15 Nov., 1877.
125	Subscribers (regular). Postmasters acting as agents only, are not subscribers. Case of Cincinnati Gazette.	31 Dec., 1877.
126	Disposition of money recovered in the mails	4 Jan., 1878.
127	Private express. Down-town Letter Office. Carrying letters outside the mails.	2 Mar., 1878.
128	Chicago, Burlington and Quincy Railroad. Protest against reduction of compensation.	15 Mar., 1878.
129	Subcontractor's lien. Construction of sections 2 and 3, act of May 17, 1878.	1 June, 1878.
130	Payment of money-orders to fictitious address. Validity of power of attorney after decease of grantor.	16 July, 1878.
131	Uniform canceling ink. Power of Postmaster-General to adopt, etc. Act of June 20, 1878.	24 July, 1878.
132	Albion Portrait Works. Fraudulent use of the mails. Section 4041, Revised Statutes.	16 Aug., 1878.
133	Silver as legal tender. To what extent, in the money-order business.	17 Aug., 1878.
134	Drafts sent through the mails for postal service are on official business, and should be registered as such.	29 Aug., 1878.
135	Sureties of postmaster liable for funds improperly credited by bank to postmaster's individual account. Case of McArthur, late postmaster at Chicago.	3 Sept., 1878.
136	Application for compensation for carrying United States mails February and March, 1866. Selma and Meridian Railroad Company.	16 Sept., 1878.
137	Correction of mistake in language of lease. Power of Postmaster-General to allow.	24 Sept., 1878.
138	Rates of postage on publications mailed to subscribers within the delivery of carrier post-offices by news-agents without the same. Construction of section 3872 Revised Statutes.	1 Nov., 1878.
139	Charges against postmaster at New London, Conn. Official misconduct and fraud of personal rights, while assistant postmaster. Mower *vs.* Tubbs.	19 Nov., 1878.
140	Ordinary postage-stamps. Can requisitions for, for Departments be filled under the act for furnishing official stamps?	3 Dec., 1878.
141	Duty of Auditor in reporting to First-Assistant, fourth-class post-offices, etc.	4 Dec., 1878.
142	Selma, Rome and Dalton Railroad Company, Reduction of 10 per cent. under act of July 12, 1876.	13 Dec., 1878.
143	Extraordinary increase in business of post-office of fourth class. Salary of postmaster, how affected by proviso, act of June 17, 1878.	16 Dec., 1878.
144	Application of Fisher A. Foster for compensation for indexing Postal Laws of 1872.	2 Jan., 1879.
145	Application for compensation for carrying the mails. Saint Louis and San Francisco Railroad Company.	11 Jan., 1879.

List of opinions given by Assistant Attorney-General for Post-Office Department—Cont'd.

No.	Subject.	Date.
146	Telegraphic rates. Construction of Postmaster-General's order fixing.	15 Jan., 1879.
147	Howe Scale Company, protest against award of contract. Question of want of consideration raised.	28 Jan., 1879.
148	Application for compensation. Leavenworth, Lawrence and Galveston Railroad Company.	31 Jan., 1879.
149	What constitutes a lease. Obligation of the government thereunder.	3 Feb., 1879.
150	Printed blanks in periodicals. Does it subject them to third-class rates?	10 Feb., 1879.
151	One month's extra pay. Are sub-contractors entitled to?	13 Feb., 1879.
152	Franking privilege. Does it extend to members-elect?	13 Feb., 1879.
153	Acquiescence in action of the Department, by claimant, what constitutes. Force and effect of a rule of the Department discussed.	18 Feb., 1879.
154	Subletting of a contract. Copy of notice required to be filed with Department.	24 Feb., 1879.
155	Claim for services rendered Special Agent	6 Mar., 1879.
156	Railroad companies refusing to carry the mails. How Postmaster-General should act.	6 Mar., 1879.
157	What constitutes a sheet primarily designed for advertising purposes.	7 Mar., 1879.
158	Sunday service. Power of the Postmaster-General to discontinue.	26 Mar., 1879.
159	Delivery of letters. Right of trustees to letters addressed to a firm, discussed.	5 April, 1879.
160	Official-penalty envelopes. Their use under section 29, act of March 3, 1879.	21 April, 1879.
161	Lease of post-office buildings. Liability of government for	23 April, 1879.
162	Mail lettings. Advertisement of, in States of Virginia and Maryland. Can an advertisement be inserted in a Washington paper?	5 May, 1879.
163	United States *vs.* Gregg. Convicted of embezzlement. Application for pardon.	6 May, 1879.
164	A regular publication designed primarily for advertising purposes. Question of discrimination raised.	8 May, 1879.
165	Missouri River, Fort Scott and Gulf Railroad. Abatement of pay from July 1, 1876, to May 25, 1878.	19 June, 1879.
166	George H. Giddings. Who entitled to custody of warrant issued in accordance with special appropriation by Congress. Effect of injunction.	21 June, 1879.

List of opinions given by Assistant Attorney-General for Post-Office Department—Cont'd.

No.	Subject.	Date.

List of opinions given by Assistant Attorney-General for Post-Office Department—Cont'd.

No.	Subject.	Date.

TITLE XIII.

ADDENDA.

CHANGES IN THE POSTAL LAWS AND REGULATIONS SINCE THE PUBLICATION OF THIS VOLUME.

IMPORTANT.

Any alterations, &c., which it may be necessary to make in this book on account of changes in the law or regulations (see page 3), and which cannot be conveniently shown in the preceding pages, should be made on the blank pages following this notice. In such cases the postmaster must take care to fill in the various columns correctly, and he should place against the section affected the number of the page in which the alteration will be found.

23 P L

No. of section altered.	Alteration in full.	Date of alteration and where noted.
605..........	An act to extend the time of special postal service until service can be obtained by advertisement. *Be it enacted by the Senate and House of Representatives of the United States of America in Congress assembled*, That in cases where special service has already been placed on new routes, the Postmaster-General may, in his discretion, extend such service until the time when service can be obtained by advertisement, not exceeding in any case one year. And whenever an accepted bidder shall fail to enter into contract, or a contractor on any mail-route shall fail or refuse to perform the service on said route according to his contract, or when a new route shall be established or new service required, or when, from any other cause, there shall not be a contractor legally bound or required to perform such service, the Postmaster-General may make a temporary contract for carrying the mail on such route, without advertisement, for such period as may be necessary, not in any case exceeding one year, until the service shall have commenced under a contract made according to law. And any provision of statute in conflict with this provision is hereby repealed. Approved June 12, 1879.	June 12, 1879. Page 143.

No. of section altered.	Alteration in full.	Date of alteration and where noted.

No. of section altered.	Alteration in full.	Date of alteration and where noted.

No. of section altered.	Alteration in full.	Date of alteration and where noted.

No. of section altered.	Alteration in full.	Date of alteration and where noted.

No. of section altered.	Alteration in full.	Date of alteration and where noted.

No. of section altered.	Alteration in full.	Date of alteration and where noted.

No. of section altered.	Alteration in full.	Date of alteration and where noted.

No. of section altered.	Alteration in full.	Date of alteration and where noted.

No. of section altered.	Alteration in full.	Date of alteration and where noted.

No. of section altered.	Alteration in full.	Date of alteration and where noted.

No. of section altered.	Alteration in full.	Date of alteration and where noted.

Alteration in full.	Date of alteration and where noted.

No. of section altered.	Alteration in full.	Date of alteration and where noted.

REFERENCE INDEX

TO THE

REVISED STATUTES OF THE UNITED STATES

FROM SECTIONS OF THE REVISED STATUTES AND SUBSEQUENT VOLUMES OF THE STATUTES AT LARGE TO SECTIONS OF THIS EDITION OF THE POSTAL LAWS AND REGULATIONS.

Act of Congress.	Title.	Chap.	Sec.	Vol.	Page.	Sec. of P. L. & R.
Revised Statutes	IV		161		26	**26**
			177		28	**3**
			183		29	**8**
	VII	3	270		45	**1150**
		4	276		46	**1139**
			277		46	**1142**
			292		49	**1144**
			293		49	**1145**
			294		49	**1146**
			295		49	**1147**
			296		49	**1148**
			298		49	**1149**
	VIII		381		63	**1221**
			382		63	**1222**
	IX		388		65	**1**
			389		65	**2**
			390		65	**4**
			391		65	**24**
			392		65	**25**
			393		65	**5**
			394		66	**5**
			395		66	**28**
			396		66	**29**
			397		67	**30**
			398		67	**31**
			399		67	**32**
			400		67	**33**
			401		67	**34**
			402		67	**35**
			403		67	**36**
			404		67	**37**
			405		67	**38**
			406		67	**39**
			407		67	**66**
			408		68	**67**
			409		68	**40**
			410		68	**41**
			411		68	**42**
			412		68	**43**
			413		68	**44**
			414		69	**47**
	XIII	3	563		95	**1206**
		7	629		111	**1206**
		14	792		148	**1225**
		17	889		168	**1223**
			890		168	**1224**
		18	919		175	**1206**
			924		176	**1207**
			925		176	**1208**
			926		176	**1209**
			927		176	**1210**
			928		177	**1211**

Act of Congress.	Title.	Chap.	Sec.	Vol.	Page.	Sec. of P. L. & R.
Revised Statutes	XIII	12	929	.....	177	1212
			930	......	177	1213
			931	......	177	1214
			932	......	177	1215
			933	......	177	1216
			952	......	180	1217
			951	......	180	1218
			958	......	181	1219
			964	......	182	1220
			1014	......	189	16
	XIX	....	1785	......	317	1253
	XL	....	3641	......	717	68
			3642	......	717	69
			3643	......	717	70
			3644	......	717	71
	XLI	....	3668	......	721	46
			3674	.....	722	65
	XLVI	1	3829	.....	750	98
			3830	......	750	101
			3831	......	750	104
			3832	......	750	51
			3833	.....	750	52
			3834	......	750	105
			3835	......	751	106
			3836	......	751	110
			3837	......	751	112
			3838	......	751	115
			3839	......	751	367
			3840	.....	751	368
			3841	......	751	657
			3842	......	752	514
			3843	......	752	1151
			3844	......	752	1152
			3845	......	752	1153
			3846	......	752	72
			3847	......	752	73
			3848	......	752	71
			3849	......	752	663
			3850	......	752	599
			3851	......	752	541
			3856	......	753	120
			3857	......	753	134
			3858	......	754	51
			3859	......	754	121
			3860	......	754	124
			3861	......	754	132
			3862	......	754	133
			3863	......	754	125
			3864	......	754	99
		2	3867	......	755	327
			3868	......	755	333
			3869	......	755	331
			3870	......	755	315
			3871	......	755	336
			3873	......	755	337
			3874	......	755	339
		3	3880	......	756	1105
			3881	......	757	182
			3882	......	757	266
			3883	.....	757	235
			3885	......	757	471
			3888	......	757	571
			3889	......	757	723
			3890	......	757	370
			3891	......	757	1233

Act of Congress.	Title.	Chap.	Sec.	Vol.	Page.	Sec. of P. L. & R.
Revised Statutes..................	XLVI	3	3892	......	758	**1231**
			3893	......	758	**225**
			3894	......	758	**226**
			3895	......	759	**566**
		4	3898	......	759	**267**
			3899	......	759	**1250**
			3900	......	759	**268**
			3901	......	759	**300**
			3902	......	759	**178**
			3904	......	759	**178**
			3912	......	760	**1127**
			3913	......	760	**255**
		5	3914	......	761	**136**
			3915	......	761	**138**
			3916	......	761	**140**
			3917	......	761	**144**
			3918	......	761	**145**
			3919	......	761	**175**
			3920	......	762	**174**
			3921	......	762	**375**
			3922	......	762	**1252**
			3923	......	762	**1252**
			3924	......	762	**1252**
			3925	......	762	**1252**
		6	3926	......	762	**806**
			3927	......	763	**812**
			3928	......	763	**824**
			3929	......	763	**875**
		7	3930	......	763	**441**
			3931	......	763	**445**
			3932	......	763	**817**
			3933	......	764	**446**
			3934	......	764	**447**
			3935	......	764	**448**
			3936	......	764	**468**
			3937	......	764	**431**
			3938	......	764	**483**
			3939	......	764	**456**
			3940	......	764	**371**
		8	3941	......	765	**573**
			3942	......	765	**607**
			3943	......	765	**607**
			3944	......	765	**580**
			3945	......	765	**581**
			3946	......	765	**582**
			3947	......	765	**587**
			3948	......	766	**588**
			3949	......	766	**601**
			3950	......	766	**589**
			3951	......	766	**603** **604** **605**
			3952	......	766	**598**
			3953	......	767	**585**
			3954	......	767	**606**
			3955	......	767	**602**
			3956	......	767	**607** **610**
			3957	......	767	**575**
			3958	......	767	**576**
			3959	......	768	**612**
			3960	......	768	**618**
			3961	......	768	**619**
			3962	......	768	**665**
			3963	......	768	**623**

Act of Congress.	Title.	Chap.	Sec.	Vol.	Page.	Sec. of P. L. & R.
Revised Statutes	XLVI	9	3964	......	768	542
			3965	......	769	543
			3966	......	769	544
			3967	......	769	545
			3968	......	769	546
			3969	......	769	547
			3970	......	769	607
			3971	......	769	548
			3972	......	769	549
			3973	......	769	550
			3974	......	769	551
			3975	......	769	552
			3976	......	769	252
			3977	......	770	253
			3978	......	770	254
			3979	......	770	1251
			3980	......	770	628
			3981	......	770	559
			3982	......	770	555
			3983	.....	770	557
			3984	......	770	558
			3985	......	770	559
			3986	......	771	560
			3987	......	771	561
			3988	......	771	562
			3989	......	771	563
			3990	......	771	564
			3991	......	771	565
			3992	......	771	567
			3993	......	772	568
			3994	......	772	369
			3995	......	772	553
			3996	......	772	554
		10	3999	......	772	645
			4000	......	773	643
			4001	......	773	637
			4002	......	773	629
			4003	......	773	630
			4004	......	773	631
			4005	......	773	632
		11	4006	......	774	649
			4007	.....	774	652
			4008	......	774	653
			4009	......	774	654
			4010	......	774	655
			4011	......	774	656
			4012	......	774	650
			4013	......	774	651
			4014	......	774	1136
			4015	......	775	1137
			4016	......	775	1138
		12	4017	......	775	6
			4018	......	776	11
			4019	......	776	7
			4020	......	776	10
			4021	......	776	19
			4022	......	776	20
			4023	......	776	21
			4024	......	776	22
			4025	......	776	23
			4026	......	776	570
		13	4027	......	777	956
			4028	......	777	976
			4029	......	777	959
			4030	......	777	982

Act of Congress.	Title.	Chap.	Sec.	Vol.	Page.	Sec. of P. L. & R.
Revised Statutes..................	XLVI	13	4031	......	777	960
			4032	......	778	983
			4033	......	778	978
			4034	......	778	980
			4035	......	778	981
			4036	......	778	1013
			4037	......	778	1014
			4038	......	778	1003
			4039	......	778	1035
			4040	......	778	1005
			4041	......	778	1012
			4042	......	779	1072
			4043	......	779	1073
			4044	......	779	1075
			4045	......	779	1074
			4046	......	779	1076
			4047	......	779	968
			4048	......	780	969
		14	4049	......	780	55
			4050	......	780	56
			4051	......	781	57
			4052	......	781	296
			4053	......	781	1249
			4054	......	781	58
			4055	......	781	59
			4056	......	781	60
			4057	......	781	61
			4058	......	782	62
			4059	......	782	63
			4060	......	782	64
			4061	......	782	478
	LX	3	4961	......	959	374
	LXV	....	5263	......	1019	1254
			5264	......	1019	1255
			5265	......	1019	1256
			5266	......	1019	1257
			5267	......	1019	1258
			5268	......	1019	1259
			5269	......	1020	1260
	LXX	5	5463	......	1059	1226
			5464	......	1059	1227
			5465	......	1060	1228
			5466	......	1060	1229
			5467	......	1060	1230
			5468	......	1060	1231
			5469	......	1060	1235
			5470	......	1061	1236
			5471	......	1061	1237
			5472	......	1061	1238
			5473	......	1061	1239
			5474	......	1062	1240
			5475	......	1062	1241
			5476	......	1062	1242
			5477	......	1062	1243
			5478	......	1062	1244
			5479	......	1062	1245
			5480	......	1062	1246
		8	5534	......	1072	1247
			5535	......	1072	1248
Act March 5, 1874	....	46	1	18	19	21, 25
Act March 18, 1874................	....	57	1	18	23	103
Act June 23, 1874.................	....	456	6	18	233	191
			12	18	235	581
				18	235	587
				18	236	585

Act of Congress.	Title.	Chap.	Sec.	Vol.	Page.	Sec. of P. L. & R.
Act March 3, 1875		128	1	18	341	**633**
			4	18	343	**1143**
			7	18	343	**247**
Act March 3, 1875		129	1	18	351	**983**
Act July 12, 1876		179	1	19	78	**573**
				19	78	**314**
				19	79	**635**
			4	19	80	**45**
			7	19	81	**116**
			9	19	82	**119**
			10	19	82	**120**
			11	19	82	**121**
			12	19	82	**122**
			13	19	82	**638**
			14	19	82	**174**
		186	1	19	90	**225**, **226**
Act August 11, 1876		260	1	19	129	**582**
				19	129	**603**, **604**, **605**, **606**
Joint resolution July 25, 1876		18	.....	19	215	**116**
Act March 3, 1877		103	2	19	335	**48**
			3	19	335	**49**
			4	19	335	**50**
			5	19	335	**249**
			6	19	335	**250**
Act March 3, 1877		110	1	19	383	**573**
				19	384	**314**
Act December 15, 1877		3	1	20	10	**245**
Act May 17, 1878		107	1	20	61	**578**
			2	20	62	**624**
			3	20	62	**625**
			4	20	62	**579**
			5	20	62	**607**
Act June 17, 1878		259	1	20	140	**6**
				20	141	**573**
				20	141	**117**, **118**
				20	142	**5**
				20	142	**636**
			2	20	143	**53**
Act February 4, 1879		45	1	20	281	**106**
Act February 21, 1879		95	1	20	317	**309**
			2	20	317	**310**
			3	20	317	**311**
			4	20	317	**312**
			5	20	317	**307**
Act March 3, 1879		180	1	20	356	**573**
				20	356	**245**
				20	356	**555**
				20	357	**46**
				20	357	**141**
				20	357	**631**
			3	20	358	**612**
			4	20	358	**632**
			5	20	358	**670**
			6	20	358	**646**
			7	20	358	**176**
			8	20	358	**177**
			9	20	358	**178**
			10	20	359	**184**
			11	20	359	**190**
			12	20	359	**209**

Act of Congress.	Title.	Chap.	Sec.	Vol.	Page.	Sec. of P. L. & R.
Act March 3, 1879		180	13	20	359	197
			14	20	359	185
			15	20	359	212
			16	20	359	206
			17	20	359	215 1134
			18	20	360	217
			19	20	360	219
			20	20	360	221
			21	20	360	229 230
			22	20	360	231
			23	20	361	233
			24	20	361	182
			25	20	361	239
			26	20	361	270
			27	20	362	271
			28	20	362	1252
			29	20	362	251
			30	20	362	602
			31	20	362	135
			32	20	362	143

INDEX

TO THE

POSTAL LAWS AND REGULATIONS.

* The title "Railway Service" refers only to the transportation of mails by railroad companies under contract or otherwise, and should not be confounded with the *Railway Mail Service*, by which is understood the distribution and dispatch of mails in transit upon railroads and steamboats in "offices" by route-agents, postal-clerks, and other postal employés denominated in these regulations "Employés of the Railway Mail Service."

GLOSSARY

OF

WORDS HAVING A TECHNICAL MEANING IN THE POSTAL SERVICE.

Acting Postmaster. A person in charge of a post-office by authority from the President in case of the removal, or by authority of the sureties of the postmaster in case of the absconding, arrest, insanity, or death of the latter, pending the appointment of a new postmaster. See sections 111, 135, 962.

Address. (Syn. *Direction.*) The superscription of mail.

Addressee. The person or care to whom matter is addressed for delivery.

Adjustment. Applied to railroad service means the fixing of the rate of compensation allowable to the amount and character of the service rendered under section 629.

Advance Signature. Used in railway mail service to designate the action of an employé in signing the record of arrivals and departures, as having departed on his run at a certain day and hour, in advance of the actual time of his departure; as, for instance, signing the night before for his morning run. This practice is strictly prohibited.

Advice of a Money-Order. A letter or notice, partly printed and partly written, bearing the same number and date as its corresponding money-order, sent by the issuing to the paying postmaster for the purpose of informing the latter as to the name and residence of the remitter and payee of the order. Used to assist the paying postmaster in the identification of the owner of the order. (Sections 981, 986, 991, 994.)

Advice-Form. The printed form, prescribed by the Postmaster-General, upon which a letter of advice is made out. (Section 991.)

Advertised. Published through the press or posted conspicuously in the post-office.

Advertised Letter. A letter which, remaining in a post-office unclaimed or undelivered, is advertised in accordance with regulations.

Agency, Route. A railroad or steamboat route on which the way service, or service for the mail supply of post-offices located thereon, or interchange between the same, is performed by an employé of the railway mail service known as a route agent.

Agent, Local Mail. An employé of the railway mail service to whom is assigned the duty of supervising transfers of mails at union depots, junctions, &c.

Agent, Route. (Syn. *Mail Agent.*) An employé of the railway mail service in immediate charge of a route agency.

Antedate. To date erroneously before the correct day, usually for fraudulent purposes; as to antedate a money-order or a remittance letter. (Section 1085.)

Application. A paper, partly printed and partly written, upon which the remitter has stated the amount for which he desires a money-order to be made out, and the particulars necessary to be known at the paying office in order to secure payment to the right person. (Sections 978, 979.)

Application, Form of. Form 6001, upon which the remitter of a money-order is required to make out his application. (Section 978.)

Badge. A mark or insignia designed to distinguish officials or employés of any branch of the post-office service.

Bag. (*See* MAIL BAG.)

Bag, Dispatch. A leather pouch with special lock, in which is forwarded the foreign correspondence of the Department of State.

Beneficiary. The payee, or person for whom the amount of a money-order is intended. Generally used to designate the payee of an international money-order. (Section 1046.)

Blind Reader. The clerk in the larger post-offices to whom is referred for final interpretation, before forwarding to the Dead-Letter Office, such mail as may be received illegibly addressed, or the proper destination of which is doubtful.

Bond of Indemnity. A bond or guaranty required by the Post-Office Department from the remitter who applies for a duplicate of a lost money-order, of which neither the payee nor his legal representative can be found. The condition of this bond is set forth in section 1006.

Box, Street-mailing. A box placed at street corners or other favorable location for the reception of mail to be taken therefrom at certain intervals to the general or branch post-office; used only in post-offices where the free delivery service is established, and generally attached to lamp-posts.

Brass Lock. A mail lock of more intricate construction than the ordinary iron lock, used only on long star routes for direct pouches, between separating post-offices, which are not to be opened *en route.*

Bulletin of Verification. A blank for the correction and the statement of the errors and irregularities of all kinds discovered in the mails exchanged between countries of the Universal Postal Union.

Bulletin, Post-Office. A printed schedule for the information of the public, of closes and arrivals of mails at post-offices.

Canceled Money-Order. A money-order, supposed to have been lost, for which an application for a duplicate has been made and forwarded to the Post-Office Department. (Section 1009.)

Canceler. (Syn. *Killer, Obliterator.*) A hand-stamp for the cancellation of postage-stamps. It sometimes forms a fixed attachment to the postmarking stamp. In all cases it should be used in connection therewith.

Case. A frame containing a number of boxes for the assorting, separation, or distribution of mail.

Case, Assorting. A piece of post-office furniture designed for a general separation of letter mail preliminary to a final disposition of the same for forwarding.

Case, General Distribution. The piece of furniture used at small post-offices for the general assorting of mails received and dispatched.

Case, Letter Carrier's. A case consisting of pigeon-holes placed over a letter carrier's table to assist him in arranging his mail for consecutive delivery.

Case, Letter-Distribution. A piece of furniture arranged and intended to facilitate the distribution of letters. Four cases, each comprising from 100 to 200 separate boxes, are usually combined in one piece of furniture.

Case, Paper-Distribution Platform. (Syn. *Platform Oven.*) The same as the last named with the exception that a working platform is raised to the level of the lower tier of boxes, thus affording greater facilities where many divisions on one case is necessary—consisting of from 300 to 550 divisions, or boxes.

Case, Paper Distribution, Upright. (Syn. *Oven.*) An upright case of horizontal tiers of boxes, ordinarily 12″ x 16″, front opening arranged to facilitate the distribution of 2d, 3d, and 4th class matter. Consisting of from 50 to 175 divisions or boxes.

Case, Registered. (*See* REGISTERED.)

Case Examination, Offices by Counties. An examination conducted in the railway mail service and distribution divisions of post-offices, consisting of the separation of cards representing the post-offices of a State or section, into boxes labeled for the counties in which such post-offices are located.

Case Examination, Offices by Scheme. An examination peculiar to the railway mail service and distribution divisions of post-offices, consisting of the separation of cards representing the post-offices in a State or section into boxes labeled for the mails directed by scheme or order to be made up for such section.

Case Examination, Transcript of Scheme. An examination somewhat similar to the above, but in which the cards represent only the offices appearing on the face of a scheme in which only a portion of the offices in such county are specifically given.

Cash-Book. The book in which the daily cash receipts and disbursements of a money-order post-office are entered. (Section 1077.)

Catch. To seize a mail while a train is in motion.

Catch-Crane. A crane erected by the side of a railroad track on which to suspend pouches containing mail to be taken by a train in motion at any rate of speed.

Catch-Pouch. (*See* MAIL-CATCHER POUCH.)

Catch-Station. A mail-station at which a mail-train does not stop, and mails are necessarily taken on trains with the catcher.

Catcher. An iron instrument used on trains in connection with the fixed catch-crane, to take on mail at mail-stations where no stop is made.

Catcher-Arm. The part of the catcher resting in sockets at either end and parallel with the side of the car at all times. The short arm of the catcher as distinguished from the trip or long arm.

Catcher-Lever. The wooden handle or lever by which the trip is worked or raised to a position on a horizontal line with the arm, for taking the pouch from the crane.

Catcher-Sockets. The sockets on either side of the car door in which the catcher works and is supported.

Catcher-Trip. The long or rather the outer arm of the catcher, which, when raised by the lever, trips the bag from the crane and secures it near the intersection with the arm.

Certificate, International. (*See* INTERNATIONAL.)

Certificate of Deposit. A receipt made out by the postmaster of a money-order post-office of the "first class" in acknowledgment of the deposit of a remittance of money-order funds. (Secs. 1082, 1083.)

Certificate of Inspection. A certificate of the Second Assistant Postmaster-General to the Auditor of the Treasury for the Post-Office Department, certifying that mail-service has been performed for a specified period by the person or by the mail-contractor named therein. This certificate also shows the amount of fines and deductions, if any, which should be charged to contractor, or person performing the service, because of failures or delinquencies during the period of time covered by such certificate, and is called a "certificate of inspection" because it is prepared after careful *inspection* of the proofs of performance of mail-service.

Certificate of Service. A certificate of a postmaster, or other officer of the department, certifying to the performance or non-performance of mail-service by a mail-contractor or other person authorized to carry the United States mails, to be filed in the office of the Second Assistant Postmaster-General, Division of Inspection. This certificate is occasionally accepted in lieu of the register of arrivals and departures

Certified List. (*See* INTERNATIONAL EXCHANGE LIST.)

Certified Money-Order. A money-order, or the listed particulars of a money-order, which has been certified by an international exchange office as correct and entitled to be paid in a foreign country. (Sections 1049, 1065.)

Charges. Amounts due and collectible at the post-office of delivery on mail insufficiently prepaid, but forwarded in accordance with regulation or treaty stipulation.

Cleat. An attachment of metal device to a sack to which the drawing-card is fastened in closing the sack.

Clerk, Chief Head—(R. M. S.) A head railway post-office clerk detailed to take immediate charge of the general details of service of a route or number of routes, to arrange for changes when necessary, &c.

Clerk, Dispatch. A clerk at a post-office to whom is assigned the special duty of dispatching and receiving mails.

Clerk, Tally. A clerk to whom is assigned the duty of tallying and checking made-up mails and making for file a permanent record of the same.

Clerk's Number. A number stamped or written on the face of a facing-slip to indicate the clerk making up the mail such facing-slip accompanies.

Close. The time specified and publicly announced as the latest that mail can be received at a post-office for dispatch by any given mail.

Closed Mail. Correspondence sent in sealed bags in transit through one or more intermediary countries.

Collector. A letter-carrier detailed to the special duty of collecting mail from street mailing-boxes, hotels, and other designated public mailing-places and conveying the same to the post-office or branch post-office.

Combined Register. (*See* REGISTER.) (Section 1062.)

Connection. A term used to indicate a transfer or continuation in transit without delay from one route to another.

Connection, Close. A term used when the difference in time between the arrival at a point of mail on one route and its departure on another is only what is requisite to make all transfers.

Connection from, Made. A term used to indicate that a connection inward or to a named mail-route has been received by the other route, understood or designated.

Connection from, Missed. A term used in the same relation to describe a failure to receive such connection.

Connection with, Made. A term used to indicate that connection outward or with a named mail route has been delivered by the route understood or designated.

Connection with, Missed. A term used in the same relation to describe a failure to deliver such connection.

Contractor. One who individually or as a firm contracts to perform certain service of the nature of transportation, in accordance with certain specifications and for a definite amount named in contract.

Contractor, Mail-Route. A contractor with the Post Office Department for transportation of the mail on a stage (star) or messenger route.

Corded Sack. (*See* JUTE CANVAS MAIL-SACK.)

Correspondence. As used in foreign mail service and in postal conventions synonymous with mail matter; any matter admitted to the mails.

Cover. Equivalent of envelope or wrapper.

Country of Destination. Same as paying country.

Country of Origin. Same as issuing country.

Coupon. A memorandum of particulars of an international money-order partly printed and partly written in the margin thereof in such a manner that it may be detached readily, and filed by itself for future reference. Sections 1047, 1049, 1085.

Credit. A specified amount of money-order funds in the custody of the postmaster at New York, N. Y., against which the postmaster at some other office has been authorized by the superintendent of the money-order system to draw drafts. (Section 1095.)

Crew. (Syn., *Set.*) The men composing a party of employés working in a car.

Dead. Such mail matter as has been advertised and remained unclaimed one month after the date of advertisement, or has been refused, or for any reason has not reached the party addressed (See Section 433.)

Deduction. The sum forfeited by a mail contractor for the failure to perform a trip or any part of a trip.

Delivery. The act of placing mail in the possession of the parties addressed or subject to their order The district contiguous to a post-office over which the postmaster at such office has immediate supervision and charge in all matters of a local nature connected with the general mail service. The mail made up in an office for the delivery of another; a direct package.

Delivery Window. The place in a post-office where delivery of letters is made, upon application to persons, not box-holders, or not receiving their mail by authorized letter-carriers.

Deposit. A remittance of money-order funds after its receipt at the designated money order post office of the "first class" to which it was addressed. Such receipt entitles the remitting postmaster to a certificate of deposit therefor from the receiving postmaster.

Depos't, Certificate of. (*See* CERTIFICATE OF DEPOSIT.) (Section 1083.)

Deposit, Office of. (*See* MONEY-ORDER OFFICE OF THE FIRST CLASS.)

Depositing Office. A post-office from which a remittance of money-order funds is received for deposit. (Section 108.)

Depositing Postmaster. (*See* REMITTING POSTMASTER.)

Depository. A post-office designated by the department for the repair of mail pouches and sacks for the receipt and storage of new pouches and sacks, and for the issue of same on order.—2 A post-office designated for the deposit of postal funds by other postmasters.

Destructive. Matter which by reason of its hurtful nature is liable to injure the persons of postal employés or damage other mail matter.

Directory Searcher. A clerk to whom is assigned the duty of searching city directories for the full proper address on mail matter, the address of which when received is incomplete or incorrect.

Direct Pouch. A pouch labeled to a post-office or route understood or named.

Discrepancy. A difference; generally used to signify a difference in number, date, or amount as stated in a money-order and in its corresponding advice. (Section 1081.)

Dispatch. A term used to indicate all the mail forwarded by a route at any one time. It includes the close, the actual leaving from the post-office, the train, boat, stage, or conveyance forwarded by, the depot or station-landing such train or boat leaves from, and the time fixed for each of these movements.

Dispatch, Advance. A dispatch made to a train or boat in advance of the last and regular dispatch for the same train or boat. The advance dispatches are numbered in reverse order or in regular numerical order from the regular (or standard) dispatch.

Dispatch, Regular. The last ordinary wagon from a post-office to a train or boat and which includes all mail deposited in the post-office to time of closing for such dispatch.

Dispatch, Schedule. A schedule showing the dispatches of mails from a post-office, with closing time, leaving time of the various wagons, route, train, and leaving time of the same, by which dispatched.

Dispatch, Supplementary. A special dispatch occasionally made after the regular dispatch.

Dispatch Number. A number indicating a certain dispatch.

Distribution. (Syn *Dis., Dist., D. P. O.*) All ordinary mail received at any post-office addressed to other post-offices, not delivery matter. 2. Matter sent to a post-office to be forwarded therefrom to other post-offices to which addressed.

Distribution Division. That portion of the service of a post-office to which is assigned the duty of arranging for and making the separation and dispatch of all mails other than those for local delivery.

Distributing Post-Offices are abolished. (*See* SEPARATING POST-OFFICES.)

Draft. An order for the payment of a sum of money. In money-order business generally used to signify an order from a postmaster drawn against his "credit" with the postmaster at New York, or an order on the postmaster at New York for an amount of money order funds drawn in favor of another postmaster by the Postmaster-General. (*See* CREDIT.) (Sections 1095, 1096 1097, 1098.)

Drop. The opening in a post-office or mail apartment of a car for the mailing of letters and other mailable matter by the public.

Drop-Letter. A letter intended for a person residing within the delivery of the post-office where it is posted.

Due Frequency. Applied to railroad service means that the Postmaster-General is to determine what number of trips per week will constitute due frequency on any route.

Due Speed. Means that the Postmaster-General shall determine what rate of speed of railroad trains will be accepted as a compliance with the law in every case.

Duplicate. An exact copy. The use of a duplicate is sometimes to supply the place of a document lost or destroyed, and sometimes to furnish or preserve information in a place from which access to the original is inconvenient or impossible. (Sections 1039, 1054.)

Duplicate Advice. (*See* SECOND ADVICE.)

Duplicate Certificate of Deposit. The copy of a certificate of deposit which the receiving postmaster is required to transmit to the superintendent of the money-order system. (Section 1082.)

Duplicate Money-Order. A second order furnished to the owner of the original by the Post-Office Department of the paying country in cases where such original has been invalidated by reason of loss, destruction, mutilation, or more than one indorsement. (Sections 1039, 1054.)

Embezzlement. Criminal use of money-order or postal funds by a person to whom they are intrusted by the post-office authority. (Section 1026.)

Employés. A general term for all connected with the railway mail service, except superintendents and local mail agents.

Equipment. All material, except that for clerical use, such as stationery, blanks, &c., necessary for the proper dispatch, security, and transportation of the mails.

Error. (Syn. X.) Indorsement made on the face of facing-slips to call attention to missent matter noted on reverse side.

Exchange. The value of the currency or money of one country expressed in the terms or denominations of another. In the transactions of the money-order system the term is used to denote the value, in the money of the United States, of a specified unit of a foreign currency as fixed by convention between the postal administrations of the two countries. Whenever the commercial value of this unit is equal to its convention value, exchange is said to be at par; when greater, at a premium; when less, at a discount. (Sections 970, 1045, 1055.)

Exchange List. (*See* INTERNATIONAL EXCHANGE LIST.) (Section 976.)

Exchange Office. (*See* INTERNATIONAL EXCHANGE POST-OFFICE.) A post-office through which the interchange of correspondence or money-orders with a foreign country is conducted.

Exchange Postmaster. The postmaster of an international exchange post-office. (Section 1045.)

Exchange, System of. A mutual agreement between the postal administrations of two countries for the issue of money-orders in either and their payment in the other country, together with detailed arrangements for the transaction of the business and for the settlement of the accounts arising therefrom. (Section 976.)

Extra National. Correspondence exchanged in the mails between two countries, which is either received from or addressed to a third country.

Facing-Slip. A piece of ordinary wrapping-paper accompanying all packages of first-class matter and circulars. The slip should be in size about 4 by 2½ inches, and bear on its face, either printed or written, the descriptive title of the mail forwarded under it, the postmark of the office or post-office in which it is made up, and the name or number of the clerk or employé of the railway mail service making up the mail. In addition to the above, facing-slips used in post-offices will indicate the hour of closing the mail forwarded under them; those used in the railway mail service will indicate the direction in which the office is moving at the time the package is made up. Employés of the railway mail service place facing-slips for direct packages inside such packages, and omit the descriptive title.

Fictitious. Matter addressed to assumed names or initials without any designated place of delivery.

Fine. The sum deducted from the pay of a mail-contractor for a violation of the terms of his contract.

Fixed Reserve. (*See* RESERVE.)

Foreign Mail Sack. Used without lock and only for dispatching mails to foreign countries. They are made of *blue* and *white* striped cotton canvas; are of four sizes, No. 0 being the largest and No. 3 the smallest. No. 0 is 50 inches in length and 64 inches in circumference. No. 1 is 43 inches in length and 62 inches in circumference. No. 2 is 41 inches in length and 48 inches in circumference. No. 3 is 32 inches in length and 38 inches in circumference.

Form. A piece of furniture arranged for the general office separation of mails received from other offices.

Frank. To exempt from postage. A signature appearing on mail-matter which exempts it from postage.

Fraudulent. Registered letters the delivery of which has been forbidden by a special order of the Postmaster-General.

Free-Delivery Division. That portion of the service of a post-office relating to the free delivery of mail by letter-carriers at residences or places of business.

General Delivery. The delivery of mail from the delivery-window of a post-office upon application of the party to whom addressed.

Hards. (Syn. *Queers, Nixes, Nondescripts, Look-ups,* and *Asides.*) Matter so addressed that the proper disposition to be made of it is not readily discernible.

Held for Postage. Matter which is not sufficiently prepaid to entitle it to transmission in the mails.

Horse Mail-Bags. Used, with lock, for horseback service only, and made of leather in saddle-bag form. There are three sizes, the largest being No. 1 and the smallest No. 3. No. 1 is 48 inches long in the longest part and 21 inches wide in the widest part. No. 2 is 45 inches long in the longest part and 18 inches wide in the widest part. No. 3 is 42 inches long in the longest part and 16 inches wide in the widest part.

Hotel. Matter returned to the post-office from a hotel, hospital, college, and other similar institutions or by a public functionary or consignee accustomed to receive mail for third parties.

Incidental Expense. An expense of occasional and irregular occurrence, not otherwise specified in instructions, which has been incurred necessarily in the transaction of postal or money-order business. (Sections 966, 971.)

Identification Check. A slip of paper given by an examining clerk in the paying-office to the owner of a money-order presented for payment, as evidence that the latter has been identified as the person he represents himself to be.

Indorsee. The person named in the indorsement, by the payee, as the one to whom payment is to be made. The person to whom the payee of a money-order transfers his right to receive payment thereof. (Section 1028.)

Indorsement. Something written across a document, previously complete, explaining, extending, or changing its scope, or as a reference. In money-order business, an instruction upon the back of the order, filled up and signed by the payee thereof, authorizing its payment to another person. (Section 1014.)

Inland Money-Order. An international money-order issued at or drawn upon an inland money-order office, as distinguished from a "certified order," or one which has been certified and numbered by an exchange office with a "certified international number."

Inland Money-Order Office. A post-office authorized to issue and pay international money-orders, as distinguished from an exchange-office, which certifies their values and affixes to them the "certified international number." (Section 1060.)

Inland Postmaster. The postmaster of an inland money-order office.

Irrespective Reserve. (*See* Reserve.)

International Certificate. A receipt, partly printed and written, on the margin of and bearing the same number as an international money-order, of which it forms a part. This receipt which is filled up, detached, and given to the remitter of the order by the inland issuing postmaster shows the amount of the order "in United States currency, the value of which the postmaster at the international exchange-office" will transmit in its currency to the paying country. (Section 1047.)

International Correspondence. Originating in and addressed to the countries between which mails are exchanged.

International Exchange Post-Office. A post-office designated in an international convention between the postal administrations of two countries to perform the office of certifying the values and the correctness of money-orders issued in either of the countries for payment in the other. Such orders are not valid or payable until so certified. (Sections 1045, 1049.)

International Exchange List. } **International List.** } A list of the numbers, amounts, dates, and other particulars of money-orders issued and certified as correct, in any country for payment to beneficiaries in a foreign country. These lists are made out, certified as correct, and transmitted by exchange-offices only. They are sent to, and for the information of, the exchange-office in the paying country in order to secure payment to the person designated in the original inland order. (Section 1050.)

Intermediary Office. An office which receives and reforwards foreign correspondence to its ultimate destination.

International Money-Order. A money-order issued in one country for payment in a foreign country. (Section 1046.)

Invalid Advice. The advice of an invalid money-order.

Invalid Money-Order. A money-order, the payment of which, by reason of its age, mutilation surplusage of indorsements, or other cause, is prohibited, except by duplicate. (Sections 1032, 1033, 1034.)

Iron Lock. The ordinary mail-lock used on pouches exchanged or interchanged between offices and routes.

Issued Order. A money-order which has been filled up and delivered to the remitter, and whose advice (or advice, coupon, and certificate) has been filled up and forwarded to destination by the issuing postmaster. (Section 986.)

Jute Canvas Mail-Sack. (Also called "Tie-Sack.") Used without lock for printed and other mailable matter not of the first class. They are made of *blue* striped jute canvas, fastened with cord. There are three sizes, the largest being No. 1 and the smallest No. 3. No. 1 is 43 inches in length and 62 inches in circumference. No. 2 is 41 inches in length and 48 inches in circumference. No. 3 is 32 inches in length and 38 inches in circumference.

Label, Card Slide. A small piece of card-board of a size to fit an attachment on the pouches of the numbered classes. When in use as a label on a pouch it bears in writing or printing the address of the office for which the pouch is intended.

Label, Wooden Printed. A small piece of hard wood bearing a printed address, for use exclusively on *sacks* containing mail.

Label, Registered Disk. A round brass label attached to each registered pouch or gold-box in transit, to indicate by the number and letters stamped thereon how many separate pouches or boxes are forwarded at any single dispatch to any one office.

Lap. Where two or more trains of cars starting from a common terminus and destined for different points are run for any distance over one railroad track.

Lap-Service. Where two or more post-routes are maintained over one railroad track.

Legal Representative. The person authorized by law to act for or in the place of another. In money-order business, used to designate the person so authorized to act for the remitter, payee, or indorser of a money-order. (Section 1028.)

Letter of Advice. (*See* Advice.)

Letter of Inquiry. A circular letter (Form 6006) addressed by the paying to the issuing postmaster asking for a second advice, or for an explanation of an alleged discrepancy between an advice and its corresponding order or the statement of the payee. (Section 995.)

Limit of Dimensions. The maximum length, breadth, and depth allowed for certain postal packets.

Limit of Weight. The maximum weight allowed for certain postal packets.

Line. Nearly a synonym of "Route." Usually applied to distinguish route-service performed during the day from that performed during the night: as Wash. & Peters. R. P. O. "Day-Line," Wash. & Peters. R. P. O. "Night-Line."

List, Weekly Canadian. A list of Canadian international money-orders certified during a given week by a Canadian international exchange post-office. (Section 1065.)

Local. Pertaining or confined to the delivery district of a post-office.

Local Mail. Used in railway mail service to indicate mail for post-offices between the initial and terminal post-offices of a railway route.

Local Post-Office. Used in railway mail service to denote post-offices supplied by a railway route between the initial and terminal post-offices of the route.

Local Service. A term used in the railway mail service to indicate the service of a route-agency or railway post-office in the making up, delivering, and exchanging mails between the terminal offices of its route, and all the duties relating to handling of such mail.

Lock. (*See* Iron Lock, Brass Lock.)

Mail. (Syn. *Post-matter.* For syn. *Correspondence, see* Correspondence.) Divided into ordinary delivery, distribution, foreign, and registered.

Mail, Advance. A mail forwarded, sent, dispatched, or received in advance of and in addition to its final regular sending or receiving.

Mail-Bag. A general term comprehending all the sorts and styles authorized to be used in conveying the mails. For the specific styles and sizes adapted to particular uses and modes of conveyance, *see* Mail-Pouch, Mail-Catcher Pouch, Through Registered Mail-Pouch, Horse Mail-Bag, Jute Canvas Mail Sack, Foreign Mail Sack, *and* Registered Foreign Mail Sack.

All mail-pouches are locked and have a *circular bottom*; all horse mail-bags are locked, *are in saddle-bag form, and have elliptical bottoms*; and all sacks are fastened with cord and have *a straight or folding bottom.*

Mail-catcher Pouch. Used exclusively for exchanging mails on railways where mail-catchers and cranes are employed therefor. They are made of cotton canvas, with leather bottoms, locked at the mouth and strapped in the middle. They are only of one size—36 inches in length and 36 inches in circumference.

Mail, Closed. (*See* CLOSED MAIL.)

Mail, Delivery. Mail for the local delivery of a post-office.

Mail, Direct. As applied to foreign exchanges, is a mail transported directly to its destination without using the intermediary service of a third country.

Mail, Direct. Mail made up direct for an office. It may be either "delivery" or "distribution" matter.

Mail, Distribution. Mail addressed to other offices than that at which it is received; not delivery mail.

Mail, Express. Mail sent by train on which there are no employés of the railway mail service.

Mail, Extra Distribution. Sometimes applied in the same sense for ordinary mail, as extra-international for freight.

Mail, Foreign. Mail received from foreign countries or colonies; or, as distinguished from "mail domestic," mail for or from foreign countries or colonies.

Mail, Local. A term used in the railway mail service to indicate mail delivered between the termini of the road as distinguished from through mail.

Mail-Messenger Service. The service to which is assigned the duty of transportation of the mails from a general post-office to adjacent depots, landings, &c., or between branch post-offices or trains, or interchangeably, under the direction of the postmaster at such general post-office.

Mail Number. A number given to a mail for convenience in scheduling or reference.

Mail, Ordinary. All mailable matter subject to domestic rates of postage and intended for the delivery of post-offices in the United States and Dominion of Canada; not registered mail.

Mail Pockets. (*See* HORSE MAIL-BAG.)

Mail-Pouch. Adapted to any mode of conveyance excepting horse-back. Has locked mouth and circular bottom. There are five sizes, the largest being No. 1, and the smallest No. 5. No. 1 is 48 inches in length and 60 inches in circumference. No. 2 is 41 inches in length and 48 inches in circumference. No. 3 is 36 inches in length and 42 inches in circumference. No. 4 is 30 inches in length and 36 inches in circumference. No. 5 is 26 inches in length and 28 inches in circumference.

Mail, Registered. Mail for which a receipt is given to the sender and by each postmaster or employé into whose hands it passes until it reaches its destination.

Mail, Regular. The mail sent out at a regular dispatch, and including all deposited in a post-office previous to the regular close therefor. (*See* DISPATCH.)

Mail, Supplementary. The mail sent at a supplementary dispatch. (*See* DISPATCH.)

Mail, Through. A term used in the railway mail service to indicate mail intended for the terminus of the route or points beyond; not local mail.

Mail, Tie. A term used in the distribution division to indicate such mails as, after being once separated or boxed, are again assorted and tied out separately for each post-office.

Maps, Post-Route. Maps prepared for the use of the Post-Office Department, showing the location of post-offices, post-routes, frequency of service, intermediate distances, &c.

Mass. To combine one or more mails with another.

Massed States. States, the mail for which is forwarded from a post-office or route without any separation or distribution.

Massing. The act of combining a mail or mails with another distinct mail, sending mail to an office or route from which it is not directly supplied.

Massing Scheme. (*See* SCHEME.)

Messenger, Mail. An employé of the department appointed at a fixed salary, to perform service somewhat similar to that performed by a contractor, the latter not being appointed and his compensation determined by contract.

Messenger, Mail-Route. An official designation for an employé of the railway mail service in immediate charge of the way service or short routes; an inferior grade of route-agent.

Messenger Service. The duties devolving upon a mail-messenger or contractor for local messenger service.

Messenger Service, Local. The wagon or transfer service between a post-office, its branch post-office, and adjacent depots, landings, &c. Usually contracted for.

Misdirected. Matter so insufficiently, illegibly, or incorrectly addressed that it cannot be forwarded to destination.

Money-Order. An order for a specified sum of money, not less than one cent nor greater than fifty dollars, made out at a money-order post-office upon a blank form prescribed by law and post-office regulations, and payable at some other money-order post-office. The purchaser of a money-order is known as the remitter, and the person to whom it is made payable as the payee or beneficiary. The tax exacted from the remitter is called the fee. (Sections 956, 957.)

Money-Order Account. An account of the cash transactions of a money-order post-office. (Section 1075.)

Money-Order Advice. (*See* ADVICE.)

Money-Order Blank. A blank form used in the transaction of money-order business. (Section 965.)

Money-Order Book. A blank book used in the transaction of money-order business. (Sections 965, 977.)

Money-Order Business. The transactions, or a portion of the transactions, of the money-order system.

Money-Order Circulars. Letters, usually printed, containing specific instructions of general application to money-order post-offices. (Section 965.)

Money-Order Clerk. An employé of a money-order post-office. (Sections 1018, 1089.)

Money-Order Convention. A written agreement between the postal administrations of two countries, approved by their respective governments, for the issue of money-orders in either country, and their payment in the other, with the general rules by which such issue and payment are to be governed. (Section 976.)

Money-Order Credit. (*See* CREDIT.)

Money-Order Division. The division of a post-office to which is assigned exclusively the direction, management, and working of the money-order system.

Money-Order Funds. Moneys received and disbursed in the transactions of the money-order business. (Section 1074.)

Money-Order Forms. (*See* MONEY-ORDER BLANKS.)

Money-Order Instructions. Instructions from the Post-Office Department relative to the transaction of money-order business. (Section 956, &c.)

Money-Order Laws. Acts of Congress relative to the money-order system or its transact[illegible] Revised Statutes, sections 958-973.)

Money-Order Office. The office of the superintendent of the money-order system in Washin[illegible] D.C.

Money-Order Post-Office. A post-office designated by the Postmaster-General to [illegible] and pay money-orders. (Sections 959, 966, 967.)

Money-Order Post-Office of the "first class." A money-order post-office designated by the Postmaster-General to receive on deposit and account for remittances of money-order funds from other post-offices. (Section 963.)

Money-Order Post-Office of the "second class." A money-order post-office which is not authorized to receive on deposit remittances of money-order funds from other post-offices. (Sections 963, 1001.)

Money-Order Proceeds. Revenues arising from the transactions of the money-order system. (Section 970.)

Money-Order System. The plan and arrangement, including the general provisions and specific details, governing the issue and payment of money-orders, the correspondence incident thereto and the settlement of all questions and accounts arising therefrom. (Sections 956, 957.)

Money-Order Transaction. An itemized unit of money-order business including all labor and material incident to or required for its completion: as, the issue of a money-order; the payment of a money-order; the receipt of a remittance of money-order funds, &c. (Section [illegible].)

Mutilated. Matter so damaged in the mails by casualties that it cannot be forwarded to destination.

Newspaper Train. A very early train, starting from a large city, for which second-class matter is made up direct at publication offices for the employés on the train, which matter is not distributed in a post-office before starting.

Nixes. Used in railway mail service to denote matter, chiefly of the first and second class, addressed to places which are not post-offices, or to States, etc., in which there is no such post-office as that indicated in the address.

Office. Used in railway mail service to denote a postal car or mail apartment in a car or on board a steamboat, which have all been designated by the Postmaster-General as post-offices for the distribution of mail in transit.

Open Mail. Correspondence sent to an intermediary country for distribution and reforwarded to the country of destination.

Paid Order. A money-order, properly receipted, which has been paid to the owner thereof at the office named thereon as the paying office. (Section 1016, etc.)

Particulars. The items of information entered in the application, advice, or coupon of a money-order, by means of which the paying postmaster is assisted in securing payment to the person to whom the order belongs. (Sections 978, 979, 994.)

Payee. The person named in the advice or coupon of a money-order as the one entitled to receive and receipt for the amount of such order. (Section 957.)

Paying Country. The country in which a money-order is due and payable.

Paying Office. The post-office at which a money-order is made payable, or upon which it is drawn.

Paying Postmaster. The postmaster of a paying office.

Penal Sum. The gross amount forfeitable by the principal and sureties thereof, as set forth in the terms of a bond of indemnity, in case of failure on the part of the former to comply with or execute the stipulations therein written. (Section 1006.)

Post-Office drawn upon. (*See* PAYING OFFICE.) (Section 1030.)

Postal Arrangement. Syn. "*Postal Convention*," but sometimes applied to an informal agreement.

Postal Code. The code of laws relating to postal matters.

Postal Card. A card with postage-stamp embossed thereon, issued by the government, used for sending short written communications.

Postal Convention. A formal agreement or arrangement with a foreign country or countries for the reciprocal exchange of correspondence at fixed rates of postage and other conditions, negotiated and concluded by the Postmaster-General, in virtue of the powers vested in him by law by and with the advice and consent of the President.

Postal Order, or Postal Money-Order. (*See* MONEY-ORDER.)

Postal Regulations. Decisions, rulings, and general orders of the Postmaster-General based on the postal laws (code).

Postal Service. Duty performed in or pertaining to the reception, distribution, and dispatch, transportation and delivery of mail-matter, including everything that is necessary to secure the safety of the mails and the celerity and certainty of their dispatch.

Postal Union, Universal. The title given to the single postal territory formed by the countries and colonies which are now, or may hereafter become, parties to the postal convention of Paris signed June 1, 1878.

Post. To put in the mail. (Syn. *Mail.*)

Postage. Established fee for the conveyance and proper delivery of mail.

Postage-Funds. Moneys derived from box-rents, postages, sales of stamps, &c., in distinction from moneys denominated money-order funds. (Section 1078.)

Postage-Rates. Defined amounts for which mail is conveyed and delivered.

Postage-Stamp. A printed form for the prepayment of postage issued and sold by the Post-Office Department to be affixed to mail matter.

Postage, Unpaid. Additional postage due and payable at delivery.

Postage Due Stamp. A printed form to be affixed and canceled upon the delivery of insufficiently prepaid matter, showing the amount of postage due and collected thereon.

Post-Bills are abolished.

Poster. (1) The sender of mail: the one who posts mail.
(2) A large printed sheet intended to be displayed in a public place as an advertise[illegible]

Poste Restante (Fr). A direction to the postmaster at the delivery office placed on mail by the sender or poster, to indicate that such mail is to be held until called for.

Postmark. Mark or stamp of a post-office on mail-matter posted thereat; sometimes [illegible] mark with a postmarking stamp or indicate the office and date of mailing in writing.

Postmark, Backing. A general term for all postmarks on the back or reverse side of mail, including transit, receiving, branch, carrier's postmark, &c.

Postmark, Branch. The postmark of a branch post-office.

Postmark, Carrier's. The postmark indicating the carrier trip on which the mail on which it appears was sent out.

Postmark, Day (of month). The portion of the general postmark indicating the day of the month.

Postmark, Directory Searcher. A postmark indicating that the mail on which it appears has been handled and treated by a certain directory searcher.

Postmark, Hour. That portion of a general postmark indicating the hour of the day.

Postmark, Month. That portion of a general postmark indicating the month of the year.

Postmark, Office. That portion of the general postmark indicating the office or post-office at which such postmark is made.

Postmark, Rating. The postmarking stamp used to indicate the amount of postage due on mail before delivery is made.

Postmark, Receiving. The postmark made on the back of mail received from other offices, to indicate the time of such receipt.

Postmark, Steamer. The postmark, usually consisting of the post-office name or abbreviation, date, and a number, used in the New York post-office to indicate by what steamer foreign mail is received.

Postmark, Transit. A backing postmark used to indicate the time letter mail in transit through an office is received at such office.

Postmark, Year. That portion of the general postmark indicating the year.

Postmaster. The officer of the Post-Office Department having immediate charge and supervision of a post-office and of all postal matters connected with its delivery district.

Postmaster, Assistant. (Syn. *Deputy.*) An officer of the Post-Office Department assisting the postmaster in the supervision of the business of a post-office, and in his absence acting as postmaster.

Post-Office. A local governmental office where mail is received, handled, and delivered, dispatched or forwarded.

Post-Office, Branch. (Syn. *Station, Sub-Post-Office.*) An outlying station in the delivery of a central or main office, located thus for convenience of the public and the service in facilitating and expediting the collection and delivery of mail.

Post-Office, First-Class. A post-office at which the salary allowed to the postmaster, based on the business transacted, amounts to $3,000 or more.

Post-Office, Fourth-Class. A post-office where the postmaster's salary is less than $1,000.

Post-Office, Free-Delivery. An office at which the free-delivery service is in operation.

Post-Office, General. A central or main post-office in cities where branch post-offices are established.

Post-Office, Head. A post-office located at a terminus or intersection of a star route, through which mail is forwarded to other post-offices on the same or connecting routes. The first post-office named in the contract for carrying the mail over a route.

Post-Office, Initial. The first office named in the terminal-route titles of the railway mail service. The office first named in contracts or proposals for service on star routes, usually designated on post-route maps by a short double turn ‖ crossing the route terminus at right angles.

Post-Office, Local. Post-office on a railroad route between the initial and terminal post-offices.

Post-Office, Money-Order. A post-office at which money-orders are issued or paid upon application or presentation.

Post-Office of Destination. The post-office to which made-up mails are labeled and where they are to be first assorted, separated, delivered, or distributed.

Post-Office of Dispatch. The office from which mails made up as received are dispatched.

Post-Office of Origin. The post-office in which mail originates or at which it is mailed.

Post-Office, Railway. (Abb. and syn., *R. P. O.*) A railway car, or portion of car, fitted and furnished for the distribution of mail, and in which such distribution is made. A route on which such cars are run and distribution made.

Post-Office, Second-Class. A post-office where the postmaster's salary is $2,000 or more, but less than $3,000.

Post-Office, Special. A post-office not located on a regular mail route, but which receives its mail from a post-office selected by the postmaster and under a schedule arranged by him as to time, frequency, and mode, the compensation of the special carrier conveying the mail to be fixed at two-thirds of the salary of the postmaster, both being paid out of the gross receipts of the post-office.

Post-Office, Terminal. The last named in the terminal-route titles of the railway mail service, and the contracts of the Post-Office Department for star service, indicated on postal railway maps by a single chart line crossing an end of a route at right angles.

Post-Office, Third-Class. A post-office where the postmaster's salary is $1,000 or more, but less than $2,000.

Post-Office, Traveling. The designation given in Europe to railway post-offices. (Styled Offices in regulations of United States railway mail service.)

Post-Roads. All railroads that are now or may hereafter be put in operation, and all letter-carrier routes established in any city or town; all the waters of the United States, all canals, and all plank or public roads during the time the mail is carried thereon.

Pouch. (*See* MAIL-POUCH.)

Premium. Excess, in commercial value, over legal or conventional value. In money-order transactions usually applied to denote the excess in the commercial value of gold coin or exchange over their legal or conventional value. (Sections 1064, 1077.)

Prepaid. Mail on which all postage-dues thereon have been paid at the office of posting.

Prepaid, Insufficiently. Mail on which only a portion of the postage-dues thereon has been paid at the office of posting.

Prepayment. The payment of all postage-dues at the post-office where mail is posted.

Prepayment, Compulsory. Full prepayment of postage fees, absolutely necessary, and without which mail cannot be forwarded.

Prepayment Optional. Payment of postage may or may not be made.

Prima Facie. On the first view. Evidence, generally documentary, which is to be taken as convincing unless rebutted. (Section 1076.)

Railway Mail Service. The service to which is assigned exclusively the immediate supervision of the transportation of domestic mails, of their distribution in transit, and of all matters pertaining to the distribution and dispatch of domestic mails beyond the delivery of a post-office, and also the weighing of mails on railroad routes.

Rate, Foreign. Rate of postage due to the foreign reforwarding office.

Rate Limit. The maximum weight for a single rate of postage.

Readjustment. Applied to railroad service means a revision of the rates of pay.

Receipt Return. A form of acknowledgment to be signed by the addressee of a registered article on its delivery, and returned by mail to the sender.

Recognized Service. The transportation of the mail by a railroad company for which no contract has been entered into, but the service is accepted by the department and payment authorized therefor under the laws and the regulations of the department.

Register of Arrival and Departure. A record kept by a postmaster or other officer of the Post-Office Department, showing the exact time of each arrival and each departure of a mail-carrier at a terminal post-office, or at a way post-office on a mail-route.

Registered Foreign Mail Sack. Used exclusively for transmitting *registered* mails to foreign countries, made of *red* and *white* striped cotton canvas. There are three sizes the largest being No. 1, and the smallest No. 3. No. 1 is 36 inches in length, and 48 inches in circumference. No. 2 is 24 inches in length, and 36 inches in circumference. No. 3 is 18 inches in length and 24 inches in circumference.

Register of Advices Received. A book kept by a paying postmaster in which he is required to make daily entries of the particulars of the advices, as received, of all money-orders drawn on his office. (Sections 979, 1017, 1020.)

Register of Money-Orders Issued. A book kept by an issuing postmaster in which he is required to make daily entries of the particulars of the advices as issued, of all money-orders drawn by him. (Sections 977, 1000.)

Register, Combined. A form of register of money-orders issued or of advices received, in which is combined the particulars of both domestic and international advices or orders. (Section 1062.)

Reissue. The issue of a new money-order in lieu of one in which some error has been discovered or in which the remitter desires some modification. (Section 1003.)

Registry Division. The division of a post-office to which is assigned the receiving, making up and dispatch of all registered mail, and the filing of records concerning the same.

Remission. The abatement of a fine or deduction, or of that part of a fine or deduction shown to have been erroneously imposed or made.

Remitter. The person who takes out or purchases a money-order. (Section 959.)

Remitting Postmaster. A postmaster who sends money-order funds for deposit at a money-order post-office of the "first class." (Section 1081.)

Remittance. A sum of money-order funds forwarded for deposit, by mail or otherwise, by a postmaster to a money-order post-office of the first class. (Section 1081.)

Repayment. The paying of the amount of a money-order at the office where it was issued. An order may be repaid to the remitter, the payee, or the indorsee. Fees are not repaid. (Sections 1035, 1039.)

Reserve. A limited amount of money-order funds allowed by the superintendent of the money-order system to be retained at certain designated money-order offices to insure the prompt payment of money-orders. Reserves are of two kinds, "Fixed" and "Irrespective." A "fixed reserve" is one which may be exceeded when the amount of unpaid advices on hand is greater than the amount of the reserve. (Sections 1080 and 1081.) An "irrespective reserve" is one which is irrespective of the amount of unpaid advices, and may not be exceeded under any circumstances.

Return. The accumulation of dead or unmailable matter transmitted at regular intervals to the Dead-Letter Office.

Return Card. A business card (except that of a hotel, college, or other public institution which furnishes envelopes for indiscriminate use of patrons), a post-office box, street and number, or other designation, printed on an envelope, by which the latter may be restored to the writer unopened.

Return Request. A request printed or written on the envelope of a letter that it be returned to the writer if not delivered.

Renewal of Credit. Where a credit has been exhausted it may be renewed by application to the Superintendent of the money-order system. (*See* CREDIT.) (Section 1095.)

Route. A post-road between any two post-offices (intermediate post-offices may or may not be included) on which transportation of the mails has been ordered and contracted for.

Route-Agents. (*See* AGENT.)

Route, Carrier's. The district within the delivery of a free-delivery office in which delivery of mails is made at residences or places of business by any one letter-carrier.

Route, Railroad. A railroad on which transportation of the mails and service has been ordered by the department.

Route, Star. A public highway or other road on which transportation of the mails has been ordered and contracted for by the Post-Office Department.

Route, Steamboat. A water-route on which transportation of the mails and service by steamboat has been ordered by the Post-Office Department.

R. P. O. (Abb. for *Railway Post-Office*.)

Run. Nearly a synonym of "Trip," but applied generally to the starting out of an employé on duty, as, "Mr. Jones takes the 'run' west to-night."

Sack. (*See* MAIL-BAG.)

Satchel. A uniform leather bag used by letter-carriers, and in which they place mail for delivery or deposit at the post-office.

Scale Number. The number assigned to any issue of authorized scales, letter-balances, &c., used in weighing or rating mail. It should be used in connection with the date of order authorizing such changed issue.

Schedule Point. A post-office on a mail-route where a specified time for the arrival and departure of the mail has been fixed by the Second Assistant Postmaster-General. Each terminus of a mail-route is always a "schedule point."

Scheme. An official and formal plan or design of distribution or assorting.

Scheme of Distribution. A scheme for the distribution division of post-offices or for employes of the railway mail service.

Scheme of Distribution, General. A distribution scheme issued by the railway mail service for general adaptation to any standpoint, and in which all routes and methods of supply are indicated.

Scheme of Distribution, General Single Supply. A distribution scheme issued by the railway mail service for general adaptation, in which only the best single supply for an office is given.

Scheme of Distribution, Massing. A supplementary scheme directing the disposition to be made of the divisions of the working office scheme.

Scheme of Distribution, Post-Office. A distribution scheme published by a post-office for its distribution division and arranged to secure a uniform casing or assorting of mail at all times.

Scheme of Distribution, Standpoint. A distribution scheme issued by the railway mail service for the direction and from the standpoint of a route or other standpoint.

Second Advice. A letter of advice, upon a distinct form, sent by the issuing postmaster in lieu of an original advice which has been mutilated or which is otherwise illegible, or which has failed to reach the paying office, or which is alleged to be defective or manifestly incorrect in any of its particulars. A second advice is not necessarily an exact copy of the original. It may be a correction thereof. (Section 995.)

Separating. A term used in the district divisions of post-offices and in the railway mail service to indicate the act of dividing mail for the convenience of a post-office or route making the final distribution of the same.

Separating Post-Offices. Post-offices where mail is received for distribution and dispatched to other post-offices. Before the introduction of the railway mail service all mail was either sent direct or to a distributing post-office, but now the larger part of the distribution is done *en route* by the employés of the railway mail service, and only mail for post-offices on star-routes is sent to separating post-offices. Distributing post-offices are abolished.

Service. A branch, division, or subdivision of the business of the Post-Office Department. The special duties of any such branch or division. The general duties of the department.

Set. (*See* CREW.)

Special Agent. A confidential agent of the department, the personal representative of the Postmaster-General, acting under special or sealed instructions in the adjustment of business which it is impossible or impracticable to adjust by means of correspondence. Special agents assigned to the money-order system receive their instructions from and report to the superintendent of the money-order system; those to the free-delivery system from the superintendent of free delivery, &c.

Special Draft. A draft on the postmaster at New York for a designated sum, furnished by the superintendent of the money-order system to meet a special emergency, to a postmaster who does not require a standing credit. (*See* CREDIT and DRAFT.) (Section 1097.)

Special Notice of Overdraft. A notice (Form 6037) sent by an issuing to a paying postmaster at a second-class office to inform him that the amount of money-orders drawn upon his office in a given day equals or exceeds $200. (Section 1001.)

Special Notice of Repayment. A notice sent by the issuing to the paying postmaster to inform him that a money-order, the advice of which has gone forward, has been repaid. (Sections 1004, 1040.)

Stamp. To impress with some mark or postmark. An instrument with which such marking is made. To affix postage-stamps to mail.

Star Service. Contracts for carrying the mail, other than by railway or steamboat, "without other reference to the mode of transportation than may be necessary to provide for the due celerity, certainty, and security thereof." So called from the fact that the printed contract forms are headed with stars in the following manner: * * * * * * * * *. The three groups of stars represent the words "celerity, certainty, security."

Sterling. The designation given to the lawful money of Great Britain. Money computed in pounds, shillings, and pence. (Sections 1049, 1050.)

Straw Bids. Bids for carrying the mail made with the intention of failing to perform service after the awarding of the contract, so that a new contract will have to be made with a higher bidder with whom a combination has been made by the lowest bidder.

Sufficient and Suitable Rooms, Fixtures, and Furniture. Applied to railroad service means that the Postmaster-General is to determine what space is required for mails and agents, what fixtures are required to facilitate distribution, and what furniture is necessary to render the department convenient and comfortable.

Superintendent of the Money-Order System. The officer at the seat of government charged by the Postmaster-General with the general supervision and management of the business of the money-order system.

Sureties. Persons who sign or indorse the bond of a postmaster as guarantors for the faithful performance, by the latter, of the duties of his office, and who bind themselves (*see* PENAL SUM) to make good the whole or a designated portion of any loss that may accrue to the postal or money-order funds by reason of the negligence or malfeasance of the postmaster, or of any of the employés of his office. (Sections 960, 964.)

Surname. The family name or designation, usually inherited from the father, as distinguished from the given or Christian name. (Section 1063.)

Terminus. One of the ends of a post-route. (*See* INITIAL OFFICE, TERMINAL OFFICE.)

Through Registered Mail Pouches. Used exclusively for domestic exchanges of through registered mails between such post-offices as are authorized to make such exchanges; made of red-striped cotton canvas of three sizes, the largest being No. 1 and the smallest No. 3. No. 1 is 48 inches in length and 60 inches in circumference; No. 2 is 41 inches in length and 48 inches in circumference; No. 3 is 36 inches in length and 42 inches in circumference.

Tracer. (Syn. *Searcher, Inquiry.*) A printed form for ascertaining the disposition made *en route* at each succeeding stage or transfer of missing ordinary or registered mail.

Transfer. The loan of funds from one account to another by authority of the Postmaster-General. (Section 1072.)

Tie-Sack. (*See* JUTE-CANVAS MAIL-SACK.)

Treaty. (*See* POSTAL CONVENTION.)

Trip. The performance of service one way over a route.

Trip, Round. The performance of service both ways over a route.

Unmailable. Matter which by law, regulation, or treaty stipulation is excluded from the mails, or which by reason of illegible, incorrect, or insufficient address cannot be forwarded to destination.

Voucher. The evidence of the payment of money upon which credit is taken in an account. Paid and repaid money-orders, receipts for stationery and incidental expenses, receipts for the salaries of clerks, and certificates of deposit are among the vouchers to a money-order account. (Sections 971, 1086, 1094.)

Way. (*See* LOCAL.) The term "way" should be applied only to post-offices on star routes and mail sent to them. The term "local" should be applied only to post-offices on railroad or steamboat routes, and to mail intended for them.

Way Mail. Mail for a way post-office.

Way Post-Office. On a star route, a post-office between the termini of the route.

Weekly List. (*See* LIST, CANADIAN.)

Weekly Statement. A detailed record of the money-order transactions of a post-office required to be sent to the superintendent of the money-order system on Saturday at the close of each week's business. The first weekly statement in each fiscal quarter includes the business of all the days of the quarter prior to the second Sunday, and the last weekly statement in each fiscal quarter includes the business of all the days subsequent to the Sunday next before the last in the quarter.

APPENDIX.

AN ABSTRACT

OF THE

FORMER POSTAL LAWS OF THE UNITED STATES,

SHOWING

THE VARIOUS CHANGES IN THE CLASSIFICATION OF MAIL MATTER, DOMESTIC RATES OF POSTAGE, AND IN THE FRANKING PRIVILEGE, FROM 1789 TO MARCH 3, 1879.

AN ABSTRACT OF THE FORMER POSTAL LAWS OF THE UNITED STATES, SHOWING THE VARIOUS CHANGES IN THE CLASSIFICATION OF MAIL MATTER, DOMESTIC RATES OF POSTAGE, AND IN THE FRANKING PRIVILEGE, FROM 1789 TO MARCH 3, 1879.

Act September 22, 1789.—For the temporary establishment of the post-office, to continue in force until the end of the next session of Congress, and no longer.

Act August 4, 1790.—Continues in force the act of September 22, 1789, until the end of the next Congress, and no longer.

Act March 3, 1791.—Continues in force the act of September 22, 1789, until the end of the next Congress, and no longer.

This act (March 3, 1791) provides that all letters to and from the Treasurer, Comptroller, and Auditor of the Treasury, and the Assistant to the Secretary of the Treasury, on public service, shall be received and conveyed by the post free of postage.

Act February 20, 1792.—Continues in force the act of March 3, 1791, until the 1st of June, 1792, and no longer, and provides that this act (February 20, 1792) shall continue in force for the term of two years from June 1, 1792, and no longer.

This act (February 20, 1792) was the first act fixing rates of postage on domestic letters, and established the following rates, to take effect June 1, 1792:

Act February 20, 1792, section 9.—By land.—For every single letter not exceeding 30 miles, 6 cents.

For every single letter over 30 miles, and not exceeding 60 miles, 8 cents.

For every single letter over 60 miles, and not exceeding 100 miles, 10 cents.

For every single letter over 100 miles, and not exceeding 150 miles, 12½ cents.

For every single letter over 150 miles, and not exceeding 200 miles, 15 cents.

For every single letter over 200 miles, and not exceeding 250 miles, 17 cents.

For every single letter over 250 miles, and not exceeding 350 miles, 20 cents.

For every single letter over 350 miles, and not exceeding 450 miles, 22 cents.

For every single letter over 450 miles, 25 cents.

For every double letter, double the said rates.

For every triple letter, triple the said rates.

For every packet weighing 1 ounce avoirdupois, to pay at the rate of four single letters for each ounce, and in that proportion for any greater weight.

Act February 20, 1792, section 10.—Letters and packets passing by sea to and from the United States, or from one port to another therein, in packet-boats or vessels, the property of or provided by the United States, shall be rated and charged as follows:

For every single letter, 8 cents.

For every double letter, 16 cents.

For every triple letter or packet, 24 cents.

For every letter or packet brought into the United States, or carried from one port therein to another by sea, in any private ship or vessel, 4 cents, if delivered at the place where the same shall arrive: and if directed to be delivered at any other place, with the addition of the like postage as on domestic letters.

Act February 20, 1792, section 13.—The postmasters to whom such letters may be delivered shall pay to the master, commander, or other person delivering the same, except the commanders of foreign packets, 2 cents for every such letter or packet.

Act February 20, 1792, section 19.—Letters and packets to be received and conveyed by post, free of postage, under certain restrictions:

President of the United States,
Vice-President of the United States, } All letters or packets to or from.

Senators,
Representatives,
Secretary of the Senate,
Clerk of the House of Representatives, } All letters or packets to or from, not exceeding 2 ounces in weight, during their actual attendance in any session of Congress, and 20 days after such session.

Secretary of the Treasury,
Assistant Secretary of the Treasury,
Comptroller,
Register,
Auditor,
Treasurer,
Secretary of State, } All letters to or from.

Secretary of War, Commissioners for settling accounts between the United States and individual States, Postmaster-General, Assistant Postmaster-General,	All letters to or from.

Provided, No person shall frank or inclose any letter or packet not his own; but public letters or packets, from the Treasury Department, may be franked by the Secretary, Assistant Secretary, Comptroller, Register, Auditor, or Treasurer.

Each person shall deliver to post-office every letter or packet inclosed to him for other persons, that postage may be charged.

Act February 20, 1792, *section* 21.—Printers of newspapers, authorized to send one paper to every other printer of newspaper, in the United States, free of postage, under regulations of the Postmaster-General.

All newspapers conveyed by mail for any distance not more than 100 miles, 1 cent; and over 100 miles, 1½ cents; if any other matter or thing be inclosed, it is subject to letter rates of postage.

Act February 20, 1792, *section* 26.—Postmaster-General to make provision for receipt of letters and packets, to be conveyed beyond the sea, or from one port to another in the United States; and for every letter so received, a postage of 1 cent shall be paid.

Act May 8, 1794.—To take effect June 1, 1794, without limit as to time. Establishes a General Post-Office. Section 9, 10, and 13 of this act re-enacts sections 9, 10, and 13 of act of February 20, 1792.

Section 19 of this act re-enacts section 19 of act of February 20, 1792, except that it omits the Assistant Secretary of the Treasury and commissioners for settling accounts between the United States and individual States, and adds the Commissioner of the Revenue and postmasters; the letters and packets of postmasters not to exceed one-half ounce in weight.

Section 26 of this act re-enacts section 26 of act of February 20, 1792.

Act December 3, 1794.—Confers franking privilege on James White, Delegate to Congress from the Territory of the United States south of the river Ohio.

Act February 25, 1795.—Confers franking privilege on purveyor of public supplies, as to letters to or from.

Act March 3, 1797.—That all letters or packets to George Washington, now President of the United States, after the expiration of his term of office, and during his life, shall be received and conveyed by post, free of postage.

Act June 22, 1798.—Extends the privilege of franking letters and packets to the Secretary of the Navy, under like restrictions and limitations as are provided in act May 8, 1794, section 19.

Act March 2, 1799, *section* 7.—Establishes a General Post-Office at the seat of Government of the United States.

For every letter composed of single sheet of paper conveyed not exceeding 40 miles, 8 cents; over 40 miles and not exceeding 90 miles, 10 cents; over 90 miles and not exceeding 150 miles, 12½ cents; over 150 miles and not exceeding 300 miles, 17 cents; over 300 miles and not exceeding 500 miles, 20 cents; over 500 miles, 25 cents.

Double letter or 2 pieces of paper, double rates.

Triple letter or 3 pieces of paper, triple rates; and for every packet composed of four or more pieces of paper, or other thing, and weighing 1 ounce avoirdupois, quadruple rate, and in same proportion for greater weights: *Provided*, No packet of letters conveyed by the water-mails shall be charged more than quadruple postage, unless containing more than four distinct letters; no package to be received weighing more than three pounds.

Act March 2, 1799, *section* 8.—Every packet or letter brought in the United States, or carried from one port to another in private ship or vessel, 6 cents, if delivered in office where received; if to be conveyed by post, 2 cents added to ordinary postage.

Act March 2, 1799, *section* 11.—Authorizes postmasters, to whom letters may be delivered by masters or commanders of any ship or vessel arriving at any port within the United States, where a post-office is established, except foreign packets, to pay two cents for each letter or packet.

Act March 2, 1799, *section* 13.—Postmasters authorized to pay mail-carriers one cent for each way-letter delivered to them, also mail-carriers authorized to demand and receive 2 cents in addition to the ordinary postage, for every letter delivered by them to persons living between post-offices on their route.

Act March 2, 1799, *section* 17.—Letters and packets to be conveyed free to and from the following:

Postmasters.—Not exceeding ½ ounce in weight.

Senators, Representatives, Secretary of the Senate, Clerk of the House,	Not exceeding 2 ounces in weight, during actual attendance in any session of Congress, and 20 days after such session.

President of the United States, Vice-President of the United States, Secretary of the Treasury, Comptroller of the Treasury, Auditor of the Treasury, Register of the Treasury, Treasurer of the United States, Commissioner of the Revenue, Supervisors of the Revenue, Inspectors of the Revenue, Commissioners, Purveyor, Secretary of War, Accountant of War Office, Secretary of State, Secretary of Navy, Accountant of Navy, Postmaster-General, Assistant Postmaster-General.	All letters and packets.

All may receive their newspapers free of postage: *Provided*, Senators, Representatives, Secretary of Senate, and Clerk of the House shall receive newspapers free during session of Congress, and 20 days after.

Letters or packets from any public officer to be franked by person sending.

All letters and packets to and from George Washington, late President, to be received and conveyed free.

Act March 2, 1799, *section* 19.—Re-enacts section 21 of act February 20, 1792.

Act March 2, 1799, *section* 20.—Fixes postage on newspapers at 1 cent each for not more than one hundred miles, and 1½ cents for any greater distance. Single newspapers from one place to another in the same State shall not exceed 1 cent.

Concealing a letter, or other thing, or any memorandum in writing in a newspaper, subjects each article in packet to a single letter postage.

Magazines and pamphlets, 1 cent a sheet, for not exceeding fifty miles; 1½ cents for over fifty miles, and not exceeding one hundred miles; and 2 cents for any greater distance.

Act March 2, 1799, *section* 25.—Postmaster-General authorized to provide for receipt of letters or packets, to be conveyed by sea to any foreign port or home port. Every letter or packet so received, subject to a postage of 1 cent.

Act January 2, 1800, *section* 1.—Confers franking privilege on William Henry Harrison, Delegate to Congress from Territory northwest of the Ohio River, to send and receive letters free of postage.

Act April 3, 1800.—Confers franking privilege to Martha Washington, to send and receive letters and packages free of postage during her life.

Act December 15, 1800, *section* 1.—Confers franking privilege on Delegate from Territory northwest of the Ohio River, to send and receive letters free of postage.

Act February 25, 1801.—Confers franking privilege on John Adams, President of the United States, after the expiration of his term of office, and during his life, on all letters and packets to him.

Act February 18, 1802.—Confers privilege of franking and receiving letters free of postage to any person admitted, or to be admitted, to take a seat in Congress as a Delegate.

Act May 3, 1802, *section* 5.—Franking privilege extended to the Attorney-General, to send and receive all letters, packets, and newspapers, free of postage.

Act March 26, 1804, *section* 3.—Letters, returns, and other papers on public service, sent by mail to or from Offices of Inspector and Paymaster of the Army, to be received and conveyed free of postage.

Act June 28, 1809.—Letters and packets from Thomas Jefferson, late President of the United States, to be received and conveyed by post, free of postage, during his life.

Act April 30, 1810, *section* 1.—Establishes a General Post-Office at the seat of Government.

Act April 30, 1810, *section* 11.—Rates of postage on letters and packets:

Single sheet of paper less than 40 miles	8 cents.
40 to 90 miles	10 cents.
90 to 150 miles	12½ cents.
150 to 300 miles	17 cents.
300 to 500 miles	20 cents.
over 500 miles	25 cents.

Double letters or two pieces of paper, double rates; triple letters or three pieces of paper, triple rates; every packet composed of four or more pieces of paper or other thing, and weighing one ounce avoirdupois, quadruple rate; and in same proportion for greater weight: *Provided*, No packet of letters, conveyed by the water-mails shall be charged more than quadruple postage, unless containing more than four distinct letters. Weight of packet limited to three pounds.

Act April 30, 1810, *section* 12.—Letters or packets brought into the United States, or carried from one port therein to another, shall be charged 6 cents, if delivered at the post-office where the same shall arrive; and if to be conveyed by post to any other place, with two cents added to the ordinary rates of postage.

Act April 30, 1810, *section* 15.—Postmasters authorized, on the receipt of letters from any ship or vessel arriving at any port within the United States, where a post-office is established, to pay to the master, commander, or other person delivering the same, except the commanders of foreign packets, two cents for every letter or packet.

Act April 30, 1810, *section* 17.—Postmasters authorized to pay mail-carrier one cent for every letter brought into their office; also mail-carrier authorized to demand and receive two cents, in addition to the ordinary postage, for every letter delivered by them to persons living between post-offices on his route.

Act April 30, 1810, *section* 24.—Letters and packets to and from the following officers of the United States to be received and conveyed through the mails free of postage:

Postmasters, not exceeding ½ oz. in weight:

Senators, Members, Delegates, Secretary of the Senate, Clerk of the House,	Limited to two ounces in weight, and during their actual attendance in any session of Congress and twenty days thereafter; excess of weight to be paid for.

President of the United States, Vice-President of the United States. Secretary of State, Secretary of Treasury, Secretary of War, Secretary of the Navy, Attorney-General, Comptroller, Treasurer, Auditor, Register, Supervisor of direct tax of district of S. C., Superintendent of Indian trade, Purveyor, Inspector and Paymaster of the Army, Accountants of War and Navy Departments, Postmaster-General, Assistant Postmasters-General, John Adams, Thomas Jefferson,	All letters and packets.

All may receive their newspapers free of postage.

Senators, Representatives, Secretary of the Senate, and Clerk of the House of Representatives shall receive their newspapers free of postage only during any session of Congress and twenty days thereafter.

Act April 30, 1810, *section* 25.—Secretaries of the Treasury, State, War, Navy, and Postmaster-General authorized to frank letters or packets on official business, prepared in any other public office, in the absence of the principal thereof.

Act April 30, 1810, *section* 26.—Printers of newspapers authorized to exchange one copy free, of newspapers, under regulations of the Postmaster-General.

Act April 30, 1810, *section* 27.—Newspapers by mail, one cent each for not more than one hundred miles; one and one-half cents for any greater distance. Single newspapers, from one place to another in the same State, not to exceed one cent.

Act April 30, 1810, *section* 32.—Postmaster-General authorized to provide for the receipt and transmission of letters and packets beyond sea, or from any port in the United States to any port therein; every letter or packet so received subject to a postage of one cent.

Act April 30, 1810, *section* 34.—Drop or local letters, one cent each.

Act April 30, 1810, *section* 39.—Adjutant-General of the militia of each State and Territory has the right to receive by mail, free of postage, from any major or brigadier general thereof, and to transmit to said generals, any letter or packet, relating solely to the militia of such State or Territory, under certain restrictions.

Act April 18, 1814, *section* 4.—Secretary of State authorized to transmit by mail, free of postage, one copy of documents ordered to be printed by either House of Congress; namely, of communications, with accompanying documents, made by the President to

Congress or either House thereof; of reports made by the Secretary of State, Treasury, War, Navy, Postmaster-General, or commissioners of the sinking-fund, to Congress, or either House thereof, in pursuance of any law or resolution of either House; affirmative reports on subjects of a general nature made to Congress, or either House thereof, by any committee respectively; for each of the judges of the Supreme Court, of the district courts, and of the Territories of the United States, to any post-office within the United States they may respectively designate.

Act December 23, 1814, *section* 2.—From and after February 1, 1815, there shall be added to the rates of postage established by law 50 per centum on the amount of such rates respectively.

Act February 1, 1816.—Repeals so much of act of December 23, 1814, as imposes 50 per centum additional postage.

Act April 9, 1816, *section* 1.—Rates of postage after May 1, 1816:

	Cents.
Every letter composed of a single sheet of paper, less than 30 miles	6
Over 30 miles and not exceeding 80 miles	10
Over 80 miles and not exceeding 150 miles	12½
Over 150 miles and not exceeding 400 miles	18½
Over 400 miles	25

Every double letter or two pieces of paper, double rates.

Every triple letter or three pieces of paper, triple rates.

Every packet containing four or more pieces of paper or one or more other articles, and weighing one ounce avoirdupois, quadruple these rates, and in that proportion for all greater rates. No packet of letters conveyed by water-mails to be charged with more than quadruple postage, unless the same shall contain more than four distinct letters.

Any memorandum written on a newspaper or other printed paper, and transmitted by mail, to be charged with letter-postage.

Act April 9, 1816, *section* 3.—Letters and packets to and from Senators, Members, and Delegates of the House, Secretary of the Senate, and Clerk of the House, to be conveyed free of postage for thirty days previous to each session of Congress and for thirty days after the termination thereof; limited to two ounces in weight; excess to be paid for.

Act March 1, 1817.—Letters and packets to and from James Madison, President of the United States, after the expiration of his term of office and during his life, to be carried by mail free of postage.

Act March 13, 1820.—Letters and packets to and from the President of the Senate *pro tempore*, and Speaker of the House for the time being, to be received and conveyed by mail, free of postage, during the session of Congress, under certain restrictions.

Act March 3, 1825.—An act to reduce into one the several acts establishing and regulating the Post-Office Department.

Section 1 establishes at the seat of government a general post-office, under the direction of the Postmaster-General.

Act March 3, 1825, *section* 5.—Authorizes the Postmaster-General to have mail carried by any steamboat or other vessel which shall be used as a packet in any waters of the United States, on such terms and conditions as shall be considered expedient: *Provided*, That he does not pay more than three cents for each letter, nor more than one-half a cent for each newspaper.

Act March 3, 1825, *section* 6.—Master or manager of any steamboat passing from one port or place to another port or place in the United States, where a post-office is established, to deliver all letters or packets addressed to such port or place, to the postmaster there, for which he shall receive of such postmaster two cents for every letter or packet so delivered, unless the same shall be conveyed under contract with the Postmaster-General.

Act March 3, 1825, *section* 13.—Rates of postage on letters and packets conveyed in the mail of the United States:

For every letter of a single sheet of paper, conveyed not exceeding 30 miles	6 cents.
Over 30 miles and not exceeding 80 miles	10 cents.
Over 80 miles and not exceeding 150 miles	12½ cents.
Over 150 miles and not exceeding 400 miles	18½ cents.
Over 400 miles	25 cents.

Every double letter or two pieces of paper, double these rates; every triple letter or three pieces of paper, triple these rates; every packet of four or more pieces of paper, or one or more other articles, and weighing one ounce avoirdupois, quadruple these rates; and in that proportion for all greater weights: *Provided*, That no packet of letters, conveyed by the water-mails, shall be charged more than quadruple postage, unless the same shall contain more than four distinct letters; weight of packet limited to three pounds.

Unbound journals of legislatures of the several States liable to same postage as pamphlets.

Memorandum written on a newspaper or other printed paper, pamphlet, or magazine, and transmitted by mail, to be charged with letter-postage.

Act March 3, 1825, *section* 15.—Every letter or package brought into the United States, or carried from one point therein to another, in any private ship or vessel, to be charged six cents, if delivered at the post-office where the same shall arrive; and if destined to be conveyed by post to any other place, with two cents added to the ordinary rates of postage.

Act March 3, 1825, *section* 18.—Postmasters authorized to pay to the master or commander of any vessel, except the commanders of foreign packets, arriving at any port in the United States where a post-office is established, two cents for every letter or packet delivered by them to the postmaster.

Act March 3, 1825, *section* 27.—Letters and packets to be conveyed by post, free of postage, to and from the following:

Postmasters limited to ½ ounce in weight.

Members, Senators, Delegates, Secretary of the Senate, Clerk of the House,	Limited to 2 ounces in weight (except documents printed by order of either House of Congress), and during their actual attendance in any session of Congress and sixty days before and after; excess of weight to be paid for.

President of the United States, Vice-President of the United States, Secretary of State, Secretary of War, Secretary of Treasury, Secretary of Navy, Attorney-General, Postmaster-General, Assistant Postmasters-General, Comptrollers of Treasury, Auditors of Treasury, Register, Treasurer, Commissioner General Land-Office, Ex-Presidents and Presidents of United States,	All letters and packets.

All of the above to receive newspapers free of postage: *Provided,* That postmasters shall not receive, free of postage, more than one daily newspaper each, or what is equivalent thereto; nor shall members of the Senate or House, Clerk of the House, or Secretary of the Senate receive newspapers free of postage after their franking privilege shall cease.

Act March 3, 1825, *section* 28.—Secretaries of Treasury, State, War, Navy, and the Postmaster-General may frank letters or packets on official business, prepared in any other public office, in the absence of the principal thereof.

Act March 3, 1825, *section* 29.—Printers of newspapers authorized to exchange one paper, free of postage, under regulations by Postmaster-General.

Act March 3, 1825, *section* 30.—Newspapers, conveyed by mail, one cent for any distance not more than 100 miles; 1½ cents for any greater distance. Single newspapers from one place to another, in the same State, one cent.

Inclosing or concealing a letter or other thing, or any memorandum in writing in a newspaper, pamphlet, or magazine, subjects it to single letter postage for each article of which the package is composed.

When mode of conveyance and size of mail will admit, magazines and pamphlets published periodically may be transported in the mail to subscribers, at 1½ cents a sheet for any distance not exceeding 100 miles, and 2½ cents for any greater distance. And such magazines and pamphlets as are not published periodically, if sent in the mail, shall be charged four cents on each sheet for any distance not exceeding 100 miles, and six cents for any greater distance. (Section 13 of this act defines a sheet to be four folio pages, 8 quarto pages, 16 octavo pages, or 24 duodecimo pages, or pages less than that of a pamphlet size or magazine, whatever be the size of the paper of which it is formed. The surplus pages of any pamphlet or magazine shall also be considered a sheet.)

Act March 3, 1825, *section* 34.—Postmaster-General authorized to make provisions for the receipt of letters and packets, to be conveyed by any vessel beyond sea, or from one port to another in the United States, and the postmaster receiving the same at the port to which such vessel shall be bound shall be entitled to a postage of one cent on each letter or packet received.

Act March 3, 1825, *section* 36.—Drop or local letters delivered at the post-office, one cent each.

Act March 3, 1825, section 40.—The adjutant-general of the militia of each State and Territory authorized to receive by mail, free of postage, from any major-general or brigadier-general thereof, and to transmit to said generals any letter or packet relating solely to the militia of such State or Territory, under certain conditions.

Act March 3, 1825, section 46.—Repeals all acts and parts of acts which have been passed for the establishment and regulation of the General Post-Office.

Act March 2, 1827, section 2.—One cent to be allowed each postmaster for every letter received from any ship or vessel and mailed by him.

Act March 2, 1827, section 4.—Authority to frank and receive letters and packets free of postage extended to the commissioners of the navy board, Adjutant-General, Commissary-General, Inspector-General, Quartermaster-General, Paymaster-General, Secretary of the Senate, Clerk of the House, Superintendent of the Patent Office.

No other person or officer, except those enumerated herein and in the act of March 3, 1825, shall be authorized to frank or receive letters by mail free of postage.

Act March 2, 1827, section 5.—One or more pieces of paper mailed as a letter and weighing one ounce avoirdupois, shall be charged with quadruple postage, and at the same rate should the weight be greater. Packages containing four pieces of paper, quadruple rates.

Every printed pamphlet or magazine, containing more than twenty-four pages on a royal sheet, or any sheet of less dimensions, shall be charged by the sheet; and small pamphlets, printed on a half or quarter sheet of royal, or less size, shall be charged with one-half the amount of postage on a full sheet. Double postage shall be charged, unless there shall be printed or written on one of the outer pages of all pamphlets and magazines the number of sheets they contain.

Act June 30, 1834.—Governors of the several States authorized to transmit by mail, free of postage, all laws and reports bound or unbound, and all records and documents of their respective States, which may be directed by the several legislatures of the States to be transmitted to the executives of other States.

Act July 2, 1836, section 8.—Auditor of the Treasury for the Post-Office Department authorized to frank and receive, free of postage, letters and packets, under regulations provided by law for other officers of the Government. All letters or packets to or from the Chief Engineer, which may relate to the business of his Office, free of postage.

Act July 2, 1836, section 20.—Postmaster General authorized to employ a Third Assistant Postmaster-General, who may receive and send letters free of postage.

Act July 2, 1836, section 36.—No postmaster shall receive, free of postage, or frank any letter or packet composed of or containing anything other than money or paper.

All letters and packets to and from Dolly P. Madison, relict of the late James Madison, shall be received and conveyed by post, free of postage, for and during her life.

Act July 4, 1836, section 1.—Patent-Office established and the Commissioner entitled to receive and send letters and packages by mail, relating to the business of his Office, free of postage.

Act September 9, 1841.—All letters and packets carried by post to Mrs. Harrison, relict of the late William Henry Harrison, to be conveyed free of postage during her life.

Act January 20, 1843, section 3.—Commissioner of Pensions authorized to send and receive letters and packets by mail, free of postage.

Act February 15, 1843, section 1.—Authorizes the chief clerk of the office of Secretary of State to frank all public and official documents sent from that Office.

Act March 3, 1845, section 1.—After July 1, 1845, Members of Congress and Delegates from Territories may receive letters not exceeding two ounces in weight, free of postage, during the recess of Congress, anything to the contrary in this act notwithstanding; and the same franking privilege which is granted by this act to the members of the two Houses of Congress is hereby extended to the Vice-President of the United States.

Postage on letters.—For every single letter in manuscript, or marks and signs, by mail, under three hundred miles, five cents; over three hundred miles, ten cents; double letter, double rates; treble letter, treble rates; quadruple letter, quadruple rates; and every letter or parcel not exceeding one-half ounce in weight shall be deemed a single letter, and every additional weight of one-half ounce or less shall be charged with an additional single postage. Drop or local letters shall be charged a postage rate of two cents each.

Act March 3, 1845, section 2.—Postage on newspapers.—Newspapers of not more than 1,900 square inches in size may be transmitted through the mails by the editors or publishers thereof to subscribers or other persons, within thirty miles of the city, town, or place in which the paper is printed, free of postage. Newspapers of less size, conveyed by mail beyond thirty miles from the place at which they are printed, shall be subject to the rates of postage chargeable under the thirtieth section, act March 3, 1825. Newspapers of greater size than 1,900 square inches subject to same rates of postage as are prescribed by this act on magazines and pamphlets.

Act March 3, 1845, section 3.—Printed or lithograph circulars, hand-bills, or advertisements, printed or lithographed on quarto-post or single-cap paper, or paper not larger than single-cap paper, unsealed, shall be charged with postage at the rate of two cents for each sheet, without regard to distance. Pamphlets, magazines, periodicals, and all other printed or other matter (except newspapers) unconnected with any writing, shall be charged with postage at the rate of two and a half cents for each copy sent, not exceeding one ounce in weight, and one cent additional for each additional ounce, without regard to distance: and any fractional excess of not less than one-half ounce above one or more ounces shall be charged for as if said excess amounted to a full ounce.

Act March 3, 1845, *section* 5.—Repeals all acts and parts of acts conferring upon any person the right or privilege to receive and transmit through the mail, free of postage, letters, packets, newspapers, periodicals, or other matter.

Act March 3, 1845, *section* 6.—All officers of the Government of the United States, heretofore having the franking privilege, shall be allowed and paid quarterly all postage on official letters, packages, or other matter received by mail.

Postage upon official letters, packages, or other matter received by the three Assistant Postmasters-General shall be remitted, and they shall be authorized to transmit by mail, free of postage, official letters, packages, or other matter under certain regulations.

Deputy postmasters allowed all postage which they may have paid or have had charged to them for official letters, packages, or other matters, and they are authorized to send by mail, free of postage, official letters and packets, under certain regulations.

Act March 3, 1845, *section* 7.—Continues in force act of June 30, 1834, authorizing the governors of the several States to transmit by mail certain books and documents, and authorizes Members and Delegates, Secretary of the Senate and Clerk of the House, to transmit by mail, free of postage, any documents printed by order of either House of Congress.

Act March 3, 1845, *section* 8.—Senators, Members, Delegates, Secretary of Senate, and Clerk of the House authorized, during each session of Congress, and for thirty days before and after every session of Congress, to send and receive through the mail, free of postage, any letter, newspaper, or packet, not exceeding two ounces in weight. Postage-charge for excess of weight on official letters, packages, &c., received during any session of Congress, to be paid out of the contingent fund of the House of which the person may be a member. Authorized to frank written letters from themselves during the whole year, &c.

Act March 3, 1845, *section* 13.—Transmission of letters by steamboats, under act of March 3, 1825, section 6, not prohibited: *Provided*, That the requirements of said sixth section shall be strictly complied with by the delivery of all letters so conveyed, not relating to the cargo or some part thereof, to the postmaster or agent of the Post-Office Department, at the port to which said letters may be delivered, and the postmaster or agent shall collect upon all letters or other mailable matter so delivered to him, except newspapers, pamphlets, magazines, and periodicals, the same rates of postage as would have been charged upon said letters had they been transmitted by mail from the port at which they were placed on board the steamboat from which they were received; weight of packet limited to three pounds.

Act March 3, 1845, *section* 15.—*Mailable matter defined.*—Letters, newspapers, magazines, and pamphlets periodically published or published in regular series, or in successive numbers, under the same title, though at irregular intervals, and all other written or printed matter, whereof each copy or number shall not exceed eight ounces in weight, except bank-notes sent in packages or bundles, without written letters accompanying them. Bound books not to be included within the meaning of these terms.

Act March 3, 1845, *section* 16.—*Newspapers defined.*—Any printed publication issued in numbers, consisting of not more than two sheets and published at short stated intervals of not more than one month, conveying intelligence of passing events, and *bona-fide* extras and supplements of any such publications.

Free exchange of newspapers between publishers as provided for by act March 3, 1825, section 29, not prohibited.

Act March 3, 1845, *section* 23.—Franking privilege conferred by former acts on the President of the United States when in office, and to all Ex-Presidents, and to the widows of the former Presidents, Madison and Harrison, continued in force.

Joint resolution of March 3, 1845.—Provides that act of March 3, 1845, shall go into effect on and after July 1, 1845.

Act May 29, 1846, *section* 3.—Same rates of postage to be charged in Texas as in other States of the United States.

Act August 6, 1846, *section* 18.—On and after January 1, 1847, postage shall be paid in gold and silver only, or in Treasury notes of the United States.

Act March 1, 1847, *section* 3.—Members and Delegates in Congress, Vice-President of the United States, Secretary of the Senate, and Clerk of the House to have power to send and receive public documents during their term of office and up to the first Monday of December following the expiration of their term of office.

Act March 1, 1847, *section* 4.—Secretary of the Senate and Clerk of the House to receive and send all letters and packages free of postage, during their term of office; limited to two ounces.

Act March 1, 1847, *section* 5.—Members of Congress to receive and send all letters and packages free of postage, up to the first Monday in December following the expiration of their term of office.

Act March 2, 1847, *section* 1.—Postmasters, whose compensation for the last preceding year did not exceed $200, to send all letters written by himself and receive all addressed to himself, on his private business, free of postage; limited to one-half ounce in weight.

Act March 3, 1847, *section* 4.—Letters, newspapers, and packets, not exceeding one ounce in weight, directed to any officer, musician, or private of the Army of the United States in Mexico, or at any place on the frontier of the United States bordering on Mexico, shall be conveyed in the mail free of postage.

Act March 3, 1847, *section* 5.—Continues in force section 4 of this Act during the present war and three months thereafter.

Act March 3, 1847, *section* 7.—Postmaster-General authorized to establish a post-office at Astoria, and other places on the Pacific:

	Cents.
All letters conveyed to or from Chagres	20
All letters conveyed to or from Havana	12½
All letters conveyed to or from Panama	30
All letters conveyed to or from Astoria	40
All letters conveyed to or from any other place on the Pacific	40

Act March 3, 1847, *section* 12.—Repeals so much of section 6 of act March 3, 1845, as requires postage to be paid on free matter from the contingent fund of the two Houses of Congress and the other Departments of the Government, and in lieu thereof provides for an annual appropriation of two hundred thousand dollars, to be paid to the Post-Office Department.

Act March 3, 1847, *section* 13.—Newspapers by mail (except exchanges between publishers), except those franked by those enjoying the franking privilege, and newspapers not sent from the office of publication, and handbills or circulars printed or lithographed, not exceeding one sheet, shall be subject to three cents prepaid postage each. Postmaster-General authorized to pay not exceeding two cents each for all letters or packets conveyed in any vessel, not employed in carrying the mail from one place to another in the United States, under such regulations as he may provide.

Publications, or books published, procured, or purchased by either House of Congress, shall be considered public documents and entitled to be franked as such.

Act March 3, 1847, *section* 14.—Repeals so much of act of March 3, 1845, and of all other acts relating to the Post-Office Department as is inconsistent with this act.

Act March 9, 1848.—Letters and packets by mail to and from Louisa Catherine Adams, widow of the late John Quincy Adams, to be free of postage during her life.

Act May 27, 1848, *section* 4.—Commissioner of Patents authorized to send by mail free of postage the annual reports of the Patent Office.

Act June 27, 1848, *section* 1.—Postmaster-General authorized to charge and collect upon all letters and other mailable matter, carried in foreign packets, the same rate of postage which the governments, to which such foreign packets belong, impose upon letters, &c., carried in American packets.

Act June 27, 1848, *section* 2.—All letters and other mailable matter conveyed by any foreign ship to or from any port of the United States, to be subject to postage charged as in above section, except letters relating to the vessel or cargo.

Act August 14, 1848, *section* 3.—Postmaster-General authorized to establish a post-office at San Diego, Monterey, San Francisco, and other places on the Pacific, in California, and all letters conveyed to or from any of the above places on the Pacific, from or to any place on the Atlantic, to be charged forty cents postage; all letters conveyed from one to any other of said places on the Pacific, twelve and a half cents.

Act March 3, 1849, *section* 1.—Rates of letters transported under the postal treaty with Great Britain:

Letters not exceeding one-half ounce, one rate of postage.

Letters exceeding one-half ounce avoirdupois, and not exceeding one ounce, two rates of postage.

Letters exceeding one ounce avoirdupois, and not exceeding two ounces, four rates of postage.

Letters exceeding two ounces avoirdupois, and not exceeding three ounces, six rates of postage.

Letters exceeding three ounces avoirdupois, and not exceeding four ounces, eight rates of postage.

And in like progression for each additional ounce or fraction of an ounce. Newspapers not sent from the office of publication to be charged with the same rates of postage as other papers; to be prepaid.

Act January 10, 1850.—Franking privilege granted Sarah Polk, relict of the late James K. Polk, during her life, to cover all letters and packages to and from.

Act May 23, 1850, *section* 17.—Marshals and their assistants, authorized to transmit papers and documents relating to the census through the post-office free.

Act March 23, 1850, *section* 19.—Secretary of the Interior required to appoint a clerk to superintend the census, who shall have the privilege of franking and receiving, free of charge, all official documents and letters connected therewith.

Act July 18, 1850.—Franking privilege granted to Margaret Smith Taylor, relict of Zachary Taylor, same as granted to widows of deceased Presidents.

Act September 27, 1850.—Third section act of August 14, 1848, extended to Territories of Utah and New Mexico, and Postmaster-General authorized to establish such rates of postage in said Territories as may to him seem proper, not to exceed those authorized in said act.

Act March 3, 1851, *section* 1.—*Rates of postage on letters*.—From and after June 30, 1851, in lieu of rates of postage now fixed by law, there shall be charged the following rates: Every single letter, in writing, marks, or signs, by mail, not exceeding three thousand miles, prepaid postage, 3 cents; not prepaid, 5 cents; for any greater distance, double these rates.

Every single letter or paper conveyed wholly or in part by sea, and to or from a foreign country over two thousand five hundred miles, 20 cents; under two thousand five hundred miles, 10 cents (excepting rates fixed by postal treaty): double letter, double rates; triple letter, triple rates; and every letter or parcel, not exceeding ½ ounce in weight, shall be deemed a single letter, and every additional weight of ½ ounce or less shall be charged with an additional rate. Drop or local letters, 1 cent each. Letters uncalled for and advertised, to be charged 1 cent in addition to the regular postage.

Act March 3, 1851, *section* 2.—Newspapers not exceeding 3 ounces in weight sent from the office of publication to *bona-fide* subscribers shall be charged with postage as follows:

Weekly newspapers free, within the county where published, and for not exceeding fifty miles out of the county where published, 5 cents per quarter; exceeding 50 miles, and not exceeding 300 miles, 10 cents per quarter; exceeding 300 miles, and not exceeding 1,000 miles, 15 cents per quarter; exceeding 1,000 miles, and not exceeding 2,000 miles, 20 cents per quarter; exceeding 2,000 miles, and not exceeding 4,000 miles, 25 cents per quarter; exceeding 4,000 miles, 30 cents per quarter.

Newspapers published monthly, sent to *bona-fide* subscribers, one-quarter of the foregoing rates; published semi-monthly, one-half of the foregoing rates; published semi-weekly, double the foregoing rates; published tri-weekly, treble the foregoing rates; and oftener than tri-weekly, five times the foregoing rates; on other papers, unsealed circulars, handbills, engravings, pamphlets, periodicals, magazines, books, and all other printed matter, unconnected with written matter, of not more than one ounce in weight, and not exceeding 500 miles, one cent: and for each additional ounce or fraction thereof, one cent; exceeding 500 miles, and not exceeding 1,500 miles, double these rates; exceeding 1,500 miles, and not exceeding 2,500 miles, treble these rates; exceeding 2,500 miles, and not exceeding 3,500 miles, four times these rates; exceeding 3,500 miles, five times these rates.

Subscribers to periodicals required to pay one-quarter's postage in advance; postage one-half the foregoing rates.

Bound books and parcels of printed matter, not over thirty ounces, made mailable matter.

Postage on printed matter, other than newspapers, and periodicals published at intervals not exceeding three months and sent from office of publication to *bona-fide* subscribers, to be prepaid.

When printed matter, on which postage is required by this section to be prepaid, shall be sent without prepayment, the same shall be charged with double the prepaid rate.

Nothing in this act shall subject to postage any matter exempted from postage by existing law.

Publishers of pamphlets, periodicals, magazines, and newspapers, which shall not exceed sixteen ounces in weight, allowed to interchange their publications free, confined to a single copy of each publication. Publishers allowed to inclose in their publications bills for subscription without additional postage. Newspapers not containing more than three hundred square inches, may be transmitted to *bona-fide* subscribers at one-fourth the rates fixed by this act.

Act March 3, 1851, *section* 8.—Provides for the annual appropriation of $500,000 to the Post-Office Department for mail-service for the two Houses of Congress, and other Departments, and officers of the government, in the transportation of free matter.

Act August 30, 1852, *section* 1.—*Rates of postage on printed matter*.—From and after September 30, 1852, postage on all printed matter passing by mail, instead of the rates now charged, shall be as follows: Each newspaper, periodical, unsealed circular, or other article of printed matter, not exceeding three ounces in weight, to any part of the United States, one cent; and for every additional ounce or fraction thereof, one cent additional.

Postage on any newspapers or periodicals paid quarterly or yearly in advance at the office of delivery, or at the office of mailing, one-half of said rates only shall be charged.

Newspapers and periodicals not weighing over 1½ ounces, when circulated in the State where published, one-half the rates before mentioned.

Small newspapers and periodicals, published monthly or oftener, and pamphlets of not more than sixteen octavo pages, sent in single packages, weighing at least eight ounces, to one address, and prepaid by postage-stamps affixed, only one-half cent for each ounce or fraction of an ounce.

Postage on all transient matter shall be prepaid or charged double the rates first above mentioned.

Act August 30, 1852, *section* 2.—*Postage on books.*—Books, bound or unbound, not weighing more than four pounds, will be deemed mailable matter and subject to postage at one cent an ounce for all distances under 3,000 miles; two cents for all distances over 3,000 miles; to which fifty per centum shall be added unless prepaid.

Publishers of newspapers and periodicals may exchange, free of postage, one copy of each publication, and may send to actual subscribers, in their publications, bills and receipts for the same free. Publishers of weekly newspapers may send to each actual subscriber within the county where their papers are printed and published one copy free of postage, under certain conditions.

Act August 30, 1852, *section* 3.—Prescribes certain conditions, which, if not complied with, subject printed matter to letter-postage.

Matter sent by mail from one part of the United States to another, the postage of which is not fixed by this act, shall, unless entitled to be sent free, be charged with letter-postage.

Act August 30, 1852, *section* 5.—Repeals so much of the second section of act of March, 3, 1851, as relates to the postage or free circulation of newspapers, periodicals, and other printed matter, and all other provisions of law inconsistent with this act.

Act August 30, 1852, *section* 8.—Postmaster-General authorized to provide stamped letter envelopes. Letters when inclosed in such envelopes (with stamps thereon equal in amount to the postage to which such letters would be liable if sent by mail) may be sent and delivered otherwise than by mail under certain conditions.

Act February 2, 1854.—The Superintendent of the Coast Survey and the assistant in charge of the Office of the Coast Survey, authorized to transmit free of postage, by the mails, all letters and documents in relation to their public duties.

Act March 3, 1855, *section* 1.—In lieu of the rates of postage now fixed by law, there shall be charged the following rates:

For every single letter, in manuscript or paper of any kind, in writing, marks, or signs, conveyed in the mail between places in the United States, not exceeding three thousand miles, three cents; and for any greater distance, ten cents; for a double letter, double rates; treble letter, treble rates; quadruple letter, quadruple rates; every letter or parcel not exceeding one-half ounce in weight shall be deemed a single letter, and every additional weight of one-half ounce or less shall be charged an additional rate; the foregoing rates to be prepaid on domestic letters, except on letters and packages to officers of the government on official business, and except on letters to or from a foreign country.

Postage on drop or local letters, one cent each.

Nothing in this act to alter the laws in relation to the franking privilege.

Act March 3, 1855, *section* 4.—Franking privilege of Vice-Presidents continued to those who have held or shall hold that office, during life.

Act March 3, 1855, *section* 5.—Books, maps, charts, or other publications, entered by copyright, and which, under act of August 10, 1846, are required to be deposited in the Library of Congress and in the Smithsonian Institution, may be sent by mail, free of postage, under regulations to be prescribed by the Postmaster-General.

Act January 2, 1857.—Repeals the provision in the act of August 30, 1852, permitting transient printed matter to be sent through the mail, without prepayment of postage; the postage on all such matter shall be paid by stamps or otherwise, as the Postmaster-General may direct.

Act April 3, 1860, *section* 1.—Modifies second clause, section 3, of act August 30, 1852, establishing the rates of postage on printed matter, so as to allow only the name, the date when the subscription expires, and the address of the person to whom sent.

Act April 3, 1860, *section* 2.—Postage on drop or local letters delivered by carriers, one cent each.

Act February 27, 1861, *section* 8.—That upon all letters returned from the dead-letter office there shall be paid the usual rate of postage; to be paid on delivery.

Act February 27, 1861, *section* 9.—That upon every letter or packet brought into the United States, or carried from one port therein to another, in any private ship or vessel, five cents if delivered at the post-office where the same shall arrive, and if destined to be conveyed by post, two cents shall be added to the ordinary postage: *Provided*, That upon all letters or packets conveyed in whole or in part by steamers over any route upon which the mail is regularly conveyed in vessels under contract with the Post-Office Department, the same charge shall be levied, with the addition of two cents a letter or packet on the domestic rates.

Act February 27, 1861, *section* 10.—Repeals all acts or parts of acts inconsistent with section 9 of this act.

Act February 27, 1861, *section* 12.—That maps, engravings, lithographs, or photographic prints, on rollers or in paper covers, books, bound or unbound, phonographic paper, and letter envelopes, shall be deemed mailable matter, and charged with postage by weight, not to exceed four pounds, at the rate of one cent an ounce or fraction of an ounce, to any place in the United States under 1,500 miles; two cents an ounce or fraction of an ounce over 1,500 miles, to be prepaid by postage-stamps.

Act February 27, 1861, *section* 13.—That cards, blank or printed, blanks in packages weighing at least eight ounces, and seeds or cuttings in packages not exceeding eight ounces, shall also be deemed mailable matter, and charged with postage at the rate of one cent an ounce, or fraction thereof, to any place in the United States under 1,500 miles, and two cents an ounce, or fraction thereof, over 1,500 miles, to be prepaid by postage-stamps.

Act February 27, 1861, *section* 14.—Modifies the act of March 3, 1855, so as to require the ten-cent rate of postage to be prepaid on letters conveyed in the mail from any point in the United States east of the Rocky Mountains to any State or Territory on the Pacific, and *vice versa*.

Drop-letters shall be prepaid by postage stamps.

Act February 27, 1861, *section* 16.—The postage over the overland route, between any State or Territory east of the Rocky Mountains to any State or Territory on the Pacific, on each newspaper, periodical, unsealed circular, or other article of printed matter not exceeding three ounces in weight, shall be one cent; and every additional ounce, or fraction thereof, one cent additional.

Act February 27, 1861, *section* 17.—Rate of letter-postage between any State or Territory east of the Rocky Mountains and any State or Territory on the Pacific, ten cents for every ½ ounce.

Act March 2, 1861, *section* 9.—Contractors on overland routes to San Francisco required to run a pony-express during the continuance of their contract or until the completion of the overland-telegraph, at certain times, carrying for the Government free of charge five pounds of mail-matter, with the liberty of charging the public for transportation of letters by said express, not exceeding one dollar for ½ ounce; to commence before the 25th day of March, 1862, and expire July 1, 1864.

Act July 22, 1861, *section* 11.—Letters written by soldiers in the service of the United States may be transmitted by mail without prepayment of postage, under regulations of the Post-Office Department; postage to be paid by the party receiving.

Act July 24, 1861.—Prepaid letters to soldiers in the service of the United States, and directed to a point where they have been stationed, may be forwarded without further charge.

Act January 21, 1862, *section* 1.—Postmaster-General authorized to return all dead-letters to writers, except those containing circulars and other worthless matter. Valuable letters to be charged treble, and all others double the ordinary rates of postage, to be collected from the writers.

Provisions of act of July 2, 1861, section 11, extended to sailors and marines in the service of the United States.

Act April 16, 1862, *section* 1.—Postmaster-General authorized to establish branch post-offices in cities, and to charge one cent in addition to the regular postage for every letter deposited in them, to be forwarded by mail, to be prepaid by stamps; and one cent for every letter delivered at such branch office, to be paid on delivery.

Act May 15, 1862, *section* 1.—Establishes the Department of Agriculture.

Act May 15, 1862, *section* 2.—Provides for the appointment of a Commissioner of Agriculture, and confers franking privileges on said Commissioner to send and receive by mail, free of postage, all communications and other matter pertaining to the business of his Department; weight limited to thirty-two ounces.

Act July 1, 1862, *section* 1.—Creates the Office of Commissioner of Internal Revenue, and confers on the Commissioner the privilege of franking all letters and documents pertaining to the duties of his Office, and of receiving free all such letters and documents.

Act July 5, 1862, *section* 6.—Chiefs of the bureaus of the Navy Department authorized to frank all communications from their respective bureaus, and all communications to their bureaus on the business thereof shall be free of postage.

Act March 3, 1863, *section* 16.—Postmasters of any office where letter-carriers are employed authorized to contract with publishers of newspapers, periodicals, and circulars, for delivery by carrier of any such publications not received by mail, at rates and terms to be agreed upon.

Contracts have no force until approved by the Postmaster-General.

Postmaster-General authorized to provide for delivery by carrier of small packets, other than letters or papers, and not exceeding the maximum weight of mailable packages; such packages to be prepaid by postage-stamps at the rate of two cents for each four ounces or fraction thereof.

Act March 3, 1863, *section* 16.—Limits weight to four ounces, except books published or circulated by order of Congress.

Act March 3, 1863, *section* 19.—Divides mailable matter into three classes. First class, letters; second class, regular printed matter; third class, miscellaneous matter.

Act March 3, 1863, *section* 20.—First-class embraces all correspondence wholly or partly in writing, except that mentioned in the third class.

Second class embraces all mailable matter exclusively in print and regularly issued at stated periods, without addition by writing, mark, or sign.

Third class embraces all other matter which is or may hereafter be by law declared mailable.

Act March 3, 1863, *section* 21.—Fixes the maximum standard weight for the single rate of letter-postage at one-half ounce avoirdupois.

Act March 3, 1863, *section* 22.—Fixes the rate of postage on domestic letters not exceeding one-half ounce in weight at three cents, and three cents additional for each additional half-ounce or fraction thereof, to be prepaid by postage-stamps affixed.

Act March 3, 1863, *section* 23.—Fixes the rate of postage on drop-letters not exceeding one-half ounce in weight at two cents, and two cents added for each additional half-ounce or fraction thereof, to be prepaid by postage-stamps affixed.

Act March 3, 1863, *section* 24.—Mailable matter wholly or partly in writing, or so marked as to convey further information than is conveyed by the original print in case of printed matter, or sent in violation of law or regulations touching the inclosure of matter which may be sent at less than letter-rates, and all matter on which no different rate is provided by law, subject to letter-postage: *Provided*, That book-manuscript and corrected proof, passing between author and publisher, may pass at the rate of printed matter: *And Provided*, That the publishers of newspapers and periodicals may print or write upon their publications sent to subscribers the address and the date when the subscription expires, and may inclose receipt for payment and bills for subscription.

Act March 3, 1863, *section* 25.—All matter not enumerated as mailable, and to which no specific rates of postage are assigned, subject to letter-postage.

Act March 3, 1863, *section* 26.—Double rates of postage to be collected on delivery on any matter on which postage is required to be prepaid at the mailing-office: *Provided*, Such matter reaches its destination without such prepayment.

Act March 3, 1863, *section* 27.—Postmaster-General authorized to provide for transmitting unpaid and duly-certified letters of soldiers, sailors, and marines, and all other letters which, from accident, appear to have been deposited without prepayment of postage; but in all cases of letters not prepaid, except certified soldiers', and naval letters, the same shall be charged with double rates of postage, to be collected on delivery.

Act March 3, 1863, *section* 29.—Postage on return dead letters, not registered as valuable, three cents for the single rate; registered as valuable, double rates.

Act March 3, 1863, *section* 30.—Letters may be forwarded from office of destination to any other office, with additional charge of postage therefor.

Act March 3, 1863, *section* 31.—Postmaster-General authorized to pay two cents each for all letters conveyed in any vessel, not employed in carrying the mail from one place to another in the United States, or from any foreign port to any port within the United States and deposited in the post-office at the port of arrival. If for delivery within the United States, double rates of postage.

Act March 3, 1863, *section* 33.—Fixes the maximum standard rate for the single rate of postage on printed matter, and also on miscellaneous matter, at four ounces avoirdupois, subject to the exception in the next section.

Act March 3, 1863, *section* 34.—The rate of postage on transient matter of the second class, and on miscellaneous matter of the third class (except circulars and books), shall be two cents for each four ounces or fractions thereof on one package to one address, to be prepaid by stamps affixed; double these rates for books. Unsealed circulars, not exceeding three in number, two cents, adding one rate for three additional circulars or less number to one address.

Act March 3, 1863, *section* 35.—Postage on matter of the second class, issued once a week or more frequently, from a known office of publication, and sent to regular subscribers, shall be as follows: For newspapers and other periodical publications, not exceeding four ounces, and passing through the mails or post-offices of the United States, the rate for each quarter shall be, for publications issued once a week, 5 cents; twice a week, 10 cents; three times a week, 15 cents; six times a week, 30 cents; seven times a week, 35 cents; and in that proportion, adding one rate for each issue more frequent than once a week. For weight exceeding four ounces and not exceeding eight ounces, at additional rate, and an additional rate for each additional four ounces or fraction thereof; postage to be prepaid for not less than one quarter nor more than one year, at either the office of mailing or delivery, at the option of the subscriber.

Weekly newspapers, to each subscriber within the county where the same are printed and published, one copy free of postage.

Act March 3, 1863, *section* 36.—Postage on mailable matter of the second class, issued less frequently than once a week, issued from a known office of publication, and sent to subscribers, shall be as follows: Upon newspapers, magazines, and other periodical publications, not exceeding four ounces, passing through the mails or post-offices of the United States, the rate for each such paper or periodical shall be one cent, and an additional rate of one cent for each additional four ounces or fraction thereof; *Provided*, That the Postmaster-General may provide for the transportation of *small* newspapers in packages, at the same rate by weight, when sent to one address; postage must be prepaid at office of mailing or delivery, at option of subscriber, for not less than one quarter nor more than one year.

Act March 3, 1863, *section* 37.—Publishers may inclose in their publications to subscribers bills for subscription, and may write or print on their publications or their wrappers name and address of subscribers and the date when subscription expires; but any other inclosure, or addition in writing or in print, shall subject the same to letter-postage.

Act March 3, 1863, *section* 39.—Postmaster-General authorized to prescribe the manner of wrapping all matter not charged with letter-postage nor lawfully franked; if not so wrapped and secured, the same shall be subject to letter-postage.

Act March 3, 1863, *section* 42.—Confers the franking privilege upon and limits it to the following persons:

President of the United States.

Vice-President of the United States.

The chiefs of the several Executive Departments.

The heads of Bureaus or chief clerks of Executive Departments, to be used only for official communications.

Senators, Representatives, and Delegates in Congress, Secretary of the Senate, and Clerk of the House; to cover correspondence to and from them, and all printed matter issued by authority of Congress, and all speeches, proceedings, and debates in Congress, and all printed matter sent to them; to commence with the term for which they are elected, and to expire on the first Monday in December following the expiration of such term.

All official communications to any of the Executive Departments, by an officer responsible to that Department, the envelope to be marked "official," with the signature of the officer thereon.

Postmasters, for their official communications to other postmasters, the envelope to be marked "official," with the signature of the postmaster thereon.

Petitions to either House of Congress, free.

The franking privilege granted by this act, limited to four ounces, except petitions to Congress, congressional or executive documents, and publications or books published, procured, or purchased by order of either House of Congress, or joint resolution of both Houses, which shall be considered as public documents, and entitled to be franked as such; and except, also, seeds, cuttings, roots, and scions, the weight of packages to be fixed by regulations of the Postmaster-General.

Act March 3, 1863, *section* 43.—Publishers of periodicals, magazines, and newspapers allowed to exchange their publications free of postage: confined to a single copy, and not to exceed sixteen ounces in weight.

This act to take effect June 30, 1863.

Act March 3, 1863, *section* 45.—Repeals all acts and parts of acts inconsistent with the provisions of this act.

Act January 22, 1864.—Clothing of wool, cotton, or linen, in packages not exceeding two pounds each, addressed to any non-commissioned officer or private in the Army, may be transmitted by mail at the rate of eight cents for every four ounces or fraction thereof, under regulations of the Postmaster-General; postage to be prepaid.

Act March 16, 1864.—The franking privilege of the President and Vice-President shall extend to and cover all mail-matter sent from or directed to either of them.

Act March 25, 1864, *section* 4.—Mailable matter conveyed by mail westward of the western boundary of Kansas, and eastward of the eastern boundary of California, subject to prepaid letter-rates, except newspapers sent from a known office of publication to subscribers, not exceeding one copy to each, and franked matter to and from the intermediate points between the boundaries named, which shall be at the usual rate.

Act June 1, 1864.—Official communications to heads of Departments or heads of Bureaus or chief clerks or one duly authorized by the Postmaster-General to frank official matter, shall be received and conveyed by mail free of postage, without being indorsed, "official business," or with the name of the writer.

Act June 30, 1864, *section* 1.—The franking privilege to the Commissioner of Internal Revenue, extended to letters and documents pertaining to the duties of his Office and to receiving free of postage all such letters and documents.

Act June 30, 1864, *section* 3.—Confers on the Deputy Commissioner of Internal Revenue the privilege of franking all letters and documents pertaining to the Office of Internal Revenue.

Act July 1, 1864, *section* 8.—The rates of postage on letters and other mailable matter addressed to or received from foreign countries and carried by vessels regularly employed in transportation of the mails, shall be as follows: Ten cents for one-half ounce or under, on letters; two cents on each newspaper, and the established domestic rates on pamphlets, periodicals, and other articles of printed matter, to be prepaid on matter sent, and collected on matter received; subject to rates established or to be established by international postal convention.

Act January 20, 1865.—Amends section 4 of act March 25, 1864, so as to insert in the proviso in said section after the word "newspapers," the words "periodicals, magazines, and exchanges."

Act March 3, 1865, *section* 20.—Privilege of franking letters and documents pertaining to the duties of the Office of Internal Revenue and of receiving free of postage all such letters and documents, is extended to the Commissioner of that Office.

Act March 3, 1865, *section* 15.—Fixes the prepaid postage on drop letters, at all offices except free delivery, at one cent.

Act February 10, 1866.—Confers franking privilege on Mary Lincoln, widow of the late Abraham Lincoln, to cover all letters and packets by mail, to and from.

Act June 12, 1866, *section* 1.—Provides for the forwarding of prepaid and free letters at the request of the party addressed, from one post-office to another without additional postage and the return of dead-letters to the writers free of postage.

Act June 12, 1866, *section* 2.—Request letters to be returned to the writers without additional postage.

Act July 13, 1866, *section* 65.—That all official communications made by assessors to collectors, assessors to assessors, collectors to collectors, collectors to assessors, assessors to assistant assessors, assistant assessors to assessors, collectors to their deputies or deputy collectors to collectors, may be officially franked by the writers thereof and transmitted by mail free of postage.

Act July 13, 1866, *section* 66.—Authorizes the Secretary of the Treasury to appoint a Special Commissioner of the Revenue; and all letters and documents to and from said Commissioner, relating to the duties and business of his Office, shall be transmitted by mail free of postage.

Act July 28, 1866, *section* 13.—Establishes the Bureau of Statistics, and authorizes the Secretary of the Treasury to appoint a Director to superintend the business of said Bureau, and provides for the transmission by mail, free of postage, of all letters and documents to and from him, relating to the business of his Office.

Act March 2, 1868.—The adjutants-general of the States and Territories authorized to transmit by mail, free of postage, any medals, certificates of thanks, or other testimonials awarded, or that may be awarded, by the legislatures of said States and Territories, to the soldiers thereof, under regulations to be prescribed by the Postmaster-General.

Act March 9, 1868, *section* 3.—Letters and documents to and from the Congressional Printer, relating to the business of his Office, shall be transmitted by mail, free of postage, under regulations to be prescribed by the Postmaster-General.

Act June 25, 1868.—That the operations of section 4, act of March 25, 1864, shall cease on and after September 30, 1868.

Act July 27, 1868, *section* 1.—Prepaid letters, having the name and address of the writer in writing, or in print on the outside, after remaining uncalled for at the post office to which directed, thirty days, or the time the writer may direct, shall be returned to the writer without additional postage.

Act July 27, 1868, *section* 3.—Weekly newspapers, sent to subscribers in the county where printed and published, to be delivered free of postage, when deposited in the office nearest the office of publication; but they shall not be distributed by letter-carriers unless postage is prepaid thereon at the rate of five cents per quarter, for not less than one quarter nor more than one year, at the office of mailing or delivery, at the option of the subscriber.

Act March 1, 1869.—Requires the franking privilege to be exercised, by persons entitled to it, by the written autograph signature upon the matter franked; letters or other mail-matter not thus franked, to be charged with postage.

Act July 8, 1870, *section* 8.—Provides that the Commissioner of Patents may send and receive by mail, free of postage, letters, printed matter, and packages, relating to the business of his Office, including Patent-Office Reports.

Act July 8, 1870, *section* 95.—Any copyright book or other art [illegible] Librarian of Congress, by mail, free of postage: *Provided*, The [illegible] matter are plainly written or printed on the outside [illegible]

Act June 1, 1872, *section* 4.—Repeals section 12, act March 3, 1847, and section 8, act March 3, 1851, so far as said sections provide for specific permanent appropriations for carrying free matter in the mails for the several Departments and Members of Congress; hereafter payment for carrying such matter shall be made out of the annual appropriations.

Act June 8, 1872, *section* 99.—The rate of postage on newspapers (excepting weeklies), periodicals not exceeding two ounces in weight, and circulars when deposited in a letter-carrier office for delivery by the office or its carriers, shall be uniform at 1 cent each; but periodicals weighing more than two ounces shall be subject to a postage of 2 cents each: these rates to be prepaid by stamps.

Act June 8, 1872, *section* 127.—Letters upon the official business of the Post-Office Department may be registered free of charge and pass by mail free of charge.

Act June 8, 1872, *section* 130.—Divides mailable matter into three classes: First class, letters; second class, regular printed matter; third class, miscellaneous matter.

Act June 8, 1872, *section* 131.—Mailable matter of the first class shall embrace all correspondence wholly or partly in writing, except book manuscript and corrected proofs passing between authors and publishers.

Act June 8, 1872, *section* 132.—Second class, to embrace all matter exclusively in print and regularly issued at stated periods from a known office of publication, without addition by writing, mark, or sign.

Act June 8, 1872, *section* 133.—Third class, to embrace all other mailable matter.

Matter of this class, except books, and other printed matter, book-manuscripts, proof-sheets, and corrected proof-sheets, shall not exceed twelve ounces in weight. Samples of metals, ores, and mineralogical specimens, limited to twelve ounces.

Act June 8, 1872, *section* 134.—Limits weight of packages to four pounds, except books published or circulated by order of Congress.

Act June 8, 1872, *section* 136.—Matter not charged with letter postage, nor lawfully franked, subject to letter-postage, unless wrapped in accordance with regulations of the Postmaster-General.

Act June 8, 1872, *section* 141.—Publishers of newspapers or periodicals may print or write upon their publications to regular subscribers the address, the date when the subscription expires, and may inclose therein bills and receipts for subscription, without extra postage.

Act June 8, 1872, *section* 142.—To inclose or cancel any letter, memorandum, or other thing, in any mail-matter not charged with letter-postage, or to write thereon, subjects such matter to letter-postage.

Act June 8, 1872, *section* 152.—Mail-matter on which postage is required to be prepaid, reaching its destination, by inadvertence, without such prepayment, shall be subject to double the prepaid rates.

Act June 8, 1872, *section* 156.—That on all matter wholly or partly in writing, except book-manuscripts and corrected proofs passing between author and publisher, and local drop letters; on all printed matter, so marked as to convey any other information than is conveyed by the original print, except the correction of a mere typographical error; on all matter sent in violation of law or regulations respecting inclosures; and on all matter to which no specific rate of postage is assigned, postage shall be 3 cents the half ounce or fraction thereof.

Act June 8, 1872, *section* 157.—Fixes the postage on drop or local letters at letter-carrier offices at 2 cents the half ounce or fraction thereof, and 1 cent the half ounce or fraction thereof at all other offices.

Act June 8, 1872, *section* 158.—Quarterly postage on newspapers and other periodical publications, not exceeding four ounces in weight, sent to subscribers, shall be at the following rates: On publications issued less frequently than once a week, 1 cent for each issue; issued once a week, 5 cents; and 5 cents additional for each issue more frequent than once a week; an additional rate shall be charged for each additional four ounces or fraction thereof.

Act June 8, 1872, *section* 160.—Small newspapers issued less frequently than once a week, in packages to one address, to subscribers, 1 cent for each four ounces or fraction thereof.

Act June 8, 1872, *section* 161.—Regular dealers in newspapers and periodicals may receive and transmit by mail such quantities of either as they may require, and pay the postage as received, at the same rates as subscribers who pay quarterly in advance.

Act June 8, 1872, *section* 163.—Postage on mailable matter of the third class shall be at the rate of 1 cent for each two ounces or fraction thereof, except that double these rates shall be charged for books, samples of metals, ores, minerals, and merchandise.

Act June 8, 1872, *section* 164.—Packages of woolen, cotton, or linen clothing, in packages not exceeding two pounds, may be sent by mail to any non-commissioned officer or private in the Army, if prepaid, 1 cent each ounce or fraction thereof.

Act June 8, 1872, *section* 166.—Letters conveyed in vessels not regularly employed in carrying the mail, shall, if for delivery in the United States, be rated with double postage.

Act June 8, 1872, section 179.—Provides for the issue and transmission by mail of postal cards at 1 cent each.

Act June 8, 1872, section 180.—Confers the franking privilege upon and limits it to the following persons:

First. The President, by himself or private secretary, to cover all mail-matter.

Second. Vice President, to cover all mail-matter.

Third. The chiefs of the several executive Departments.

Fourth. Senators, Representatives, Delegates, Secretary of the Senate, Clerk of the House, } To cover their correspondence, all printed matter issued by authority of Congress, and all speeches, proceedings, and debates in Congress.

Fifth. Such heads of Bureaus or chief clerks as the Postmaster-General may designate, to cover official communications only.

Sixth. Postmasters, to cover official communications to other postmasters only.

Written autograph signatures, of all persons entitled to frank, required: mail-matter not thus franked to be charged with postage.

Act June 8, 1872, section 181.—The franking privilege of Senators, Representatives, Delegates, Secretary of the Senate and Clerk of the House, to commence with the term for which they are elected and expire the first Monday in December following such term.

Act June 8, 1872, section 182.—Books or publications, procured or published by order of Congress, to be public documents, and may be ranked as such.

Act June 8, 1872, section 183.—Maximum weight for franked and free matter shall be four ounces, except petitions to Congress, Congressional and Executive public documents, periodical publications interchanged between publishers, and packages of seeds, cuttings, roots, and scions, the weight of which latter may be fixed by the Postmaster-General.

Act June 8, 1872, section 184.—*Free mail-matter.*—The following mail-matter shall be allowed to pass free in the mail:

First. All mail-matter sent to the President or Vice-President.

Second. Official communications to chiefs, heads of Bureaus, chief clerks, or franking-officer of any of the Executive Departments.

Third. Letters and printed matter sent to Senators, Representatives, Delegates, Secretary of the Senate, and Clerk of the House.

Fourth. Petitions to Congress.

Fifth. Copyright matter to the Librarian of Congress, if marked "copyright matter."

Sixth. Publications sent and received by the Smithsonian Institution, if marked "Smithsonian exchange."

Seventh. Newspapers, periodicals, and magazines, exchanged between publishers, not exceeding sixteen ounces in weight.

Eighth. Weekly newspapers, one copy to each subscriber within the county where the same is printed and published.

Ninth. Notice to the publishers of the refusal or neglect of subscribers to take newspapers, magazines, or other periodicals from the post-office.

Tenth. Dead-letters returned to the writers.

Eleventh. Medals, certificates of thanks, or other testimonials awarded by the legislatures of States and Territories, to the soldiers thereof.

Act June 8, 1872, section 185.—All mail-matter to or from Mary Lincoln, widow of late President Lincoln.

Act January 9, 1873.—Amends section 133 of act of June 8, 1872, so as to authorize the transmission by mail of packages of seeds, cuttings, bulbs, roots, and scions, of any weight. For each package not exceeding four pounds, the postage shall be 1 cent for each two ounces or fraction of an ounce; to be prepaid in full.

Act January 31, 1873.—Abolishes the franking privilege from and after July 1, 1873.

Act March 3, 1873.—Repeals, from and after June 30, 1873, all laws and parts of laws permitting the transmission by mail of any free matter whatever.

Act June 23, 1874, section 5.—On and after January 1, 1875, all newspapers and periodical publications mailed from a known office of publication or news agency, and addressed to regular subscribers or news agents, postage shall be charged at the following rates: On newspapers and periodical publications issued weekly and more frequently, 2 cents a pound or fraction thereof; and on those issued less frequently than once a week, 3 cents a pound or fraction thereof: *Provided,* That nothing in this act shall be held to change section 99 of the act of June 8, 1872.

Act June 23, 1874, section 7.—Newspapers, one copy to each subscriber residing in the county where same are printed in whole or in part, and published, shall go free in the mails: but they shall not be delivered at letter-carrier offices, or be distributed by carriers unless postage is paid thereon.

Act June 23, 1874, section 8.—Mailable matter of the third class referred to in section

133 of act of June 8, 1872, may weigh not exceeding four pounds to each package, and postage shall be charged thereon at the rate of 1 cent for each two ounces or fraction thereof.

Act June 23, 1874, section 13.—Fixes the postage on public documents mailed by any member of Congress, the President, or head of any Executive Department, at 10 cents for each bound volume, and unbound documents the same rate as that on newspapers mailed from a known office of publication to subscribers; and the postage on the daily Congressional Record, mailed from the city of Washington as transient matter, at one cent.

Act March 3, 1875, section 3.—Extends the provisions of section 13 of act of June 23, 1874, to ex-Members of Congress and ex-Delegates, for nine months after the expiration of their terms, and postage on public documents mailed by them shall be as provided in such section.

Act March 3, 1875, section 5.—The Congressional Record, or any part thereof, or speeches or reports therein, shall, under the frank of a Member or Delegate, written by himself, be carried in the mail free of postage; and public documents, printed or ordered to be printed for the use of either House of Congress, may pass free by mail upon the frank of any Member or Delegate of the present Congress, written by himself, until the first day of December, 1875.

Act March 3, 1875, section 7.—Seeds transmitted by the Commissioner of Agriculture, or by any Member or Delegate receiving them for distribution from said Department, together with the Agricultural Reports, shall pass free in the mails under regulations of the Postmaster-General, and the provisions of this section shall apply to ex-Members and ex-Delegates for the period of nine months after the expiration of their term.

Act March 3, 1875, volume 18, page 377.—Amends section 8 of act of June 23, 1874, by inserting the word "ounce" in lieu of the words "two ounces."

Act July 12, 1876, section 15, volume 19, page 82.—Rates on all printed matter of the third class, except unsealed circulars, fixed at one cent for each two ounces. Permits limited inscriptions and addresses on third-class matter.

Act March 3, 1877, sections 5 and 6, volume 19, page 335.—Provides for official penalty envelopes and free transmission of same in mails when sent by Executive Departments, and containing inclosures relating to Government business.

Act March 3, 1879, section 29, volume 20, page 362.—The provisions of the preceding act extended to the Smithsonian Institution and to all Government offices.

Act March 3, 1879, sections 7–27, volume 20, pages 358–362.—General act repealing all former laws relating to classification of mail-matter and rates of postages. Makes four classes of mail-matter, to wit: First-class, written matter at three cents each half ounce; second class, periodical publications regularly issued for general information at two cents per pound, including sample copies; third class, miscellaneous printed matter at one cent for each two ounces; and fourth class, merchandise, all matter not included in the other three classes, at one cent each ounce. Liberalizes the provisions of former laws respecting written inscriptions on printed matter, defines printed matter generally, and permits second-class matter to be delivered through the boxes or general delivery at letter-carrier post-offices at two cents per pound.

○

www.ingramcontent.com/pod-product-compliance
Lightning Source LLC
Chambersburg PA
CBHW031825270326
41932CB00008B/553

* 9 7 8 3 3 3 7 2 3 6 4 3 4 *